ELEMENTARY SCIENCE METHODS

A CONSTRUCTIVIST APPROACH

Fifth Edition

David Jerner Martin
Kennesaw State University

WADSWORTH
CENGAGE Learning™

Australia • Brazil • Japan • Korea • Mexico • Singapore • Spain • United Kingdom • United States

Elementary Science Methods:
A Constructivist Approach,
Fifth Edition
David Jerner Martin

Education Editor: Dan Alpert
Development Editor: Tangelique
Williams
Assistant Editor: Caitlin Cox
Editorial Assistant: Stephanie Rue
Technology Project Manager: Julie
Aguilar
Marketing Manager: Karin
Sandberg
Marketing Assistant: Ting Jian Yap
Marketing Communications
Manager: Shemika Britt
Project Manager, Editorial
Production: Tanya Nigh
Creative Director: Rob Hugel
Art Director: Maria Epes
Print Buyer: Karen Hunt
Permissions Editor: Roberta
Broyer
Production Service: Newgen,
Laura Horowitz
Text Designer: Gary Harman/The
Artworks
Photo Researcher: Don Schlotman
Copy Editor: Eric Wesley Morrison
Cover Designer: Bartay Studio
Cover Image: David Roth/Taxi/
Getty Images
Compositor: Newgen

For product information and technology assistance, contact us at
Cengage Learning Academic Resource Center, 1-800-423-0563

For permission to use material from this text or product, submit all
requests online at **www.cengage.com/permissions.**
Further permissions questions can be e-mailed to
permissionrequest@cengage.com.

Library of Congress Control Number: 2007943267

ISBN-13: 978-0-495-50675-1

ISBN-10: 0-495-50675-3

Wadsworth Cengage Learning
10 Davis Drive
Belmont, CA 94002-3098
USA

Cengage Learning products are represented in Canada by
Nelson Education, Ltd.

For your course and learning solutions, visit
academic.cengage.com.

Purchase any of our products at your local college store
or at our preferred online store **www.ichapters.com.**

Printed in the United States of America
1 2 3 4 5 6 7 12 11 10 09 08

CONTENTS IN BRIEF

CONTENTS

ABOUT THE AUTHOR

David Jerner Martin is author of *Elementary Science Methods: A Constructivist Approach* (Thomson Wadsworth), *Constructing Early Childhood Science* (Thomson Delmar) and *Building Teachers: A Constructivist Approach to Introducing Education* (Thomson Wadsworth) which he co-authored with Kimberly S. Loomis. He has been educational consultant to The Weather Channel and numerous schools in the United States and abroad. *Elementary Science Methods: A Constructivist Approach* has been translated into Korean and Chinese, and has been recognized with the prestigious "Flame of Excellence" Award of the KSU Foundation of Kennesaw State University.

PREFACE

Children learn science by doing science . . . by asking their own questions about things that interest them, exploring answers to their questions through applying the processes of science in open-ended inquiries, and combining new experiences with information they already possess as they form personally constructed meanings. This is the essence of constructivism—building personal knowledge from one's own experience and thought.

This text prepares students to teach science from a constructivist perspective in preschool through eighth grade. It uses a constructivist approach to teach students to teach in a constructivist manner. A wealth of open-ended inquiry activities are suggested for students to do in class to construct their own personal conceptualizations about teaching science in the elementary and middle schools. Students pursue these activities and discuss their outcomes in small groups and with the whole class—much as teachers conduct their elementary science classes.

In the end, teachers must be able to apply the methodology they have constructed in their classrooms. More than 200 process-oriented inquiry activities are suggested, each keyed to a range of grade levels, and each open-ended so teachers can encourage children to develop and perform their own investigations. The activities are placed in the text where the concepts they illustrate are discussed so students can see immediately how to apply the concepts in the classroom. Children's literature is referenced extensively to encourage the tandem construction of scientific understandings and literacy.

The text is divided into three parts. In Part 1, students construct basic understandings of how they will teach science. They consider a number of concepts including the nature of science, goals and objectives of quality science education, the processes of science, the role of content in teaching the processes, the constructivist paradigm, methods of encouraging student inquiry, ways of accommodating learner differences including English language learners and multicultural dimensions, and methods of assessing authentically.

Part 2 extends the students' explorations of the basic science program to include literature and other interdisciplinary topics, technological applications, concept mapping, and professional aspects of science teaching.

Part 3 describes a model of science that may represent the ultimate in constructivist science education.

The text is suitable for both undergraduate and graduate work. The inexperienced undergraduate student will construct sound conceptualizations of constructivist, inquiry-oriented science teaching through the use of this text. The graduate student will consider advanced models of inquiry and interdisciplinary studies including science-technology-society, issues of content and methodology, ways of contributing to the profession through action research, and the sophisticated model of teaching by listening.

There are several significant new features in this fifth edition.

- Emphasis on science content is increased.

- National Science Education Standards in the margins have been expanded to include the content of each standard in addition to its number.

- Teacher notes that explain the content needed for implementing activities are highlighted.

- Appendix A references each activity by its content area.

- The Supplemental chapter on the companion Web site details the basic concepts and principles of science typically needed by teachers.

- Material on the Nature of Science has been expanded and is more prominent.

- Material and activities appropriate for 7th and 8th grades has been added.

- Safety precautions have been emphasized and have been highlighted with safety icons in the margins.

- The chapter on Learner Differences has been expanded into two chapters dealing with differences in perspectives and learning differences.

- An extensive section on teaching science to English Language Learners has been included in Chapter 7.

- The number of nonfiction children's literature titles has been increased.

- Bloom's cognitive taxonomy has been updated to the new version.

- Technology applications have been updated.

- The Student Book Companion Web Site has been updated to include current references. The Web site can be accessed through the following URL: http://academic.cengage.com/education/martin5

- A new science teaching vignette has been included on the DVD.

Two recent developments in education are noteworthy. One is the emphasis on high-stakes standardized testing that has permeated every state in the nation, affecting virtually every teacher in every school. The other is the *No Child Left Behind Act* signed into law by President George W. Bush in January, 2002 and scheduled for reauthorization in 2007 which, among other provisions, promotes continued standardized testing. This emphasis on high-stakes testing has had the effect of discouraging teachers from taking the time to foster children's explorations into scientific investigations. It has sent teachers back to teaching the facts, principles, concepts, and laws that others deem essential for children to demonstrate they have learned. In other words, the tendency is to revert to teaching *about* science rather than teaching *how to do* science. Of course, this high-stakes testing situation must be taken into consideration as teachers develop their science programs. However, I sincerely hope teachers will use their convictions of the value of the constructivist approach to science education as the primary basis for their science programs and will implement a science education they *know* works. The current focus on standardized testing is real, but that doesn't make it right.

In over 30 years in the field of science education at all levels from kindergarten through college, it has been my experience that the only science children learn is the science they do themselves. In this practical text, I have taken the bold and uncompromising position that hands-on, process-oriented, constructivist-focused inquiry must be fostered in science education in the elementary schools. Preservice and inservice teachers who construct their science education conceptualizations and methodologies through the guidance offered in this text will find science teaching to be fun, stimulating, rewarding, and extremely successful.

When Carl Sagan received a copy of the first edition of this book, he wrote a short note to me that concluded, "I hope all goes well with your effort to change the teaching of science."

His response is more important now than ever. But, I won't be the one who changes science education. You will. For it is the students who construct their own conceptualizations of the way science can be taught most effectively who will change the teaching of science.

David Jerner Martin
December, 2007

ACKNOWLEDGMENTS

This work would not have been possible without the support and help of many people. I am especially grateful to the following people:

Dr. Linda Webb who reviewed and critiqued countless drafts and whose encouragement and support has kept me going.

Mr. Paul Hultberg who understands both children and education and took the photographs that so skillfully bring the two together.

The staff and students at Sedalia Park Elementary School in Cobb County, Georgia who welcomed me as a colleague, provided me with much valuable experience, and allowed us to take the photographs there.

Professor Ernst vonGlasersfeld for his critical review of the material in Chapter 4.

Dr. Mira Han, Professor of Early Childhood Science Education at Kyungnam University, Masan, South Korea, who provided much input to the material on science education for preschoolers and kindergarteners and who shared the teachings of Vygotsky.

Dr. Traci Redish who reviewed, critiqued, and provided much valuable input to the material on educational technology.

Dr. Mark Warner who critiqued the material on the *No Child Left Behind* act and the problem-solving approach and who introduced me to WebQuests.

Dr. Debra Coffey who reviewed, critiqued, and provided much valuable input to the material on reading, writing, and interdisciplinary approaches.

Dr. Loretta McMillon Howell who reviewed, critiqued, and provided much valuable input to the multicultural material.

Dr. Tony Strieker who reviewed, critiqued, and provided much valuable input to the material on children with disabilities.

Ms. Denise Grant who provided help with the material dealing with gifted and talented students.

Dr. Pam Rhyne and Dr. Gary Lewis who reviewed, critiqued, and provided much valuable input to the material on basic scientific concepts and principles in the Supplementary Chapter.

Dr. Anita VanBrackle who provided help on the material dealing with mathematics.

Dr. Edward C. Lucy, professor, mentor, colleague, and friend, who reviewed, critiqued, and provided much valuable input.

Editors Dan Alpert and Tangelique Williams of Wadsworth/Cengage Learning who provided much support for this edition, kept encouraging, and knew just when to say what.

All the many professional colleagues who have supported my work through the years in many diverse ways.

The undergraduate and graduate students in my college classes who have shown me what works and what doesn't. I have used many of their ideas and vignettes in this text.

The many professional colleagues who provided critique through their reviews:

LaVerne Logan,
Western Illinois University

Linda Carter,
Columbia College, Chicago

Dale A. Banks,
Saint Mary's College

Bruce Patterson,
Central Michigan University

Pamela J. Riggs,
Missouri Valley College

Patricia Stinger-Barnes,
Carson-Newman College

Steve Murphee,
Belmont University

Chelly Templeton,
Palm Beach Atlantic University

Frances H. Squires,
Indiana University, Southeast

Philip J. Natoli,
State University of New York,
　Geneseo

William R. Veal,
College of Charleston

Allen Larson,
Western Illinois University

David Boger,
North Carolina A&T State
　University

Phyllis Miller,
Kutztown University

Julie Saam,
Indiana University Kokomo

Melody L. Russell,
Auburn University

Amy J. Vena,
Bridgewater State College

Pamela B. Blanchard,
Louisiana State University

To all these people, and many more, "Thank you."

TO THE STUDENT

Welcome to this exploration of elementary science education!

Teaching science need not be difficult. Science is one of the most fascinating pursuits children experience. Children love to tinker, to explore, to try things out, to observe things, to talk about what they observe, to find out what makes things work. They love to play with magnets, discovering that some things are attracted to magnets and some things are not—even through water, plastic, and sand—discovering the idea that some ends of straight magnets attract each other and some ends repel. They are enthralled by the metamorphosis of a caterpillar into a beautiful butterfly. They get excited exploring why things swing and why things balance, the movement and variety of the stars and the planets in the night sky, and the different characteristics of rocks.

However, despite children's natural fascination with exploring on their own, for many years the teaching of science has consisted of the skillful impartation of scientific knowledge to students. Textbooks have contained information for children to learn, and it has been the job of the teacher to interpret the textbook and augment it as necessary to ensure that every child learns the material presented.

Science education of the 21st century moves from this teacher-focused approach to one that is radically different. It encourages children to construct information in ways that are meaningful to them. It comprises experiences for children to undertake themselves. The focus of science education today is on doing rather than acquiring.

Children learn science by doing science, and children do science by using the processes of science in personally constructed inquiries. Therefore, this book is about constructing the process-oriented inquiry method of science teaching. It emphasizes process skills and hands-on experiences through which children develop their own questions about phenomena that interest them and seek their own answers to those questions through activities that they themselves devise. As you will see, inquiry is the agent of constructivism.

The text uses a constructivist approach; you will learn to teach science in the same manner as the children in your classroom will learn how to do science. You will develop your own personally constructed conceptualizations about teaching science. Many questions and issues are raised for you to grapple with; there are many more questions than answers, for you have to come to your own conclusions.

Each topic begins with one or more case studies or activities to help you begin to construct your conceptualizations. Topics are treated inductively, which means you will explore a variety of specific situations pertaining to a phenomenon before the concept is introduced or defined. In this way, you will construct your own generalizations and conclusions as you move through a topic, rather than rely on the preconstructed conclusions of the author. Periodically, you will be asked to compare your conclusions with the author's. Hopefully there will be a degree of congruence.

Disagreement and debate are encouraged. This is the only way people can crystallize their own ideas. This is the essence of constructivism.

Many class activities, called *Constructing Your Ideas,* are suggested throughout the text. They are designed to help you construct your conceptualizations.

The many *In the Schools* activities throughout the text illustrate the concepts under consideration and show how they are actually used in classrooms.

Suggested children's activities called *Constructing Science in the Classroom* occur throughout the text near the science learning principle they can be used to teach. They are provided as suggestions only, points of departure—they are not intended to be duplicated. The icon suggests the range of grade levels for the activity. Most of the activities contain suggested literature connections.

Safety precautions are highlighted with safety icons in the margins. In addition to safety notes in many of the activities, an entire section in Chapter 9 is devoted to safety in science education.

Many Internet sites are referenced in the text. We have put direct links to the Web sites on the Student Book Companion Web site. All you need to do is access the book Web site and then click on the desired link. To access this Web site, type the following URL in your Internet browser:

http://academic.cengage.com/education/martin5

In addition to the direct links, there is much more:

- Links to other interesting Web sites

- The Supplemental Chapter, "Basic Concepts and Principles for the Elementary Science Education Program"

- A list of prominent women in science

- Direct links to text references that came from websites

The accompanying DVD has several video clips that show examples of discrepant events and constructivist science teaching. Individual video clips are referenced in appropriate places in the text.

NSES Content
Standard B. Physical
Science: Properties of
Objects and Materials

Throughout this book, margin notes refer to specific National Science Education Standards applicable to the topic under discussion. They show the content areas and can help guide your construction of the many aspects of science education.

Be sure to make use of the appendices; they will help you immensely in your construction of your science education system. Appendix A contains cross-references of activities to basic scientific principles and concepts. Appendix B is a list of the children's literature cited in the text. A glossary of terms highlighted in **bold face** in the text is provided to help you define words or phrases that may be new to you.

The goals of this book are for you to construct your own personal philosophy of teaching science, lose any fears or lack of confidence that may have accompanied you into this course, and construct a methodology and curriculum base that will enable you to enter the classroom a competent teacher of science.

Enjoy your explorations!

David Jerner Martin
December, 2007

PART 1 CONSTRUCTING THE ELEMENTARY SCIENCE PROGRAM

CHAPTER · · · · · 1

THE SCIENCE EDUCATION IMPERATIVE

Except for children (who don't know enough not to ask the important questions), few of us spend much time wondering about why nature is the way it is; where the cosmos came from, or whether it was always here; if time will one day flow backward and effects precede causes; or whether there are ultimate limits to what humans can know . . . In our society it is still customary for parents and teachers to answer most of these questions with a shrug.

Carl Sagan, in S. W. Hawking, *A Brief History of Time* (New York: Bantam Books, 1988), ix

Children are natural-born scientists. They begin recognizing and sorting out their world from the moment of birth, and perhaps even earlier. They exhibit natural curiosity about what things are, how things work, and how things are related to each other. They wonder where the wind, rain, snow, and hail come from. They wonder why mold grows on strawberries. They wonder why fish can breathe in water and why birds can fly. They wonder why feathers fall more slowly than rocks. They wonder what makes a truck go and how toys work. They have a wonderful time exploring these questions and coming to their own conclusions.

Thus, children come to school with a multitude and a great variety of experiences and adventures acquired from this natural inquisitiveness and their innate desire to find out why things happen and how things work. The teacher of science in the elementary grades has a wonderfully rich palate to work with. When teachers give their students encouragement, sensitivity, and developmentally appropriate teaching; the power to ask and investigate their own questions;

and ownership of their own constructions, this curiosity and desire to explore continues through the elementary grades and even into adulthood.

The goal of this chapter is to stimulate your thinking about elementary science education. The constructivist viewpoint suggests that learning occurs best when you question your own preconceived ideas and that the best way for this to occur is through exposure to experiences you cannot reconcile readily in your own mind with the understandings and experiences available to you. Thus, in this first chapter, the stage is set for you to begin to question your current understandings about science education.

A fundamental issue is raised: How much science does a competent elementary science teacher need to know? Teachers often perceive their intellectual authority as dependent on their knowledge of "the truth." The issue of content is examined from several viewpoints, and the proposition is offered that competent teachers of elementary science do not have to know as much science content as they may have thought but, instead, need such skills as observing, predicting, and hypothesizing.

Attention is given to the nebulosity of "right" and "wrong" answers. Answers that teachers may consider to be wrong may, to some degree, be "right." Thus, it is suggested that it is more important for teachers to listen to children and elicit from them their reasons for their responses rather than to declare their responses either right or wrong.

The processes of science are introduced as the most important outcome of science education in elementary grades, because using the processes in inquiry investigations is the means by which new knowledge can be produced. It is suggested that quality elementary science education programs use basic scientific concepts and facts as the *vehicles* to teach the processes.

Preconceived notions about science and science teaching are examined. You are encouraged to identify your own preconceptions so you can begin your study of elementary science teaching with an open mind.

In summary, the goal of the first chapter is to stimulate your questioning about the best way to teach science to elementary children. In keeping with the constructivist inquiry **paradigm** promoted in this text, you are encouraged to answer your own questions.

How Much Science Does the Elementary Science Teacher Need to Know?

NSES Professional Development Standard A. Learning Content Through Inquiry

What do you remember from your own science experiences in school?

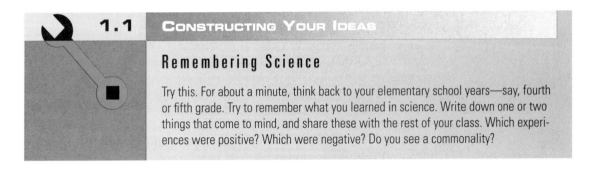

1.1   CONSTRUCTING YOUR IDEAS

Remembering Science

Try this. For about a minute, think back to your elementary school years—say, fourth or fifth grade. Try to remember what you learned in science. Write down one or two things that come to mind, and share these with the rest of your class. Which experiences were positive? Which were negative? Do you see a commonality?

NSES Content Standard A. Scientific Inquiry: Understanding About Scientific Inquiry

Here are some of the things students have said in classes like yours: "Going on a field trip to the river bed," "Dissecting frogs," "Watching caterpillars hatch into butterflies," "Collecting rocks."

Chances are that neither you nor other members of your class listed such notions as the composition of an atom of oxygen, the hardness of quartz, the probability of obtaining yellow pea plants from crossing two hybrids, the number of chromosomes in a normal human cell, the nature of **friction,** the class of lever represented by a pair of scissors, or the freezing point of water in degrees Celsius.

If you were to think back to your more recent high school years, or even to your college years, in all probability you would not include this kind of factual information in a list of things you remember having learned in science. Yet, without doubt, this material was taught!

This little exercise, of course, suggests a very important question. If we cannot remember those facts, concepts, and pieces of information that undoubtedly were taught to us during our school days, why were they taught? (Maybe we also need to ask *how* they were taught.) It appears that teaching factual material does not promote either lasting learning of science or enjoyment and appreciation of science.

You are undertaking to learn how to teach science to children. You want your children to remember what they have learned. If 14 or 15 years from now they are asked the question "What do you remember learning in science?" you will want them to be able to list some of what they learned in *your* classes! You also will want them to remember experiencing joy in learning science.

Teachers of elementary science typically perceive their job as directly related to the amount of scientific content to which they can expose children. It generally is believed that science is factual in nature and that there are certain facts, concepts, theories and bits of information that every elementary school child must know. It is the purpose of this section to examine how realistic this belief is.

Amount of Science Known Today

One of the difficulties with focusing on factual information in science education is the sheer volume of information currently known. The amount of science known today is enormous. The discipline of biology alone comprises more than 1400 specific fields, each with its own distinctive characteristics (Hurd, 2002). Costa and Liebman (1995) estimated that by the year 2020, the amount of knowledge in the world will double every 73 days. That means the amount of knowledge available to the world in mid-March will be twice the amount that was available on New Year's Day! Stephen Hawking, in his White House Millennium Evening address of 1998, said that if knowledge were to keep growing at the current rate, by the year 2600, "if you stacked the new books being published next to each other, you would have to move at 90 miles an hour just to keep up with the end of the line. Of course," he continued, "by 2600 new artistic and scientific work will come in electronic forms rather than in physical books. Nevertheless, if the exponential growth continued, there would be ten papers a second in my kind of theoretical physics, and no time to read them" (Hawking, 1998).

As you can tell, there is a huge amount of science known today, and the amount of scientific knowledge is increasing at an unprecedented rate.

Because so much science is known, we should not be surprised that children may very well ask questions to which we do not know the answers. Let us say, for example, you decide that someday you might have to teach **metamorphosis** to children in your elementary class. So, you study the stages in the metamorphosis of caterpillars in your college science classes, committing them to memory, and you observe the application of these stages in beetles, moths, and butterflies. You are all set to teach metamorphosis. Now, let us say you are presenting a well-prepared lesson on the metamorphosis of caterpillars into butterflies. Unexpectedly, some child asks a question about **earwigs** (see Figure 1.1), perhaps because the child's family has just discovered a colony of these pests. Now what? You know a lot about your subject, but you do not know about earwigs. How do you respond?

Here is another scenario: This time, suppose you are dealing with simple machines. As you are having the children "invent" their own machines, a child asks about cranes. Not having studied cranes, you are in a quandary. What do you do?

By now, you see the problem: *No matter how much science you study and learn, it will never be enough.*

Earwig

FIGURE 1.1

Obsolescence of Scientific Knowledge

There is another difficulty with focusing on factual information in science: *Scientific knowledge may become obsolete.* What we know today may be replaced in a few years by different information. For example, before 1956, biology teachers insisted their students memorize the *fact* that the normal cells in the human body had 48 **chromosomes** (24 pairs). Woe unto any student who did not know this indisputable fact! In 1956, however, it was discovered that the number of human chromosomes is 46, not 48 (Therman, 1986, p. 8). Better techniques enabled a more precise separation of the chromosomes and, thus, a more accurate count. What happens to all those pre-1956 students of biology who are roaming the globe with the so-called indisputable knowledge that the human body has 48 chromosomes in each normal cell? What can we do about that factual error?

Changing Scientific Knowledge

There is yet another difficulty with focusing on factual information in science: *Scientific knowledge changes.* Scientific inquiry often results in the rejection of one previously accepted theory and the adoption of another. Our understandings of basic phenomena change with additional research, new technology, refined investigations, and deeper probing. A good example of this is the modern concept of **plate tectonics,** which suggests the earth's continents and oceans lie on plates that move. This theory is less than 40 years old and replaces the previously well-established view that continents and ocean basins are permanent.

In another example, **DNA** was discovered in 1953 by Francis Crick, a British researcher, and James Watson, an American, working together at Cambridge University. This discovery has completely revolutionized the way people think about life and has opened up entirely new areas of inquiry (see Figure 1.2).

New species of plants and animals are discovered every year. For example, more than 400 new species of plants and animals have been discovered on the island of Borneo since 1996 (Engeler, 2007), and 20 new species of ocean sharks and rays have been discovered in Indonesia since 2001 (Casey, 2007).

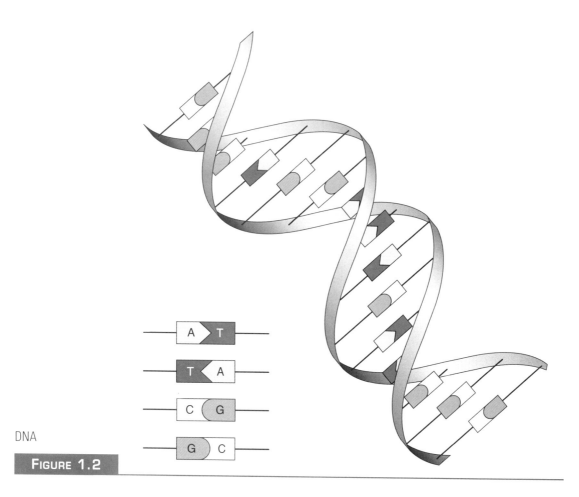

DNA

FIGURE 1.2

Major changes also have occurred in the field of astronomy during the past few years. For one, the way that we describe our planetary system is changing. In 2006, the International Astronomical Union, a professional society of about 10,000 astronomers from throughout the world, approved new definitions of objects in our solar system. This action was necessary because the word *planet* had no formal definition (Riddle, 2007), and it resulted in the "demotion" of Pluto from being a planet to being a *dwarf planet,* thus leaving only the first eight as recognized planets in our solar system (instead of the previous nine or even ten if Sedna was considered to be a planet). The new classification of objects that revolve about stars such as our sun fall into three categories as follows (Gingerich, 2006):

Planet

- Must be in orbit around the sun (but not be a star itself).

- Must be nearly spherical in shape.

- Must have "cleared the neighborhood" around its orbit.

- Cannot be a satellite.

Dwarf Planet

- Has all of the characteristics of a planet except that it is too small to attract other things in its orbit and, thus, cannot clear its neighborhood.

Small Solar System Bodies

- Includes all other objects that revolve about the star; this includes Sedna, tentatively classified as a planet when it was discovered, and many other fairly large bodies that are close to the size of Pluto and Sedna as well as comets and asteroids.

There is widespread public opposition to the demotion of Pluto because of historic and sentimental reasons. Britt (2006) notes that only 424 astronomers (less than 5 percent of those who were eligible) voted on the proposed revisions. However, "No one could deny that Pluto was unlike other known planets" (Bartlett, 2006, p. 829). It exhibits several nonplanetary characteristics: its mass is less than 1 percent of the earth's mass; its orbit is sharply inclined to the orbits of the other planets; and it occasionally is closer to the sun than Neptune.

The debate about whether to call Pluto a planet is likely to continue, and a group of American astronomers is planning to call a special meeting of the International Astronomy Union in 2007, two years in advance of its next scheduled meeting, to correct what they believe is a mistake (Adler, 2006).

You can keep up with the debate about the status of Pluto through several Web sites hot-linked on the Student Book Companion Web Site.

Whichever way the debate is resolved, at the present time, there are eight official planets, not nine.

Exploration of our solar system continues to be expanded and refined. In January 2006, a spacecraft named *New Horizons* was launched on a 9½-year, 2½-billion mile trip to Pluto (see Figure 1.3). The purpose of this mission is to help us understand worlds that are in a region at the edge of our solar system thought to be populated largely by icy bodies. The spacecraft will fly past Pluto and gather information about the materials from which life evolves that are abundant on Pluto and other distant objects, thereby enriching our understanding about the evolution of life. Astronomers also hope to learn more about the evolution of the earth's atmosphere by comparing it to the atmosphere of Pluto, which is thought to be similar to the earth's original atmosphere of hydrogen and helium.

Two direct links to *New Horizons* Web sites are provided on the Student Book Companion Web Site.

On January 3, 2004, the unmanned exploration vehicle *Spirit* landed on Mars after a journey of 300 million miles that took almost seven months (see Figure 1.4). This was followed by the *Mars Reconnaissance Orbiter* (see Figure 1.5), which began orbiting Mars in 2006 and taking photographs through a powerful telescope for transmission to earth. A new Mars

Drawing of *New Horizons* over Pluto (Courtesy NASA/JPL-Caltech)

FIGURE 1.3

A direct link to the official Saturn exploration Web site is available on the Student Book Companion Web Site. This site provides information about the *Cassini-Huygens* mission and teacher materials for school children.

exploration vehicle, the *Phoenix Mars Lander,* is scheduled for launch in the summer of 2007 and will land on Mars in May 2008 (Phoenix Mars Lander, 2007). The purpose of these continuing explorations is to look for clues about whether Mars ever had a watery environment suitable for sustaining life as we know it; to study the Martian atmosphere, weather, and climate; and to assess the viability of sending manned expeditions to the planet. Much information will be added to what we already know about Mars and space science, and some of what we already know will be replaced with new information.

On June 30, 2004, the *Cassini* spacecraft arrived at Saturn after a journey of 2.2 billion miles that took nearly seven years at a speed of 34,000 miles per hour. The *Cassini-Huygens* mission has photographed Saturn, its rings, and its moons to seek information that will help our understanding about the origin of life and the evolution of the planets (see Figure 1.6.)

One of the most exciting recent developments in the field of life science is the human **genome** project. A genome is the full set of all the **genes** in the chromosomes of each cell in an organism. The human genome project has identified approximately 32,000 genes and the traits they determine (International Human Genome Sequencing Consortium, 2001). The project has opened the doors to much new research into such topics as how genes express their traits (Human Genome Study, 2007); developing treatments and, possibly, cures for diseases such as lupus (GlaxoSmithKline, 2007), Lou Gehrig's Disease (Scan of Entire Human Genome, 2006), diabetes

(a) NASA illustration of *Spirit,* the Mars exploration robot

(b) Martian landscape photographed by a camera on *Spirit*

Mars exploration by *Spirit* (Courtesy National Aeronautics and Space Administration/ Jet Propulsion Laboratory–California Institute of Technology)

FIGURE 1.4

Mars Reconnaissance Orbiter (Courtesy National Aeronautics and Space Administration/ Jet Propulsion Laboratory–California Institute of Technology)

FIGURE 1.5

(Russo, 2007), and certain kinds of cancer (Shute, 2007); and analyzing genetic evidence related to human evolution (Hoare, 2006; Kellis, 2006; Wade, 2006).

These are but a few examples of the continual change in scientific knowledge.

Saturn and its rings photographed from *Cassini*, approximately 999,000 kilometers (621,000 miles) from Saturn (Courtesy National Aeronautics and Space Administration/ Jet Propulsion Laboratory–California Institute of Technology)

FIGURE 1.6

Scientific Controversies

There are many controversies in science. Examples include the definition of a planet, the preservation of certain species of wildlife, and stem cell research. Among the more controversial topics are global warming and the debate over evolution versus intelligent design. In both, there are sound arguments supporting each view. Scientists who exhibit low concern over global warming say that we are simply undergoing a temperature cycle that has been occurring periodically for **eons**; those who exhibit high concerns cite the alarming rate of iceberg and ice sheet melting, which is more rapid than in previous occurrences. Those in favor of evolution cite evidence from geology and species adaptations; those in favor of intelligent design feel God ought to be able to do anything, including ordering the universe and all its parts and inhabitants according to His plan.

You can find a huge amount of information about scientific controversies on the Internet and in other resources. It is worth investigating them to gain an understanding of how science is done and how different interpretations can be formed from the same data. You should use caution before introducing controversial topics in your class. Discuss them only if you feel they are appropriate to your curriculum and the students' level of development and if school policy permits.

How Much Science Does the Elementary Teacher Need to Know?

This discussion has shown that elementary science teachers face at least three difficulties in learning "enough" content:

1. The amount of science known today is far too large for any one person to be able to know it all—or even a small part of it.

2. Scientific knowledge considered to be factual today may become obsolete in the future.

3. Scientific conceptualizations tend to change with time.

Because this is the case, what science should the elementary science teacher know? We stated in the beginning of this book that there would be more questions than answers. This is the first such instance. There is absolutely no answer to the question "What science should the elementary science teacher know?" Nor is there any universally agreed-on answer to the question "What is the *minimum* amount of science the elementary science teacher needs to know to be a competent science teacher?"

The National Science Education Standards (see Chapter 2) suggest that "teachers of science must have a strong, broad base of scientific knowledge extensive enough for them to:

NSES Professional Development Standard A. Learning Content Through Inquiry

- Understand the nature of scientific inquiry, its central role in science, and how to use the skills and processes of scientific inquiry;

- Understand the fundamental facts and concepts in major science disciplines;

- Be able to make conceptual connections within and across science disciplines as well as mathematics, technology, and other school subjects;

- Use scientific inquiry and ability when dealing with personal and societal issues" (National Research Council, 1996, p. 39).

The National Science Teachers Association's *NSTA Standards for Teacher Preparation* suggests that elementary science teachers should study content that is balanced among the main fields of science and that they should study this material in the context of student-focused, laboratory-centered investigations (National Science Teachers Association, 2003). Gerald Wheeler, Executive Director of NSTA, says that "[a] nation's ability to remain an economic and technological leader in a global marketplace relies on how well that nation educates its students in science, technology, engineering, and math" and that "teachers need to know the science they teach" (Wheeler, 2006, p. 30, 31).

It seems a good idea for elementary science teachers to have studied the three basic content fields: life science, physical science, and earth–space science. Life science includes the study of cells, plants, animals, life cycles, **genetics,** evolution, and **ecology.** Physical science includes topics related to matter, energy, and chemistry. Earth–space science includes topics related to **geology,** rocks and minerals, the earth, the seas, weather and other forces that shape the earth, and space. Summaries of basic concepts in these areas are presented in the Supplemental Chapter available on the Student Book Companion Web Site.

Concern is growing that our youth are insufficiently prepared in science—that they don't know enough science to be successful in today's world. This concern has been bolstered by poor 8th- and 12th-grade science test scores on the Third International Mathematics and Science Study (TIMSS) given in 1995 and poor 8th-grade science test scores on the repeat of TIMSS (TIMSS-R) given in 1999 and, again on the TIMSS given in 2003 (TIMSS-2003) (see Figure 1.7). TIMSS is a test of mathematics and science understanding given to students in many countries during grades 4, 8, and 12. Its purpose is to enable countries to assess the state of mathematics and science education in their own country and in comparison with other countries. TIMSS was administered in 2007. However, as Holliday and Holliday (2003), Wang (2001), and numerous others have observed, many problems are associated with the uniform administration of the test to all children in all participating countries and with the interpretations of the test findings. (See Chapter 8 for more information on these assessments.)

The concern about the science preparedness of our youth also has been strengthened by the science scores on the Nation's Report Card. The National Center for Educational Statistics, a division of the U. S. Department of Education, has conducted national assessments in science, mathematics, and reading since 1969 to show overall achievement of U. S. students. The *National Assessment of Educational Progress* (NAEP), also known as the Nation's Report Card, compiles the results. Trends in science achievement are as follows (National Assessment of Educational Progress, 2006; National Center for Educational Statistics, 2005):

- Nine-year-olds: Scores declined during the 1970s, began to rise between the early 1980s and the mid-1990s, and rose again in 2005.

The Student Book Companion Web Site contains the Supplemental Chapter "Basic Concepts and Principles for the Elementary Science Program," a review of science concepts and principles appropriate for the elementary school science teacher. The various topics referred to in this text are expanded and explained in the Supplemental Chapter.

A direct link to a Web site where you can find details about the TIMSS, TIMSS-R, and TIMSS-2003 is available on the Student Book Companion Web Site.

		Number of Countries with Science Scores Significantly Higher than the United States	Number of Countries with Science Scores Not Significantly Different from the United States	Number of Countries with Science Scores Significantly Lower than the United States
Fourth-Grade Science	1995 (26 countries)	1	6	19
	1999 (not tested)			
	2003 (25 Countries)	3	6	16
Eighth-Grade Science	1995 (41 countries)	9	17	15
	1999 (38 countries)	14	6	18
	2003 (45 countries)	7	6	32
High School Seniors: General Science	1995 (21 countries)	11	8	2
High School Advanced Mathematics and Science Students Taking Physics	1995 (16 countries)	14	2	0

Note: The term *significance* refers to statistical significance—the likelihood that the scores are true representations of students' knowledge and understandings.
Data from Office of Educational Research and Improvement, 1999; National Center for Education Statistics, 2001; and National Center for Education Statistics, 2004.

Number of countries scoring above, at, and below the United States on the TIMSS tests of science (adapted from Martin & Loomis, 2007).

FIGURE 1.7

- Thirteen-year-olds: Scores declined during the 1970s, rose during the 1980s and early 1990s to the 1970 level, and since then, have remained relatively unchanged.

- Seventeen-year-olds: Scores declined during the 1970s and early 1980s, rose between 1986 and 1992, and have declined since 1996.

Direct links to the Nation's Report Card reports are available on the Student Book Companion Web Site.

These data are shown in graphical form in Figure 1.8.

In addition to concerns about preparedness in science, there is a growing fear that the United States is in danger of losing its competitive edge in the global economy, spurred by a decline in scientific, mathematical, and technological competence (Bybee & Fuchs, 2006). In *The World is Flat,* Friedman (2005) reports that many countries are working to upgrade their citizens' understanding of science, mathematics, and technology, with the result that American firms are finding it increasingly attractive to outsource much of their manufacturing and technological support.

1.2   CONSTRUCTING YOUR IDEAS

Trends in Science Achievement

Compare the trends in science achievement exhibited by 4th, 8th, and 12th graders on the TIMSS science tests and the NAEP science tests. What similarities do you observe? What differences do you observe? What trends do you observe? What questions or conclusions can you make from these trends?

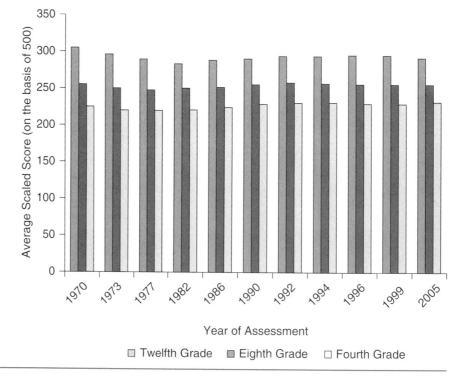

Average achievement in science by fourth graders, eighth graders, and twelfth graders on the National Assessment of Educational Progress, 1970–2005 (Data from National Assessment of Educational Progress, 2006)

FIGURE 1.8

It is widely suggested that the solution to this perceived lack of science knowledge and understanding lies in teachers knowing more science content and imparting this content to children. Addressing this concern, the National Research Council has asserted that teachers must be prepared with deeper understandings of science, mathematics, and technology than is currently the case and that content knowledge must be a central focus of teacher preparation programs (NRC Report, 2000).

In her analysis of state policies and teacher quality, Darling-Hammond (2000) found that content proficiency is a necessary, but not sufficient, requirement for good teaching and that the lower the grades being taught, the more important the pedagogical expertise. Similarly, Schibeci and Hickey (2000) argue that "science content alone is not a sufficient basis for good [science] teaching. Effective teachers need *both* subject matter knowledge *and* pedagogical content knowledge" (p. 1166). Nonetheless, both suggest that when teachers possess a deeper understanding of content, they are better equipped to employ a range of teaching strategies to facilitate children's development of their own constructions.

Despite the current focus on teachers acquiring science content so they can be better prepared to teach science, it seems prudent to offer the following proposition: *Elementary science teachers do not need to have extensive knowledge about science to be able to teach it well.*

Before you throw this book away on charges of blasphemy, let me hasten to add that there most definitely are certain basic, fundamental, overarching principles of science with which all teachers—and, for that matter, all citizens of the world—should be familiar. However, elementary teachers do not need to master a huge collection of facts, concepts, and theories about science. Rather, they need to know how children learn science and how to teach children. As Yager (1993) said, "Apparently what a teacher does and how he/she does it in the classroom is far more important than what a teacher knows or the curriculum he/she uses" (p. 146).

Rather than learning vast amounts of scientific information, children must learn how to *do* science. They must learn how to observe, how to create, how to come up with new ideas, how to analyze, how to evaluate, and how to create. They must be able to construct their own conceptualizations. They must be able to ferret out for themselves what is important and what is unimportant *for them.*

It is not necessary for teachers to clutter children's minds with myriad facts, principles, and concepts to be learned under the mistaken impression that these are essential for survival in tomorrow's (or today's) society. Children must learn how to *do* science.

RIGHT AND WRONG

In the traditional **paradigm** of education, teachers present information for children to learn, and children demonstrate they have learned this

NSES Teaching Standard A. Inquiry-Based Program

information with their responses to questions and situations. Some responses are considered "right," and others are considered "wrong."

Let us consider two questions that are fundamental for all of elementary science education. *Are there right answers? Are there wrong answers?*

THE GUMMY BEARS LESSON

A student teacher had developed a fine **multidisciplinary** math and science lesson for first grade using gummy bears. The object of the lesson was for children to sort gummy bears given to them in individual plastic bags by color, lay them head-to-toe on vertical columns previously drawn on chart paper, and draw an elementary histogram of the numbers of each gummy bear color in their bags (see Figure 1.9). The student teacher passed out bags of different-colored gummy bears, one bag to each student. Seizing on a "teachable moment," she asked each child to estimate how many gummy bears were in the bag as she handed it to him or her. (Before this lesson, the class had explored estimation using common classroom objects.) It was obvious that there were 15 to 20 gummy bears in each bag. The student teacher went from child to child asking, "How many gummy bears do you suppose there are in your bag?" "Twenty," said one child. "Twenty-five," said another. "Seventeen." "Twenty." "Thirty." "Twenty-five." "Five." "Eighteen." Wait a minute! Didn't Melissa just say "five"? Wisely, the student teacher moved on to the rest of the children, not commenting on what Melissa or anyone else had estimated. The class did the lesson while the student teacher facilitated. No one commented on the estimating activity. When they were finished, Melissa raised her hand. "I said there were five gummy bears in the bag," she said. "I thought you meant, 'How many colors?'"

This anecdote illustrates a principle that is found over and over again in all education, not only in science education: *There are no right answers!*

Suppose a teacher asks a child in her second-grade class how much 5 plus 2 is. She expects the answer to be 7, of course. Suppose the child answers "10." Is that wrong? She asks the child, "How did you get 10?" From what the child says, the teacher infers that the child employed multiplication rather than addition. This was an error in operation, and the teacher can easily tell what happened to produce the "wrong" answer. Suppose the answer given is 3. Obviously, the child must have subtracted. How about "52?" We all know the magnificent riddle that asks, "How much is 5 plus 2?" "It's 52!" Again the child's answer is understandable. Suppose the child answers "9." The teacher searches her mind for a way the child could come up with "9" for an answer, but she cannot find a single

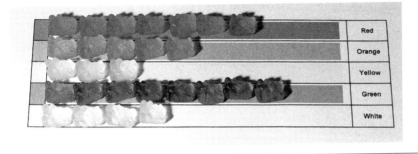

Gummy bears
histogram

FIGURE 1.9

possible way, so the typical teacher dismisses the answer because it is not convincing. This dismissal does not occur when the responses of "10," or "3," or "52" are heard, because the teacher can construct in her own mind the way the child probably was thinking. However, the teacher finds it impossible to construct a method in her mind by which one can obtain the answer of "9." Does that make "9" wrong? This question is left for you.

Recognizing the Unexpected

Albert Einstein (1954) wrote:

NSES Content Standard F. Science in Personal and Social Perspectives: Science and Technology in Local Challenges

> It is in fact nothing short of a miracle that the modern methods of instruction have not yet entirely strangled the holy curiosity of inquiry . . . It is a very grave mistake to think that the enjoyment of seeing and searching can be promoted by means of coercion and a sense of duty.

New knowledge is produced as a result of new thinking—thinking that rejects the limitations of "right" and "wrong." Scientists doing science are not locked into right and wrong answers. Rather, they continually search for new and unexpected occurrences that do not fit previously conceived patterns. To illustrate this point, let us consider stories of some famous inventions and discoveries.

The telephone was developed from an accidental occurrence. Alexander Graham Bell and his associate, Thomas Watson, were experimenting with the possibility that a vibrating membrane might be made to produce changes in electric current similar to the way the human eardrum transmits vibrations to the hammer, anvil, and stirrup—the tiny sound-conducting bones in the inner ear. One day in 1875, Watson was working on the transmitting part of the apparatus while Bell was in another room listening at the receiving end. Suddenly, Bell heard a twang over the receiver. One of the springs in the transmitter had become stuck, and Watson had caused it to twang while trying to get it free, generating a small electric current that was transmitted along the wire to the receiver. This accident ultimately resulted in the development of the telephone (Evans, 1966).

The production of penicillin can be traced to a chance observation by Sir Alexander Fleming in 1928 that some airborne material, later shown to be mold, had contaminated **Petri dishes** of **culture medium** on which colonies of staphylococcal bacteria were growing, killing the bacteria (Macfarlane, 1984).

Jack St. Clair Kilby won half of the 2000 Nobel Prize in Physics for "his part in the invention and development of the integrated circuit, the chip" (Nobel e-Museum, 2000). This silicon microchip has made possible the development of the personal computer, cell phones, electronic toys, heart pacemakers, and thousands of other applications—even lavish fireworks displays! It has virtually defined the field of electronics. Kilby, an electrical engineer, was unable to take the advanced theoretical physics courses offered at MIT, because his application was rejected as a result of low math entrance exam scores. He says of his microchip invention that, because he had not received advanced education in theoretical physics, "I didn't know what everybody else considered impossible, so I didn't rule anything out" (Reid, 2001, p. 134).

NSES Teaching Standard E. Developing Learners who Reflect Intellectual Rigor and Attitudes Conducive to Science Learning

In each of these cases, the discovery was made because people were able to recognize the significance of something they had never seen before! This is one of the primary characteristics of scientists. New knowledge is not produced simply by committing old knowledge to memory, although some previous knowledge certainly is necessary as a foundation. New knowledge is produced by being able to observe what others have not observed, ask questions no one has thought to ask, try things no one has thought to try, make inferences no one has thought to make, sort things in ways no one has sorted them, and focus less on *right* answers and more on *sensible* answers. New knowledge is produced as the result of being able to *do* science.

Perception

NSES Professional Development Standard B. Integrating Knowledge of Science, Learning, Pedagogy, and Students

The way people make sense of a happening or an observation is a direct result of the way they perceive it.

1.3   **CONSTRUCTING YOUR IDEAS**

Meanings of a Word

Try this. Pick a word that is a little unusual but is known to everyone, and ask the rest of the class to write the first word that comes to mind. For example, you might ask the students to write the first thing that comes to mind when you say the word *jaguar.*

Responses might include "tiger," "animal," "car," "silver," "money," "rich," and "cat." Each response represents the initial association made with the word. Notice the different ways people in your class perceive the same stimulus.

1.4   CONSTRUCTING YOUR IDEAS

Meanings of Pairs of Words

Try this. Create pairs of words from the following list, and tell *why* you paired them:

ants — cats — monkeys — buildings —
plastic — rocks — bananas — tacks

Pair #1: _____ and _____

Why? _____

Pair #2: _____ and _____

Why? _____

Compare the responses of different members of your class. Who paired something with the word *monkeys?* Perhaps someone paired *bananas* with *monkeys,* because monkeys eat bananas. Perhaps someone else paired *rocks* with *monkeys,* because monkeys like to climb rocks. Did anyone pair *buildings* with *monkeys?* Who paired something with the word *cats?* A student once paired *tacks* with *cats,* because these words had four letters in common. How about other pairs? Different people perceive these words in different ways.

1.5   CONSTRUCTING YOUR IDEAS

Meanings of a Sentence

Try this. Read the following sentence aloud to a group of people, and ask them to write down the first thing that comes to mind:

There is a man at home with a mask,
and another man coming home.

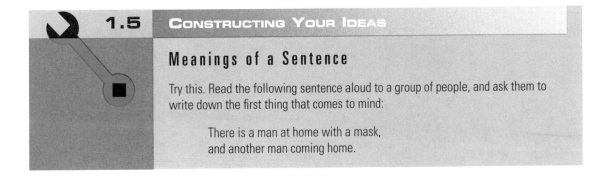

Some of the responses might include "robbers," "Halloween," "rape," and so on. One student wrote "baseball." All individuals in your group heard precisely the same thing (the sentence), yet they perceived the meaning in a variety of different ways.

Optical illusions also show that different people perceive the same stimulus in different ways. What do you see in Figure 1.10? Do other people see the same things?

Perception is "the detection and interpretation of sensory stimuli" (Solso, 1988, p. 6). It is the mental image formed when information is received through the senses and attended to. No two people, when exposed to the same stimulus, perceive it in the same way. This is because we all have different previous experiences, of different strengths, that influence how we perceive things. Different people in your class probably associated the word *jaguar* with different phenomena. Different people formed different pairs of words from the same list. Different people attached different meanings to the "man with a mask."

 Several "moving" optical illusions are available on the Student Book Companion Web Site.

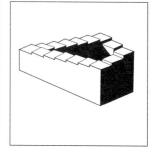 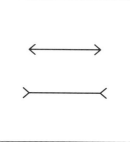 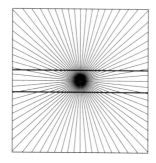

a. Are these lines straight?

b. Are these lines of different lengths?

c. Where is the top of the stairs?

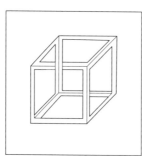 

d. Can you build this box?

e. How many legs does this elephant have?

f. Are the horizontal lines parallel? Or do they slope?

Optical illusions

FIGURE 1.10

If this is true with simple things like words, then it also is true with more complex concepts like *volcano eruption.* Ask a class of third graders to respond to the word *volcano,* and the children will talk about all sorts of things, from explosions, lava, and cones, to Mount St. Helens (if they have a relative who lives in Washington State) and Hawaii (if they have visited there, have relatives there, or have become interested in Hawaii). Is any one of these responses the *right* one? Is any one of these responses *wrong?* How about *jaguar?* Which response is right? Which is wrong? It would be very difficult, indeed, to say that any of these responses is either *right* or *wrong.* The best we can say is that the response is right *to the individual.* Students are likely to respond in very different ways from what we teachers expect. That does not make students' responses wrong; it simply makes these responses *theirs.*

Listening

It is a fundamental premise of this text that teachers of elementary science must listen to children—listen to their responses—so they can understand what *the children's* previous experiential bases are, what *their* perceptions are, how *they* are combining new information with their prior experiences and perceptions, and how *they* are constructing information. Listening to children involves tuning oneself into what the children are communicating. It involves being aware of children's responses, both verbal and nonverbal. It involves recognition of the much sought after "ah-hah's" and acknowledgement and understanding of children's perplexities and confusions. It involves continuous effort toward understanding what is going on in children's minds.

NSES Teaching Standard A. Inquiry-Based Program

Listening to children not only provides the teacher insight regarding what is going on in children's minds, it also can provide very interesting and unique results, such as totally unexpected but sensible responses and totally novel explanations that make sense but that you never thought of before.

Thus, we see that there are no "right" answers and no "wrong" answers. Instead, we see that the answers children offer are representative of the ways they are thinking. It is far more important for teachers to listen to children and elicit from them the reasons for their responses than it is for teachers to declare their responses either right or wrong.

As the cob said to Louis in *The Trumpet of the Swan,* "I assure you that you can pick up more information when you are listening than when you are talking" (White, 1970, p. 50).

THE PROCESSES OF SCIENCE

We have tried to make the point that it is better for children to learn how to do science than it is for them to learn the facts, concepts, and

NSES Content Standard G. History and Nature of Science: Nature of Science

theories that someone else has concluded—in other words, that it is better for children to learn to *do* science than to learn *about* science. What does it mean to *do science?* What do children do when they do science?

To answer these questions, we turn our attention to the *processes of science.*

1.6   CONSTRUCTING YOUR IDEAS

What Did You See on Your Way to School Today?

Try this. Take about one minute and think about what you saw on your way to school today. Then, write down one or two things, and share them in your class.

What did you see? Responses in other classes have included "traffic," "signal lights," "rain," "fog," and "an accident." However, many people have difficulty recalling what they saw on the way to school. Why is that? Certainly, there were countless stimuli. But we do not always pay attention to what we are seeing. We have not sharpened our powers of *observation.* Observations are made by employing our senses, and observing is the first and most fundamental of the *processes of science.*

The dictionary defines the term *process* as a series of actions or operations directed to some end (Merriam-Webster, 2003). In science, the processes are directed to the end of understanding a phenomenon, answering a question, developing a theory, or discovering more information about something. Twelve processes make up the scientific endeavor:

- Observing
- Classifying
- Communicating
- Measuring
- Predicting
- Inferring
- Identifying and controlling variables
- Formulating and testing hypotheses
- Interpreting data
- Defining operationally

- Experimenting
- Constructing models

Using the Processes of Science

Many of us committed to memory the *scientific method:* problem, hypothesis, experimentation, observation, data collection, and conclusion. Unfortunately, this is not the way scientists do science (Crowther et al., 2005). A scientist normally starts out with one or more observations or reflections that provoke one or more questions. It is these questions, arising from initial observations and reflections, that scientists experiment with in a variety of ways—not always (maybe not even usually) in the form of formally stated hypotheses.

The fact is that there is no single "right" way to do science. However, certain features do characterize good scientific inquiry. Scientists need to identify and control variables that they believe may contribute to an effect. They need to collect data through a variety of instruments that measure the various factors, and they need to interpret this data through inferring and sound reasoning. They often formulate and test hypotheses. They communicate the results of their inquiries, the methods used to obtain these results, and their interpretations of these results to others, either to be validated or to be challenged.

Do these characteristics of doing science sound familiar? They should, because they are the processes of science. Scientists do science through careful and appropriate application of the scientific processes to questions that were generated as a result of wondering about something. Science is the process of obtaining and verifying knowledge, and scientists do science through the processes of science. The resulting knowledge may be theoretical (subject to verification, validation, and revision), may involve discoveries of new facts (like the discovery of new elements or the discovery of a new species of insect), or when technologically developed, may result in new gizmos.

In short, learning to do science means learning to do the processes in inquiry situations. The processes are explored in detail in Chapter 3.

History of the Process Approach to Science Education

Let us take a short historical excursion to see how the processes of science came to be recognized as the foundation for scientific activity. In October 1957, the United States felt deeply humiliated by the launch of the Soviet satellite *Sputnik* (see Figure 1.11). American scientists had been working on launching an American satellite for a number of years, yet the Soviets were first. Great was the gnashing of teeth and long were the faces

NSES Content Standard G. History and Nature of Science: Nature of Science

of the scientists, the citizenry, and the government. The question was asked, "How did this happen? How did the United States, with all its technological capabilities, all its talent, and all its money, not achieve the goal of being first in space?" As so often happens, education took much of the blame. This was a turning point in science education.

Two years later, in 1959, Jerome Bruner, a renowned professor of psychology at Harvard, chaired the now-famous, 10-day Woods Hole conference in Woods Hole, Massachusetts. The conference was held at the request of the National Academy of Sciences, which had been examining the state of science education in America for several years. The intent of the conference was "not to institute a crash program, but rather to examine the fundamental processes involved in imparting to young students a sense of the substance and method of science" (Bruner, 1965, p. vii). The conference was unprecedented in that it dealt with education yet was chaired by a psychologist and was attended by experts in several scientific disciplines (psychology, mathematics, and cinematography) in addition to education. Among the participants were Robert Gagne, Bärbel Inhelder (representing Jean Piaget), and B. F. Skinner.

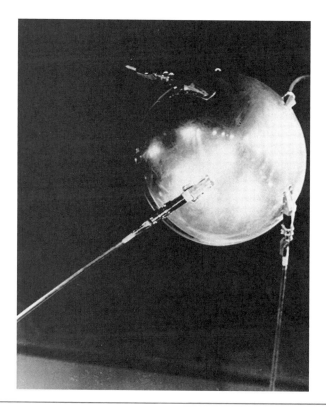

Sputnik (Courtesy National Aeronautics and Space Administration)

FIGURE 1.11

The question was asked, "How do scientists *do* science?" Although there had been brief forays into process-oriented science curricula before the conference, science education had largely consisted of imparting those facts, concepts, theories, and laws of chemistry, biology, physics, geology, astronomy, and other scientific fields deemed to be important for children to learn. At the Woods Hole conference, the participants reached the conclusion that students should learn science in the way science is done. Chemistry should be learned in the way chemists practice their profession, physics in the way physicists explore the physical world, and biology in the way biologists examine life processes.

These convictions manifested themselves in the expansion of bold new approaches to science education that focused more on process than on content. As the process approach to science education rippled to the lower grades, a host of new elementary science curriculum programs became available (see box titled "Hands-On Elementary Science Approaches of the 1960s"). These were hands-on programs that encouraged students to predict and experiment first and to conclude later. This approach was in direct contrast to the verification model of laboratory "experiments" in which the teacher explained what was supposed to happen based on some theory or principle, then set the students to work on a carefully outlined laboratory activity designed to demonstrate that the theory or principle was correct.

For example, you may recall adding a drop of iodine to various food materials in biology class. You had already learned that iodine turns blue-black in the presence of starch and that this is the test for starch. So, in the laboratory activity, you were directed to place one drop of iodine on each of several foods, such as potato, sugar, cornstarch, and bread, and record the resulting color. Then, you were to record your conclusions, which in this case were that the potato, cornstarch, and bread contained starch. In essence, you *verified* what someone else had already concluded.

In time, educators began to dissect the ways scientists do science to find its roots. This resulted in the identification of the processes of science.

Because the processes of science are the fundamental building blocks of the scientific enterprise, it is essential that our children develop facility in these processes. Scientific facts and concepts are springboards for children to use as they explore the processes. Processes are mastered using content as the vehicle. For example, the process of *observing* can be learned using plants, animals, rocks, and moving objects. Children can learn to *classify* using leaves, pictures of seasons, shells, and minerals. They *communicate* the results of their scientific inquiries, *measure* items they use in their experiments, *predict* what would happen if a plant were deprived of light, and *infer* why soil is composed of many different things.

Once again, a fundamental premise of this text is that it is far more important for children to learn the process skills than to learn facts. In other

NSES Content Standard F. Science in Personal and Social Perspectives: Personal Health words, it is far more important that they learn to *do* science than learn *about* science.

HANDS-ON ELEMENTARY SCIENCE APPROACHES OF THE 1960s

In the new hands-on elementary science approaches of the 1960s, children were led through a series of activities to make discoveries for themselves. The whole idea was for children to master the processes of science—to learn how to *do* science. These new science programs rapidly replaced the former content-oriented programs. They became the solution to the perceived deterioration of science knowledge and scientific expertise of America's youth.

Notable among the programs that fostered process-oriented inquiry science education were Elementary Science Study (ESS) and Science Curriculum Improvement Study (SCIS).

The Elementary Science Study program was a hands-on discovery approach to elementary science education. Many units were developed to foster children's development of the scientific processes to guide their own investigations. Units ranged from "Growing Seeds," "Match and Measure," and "Primary Balancing," which were suitable for early elementary grades, to "Water Flow," "Mapping," and "Kitchen Physics," which were suitable for upper elementary grades. The emphasis was on free discovery, with the teacher facilitating each child's explorations of phenomena according to the child's needs, interests, and background. Teacher guides for the ESS units are available from Delta Education.

The Science Curriculum Improvement Study was developed through the efforts of Dr. Robert Karplus, a theoretical physicist at the University of California, Berkeley. He was dissatisfied with the textbook-based, content-oriented science instruction that his daughter and other children in elementary classrooms were receiving. He developed SCIS as an inquiry approach to science education that encouraged children to make their own observations and formulate their own conclusions in the same manner that scientists do science. Karplus and his colleagues with the SCIS project developed the now-famous "learning cycle" to guide teachers in facilitating children's inquiries (see Figure 1.12). Grounded in the constructivist approach to education, the learning cycle is a three-phase approach to teaching: (1) exploration, (2) concept introduction, and (3) concept application (Karplus, 1977, 2000). In this widely used instructional model, students first explore a concept presented by the teacher to see what they can figure out (exploration phase). Their hands-on explorations are facilitated, but not directed, by the

A direct link to the home page of Delta Education is available on the Student Book Companion Web Site.

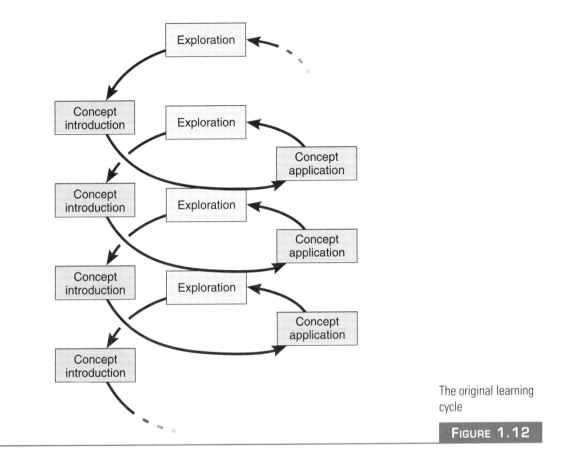

The original learning cycle

teacher. After children have had a chance to explore, their discoveries are used to derive the concept (concept introduction phase); the concept may be consolidated with current scientific knowledge under the teacher's direction. Finally, children are encouraged to investigate the usefulness and applications of the concept (concept application phase). Again, the teacher serves as facilitator more than director. These investigations logically lead to the exploration phase of a new concept, and the cycle begins again. There are many contemporary variations of the learning cycle, and some include an evaluation phase. One commonly used variation is the "5E" learning cycle developed by the Biological Sciences Curriculum Study (1989). Its sequence is as follows: (1) *E*ngage, (2) *E*xplore, (3) *E*xplain, (4) *E*laborate, and (5) *E*valuate. An updated version of SCIS (SCIS 3) is available from Delta Education.

OWNERSHIP OF KNOWLEDGE AND THOUGHT

NSES Professional Development Standard B. Integrating Knowledge of Science, Learning, Pedagogy, and Students

Science education, as all education, should lead to independent self-activity. It should empower individuals to think and act. (DeBoer, 1991, p. 249)

To be self-empowered, children must develop confidence in their thinking abilities. They must take ownership of both their knowledge and their thinking. Even before they enter school, children know a great deal of science, such as the properties of toys, the characteristics of seasons, the difference between heat and cold, what cooking does to food, and so on. They need to be told that they know a lot of science so that they can develop confidence and begin to take ownership of their abilities to learn.

Mystery Box

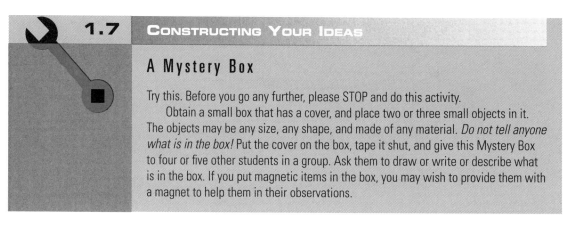

1.7 CONSTRUCTING YOUR IDEAS

A Mystery Box

Try this. Before you go any further, please STOP and do this activity.

Obtain a small box that has a cover, and place two or three small objects in it. The objects may be any size, any shape, and made of any material. *Do not tell anyone what is in the box!* Put the cover on the box, tape it shut, and give this Mystery Box to four or five other students in a group. Ask them to draw or write or describe what is in the box. If you put magnetic items in the box, you may wish to provide them with a magnet to help them in their observations.

A typical box might contain a 1-inch washer taped to the bottom of the box, a loose metal screw, and a small and irregularly shaped stone (see Figure 1.13). You may wish to include coins or marbles. *Do not put too many items in the box!*

What do you have to do to figure out what is in the box? Probably, you will shake it. You will tilt it—sometimes rapidly, sometimes very slowly, and sometimes at different angles. You will listen to what is happening inside as you tilt it. You will try to balance it. You will try the magnet to see if there is anything magnetic inside it. Can you feel a magnetic force? You have been using the sense of feel (magnetic pull), sound (listening to what happens when you tilt the box), and sight (checking for balance). What other senses can you use? Try smelling it. Any odors? As you proceed with your investigation, you will get more and more refined in focus. You will discuss your ideas with others in your group—arguing, defending, changing your mind in response to the input of others, and so on.

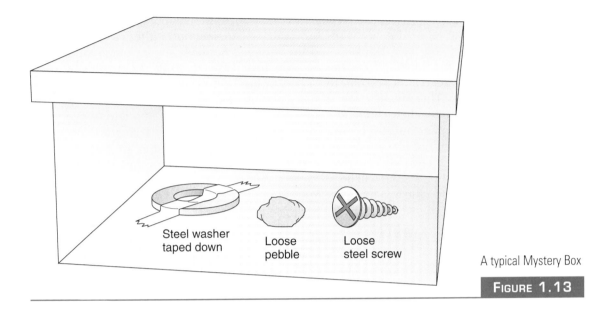

Steel washer taped down

Loose pebble

Loose steel screw

A typical Mystery Box

FIGURE 1.13

Notice that you used several processes in this activity: observation, classification (identifying objects as magnetic or nonmagnetic), communication (with members in your group), maybe some measurement (locations of permanent objects, relative strength of magnetic pull), prediction, inference, formulation and testing of hypotheses (if you compared the magnetic strength of known objects with the magnetic strength of objects in the box), interpretation of data, and possibly, construction of models.

Now, you can make some preliminary generalizations about what is inside the box. Let us refine these conclusions. How big is each item? What shape? How thick? What color?

Keep pursuing your investigation. In an elementary science classroom, the teacher might keep the box or boxes in the science center for several weeks, continually challenging the children to refine their conclusions about what is in the box. Children would work in cooperative groups, challenging each other's perceptions and asking for reasons why they inferred what they did.

Eventually, you will have formulated your very best idea. Are you *right?* How sure are you? What is your confidence percentage? How could you increase your confidence percentage? You could make a model—create an identical box with the same things in yours that you think are inside the Mystery Box—and compare the two boxes carefully to see if they exhibit the same characteristics.

Your classmates will probably have several notions regarding what is in the box. Who is right? Who is wrong? Remember, the box is closed.

"Rightness" and "Wrongness" take on different perspectives—they are no longer functions of correctness of answer but, rather, are the function of your best thinking and the way you interrelate your observations and your thinking to form your conclusions. Each student's conclusion is accepted as representative of his or her best thinking.

This Mystery Box activity also is analogous to children's minds. You, the teacher, can never know with certainty what is in a child's mind. You can ask questions. You can listen. You can ask for clarification, drawings, logic, observations, and personal feelings in an effort to discover what and how children are thinking. However, your conclusion as to what is in a child's mind will be no more accurate than your conclusion as to what is inside the Mystery Box. You can only *infer*.

Ownership

Should you open the boxes? Suppose they were sealed shut, never to be opened! How would you feel? Frustrated? Cheated? You would never know if you were right or wrong. If you do not open the boxes, you will be required to rely on your own powers of observation, your own reasoning and inferring, and your own conclusions drawn from your own thinking and others' input. You will be forced to *validate* your conclusions from your own thinking. You will be forced to *assume ownership* of your observations, thoughts, and conclusions.

Suppose, however, that you know you will be allowed to open the box at some point in time. Suddenly, *your* thinking is devalued. Instead of observing and inferring and reasoning, you are trying to "guess." Your motivation becomes comparing your answer with the "right" answer, not reaching your own conclusion. There is a "right" answer, and you compare your answer with it. If you guessed correctly, great! If not, oh well!

Should you open the box? Do you have faith in the ability of the scientific processes you used in this activity to provide a "best" answer? Each class will have to decide for itself. As you are deciding, please cite your arguments.

Valuing Children's Thinking

1.8   CONSTRUCTING YOUR IDEAS

Whose Knowledge Is Valued?

Here is a question for you to wrestle with. Is it more important that elementary school children value the teacher's knowledge or their own?

Many students answer "their own." This response comes from a belief that one of the primary jobs of the teacher is to help children think for themselves. But what about the teacher? Isn't the teacher's thinking more valid than the children's? Doesn't the teacher have the benefit of many years of education in learning how to think? Shouldn't the teacher teach the children how to think? Shouldn't the teacher encourage the children to emulate correct thinking? These are questions for you to ponder.

If you truly believe it is important for children to take ownership of their own knowledge, then you will be asking how teachers can foster children's beliefs that their thinking is valuable.

Let us digress briefly. The typical elementary teacher asks between 64 and 348 questions a day in elementary school (Orlich et al., 1985). The reason is that questioning, as a teaching-learning strategy, stimulates student thinking, enables teachers to better understand what children are thinking, and helps teachers to know where to provide clarification.

Consider a typical series of questions a kindergarten teacher might ask in introducing a lesson on animals:

"Name one animal."

"Name another kind of animal."

"Name an animal that flies."

"Name an animal that has four legs."

"Name an animal that lives at home."

"Name an animal that lives in the forest."

"Name an animal that lives in water."

"Name an animal with fur."

It is easy to see how a teacher can fit 348 such questions in the course of a day.

Let us take a look at another set of questions. Each of these teacher questions implies there are right answers and that any other answers are wrong:

"Name an animal that flies."

"Bird?"

"Right!"

"Duck?"

"Right!"

"Dog?"

"Wrong!"

"Name an animal that has four legs."

"Dog?"

"Right!"

"Spider?"

"Wrong!"

"Name an animal that lives at home."

"Cat?"

"Right!"

"Lion?"

"Wrong!"

You get the idea: For each question, there are Right answers and there are Wrong answers. Who knows the Right answers? The teacher, of course. Note that in the above scenario, the children answered in a questioning tone of voice, and the teacher told them whether they were right or wrong. Teachers indicate "right" or "wrong" answers in a variety of subtle ways, with comments like "Oh, really?" "That's a good answer," "Thank you for answering," and so on until, finally, a right answer comes along. Then, the teacher says "Right," or "That's what I was looking for," or "The other answers were good ones, but that is the one I wanted to hear."

In this type of situation, it is the teacher who owns the knowledge. The teacher encourages the children to compare their answers (maybe right and maybe wrong) with the teacher's (always right), thereby giving the children the unmistakable notion that their job is to supply the answers the teacher wants to hear. The teacher owns the knowledge. The teacher is in charge. It is the teacher's thinking that is valued. The same thing happens in hands-on settings involving children doing activities whose end results are already known, where it is the job of the child to come up with the result the teacher expects. A teacher comment like "I don't think that's quite right; try it again and see what you get" translates to "You haven't yet gotten the result I wanted you to get."

How can that be reversed? As we will see in Chapter 5, using Bloom's higher cognitive levels in questioning promotes discussion, whereas using Bloom's lower cognitive levels leads to right and wrong answers (Bloom et al., 1956). In addition, using **open-ended questions** with longer wait time and longer think time rather than **closed questions** that require only short answers goes a long way toward fostering children's beliefs that their own thinking is important. But, of course, you can't ask 348 questions a day in that manner. (You will explore the use of informal and formal questioning as a method of assessing children's comprehensions in Chapter 8.)

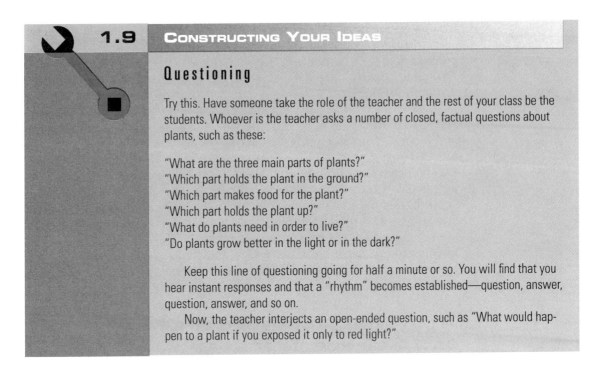

1.9   **CONSTRUCTING YOUR IDEAS**

Questioning

Try this. Have someone take the role of the teacher and the rest of your class be the students. Whoever is the teacher asks a number of closed, factual questions about plants, such as these:

"What are the three main parts of plants?"
"Which part holds the plant in the ground?"
"Which part makes food for the plant?"
"Which part holds the plant up?"
"What do plants need in order to live?"
"Do plants grow better in the light or in the dark?"

Keep this line of questioning going for half a minute or so. You will find that you hear instant responses and that a "rhythm" becomes established—question, answer, question, answer, and so on.

Now, the teacher interjects an open-ended question, such as "What would happen to a plant if you exposed it only to red light?"

The response to the last question is slower to come. First, there are a few "silly" responses; that is because people don't want to interrupt the rhythm and because they want to fill the awkward silence required for thinking with some sort of sound. However, most students will remain silent as they try to gather their thoughts. After a suitable wait period (say, 15 seconds), the teacher again asks for the responses and listens to them without comment. Students will offer their best thinking on the subject, thereby taking ownership of their responses.

When asking questions of children, if you, the teacher, resist the temptation to offer "words of great wisdom" (or, better yet, if you don't know the answer to the question), the children will have to work it out for themselves. They will own the thought processes as well as the conclusion. They will be well on their way to learning that their knowledge is valuable and is valued by the teacher.

Another way to encourage children's ownership of their own thought processes and knowledge is to reduce the number of affirmations, such as "right," "good try," "wonderful," and so on, that are offered, because these responses lead the child to believe that responses are given for the teacher's judgment. To foster children's ownership of their thinking, you can replace these responses with simple statements thanking children for their responses or with nonverbal responses, such as smiles or head nods. Responses to children's answers that foster the highest degree of ownership are those that probe the children's thinking: "Why did you say that?" "How do you know?" "Give an example of what you just said," "Can you add to Jane's response?" "Do you agree?" "Do you disagree?" "What would happen if . . ." "Tell us how you came up with that idea," "Can you explain your thinking?"

During this course, you will construct a way of teaching elementary science that places ownership of thought as well as scientific facts, concepts, and theories squarely in the laps (or heads) of your children—a *process-oriented inquiry methodology*. Under the guidance of the teacher, children ask their own questions, devise their own ways to explore their questions, and develop their own answers to their questions. It is not within the scope of this book to discuss at length how children learn, but if children are to learn and retain anything, they must own and value what *they* do, not what *we* do. Our job is to lead them to their own sound thinking. We must set a tone in the class that lets all children know their answers are at least as important as anyone else's—including the teacher's.

ATTITUDES ABOUT SCIENCE AND SCIENCE TEACHING

NSES Professional
Development Standard
C. Lifelong Learning

All people have preconceived notions shaped by their own prior experiences and learning. Some of these notions are congruent with generally accepted knowledge, and some are not. Some are positive, and some are negative. Many teachers have preconceived ideas about the ability of children to learn and about the amount of scientific information our children possess before coming to school. Preconceived ideas about the natural world strongly influence what people learn; we will discuss this phenomenon and its implications for teaching elementary science in Chapter 4. Similarly, a teacher's preconceptions about the ability of children to learn strongly influence the way he or she teaches.

Teacher Beliefs

Combs (1993) has investigated what makes good "helpers" (which include teachers as well as counselors, clergy, nurses, therapists, and the like). He has concluded that what makes an effective helper is *not* knowledge and is *not* methodology. Rather, the effectiveness of a helping professional is a result primarily of the *beliefs* of the individual. Teachers, who are helping professionals, behave in terms of their beliefs. Combs identified five areas of beliefs:

1. *Beliefs about the kind of data to which we should be tuned:* Good helpers tune into data concerned with *people* questions; poor helpers tune into data concerned with *things* questions.

2. *Beliefs about what people are like:* Good helpers believe people are *able;* poor helpers *doubt* that people are able.

3. *Beliefs about self (self-concept):* Good helpers see the self in essentially *positive* ways and are self-actualizing; poor helpers see the self in essentially *negative* ways.

4. *Beliefs about purpose (what is truly important):* Good helpers see their purpose to be essentially a *freeing* behavior; poor helpers see their purpose to be essentially a *controlling* behavior.

5. *Beliefs about methods:* Good helpers use *self-revealing* methods; poor helpers use *self-concealing* methods.

Thus, we see that teachers' beliefs about science, about science teaching, and about children's ability to succeed in science strongly influence their teaching of science.

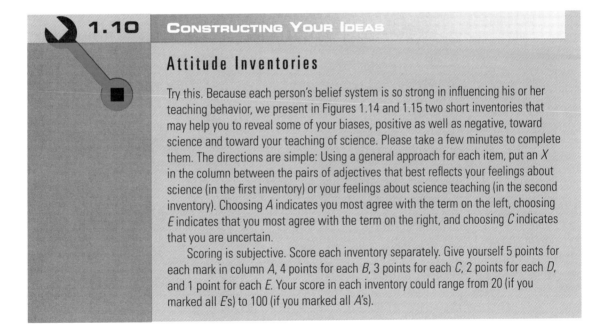

1.10 CONSTRUCTING YOUR IDEAS

Attitude Inventories

Try this. Because each person's belief system is so strong in influencing his or her teaching behavior, we present in Figures 1.14 and 1.15 two short inventories that may help you to reveal some of your biases, positive as well as negative, toward science and toward your teaching of science. Please take a few minutes to complete them. The directions are simple: Using a general approach for each item, put an *X* in the column between the pairs of adjectives that best reflects your feelings about science (in the first inventory) or your feelings about science teaching (in the second inventory). Choosing *A* indicates you most agree with the term on the left, choosing *E* indicates that you most agree with the term on the right, and choosing *C* indicates that you are uncertain.

Scoring is subjective. Score each inventory separately. Give yourself 5 points for each mark in column *A*, 4 points for each *B*, 3 points for each *C*, 2 points for each *D*, and 1 point for each *E*. Your score in each inventory could range from 20 (if you marked all *E*'s) to 100 (if you marked all *A*'s).

These inventories may give you a general idea about your current attitudes toward science and the teaching of science. If you scored on the positive side (80–100), you are well on your way to enjoying teaching elementary science. If your score was low, indicating negative attitudes, you may want to look at what you can do to develop a more positive general attitude. You are the only one who knows; no one can tell you what your attitude is.

MY ATTITUDES ABOUT SCIENCE

	A	B	C	D	E	
1. GOOD	___	___	___	___	___	BAD
2. PLEASURABLE	___	___	___	___	___	PAINFUL
3. MEANINGFUL	___	___	___	___	___	MEANINGLESS
4. IMPORTANT	___	___	___	___	___	UNIMPORTANT
5. POSITIVE	___	___	___	___	___	NEGATIVE
6. SIMPLE	___	___	___	___	___	COMPLEX
7. BENEFICIAL	___	___	___	___	___	HARMFUL
8. INTERESTING	___	___	___	___	___	BORING
9. EASY	___	___	___	___	___	DIFFICULT
10. OBJECTIVE	___	___	___	___	___	SUBJECTIVE
11. SAFE	___	___	___	___	___	DANGEROUS
12. USEFUL	___	___	___	___	___	USELESS
13. EFFORTLESS	___	___	___	___	___	LABORIOUS
14. ORDERLY	___	___	___	___	___	DISORDERLY
15. COMFORTABLE	___	___	___	___	___	UNCOMFORTABLE
16. VALUABLE	___	___	___	___	___	WORTHLESS
17. STIMULATING	___	___	___	___	___	MONOTONUS
18. COMFORTING	___	___	___	___	___	THREATENING
19. PRODUCTIVE	___	___	___	___	___	UNPRODUCTIVE
20. UNCLUTTERED	___	___	___	___	___	CLUTTERED

Inventory of attitudes toward science

FIGURE 1.14

You also may want to look at individual items. Which ones did you mark *D* or *E?* Which ones were you unsure of, thus marking a *C?* These may indicate areas to which you might want to pay attention as you develop your competence in teaching elementary science—fears, likes, dislikes, areas of discomfort, and so on. Using a different survey, Cobern and Loving (2002) showed that preservice elementary teachers had mixed beliefs about the value of science. The students sampled believed science is a positive force for public health and the economy and supported the theme of *Science for All.* However, they were a little less certain about

MY ATTITUDES ABOUT ME TEACHING SCIENCE

	A	B	C	D	E	
1. SAFE	_____	_____	_____	_____	_____	DANGEROUS
2. HAPPY	_____	_____	_____	_____	_____	SAD
3. COMFORTABLE	_____	_____	_____	_____	_____	UNCOMFORTABLE
4. SUCCESSFUL	_____	_____	_____	_____	_____	UNSUCCESSFUL
5. CLEAN	_____	_____	_____	_____	_____	DIRTY
6. ORDERLY	_____	_____	_____	_____	_____	DISORDERLY
7. USEFUL	_____	_____	_____	_____	_____	USELESS
8. CONTENTED	_____	_____	_____	_____	_____	DISCONTENTED
9. PLEASURABLE	_____	_____	_____	_____	_____	PAINFUL
10. IMPORTANT	_____	_____	_____	_____	_____	UNIMPORTANT
11. REFRESHED	_____	_____	_____	_____	_____	WEARY
12. ORGANIZED	_____	_____	_____	_____	_____	DISORGANIZED
13. BENEFICIAL	_____	_____	_____	_____	_____	HARMFUL
14. OPTIMISTIC	_____	_____	_____	_____	_____	PESSIMISTIC
15. EAGER	_____	_____	_____	_____	_____	INDIFFERENT
16. STRONG	_____	_____	_____	_____	_____	WEAK
17. GOOD	_____	_____	_____	_____	_____	BAD
18. SUFFICIENT	_____	_____	_____	_____	_____	INSUFFICIENT
19. INFLUENTIAL	_____	_____	_____	_____	_____	UNINFLUENTIAL
20. STIMULATING	_____	_____	_____	_____	_____	MONOTONOUS

Inventory of attitudes toward teaching science

FIGURE 1.15

the role of science relative to the environment. Remember what Combs said: The most important factor influencing people to be good in the helping professions is their beliefs. These beliefs are manifested in attitudes. The successful elementary science teacher enters the field with a positive attitude and a truly open mind.

Often, discovering your current beliefs about science and the teaching of science and being aware that you do have preconceived beliefs about the natural world are all that is necessary to open new areas of inquiry to you.

I did not start out in the professional world as a teacher; I began in sales and customer service. For the first four years of my teaching career, I was a teacher in a self-contained, fifth-grade classroom. I taught the whole curriculum, including science. As a student, I did not like science. Now, as an adult, I realize that this lack of love for science was due to the negative experiences I had throughout my schooling. Being told I was "wrong" in my thinking brought on these negative experiences. When I knew I would have to teach science, I was petrified. I did not feel that I had enough background knowledge to teach science effectively.

What I have realized since is that children naturally seek answers to problems. Once a teacher relinquishes the prescriptive control of "cookbook" science and *truly* allows the students to explore, she will see amazing things. Students, encouraged through inquiry teaching, begin to find the concepts on their own. The concepts they discover are the very concepts the teacher wants them to learn. In inquiry teaching, students take ownership of their learning. Journaling is one technique I find necessary in inquiry teaching. The teacher uses the students' journals to help her make sense of how the students are thinking. This also promotes students taking ownership of their learning. For example, a student may not be able to tell a teacher in terms of technical vocabulary that the system that he has built is a parallel circuit, but he *can* provide a description of the circuit that was built and how it is different from the other circuits. Then, the teacher can assign the proper vocabulary terms and definitions, again helping the student to take ownership of the learning experiences.

Through this natural inquiry of science learning, teachers are guiding students to discoveries, not discovering for them. It is more important to ask the kinds of questions that will allow students to find their own answers and, in turn, ask more questions than it is to provide textbook answers. This creates a continuous style of natural learning.

Good science teaching is not about "knowing it all." It is about how you get your students to learn successfully on their own with minimal guidance and direction. It is truly an amazing experience to watch students take ownership of their own learning!

Stefanie Gerron

Fourth- and Fifth-Grade Teacher
Snow Heights Elementary School
North Richland Hills, Texas

METAPHORS

One last comment about previous beliefs involves the use of **metaphors**. Researchers have looked at metaphors and teachers' latent beliefs about teaching as indicated by the metaphors they choose to characterize their role as a teacher (BouJaoudi, 2000; Munby, 1986; Pajares, 1992; Pittman & O'Neill, 2001; Tobin, 1990). For example, teachers characterizing themselves as "captain of the ship" may be very strong leaders and reluctant to transfer responsibility for learning to children.

NSES Professional Development Standard C. Lifelong Learning

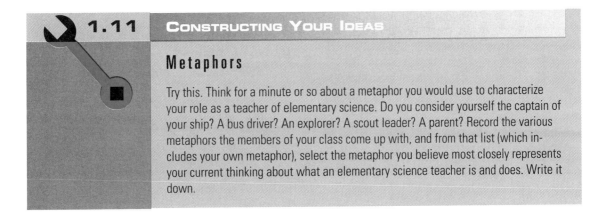

1.11 CONSTRUCTING YOUR IDEAS

Metaphors

Try this. Think for a minute or so about a metaphor you would use to characterize your role as a teacher of elementary science. Do you consider yourself the captain of your ship? A bus driver? An explorer? A scout leader? A parent? Record the various metaphors the members of your class come up with, and from that list (which includes your own metaphor), select the metaphor you believe most closely represents your current thinking about what an elementary science teacher is and does. Write it down.

Refer to the metaphor you chose frequently during this course; see if you want to change it. This may be one of the better indicators of how you are constructing the content of the course.

RESEARCH IN SCIENCE EDUCATION

Educational research takes many forms and serves many functions. Its primary purpose is to inform the educator on issues of best practice. Research in science education serves the same purpose as general educational research and essentially centers on issues of curriculum, methodology, assessment, and the learner.

NSES Professional Development Standard D. Coherent and Integrated Programs

Much research is referred to in this text; the student is advised to study the referenced material, question its **validity** and its application to the classroom, and become a proactive consumer of the research. Questioning is the key to intelligent consumption of research. Research provides a springboard for discussion and a catalyst for questions.

Conclusion

The goal of the first chapter has been to promote your personal inquiry into the "best" ways of teaching science to elementary children. You have examined a number of issues and have drawn tentative conclusions. You have started to ask important questions about content, process, goals, outcomes, and methodology of elementary science teaching. As you progress through this course, make it your goal to formulate answers to these questions, resolve your concerns, and develop a system of science education that meets the needs of today's children as we prepare them to live in the twenty-first century. No one can do this for you; to try to do so would be to do the same thing we are suggesting you *not* do with children—pump them full of previously digested information. You have to make up your own mind; you have to construct this business of elementary science education so that it makes sense to you.

The rest of the text will help you in your quest.

CHAPTER 1

Additional Questions for Discussion

1. How much science do you need to know to teach science?

2. How much known science do children in elementary grades need to learn?

3. In his book *Horace's Compromise,* Sizer (1985) states, "Good teachers and wise students know how to separate performance (you flunked) from person (you're O.K.). Making a child feel stupid is stupid and cruel, but pretending that $2 + 2 = 5$ in order to massage the student's ego is cruel, and dishonest in addition" (p. 175). Contrast this proposition with the constructivist viewpoint of no right answers and no wrong answers suggested in this chapter.

Internet Activities

There are many references on the Internet that deal with plate tectonics, DNA, inter-planetary spacecraft, the human genome project, and other exciting and important projects. Use the search engines to find additional information about these topics. You can find information about other new scientific work by searching "science" and then narrowing your search in accordance with your interests.

CHAPTER 2
SCIENCE EDUCATION TODAY

The task of science is to both extend the range of our experience and reduce it to order.

Niels Bohr, in G. Holton & H. D. Roller, *Foundations of Modern Physical Science* (Reading, MA: Addison-Wesley, 1958), p. 214

You have been exploring a number of factors related to teaching science to elementary school children. You have considered the propositions that it is better for children to learn to *do* science through mastering the processes than to learn *about* science, that scientific content is the vehicle through which the processes can be taught, and that children should learn science in a manner similar to the way scientists actually do science.

Thus far, we have not said very much about science itself or about how scientists do science. So, in this chapter, you will inquire into the nature of science—the scientific enterprise, products, applications, and attitudes—and you will explore goals and objectives that are appropriate for the quality elementary science program.

THE NATURE OF SCIENCE

2.1   CONSTRUCTING YOUR IDEAS

Portraying Scientists and Science

Try this. In groups, draw a picture of a scientist or of some other scene that portrays your feeling of what science is. Using the picture as a guide, describe to the class your group's feeling about science.

NSES Content
Standard G. History
and Nature of Science:
Nature of Science

Directions for the "Draw-a-Scientist" activity and rubrics for scoring can be found on Web sites that are linked at the Student Book Companion Web Site.

What we know today as *science* was originally called *philosophy*. The word *philosophy* was coined during the time of Aristotle from two words, *philos* (love) and *sophia* (wisdom). Thus, the term *philosophy* literally means "love of wisdom." The term *science* comes from the Latin word *scientia* (to know). The dictionary grounds its primary definition of *science* in the Latin derivative: "A state of knowing; knowledge as distinguished from ignorance or misunderstanding" (Merriam-Webster, 2003).

The National Science Teachers Association (NSTA) describes science as "characterized by the systematic gathering of information through various forms of direct and indirect information and the testing of this information. . ." (National Science Teachers Association, 2000). Alan Leshner, Chief Executive Officer of the American Association for the Advancement of Science (AAAS), says, "The purpose of science is to answer our questions about the nature of the world—whether we like the answers or not" (Perkins-Gough, 2006, p. 9). This means that "whatever science content you are teaching, you are also teaching about the scientific enterprise" (ibid., p. 15).

The nature of science is better described by its components rather than by a concise definition (Crowther, Lederman, & Lederman, 2005); the nature of the scientific enterprise includes not only its methods, rigor, and beliefs but also its limits, perils, and pitfalls (Perkins-Gough, 2006). In this section, you will investigate major components of the nature of science.

Characteristics of the Scientific Enterprise

NSES Content
Standard G. History
and Nature of Science:
Nature of Science

Science has several unique characteristics. In the quality elementary science program, children embrace these characteristics during their inquiries and investigations as they do science.

1. *Science rejects authority and authoritarianism.* Many people believe the primary work of scientists is to show that hypotheses are true. Although this occurs in many laboratories, most scientific work tries to *disprove* hypotheses rather than to prove hypotheses correct. If, over a period of time, no one succeeds in disproving a given hypothesis, it becomes increasingly acceptable.[1]

A good example of this involves the controversy surrounding the work of Jean Piaget, who studied a very limited sample of subjects— namely, children who attended private schools in Switzerland. Many researchers cast aspersions on Piaget's work, because the sample was not representative of the population to which he generalized his conclusions. However, as other researchers tried to *disprove* Piaget's theories, they found they were unable to do so. It is this lack of contradiction, as much as the affirmation of the theories in subsequent studies, that has led to wide acceptance of his theories. (See Chapter 4 for a discussion of Piagetian principles applied in the elementary science classroom.)

2. *Science is honest.* Scientists publish their research findings, and these publications encourage others to duplicate experiments and either disprove or fail to disprove the hypotheses. A good example of this occurred in 1989, when scientists from two universities announced their research on developing a process to produce cold fusion.

Fusion is the nuclear reaction that provides the energy in the sun. Fusion occurs when the nuclei of four hydrogen atoms combine to form the nucleus of a single helium atom (see Figure 2.1). In this process, a great deal of energy is released, because it takes less energy to hold together the nucleus of a single helium atom than it takes to hold together the nuclei of each of the four hydrogen atoms. The process of fusion would be an ideal source of energy for automobiles, power plants, and factories, because it uses hydrogen, an element found in water and thus plentiful on earth, to produce enormous amounts of energy. However, the reaction is too radioactive and too hot for these applications. It would be extremely desirable, therefore, to develop a safer system for fusion, a system termed "cold fusion."

Several university researchers who had been investigating cold fusion announced they had discovered methods for producing nuclear fusion at room temperatures and provided details of their experimental procedures. However, as other researchers tried to develop experiments to duplicate the systems described by the university researchers, they were unable to do so. It was with some embarrassment that the universities retracted the scientists' original findings, for it became apparent their research had been flawed (Wade, 1993, p. 477). Scientists are continuing to work at developing cold fusion systems that can be used as energy sources for automobiles and other practical applications by harnessing the potential energy that hydrogen releases in fusion reactions.

 A direct link to the online newsletter, *Cold Fusion Times,* which reports advances in cold fusion research, is available on the Student Book Companion Web Site.

3. *Science rejects supernatural explanations as primary explanations for observed phenomena.* Examples include witchcraft, astrology,

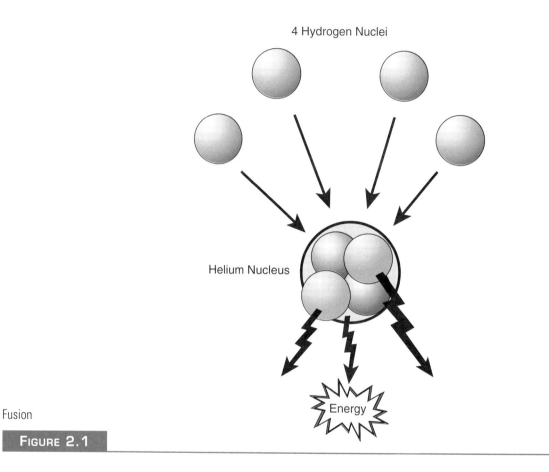

4 Hydrogen Nuclei

Helium Nucleus

Energy

Fusion

FIGURE 2.1

alien abductions, extrasensory perception (ESP), plant emotions, bio-rhythms, and alternative medicine such as magnetic therapy. Often referred to as *pseudoscience,* these beliefs lack the support of systematic observational data and frequently have been arrived at through faulty reasoning or poor scientific methodology. Significant proportions of Americans hold pseudoscientific beliefs. Although the numbers declined between 2001 and 2005, belief in pseudoscience continues to be wide-spread, with at least 25 percent of Americans expressing a belief in astrol-ogy, half believing in the existence of ESP, and 30 percent believing in the existence of UFOs and that aliens have landed on earth (National Science Board, 2006). Walker, Hoekstra, and Vogl (in *Skeptic* 2002) suggest that "the inability [to evaluate pseudoscientific claims] stems in part from the way that science is traditionally presented to students: "Students are taught what to think but not how to think" (p. 2). Leshner (in Perkins-Gough, 2006) says that if people understood the nature of science, they could avoid these kinds of pitfalls—that understanding the nature of sci-ence is more important than mastering its details.

Science searches for natural rather than supernatural explanations. For scientific breakthroughs to be accepted, they must be tested against existing knowledge. However, even though pseudoscientific phenomena have not been successfully subjected to the rigors of scientific inquiry, this does not make them "wrong." Many of our most significant scientific discoveries were first met with skepticism. A great deal of current scientific activity is being devoted to finding the truth about the fringe areas (Herbert, 2001).

Carl Sagan (1995) offers a "baloney detection kit," a set of "tools for skeptical thinking," that shows how the characteristics of the scientific enterprise are applied in reasoned and skeptical thinking about such phenomena as UFOs, extrasensory perception, and horoscopes (pp. 210–211). This "kit" is extremely useful in establishing at least tentative validity in any scientific endeavor.

4. *Science is skeptical and rejects the notion that it is possible to attain absolute truth.* Scientists accept that in the natural world, some degree of uncertainty will always exist. Even Newton's laws of motion, once considered to be truths, are subject to a degree of skepticism; indeed, Einstein's theories of relativity have shown exceptions to the Newtonian laws.

5. *Science is parsimonious.* Occam's Razor says, "Entities shall not be multiplied beyond necessity," meaning that the simpler explanation is preferred to the more complex explanation. In science, if several different explanations for an observation are possible, the simplest one is chosen. **Parsimony** is evident throughout science: Newton's laws are very simple (although not simplistic) statements of how things move. For example, Newton's first law states that an object at rest stays at rest, and that an object in motion stays in motion in a straight line, unless that object is acted on by an external, unbalanced force. Einstein's general theory of relativity has been reduced to a single, simple, and famous equation: $e = mc^2$. Darwin's theory of evolution is reduced to a simple and very descriptive phrase: *survival of the fittest.*

6. *Science seeks consistency.* Science presumes that the things and events in the natural world occur in consistent patterns and that the basic rules are the same everywhere in the universe. For example, scientists believe that everything in the universe is composed of the same elements that are found on earth.

Teaching the Nature of Science

The nature of science includes concepts that are abstract for many students—concepts that they do not seem to understand until they actually do activities and see the concepts for themselves. Akerson (2005) found that the nature of science needs to be taught explicitly, and he

NSES Content
Standard G. History
and Nature of Science:
Nature of Science

recommends that this teaching should be included within the context of inquiry. Teachers need to ask students whether their results mean that their inquiries are complete or if more work can be done, emphasizing the usefulness of further investigation to either affirm or, perhaps, change the claims the students made on the basis of the evidence they gathered. Matkins and Bell (2007) also found that the nature of science is best taught within the context of subject matter inquiries through questioning opinions, introducing controversial topics such as global climate change, showing the connections between process skills and the nature of science, and discussing the interpretation of evidence in inquiries.

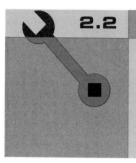

2.2   CONSTRUCTING YOUR IDEAS

Teaching the Nature of Science

The National Science Education Standards call for students to study the nature and history of science so that they develop an understanding of science as a human endeavor. In a group, sketch out a lesson you might teach that focuses on these objectives.

Products of Science

We defined *science* as a process by which knowledge is produced. Thus, the scientific enterprise is comprised of at least two factors—processes and products. Let us look at the products.

The products of science include the applications, facts, concepts, theories, laws, and attitudes that occur as a result of doing science—that is, scientific content.

Applications as Products of Science

NSES Content
Standard E. Science and
Technology: Understanding About Science and
Technology

Among the more conspicuous products of science are the applications—jet planes, interplanetary rockets, video cell phones, blackberries, plasma TV screens, remote controls, computers, fax machines, frost-resistant strawberries, cloned plants and animals, laser surgery, and countless other advances that we so often take for granted (see Figure 2.2). These products are the outcomes of the interaction between scientific thought and theory and the technological applications devised by engineers and inventors. They are the result of the interface between science and technology, a distinction that is becoming increasingly difficult to make.

Technology can be described as the means by which humans control or modify their environment, and it can be traced to Paleolithic cultures, when humans shaped tools out of stone. In increasingly sophisticated

Modern gizmos

FIGURE 2.2

ways, humankind has been using technological enterprise to change our world to accommodate our needs—better stone tools, new metal alloys, devices for agriculture, transportation, health, and communication, and countless other technological advances.[2]

As we have said, products of science include not only applications but also facts, concepts, theories, laws, and attitudes. Let us investigate how children can construct these scientific products as a result of doing science.

Scientific Facts

Here are some notions considered to be facts:

1. The earth rotates on its axis once about every 24 hours.

2. Seventy-six percent of all animal species are insects.

NSES Content
Standard G. History
and Nature of Science:
Nature of Science

3. Green plants contain chlorophyll in the cells of their leaves.

4. Water molecules are made of hydrogen and oxygen atoms.

5. A freely falling object accelerates toward earth at the rate of 9.8 meters per second every second.

6. The temperature at which pure water freezes is 0° Celsius or 32° Fahrenheit.

As you can tell, a fact is a piece of information that has actual existence and usually is concrete and observable.

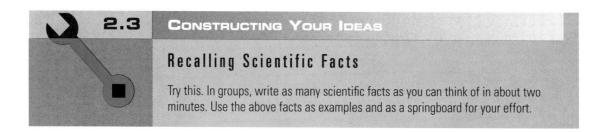

2.3   CONSTRUCTING YOUR IDEAS

Recalling Scientific Facts

Try this. In groups, write as many scientific facts as you can think of in about two minutes. Use the above facts as examples and as a springboard for your effort.

You probably accumulated quite a number of facts. How long were your lists? How hard did you have to think?

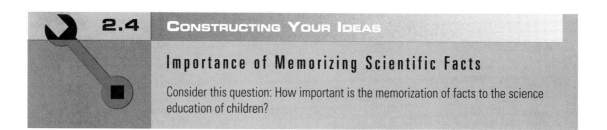

2.4   CONSTRUCTING YOUR IDEAS

Importance of Memorizing Scientific Facts

Consider this question: How important is the memorization of facts to the science education of children?

We have suggested that in quality science programs, children learn how to do science rather than learn about science. However, many factual pieces of information make up scientific concepts, theories, and laws, and this naturally raises the question "Can children discover scientific facts for themselves?"

Discovering Facts About Soil

A teacher in a first-grade class brought to school a pail of soil from her backyard. She spooned samples of the soil onto paper plates and asked the children to examine the specimens and list what they found in the soil. The objective was for the children to observe the soil and identify what was in it. They were encouraged to use whatever they needed—fingers, magnifying glasses, sieves, pencils, and the like. The teacher moved from group to group, asking what they had found so far and suggesting additional ways of observing. When the children were finished, the teacher made a class list of what the groups had found in the soil; some of the items identified were leaves, sticks, sand, little stones, bugs, tiny worms, and mud. Children had discovered a basic fact about soil— soil is composed of many different things.

In conjunction with this lesson, the teacher read the book *Lots of Rot* by Vicky Cobb (Lippincott, 1981), which discusses how rot is formed in food and soil and how people can grow their own rot. The book also suggests activities children can do to discover information about mold, bacteria, and mildew.

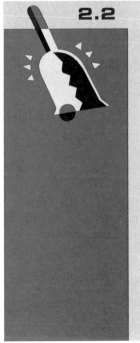

Discovering Facts About Minerals

In a fourth-grade class, a teacher set out specimens of quartz at four workstations around the room. In groups, children were to test the hardness of quartz using their fingernail, a penny, and a nail. They were instructed to observe whether each of these items would scratch the quartz and whether the quartz would scratch the item. From this activity, the children were able to find out for themselves that quartz is harder than any of the other materials supplied. The children were discovering facts about minerals. (**Teacher Note:** Quartz is the hardest of these materials and will scratch the fingernail, the penny, and the nail. This hardness test is a primary test for quartz.)

The teacher then provided each group of children with a bag containing specimens of several rocks of different hardnesses (such as gypsum, coal, quartzite, shale, sandstone, soapstone, talc, slate, obsidian, and limestone) and a penny, a piece of black construction paper, and a piece of white paper. Children tested the hardness of each rock by seeing if it scratched the penny and if the penny scratched the rock. Children also rubbed each rock on the black and white papers to see what happens. From the results of the activity, children classified the rocks in descriptive ways, such

Continued on next page

as "harder than the penny" and "softer than the penny," "writes on black paper," "doesn't write on black paper," and so on.

Teacher Note: Strictly speaking, rocks do not have specific hardnesses, because they are made of mixtures of different minerals, each of which has its own hardness. However, for the purposes of this activity, this distinction can be disregarded.

The teacher then read *The Magic School Bus Inside the Earth* by Joanna Cole (Scholastic, 1987). In this book, children investigate rocks and minerals—their characteristics, how they formed, where they are found, and what they are used for.

Additional Literature Connections

The Big Rock by Bruch Hiscock (Atheneum, 1988) traces the origin of a huge granite rock in the Adirondack Mountains that is worn down over the years by outside elements.

Rocks In His Head by Carol Otis Hurst (Greenwillow Books, 2001) is the story of a man who lived during the 1920s who had a lifelong love of collecting and identifying rocks and minerals.

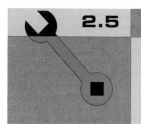

2.5　CONSTRUCTING YOUR IDEAS

Activity for Discovering a Scientific Fact

Now it's your turn. In a group, select one fact from the list you made earlier, and devise an activity children could do to discover this fact for themselves

---

Scientific Concepts

NSES Content Standard G. History and Nature of Science: Nature of Science

Scientific concepts are ideas that combine several facts or observations. A concept is an "observed regularity in events or objects" (Novak & Gowan, 1984, p. 4). For example, the statement "Green plants need light to grow" relates the two observations of light and amount of growth of green plants. Here are some concepts:

1. Green plants bend toward light.

2. The human body uses food for energy and growth.

3. Some chemicals fizz when they come into contact with other chemicals.

4. It takes more force to slide a book on sandpaper than on smooth paper.

5. Running water cuts gullies in soft rock.

6. Heavy marbles roll farther than light marbles when both are given the same push.

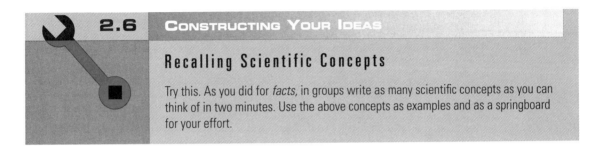

2.6 CONSTRUCTING YOUR IDEAS

Recalling Scientific Concepts

Try this. As you did for *facts,* in groups write as many scientific concepts as you can think of in two minutes. Use the above concepts as examples and as a springboard for your effort.

How long were your lists?

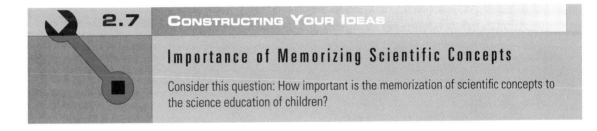

2.7 CONSTRUCTING YOUR IDEAS

Importance of Memorizing Scientific Concepts

Consider this question: How important is the memorization of scientific concepts to the science education of children?

As we saw with scientific facts, there are many scientific concepts. Because quality science education programs ask children to do science instead of learning about science, is it possible for children to develop scientific concepts for themselves?

2.3 IN THE SCHOOLS   NSES Content Standard B. Physical Science: Light Energy

Developing Concepts About Shadows

In an elementary classroom, a teacher supplied a flashlight, a large sheet of white paper, and several solid, wooden shapes for each group. The students were asked to use the flashlight to make shadows from the wooden shapes and to trace the shadows formed as the flashlight was held at various angles. Children observed that as the angle of the flashlight changed, so did the length of the shadow of each shape.

Continued on next page

The children were developing a concept about the relationship between shadow length and the angle of the light source.

The teacher read the poem "My Shadow" by Robert Louis Stevenson to show the phenomenon in literature.

Additional Literature Connections

There's a Nightmare in My Closet by Mercer Mayer (Dial Press, 1968) tells the story of a boy who faces monsters in the night.

Shadows Here, There, and Everywhere by Ron and Nancy Goor (Crowell, 1981) presents information about shadows, including how they are formed, why they can have different lengths, and how they reveal the shapes of things.

Shadow by Blaise Cendrars and Marcia Brown (Charles Scribner's Sons, 1982) describes how village storytellers and shamans from Africa inspire poetic images of shadows that call on present beliefs and spirits of the past.

2.4   IN THE SCHOOLS

NSES Content Standard F. Science in Personal and Social Perspectives: Personal Health

Developing Concepts About Pulse and Rate of Respiration

In a third-grade class, the teacher taught the children how to take their own pulse by placing two fingers lightly on the wrist or on the side of the neck. She also taught them how to count their respirations. She asked the children to measure and record their own pulse and respiration while seated at their desks. Next, she asked them to undergo light exercise (such as marching in place) for two minutes and then to measure and record their pulse and respiration again. Finally, she asked them to undergo heavy exercise (such as jumping or running in place) for two minutes and, again, to measure and record their pulse and respiration. The children compared the data and made graphs of the data for pulse and for rate of respiration (see Figure 2.3). They came to the conclusion that the more one exercises, the higher one's pulse rate goes and the faster one breathes. They had developed this concept for themselves.

The teacher then read *The Heart: Our Circulatory System* by Seymour Simon (Morrow Junior Books, 1996), a nonfiction book that describes the human heart and circulatory system and how it works. The teacher also read *Exercise* by Sharon Gordon (Children's Press, 2002), a nonfiction book that discusses the importance of exercise and describes different ways of keeping personally fit.

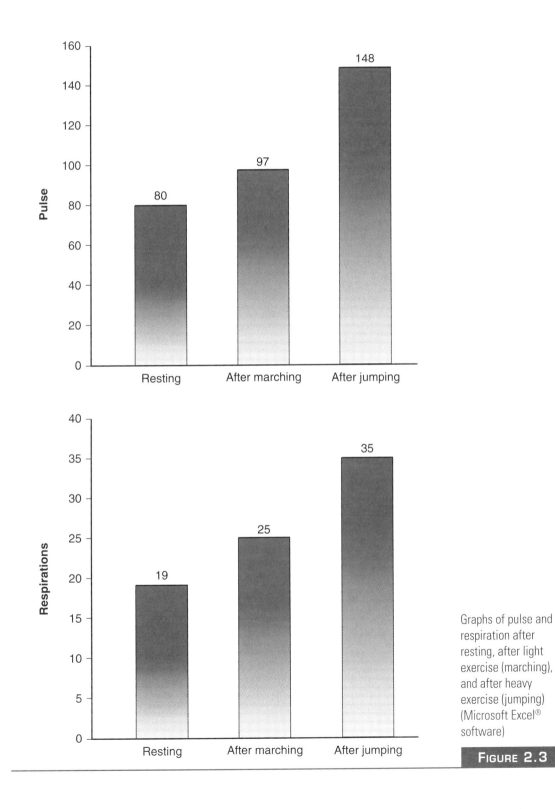

Graphs of pulse and respiration after resting, after light exercise (marching), and after heavy exercise (jumping) (Microsoft Excel® software)

FIGURE 2.3

Developing Concepts About Parachutes

In a sixth-grade class, a teacher asked the children to experiment with parachutes to see if the area of a parachute affects the rate at which it falls. She provided the same weight for each group (a small car), and she gave directions for making the parachutes. Children made parachutes of different sizes. They measured the side of the square that formed their parachute and calculated its area using the formula: area $= s^2$ (where s equals the length of one side). They then climbed onto tables and held the parachutes the same distance above the floor. At a given signal, they let them drop. The larger ones reached the floor later than the smaller ones, thus suggesting that the larger the area of the parachute, the slower it falls (see Figure 2.4). The children were encouraged to try many variations on the same basic activity—timing the length of fall using stopwatches, starting the parachutes from higher places (such as the top of a ladder), using different materials for the parachute, and so on. In each case, the results were the same: The larger the area of the parachute, the slower it fell. Children were developing concepts about the effect of the area of a parachute on how fast it falls.

Children experimenting with parachutes

FIGURE 2.4

2.6   IN THE SCHOOLS   NSES Content Standard B. Physical Science: Sound Energy

Developing Concepts About Sound

In a second-grade class, the teacher filled empty soda bottles with water to various heights. She tapped each bottle with a wooden stick, and the children noticed that the more water in the bottle, the lower the pitch of the sound. The teacher then provided each group with three empty soda bottles and instructed them to experiment with the phenomenon some more, doing what they wanted to see if the pitch of a sound depends on the amount of water in the bottle. Groups tapped the sides of the bottles as they filled them with water, noting the changes in pitch as they proceeded. Other groups borrowed enough bottles to set up a musical scale and were able to play "Mary Had a Little Lamb" on their bottles. When the activity was concluded, the whole class discussed their results. It seemed that everyone noticed the same phenomenon: The more water in the bottles, the lower the pitch. These students were now in a position to formulate a concept: The pitch of the sound made by tapping the sides of soda bottles depends on the depth of the water in the bottles. The music teacher was invited to hear children's explanations of their explorations.

View the video clip "The Pitch of Sound" on the companion DVD.

Literature Connection

Ty's One-Man Band by Mildred Pitts Walter (Scholastic, 1980). Ty uses several everyday objects (a washboard, a comb, wooden spoons, and a pail) as musical instruments.

It is useful to compare this activity with Constructing Science In The Classroom 3.40, *The Pitch of Sound,* in which children explore the effects of the pitches of sound that are produced when they blow across the tops of soda bottles with varying amounts of water in them.

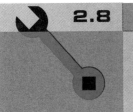

2.8   CONSTRUCTING YOUR IDEAS

Activity for Developing a Scientific Concept

Now it's your turn. In a group, select one concept from the list you made earlier, and devise an activity children could do to develop this concept for themselves.

Scientific Theories

Scientific theories are developed to explain concepts or other observed regularities. Theories appear to be true but cannot be proved. For example,

NSES Content Standard G. History and Nature of Science: Nature of Science

suppose you notice one day that the tires on your car are soft. The weather is colder than it has been, and you wonder if the tires became soft because it got cold. You set up an experiment in which you fill balloons with air and put them in the refrigerator, measuring the diameter of the balloons before and after they are chilled. If all the balloons shrink, you begin to form the theory that air contracts when it is cold.

Hawking and Mlodinow (2005) write that a good theory satisfies two requirements: It must provide an accurate description based on a small number of elements, and it must make definite predictions about the results of future observations. A famous example of theories is the atomic theory. According to the atomic theory, the atom contains a dense **nucleus** made of **protons** (with positive electric charges) and **neutrons** (with no electric charges) and a vast external space filled by rapidly moving **electrons** (with negative charges and almost no mass) (see Figure 2.5). This theory is based on indirect evidence; no one has actually seen an atom. However, if it is true that atoms are constructed in the way described by the atomic theory, they should behave in certain ways when undergoing chemical or nuclear reactions. Huge numbers of experiments have shown that atoms do behave as expected. So, even though no one can say they have seen an atom, and even though no one can verify the structure of an atom from direct observation, the atomic theory tells us what an atom ought to look like.

Here are some examples of theories:

1. *The **kinetic** theory of matter:* Molecules are in motion, and the rate of motion varies with temperature.

2. *The molecular theory:* Compounds are formed by the interaction of electrons of atoms.

3. *Einstein's general theory of relativity:* The faster an object goes, the greater its mass becomes.

4. *Theory of evolution:* Species adapt to their environments, and those that are most fit survive.

5. *Theory of plate tectonics:* The outer shell of the earth consists of several moving plates on which the oceans and continents lie.

6. *Cellular theory of life:* Living things are made of cells.

During the course of doing science, children develop numerous theories. They use the processes of scientific inquiry in rigorous investigations as they explore and investigate. Although their theories may not always be congruent with currently accepted science, they represent the children's own constructions and best scientific thinking. They are the result of children *doing* science.

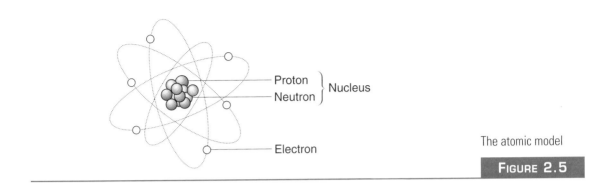

Proton ⎫
Neutron ⎭ Nucleus

Electron

The atomic model

FIGURE 2.5

Scientific Laws

Scientific laws are theories that appear to be so true that it is believed they can never be disproved. According to the National Science Teachers Association, laws are generalizations or universal relationships that are related to the way in which some aspect of the natural world would behave under certain conditions (National Science Teachers Association, 2000). Well-established laws and theories must be internally consistent and compatible with the best available evidence, must be successfully tested against a wide range of applicable phenomena and evidence, and must possess appropriately broad and demonstrable effectiveness in further research (National Science Teachers Association, 2000).

We have mentioned several laws already. Here are some examples of scientific laws:

1. *Newton's third law of motion:* For every force, there is an equal and opposite force.

2. *The law of universal gravitation:* All objects attract all other objects with a force that depends on their masses and the distance between them.

3. *The law of conservation of matter:* Matter can neither be created nor destroyed.

4. *The law of conservation of energy:* Energy can neither be created nor destroyed.

5. *The law of conservation of matter and energy:* The sum of the matter and the energy in the universe is constant.

6. *The law of segregation:* During reproduction, the two factors that control each trait separate (segregate), with one factor from each pair being passed to the offspring.

NSES Content Standard G. History and Nature of Science: Nature of Science

Most scientists are reluctant to acknowledge laws as the absolute truths implied by the term *law;* remember that science shuns authority and maintains a skeptical attitude. Laws imply an invariant consistency and an absolute truth that scientists are disinclined to accept. There are very few laws in the world of science. In fact, many contemporary texts leave out the term *law* entirely.

Attitudes Toward Science

NSES Teaching Standard E. Developing Learners Who Reflect Intellectual Vigor and Attitudes Conducive to Science Learning

There is another product of science that we cannot investigate as concretely as we can facts, concepts, theories, and laws. This product is *attitude.* People's attitudes about science range from positive when good things happen (such as a life saved by a miracle drug) to negative when something bad happens (such as your computer crashing). In Chapter 1, you assessed your attitudes about many characteristics of science and about the teaching of science. The attitudes that people possess about science and technology are formulated from their own experiences and explorations. For young children, having fun in science; having successful experiences; inquiring; asking their own questions; and developing, challenging, and formulating their own sound conclusions all foster positive attitudes about science that hopefully will remain with them throughout their lives.

Interdisciplinary Nature of Science

NSES Teaching Standard A. Inquiry-Based Program
NSES Program Standard B. Relevant, Inquiry-Based, and Connected with Other Subjects

There are thousands of discipline-centered specialties in science. However, in the broad scheme of the scientific enterprise, it is impossible to isolate a single discipline from all the others. To try to do so would be like trying to cook without using anything to measure ingredients, without controlling temperatures, and without paying attention to the selection of proper pans. All disciplines in science depend on other disciplines. For example, it is impossible to study how cells work (traditionally a life science topic) without also investigating the chemical changes that take place, the electron densities at the cell membranes, and the diffusion of substances across cell membranes—all of which, traditionally, are physical science topics. One cannot study the nature of minerals, an earth science topic, without considering the chemistry and physics of their crystalline structures. Those who study the universe rely heavily on the physics of optics and wave motion to obtain an understanding of their data. The study of ecosystems relies on all the scientific disciplines: physical science, life science, and earth and space science (see Figure 2.6).

Not only does the term *interdisciplinary* refer to integration of the various sciences, it also refers to discarding traditional subject area borders. One cannot imagine studying science without also having an appropriate facility in language, and much data interpretation from scientific experi-

The study of coastal ecosystems is interdisciplinary in nature.

FIGURE 2.6

ments is arrived at mathematically. If science is to be meaningful, it must be learned in social contexts; indeed, technology is largely a socially motivated discipline. Studies of conservation, health care, weather forecasting, genetic engineering, and sources of energy are all deeply rooted in social contexts.

Many theorists advocate teaching science from a science–technology–society (STS) perspective, a scheme that integrates the studies of science, technology, and society in project or thematic approaches. The issue of interdisciplinary, cross-disciplinary, and integrated approaches to science is addressed more completely in Chapter 10.

GOALS OF ELEMENTARY SCIENCE EDUCATION

Now that we have looked at the nature of science and the ways that scientists do science, let us turn our attention to the goals inherent in a quality elementary science education program.

Sagan (1989) wrote, "We live in a society exquisitely dependent on science and technology, in which hardly anyone knows anything about science and technology." The ability to understand science and technology in its day-to-day context is called **scientific literacy;** the development of scientific literacy is the basic goal of all science education. Scientific

NSES Program Standard A. Consistent Goals Across Grades

literacy is the knowledge and understanding of the scientific concepts and processes required for personal decision-making, participation in civic and cultural affairs, and economic productivity (National Research Council, 1996). It involves developing the information base necessary to arrive at reasoned decisions about scientific and technological issues. Scientifically literate people know how and when to ask questions, how to think critically, and how to make decisions based on reason rather than on emotion or superstition.

DeBoer (2000) argues that there are many routes to scientific literacy and that "local school districts and individual classroom teachers should pursue the goals that are most suitable for their particular situations along with the content and methodologies that are most appropriate for them and their students" (p. 582).

A number of national organizations have taken positions on goals of science education, which have become widely disseminated. Three of these organizations have written position statements: the National Science Teachers Association, the American Association for the Advancement of Science and the National Commission on Science Education Standards and Assessment. (Details about the major science education professional organizations are given in Chapter 13.) Although the position statements are in a constant state of evolution, it is useful to become familiar with what these organizations say about science education. The material in this book is grounded, in part, in the philosophies and positions of these national organizations. All three position statements are similar: They all stress teaching less content, teaching more investigation skills, teaching in the inquiry mode, teaching from an interdisciplinary perspective, teaching *all* children, stimulating children's interest in science, and, especially, developing scientifically literate citizens.

 Direct links to the Web sites of science education organizations are provided on the Student Book Companion Web Site in the listings for Chapter 13.

National Science Teachers Association

NSES Program Standard A. Consistent Goals Across Grades

The National Science Teachers Association (NSTA), the largest organization of science teachers in the nation, is extremely active in the reform of science education at all levels. In 1990, the NSTA adopted a position paper on science education in which two major goals of science education were identified: to achieve scientific literacy for all citizens and to ensure an adequate supply of scientists, engineers, and science teachers (National Science Teachers Association, 1990). The NSTA says that to achieve these goals, elementary science should emphasize learning the concepts and processes of science through activities; curricula should be organized around conceptual themes; students should see applications of science and technology in everyday life; and programs should integrate science, technology, mathematics, humanities, and the social sciences and be responsive to the needs of underrepresented students.

This position was reaffirmed in the 2003 position statement, "Beyond 2000—Teachers of Science Speak Out: An NSTA Lead Paper on How All Students Learn Science and the Implications to the Science Education Community" (National Science Teachers Association, 2003). In this paper, NSTA reiterated the importance of science literacy for *all* students and emphasized the need for technological literacy. Referring specifically to elementary science education, NSTA says, "The elementary science program must provide opportunities for students to develop understandings and skills necessary to function productively as problem-solvers in a scientific and technological world" (National Science Teachers Association, 2002, p. 1). To do this:

1. Students must be involved in first-hand exploration and investigation through employing inquiry and process skills.

2. Instruction must build on students' conceptual frameworks.

3. Content must be organized on the basis of broad conceptual themes.

4. Mathematics and communication must be made an integral part of science instruction.

American Association for the Advancement of Science

The American Association for the Advancement of Science (AAAS), the world's largest federation of scientific and technological societies, engages in a wide variety of activities to advance science and human progress. Responding to grave concerns about the state of science education in the United States, the AAAS embarked on "Project 2061," named for the year when Halley's comet will make its next pass near the earth. The project resulted in the publication of *Science for All Americans* (Rutherford & Ahlgren, 1990) as a first step toward improving scientific literacy. This book suggests that teachers should treat science topics from an interdisciplinary perspective and should focus on systems and interrelationships among the scientific disciplines rather than on isolated facts and concepts from isolated fields of study. Teachers should proceed from the concrete to the abstract, start with questions rather than answers, help children look for information they have previously acquired, and engage students in collecting evidence and interpreting data to answer the questions.

To augment *Science for All Americans,* the AAAS published a companion volume, *Benchmarks for Science Literacy: Project 2061* (American Association for the Advancement of Science, 1994), which expands the concepts and shows the integration among the scientific disciplines as

NSES Program Standard A. Consistent Goals Across Grades

well as the integration of science, mathematics, and technology. This companion volume has had a huge impact on contemporary science education, and many school districts have developed science programs based on the principles and suggestions outlined.

A direct link to the Project 2061 Web site and the available AAAS materials and programs is available on the Student Book Companion Web Site. You can access many full text versions of the AAAS publications through a direct link available on the Student Book Companion Web Site.

The AAAS also has published several additional volumes to help teachers design and implement meaningful and relevant science programs. *Designs for Science Literacy* (American Association for the Advancement of Science, 2001b) is intended to assist educators in developing curricula. The AAAS and NSTA teamed together to develop the *Atlas of Science Literacy,* Volume 1 (American Association for the Advancement of Science, 2001a), and the *Atlas of Scientific Literacy,* Volume 2 (American Association for the Advancement of Science, 2008). These volumes are collections of curriculum maps that show the anticipated growth over time of students' understandings of science and help teachers to organize recourses and plan coherent instruction. *Resources for Science Literacy* (American Association for the Advancement of Science, 1997) is a CD-ROM designed to help teachers understand and use science literacy goals.

The AAAS has continued to help strengthen science education by embarking on new programs, providing online professional development workshops, preparing curriculum materials, and publishing newsletters.

National Science Education Standards

NSES Program Standard A. Consistent Goals Across Grades

The National Commission on Science Education Standards and Assessment was formed at the request of NSTA and other professional scientific societies to take the lead in developing national standards for science education. The result is the *National Science Education Standards* (National Research Council, 1996), a document that describes what students should know, understand, and be able to do as a result of their learning experiences in science. The primary goal is scientific literacy for *all* students. "All students regardless of age, sex, cultural or ethnic background, disabilities, aspirations, or interest and motivation in science should have the opportunity to obtain high levels of scientific literacy" (p. 20). The standards are guided by four principles:

1. Science is for all students.

2. Learning science is an active process.

3. School science reflects the intellectual and cultural traditions that characterize the practice of contemporary science.

4. Improving science is a part of systemic education reform. (p. 19)

The science education standards are not federal mandates, nor do they represent a national curriculum. Rather, they offer a vision of what it means to be scientifically literate and a set of criteria for content, science teaching, professional development, assessment, science programs, and systems that support science education. The science teaching standards call for inquiry-based science education programs in which teachers facilitate learning rather than impart information, use multiple authentic methods of assessment, provide learning environments conducive to inquiry learning, maintain standards of intellectual rigor, and actively participate in the development and planning of their science programs.

The science content standards describe desirable student outcomes for levels K–4, 5–8, and 9–12. The content is identified in eight categories (National Research Council, 1996, p. 104):

1. Unifying concepts and processes in science

2. Science as inquiry

3. Physical science

4. Life science

5. Earth and space science

6. Science and technology

7. Science in personal and social perspectives

8. History and nature of science

These standards, together with Project 2061, are the driving force behind today's science education at all levels. Both are promoted by NSTA, and both describe the nature of contemporary science education. Themes common to both (Sandall, 2003) include:

- Scientific literacy is for all students.

- Science education comprises active, hands-on learning and in-depth study of fewer topics.

- Science education should emphasize critical thinking, problem solving, and developing mathematics and science as a way of thinking and reasoning.

- Science education should emphasize integration and interdisciplinary activities.

- Science education should emphasize application of science, mathematics, and technology to real-life situations.

It is extremely important that you become familiar with the National Science Education Standards as you develop your individual teaching style and plan science instruction. Individual standards are shown in abbreviated form in the margins throughout this text to help you see the relationships between the National Science Education Standards and the conceptualizations you are constructing as you progress. You will note that the content standards are somewhat detailed. The National Research Council has indicated that the next generation of content standards should focus on a few core ideas that link the concepts and develop them over successive grades (Getting to the Core, 2007). The complete standards are reproduced inside the front and back covers of this text.

A prominent feature of the National Science Education Standards is its focus on inquiry. To help educators implement inquiry approaches to teaching science, the National Research Council published a companion volume, *Inquiry and the National Science Education Standards: A Guide for Teaching and Learning* (National Research Council, 2000). The book is intended to serve as a practical guide for educators, and it includes much practical information about inquiry science teaching and ways to implement the inquiry methodology in the classroom. Chapter 5 in this text is devoted entirely to an exploration of inquiry teaching.

A direct link to the full text of the National Science Education Standards is available on the Student Book Companion Web Site.

No Child Left Behind

NSES Program Standard A. Consistent Goals Across Grades

On January 8, 2002, President George W. Bush signed into law the *No Child Left Behind Act of 2001* (often referred to as NCLB), the most recent reauthorization of the *Elementary and Secondary Education Act* (ESEA) first established in 1965. The now-familiar law is based on four principles: increased accountability for student achievement; greater choice for parents and students; more flexibility for states, local school districts, and schools in the use of federal funds; and a stronger emphasis on reading, especially for younger children (U.S. Department of Education, 2002). The Act also mandates that by 2006, all teachers teaching in core academic subjects must be highly qualified (U.S. Department of Education, 2004).

According to President Bush (2004), "[W]e are asking states and schools to set higher standards so that we can make sure that every student is learning" (p. 119). The core of the Act is its focus on student achievement and the accountability of teachers, schools, and states for continued increase in achievement. These provisions call for challenging state standards and annual testing for all students. In accordance with the terms of the Act, by the 2005–2006 academic year, states receiving federal education funds tested all students in grades 3–8 annually in reading and mathematics; and by the 2007–2008 school year, states receiving federal funds must also test all students in science at least once in the elementary, middle, and high school grades (Rebora, 2004). The tests are standardized and are based on the standards of individual states; the same test is given to many children in the same grade throughout the state or, in some cases, throughout the nation.

You can access the entire *No Child Left Behind Act of 2001* and the *"No Child Left Behind Toolkit for Teachers"* online through a direct link available on the Student Book Companion Web Site.

If the students in a given school fail to show they are making *adequate yearly progress* (AYP) based on their scores on the standardized achievement tests, these schools are subject to corrective action and restructuring measures aimed at getting them back on course to meet the state standards. If they fail to demonstrate the required improvements in student achievement over time, they may be identified as *inadequate,* opening several options to parents, including school choice, supplemental education services, and tutoring—all at the "inadequate" school's expense. Schools not making adequate yearly progress after receiving extra help may be "reformed" by the state or even disbanded. On the other hand, schools in which students do well on the tests and their teachers, may be rewarded financially. Students who fail the achievement tests may be retained in the grade during which the test was given (say, third grade); when significant numbers of failing students are taught by the same teacher, that teacher is subject to corrective and disciplinary action.

Thus, the standardized achievement tests have assumed monumental importance. On the results of these tests lie student progress in school, teacher rewards or sanctions, administrator freedoms, school funding, and even the continued existence of the school itself. Because of this, the term "High Stakes Testing" has risen to prominence in educational discussions. Yet, it is well known that standardized achievement tests are not necessarily accurate measures of student achievement (see, for example, Goldberg, 2004; Kohn, 2000; Linn, Baker, & Betebenner, 2002). This issue is multifaceted, and you will have the opportunity to examine it in greater depth in Chapter 8.

There are additional concerns with the Act. The National Education Association (NEA) believes it presents obstacles to helping students, because it focuses on punishments rather than on assistance, mandates rather than support, and privatization rather than teacher-led, family-oriented solutions (National Education Association, 2004). The American Federation of Teachers (AFT) has cited similar concerns (Feldman, 2003). The law is seen by many as challenging the independence of schools, stifling the creativity and teaching abilities of teachers, and placing tremendous pressure on schools and teachers to demonstrate increasing standardized achievement test scores. As we indicated above, teachers are greatly concerned with the huge reliance placed on standardized achievement tests. Many teachers feel they must teach for the test at the expense of teaching the desired curriculum. Furthermore, in many cases, little, if any, school time is allocated to subjects that are not tested—including science.

In addition, there are concerns about the current practice of holding students who are struggling with poverty and transience issues, learning disabilities, behavioral disorders, and non-English native languages to the same standards as those who do not face such difficulties (Thomas, 2005), because the accountability requirements seem to demand that all subgroups, including high-poverty and racially diverse schools, meet the same goals (Kim & Sunderman, 2005).

On the other hand, Griswold (2005) has shown that there may be a relationship between standardized tests scores in lower grades and achievement scores made by those same students in high school, suggesting that standardized tests of the sort advocated by the Act may alert educators to students who may be at risk in the early years.

Community members have concerns about the Act but support some of its aspects. The result of a four-year project that sought the input and opinion of community stakeholders about the Act showed that community members have the following thoughts (Lefkowits & Miller, 2006):

1. Communities must share in the responsibility; accountability cannot rely only on tests scores.

2. Community members rejected the "one-size-fits-all" notion and made it clear that they believe no single approach will close the achievement gap.

3. Community members believed that standardized achievement tests give only the broadest view of student performance and that standardized test results do not give parents the information they want.

4. Community members agreed that schools should be held accountable for meeting student performance goals, providing these goals are developed with community input. However, there was no clear sense of how and to whom this accountability should proceed.

The 38th Annual Phi Delta Kappa/Gallup Poll of the Public's Attitudes Toward the Public Schools reflected similar opinions and showed that the majority of the public supports seeking school improvement through existing schools and the existing system, urging educators to keep close to the community and use community input (Rose & Gallup, 2006).

The Center on Education Policy has collected information about the Act during its first four years and has summarized their conclusions as follows (Jennings & Rentner, 2006):

1. Officials report that student achievement on state tests is rising, but it is not clear that students are gaining as much as the test scores would suggest.

2. Schools are spending more time on reading and mathematics, sometimes at the expense of subjects not tested.

3. Schools are paying much more attention to the alignment of curriculum and instruction and are analyzing test data much more closely.

4. Low-performing schools are undergoing makeovers rather than restructuring.

5. Schools and teachers have made considerable progress in demonstrating that teachers meet the law's academic requirements, but many educators are skeptical that this will improve the quality of teaching.

6. Students are taking a lot more tests.

7. Schools are paying much more attention to achievement gaps and the learning needs of particular groups of students.

8. The percentage of schools on state "needs improvement" lists has been steady but is not growing.

9. The federal government is playing a bigger role in education.

10. The Act's requirements have meant that state governments and school districts have expanded roles in school operations, but without adequate funds.

On the fifth anniversary of the Act (2006), U.S. Secretary of Education Margaret Spellings said that test results show the law is working: The achievement gap between minorities and whites has shrunk to its smallest size in history, and the most recent Nation's Report Card has shown gains in reading and mathematics for fourth graders as well as gains in mathematics for eighth graders (Landmark Legislation, 2007).

NCLB is scheduled for reauthorization by Congress in 2007. As the Act is getting ready to be debated in Congress, politicians and educational organizations, such as the Association for Supervision and Curriculum Development, the National Education Association, and the American Federation of Teachers, have identified some primary issues they hope will frame the debate. These issues include the following (Franklin, 2006; Wilcox, 2007):

- Full funding is lacking.

- The law's 100 percent student proficiency is impossible to meet.

- The focus on reading and mathematics takes time away from the rest of the curriculum.

- NCLB judges school performance on the basis of reading and mathematics scores only.

- NCLB limits how test scores can be used.

- NCLB is drastic with respect to how it measures "failure" in certain subgroups.

- Accountability measures are not fair.

- NCLB does not provide flexibility to innovate.

- Multiple measures of student achievement are not provided.

However, Kati Haycock, director of The Education Trust (an organization that advocates for policies that help close the achievement gap), defends the law as being fundamentally about helping the "hidden kids." She says that even though a lot of people don't like all the features of the law, the law is "putting wind behind the sails of people who are trying to bring about change for all kids" (Franklin, 2006, p. 8).

In general, critics seem to agree that reauthorization needs "to do more than tinker around the margins of NCLB" (Wilcox, 2007, p. 1), and that providing school choice, providing supplementary education services for students needing extra help, and restructuring or disbanding failing schools are not working.

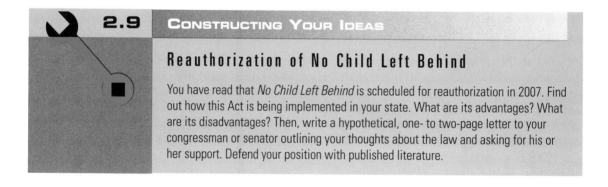

2.9   **CONSTRUCTING YOUR IDEAS**

Reauthorization of No Child Left Behind

You have read that *No Child Left Behind* is scheduled for reauthorization in 2007. Find out how this Act is being implemented in your state. What are its advantages? What are its disadvantages? Then, write a hypothetical, one- to two-page letter to your congressman or senator outlining your thoughts about the law and asking for his or her support. Defend your position with published literature.

Goals 2000: Educate America Act

NSES Program
Standard A. Consistent
Goals Across Grades

In 1990, President George H. W. Bush and the nation's governors met for the first time in the history of the United States to discuss national educational policy. Their discussion was summarized in six national goals for public education. Two additional goals were added to the original six, resulting in an expanded *Goals 2000: Educate America Act* that was passed into law in 1994. As listed in the *Goals 2000* law, the goals are as follows:

1. *School readiness.* By the year 2000, all children in America will start school ready to learn.

2. *School completion.* By the year 2000, the high school graduation rate will increase to at least 90 percent.

3. *Student achievement and citizenship.* By the year 2000, all students will leave grades 4, 8, and 12 having demonstrated competency over challenging subject matter, including English, mathematics, science, foreign languages, civics and government, economics, arts, history, and geography, and every school in America will ensure that all students learn to use their minds well so they may be prepared for responsible citizenship, further learning, and productive employment in our nation's modern economy.

4. *Teacher education and professional development.* By the year 2000, the nation's teaching force will have access to programs for the continued improvement of their professional skills and the opportunity to acquire the knowledge and skills needed to instruct and prepare all American students for the next century.

5. *Mathematics and science.* By the year 2000, U.S. students will be first in the world in mathematics and science achievement.

6. *Adult literacy and lifelong learning.* By the year 2000, every adult American will be literate and will possess the knowledge and skills necessary to compete in a global economy and exercise the rights and responsibilities of citizenship.

7. *Safe, disciplined, and alcohol- and drug-free schools.* By the year 2000, every school in the United States will be free of drugs, violence, and the unauthorized presence of firearms and alcohol and will offer a disciplined environment conducive to learning.

8. *Parental participation.* By the year 2000, every school will promote partnerships that will increase parental involvement and participation in promoting social, emotional, and academic growth of children.

Goal 5 states that U.S. students will be first in the world in mathematics and science achievement. Factors such as how science and mathematics are taught, availability of quality instructional materials, and time spent on learning science and mathematics influence how well this objective will be accomplished. The goal suggests a worldwide comparison, one that often is interpreted in terms of content acquisition. The assessments used to measure progress on Goal 5 are discussed in Chapters 1 and 8.

A direct link to the full text of *Goals 2000*, progress reports, and supplemental material is available on the Student Book Companion Web Site.

WHAT DO YOU THINK?

It is time now for you to consolidate the thoughts you have constructed thus far about elementary science education.

NSES Professional Development Standard C. Lifelong Learning

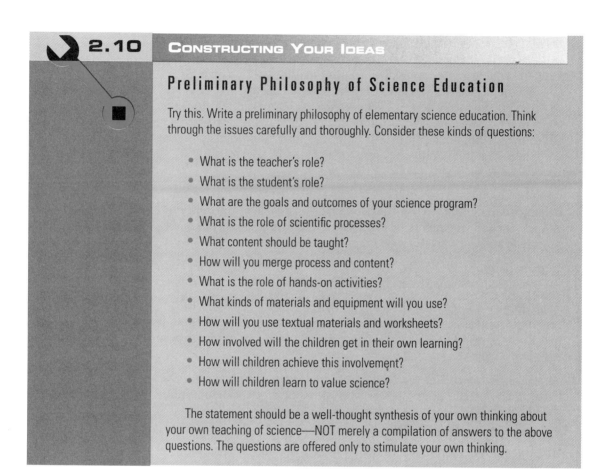

2.10　CONSTRUCTING YOUR IDEAS

Preliminary Philosophy of Science Education

Try this. Write a preliminary philosophy of elementary science education. Think through the issues carefully and thoroughly. Consider these kinds of questions:

- What is the teacher's role?
- What is the student's role?
- What are the goals and outcomes of your science program?
- What is the role of scientific processes?
- What content should be taught?
- How will you merge process and content?
- What is the role of hands-on activities?
- What kinds of materials and equipment will you use?
- How will you use textual materials and worksheets?
- How involved will the children get in their own learning?
- How will children achieve this involvement?
- How will children learn to value science?

The statement should be a well-thought synthesis of your own thinking about your own teaching of science—NOT merely a compilation of answers to the above questions. The questions are offered only to stimulate your own thinking.

This activity is deliberately suggested at the beginning of the course, to give you a chance to reflect on your own thinking and to review your thoughts as you move along. As such, your statement will not be an all-inclusive opus, nor will it be definitively refined. Rather, it will be an expression of your ideas about the science teaching–learning experience as you see it at the beginning of your investigations. You will use this statement, together with the metaphor you selected for "science teacher" in Chapter 1, to guide you in your construction and reconstruction of your own thinking about appropriate methodology in quality elementary science education. Toward the end of the course, review this statement and your metaphor to compare your thoughts at the beginning of the course with your thinking at the end to see if there are any changes.

Conclusion

Science education today focuses on inquiry and process, with the primary goal of enabling students to achieve scientific and technological literacy. The nature of science is characterized by systematic gathering of information and the formation of evidence-based conclusions through rigorous investigation, honesty, skepticism, parsimony, and consistency. Science rejects authoritarianism, supernatural explanations, and absolute truth. The products of science include applications, facts, concepts, theories, and laws. Contemporary science education is informed and supported by science-oriented professional organizations. Federal government programs are thought to have both positive and challenging influences on contemporary science education.

CHAPTER 2

Additional Questions for Discussion

1. When children work to discover scientific facts, concepts, and theories for themselves, they may come to unexpected conclusions. To what extent should teachers ensure that children's conclusions are congruent with accepted scientific information?

2. It has been said that teaching is both a science and an art. How does the science of teaching parallel the nature of science as described in this chapter?

3. How can you tell if a person is scientifically literate?

4. John Dewey (1938) discussed the "importance of the participation of the learner in the formation of the purposes which direct his activities in the learning process" (p. 67). How are Dewey's vision and the National Science Education Standards compatible? How are they incompatible?

*5. What are the most important goals of science education?

6. What are some advantages and some disadvantages of *No Child Left Behind* relative to elementary science education?

Internet Activities

Use the Internet to access material on cold fusion. Check this topic regularly for dated information.

Use the Internet to find material on pseudoscience topics. Browse the general subject heading, pseudoscience; individual subjects, such as ESP, superstition, and astrology; and specific journals, such as *Skeptical Inquirer* and *The Futurist*.

Use the Internet to find the latest discussions and information about the reauthorization of *No Child Left Behind*.

Notes

1. Thomas Kuhn (1970) writes, "Mopping-up operations are what engage most scientists throughout their careers . . . No part of the aim of normal science is to call forth new sorts of phenomena; indeed those that will not fit the box are often not seen at all. Nor do scientists normally aim to invent new theories, and they are often intolerant of those invented by others. Instead, normal scientific research is directed to the articulation of those phenomena and theories that the paradigm already supplies" (p. 24).

2. There are those who believe science and technology have gone too far—that we would be much better off if we stopped acquiring new knowledge, stopped developing new gizmos, and stopped exploration into space and the oceans. Jacques Ellul (1964) argues that technology is the curse of human life—that "technique" and standardization have become the way of life and efficiency is the primary measure of all aspects of culture.

THE PROCESSES OF SCIENCE

The shrewd guess, the fertile hypothesis, the courageous leap to a tentative conclusion—these are the most valuable coins of the thinker at work.

Jerome Bruner, *The Process of Education* (Cambridge, MA: Harvard University Press, 1960), p. 14

You have been investigating the nature of science, the difference between children learning about science and children doing science, the difference between process and product, and the positions taken by the national organizations on science education. We have suggested that it is better for children to learn to do science than to learn the facts, concepts, and theories someone else has concluded; that it is far more important for children to master process skills than to learn facts; and that children should do science the way scientists do. You have discovered that scientists do science through careful and appropriate application of the scientific processes to questions that were generated as a result of wondering about something. We have suggested that in a quality elementary science program, children ask their own questions, devise their own ways to explore their questions, and develop their own answers to their questions. They consider themselves scientists.

Science process skills are what scientists employ when they do science. They are "a set of broadly transferable abilities, appropriate to many science disciplines and reflective of the behavior of scientists" (Padilla, 1990). Elementary school children use process skills to find out how scientists think and work and to investigate their own questions in a manner similar to the way that scientists conduct their inquiries. Children use process skills to construct knowledge by asking questions, making observations, taking measurements, collecting data, organizing and interpreting the data, predicting the outcomes of manipulating one **variable** while keeping the other variables constant, formulating and testing hypotheses, developing experiments, inferring reasons for what they observe, and communicating their models to others. *Doing* science means applying the process skills that form the core of inquiry-based, hands-on science learning. To apply the processes, children first have to master them.

In this chapter, you will investigate twelve processes that have been identified as basic to scientific investigation. We divide the processes into two groups: the basic processes, which form the foundation for scientific investigation, and the integrated processes, which form the method of actual scientific inquiry. The basic processes are the fundamental activities required in scientific inquiry—the key skills that underlie all scientific investigations. The integrated processes are complex activities that extend the basic processes into problem-based scientific explorations.

The *basic processes* include:

Observing
Classifying
Communicating
Measuring
Predicting
Inferring

The *integrated processes* include:

Identifying and controlling variables
Formulating and testing hypotheses
Interpreting data
Defining operationally
Experimenting
Constructing models

OBSERVING

Let us take a short foray into the world of rocks.

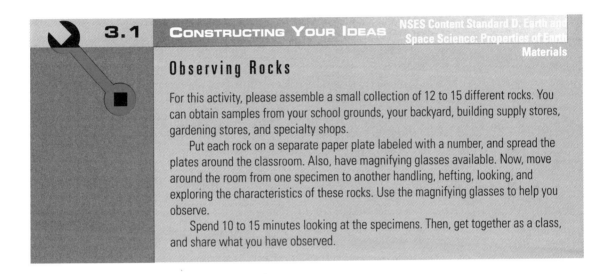

3.1 CONSTRUCTING YOUR IDEAS

NSES Content Standard D. Earth and Space Science: Properties of Earth Materials

Observing Rocks

For this activity, please assemble a small collection of 12 to 15 different rocks. You can obtain samples from your school grounds, your backyard, building supply stores, gardening stores, and specialty shops.

Put each rock on a separate paper plate labeled with a number, and spread the plates around the classroom. Also, have magnifying glasses available. Now, move around the room from one specimen to another handling, hefting, looking, and exploring the characteristics of these rocks. Use the magnifying glasses to help you observe.

Spend 10 to 15 minutes looking at the specimens. Then, get together as a class, and share what you have observed.

Most people have a difficult time making careful observations of things the first time they see them, so you may wish to use the sheet in Figure 3.1 to help guide you in what to look for. Do not feel compelled to fill in all the boxes; use the sheet only as a guide. "Color" is self-explanatory. "Texture" is simply how the rock feels in your hand: rough, slippery, smooth,

NSES Teaching Standard A. Inquiry-Based Program
NSES Program Standard B. Relevant, Inquiry-Based, and Connected with Other Subjects
NSES Content Standard A. Science as Inquiry: Abilities Necessary To Do Scientific Inquiry

Rock Number	Color	Texture	How Heavy	How Shiny	Other Properties
1					
2					
3					
4					
5					
6					

Data sheet for rock-observation activity

FIGURE 3.1

grainy, and the like. "How heavy" refers to whether it feels heavier that you expected, lighter than you expected, or just about right as you "heft" the specimen in the palm of your hand. "How shiny" is self-explanatory. "Other properties" refers to those properties that will be readily apparent as you look at the specimens.

The purpose of this activity is for you to observe. It is *not* intended that you identify the rocks; tell the differences among **igneous, sedimentary,** and **metamorphic** rocks; or learn their names. The sole purpose of this activity is for you to *observe*.

What senses did you use? Certainly, you used the sense of sight as you observed the various colors and different subtleties of color. You probably used the sense of touch as you felt how smooth or how rough the specimens are. You probably did *not* use the sense of taste. *Safety note*: It is important that people be cautioned *not* to taste things unless the instructor specifically says it is okay to do so. Did you use the sense of smell or hearing? How about other senses? What sense did you use to compare relative weights by hefting the specimens? It probably was more of an internal muscular sense than the sense of touch as we commonly know it.

As an interesting sidelight to this activity, there might have been one or two students—maybe even you—who were not interested in the rocks. This is important to notice, and it is useful to compare how much these uninterested individuals observed with how much those who were interested observed. It seems that we are much better observers when we are interested than when we are not.

3.1   IN THE SCHOOLS   NSES Content Standard A. Science as Inquiry: Abilities Necessary To Do Scientific Inquiry

Observation Activities

Activities patterned after this rock-observing activity provide excellent ways for children to begin observing. Use pictures, leaves, cowbells, coins, stamps, buttons, hardware, or just about anything else. Place the specimens on paper plates, and put the plates around the room. Children then move around and make observations to report back to the class. Do you have a collection? Use it. If you don't have a collection, remember the old dictum, "If you're going to be a teacher, never throw anything away," and use things you have saved.

In observing, we learn to use all our senses. Physiologists tell us we have many more than the five basic senses of sight, sound, taste, smell, and touch. We also have the sense of balance, the sense of muscle contraction, the sense of muscle memory, the sense of direction, the muscular senses we use when we investigate how heavy something is, and other internal senses. In our skin, we have four different kinds of receptors—those for cold, heat, deep pressure, and surface pressure. In all, the human body has some 30 different kinds of receptor systems; thus, one can say the human body has more than 30 different kinds of senses.

In developing the skill of observation, children learn to use all their senses to attend to stimuli that will be recorded in the sensory register and, from there, will move on for processing. Connections with the memory bank in the long-term memory help people recognize stimuli, making it easier for them to make perceptual sense. Because children do not have the wealth of experience that older children and adults have, it is important for them to begin obtaining this experiential base. The more observation activities they perform, the more experiences they will add to their long-term memory stores, thus becoming better able to make connections with new things they observe.

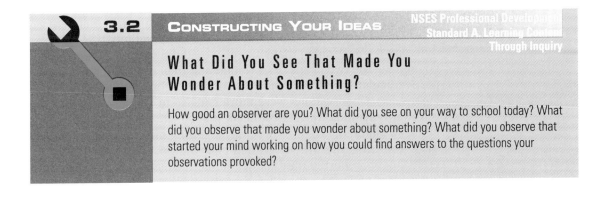

3.2   **CONSTRUCTING YOUR IDEAS**

NSES Professional Development Standard A. Learning Content Through Inquiry

What Did You See That Made You Wonder About Something?

How good an observer are you? What did you see on your way to school today? What did you observe that made you wonder about something? What did you observe that started your mind working on how you could find answers to the questions your observations provoked?

A CASE OF MOON WATCHING

A class of elementary science methods students was asked to describe the moon as they had seen it the night before. Many students had not seen it, and those who had gave different descriptions of what they had seen. Some said the curve of the moon pointed to the right, some said it pointed to the left, and some said it pointed straight up. To clarify the verbal descriptions, several students drew on the board what they had seen. Because there were so many different descriptions, the question was posed, "How could you make accurate observations of the moon?" The class decided they needed to draw the moon exactly as they saw it. The next day, several students shared the moon drawings they had made the previous night. Again, there were discrepancies, such as left

NSES Professional Development Standard A. Learning Content through Inquiry NSES Content Standard D. Earth and Space Science: Changes in Earth and Sky

Moon-watching drawing for showing what direction the moon is facing

FIGURE 3.2

versus right, the angle at which the concave part pointed upward, and whether the "dark" part of the moon had been partially visible. The class decided that still more accurate observations were needed, because the moon itself obviously could not be different from one student to another—it was the observations that were different. It was decided that students could draw an imaginary line connecting the two cusps of the moon and then draw an imaginary perpendicular bisector to show the direction the moon faced (see Figure 3.2). Observations were more consistent the following day, but new questions were introduced: it seemed that the moon had changed shape during the three days, getting more and more full. Also, it seemed that the moon had changed position. Indeed, several students reported they could not find the moon, even though it was a clear night.

It became a class project to record observations of the moon every clear night. Concerning the process of observation, the class discovered that they had to record their observations in the form of drawings with detailed descriptions to be able to compare what they had seen over the span of several nights. As the class progressed, several concepts were made from the moon observations: (1) The moon changes shape. (2) The moon changes position in the sky. (3) The way you see the moon depends on where you are. (4) The moon is sometimes visible during the day. In addition, a number of questions were generated by the observations: (1) Why does the moon change shape? (2) Where does it go when it disappears? (3) Why does it move? (4) Why does the moon look different in different places? Although these questions were not answered, several members of the class undertook investigations to try answering the questions for themselves.[1]

The essence of all science is observation. Ultimately, observation is what determines the procedure and the outcome of any scientific inquiry. It is impossible to inquire scientifically without observing accurately. We must be able to observe not only expected things but also unexpected things. Recall that in Chapter 1, several inventions were described as having come from unexpected observations.

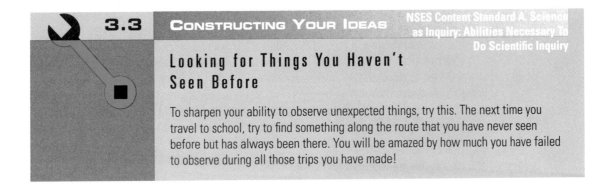

3.3 **CONSTRUCTING YOUR IDEAS** NSES Content Standard A: Science as Inquiry: Abilities Necessary To Do Scientific Inquiry

Looking for Things You Haven't Seen Before

To sharpen your ability to observe unexpected things, try this. The next time you travel to school, try to find something along the route that you have never seen before but has always been there. You will be amazed by how much you have failed to observe during all those trips you have made!

Observation may be **qualitative,** and observation may be **quantitative.** Your observations were qualitative when you observed the rocks; qualitative observations do not require measurement. In quantitative observation, measurements are required to attach specific facts to the observations. For example, measuring the volume and the weight of a certain rock are quantitative observations; from these measurements, you would be able to calculate its **density,** which is a measure of its weight per volume. The most appropriate type of observation for young children is qualitative; quantitative factors are introduced as the children become ready for the mathematical abstractions involved.

Once again, observation is the first and, without doubt, the most important scientific process skill for elementary school children to master. Elementary teachers must give children the maximum possible opportunity to observe. Observation must be built into every aspect of the daily program. It is our responsibility to help young children develop, sharpen, and master their powers of observation. Observation is the cornerstone of all scientific work.

Several observation activities are suggested in Constructing Science in the Classroom 3.1–3.7. Some are appropriate for young children, and some are more appropriate for older children. The activities suggest ways of providing practice using each of the five basic senses.

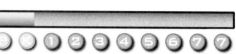

3.1 — CONSTRUCTING SCIENCE IN THE CLASSROOM

WHAT'S IN THE SOCK?

Observation Activity Using a Variety of Senses

NSES Content Standard A. Science as Inquiry: Abilities Necessary To Do Scientific Inquiry

Objective

The student will use various senses to identify unknown objects placed in a sock.

Secretly put into a sock an object that requires more than one sense to identify. Suggestions include a banana, an apple, a pear, a handful of grapes, a lemon, an onion, a potato, or the like. Hold the sock in front of the children, and ask them to guess what they think is in the sock by looking at it and tell why they guessed what they did. Then, ask what other ways they could use to discover what is in the sock without looking. Pass the sock around, and allow the children to use their senses to explore the object inside, again emphasizing that they cannot look in the sock. Next, ask for their guesses as to what is inside the sock and their reasons for those guesses. Reveal the surprise object, and discuss how it feels, smells, sounds, looks, and tastes.

Literature Connections

My Five Senses by Aliki (Crowell, 1989) is a simple text with clear illustrations of how we use our five senses. "When I bounce a ball, I use three senses. I see, hear, touch."

There Are Rocks in My Socks Said the Ox to the Fox by Patricia Thomas (Lothrop, 1979) describes how the ox felt with rocks in his socks.

3.2 — CONSTRUCTING SCIENCE IN THE CLASSROOM

WHAT'S IN THE BAG?

Observation Activity Using the Sense of Touch

NSES Content Standard A. Science as Inquiry: Abilities Necessary To Do Scientific Inquiry

Objective

The student will use the sense of touch to identify materials in a bag.

Pass out "feely bags" to each child. A feely bag is a paper bag in which you have secretly put a familiar object. Children must put their hands in the bag and describe what they feel, but they are not allowed to look inside. They guess what the object is from how it feels. Then, they verify their guesses by looking.

Next, give each child an empty paper bag and a plastic bag with a variety of small objects, such as wooden letters, wooden beads, pencils, pieces of cloth, cotton balls, cotton swabs,

Continued on next page

paper clips, strands of beads, ribbon, wooden shapes, and the like. Each child puts two or three items (some easily identifiable, and some less easily identifiable) into the paper feely bag and exchanges bags with a partner. Observation and identification proceeds as before.

Children can prepare their own bags at home and bring them to school the next day or play the game with family members.

Literature Connections

The poem "What's in the Sack," in *Where the Sidewalk Ends* by Shel Silverstein (Harper and Row, 1974), is a humorous account of a man carrying a huge sack on his back. It tells of the man's frustrations when people do not really care about him, only about what's in the sack.

Find Out by Touching by Paul Showers (Crowell, 1961) encourages children to find something made of wood, metal, cloth, plastic, and rubber and place the objects in boxes. Using their sense of touch, children determine what is in the boxes.

The Five Senses by Keith Faulkner (Scholastic/Cartwheel Books, 2002) has bright, bold pictures of animals using their senses to explore the world.

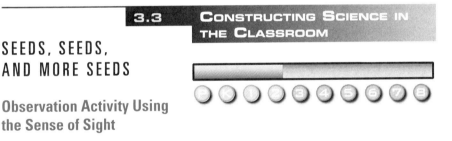

| 3.3 | **CONSTRUCTING SCIENCE IN THE CLASSROOM** |

SEEDS, SEEDS, AND MORE SEEDS

Observation Activity Using the Sense of Sight

Objective

The student will observe seeds.

NSES Content Standard C. Life Science: Life Cycles of Organisms

Obtain a collection of several different kinds of bean and pea seeds; these are all seeds that come in two parts. (If they haven't been cooked or frozen, you could plant them, and they would grow.) Soak them in water for a few hours to loosen up their skin.

Ask children to describe or draw the outsides of the seeds. Then, cut the seeds open. Children should be able to split them with plastic knives; otherwise, you can let them stand in a glass of water until they split open by themselves. Ask children to describe (or draw) what the insides look like. Provide magnifying glasses to aid children in their observations (see Figure 3.3).

To help children sharpen their skills of observation, ask them to compare cooked, packaged, fresh, and frozen vegetables.

Literature Connections

All About Seeds by Melvin Berger (Scholastic, 1992) suggests several activities for collecting, planting, and cooking seeds.

Continued on next page

Examining the insides
of seeds

FIGURE 3.3

Eat the Fruit, Plant the Seed by Millicent Selsam (Morrow, 1980) is an easy, how-to book that shows various stages of development from seed to plant in six different fruits.

3.4 **CONSTRUCTING SCIENCE IN THE CLASSROOM**

WHAT'S THAT SOUND IN THE EGG?

Observation Activity Using the Sense of Hearing

NSES Content
Standard A. Science as
Inquiry: Abilities Neces-
sary To Do Scientific
Inquiry

Objective

The student will use the sense of hearing to identify unknown materials.

Put various items in a dozen plastic eggs. Seal them, and label them with numbers. Suggested items include tiny marshmallows, rice, beans, pins, cotton, dice, paper clips, a key, matches, a bottle cap, pennies, toothpicks, macaroni, thread, crayon pieces, machine nuts, machine screws, M&M's®, and a marble. Also, have available a few empty eggs as well as samples of each item that you put in the eggs.

To be sure that young children can distinguish between loud and soft sounds and between sounds of different qualities, have children close their eyes while you drop familiar objects on the table or floor. Children listen to the sounds that are made and try to identify the object from its sound.

Pass out the eggs, and ask the children to shake them and try to identify what is in each egg from the sounds it makes when shaken. Typical inquiry questions for young children might include "Which eggs have hard sounds?" "Which eggs have soft sounds?" "Which eggs seem empty?" "Which eggs have similar sounds, like metal, glass, and plastic?" "Are some sounds easy to recognize?" "Are some sounds difficult to recognize?" "Are there certain sounds with which we are all familiar?"

Continued on next page

If children are uncertain of what is in a particular egg, suggest that they put a sample of what they think might be in the egg into an empty egg and compare the sounds made when they are both shaken. (In this way, they are constructing *models* of the unknown eggs.)

Literature Connections

Click, Rumble, Roar: Poems About Machines by Lee Bennett Hopkins (Crowell, 1987) is a book of poetry about the different sounds that machines make.

Just Listen by Winifred Morris (Atheneum, 1990) is a moving story of a young girl's visit to her grandmother's house. The two ladies spend time together outside and listen to the "special song" of nature.

Frogs Sing Songs by Yvonne Winer (Charlesbridge, 2003). Each page in this nonfiction book features a frog in its natural habitat. Readers learn when, where, how, and why frogs sing.

3.5   **CONSTRUCTING SCIENCE IN THE CLASSROOM**

WHAT DID YOU SEE TODAY?

Ongoing Observation Activity

Objective

The students will observe their natural surroundings.

"What did you see on your way to school today?" Ask this question each day. As time goes on, children will start looking for things to report, sharpening their awareness and their observational skills.

"Did you see the same things on the way home?" Children discuss with their parents what they see on their way to and from school.

NSES Content Standard A. Science as Inquiry: Abilities Necessary To Do Scientific Inquiry

Literature Connections

I'm in Charge of Celebrations by Byrd Taylor (Scribner, 1986) is a story about a Native American girl who makes celebrations of beautiful everyday happenings, such as seeing rainbows or coyotes.

Footprints and Shadows by Anne Wescott Dodd (Simon & Schuster, 1992) contains beautiful watercolor illustrations and lyrical text that will capture children's attention as the footprints and shadows play their game of hide-and-seek.

Shadows and Reflections by Tana Hoban (Greenwillow, 1990) contains a collection of pictures that offers an opportunity for comparing and contrasting objects with their shadows and reflections.

Journey into the Desert by John Brown (Oxford University Press, 2002) describes characteristics of the desert, its vegetation and wildlife, and the people of the desert. This nonfiction book also offers survival tips.

3.6 CONSTRUCTING SCIENCE IN THE CLASSROOM

WHAT'S THAT SMELL?

Observation Activity Using the Sense of Smell

NSES Content
Standard A. Science as
Inquiry: Abilities Neces-
sary To Do Scientific
Inquiry

Objective

The student will use the sense of smell to identify materials in film canisters.

Obtain used film canisters from a local photo finishing shop (they are normally free), and number each one. Put a small piece of cotton or a tissue in each, and place a few drops of substances with different odors in each one (for example, perfume, cinnamon, soap, lemon juice, apple juice, orange juice, chopped onion, instant coffee, and herbal tea). Cover the canister with plastic wrap, and poke two or three holes in it. Ask children to describe the odor and try to identify the material in the canister.

Literature Connections

Mucky Moose by Jonathan Allen (Macmillan, 1990) is a humorous story of a foul-smelling moose. All the animals in the forest avoid this moose except for the skunks. When a notorious wolf attempts to capture and eat the moose, several hilarious fiascoes occur.

Dog Breath by Dav Pilkey (Blue Sky, 1994) is a story about Hally, the family dog, who is about to be given away because she has bad breath. Fortunately, Hally proves to be indispensable when she foils a robbery attempt.

Breathtaking Noses by Hana Machotka (Morrow Junior Books, 1992) is a nonfiction book that describes specialized animal noses.

3.7 CONSTRUCTING SCIENCE IN THE CLASSROOM

OBSERVING ROCKS AND MINERALS

Observation Activity Using All Senses

NSES Content
Standard D. Earth
and Space Science:
Properties of Earth
Materials

Objective

The student will make observations of rocks and minerals.

This activity expands the initial rock observation activity described in Constructing Your Ideas 3.1 and is suitable as an introduction to a unit on rocks and minerals.

Assemble a small collection of several different samples of about 15 different rocks and minerals. Here are some suggestions:

Continued on next page

Feldspar—two or three different colors
Sandstone—one or two specimens (showing layering of different colors, if these specimens are available)
Shale—several colors; some specimens with fossils and some specimens without
Granite—one or two good-sized specimens of different colors
Conglomerate
Quartz—8 to 10 different kinds of quartz, such as clear crystalline quartz, tiger's eye, bloodstone, jasper, geodes, agate, rose quartz, and amethyst
Magnetite and/or lodestone
Gypsum—several varieties, including Iceland Spar if you can get a specimen
Pyrite
Chert
Limestone—several different types
Gneiss
Fluorite
Soapstone
Pumice
Obsidian
Coal

You will be able to think of many more. Use what you have available locally, or use your own personal collection.

Put the specimens of each different kind of rock or mineral on paper plates, appropriately labeled with what kind it is and spread these around the classroom. Have magnifying glasses available. Also, put a magnet by the lodestone, and tie a string around the lodestone so it can dangle. Children move around the room from one specimen to another handling, hefting, looking at, and exploring the characteristics of these rocks and minerals. You may wish to develop a guide sheet similar to that in Figure 3.1 to help children in their observations. For a more structured investigation, you can discuss properties of rocks and minerals, such as hard, soft, shiny, glossy, round, flat, and so on, before children investigate on their own.

After children have spent 20 to 30 minutes observing and discussing the specimens, get together as a class, and have the children share what they observed. Here are a few typical observations:

Some specimens of the same mineral come in different colors.
Some minerals look alike even though they are different minerals.
Some minerals are very heavy; some are very light.
The magnetite is magnetic and is attracted to the magnet. The lodestone has poles just like a magnet.
Some rocks are made of tiny grains; others are made of crystals that are very large.

Children will notice many more characteristics about the specimens.

Literature Connections
Everybody Needs a Rock by Byrd Baylor (Aladdin, 1974) is a poetic story that prescribes 10 rules for finding your own special rock. One of the rules is to sniff a rock. "Some kids can

Continued on next page

Examining specimens
of rocks and minerals

FIGURE 3.4

tell by sniffing whether a rock came from the middle of the earth or from an ocean or from a mountain where the wind and sun touched it every day for a million years."

Rocks and Rills—A Look at Geology by A. Harris Stone and Dale Igmanson (Prentice-Hall, 1968) poses many questions about rocks, minerals, and other geologic phenomena. This nonfiction book suggests several experiments designed to let students discover their own answers.

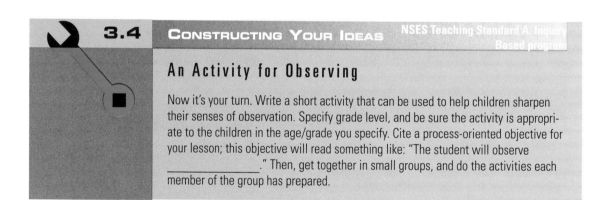

3.4   **CONSTRUCTING YOUR IDEAS**   NSES Teaching Standard A, Inquiry Based program

An Activity for Observing

Now it's your turn. Write a short activity that can be used to help children sharpen their senses of observation. Specify grade level, and be sure the activity is appropriate to the children in the age/grade you specify. Cite a process-oriented objective for your lesson; this objective will read something like: "The student will observe _____." Then, get together in small groups, and do the activities each member of the group has prepared.

CLASSIFYING

Before you start this section, please assemble a fairly large collection of something: shells, feathers, foreign coins, buttons, stamps, pieces of hardware, rocks and minerals, or the like. Once you have assembled a collection of, say, 50 to 60 specimens of the same kind of thing for each group in your class, you are ready to do some activities on classification.

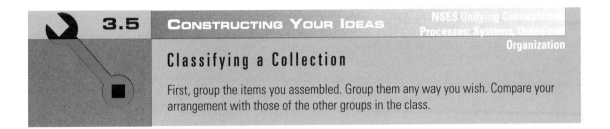

3.5 **CONSTRUCTING YOUR IDEAS** NSES Unifying Concepts and Processes: Systems, Order, and Organization

Classifying a Collection

First, group the items you assembled. Group them any way you wish. Compare your arrangement with those of the other groups in the class.

How many different ways were there of sorting the collection? What kinds of arrangements did each group form?

If you had used a collection of foreign coins, you might have formed groups of square coins, round coins, coins with holes in them, coins with pictures of animals, coins with nothing but writing on them, tiny coins, and so on. This is a simple form of classification that young children can do. It requires the ability to abstract common properties of similar objects.

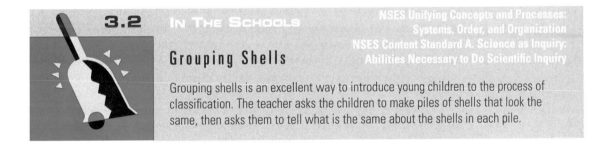

3.2 **IN THE SCHOOLS** NSES Unifying Concepts and Processes: Systems, Order, and Organization
NSES Content Standard A. Science as Inquiry: Abilities Necessary to Do Scientific Inquiry

Grouping Shells

Grouping shells is an excellent way to introduce young children to the process of classification. The teacher asks the children to make piles of shells that look the same, then asks them to tell what is the same about the shells in each pile.

Observing and grouping shells

FIGURE 3.5

Young children have the ability to group objects by *single* characteristics that are readily apparent. For example, a preschool teacher may put six red squares, six yellow squares, and six green squares cut out of tag board in a paper bag, shake them up, and then dump them out on the desk in front of the child. Children will be able to sort the squares by color into three piles: red ones, yellow ones, and green ones. Next, the teacher may put six yellow squares, six yellow triangles, and six yellow circles in a paper bag, shake them up, and then dump them out on the desk. Children will be able to sort the pile of yellow shapes into three groups: squares, triangles, and circles. (Shapes cut out of Velcro® provide a tactile stimulus especially useful for young, visually impaired children.) Each of these sorting activities requires recognition of a single characteristic—color or shape. However, if the teacher puts three each of red, yellow, and green squares; three each of red, yellow, and green triangles; and three each of red, yellow, and green circles in a bag and does the same thing, the average preschooler will sort them *either* by shape or by color. Those who sort them by shape will not readily understand that those who sorted them by color are also correct; preoperational children do not yet have the ability to recognize that the same object can have more than one attribute.

Piaget describes an activity that illustrates this point. An experimenter shows a preoperational child 20 wooden beads, including 17 brown ones and 3 white ones. The child is asked, "Can you make a longer necklace with the brown beads or the wooden beads?" The preoperational child typically replies "brown beads," unable to recognize that each bead has two attributes—its color and the material it is made of (Bybee & Sund, 1982). Preoperational children can deal with only one attribute at a time (Salkind, 1985).

Classifying objects by considering relationships that are subordinate to a larger group as a whole is called **class inclusion,** and this skill is learned during the early concrete operational stage of cognitive development. Early concrete operational children recognize that the same object may have more than one attribute—for example, the beads are all wooden and also have different colors, or each of the cut-outs in the paper bag not only has a certain shape but also a certain color. When children are ready, they are able to start sorting things into two groups that have mutually exclusive attributes using class inclusion skills. Readiness for attempting work requiring more complex thinking often is inferred from children's performance on the Piagetian conservation tasks.[2]

It is important to note that the ability to sort (or classify) does not come spontaneously to children; they must be exposed to the phenomenon. They must be encouraged to do many sorting activities using many different kinds of things to gain experience in the skill of classification. It is a good idea to include classification activities together with observation activities in daily learning centers.

▶ Now, return to the collection you have been working with, and mix it up. This time, sort the collection into two groups, and label each group with a descriptive word or drawing. Again, compare your groups with those of other groups in the class.

What different ways did people have of sorting the collection into two sets? Ask each group to explain why they sorted the way they did. Were any of these ways "righter" than any other? Were any wrong? Note that the names given to the classified sets often show the reason why the people arranged the collection the way they did. Can you tell why?

Take another look at the two sets the groups in your class devised. Each group of students devised two clusters, each labeled with a descriptive word or drawing. Are the two clusters *parallel* in construction? In other words, are the two clusters close to being opposites of each other? Suppose, for example, the two clusters identified in the foreign coin collection were (1) copper-colored coins and (2) silver-colored coins. These two clusters are "opposite" to each other with regard to the color attributes. Suppose, however, the two clusters were (1) copper coins and (2) coins with faces. These two clusters are NOT "opposites." In grouping the coins this way (copper coins and coins with faces), there could be coins that are copper-colored and also have faces on them. The clusters are not *mutually exclusive.* There is no clear line of demarcation between them.

For children to devise parallel classification systems, they must be able to abstract the general attributes that are common to objects in a collection as well as the specific cases of these attributes possessed by each item that make some different from the others. This ability occurs during the mid-concrete operational stage. Children need practice developing parallel classification systems, and the more activities they can be provided, the better they will learn this skill. These types of classification activities also can be included in the learning centers.

▶ The next step is for you to form two subgroups within each mutually exclusive group that you formed above. (If you didn't form mutually exclusive groups, please rearrange the objects so that you have two mutually exclusive groups.) Name each of the subgroups with a word or a drawing. As before, share your arrangements with the class to compare the various ways that people had of grouping similar objects.

You will end up with a grouping something like this:

Main Group A	**Main Group B**
Subgroup 1	Subgroup 1
Subgroup 2	Subgroup 2

Pay special attention to the subgroups. Are Subgroup 1 and Subgroup 2 mutually exclusive within each main group? If not, you will want to rearrange them. Look at each Subgroup 1 under Main Group A and Main Group B. Are they the *same* subgroup? Do the same for each Subgroup 2. For example, if you used the foreign coin collection, you might have a classification system that looks like this:

Copper-Colored Coins	Silver-Colored Coins
Large	Large
Small	Small

In this arrangement, the subgroups under each of the main groups are the same. You can have large copper coins, small copper coins, large silver coins, or small silver coins. Assuming you had defined "large" and "small" fairly precisely, it would be easy to take a new coin that had not been part of the collection and place it in one of the four groups. However, consider the following classification:

Copper-Colored Coins	Silver-Colored Coins
Large	With faces
Small	Without faces

What do you think about this system? The subgroups under each main group are mutually exclusive; indeed, it would be possible to take a new coin and place it accurately into one of the four groups: (1) large copper, (2) small copper, (3) silver with faces, or (4) silver without faces. However, there is something unsettling about the system. Again, the problem is the lack of parallelism. The subgroupings under the main groups are not parallel to each other. Furthermore, this classification system suggests that the same attributes are not being recognized in *all* the items of the collection. The primary attribute recognized in the copper coins is size, and the primary attribute recognized in the silver coins is decoration. However, the absence of parallelism in the subgroups does not make the classification system wrong or even necessarily weak. Indeed, in some instances, it is more descriptive of a collection to have nonparallel classification systems. For example, a collection of leaves might include broad leaves and pine needles. The attributes found in the broad leaves are different from those found in the pine needles, so the classification system would necessarily be nonparallel. Such a system might look like this:

Broad Leaves	Pine Needles
Straight edges	Fat
Crooked edges	Thin

The important consideration in assessing a system of classification is whether it accurately describes the differences among the specimens in the collection. It is critical to *ask* children why they grouped items the way they did to discover their thinking about the process of classification.

▶ Take your classification activity one step further. For each subgroup, form two or more sub-subgroups. Watch for the use of similar attributes, mutual exclusivity, and parallelism. Check each other's classification systems. As an added challenge, select the "weirdest" item from your own collection, one that you had a hard time deciding where to place, and give this item to a different group, challenging them to place it in their classification system. If their system does the job, they should be able to accomplish this task immediately.

You will end up with a grouping something like this:

Main Group A	Main Group B
Subgroup 1	Subgroup 1
a	a
b	b
Subgroup 2	Subgroup 2
a	a
b	b

The leaf classification system described above might look like this:

Broad Leaves	Pine Needles
Straight edges	Fat
Straight veins	Round tips
Radiating veins	Pointed tips
Crooked edges	Thin
Straight veins	Round tips
Radiating veins	Pointed tips

These multiple groupings are hierarchical systems of classification that require higher levels of cognitive skills than simpler class inclusion systems do. Children are in the late concrete or early formal operational stage of cognitive development when they are able to master these more complex systems of classification.

3.3   IN THE SCHOOLS

NSES Unifying Concepts and Processes:
Systems, Order, and Organization
NSES Content Standard A. Science as Inquiry:
Abilities Necessary To Do Scientific Inquiry

Grouping Noodles

A kindergarten teacher provided each child with a bag full of red-, yellow-, green-, and blue-dyed pasta. Pasta comes in a variety of sizes and shapes, and she chose several different kinds. Previously, she had dyed the pasta by putting some in a plastic, closable bag and adding about a half-cup of rubbing alcohol and the contents of a small bottle of food coloring. She shook the bag a few times to coat the pasta, drained the alcohol into the sink, and spread the colored pasta on newspaper outdoors to dry for an hour or so. (Note that the new color gels do not dye the pasta as well as the liquid food coloring.) *Safety note:* **Rubbing alcohol is poisonous to consume!** The children were asked to sort the colored pasta in whatever way they could think of and then describe their grouping systems to the class. They made necklaces of the pasta, stringing them in patterns of their own determination on yarn, and were asked to explain their patterns to the class.

The teacher then read *The Color of Noodles* by Amy Knapp (Sandpiper Press, 1998), a whimsical demonstration that colors are not always what they seem to be.

3.4   IN THE SCHOOLS

NSES Unifying Concepts and Processes.
Systems, Order, and Organization
NSES Content Standard A. Science as Inquiry:
Abilities Necessary To Do Scientific Inquiry

The Hardware Store

A fourth-grade teacher brought a bag of assorted hardware items to school: several kinds of washers, nails, screws, bolts, nuts, and other small items. Groups were provided about 50 of the items and asked to develop a system of organizing them so that customers would be able to readily find what they needed. They also were asked to label the groups to facilitate a customer's search. The teacher then played the role of a customer and asked each group to locate a specific item.

Literature Connection

Aunt Ippy's Museum of Junk by Rodney Greenblat (HarperCollins, 1991). Two children visit their aunt's museum of junk and discover many reusable materials. This is an interesting introduction to the process of classification.

3.5   IN THE SCHOOLS

NSES Unifying Concepts and Processes.
Systems, Order, and Organization
NSES Content Standard A. Science as Inquiry:
Abilities Necessary To Do Scientific Inquiry

Fingerprinting

A third-grade teacher challenged children to be "detectives" by classifying the fingerprints of the class members. Children blackened 5" × 7" cards thoroughly with soft lead pencils, rubbed their fingertips on the pencil smears, and rolled their fingertips on the sticky side of transparent tape. They taped the lifted fingerprints onto a sheet of paper and labeled each with the finger number and the hand (right or left). They then compared the primary patterns of their fingerprints with the three primary fingerprint patterns: *arches* (lines that start on one side, travel up the fingerprint, and exit on the other side), *loops* (lines that enter and exit on the same side of the fingerprint), and *whorls* (circles that do not exit on either side of the fingerprint). They classified their fingerprints according to the three main patterns (see Figure 3.6) and constructed histograms of the number of children whose fingerprints were classified in each category.

Literature Connection

Ed Emberly's Great Thumbprint Drawing Book by Ed Emberly (Little, Brown & Co., 1994) is a nonfiction book that contains directions for creating a variety of shapes and figures using thumbprints.

 A direct link to the FBI Kids Page, where detailed information about fingerprinting can be accessed, is available on the Student Book Companion Web Site.

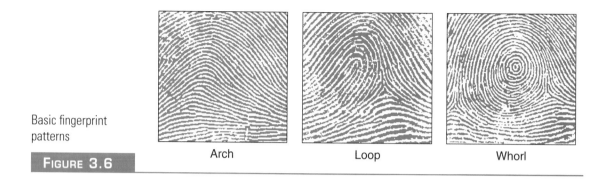

Basic fingerprint
patterns

FIGURE 3.6

Arch   Loop   Whorl

Classification is a skill that is used throughout the scientific enterprise. It is a skill needed by children to put facts together to form concepts, and it is essential in identifying variables as children form hypotheses and design experimental procedures.

Several classification activities appropriate for different age groups of children are suggested in Constructing Science in the Classroom 3.8–3.13.

3.8   **CONSTRUCTING SCIENCE IN THE CLASSROOM**

WHAT'S MAGNETIC? WHAT'S NOT MAGNETIC?

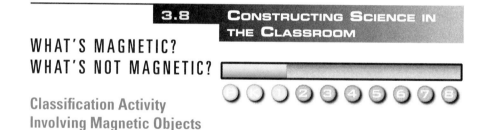

Classification Activity Involving Magnetic Objects

Objective

NSES Content
Standard B. Physical
Science: Magnetism

The student will classify common objects as magnetic or nonmagnetic.

Provide each child with a magnet, and allow time to explore items in the classroom to see which are attracted to the magnet. *Safety Note:* Caution children *not* to bring magnets close to computers, computer monitors, or TV screens. To do so runs the risk of electric shock and is likely to damage the computer or TV permanently. Similarly, caution children *not* to bring magnets close to any electronic device or CD/DVD to avoid permanent damage. Then, place a number of objects, both magnetic and nonmagnetic, on a tray (for example, a nail, a paper clip, scissors, a rubber band, a piece of wood, a crayon, a leaf, a key, a screw, a metal washer, a penny, a nickel, a dime, a quarter, a piece of paper, and the like). Ask children to select one item at a time and tell whether the magnet picks it up. Have a chart available with two columns, labeled "Magnet Attracted" and "Magnet Did Not Attract" or suitable pictographs. After testing each item, children place it on the appropriate half of the chart.

Child-constructed bulletin boards showing objects that are magnetic and objects that are not magnetic can culminate the lesson.

Continued on next page

Even batteries are attracted to magnets!

FIGURE 3.7

This lesson also can be used as a prediction activity. Children select one object at a time and predict whether it will be attracted to the magnet. Then, they try it with the magnet and place the object on the appropriate half of the chart. It is a good idea to have "prediction" and "actual" charts so children can compare their predictions with what actually happened.

Literature Connections

Mickey's Magnet by Franklin Branley and Eleanor Vaughn (Scholastic, 1956). Mickey discovers some of the properties of magnets when he accidentally spills a box of straight pins and has to pick them up.

Magnets (Delta Science Reader, 2004) is a nonfiction book about magnets, magnetic energy, electromagnetism, and how magnets are used.

 See the video clip "Where are the Poles of a Refrigerator Magnet?" on the companion DVD.

3.9 **CONSTRUCTING SCIENCE IN THE CLASSROOM**

CLASSIFYING SEEDS

Classification Activity Involving Seeds

Objective

The student will devise classification systems for seeds.

Use the collection of different kinds of bean and pea seeds that you used in the observation activity shown in Constructing Science in the Classroom 3.3. Children have described or drawn the outsides and the insides of the seeds. Now, ask them to group them and name the groups. Add other seeds, such as corn, marigold, pansy, radish, and the like, and ask children to group the seeds again. Older children can be asked to form subgroups in their classification

NSES Content Standard C. Life Science: Life Cycles of Organisms

Continued on next page

system. Have children identify each main group and subgroup with a descriptive name or drawing, and describe their groupings.

As an extension activity, ask children to estimate the number of seeds in each collection.

Literature Connections

Is It Red? Is It Yellow? Is It Blue? An Adventure in Color and *Is It Rough? Is It Smooth? Is It Shiny?*, both by Tana Hoban (Greenwillow, 1978, 1984), provide vibrant photographs and wordless text that offer many opportunities for introductory classification activities.

Seeds and More Seeds by Millicent Selsam (Harper & Row, 1959) follows an inquisitive young boy who discovers, through experimentation, how to find and plant seeds that grow into beans, fruits, trees, and flowers. The story uses the processes of observation, classification, communication, and measurement.

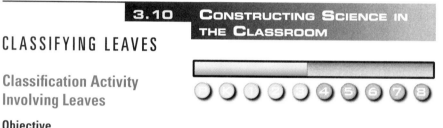

3.10 **CONSTRUCTING SCIENCE IN THE CLASSROOM**

CLASSIFYING LEAVES

Classification Activity Involving Leaves

NSES Content Standard C. Life Science: The Characteristics of Organisms

Objective

The student will classify leaves according to self-identified criteria.

Take children for a walk around the school to collect leaves. *Safety note:* Be sure to inspect the area before you take children to it to be sure there are no dangerous plants, such as poison ivy or poison oak. Also, caution children not to taste or chew on the leaves, because many leaves are poisonous. When you return to the classroom, ask children to group the leaves according to one or more characteristics they themselves identify. Share the classification systems with the class as a whole.

To enable children to explore other groupings later, you may preserve the leaves. Place them between squares of waxed paper (waxed sides toward the leaf), put a cloth over the squares, and iron with a hot iron. Add the preserved specimens to the science center.

Literature Connections

Crinkleroot's Guide to Knowing the Trees by Jim Arnosky (Bradbury, 1992) is a nonfiction book that takes a tour through a forest, during which Crinkleroot introduces broad-leafed and evergreen trees.

Why Do Leaves Change Color? by Betsy Maestro (HarperCollins, 1994) is a nonfiction story of how leaves change color when they are exposed to less water and sunlight.

SunSprouts®: Snails and Slugs by Jill McDougall (ETA/Cuisenaire, 2002) is a nonfiction book about things that are the same and things that are different between a snail and a slug.

3.11 CONSTRUCTING SCIENCE IN THE CLASSROOM

CLASSIFYING MATERIALS IN SOIL

Classification Activity Involving Soil

Objective

The student will devise classification systems for materials found in soil.

Provide several bags of soil from your home or the schoolyard. Put a spoonful of each kind of soil on a paper plate for each group, and give each group a magnifying glass. Ask the children to group (or classify) the materials they find in the soil. When they find something recognizable in the soil, such as sand, rocks, bark, leaves, worms, roots, or seeds, they name it and put it on a piece of paper. If children find something they aren't sure of, they place it on a different sheet of paper labeled with a question mark. Typical questions the teacher asks while circulating around the room might include "Which things are alive?" "Which things used to be alive?" "Which things never were alive?" "Which things are the largest?" "Which things are the smallest?" Having separated and identified the different things in the soil, children can group them on some basis and describe their classification system to the rest of the class.

NSES Content Standard D. Earth and Space Science: Properties of Earth Materials

Groups of similar things found in soil

FIGURE 3.8

Literature Connections

My Feet by Aliki (Crowell, 1990) is a delightful story in which Aliki explains how we use feet and describes the many variations in size and appearance. This is a great introduction to classification for younger children.

Continued on next page

Benny's Animals and How We Put Them in Order by Millicent Selsam (Harper & Row, 1966). A young boy with a passion for neatness and order learns how to classify animals.

CLASSIFYING SMELLS

Classification Activity Involving Sense of Smell

NSES Content Standard A. Science as Inquiry: Abilities Necessary To Do Scientific Inquiry

Objective
The student will classify smells according to self-generated criteria.

Extend the film canister odors observation activity (Constructing Science in the Classroom 3.6) by asking children to sort canisters through matching the odors in some way. Suggestions include "pleasant and unpleasant odors," "those that are easy to identify and those that are difficult to identify," and "fruit-like odors and nonfruit-like odors." Have children come up with their own categories, and ask them to describe their classification systems to the class.

Literature connections:
The Nose Knows by Ellen Weiss (Kane Press, 2002) follows a boy with an amazing sense of smell who becomes the "family nose" when his parents and siblings all come down with colds and can't detect gas from the stove, bad orange juice, and decaying flowers.

What's That Awful Smell? by Heather Tekavec (Dial, 2004). Several farm animals try to solve the mystery of the awful smell coming from the barn.

3.13   CONSTRUCTING SCIENCE IN THE CLASSROOM

CLASSIFYING BUGS

A Classification Activity

Objective
The student will classify insects according to observed characteristics.

NSES Content Standard C. Life Science: The Characteristics of Organisms

Take students on a field trip to the school grounds, and ask them to collect the insects they find. ***Safety note:*** Teach students how to capture insects in jars *without touching them.* Be sure they stay away from fire ants and spiders—cautioning them especially not to probe under things or in dark warm areas. Also, be sure that the students can recognize poison oak, poison ivy, and poison sumac and that they stay away from these plants. Give students photographs of insects to supplement the insects they collected on the school ground so that each group has 15 to 20 actual insects or photographs of insects.

Continued on next page

Ask students to identify characteristics seen in the insects (both real and photographs) and to classify their collection according to these characteristics. Then give a descriptive name to each group and explain why they formed their groups.

Teacher Note: Insects are the earth's most diverse group of living organisms, with some 900,000 different kinds of insects known. Of these, 250,000 to 350,000 are beetles, the most populous living organism on earth, accounting for a fifth of all known living organisms. New species of insects are being discovered regularly. Spiders, however, are not insects. Spiders have eight legs, no antennae, two body sections (head and abdomen), and no wings; insects have six legs, antennae, three body sections, and usually, wings.)

Literature Connection

Simon and Schuster's Guide to Insects by Dr. Ross H. Arnett and Dr. Richard L. Jacques, Jr. (Simon and Schuster, 1981), is an outstanding and authoritative guide to insect species commonly found in North America.

 Web sites with pictures of insects suitable for this activity can be accessed directly through links on the Student Companion Book Web Site.

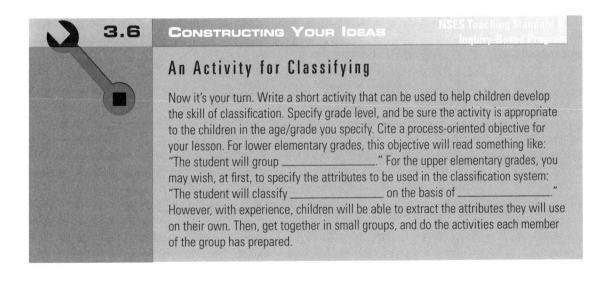

3.6   **CONSTRUCTING YOUR IDEAS**   NSES Teaching Standard A
                                                                    Inquiry-Based Program

An Activity for Classifying

Now it's your turn. Write a short activity that can be used to help children develop the skill of classification. Specify grade level, and be sure the activity is appropriate to the children in the age/grade you specify. Cite a process-oriented objective for your lesson. For lower elementary grades, this objective will read something like: "The student will group _____." For the upper elementary grades, you may wish, at first, to specify the attributes to be used in the classification system: "The student will classify _____ on the basis of _____." However, with experience, children will be able to extract the attributes they will use on their own. Then, get together in small groups, and do the activities each member of the group has prepared.

COMMUNICATING

Communication is enormously important in science (as it is in all of life). Without communication, others would not know what a person did or plans to do or how a person reasons and thinks. You looked at the importance of communication in Chapter 1, when you considered the necessity of listening to students, and again in Chapter 2, when you looked at the role of communication in the nature of science.

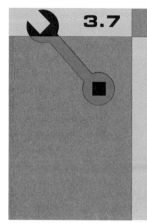

3.7   CONSTRUCTING YOUR IDEAS

Directions for Putting on a Jacket

Try this. Select a partner, and pretend your partner is from a far-away planet and has never seen a jacket or a human put one on. Obtain a jacket or a sweater, and give instructions to your partner as to how to put it on. (To the partner: *Be sure to follow the directions EXACTLY as told to you.*)

How do you start? Do you first tell your partner to be sure the jacket is right-side out? Then what? "Put your right arm into the right sleeve of the jacket." Great, but you didn't say what end of the sleeve your arm goes into. Try this for a few minutes, and then switch roles with your partner.

NSES Teaching
Standard A. Inquiry-
Based Program
NSES Program
Standard B. Relevant,
Inquiry-Based, and
Connected with Other
Subjects
NSES Content
Standard A. Science as
Inquiry: Abilities
Necessary To Do
Scientific Inquiry

This exercise shows what a precise and exquisitely difficult matter it is to communicate accurately. Did you ever have to follow someone's directions to their house? Joke books are filled with such directions as "Turn right about four fenceposts before you get to the large maple tree." The skill of accurate and precise communication is essential in all walks of life, including the scientific enterprise.

Communication can be defined as any and all ways that people let others know their thoughts. We have already employed the skill of communication in activities involving observation and classification. When children observe something, they let others know what they observed by communicating. Children communicate their explanations for their systems of classification. When children discover something, they let others know what they have discovered by communicating. In fact, probably the only way teachers can discover how children are understanding information is to ask them about it and then listen to what they have to say.

Communication includes verbal as well as nonverbal behavior; people communicate by speaking, gesturing, writing, sharing, drawing, telling stories, giving oral presentations, playacting, pantomiming, singing, puppeteering, and so on. In the classroom, children communicate in small groups, in large groups, in individual conversations with each other, in conferences with the teacher, and so on. Graphs, charts, concept maps, graphic organizers, diagrams, posters, symbols, maps, and mathematical equations are ways to communicate data gathered during an investigation. A graph of daily maximum and minimum temperatures tells legions about temperature trends; a chart of daily food groups eaten by children tells legions about their nutrition habits.

The Sandwich

A third-grade teacher set up a table with several different kinds of sandwich items: a wrapped loaf of bread, a closed jar of peanut butter, a closed jar of jelly, a box of raisins, a bag of small marshmallows, a bag of M&M®s plastic knives, plastic spoons, and paper plates. Children were divided into pairs. One child in each pair went to the table, surveyed the sandwich-making items that were available, and wrote down the precise steps for making a sandwich. These children were to pretend that the other person of the pair had never seen a sandwich, had no idea what a sandwich was, and was completely unfamiliar with the ingredients available. The directions were to be so specific that they would even include opening the peanut butter jar.

The team member then gave the written instructions to the other team member, who was asked to follow the directions *exactly* and make the sandwich.

The teacher read *The Giant Jam Sandwich* by John Vernon Lord (Houghton Mifflin, 1987). In this humorous book, four million wasps invade the village, so the citizens make a giant jam sandwich to trap them.

Funny Figures

Children provide oral descriptions of unknown objects, such as the funny figures pictured in Figure 3.9. One child holds a funny figure such that the partner cannot see it and then describes it so that the other child can make an accurate drawing of the figure.

A wide variety of such activities designed to foster full and accurate understanding should be included in the science program so that children can be given the maximum opportunity to develop accurate communications skills. They can write descriptions of activities for publication in class books. They can write in their science journals regularly, describing and illustrating their science activities. They can share their journals with each other and with the teacher to see if their descriptions are clear and accurate. They can describe their activities and the results of their investigations orally with each other, with the teacher, and in the form of class presentations. The more opportunities children are given to discuss, describe, and explain, the better their communications skills will become.

See the Student Book Companion Web Site for a direct link to the Delta Education site.

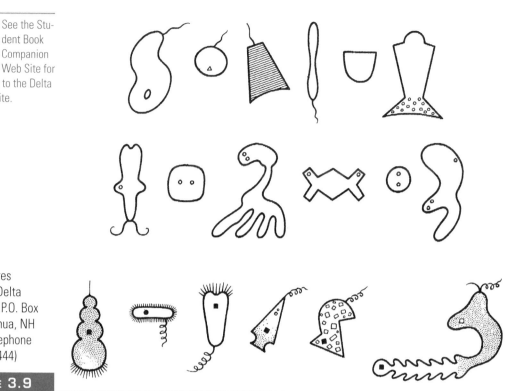

Funny figures (Courtesy Delta Education, P.O. Box 3000, Nashua, NH 03061. Telephone 800-442-5444)

FIGURE 3.9

Additional communications activities for you to consider using in your classroom are shown in Constructing Science in the Classroom 3.14–3.16

| 3.14 | CONSTRUCTING SCIENCE IN THE CLASSROOM |

TWENTY QUESTIONS

Communication Game

NSES Content Standard A. Science as Inquiry: Abilities Necessary To Do Scientific Inquiry

Objective

The student will communicate characteristics of unknown objects and events.

The game "Twenty Questions," which can be played using all kinds of objects and events, is an excellent way of sharpening children's communications skills. Possible ways of communicating include the following:

Oral descriptions
Drawings

Continued on next page

Charts
Concept maps
Graphs
Posters
Written descriptions
Pantomimes

Literature Connections

The Wise Woman and Her Secret by Eve Merriam (Simon & Schuster, 1991) tells of many people seeking the advice of a wise woman who says, "The secret of wisdom is to be curious; to take the time to look closely; to use all your senses to see and touch and taste and smell and hear; to keep wandering and wondering."

Communication by Aliki (Greenwillow, 1993) uses attractive illustrations and simple language to describe the many ways and reasons that people and animals communicate. The inside cover of this nonfiction book includes drawings of sign language and the Braille alphabet.

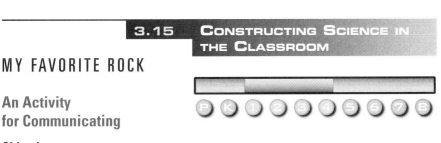

3.15   CONSTRUCTING SCIENCE IN THE CLASSROOM

MY FAVORITE ROCK

**An Activity
for Communicating**

Objective

The student will describe a rock accurately.

> NSES Content
> Standard D. Earth and
> Space Science: Proper-
> ties of Earth Materials

Obtain a collection of 10 to 12 similar rocks. One by one, have students select one that they would consider to be their favorite, but without removing it from the collection. The student should decide why this is his or her favorite. Without removing it from the collection, the student describes his or her favorite rock to a partner and then asks the partner to pick out the right one. If the partner picks out the wrong one, the student should *not* tell which is the right one; instead, the student should describe the right rock better. When the partner selects the right rock, reverse roles.

Ask students whether they thought it was easy to describe their favorite rocks and whether it was easy to pick out the right rock from the partner's description. What could they do better?

For a greater challenge, use unshelled peanuts instead of rocks.

Continued on next page

Literature Connections

I Love Rocks by Cari Meister (Children's Press, 2001) provides factual information about rocks and follows a girl's infatuation with her pet rock.

Queen Nadine by Maryann Kovalski (Orca Book Publishers, 1998) is a story of a girl who lives on a farm and collects rocks, one of which is her pet rock.

The Big Alfie Out of Doors Storybook by Shirley Hughes (Lothrop, 1992) is the story of Alfie, who finds fascination in small things and who suffers the loss of his favorite rock.

3.16   **CONSTRUCTING SCIENCE IN THE CLASSROOM**

CHARTING FOOD GROUPS

An Activity for Communicating with Charts

NSES Content Standard F. Science in Personal and Social Perspectives: Personal Health

A direct link to the U.S. government food pyramid is located on the Student Book Companion Web Site. From the main site, you can access materials suitable for children, including a game and a reproducible poster. Children also can access a page (select "MyPyramid Plan") where they can find a nutritional and exercise plan customized to their needs.

Objective

The student will construct a chart showing the foods eaten in a lunch meal.

First, discuss the U.S. government food pyramid and its food groups with the children. The foods identified are grains, vegetables, fruits, oils, milk, and meats and fish. In addition, the pyramid recognizes "discretionary calories" (including sugars, higher calorie forms of foods, fats, and eating more from the food groups) and exercise. Show children the pyramid, and explain that the thickness of each stripe on the pyramid is an indicator of how much of that food they need to eat to maintain healthy eating habits. If they are familiar with the earlier form of the food pyramid, relate the new pyramid to the former one (see Figure 3.10.) (The 1992 food pyramid focuses on food groups and on the relative amounts that people should eat from each. The 2005 food pyramid focuses more on overall nutrition and less on food groups, and emphasizes the need for exercise.)

For a few days before the activity, ask children to describe the foods they ate at various meals and to show in which of the groups of the pyramid these foods can best be placed. Most of what we eat contains elements of more than one food group, so children should categorize given foods according to the predominant food group—for instance, a hamburger would contain grains (the bun) and meat (the meat).

On the appointed day, ask children to analyze the food they eat for lunch relative to the basic food groups. Give each child a blank food pyramid, and ask them to mark the names of the foods they ate (such as hamburger, hamburger bun, lettuce, and so on) in the proper places on the pyramid. Ask children to use these pyramids to show the rest of the class the degree to which they ate foods from *each* of the food groups during lunch.

This is a good opportunity to discuss childhood obesity as a very serious national health problem—for example, the health risks of childhood obesity, ways of curbing it, and the relationship between obesity and the foods eaten as shown in the food pyramid. Have children

Continued on next page

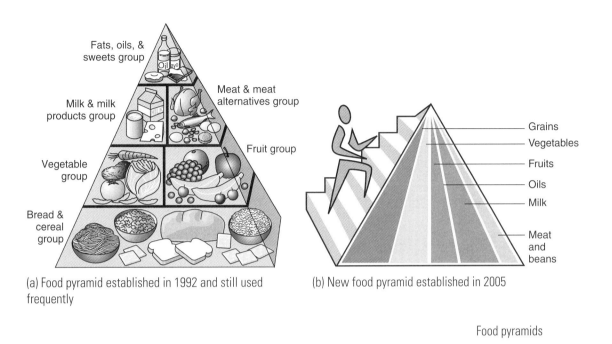

(a) Food pyramid established in 1992 and still used frequently

(b) New food pyramid established in 2005

Food pyramids

FIGURE 3.10

access the *MyPyramid.gov* site and click on *MyPyramid Plan,* input their age, weight, and exercise habits, and find a customized nutritional and exercise plan that they can compare with their current habits.

Because fat intake is a major contributor to obesity, you might ask children to test foods for fat. Have them place the same amount of each of several different kinds of foods on a piece of brown paper bag. Try such foods as raw and cooked hamburger, rice, French fries, apples, banana, cauliflower, various kinds of bread, various kinds of cookies, ice cream, and the like. The fat leaves a grease spot, and the greater the fat content, the larger the grease spot (providing the other variables, such as size, are the same).

Literature Connections

Gregory, the Terrible Eater by Mitchell Sharmat (Simon & Schuster, 1984) follows Gregory, the goat, who is a very picky eater, preferring fruits, vegetables, eggs, and orange juice to shoes and tin cans.

The Edible Pyramid: Good Eating Every Day by Loreen Leedy (Holiday House, 1996) describes animal characters in a restaurant who are offered foods grouped in sections of the food pyramid and who learn how many servings of each they need every day.

*Several sources have suggested that the current U.S. government food pyramid is flawed (Harvard School of Public Health, 2002; Willett & Stampfer, 2002)—that not all fats are bad for you and not all complex carbohydrates are good for you.

The Harvard School of Public Health has many authoritative articles on virtually all aspects of nutrition. You can access this site through a direct link on the Student Book Companion Web site.

3.8

CONSTRUCTING YOUR IDEAS   NSES Teaching Standard A
                                               Inquiry-Based Program

An Activity for Communicating

Now it's your turn. Write a short activity that can be used to help children develop skill in communication. Specify grade level, and be sure the activity is appropriate to the children in the age/grade you specify. Cite a process-oriented objective for your lesson; this objective will read something like: "The student will communicate _____." Then, get together in small groups, and do the activities each member of the group has prepared.

MEASURING

NSES Teaching
Standard A. Inquiry-
Based Program
NSES Program
Standard C. Coordinated
with Mathematics
NSES Content
Standard A. Science
as Inquiry: Abilities
Necessary To Do
Scientific Inquiry

Elementary school children measure five basic entities in science: (1) length, (2) volume, (3) weight or mass, (4) temperature, and (5) time.

Length

Length is defined as the distance between two points. Examples are the length of a tabletop, the height of a door, the distance between two cities, the circumference of a beach ball, and so on. Length is the fundamental measurement needed to find area, which is calculated by applying various area formulas, such as length times width (for the area of a rectangle) or one-half base times height (for the area of a triangle). Length also may be used to find volume by applying various formulas, such as length times width times height (for the volume of a rectangular box).

Length may be measured either in metric units or in conventional units. The basic metric unit of length is the meter, which originally was defined as one ten-millionth of the distance from the North Pole to the equator as measured along a great circle passing through Lyons, France. Today, the meter is defined in more precise terms—namely the distance that light travels in 1/299,792,458th of a second.

The meter is divided into 10 centimeters, and each centimeter is divided into 10 millimeters. Thus, there are 1,000 millimeters in a meter. One thousand meters makes a kilometer. (See Figure 3.11 for a table of metric prefixes.)

The basic unit of length in the conventional system is the foot. Three feet equal a yard. A meter is a little longer than a yard. If you put an inch ruler next to a centimeter ruler, you will find that it takes about 2½ centimeters to make 1 inch.

Prefix	Meaning
kilo-	1,000 times
hecto-	100 times
deca-	10 times
deci-	1/10th
centi-	1/100th
milli-	1/1,000th

Table of metric prefixes

FIGURE 3.11

Children should be encouraged to measure such things as desktops, the length and width of the room, the height of the door, their own heights, and anything else in their physical environment. Many instruments are available to assist in measuring such as rulers, yardsticks, meter sticks, and calipers. When young children find the length of an object they are measuring to be between whole numbers of the units they are using, you can ask them to record the number of *whole* units they measured and to disregard the additional fractional part.

Children can measure length in terms of number of LEGOs®, plastic bears, blocks, paper clips, lengths of string, nose-to-fingertips span, length of feet, and so on. The important thing is that they gain the idea that length can be quantified and things can be measured; this is more important than memorizing the rubrics of the metric system or the number of inches in a foot.

Children measure everything, including walls and their own heights

FIGURE 3.12

3.8

NSES Program Standard C. Coordinated with Mathematics
NSES Content Standard C. Life Science: The Characteristics of Organisms

Graphing Plant Growth

Plant height can be measured in terms of the number of squares on a piece of graph paper. Children place strips of graph paper behind the plants they want to measure, then cut off the strips at the top of the plant. They paste the strips onto a large chart and count the number of squares, showing the relative heights of the plants in graphical form. This procedure also can be used to display plant growth over time.

Literature Connection

The Carrot Seed by Ruth Krauss (Harper & Row, 1945). A little boy plants a carrot seed and cares for it regularly. The seed grows into a huge plant despite everyone telling him it won't come up.

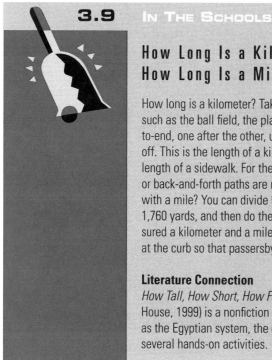

3.9

NSES Program Standard C. Coordinated with Mathematics
NSES Content Standard A. Science as Inquiry: Abilities Necessary To Do Scientific Inquiry

How Long Is a Kilometer?
How Long Is a Mile?

How long is a kilometer? Take a few meter sticks outside to a large but safe region, such as the ball field, the playground, or the sidewalk, and lay the meter sticks end-to-end, one after the other, until 1,000 separate meter lengths have been counted off. This is the length of a kilometer. It may be possible to measure a full kilometer's length of a sidewalk. For the ball field or playground, keep track of how many circular or back-and-forth paths are required to equal one kilometer. How does it compare with a mile? You can divide 5,280 feet in a mile by 3 feet in a yard, obtaining 1,760 yards, and then do the same thing with yardsticks. In one class, children measured a kilometer and a mile along the street in front of their school and put markers at the curb so that passersby could check the accuracy of their car odometers.

Literature Connection

How Tall, How Short, How Far Away? By David A. Adler and Nancy Tobin (Holiday House, 1999) is a nonfiction book that introduces several measuring systems, such as the Egyptian system, the conventional system, and the metric system. It contains several hands-on activities.

Volume

The *volume* of something is how much space it takes up. Volume can be measured in terms of length (as mentioned above) or in terms of its own units. The basic metric unit for volume is the liter, which is about the same as a quart. One liter contains 1,000 milliliters. Because the volume of a milliliter is the same as the volume of a cubic object that is 1 centimeter on each side, the term *cubic centimeter,* or *cc,* is used more commonly than milliliters. It takes 1,000 cc to equal one liter. The basic unit of liquid volume in the conventional system is the quart, which contains 4 cups; the cup is equivalent to 8 ounces of liquid. Four quarts make a gallon.

As with length, it is not only possible, but also desirable, for children to invent their own units of volume; a paper cup, coffee can, and the like are ideal for measuring amounts of liquid.

NSES Teaching Standard A. Inquiry-Based Program
NSES Program Standard B. Relevant, Inquiry-Based, and Connected with Other Subjects
NSES Content Standard A. Science as Inquiry: Abilities Necessary To Do Scientific Inquiry

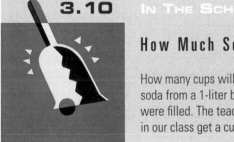

3.10   IN THE SCHOOLS

NSES Program Standard C. Coordinated with Mathematics
NSES Content Standard A. Science as Inquiry: Abilities Necessary To Do Scientific Inquiry

How Much Soda Is in a Liter?

How many cups will a liter of soda fill? A kindergarten teacher asked a child to pour soda from a 1-liter bottle into cups. Other children counted the number of cups that were filled. The teacher asked, "If we buy one 1-liter bottle of soda, will every child in our class get a cup of soda?"

In dealing with young children and the concept of volume, let us recall the Piagetian experiments relative to **conservation.** When a ball of clay is rolled into a cigar-shaped cylinder, preoperational children are not able to perceive that the volume of clay stays the same. Instead, they perceive that there is *more* clay, because it occupies greater length. The same is true when water is poured from a tall, thin glass into a large tank; because it occupies less depth in the tank than in the glass, young children perceive that there is less water. These experiments show that preoperational children have difficulty in conserving volume. They do not understand that the amount of material in something does not change when the shape changes. These tasks are sometimes used to determine whether children are ready for concrete operational thought.[3] (The Piagetian stages and their application to elementary science education are discussed in Chapter 4.)

Because preoperational children have difficulty with tasks involving conservation of volume, it is inappropriate to ask them to compare volumes of different materials or to do activities that require them to recognize that the volume of a material does not change when its shape does. In kindergarten, volume activities should consist of counting tasks, such as finding the number of cups of sand it takes to fill or empty a pail.

Calculating volume by **displacement** is an advanced concept, and many children in upper elementary grades cannot understand it. Displacement is a method of determining the volume of an irregularly shaped object by placing it in a container of a known volume of water and then measuring the apparent increase in the volume of water when the object is immersed in the water. This is similar to what you do when you want to measure ½ cup of shortening for a cookie recipe. You put, say, 1½ cups of water in a 2-cup measuring cup, then completely submerge the shortening in the water until the level of water reaches the 2-cup mark. In this way, you have measured ½ cup of shortening. This concept is difficult for children to understand. Not only do they have to understand that the volume of water is conserved (none is added, and none is taken away) and that the volume of shortening is conserved, they also have to understand that two things cannot occupy the same place at the same time and they have to conceive of the subtraction process necessary for calculating the volume. Many fifth-grade teachers have reported that even though this concept is presented in the curriculum, their students simply do not understand it. This, of course, is to be expected: Many fifth-grade children do not yet have the level of conservation reasoning required to understand displacement. (The concept of displacement is used in Constructing Science in the Classroom 3.44 ("Why Do Some Things Sink and Some Things Float in Water?"))

Weight or Mass

There is a difference between weight and mass. *Weight* is the *pull* of gravity on something, and *mass* is the *amount* of material in that something. Weight depends on the strength of gravity. Gravity on the moon is about 1/6 of the gravity on the earth, so things weigh about 1/6 as much on the moon as they do on the earth. People can jump higher and hop farther on the moon than they can on the earth because there is less gravity to hold them down. However, people have the same amount of mass (material) in them whether they are on the earth or on the moon. Weight varies from place to place, but mass does not.

Mass and weight are measured in different ways and have different units. The most common unit of mass is the kilogram, a metric unit. The most common unit of weight is the pound, a conventional system unit. Unfortunately, these units are often used interchangeably in modern society. For example, at home, we weigh 125 pounds; when we get to the doctor's office, the nurse tells us we weigh 57 kilograms. The label on a pound package of butter says "net weight 1 pound (454 grams)." Yet, the pound is a unit of weight, and the kilogram and gram are units of mass. The reason people tend to interchange the pound and the kilogram is that for all practical purposes, the weight of a given mass stays the same everywhere on earth. If a rock has a mass of 5 kilograms, it will weigh 11 pounds on earth (2.2 times its mass in kilograms) no matter where you take it. Of course, there may be slight variations in weight depending on altitude, because the force of gravity decreases the higher you go. However, this change in weight is insignificant. As you can imagine, it is difficult for children to understand that mass and weight are two different things. Because of this common, yet technically erroneous, interchangeability of the units for mass and weight, it is suggested that elementary teachers not expend much effort trying to get children to understand the difference between the two. This concept will certainly come later.

The basic unit of weight is the pound; there are 16 ounces in a pound and 2,000 pounds in a ton. There are many units in the conventional system to measure large and small amounts of weight, such as tons, ounces, and drams.

The basic unit of mass is the kilogram. A kilogram is defined as the mass of a cylinder made of an alloy of platinum and iridium and kept in Paris, France. A mass of 1 kilogram weighs 2.2 pounds on the earth at sea level. A gram is 1/1,000 of a kilogram and equals the mass of 1 cubic centimeter of pure water; it is about the mass of a good-sized mosquito. The prefixes shown in Figure 3.11 apply to the gram; the most commonly used subunits are the milligram (1/1,000 of a gram) and the kilogram (1,000 grams).

It is not necessary for young children to weigh things in terms of grams or ounces or pounds; these concepts are abstract and are developed in later grades. Instead, they should be encouraged to weigh things in terms of small plastic bears, paper clips, LEGOs®, blocks, and the like. Simple balances are available that use tiny plastic bears, plastic cubes, or paper clips as units of weight. Children also can compare weights of similar things relative to each other, such as large rocks versus small rocks, heavy books versus light books, and large metal washers versus small metal washers.

USING A TWO-PAN BALANCE

Balances and scales are available in single-pan or two-pan forms. The two-pan form is the most appropriate type for elementary science. In this balance, the object to be weighed is placed on one pan, and weights are added to the other pan until balance is achieved. This normally is shown by a pointer that points to lines on both sides of a middle line as the balance swings to and fro. When the pointer stops at the middle line, balance has been achieved. However, because of friction, it is possible that the pointer may come to rest slightly before or slightly after balance has been achieved. To avoid this imbalance, we take the reading "on the swing," which means that balance has been achieved when the pointer loses the same amount of each side of the middle line as it passes it. We do not wait for the balance to stop swinging. Figure 3.13 shows several two-pan balances.

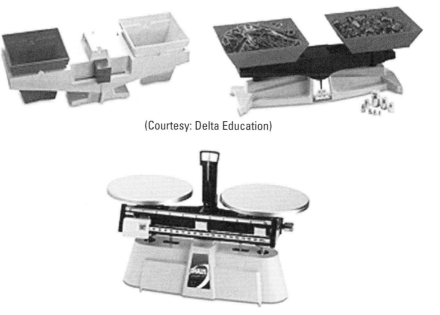

(Courtesy: Delta Education)

Two-pan balances

FIGURE 3.13

(Courtesy: Ohaus Corporation)

3.11 IN THE SCHOOLS NSES Content Standard A. Science as Inquiry: Abilities Necessary To Do Scientific Inquiry

Weighing Cookies

In a second-grade class, the teacher gave each child a chocolate chip cookie and asked the children how they could tell who has the biggest one. Children compared diameters and then thickness. At the teacher's suggestion, they compared the weights of each other's cookies on the balance. Children were then given untouched cookies for a snack.

Literature connections

If You Give a Mouse a Cookie by Laura Joffe Numeroff (Harper & Row, 1985). The consequences of giving a cookie to an energetic mouse run the young host ragged.

The Misfortune Cookie by Dan Greenburg and Jack E. Davis (Grosset & Dunlap, 1998) tells the story of Zak, who visits a very strange Chinese restaurant and finds that the fortunes in his fortune cookie start coming true.

Temperature

Temperature can be measured either in degrees Celsius (the metric system) or in degrees Fahrenheit (the conventional system). Of course, a certain temperature is the same whether it is expressed in Fahrenheit or Celsius. Children should become familiar with both the Fahrenheit system and the Celsius system. The points of reference in each system are the freezing point and the boiling point of water (at sea level). The freezing point of water is 0° Celsius or 32° Fahrenheit. The boiling point of water is 100° Celsius or 212° Fahrenheit. The advantage of the Celsius scale is that the difference in temperature between freezing water and boiling water is divided into 100 degrees, whereas in the Fahrenheit scale, this difference is divided into 180 degrees.

Common temperatures in both Celsius and Fahrenheit are given in Figure 3.14.

	Celsius	Fahrenheit
Boiling point of water	100°	212°
Human body normal temperature	37°	98.6°
Hot day outside	32°	90°
Comfortable room temperature	21°	70°
Freezing point of water	0°	32°
Cold day outside	−18°	0°

Common temperatures in degrees Celsius and degrees Fahrenheit

FIGURE 3.14

Temperature is an abstract concept, one that young children have difficulty understanding. Thus, young children might be encouraged to compare temperatures of objects with their own body temperature: How do things feel? Does a cup of water feel hot? Warm? Cool? Cold? Is sand hot in the summer? How hot? Too hot to walk on? How about the blacktop on the streets? How about the concrete of the sidewalks? Is a room hot? Cold? Just right? What do you like hot? Soup? Cocoa? Pizza? What do you like cold? Soda? Ice cream?

3.12 IN THE SCHOOLS   NSES Content Standard A: Science as Inquiry: Abilities Necessary To Do Scientific Inquiry

Recording Daily Temperatures

Children can be introduced to the conceptual meaning of temperature by recording temperature readings taken from television or radio weather broadcasts on the daily classroom calendars.

As children grow older, they learn to read the thermometer, but because this may require **interpolation** (inferring numbers that are not printed on the scales), skill in estimation is required. Thus, temperature readings could be deferred until children can estimate the distance between two known positions. Then, they will be able to count the lines between degrees that are marked on the thermometer and interpolate the actual reading. Digital thermometers provide accurate temperature readouts and can be used until children learn how to read regular thermometers.

3.13   IN THE SCHOOLS   NSES Content Standard A. Science as Inquiry: Abilities Necessary To Do Scientific Inquiry

Varying Temperatures

A fifth-grade teacher read the story of *Goldilocks and the Three Bears* and asked her students what variables might have caused the three bowls of porridge to vary in temperature. Each group selected one of the variables cited and devised ways to test the effect of that variable on temperature. Because time was a factor in the story, students recorded the temperature every minute or so until it remained the same for three consecutive readings.

Time

There are two aspects to measuring time—time of day and time intervals. One of the skills children learn in the early elementary grades is to tell time using clocks. Time is recorded from the wall clocks for many daily

3.14   IN THE SCHOOLS   NSES Content Standard D. Earth and Space Science: Objects in the Sky

Recording Time and Temperature

Children record the outdoor temperature at, say, 11:30 AM each day and construct a histogram to show how the outdoor temperature changes from day to day.

Literature Connection
Temperature and You by Betsy and Guilio Maestro (Lodestar, 1990) is an introductory story of what temperature is and how it is measured. This book is appropriate for lower grades.

routines. Children should be discouraged from using digital clocks until time concepts have been explored using regular clocks. Many science activities involve recording the time of day.

A different aspect of time involves measuring intervals of time rather than time of day. The unit for time intervals is the second; this is a universal unit and is the same in the conventional system and the metric system. The second was first defined as 1/86,400th of the mean solar day (the average length of the day over a period of one year). Now, however, the second is defined in terms of a type of radiation that is emitted by the element cesium-133.

Intervals of time can be measured using stopwatches or the second hand on a clock. Time intervals also can be measured using systems devised by the teacher and students. The length of a second is about the length of time that it takes to say "one-one-thousand." Intervals of time measured in many science activities can be approximated by having children count "one-one-thousand, two-one-thousand, three-one-thousand, ..." rhythmically. As children gain skill in this rhythmic method of counting seconds, they can compare their counting with the sweep second hand on the wall clock to demonstrate for themselves that their method is, in fact, very close to "real" time.

Hourglasses, which come in many sizes, can be used to measure intervals of time by recording the number of flips of the hourglass it takes for a given occurrence, such as popping popcorn, to happen. One teacher used paper funnels available at gas stations; she put a given amount of sand in the funnel and let it run out to act like an hourglass.

3.15   IN THE SCHOOLS

NSES Content Standard A, Science as Inquiry: Abilities Necessary To Do Scientific Inquiry

How Long Does It Take to Run Across the Playground?

How long does it take a person to run from one end of the playground to the other? One child does the running, and another child operates a stopwatch, counts seconds on a clock, or uses some nonconventional timing system devised by the class.

Literature Connection

Clocks and More Clocks by Pat Hutchins (Macmillan, 1970). Mr. Higgins buys many clocks, but they all show different times when he moves from room to room. He consults a clockmaker, who teaches him about elapsed time.

Toasting Marshmallows

A seventh-grade teacher asked the students how long it takes to toast marshmallows over a fire. After some discussion, the class decided that the time it takes depends on how far away the marshmallow is above the fire. The teacher procured some regular-sized marshmallows, some skewers, and a can of Sterno®. Students held each marshmallow directly over the flame at measured distances above the can (so it would be easier to measure) and recorded the time it took for the marshmallow to become toasted. They decided to define "toasted" as the moment just before the marshmallow caught fire.

They graphed their data with the distance above the Sterno® can on the *x*-axis (horizontal axis) and the time on the *y*-axis (vertical axis) using a graphing program. They formed their conclusions from their observations and the graph (see Figure 3.15). (Adapted from an activity developed by Wendy Hobbs, a graduate student at Kennesaw State University.)

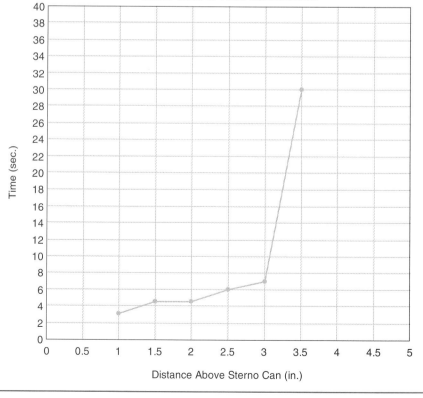

Graph of the time it takes to toast marshmallows held at different heights above a flame (Graph Master software)

FIGURE 3.15

As is true for all units of measurement, time is an abstract concept, and children have to build meaning for the concept by doing activities that involve the use of time. Kindergarten is not too early for children to start.

Metric Versus Conventional Units

Many science educators have written about educating our young people in the metric system. The United States is one of very few countries that still use the conventional system. Even Canada and Mexico, our closest neighbors, use the metric system. The U.S. Congress has tried for many years to legislate use of the metric system but has consistently failed to secure the needed support. (However, in 1988, a law was passed requiring federal agencies to use the metric system, whenever practical, to make the United States more competitive in international trade.) So, in the United States, a person is still 5 feet 3 inches tall and weighs 120 pounds, and the temperature is still 72° Fahrenheit.

It is useful to examine the arguments for and against using the metric system. The world of science uses the metric system. Therefore, in keeping with our premise that children should learn science the way that scientists do science, children should make all measurements in science using the metric system. The metric system is easier to use than the conventional system, and children enjoy working with it. However, learning theory suggests that children learn best that which is meaningful to them. Children are familiar with the conventional system and use terms like inches, miles, pounds, ounces, and degrees Fahrenheit. Children do not measure everyday things in meters, weigh things in kilograms, or record temperatures in degrees Celsius. To insist that the metric system be used in elementary science education, even though it is not used in the daily lives of the children, is asking children to think in terms of units that are less meaningful to them than the conventional units are. It also may place an aura of mysticism and elitism around the study of science. This is one of the many ambiguities in the field of education with which you must wrestle. So, it is your decision whether the metric system should be used in your science program. You will have support either way, although the National Science Teachers Association encourages the use of the metric system whenever possible (National Science Teachers Association, 1999). If you use the metric system because of its ease of conversion among subdivisions of the scales and because of its universal use in the scientific enterprise, you have a very strong argument for choosing the metric system. If you use conventional units to foster meaning based on previous experiences and familiarity, you have a very strong argument for choosing conventional units. Most units in this text are provided in both metric and conventional units.

NSES Teaching Standard E. Developing Learners Who Reflect Intellectual Rigor and Attitudes Conducive to Science Learning

Comparing Metric and Conventional Units

To help children understand that both metric and conventional units are in common use, a teacher asked children to list items sold in grocery stores together with the units of measurement used. Children discovered that flour and sugar are sold by the pound and that soda is sold by the liter.

Several measurement activities appropriate for various grade levels are suggested in Constructing Science in the Classroom 3.17–3.23.

3.17   CONSTRUCTING SCIENCE IN THE CLASSROOM

HOW MANY PENNIES?

Activity For Measuring Length

NSES Content Standard A. Science as Inquiry: Abilities Necessary To Do Scientific Inquiry

Objective

The student will measure length using common objects.

Provide each child with a number of pennies and several objects to be measured, such as a clothespin, napkin, paper clip, sheet of construction paper, and the like. Explain to the children that the unit of measure is "one penny," and ask them to select an object and estimate how many pennies long it is. Then, have the children lay the pennies end-to-end, obtaining an actual length measurement in terms of number of pennies (see Figure 3.16).

Estimated and actual penny-lengths are recorded on a chart. Children continue measuring objects in terms of pennies, thereby gaining an understanding about the meaning of measurement of length. In addition, their estimates become more and more accurate.

For follow up, ask children what other items can be used for measurement.

Literature Connections

How Big Is a Foot? by Rolf Myller (Atheneum, 1962) is a comical story about the use of nonstandard measurement. The king orders a carpenter to build a bed based on the length of the king's foot; however, the carpenter builds the bed based on the length of his own foot.

The Hundred Penny Box by Sharon Bell Mathis (Puffin, 1986). An elderly woman explains to her grandson that a penny is placed in a box every year of her life. The passage of time is well explained in this moving story.

Measuring the length
of a sheet of paper
with pennies

FIGURE 3.16

3.18   CONSTRUCTING SCIENCE IN THE CLASSROOM

HOW MUCH DOES A PENNY WEIGH?

Activity for Measuring Weight

Objective

The student will measure the weight of objects using nonconventional units.

First, show children how to use the two-pan balance (see the box "Using a Two-Pan Balance").

Put a penny in one pan of the balance, and add paper clips to the other pan until the scale is balanced. Children record the number of paper clips used. Encourage children to experiment with how much two, three, and four pennies weigh. Also, encourage them to explore the weights of many different things using different items as weights on the balance.

Literature Connection

Let's Find Out About What's Light and What's Heavy by Martha and Charles Shapp (Franklin Watts, 1975) uses attention-getting pictures and humorous text to help children discover that what may be light for one person may be heavy for another.

NSES Content
Standard A. Science as
Inquiry: Abilities
Necessary To Do
Scientific Inquiry

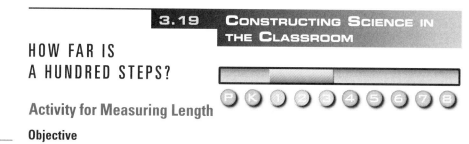

HOW FAR IS A HUNDRED STEPS?

Activity for Measuring Length

NSES Content Standard A. Science as Inquiry: Abilities Necessary To Do Scientific Inquiry

Objective
The student will walk 100 paces and will measure the distance.

First, show children how to make uniform paces by walking normally. Take them to the hall, and one at a time, ask children to walk 100 paces in a straight line. They are to mark where they end with a piece of masking tape labeled with their name. They measure the distances they walked with a foot ruler, yardstick, or meter stick and record these on paper. Children then compare distances to see the differences in lengths of strides.

Literature Connection
Is It Larger? Is It Smaller? by Tana Hoban (Greenwillow, 1985) introduces comparisons of different sizes of the same object and explores the concepts of length, weight, volume, area, time, and money.

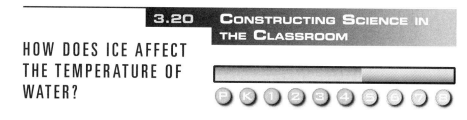

HOW DOES ICE AFFECT THE TEMPERATURE OF WATER?

Activity for Measuring Temperature

NSES Content Standard B. Physical Science: Heat Energy

Objective
The student will measure the temperature of water.

Fill a glass partly full of water, and record its temperature. Add an ice cube to the water, and predict how long it will take to melt. Every minute, record the temperature and the time on a chart. Keep recording temperature and time readings until the last three readings stay the same.

Literature Connection
Winter Barn by Peter Parnall (Macmillan, 1986). The winter barn is a safe haven for all the creatures that seek shelter from the brutal, subzero winds as they wait for the first signs of spring.

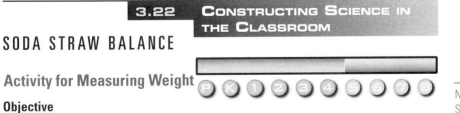

3.21   CONSTRUCTING SCIENCE IN THE CLASSROOM

HOW MUCH DOES AIR WEIGH?

Activity for Measuring Weight

Objective
The student will weigh a given amount of air.

Air is a difficult phenomenon for young children to grasp, because we cannot see it or smell it. However, we can feel it when the wind blows, so we know air is all around us. Does air weigh anything? Because it is a material (we know this because we can feel it when it blows), it must be matter, and because it is matter, it must have some weight.

Take an empty balloon, and put it on the right-hand pan of a pan balance. Add weights, paper clips, and tiny pieces of paper to the left-hand pan until the mechanism is balanced. Now, fill the balloon with air by blowing it up. (We understand that what you blow into the balloon isn't strictly air; it contains higher amounts of carbon dioxide and water vapor, because it comes from your lungs. However, it still is air.) Tie a knot in the filled balloon, and put it back on the right-hand pan. The scale will be off-balance because of the added weight of the air in the balloon. The weight of the air is very small, probably less than a gram. Cut strips of graph paper, and add them to the left-hand pan of the scale until perfect balance is regained. The weight of the strips of paper is equal to the weight of the air in the balloon.

To find out how much weight this is, weigh a whole sheet of the graph paper, and divide by the number of squares in the sheet. This gives the weight of one square. Multiply this by the number of squares it took to balance the full balloon, and you will have calculated the weight of air in the balloon.

Literature Connection
Air Is All Around You by Franklyn M. Bradley (Crowell, 1986) is a nonfiction book that describes the various properties of air and shows how to prove that air takes up space and that there is air dissolved in water.

NSES Content Standard D. Earth and Space Science: Structure of the Earth System

3.22   CONSTRUCTING SCIENCE IN THE CLASSROOM

SODA STRAW BALANCE

Activity for Measuring Weight

Objective
The student will measure weights of very small objects using the soda straw balance.

With this soda straw balance, children can weigh extremely light objects, such as a mosquito, a hair, a blade of grass, and a square of graph paper. Obtain a plastic or paper

NSES Content Standard A. Science as Inquiry: Abilities Necessary To Do Scientific Inquiry

Continued on next page

soda straw, a bolt or screw that will fit snugly into one end of the straw, a pin, and two wooden blocks. Cut one end of the straw at an angle to form a "pan." Put the bolt in the other end, and screw it partway into the straw. Run the pin through the straw *just barely forward* of the screw and a little bit above the center of the straw. Balance the straw between the two blocks of wood, and screw the bolt in or out very slowly until the straw rests at a suitable incline. This balance can measure weights as little as 1/1,000 of a gram (see Figure 3.17).

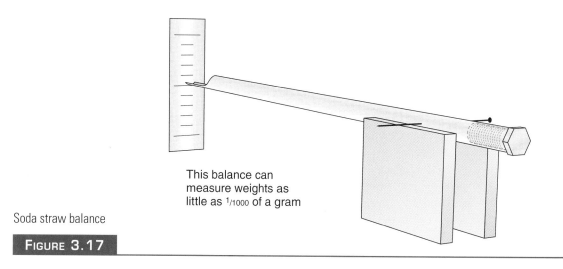

This balance can measure weights as little as $^1/_{1000}$ of a gram

Soda straw balance

FIGURE 3.17

To find the weights of things using this balance, weigh a sheet of graph paper on a gram balance. Count the number of squares in the sheet, and divide the weight by the number of squares to obtain the weight of one square. Cut out one square, and place it in the pan of the soda straw balance. Set up a tongue depressor next to the tip of the balance, and record the positions of the tip of the balance both without the square of graph paper and with the square of graph paper. Divide the space between these two positions into 10 equal segments, and calculate the weight represented by each segment. (Each division is equal to 1/10th of the weight of the square of graph paper.)

Now, use the soda straw balance to measure all sorts of very light things!

Literature Connection

8,000 Stones: A Chinese Folktale retold by Diane Wolkstein (Doubleday, 1972) explains the use of nonstandard units of measure and how to weigh something very large.

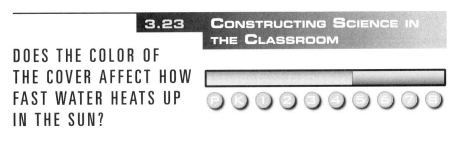

DOES THE COLOR OF THE COVER AFFECT HOW FAST WATER HEATS UP IN THE SUN?

3.23   CONSTRUCTING SCIENCE IN THE CLASSROOM

Activity for Measuring Temperature

Objective

The student will measure temperature of water under different conditions.

Provide children with large Styrofoam cups, a bucket of tap water, thermometers, an assortment of papers of differing colors (including white and black), and a piece of aluminum foil.

Children fill their cups about three-quarters full with tap water. Then, children cover the top of the cup with a piece of colored or white or black paper or aluminum foil, insert the thermometer through the cover so it is in the water, and record the initial temperature. They place the cups in the sun, and record the temperatures every minute and for a predetermined period of time—say, 10 minutes.

Back in the classroom, children graph their data on a bar graph showing the temperature of the water for each color and type of cover after the same period of time. If several children selected the same cover, the temperatures should be averaged and then plotted on the graph.

Children look at the data and the graphs to answer the question, "Does the color of the cover affect how fast the water in the cups heats up in the sun?"

NSES Content
Standard B. Physical
Science: Heat Energy

3.9   CONSTRUCTING YOUR IDEAS

An Activity for Measuring

Now it's your turn. Write a short activity that can be used to help children develop one of the measurement skills. Specify grade level, and be sure the activity is appropriate to the children in the age/grade you specify. Cite a process-oriented objective for your lesson; this objective will read something like: "The student will measure _____." Then, get together in small groups, and do the activities each member of the group has prepared.

PREDICTING

A great deal of scientific inquiry begins with predicting the result of an investigation and then testing that predicted result to see if it occurs.

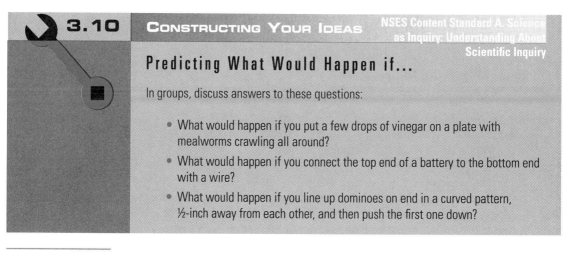

3.10   CONSTRUCTING YOUR IDEAS

NSES Content Standard A. Science as Inquiry: Understanding About Scientific Inquiry

Predicting What Would Happen if...

In groups, discuss answers to these questions:

- What would happen if you put a few drops of vinegar on a plate with mealworms crawling all around?
- What would happen if you connect the top end of a battery to the bottom end with a wire?
- What would happen if you line up dominoes on end in a curved pattern, ½-inch away from each other, and then push the first one down?

NSES Teaching Standard A. Inquiry-Based Program
NSES Program Standard B. Relevant, Inquiry-Based, and Connected with Other Subjects
NSES Content Standard A. Science as Inquiry: Abilities Necessary To Do Scientific Inquiry

These are questions that involve prediction.

Prediction is an individual's best guess as to what will happen next in a given situation—what would happen if you did something.

It has been said that the most important question elementary science teachers (or any science teacher, for that matter) can ask their students is "What would happen if _____?" When this question is asked, it seems to require an answer. These "What would happen if _____?" questions stem from observations and curiosity, with the observations leading to questions that someone wants to investigate, and they all involve the process of prediction.

3.18   IN THE SCHOOLS

NSES Content Standard D. Earth and Space Science: Earth in the Solar System

Predicting Times of Sunrise and Sunset

A class of second-grade students recorded sunrise and sunset data every day for 10 school days. Then, they made a graph of this data and, from their graph, predicted the times the sun would rise and set the next school day. They compared their predictions with actual data in the newspaper. The children also predicted the maximum and minimum temperatures and the weather for the next day and compared their predictions with what actually happened.

3.19   IN THE SCHOOLS

Fading Paper

A third-grade teacher taped cardboard shapes onto squares of construction paper of different colors. Children predicted which color would fade the most when left in the sun. They taped the colored squares to the window with the cardboard shapes facing outside. After three days, they checked their predictions by removing the cardboard shapes and comparing the colors of the portions of the squares exposed to the sun with the unexposed areas that had been covered by the shapes.

There are certain things we can predict somewhat accurately. We can predict with reasonable certainty the times of sunrise and sunset. We can predict that in winter, the weather will be cold, and that in summer, it will be hot. From complex calculations involving speed and orbit, we can predict that Halley's comet will return in the year 2061.[4]

Some predictions, however, are less accurate. For example, meteorologists attempt to provide the public with their best guess as to what will happen to our weather given the information they have. But many unpredictable variables, such as sudden shifts in atmospheric pressure, wind direction, or atmospheric temperature, cause unexpected changes in weather.

Prediction is essential in doing science, and children should be encouraged to predict before they test. For example, children should predict whether an item will sink or float before they try it. They should predict whether an item will be attracted or will not be attracted to a magnet before they try it. In this way, children learn to compare what actually happens with what they thought would happen rather than merely accepting what happened without thinking about it. The discrepancies between predicted and actual occurrences are areas worthy of further investigation. For example, if a child predicts that a coin will be attracted to a magnet and then finds that it is not, the child may want to investigate why this is so.

Children may be reluctant to be wrong in their predictions, and they may hesitate to make a prediction unless they are sure they will be right. When you encounter this situation, explain that it is when predictions are not accurate that the real opportunity for scientific investigation presents itself.

THE CASE OF THE MYSTERIOUS CRAYONS

Often, an activity can have unexpected results, thus opening up whole new avenues of inquiry no one had thought of before. In a

NSES Teaching Standard E. Developing Learners Who Reflect Intellectual Rigor and Attitudes Conducive to Science Learning

first-grade class, a teacher was engaging his students in a "sink or float" prediction activity. Included in the assemblage of items for children to predict and then try were several kinds of crayons. The activity proceeded as expected with the wooden objects, the buttons, the Ivory® soap, the paper clips, and so on. However, a most remarkable thing was observed by the children: Some of the crayons sank, and some of the crayons floated. Attempting to understand this newly discovered phenomenon, the teacher asked the children to suggest reasons why some crayons would sink and others float. "Maybe it's the paper." So, they removed the paper from all the crayons. Some sank, and some floated. "Maybe it's the length." So, the children gathered several crayons of the same length with the papers removed. Some sank, and some floated. "Maybe it's how fat they are." So, the children tried crayons of the same length, but of different thicknesses, with their papers removed. Some sank, and some floated. After some time spent trying several things, someone noticed that the orange and black colors floated while the white and purple colors sank. More experimentation showed that this, indeed, was the case. The darker colors of the same brand of crayon sank, and the lighter colors floated. In fact, some of them, the middle colors, floated halfway between the top and the bottom of the water.

Why did this happen? I don't know.

 See the video clip, "Do Crayons Sink? Or Float?" on the companion DVD.

Why do *you* think this might happen? How would you find out? Try out your ideas. Compare your findings with the Crayola explanation.

The Crayola® Company has addressed this problem on their Web site. See the Student Book Companion Web Site for a direct link.

Constructing Science in the Classroom 3.24–3.27 describe some activities that focus primarily on the process skill of prediction. Note that all require observation, and some require classification and measurement as well.

3.24   CONSTRUCTING SCIENCE IN THE CLASSROOM

SINK? OR FLOAT?

NSES Content Standard B. Physical Science: Properties of Objects and Materials

A Prediction Activity

Objective
The student will predict whether given objects sink or float.

Continued on next page

Provide a tray with a number of different kinds of objects, some of which sink and some of which float. Suggestions include a metal spoon, a plastic spoon, a metal fork, a plastic fork, a piece of wood, a penny, a dime, a nickel, a quarter, an empty shampoo bottle, liquid soap, regular soap, a wooden clothespin, a pencil, a wooden spoon, a paper clip, and crayons. Also, provide a data sheet for children to record their results. The data sheet might look like this:

Sink? Or Float?

Object	Prediction		Result	
	Float	Sink	Float	Sink

Children select objects from the tray, predict whether they will sink or float, and record their predictions on the data table. Then, they try the item and record their results. Ask inquiry-oriented questions, such as "What would happen if we changed the shape of an object?" Let children try changing the shapes of the paper clip, the lengths of the crayons, and other things. Try a flat piece of aluminum foil. "What would happen if we changed its shape into a boat, a cup, or a tight ball?" What actually does happen? "What would happen if we changed the size of things?" Encourage children to try.

(A more sophisticated version of this activity, involving the calculation of densities, is shown in Constructing Science in the Classroom 3.44.)

Literature Connections

Mr. Gumpy's Outing by John Burningham (Henry Holt, 1970) is a humorous tale of an outdoor adventure on a boat on a river. One by one, children and animals join Mr. Gumpy in the boat. Everything is fine until they upset the balance of weight in the boat.

The Magic School Bus: Ups and Downs by Jane Mason, Bruce Degen, and Joanna Cole (Scholastic, 1997) explores several instances of sinking and floating.

Sink or Float? (Delta Science Reader, 2004) is a nonfiction book about basic facts of what sinks and what floats and why.

TRANSPARENT— TRANSLUCENT—OPAQUE

A Prediction Activity

NSES Content
Standard B. Physical
Science: Light Energy

Objective

The student will predict whether given materials are transparent, translucent, or opaque.

When we shine a light on an object, one of three things can happen: (1) All the light can go through the material, and the material is said to be **transparent.** (2) Some of the light can go through the material, and the material is said to be **translucent.** (3) None of the light goes through the material, and the material is said to be **opaque.** (These definitions are not precise, but for purposes of this activity they are fine.)

Provide transparent, translucent, and opaque materials, such as a clear plastic jar, a sheet of white paper, overhead transparency film, cardboard, poster board, aluminum foil, waxed paper, tissue paper, facial tissue, a glass of water, a mirror, plastic wrap, an eyeglass lens, Scotch® tape, and a magnifying glass. Children predict whether each object is transparent, translucent, or opaque. Then, they shine flashlight beams at each object to check their predictions. A data table to help children in their exploration might look like the one below; children can either write or draw their predictions.

TRANSPARENT—TRANSLUCENT—OPAQUE

Item	Transparent		Translucent		Opaque	
	Predicted	Actual	Predicted	Actual	Predicted	Actual

(This activity can be integrated with language study as children investigate other words beginning with the prefix *trans-*.)

Literature Connections

Keep the Lights Burning, Abbie by Peter Roop (Carolrhoda, 1985). Abbie keeps the light on in the lighthouse during a storm.

Bouncing and Bending Light by Barbara Taylor (Watts, 1990) is a nonfiction book that presents projects to demonstrate the effects of mirrors and lenses on light rays.

3.26   CONSTRUCTING SCIENCE IN THE CLASSROOM

WHAT KINDS OF MATERIALS ABSORB WATER?

A Prediction Activity

Objective

The student will predict whether given materials absorb water.

    Provide an assortment of materials, such as waxed paper, paper towels, paper bags, napkins, typing paper, plastic wrap, cloth, and oilcloth. Children place the material on a piece of cardboard held at an angle. Using an eyedropper or a straw, children place one or two drops of water on the material at the top of the incline. You might want to demonstrate this with one of the materials to show that the water runs down the incline quickly or slowly, depending on how rapidly it is absorbed by the material.

    Ask children to predict which materials will allow the water to run down the incline rapidly and which will cause the water to run down the incline slowly. Children record their predictions and then test them. There are many variations children should be encouraged to explore: "What if the material is flat on the table?" "What if the material is held over the top of an open coffee can?" "What if we use oil instead of water?" Encourage children to try many different substances.

Literature Connections

Desert Giant: The World of the Saguaro Cactus by Barbara Bash (Sierra Club/Little, Brown & Co., 1989) is a wonderful nonfiction book about the life cycle of the saguaro cactus and the haven it provides for desert life. The book has an abundance of information, such as how the cactus skin expands to store rainwater for the dry spells.

    A Day in the Desert, written and illustrated by a first-grade class at Robert Taylor Elementary School in Henderson, Nevada (Willowisp, 1994), is a wonderful example of children expressing their observations of what they saw in the desert.

> NSES Content Standard B. Physical Science: Properties of Objects and Materials

---

3.27   CONSTRUCTING SCIENCE IN THE CLASSROOM

HOW DO EARTHWORMS BEHAVE?

A Prediction Activity

Objective

The student will predict the reaction of earthworms under various conditions.

> NSES Content Standard C. Life Science: Organisms and Environments

Continued on next page

Provide each group with one or two earthworms, and ask the children to find out how earthworms behave. You can obtain earthworms at bait-and-tackle shops. Children may do whatever they want to answer the question, but with the proviso that they may not cause bodily harm to the earthworms. Let children predict, test their predictions, and write down their conclusions and the reasons for their conclusions. Then, have the children share these with the class.

Literature Connections

Secrets of a Wildlife Watcher by Jim Arnosky (Lothrop, Lee & Shepard, 1983) is a beautifully illustrated, nonfiction guidebook that shares the techniques of finding and observing wildlife behavior.

How to Eat Fried Worms by Thomas Rockwell (Random House, 2000) is a delightfully repulsive story of a boy who, to win a bet, agrees to eat 15 worms in 15 days.

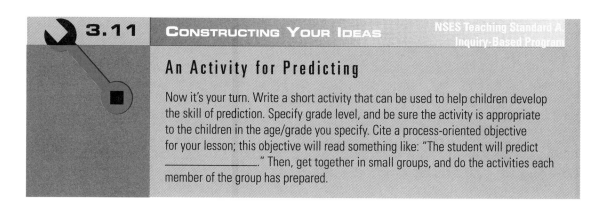

3.11 | **CONSTRUCTING YOUR IDEAS**

NSES Teaching Standard A: Inquiry-Based Program

An Activity for Predicting

Now it's your turn. Write a short activity that can be used to help children develop the skill of prediction. Specify grade level, and be sure the activity is appropriate to the children in the age/grade you specify. Cite a process-oriented objective for your lesson; this objective will read something like: "The student will predict _____." Then, get together in small groups, and do the activities each member of the group has prepared.

INFERRING

Very often, we form conclusions based on inferring, and in science, inferential reasoning is used extensively.

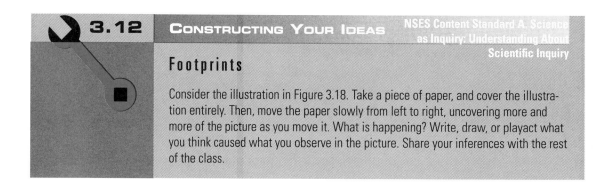

3.12 | **CONSTRUCTING YOUR IDEAS**

NSES Content Standard A: Science as Inquiry: Understanding About Scientific Inquiry

Footprints

Consider the illustration in Figure 3.18. Take a piece of paper, and cover the illustration entirely. Then, move the paper slowly from left to right, uncovering more and more of the picture as you move it. What is happening? Write, draw, or playact what you think caused what you observe in the picture. Share your inferences with the rest of the class.

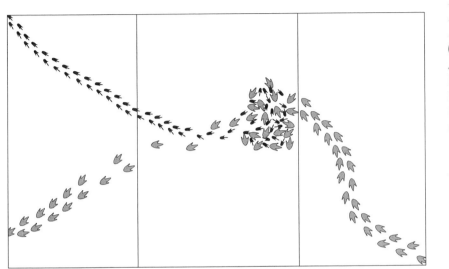

FIGURE 3.18

Remember, there is no right answer. Some people will say that a small bird and a large bird were coming from opposite directions. The large bird spied the small one, attacked it, and after a scuffle, ate it and then continued on its own trip. Others will infer that the small bird managed to fly away after the scuffle. Still others will suggest that the small bird hopped onto the back of the larger animal and went for a ride. Are these inferences consistent with what is in the picture?

▶ What do you think about the following interpretation?
A small monster was blithely walking down a hill, minding its own business, when all of a sudden, it spied a huge monster strolling from the opposite direction. At just that moment, a gigantic snowball rolled down from the top of the hill, and both monsters panicked. The snowball swallowed up the little monster, but the big monster managed to get away. Tired, disoriented, and still panting from its successful attempt to avoid being swallowed up by the huge snowball, the big monster walked away.

The following are actual inferences written by fourth- and fifth-grade children. As you read each one, check it for validity.

"Two animals were walking. They came together and hit heads because they weren't looking where they were going. They got dizzy and were walking around in circles. Then the dizziness went away. Then they saw each other and started fighting. The bigger one got the smaller one and carried him off."

"The Dance. One night the Gleep and the Glorg were walking through the Pluto Prairie and they met each other and fell in love. Then the Gleep and the

NSES Teaching Standard A. Inquiry-Based Program
NSES Program Standard B. Relevant, Inquiry-Based, and Connected with Other Subjects
NSES Content Standard A. Science as Inquiry: Abilities Necessary To Do Scientific Inquiry

Glorg had a romantic weird dance together. After that the Gleep jumped on the Glorg's back and walked off in the night and got a free piggy back ride."

"There was this Apatosaurus and an Archaeopteryx that were walking in the same direction, and the Apatosaurus saw the Archaeopteryx. He tried to get away by taking big steps. The bird saw the dinosaur, ran to him, and they got into a fight. The bird scratched and the dinosaur stomped. The fight finally ended and the Apatosaurus won. However, he didn't eat meat so he walked away."

"The Pot of Gold. A lepercon [*sic*] was walking to a pot of gold. So was a giraffe. They got there at the same time and started to argue about it. The giraffe ran to the lepercon but the lepercon disappeared with the gold. The giraffe stomped off angrily."

"The Universe formed as a ball and then exploded into big foot-shaped galaxies and spread into little paths. Then all the galaxies got sucked together and the process started again."

Inference is a person's best guess as to *why* something happened. This is contrasted with prediction, which is a person's best guess as to *what* will happen next. In inference, we have to guess what caused something to happen. Our guess must be based on the evidence we have. Criminal trials often are based on inferential reasoning: the evidence is presented, and the cause of the evidence is inferred from assembling all the evidence.

Inferential reasoning is basic to all scientific understanding. Many times, we can observe directly what happens in a scientific activity. For example, we can observe that when we put a drop of vinegar on a piece of limestone, the vinegar fizzes. We can draw the conclusion directly from the evidence that vinegar fizzes on limestone. Often, however, we cannot observe what happens directly, and we must infer.

3.20   IN THE SCHOOLS   NSES Content Standard B. Physical Science: Properties and Changes of Properties in Matter

Burning a Candle in a Goldfish Bowl

A fourth-grade teacher fastened a candle to the bottom of a goldfish bowl with wax and lit the candle. She then filled the bowl with water, inverted a jar over the candle, and lowered the jar so that its rim was below the level of the water. Shortly, the flame went out. Children observed the flame being extinguished, but they could not observe why this happened. They also observed that water rose into the jar. They put these two observations together—that the candle went out, and that the water rose in the jar—and inferred that the reason the candle went out was that it had used up the oxygen in the air.

This was an inference.

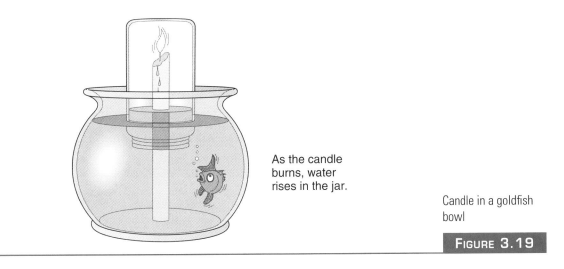

As the candle burns, water rises in the jar.

Candle in a goldfish bowl

FIGURE 3.19

Children's literature is a great source of opportunities for children to reason inferentially.

3.21   IN THE SCHOOLS   NSES Content Standard A. Science as Inquiry: Abilities Necessary To Do Scientific Inquiry

Inferring Through Children's Literature

The Mitten: A Ukrainian Folktale, adapted by Jan Brett (G. P. Putnam, 1989), is a logical choice to accompany the footprints activity in Constructing Your Ideas 3.12. As each animal comes to crawl inside the lost mitten, it walks across the snow, leaving its footprints. A good activity is for children to infer whether the tracks pictured are those of the animal that has just made its way to the mitten.

Animal Tracks and Traces by Kathleen Kudlinski (Franklin Watts, 1991) also is an excellent accompaniment to the footprints activity in Constructing Your Ideas 3.12. The book encourages children to become good detectives by discovering where to look for animal clues, including tracks, nests, skin, feather or fur coverings, and food remnants.

Tracks in the Snow by Wong Herbert Yee (Holt, 2003). A little girl discovers tracks outside her window and tries to find out what animal made those tracks.

Several activities are shown in Constructing Science in the Classroom 3.28–3.33 that can be used to help children develop the process skill of inference. All require observational skills, and several require other process skills as well.

THE ORIGIN OF SOIL

An Inferring Activity

NSES Content
Standard D. Earth
and Space Science:
Properties of Earth
Materials

Objective

The student will infer the origin of a sample of soil.

As you did in the activity on classifying materials in soil (Constructing Science in the Classroom 3.11), bring a bag of soil from your home or from the schoolyard, and put a spoonful of the soil on a paper plate for each child or group of children. Provide magnifying glasses, and tell children they are going to be detectives. Ask the children to look at the soil carefully to try to identify the different kinds of things they can find in it. Ask the children to describe what they see in the soil, to infer where these things came from, and to cite their reasons for their inferences. Finally, ask them to infer where the soil sample came from based on what they found in it.

Literature Connection

Who Is the Beast? by Keith Baker (Harcourt Brace, 1990). Several animals identify various parts of a beast, and children infer what the beast is from the progressive clues.

CAUSE OF BANDING IN SEDIMENTARY ROCKS

An Inferring Activity

NSES Content
Standard D. Earth and
Space Science: Earth's
History

Objective

The student will infer the cause of banding in sedimentary rocks.

Provide each group with several specimens of banded sedimentary rocks, and ask them to examine them carefully and describe them (see Figure 3.20). Provide each group with a clear plastic jar, about the size of a mayonnaise jar; enough water to fill the jar about half-full; and a plastic bag containing a mixture of fine rocks, sand, and dried mud. Ask them to empty the contents of the plastic bag into the jar, stir or shake it, and let it settle. Ask them to infer from the results of this activity how the bands were formed in the sandstone and then share this with the class, giving the reasons for their inferences. (Note that in this activity, children are constructing models of sedimentary rock formation.)

Continued on next page

Literature Connection
A River Ran Wild by Lynn Cherry (Harcourt Brace Jovanovich, 1992) is a true story of the Nashua River Valley in Massachusetts and the impact of the Industrial Revolution on the river. The book explains how the riverbed changed when the settlers built dams and sawmills.

Banded sedimentary rock (Courtesy Mineral Information Institute)

FIGURE 3.20

3.30   CONSTRUCTING SCIENCE IN THE CLASSROOM

THE CAUSES OF SOIL EROSION

An Inferring Activity

Objective
The student will infer the causes of soil erosion in the environment around the school.

Take the class of children outside, and help them find examples of soil erosion around the school. Ask them for their observations about the soil, the general area, the slope of the ground, and the like. Also, ask them to form inferences as to what caused the soil to erode in the way that they observed and to provide the reasons for their inferences.

In urban settings, it may be more appropriate for children to look for examples of plants growing in unusual places such as coming up through concrete, and infer reasons for what they observe.

This would be a good place to engage children in discussions of the damage done by hurricanes and tornadoes, especially Hurricane Katrina. Have the children compare the hurricane's devastation with school ground erosion and infer the similarities and differences between their causes and results.

Literature Connections
Follow the Water from Brook to Ocean by Arthur Dorros (HarperCollins, 1991). This nonfiction story describes the journey of water and the erosion that water causes in the rivers, waterfalls, canyons, dams, and oceans..

NSES Content Standard D. Earth and Space Science: Changes in Earth and Sky

Continued on next page

Come a Tide by George Lyon (Orchard Books, 1990). When the snow melted, the water overflowed the banks of the creeks and river, and a little rural town flooded. Gardens were washed away, and homes were filled with water. However, the townspeople began the slow process of rebuilding their homes.

Hurricane Katrina Strikes the Gulf Coast: Disaster & Survival by Mara Miller (Enslow, 2006) describes one of the most devastating natural disasters in American history.

3.31   CONSTRUCTING SCIENCE IN THE CLASSROOM

WHAT IS THAT UNKNOWN SUBSTANCE?

An Inferring Activity

Ⓟ Ⓚ ① ② ③ ④ ⑤ ⑥ ⑦ ⑧

Objective

NSES Content Standard B. Physical Science: Properties of Objects and Materials

The student will infer the identity of an unknown substance.

Provide each group with a small cup of salt and a small cup of sugar; ask them to describe the similarities and differences between the salt and the sugar. Then, give each group a cup of water, some plastic spoons and small cups, magnifying glasses, and a cup of either salt or sugar—unknown to the children—and ask them to use these tools to infer whether their unknown substance is salt or sugar. Tasting is specifically prohibited except as a last resort. Children then report to the class what their inference was and why they made their inference.

Literature Connections

Sense Suspense: A Guessing Game for the Five Senses by Bruce McMillan (Scholastic, 1994) provides close-up pictures and requires the reader to figure out what the whole picture is and what senses can be used to solve the mystery. The beautiful pictures are from the Caribbean; the text is in both Spanish and English.

Bartholomew and the Oobleck by Dr. Seuss (Random House, 1949) describes a king who is bored with the regularity of rain and snow falling from the sky, so he commands his magicians to change the precipitation. "Oobleck" falls from the sky and causes some amusing situations.

(You can make your own "Oobleck" by mixing one 1-pound box of cornstarch, $1\frac{2}{3}$ cups of water, and a few drops of green food coloring. Children explore the properties of this m aterial for themselves by rolling it into a ball and squeezing it, smashing it with a hammer, letting it set, freezing it, heating it, and so on.)

3.32   **CONSTRUCTING SCIENCE IN THE CLASSROOM**

HOW OLD IS THAT TREE?

An Inferring Activity

NSES Content Standard C. Life Science: Organisms and Environments

Objective

The student will infer the age of trees from tree rings.

A tree ring is a layer of wood produced by the tree in one year. One ring normally contains a thin layer (produced early in the growing season) and a thicker layer (produced later in the growing season). After a discussion about the nature of tree rings and the seasonal growth of trees that results in tree rings, give children cross-sectional pieces of a tree trunk, and ask them to infer the age of the tree from the number of rings. Also, give children cross-sectional pieces of several branches of the same tree. From the count of the number of rings, ask them to infer which of the branches is the oldest, which is the youngest, and from where on the tree they came. Depending on the nature of the rings, they also may be able to infer the length and weather conditions of the seasons during which the tree grew. Wide rings suggest a growing season with plentiful rainfall; narrow rings suggest hard times, such as drought. (For more information, children can access Web sites on **dendrochronology.**)

Much information about tree rings and their interpretations can be accessed from the University of Tennessee at Knoxville "Principles of Dendrochronology" Web site. See the Student Book Companion Web Site for a link to this site.

Literature Connection

Outside and Inside Trees by Sandra Markle (Bradbury, 1993) is a beautifully illustrated book that encourages children to look at trees from a new and different perspective.

3.33   **CONSTRUCTING SCIENCE IN THE CLASSROOM**

PAPER CHROMATOGRAPHY

An Inferring Activity

NSES Content Standard B. Physical Science: Properties of Objects and Materials

Objective

The student will infer the colors that make up black ink.

First, give each group of children a black felt-tip pen. Ask them to make a mark with it on a sheet of white paper and describe what they see. Ask them to infer whether the black ink is one color or a mixture of several colors.

Next, ask children to test their inferences. Provide each group with a cup that is approximately half-full of water and a few strips of white paper towel or coffee filter paper about ½ inch wide. Children draw a line with the black pen across the strip of paper towel about 3 inches above the bottom. They hold the strip so that the bottom edge is just below the surface of the water, being careful not to let the ink line sink into the water. The water travels up the paper towel and, as it passes the black line, separates the ink into its component colors.

Continued on next page

Children can try this with different black inks and with inks of different colors.

Challenge

Paper chromatography can be used to identify the color pigments in plant leaves; from the colors, students can predict the color the plant's leaves will become in the fall. Children gather one leaf from each of several different plants (including trees) and record the name of the plant or tree on a data sheet. They break off a piece of the leaf and grind its open end against one end of the paper towel or coffee filter paper strip in a circular motion, using a spoon or a fingernail to press the pigment into the strip. They suspend the end of the paper strip in water as described above and observe the colors that travel up the strip. On their data sheet, they record these colors and their predictions of what color each leaf will change to in the fall. When the leaves change color, check the actual colors against the predictions.

(**Teacher Note:** Leaves turn color in the fall because the green chlorophyll disappears and we begin to see the other colors, most of which have been there all along but have been covered up by the intense color of the chlorophyll.)

Literature Connection

The Mystery of the Stranger in the Barn by True Kelley (Dodd, Mead and Co., 1986). Items seem to be disappearing from a barn, but a hat was left behind. Is a mysterious stranger hiding in the barn? This is a good story to demonstrate the difference between evidence and inference.

3.13   **CONSTRUCTING YOUR IDEAS**   NSES Teaching Standard A. Inquiry-Based Program

An Activity for Inferring

Now it's your turn. Write a short activity that can be used to help children develop the skill of inferring. Specify grade level, and be sure the activity is appropriate to the children in the age/grade you specify. Cite a process-oriented objective for your lesson; this objective will read something like: "The student will infer the reason for _____." Then, get together in small groups, and do the activities each member of the group has prepared.

NSES Teaching Standard A. Inquiry-Based Program
NSES Content Standard A. Science as Inquiry: Abilities Necessary To Do Scientific Inquiry

INTERRELATIONSHIPS AMONG THE BASIC PROCESSES

Most of the activities that you have done in this chapter have used more than one process. For example, you combined the processes of observation and communication to accomplish the rock-observing activity. Moon watching required measurement and communication, together with observation. In classifying, you also used communication. Many different types of communication accompanied inferring in the footprints activity.

The processes of observing, classifying, communicating, measuring, predicting, and inferring are the focus of the early elementary science program. They are interdependent and almost never taught in isolation. The scientific content appropriate to elementary science is used as the vehicle through which mastery of these processes can be attained. After children have acquired facility in the basic processes, they are able to explore scientific concepts the way scientists do.

THE INTEGRATED PROCESSES

The scientific processes we have discussed thus far are the basic processes. They form the foundation for scientific investigation and are prerequisites to the more complex integrated processes. The integrated process skills form the method of actual scientific investigation and are as follows:

Identifying and controlling variables

Formulating and testing hypotheses

Interpreting data

Defining operationally

Experimenting

Constructing models

NSES Teaching Standard A. Inquiry-Based Program
NSES Program Standard B. Relevant, Inquiry-Based, and Connected with Other Subjects
NSES Content Standard A. Science as Inquiry: Abilities Necessary To Do Scientific Inquiry

There is little doubt that these process skills require deeper levels of thought than the basic skills of observing, classifying, communicating, measuring, predicting, and inferring do. Popular beliefs about elementary science education hold that children should focus on classification, description, and manipulation of concrete materials rather than on experimenting and using the integrated processes. However, many children are capable of investigating the integrated skills during the early grades. Metz (1995), Tytler and Peterson (2004), and Martin, Jean-Sigur, and Schmidt (2005) argue that research shows elementary school children are, indeed, capable of manipulating variables, developing and executing true experiments, and citing evidence for knowledge claims. Of course, we must be careful not to ask children to do something they are not cognitively capable of doing, and several examples of this have been cited in this chapter. For example, in general, children in the lower grades cannot devise complex classification systems, nor can they apply complex principles of conservation. We leave these concepts for later years, when the children are ready for them. However, this does not mean that *no* child is ready for these principles in the early grades—it means we must be on the lookout for those who *are* ready and who demonstrate appropriate comprehension before we introduce them. It is the same way with the integrated process skills. Many children in early elementary grades are not capable of the thinking associated with true comprehension of variable identification, variable isolation, hypothesis formulation and testing, operational definition, experiment planning and execution, data interpretation, and model development. However, many elementary children *are* ready to work with these processes. Thus, it is appropriate to encourage children to explore these processes, assess the results of their explorations, share their conclusions with others, and in general, validate their perceptions of their application of these skills.

THE PENDULUM

Let us begin with an activity that illustrates the application of all the integrated processes.

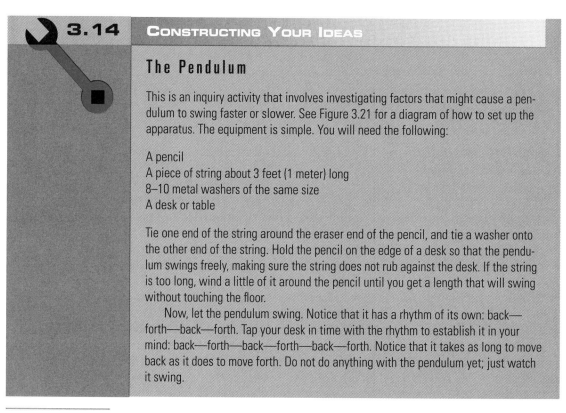

3.14   CONSTRUCTING YOUR IDEAS

The Pendulum

This is an inquiry activity that involves investigating factors that might cause a pendulum to swing faster or slower. See Figure 3.21 for a diagram of how to set up the apparatus. The equipment is simple. You will need the following:

A pencil
A piece of string about 3 feet (1 meter) long
8–10 metal washers of the same size
A desk or table

Tie one end of the string around the eraser end of the pencil, and tie a washer onto the other end of the string. Hold the pencil on the edge of a desk so that the pendulum swings freely, making sure the string does not rub against the desk. If the string is too long, wind a little of it around the pencil until you get a length that will swing without touching the floor.

Now, let the pendulum swing. Notice that it has a rhythm of its own: back—forth—back—forth. Tap your desk in time with the rhythm to establish it in your mind: back—forth—back—forth—back—forth. Notice that it takes as long to move back as it does to move forth. Do not do anything with the pendulum yet; just watch it swing.

NSES Professional Development Standard A. Learning Content Through Inquiry NSES Content Standard B. Physical Science: Motions and Forces

How would you define a *swing?* Some will define it as the total back-and-forth movement (a full cycle) and others will define it as either back or forth (a half-cycle), because they both take about the same time.

▶ While you are watching the pendulum swing, discuss this question: What do you suppose will make this pendulum move faster or slower? Brainstorm responses to the question as a class, writing all responses on the board.

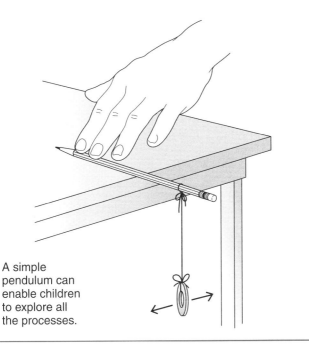

A simple pendulum can enable children to explore all the processes.

The pendulum

FIGURE 3.21

Here are some typical responses:

How hard we push it to get it started

The weight of the bob

The color of the string

The length of the string

How far we pull it back to get it started

How much wind there is

How thick the air is

You are sure to come up with more.

All these ideas as to what might make the pendulum swing faster or slower are called *variables*. In brainstorming the factors that might influence the speed of a pendulum's swing, you have identified variables. It is not necessary to identify *all* variables that could possibly affect the swing of the pendulum; there are bound to be some you don't think of.

Think of how you can change the values of the variables you identify. For example, you can change the weight of the bob by adding washers. You can change the length of the string by winding some of it onto the pencil. You can change how far you pull the bob back by letting it drop from different heights measured from the floor or from different angles measured from the perpendicular.

▶ Next, for each of the factors you have identified as a class, identify the effect you think it will have on the speed of the pendulum. For instance, for the variable *how far back we pull it,* you might guess that the farther back you pull it, the faster it will swing. For each factor, write what you think will happen. If you don't know what will happen or there is disagreement, write that down as well.

Of course, if we *knew* what would happen, there would not be much point in investigating the phenomenon. Your statement of what you think will happen to the pendulum's speed when you change a given variable is called a **hypothesis;** it takes the form of a statement that says, essentially, "If I do *this* to the pendulum, it will *speed up* or *slow down.*" Whether it is written this way or not, it will be thought of this way.

We have one more factor to consider before we can investigate. Our inquiry centers on the question "What will make the pendulum move faster or slower?" That means we are investigating the speed of the swinging pendulum, and we will have to measure its speed. This is difficult to do, because speed is measured in terms of distance per unit of time, such as miles per hour, feet per second, or meters per second. To measure speed, we would have to find the distance the pendulum travels and the time it takes to travel that distance. However, we already have discovered that it has a definite back-and-forth rhythm. Could we measure the *time* without the distance? That would give us a measure that is proportional to speed. The time a pendulum takes to complete one full swing—back *and* forth—is called its **period.** How could we measure the period? Well, we could use a stopwatch, starting it as soon as we let the pendulum go and then stopping it as soon as the pendulum returns, but there are likely to be inaccuracies with this method. On the other hand, we could count the number of swings in a certain period of time—say, 1 minute. If you try letting it swing for 1 minute, you will find that a minute is a long time, and the pendulum tends to wander from its original path. How about counting the number of swings in 15 seconds? That way, we can finish our swing counting before the pendulum starts to wander.

For purposes of this investigation, let us use the number of swings in 15 seconds as the indication of the speed.[5]

Now you are ready to plan your experiment. Each group can select one of the variables to test, or each group can test them all. Whichever way you choose, it is critical that while you are experimenting with one variable, you keep all the other variables constant. If, for example, you are investigating the effect of the height of the pull, you must keep the length of the string, the weight of the bob, and all other factors the same throughout your investigation.

▶ Discuss this question: What would happen if you did not keep the variables constant?

How many different values of the variable you are investigating will you need to test? Certainly, you will need to experiment with at least three or four different values. In our example, you will want to set the pendulum swinging from at least three or four different heights. How many times will you need to try the same value of the variable? Most scientists do at least three trials for each value of each variable. That is, you would count the number of swings for each different height of drop three different times. Many factors can influence your count on any trial—you may miscount; you may count in different ways (starting with "1" when you first let it go, or starting with "1" after a full swing has been completed); you may round up to the next whole number of swings one time and round down a differ-ent time; you may ignore a quarter of a swing one time and count a quar-ter of a swing another time, and so on. So, it is desirable to test each value three times and then average the three results.

▶ Now, go ahead and do the investigation. Collect the data, and write it down in raw form. Do any averaging that is needed after you have the raw data. Your data can be recorded in a data table similar to the one shown below. (See Chapter 11 for an example of using a computer spreadsheet to record the data from the pendulum inquiry.)

Pendulum Data Table

Variable _____

Value of Variable	**Number of Swings in 15 Seconds**	
1. Value _____	Trial 1	_____
	Trial 2	_____
	Trial 3	_____
	Average	_____
2. Value _____	Trial 1	_____
	Trial 2	_____
	Trial 3	_____
	Average	_____
3. Value _____	Trial 1	_____
	Trial 2	_____
	Trial 3	_____
	Average	_____

▶ When all groups are finished, record your averaged data next to the variable you investigated. You might want to set up a summary data table, something like the one shown below.

Consolidated Data for Pendulum Swing Investigation

Variable _____

    Value 1 _____   Average swings _____

    Value 2 _____   Average swings _____

    Value 3 _____   Average swings _____

Variable _____

    Value 1 _____   Average swings _____

    Value 2 _____   Average swings _____

    Value 3 _____   Average swings _____

Variable _____

    Value 1 _____   Average swings _____

    Value 2 _____   Average swings _____

    Value 3 _____   Average swings _____

▶ Look at the class data. What can you conclude? What effect did changing the height of the drop have on the number of swings in 15 seconds? What effect did the weight of the bob have? How about the length of the string?

Was there any set of data that seemed to be inconclusive? Here is an example:

Data for Height of Pendulum Drop

Variable   Height of Drop _____

    Value 1 ____3 centimeters____   Average swings ____15____

    Value 2 ____4 centimeters____   Average swings ____14____

    Value 3 ____5 centimeters____   Average swings ____15____

In this case, it could be suggested that the number of swings seems to depend on the height of the drop, but one item of data seems to be **anomalous.** If the average number of swings for Value 3 had been 13, we would have been able to conclude that the higher the drop, the slower the pendulum swings. Maybe we need to do a few more trials with a few more values. The data indicate that the effect that seemed to be observed might very well be a function only of the accuracy with which we did the experiment; the data does not tell us conclusively that there was any effect.

You may have decided that each group would explore a different variable. If so, data from different groups cannot be combined, because each group kept constant the variables they were not investigating, but at different values from those of other groups. For example, one group may have had a constant string length of 8 inches, while another group may have kept its string length constant at 12 inches. The data from all groups could be combined only if each group investigated all the variables and used the same values for each constant variable. In an actual class setting, it would be preferable for all the groups to investigate all the variables. This gives much more data for each variable, because the data can be combined. The more data we have, the easier it is to interpret the results.

This investigation into the pendulum leads us to our exploration of the integrated science process skills; you used all of them in the pendulum inquiry. You identified the variables that would affect the swing of the pendulum. You controlled (kept constant) all the variables except the one you were exploring. You formulated hypotheses for each variable ("If I increase the height of the drop, the pendulum will swing faster"). You tested the hypotheses by changing the value of the variable and collecting data from at least three separate trials. You defined operationally when you decided to measure how long it takes the pendulum to make one complete swing in terms of the number of swings it makes in 15 seconds rather than timing how long each swing takes. You planned the experiment when you decided how you were going to set up the apparatus to investigate the problem, how you were going to investigate all the variables, and how you were going to collect the data. You interpreted data when you looked at the results to see if your variable had any effect. And the pendulum itself is a model of many kinds of back-and-forth movement, such as the grandfather clock.

IDENTIFYING AND CONTROLLING VARIABLES

In any scientific investigation, the system we are investigating will have many variables. It is essential that we know what variable is causing the effects that we observe.

NSES Teaching Standard A. Inquiry-Based Program
NSES Program Standard B. Relevant, Inquiry-Based, and Connected with Other Subjects
NSES Content Standard A. Science as Inquiry: Abilities Necessary To Do Scientific Inquiry

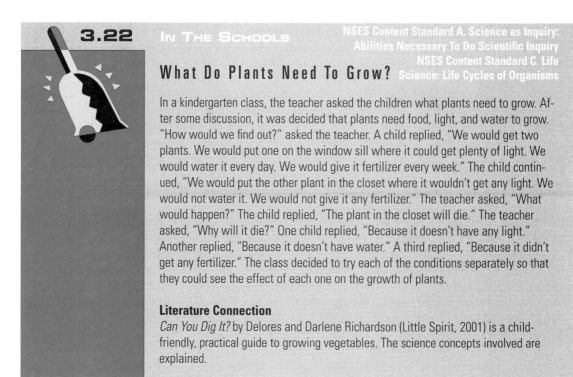

3.22

NSES Content Standard A. Science as Inquiry: Abilities Necessary To Do Scientific Inquiry
NSES Content Standard C. Life Science: Life Cycles of Organisms

What Do Plants Need To Grow?

In a kindergarten class, the teacher asked the children what plants need to grow. After some discussion, it was decided that plants need food, light, and water to grow. "How would we find out?" asked the teacher. A child replied, "We would get two plants. We would put one on the window sill where it could get plenty of light. We would water it every day. We would give it fertilizer every week." The child continued, "We would put the other plant in the closet where it wouldn't get any light. We would not water it. We would not give it any fertilizer." The teacher asked, "What would happen?" The child replied, "The plant in the closet will die." The teacher asked, "Why will it die?" One child replied, "Because it doesn't have any light." Another replied, "Because it doesn't have water." A third replied, "Because it didn't get any fertilizer." The class decided to try each of the conditions separately so that they could see the effect of each one on the growth of plants.

Literature Connection

Can You Dig It? by Delores and Darlene Richardson (Little Spirit, 2001) is a child-friendly, practical guide to growing vegetables. The science concepts involved are explained.

In our everyday lives, we tend to formulate generalizations without controlling the variables. Consider the person who is coming down with flu-like symptoms. Someone tells her that she ought to take aspirin. Someone else suggests eating chicken soup. A third person suggests getting plenty of rest. So, the afflicted person goes home, takes two aspirins, eats a bowl of chicken soup for dinner, and goes to bed early. The next day, she feels much better. Of the things she did, which cured her cold?

In many scientific inquiries, we investigate to find out what causes something to happen—to find the effect of one variable on another. To pinpoint the cause, we must keep all the variables constant except the one with which we are experimenting.

Suppose we want to know what causes a toy truck to roll faster or slower down an inclined board. We brainstorm the various conditions that could make a difference (angle of the board, surface of the board, length of the board, and so on) to isolate the variables that can have an effect on the speed of the toy truck. When we do the investigation, we investigate the effect of changing only one of the variables; we must keep the other variables constant. In this way, we can tell whether a single variable has an effect. (See Constructing Your Ideas 3.16.)

Suppose we have reason to believe that more than one variable has an effect. For example, we may suspect that both the surface and the angle

NSES Content Standard B. Physical Science: Motions and Forces of the board affect the speed of the toy truck. We investigate the variables one at a time, and we look at the data for each variable. If both variables have effects, we may want to carefully devise an experiment that would include manipulating the two variables simultaneously to investigate the double effect.

The idea behind identifying and controlling variables is that we must be sure that what we *think* caused an effect *did,* in fact, cause it. We must be able to confirm the cause-and-effect relationship between the two phenomena.

Children do not intuitively know that they must identify and control variables during an investigation. Such knowledge requires the ability to perceive that there is more than one attribute to given objects and that the attributes are seen not only in the object's physical characteristics (as we described in the section on classification) but also in the object's behavior. For example, in the toy truck investigation, children must be able to perceive that the same toy truck may go faster or slower. It also requires the perception of interaction between two occurrences—for example, the understanding that the roughness of the board's surface interacts with the toy truck in such a way as to affect the speed of the truck. When children acquire the ability to perceive multiple physical attributes, multiple behavioral attributes, and interactions both between and among events, they can begin to reason that there may be several distinct variables that can influence a particular happening.

Several activities that focus on identifying and controlling variables are provided in Constructing Science in the Classroom 3.34–3.38.

NSES Professional Development Standard B. Integrating Knowledge of Science, Learning, Pedagogy, and Students

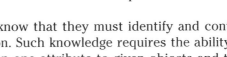

3.34   CONSTRUCTING SCIENCE IN THE CLASSROOM

WHAT DO SEEDS NEED IN ORDER TO SPROUT?

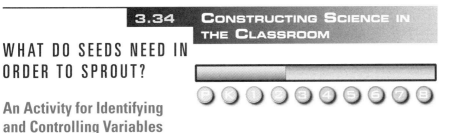

An Activity for Identifying and Controlling Variables

Objective

The student will identify and control variables involved with stimulating seeds to sprout.

Provide children with a half-dozen lima bean seeds. Also, show them lima bean seeds that have sprouted (which you prepared ahead of time). Ask them to tell what they think would cause the lima beans to sprout. Children might suggest such factors as water, amount of water, light, fertilizer, soil, and so on. Record the factors they identify, and ask them to apply each variable to a different lima bean seed which they will "plant" in a paper cup with facial tissues in the bottom for the seed to rest on. Some cups might be filled to the top with

NSES Content Standard C. Life Science: Life Cycles of Organisms

Continued on next page

water. Some might merely keep the tissue moist. Some might have water with fertilizer, and some might have water without fertilizer. Some might be placed in the sunlight and others in a dark place.

Children observe the results of their activities and record the conditions under which the lima beans sprouted.

Literature Connections

The Tiny Seed by Eric Carle (Simon & Shuster, 1991). Flower seeds blow away in the autumn and land in many different places. When the conditions are right, they grow. The following autumn, the seeds from these plants blow away, and the cycle starts again.

The Dandelion Seed by Joseph Patrick Anthony (Dawn Publications, 1997) follows a dandelion seed that is blown away and begins the cycle of life.

The Magic School Bus Plants Seeds by Joanna Cole (Scholastic, 1995) takes children on a trip to the interior of flowers to see how seeds are made.

The Plant that Kept on Growing by Barbara Benner (Gareth Stevens Publishing, 1996) describes two children who plant seeds in the hope of growing the very best plant for the 4-H show. However, all the seedlings get eaten except one, which grows into a huge tomato worthy of first prize.

3.35   CONSTRUCTING SCIENCE IN THE CLASSROOM

BREAD MOLD

An Activity for Identifying and Controlling Variables

NSES Content Standard C. Life Science: Structure and Function in Living Systems

Objective

The student will identify and control variables that cause bread to mold.

First, obtain a piece of bread that is moldy, and show it to the children. Then, provide for each group a slice of fresh bread, some water, and some plastic wrap. Have them tear the slice of bread into several pieces. Children wet one piece and keep another piece dry. Ask them which piece they think would mold first; allow time to see the results (2–3 days). Then, ask the children to come up with as many variables as possible that might influence how fast their pieces of bread will develop mold. Variables might include keeping the bread moist or dry, wrapping it in plastic wrap or leaving it in the open air, and keeping it in the light or in the dark. Children will come up with others.

Children devise ways of testing the effects of the variables they come up with and then implement the tests.

Literature Connection

Tony's Bread: An Italian Folktale by Tomie DePaola (Putnam, 1996) is the story of Tony, who dreams of becoming the most famous baker in northern Italy.

3.36 CONSTRUCTING SCIENCE IN THE CLASSROOM

HOW LONG CAN YOU KEEP AN ICE CUBE FROZEN?

An Activity for Identifying and Controlling Variables

Objective
The student will identify and control variables involved in keeping an ice cube frozen.

Hold a contest in which children wrap ice cubes in such a way as to keep them from melting; the one whose ice cube lasts the longest is the winner. What Influences the melting of the ice cube? Heat, of course. How about pressure? What can we do to keep it from melting? What variables need to be controlled so that all children have the same advantage? How about opening their apparatus to check whether the ice cube is still frozen? As children develop the rules for the competition, they are actually listing the variables.

Literature Connections
The Frozen Man by David Getz (Henry Holt, 1994) and *Iceman* by Don Lessem (Crown, 1994) are both nonfiction books about the discovery of a 5,000-year-old body in a glacier of the Swiss Alps.

Einstein Anderson Shocks His Friends by Seymour Simon (Viking, 1980) has one chapter that deals with Einstein wrapping a snow sculpture in a blanket so that it will not melt before a contest.

NSES Content
Standard B. Physical
Science: Heat Energy

3.37 CONSTRUCTING SCIENCE IN THE CLASSROOM

HOW DOES TEMPERATURE AFFECT THE MOVEMENT OF BLUE FOOD COLORING IN WATER?

An Activity for Identifying and Controlling Variables

Objective
The student will identify and control the variables in an activity relating heat and rate of distribution of food coloring in water.

NSES Content
Standard B. Physical
Science: Heat Energy

Continued on next page

The idea is for children to devise their own inquiries to investigate the effect of water temperature on the movement of blue food coloring in the water. Essentially, they put blue food coloring in transparent cups of water at different temperatures, then record the amount of time it takes for the water to become completely colored. Before this can be done, children will need to list the variables that can affect the results of the investigation. Some variables are density and type of the blue food coloring, how still we hold the cup, temperature of the water, when the food coloring is added, and how the food coloring is added (directly onto the surface of the water, or down the inside of the cup). Children also will need to determine how they will be able to tell when the blue color is evenly distributed.

Literature Connection

Einstein Anderson Tells a Comet's Tale by Seymour Simon (Viking, 1981). Using the scientific process of identifying and controlling variables, Einstein is able to make changes to his soapbox derby vehicle, which enables his team to win the race.

3.38 **CONSTRUCTING SCIENCE IN THE CLASSROOM**

LET'S MAKE A CLOUD

An Activity for Identifying and Controlling Variables

Objective

NSES Content Standard D. Earth and Space Science: Objects in the Sky

The student will identify the variables that influence cloud formation.

Meteorologists tell us that for clouds to form, we need moisture, a distinct temperature **gradient** (difference in temperatures between two regions), and small particles on which tiny droplets of water form. Children can investigate this themselves. Provide each group of children with a transparent plastic cup, some hot water, a plastic bag of ice cubes, some matches, and a square piece of black paper about 4 inches on each side. Fill the cup to about 1 inch deep with hot water. Light the match, and drop it into the cup. It will go out, of course, when it hits the water. (Alternatively, children can rub two chalkboard erasers together and let the chalk dust fall into the cup.) IMMEDIATELY cover the top of the cup with the plastic bag of ice. Observe what happens inside the cup. (A cloud will form.) Hold the black paper behind the cup to make what happens easier to see.

Consider these questions: How do we know the visible vapor in the cup is a cloud and not just smoke from the match? Is match smoke (or chalk dust) necessary for the cloud to form? How could we find out? What would happen if we reversed the temperatures (had ice in the bottom of the cup and put a bag with hot water on the top)? What happens if the temperatures at the top and the bottom of the cup get closer together? From these investigations, children will isolate the variables needed for clouds to form.

Continued on next page

Literature Connections

Splish, Splash by Joan Bransfield Graham (Ticknor and Fields, 1994) is a collection of poetry about water in its various states. "Water is a magic potion; it can fill a glass, an ocean, raging river, tiny tear, drops of dew that disappear."

The Snowflake: A Water Cycle Story by Neil Waldman (The Milbrook Press, 2003) is a nonfiction book that describes a snowflake traveling through the water cycle month by month and changing form.

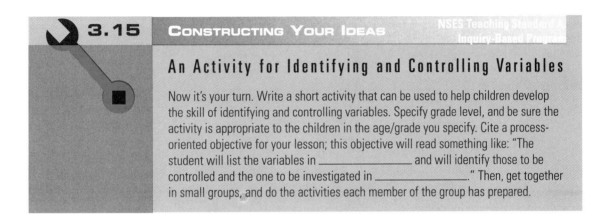

3.15   CONSTRUCTING YOUR IDEAS   NSES Teaching Standard A: Inquiry-Based Program

An Activity for Identifying and Controlling Variables

Now it's your turn. Write a short activity that can be used to help children develop the skill of identifying and controlling variables. Specify grade level, and be sure the activity is appropriate to the children in the age/grade you specify. Cite a process-oriented objective for your lesson; this objective will read something like: "The student will list the variables in _____ and will identify those to be controlled and the one to be investigated in _____." Then, get together in small groups, and do the activities each member of the group has prepared.

FORMULATING AND TESTING HYPOTHESES

In the pendulum activity, you formulated hypotheses regarding what would happen to the period of the pendulum if you varied each of several factors. This was a good example of the science process skill of formulating hypotheses.

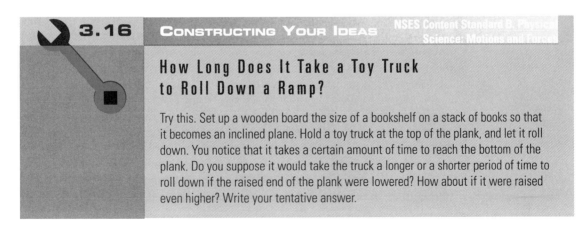

3.16   CONSTRUCTING YOUR IDEAS   NSES Content Standard B: Physical Science: Motions and Forces

How Long Does It Take a Toy Truck to Roll Down a Ramp?

Try this. Set up a wooden board the size of a bookshelf on a stack of books so that it becomes an inclined plane. Hold a toy truck at the top of the plank, and let it roll down. You notice that it takes a certain amount of time to reach the bottom of the plank. Do you suppose it would take the truck a longer or a shorter period of time to roll down if the raised end of the plank were lowered? How about if it were raised even higher? Write your tentative answer.

How long does it take the cart to roll down the ramp?

FIGURE 3.22

NSES Content
Standard B. Physical
Science: Motions and
Forces
NSES Teaching
Standard A. Inquiry-
Based Program
NSES Professional
Development
Standard A. Learning
Content Through Inquiry

You will notice that you are considering two separate variables in this activity: (1) the length of time it takes the truck to roll down the plank and (2) the height of the raised end of the plank. In suggesting a tentative answer to the question "Will it take the toy truck a longer or a shorter period of time to roll down the plank if the raised end were lowered?" you were formulating a hypothesis. You were saying something like this: "If I increase the incline of the plank, the truck will take less time to roll down, and if I decrease the incline, it will take more time." This is a statement of hypothesis.

A hypothesis is a statement of your best guess as to the *relationship between two variables*. In the case of the toy truck on the plank, it is your best guess as to the relationship between the time it takes the truck to roll down the plank and the height of the raised end of the plank. Hypothesis formulation is different from prediction. In prediction, we simply ask what would happen if we did something ("I wonder what would happen if I put a drop of vinegar on limestone."). Here, there is only one variable: the vinegar. In hypothesis formulation, we ask what would happen to one variable if we change an interacting variable ("I wonder what would happen to the rate of plant growth if I played music to it.").

Let us return to the plank and the toy truck. How can you obtain a measure of the time it takes for the toy truck to roll down the plank? Maybe you can use a stopwatch, starting it the instant you let the truck go and stopping it the instant the front wheels touch the floor. If you do this the same way every time, you will probably have a good indication of the time it takes for the truck to roll down the plank. Alternatively, you could define the time in terms of some other variable, such as the number of clicks on a metronome or the number of handclaps done in a steady, rhythmic fashion. You can raise or lower the raised end of the plank simply by varying the number of books that support it, and you can measure the resulting height of the raised end.

▶ Go ahead and do this activity. Write down your hypothesis. Decide what kind of information you need to investigate it, and then test your hypothesis. Record your results, and examine the data after you are finished. What can you conclude?

You probably will need only two items of information for this investigation, because everything else will stay the same. You will need to know the height of the raised end of the plank, and you will need to know how long it takes the truck to roll down the plank. The height of the plank can be measured with a ruler; the time can be measured with a stopwatch or using some other method of your choice. Let us set up a data table to help us record the data. It might look something like this:

Data Table

Height	Time	
_____	Trial 1	_____
	Trial 2	_____
	Trial 3	_____
	Average	_____
_____	Trial 1	_____
	Trial 2	_____
	Trial 3	_____
	Average	_____
_____	Trial 1	_____
	Trial 2	_____
	Trial 3	_____
	Average	_____

NSES Content Standard A. Science as Inquiry: Abilities Necessary To Do Scientific Inquiry

You will want to place the board at several different heights, and you will want to do at least three trials for each height and average the results.

When we test hypotheses, we assure ourselves that we have identified all the variables, have taken steps to control all except the one we are experimenting with, have planned what we are going to do to test our hypothesis, and have identified the information we need to obtain so that we can make conclusions about our hypothesis. Often, this includes recording data. In many cases, we can anticipate what kinds of data we will be recording before we ever get started, but often, we simply have to tinker with the setup for a while before we can decide how to proceed.

Let us look at another activity that involves formulating and testing hypotheses. We know that the moon has craters on its surface. How do they form? Astronomers tell us that **meteoroids** rushing through space crash into the moon when they come close enough to be attracted by the moon's gravity, and the resulting impact forms a crater. Can we investigate this?

3.17 CONSTRUCTING YOUR IDEAS

Moon Craters

NSES Professional Development Standard A

Learning Content Through Inquiry NSES Content Standard D. Earth and Space Science: Earth in the Solar System

Obtain an aluminum pan or a plastic box 6-8 inches deep, and fill it with flour. Obtain rocks or marbles of different sizes and weights. One at a time, hold a rock or a marble above the flour in the plate, and drop it. Try dropping the objects from different heights. What do you notice? If you sprinkle a little ground cinnamon on the surface of the flour, you might be able to see what happens better (see Figure 3.23). Discuss the effects of your initial investigation with your classmates.

What variables might affect the size of the craters on the moon? Develop a hypothesis, and plan how to test it. Then, execute your plan, and report back to the class.

 Direct links to NASA Web sites where you can find photographs and many details concerning the moon are available on the Student Book Companion Web Site.

Dropping a ball into a pan of flour

Measuring the depth of the crater

Measuring the diameter of
the crater

Simulating the
formation of moon
craters

FIGURE 3.23

Additional activities designed to aid children with developing the process skill of formulating and testing hypotheses are suggested in Constructing Science in the Classroom 3.39–3.41

3.39   CONSTRUCTING SCIENCE IN THE CLASSROOM

WHICH BUBBLES LAST LONGEST?

An Activity for Formulating and Testing Hypotheses

NSES Content Standard A. Science as Inquiry: Abilities Necessary To Do Scientific Inquiry

Objective

The student will formulate and test a hypothesis concerning how to keep bubbles intact the longest.

The teacher may start the activity by blowing some bubbles and asking such questions as "What is inside a bubble?" "How do you know?" "What are bubbles made of?" Provide each group with pipe cleaners or pieces of wire, plastic plates, straws, and "bubble juice" made of 1 cup of water, 2 tablespoons of liquid detergent, 1 tablespoon of glycerin (available in most drug stores), and 1 teaspoon of sugar. Encourage children to play with making bubbles for a few minutes, blowing bubbles on the plates using the straws and blowing bubbles using the pipe cleaners or wire. Once they get the hang of how to blow bubbles, ask them to formulate a hypothesis as to what method will produce the longest-lasting bubble and to devise a way to test their hypotheses. Then, ask them to test their hypotheses to see which are supported by evidence.

Literature Connections

Mr. Archimedes' Bath by Pamela Allen (HarperCollins, 1980). Mr. Archimedes is upset when his bathtub overflows and the water level changes, so he decides to use the scientific processes to find answers to his questions.

A Children's Museum Activity Book: Bubbles by Bernie Zubrowski (Little, Brown & Co., 1979) is one in a series of nonfiction books written by Zubrowski, a staff member at the Children's Museum in Boston, to promote the natural curiosity that children have about experimenting with objects.

Ultimate Bubble Book: Soapy Science Fun by Shar Levine and Leslie Johnstone (Sterling, 2003) is a nonfiction book that contains a collection of free-exploration and guided-inquiry investigations into bubbles using dish soap, water, and glycerin.

3.40 CONSTRUCTING SCIENCE IN THE CLASSROOM

THE PITCH OF SOUND

An Activity for Formulating and Testing Hypotheses

Objective

The student will formulate and test a hypothesis that describes the relationship between the length of an air column and the pitch of the sound it produces when one blows across its top.

First, model the activity with bells, a pitch pipe, or a guitar to be sure that children can recognize different pitches. Then, give each group eight identical soda bottles filled with varying amounts of water. Ask children to hypothesize the relationship between the length of the air column and the pitch of the sound that results from blowing across the bottle tops. To test their hypotheses, children blow across the mouth of each bottle and observe the pitch of the sound.

See the video clip "The Pitch of Sound" on the companion DVD.

NSES Content Standard B. Physical Science: Sound Energy

Literature Connections

The Magic School Bus in the Haunted Museum: A Book About Sound by Joanna Cole (Scholastic, 1995), based on an episode of the animated TV series, describes how children discover the way sound is produced and how it travels.

The Sound of Bells by Eric Sloane (Doubleday, 1966) is a nostalgic look at the history of bell ringing in our country, from the tinkle of cowbells to the thunderous tones of the town hall bell.

3.41 CONSTRUCTING SCIENCE IN THE CLASSROOM

STRENGTH OF ELECTROMAGNETS

An Activity for Formulating and Testing Hypotheses

Objective

The student will formulate and test a hypothesis describing the relationship between the number of coils of wire wound around a nail and the strength of the resulting electromagnetic field.

Have children wind five or six coils of wire around a nail and connect the free ends of the wire to a 9-volt battery to form an electromagnet (see Figure 3.24). Then, have the children use the electromagnet to pick up some paper clips. "How many can you pick up?" Now, have the children wind more wire around the nail and see how many paper clips they can pick up. Ask the children to formulate a hypothesis showing the relationship between the number of coils of wire and the strength of the electromagnet. Then, ask them to test their hypotheses.

NSES Content Standard B. Physical Science: Magnetism

Continued on next page

Children observe that the number of paper clips the electromagnet will pick up depends on the number of times they wind the wire around the nail. From these observations, they may infer that the strength of the electromagnet depends on the number of times the wire is coiled around the nail. From this inference, they can predict that if they increase the number of coils around the wire, they will be able to pick up more paper clips. To record their data, children could make a data table that looks something like this:

Initial Observations

Number of Coils	Number of Paper Clips

Predictions

Number of Coils	Predicted Number of Paper Clips	Actual Number of Paper Clips

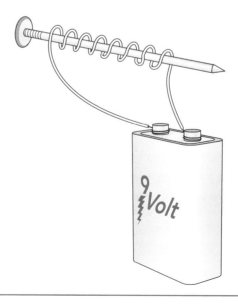

An electromagnet

FIGURE 3.24

Continued on next page

Literature Connection

The Secret Life of Dilly McBean by Dorothy Haas (Bradbury, 1986). With the help of a professor, Dilly develops secret magnetic powers.

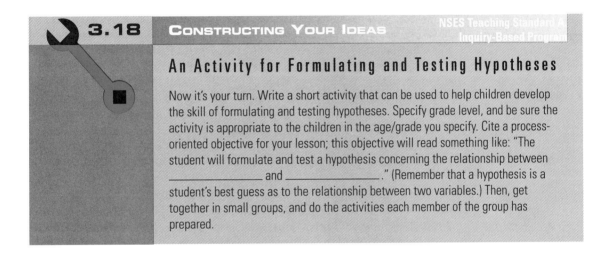

3.18 CONSTRUCTING YOUR IDEAS

NSES Teaching Standard A: Inquiry-Based Program

An Activity for Formulating and Testing Hypotheses

Now it's your turn. Write a short activity that can be used to help children develop the skill of formulating and testing hypotheses. Specify grade level, and be sure the activity is appropriate to the children in the age/grade you specify. Cite a process-oriented objective for your lesson; this objective will read something like: "The student will formulate and test a hypothesis concerning the relationship between _____ and _____ ." (Remember that a hypothesis is a student's best guess as to the relationship between two variables.) Then, get together in small groups, and do the activities each member of the group has prepared.

INTERPRETING DATA

In many activities, students gather data. The data can be qualitative, quantitative, or in many cases, a combination of both.

3.23 IN THE SCHOOLS

NSES Content Standard D: Earth and Space Science: Structure of the Earth System

Water Quality

A middle grades science teacher led a class of students in an investigation of the quality of the water in a stream behind the school. Students used probes, digital cameras, and other technological devices to gather information about the water's **pH,** temperature, dissolved oxygen, and **turbidity.** The information was both qualitative and quantitative. The pH, temperature, and percentage of dissolved oxygen were measured at different positions and depths of the stream. Turbidity was estimated in terms of the depth to which the end of a meter stick could be seen.

The teacher helped the students analyze the data and formulate conclusions based on the data about the quality of the water in the stream.

(Adapted from Wu & Krajcik, 2006)

NSES Teaching
Standard A. Inquiry-
Based Program
NSES Program
Standard B. Relevant,
Inquiry-Based, and
Connected with Other
Subjects
NSES Content
Standard A. Science
as Inquiry: Abilities
Necessary To Do
Scientific Inquiry

During the investigation in which you dropped rocks on a pan of flour (Constructing Your Ideas 3.17), you collected some data. You probably recorded such items of data as (1) weight of rock, (2) size of rock, (3) height of drop, (4) depth of crater, and (5) diameter of crater. You also may have collected some qualitative data, such as noticing that the flour displaced from the crater spewed out like rays.

Had you planned to gather all this data? Had you previously set up data tables to record the results?

The first step in interpreting data is to decide what data you want to gather. This comes from the hypothesis you devise. You may do the investigation mentally, visualizing what will happen and deciding what kinds of information you will need to have to tell why it happened. Or, you may want to tinker with the experiment itself to see what happens.

For example, in the moon craters investigation, you could state as a hypothesis that the higher you hold the rock, the deeper the crater will be. You will need to measure how high the rock is held and how deep the resulting crater is. You could also hypothesize that the higher the rock is held, the wider the crater will be. Now, you will also need to measure the diameter of the crater. In addition, you could hypothesize that the heavier the rock, the deeper and wider the crater will be. In this case, you will need to weigh the rocks, and you will investigate the effects of two separate variables for each rock: (1) height of drop, and (2) weight of rock. How will you organize your investigation so you can interpret the results?

Let us take the hypothesis that the heavier the rock and the higher the drop, the deeper and wider the crater will be. You will need to duplicate the procedure you follow with one rock for all the other rocks of different weights. Then, when you have all the data, you will be able to look at the results for each rock to see if the weight of the rock and the height of the drop influence the depth and the diameter of the crater. You might set up a data table like this:

Data Table for the Moon Crater Investigation

Weight	Height of Drop		Depth	Diameter
#1 _____	1 _____	Trial 1	_____	_____
		Trial 2	_____	_____
		Trial 3	_____	_____
		Average	_____	_____

Continued on next page

Weight	Height of Drop		Depth	Diameter
	2 _____	Trial 1	_____	_____
		Trial 2	_____	_____
		Trial 3	_____	_____
		Average	_____	_____
	3 _____	Trial 1	_____	_____
		Trial 2	_____	_____
		Trial 3	_____	_____
		Average	_____	_____
#2 _____	1 _____	Trial 1	_____	_____
		Trial 2	_____	_____
		Trial 3	_____	_____
		Average	_____	_____
	2 _____	Trial 1	_____	_____
		Trial 2	_____	_____
		Trial 3	_____	_____
		Average	_____	_____
	3 _____	Trial 1	_____	_____
		Trial 2	_____	_____
		Trial 3	_____	_____
		Average	_____	_____
#3 _____	1 _____	Trial 1	_____	_____
		Trial 2	_____	_____
		Trial 3	_____	_____
		Average	_____	_____
	2 _____	Trial 1	_____	_____
		Trial 2	_____	_____
		Trial 3	_____	_____
		Average	_____	_____

Continued on next page

Weight	Height of Drop		Depth	Diameter
3 _____	Trial 1		_____	_____
	Trial 2		_____	_____
	Trial 3		_____	_____
	Average		_____	_____

NSES Content Standard D. Earth and Space Science: Earth in the Solar System
NSES Teaching Standard A. Inquiry-Based Program
NSES Program Standard C. Coordinated with Mathematics

Once the data is in a form you can read, you can look at the numbers to see what they tell you. Focusing on only one rock, you can see if the depth of the crater increased, decreased, or remained the same when the height of the drop was increased; you can do the same thing with the diameter of the crater. You can analyze the data from each rock in the same manner. This enables you to make conclusions about the relationship between height of drop and the depth and diameter of crater. Next, you can focus on the different kinds of rocks and find the data for the same height of drop for each rock. Comparing the crater depths and diameters made by different rocks dropped from the same height enables you to make conclusions about the effect of the weight of the rock on the crater. Having done this, you can put the two conclusions together to derive a concept—for example, "Craters are deeper and wider when the rock is heavier and is dropped from greater heights."

One of the best ways to organize data for interpretation is to put the data in visual form, such as a graph, chart, or histogram. Sample data tables from the moon crater investigation, together with computer-generated graphs of the data, are shown in Figures 3.25 and 3.26. Calculators and computers are very useful aids to constructing graphs. (The use of technology is discussed in Chapter 11.)

Young children should be encouraged to create graphs of plant size, numbers of children with certain hair color or eye color, and so forth. Children can line up in rows according to color of sweater (or some other characteristic) to form a "living graph."

Interpreting data is not difficult once you have decided what kind of data you need. However, suppose you don't know what kind of data to collect. In that case, you simply tinker with the activity to get an idea of what is happening, and then you decide what you need to find out to be able to answer the question.

In the moon crater investigation, we talked about quantitative data—the kind of data associated with numbers or measurements. Qualitative data also can be collected. The presence or absence of rays from the

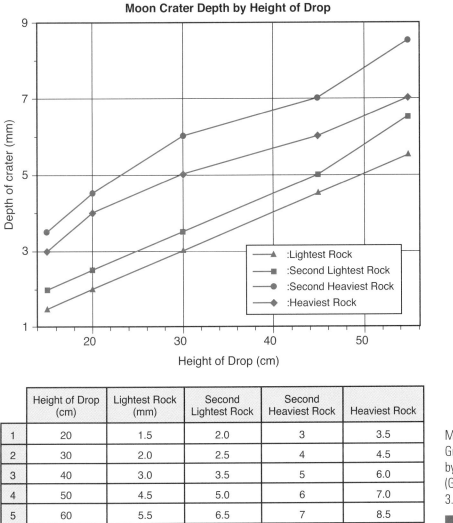

Moon Crater Depth by Height of Drop

	Height of Drop (cm)	Lightest Rock (mm)	Second Lightest Rock	Second Heaviest Rock	Heaviest Rock
1	20	1.5	2.0	3	3.5
2	30	2.0	2.5	4	4.5
3	40	3.0	3.5	5	6.0
4	50	4.5	5.0	6	7.0
5	60	5.5	6.5	7	8.5

Moon crater depth—
Graph and data table
by height of drop
(Graphical Analysis
3.2, Vernier Software)

FIGURE 3.25

craters in the pan of flour is a good example of qualitative data. You might decide that you want to see if the size of the rocks or the height of the drop had any effect on the formation of rays. If the information you gather is either "Yes, rays are formed" or "No, rays are not formed," you are collecting qualitative data.

In many life science activities, qualitative data is the only kind of data available.

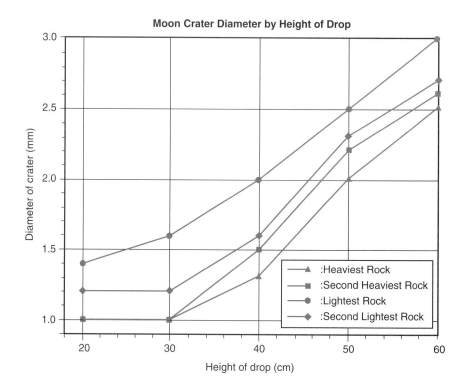

Moon crater
diameter—Graph and
data table by height
of drop (Graphical
Analysis 3.2, Vernier
Software)

FIGURE 3.26

	Height of Drop (cm)	Lightest Rock (mm)	Second Lightest Rock	Second Heaviest Rock	Heaviest Rock
1	20	1.4	1.2	1.0	1.0
2	30	1.6	1.2	1.0	1.0
3	40	2.0	1.6	1.5	1.3
4	50	2.5	2.3	2.2	2.0
5	60	3.0	2.7	2.6	2.5

3.24   IN THE SCHOOLS   NSES Content Standard C. Life Science: Organisms and Environments

Mealworms

A fourth-grade teacher asked the children to investigate whether mealworms move toward or away from a stimulus. (Mealworms, the larvae of a beetle, are available at most pet stores.) Children were asked what stimuli they would want to investigate,

Continued on next page

and they suggested light, sugar, vinegar, and hilly terrain. Children set up the various stimuli on paper plates and watched the mealworms interact with them. The data they collected was qualitative rather than quantitative. For example, children observed that the mealworms moved away from vinegar but moved toward the sugar, the light, and the bottom of an incline. From their observations, they decided to investigate other questions: Do mealworms crawl in a straight line? How far can a mealworm crawl in one minute? (See Figure 3.27.)

Literature Connections
Mealworms by Donna Schaffer (Capstone, 1999) is a nonfiction book for young children that describes the physical characteristics, habits, and stages of development of mealworms.

The Icky Bug Alphabet Book by Jerry Pallotta (Charlesbridge Publishing, 1989) is a nonfiction picture book about insects and arachnids—one for each letter of the alphabet.

Bizarre Bugs by Doug Wechsler (Boyds Mills Press, 2003) has excellent pictures of and strange but true information about insects.

Watching the behavior of mealworms

FIGURE 3.27

Additional investigations that children can explore to gain facility with interpreting data are shown in Constructing Science in the Classroom 3.42–3.44. In these activities, children collect and graph data to reach their conclusions.

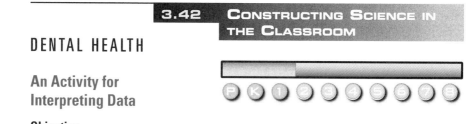

DENTAL HEALTH

An Activity for Interpreting Data

NSES Content
Standard F. Science in
Personal and Social
Perspectives: Personal
Health

Objective

The student will interpret data concerning the effect of time spent brushing teeth and cleanliness of teeth.

Note: *This activity requires advance permission of parents.*

Children will use *red disclosing tablets* (available from dentists and dental hygienists) to reveal which teeth are clean and which are not after brushing. Give children a sticky snack such as peanut butter and crackers, a toothbrush, a small tube of toothpaste, and a red disclosing tablet. In the interest of promoting dental health, local dental offices often are eager to provide the toothbrushes, tubes of toothpaste, and disclosing tablets. You may even want to ask a dental hygienist to participate in this lesson. Have children eat the snack, and then ask them to brush until they feel their teeth are clean. Have a partner record amount of time spent brushing. When all are done, record the time spent brushing by each child's name on a sheet of chart paper. Then, ask each child to chew on a red disclosing tablet (they are nontoxic) and rinse thoroughly. Teeth that retain the red color are still not clean. Have each child's partner count the number of teeth that are clean (not stained red), and record that number by each student's name next to the time that child spent brushing.

Ask children to look at the data and form conclusions. You also may wish to have children develop a graph of the data so it can be portrayed visually.

Data Table

Name	Time Spent Brushing	Number of Clean Teeth

Challenge

Ask children to research and develop a dental hygiene forum in which they present the anatomy of a tooth; descriptions of various dental problems such as plaque buildup, cavities, and gum disease; and descriptions of proper dental care and its effects. Contact your local or state dental association for suggestions and assistance.

Continued on next page

Literature Connections

I Know Why I Brush My Teeth by Kate Rowan (Candlewick Press, 1999) is a story about the importance and proper way of caring for teeth.

Teeth by Beth Ferguson (Benchmark Books, 2004) is a nonfiction book that provides easy-to-read, illustrated information about teeth and ways of taking care of them.

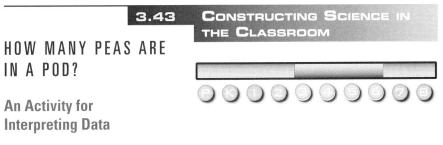

3.43 **CONSTRUCTING SCIENCE IN THE CLASSROOM**

HOW MANY PEAS ARE IN A POD?

An Activity for Interpreting Data

Objective

The student will interpret data concerning the number of peas in pea pods.

Provide each group of children several whole pea pods. Ask children to collect data about the length, width, thickness, color, and other external characteristics of the pods. Children then open the pods one by one and count the number of peas in each. They record their data on the board along with the data collected by other groups. Children then graph the data in such a way as to be able to interpret it. The graph might look like the one shown in Figure 3.28.

Graphs are interpreted in terms of the relationship between two variables—for example, the longer the pod, the more peas.

As a seasonal alternative, children can predict and then count the number of seeds in pumpkins, graphing the number of seeds against the circumference (distance around) the pumpkin.

NSES Content Standard C. Life Science: Life Cycles of Organisms

Literature Connections

Black and White by David Macaulay (Houghton Mifflin, 1990) would be an exciting introduction to the process of interpreting data. The book contains four stories, but in reality, it may contain only one story. Attention must be given to interpreting clues provided in the story.

The Pumpkin Book by Gail Gibbons (Holiday House, 1999) describes the different sizes and shapes of pumpkins, how they grow, and their traditional uses and cultural significance.

From Seed to Pumpkin by Jan Kottke (Children's Press, 2000) illustrates how a pumpkin seed grows into a plant that is used for pies and jack-o'-lanterns.

Pumpkin Patch by Elizabeth King (Viking Penguin, 1996) traces the cultivation and growth of pumpkins through photographs.

How Many Peas in a Pea Pod?

How Long?	How Many?
6 cm	4
6.5 cm	4
7 cm	6
9 cm	9
11 cm	13
11.5 cm	14
12 cm	14
13 cm	15

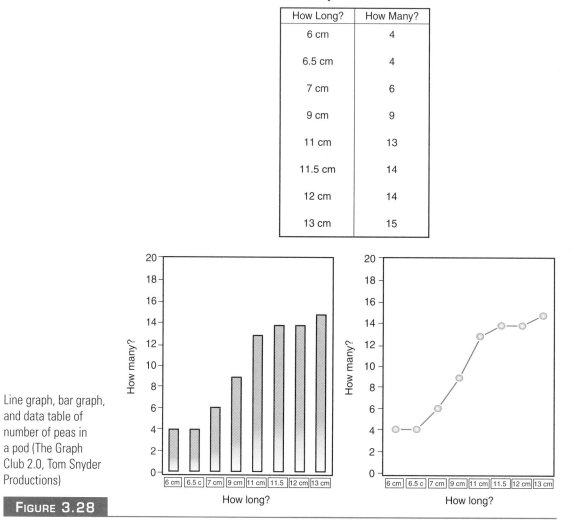

Line graph, bar graph, and data table of number of peas in a pod (The Graph Club 2.0, Tom Snyder Productions)

FIGURE 3.28

3.44   CONSTRUCTING SCIENCE IN THE CLASSROOM

WHY DO SOME THINGS SINK AND SOME THINGS FLOAT IN WATER?

An Activity for Interpreting Data

Objective

The student will measure the mass and volume of objects and will find a relationship that explains why some things sink and some things float in water.

NSES Content Standard B. Physical Science: Properties and Changes of Properties in Matter

Provide a bucket of water and a number of objects that children can test for sinking and floating. Encourage children to bring small objects from home to test. If possible, provide a piece of ebony (a wood that sinks) and a piece of pumice (a rock that floats). Try to provide a few objects that are rectangular in shape.

Select 6-8 objects, and ask the students to predict whether each will sink or float. Then, try each object. Have the children record both the predictions and the results of the tests.

Have students find the mass and volume of each object. They find the mass by weighing the object on a pan balance. They find the volume either by measurement of its length, width, and height, or by displacement. (To find the volume of an object by displacement, partly fill a graduated cylinder with water, and record the volume. Put the object in the cylinder, and submerge it completely. Record the new level of the water. The difference between the new level and the beginning level is the volume of the object).

Students construct a graph with mass on the vertical (y) axis and volume on the horizontal (x) axis. Use a graphing program if one is available. Each object will have a unique mass and volume. Use different colors to graph objects that sink and objects that float.

Finally, have students develop a concept for explaining why some objects sink and some objects float in water. Students should base this concept on the information they have obtained and the graph they have constructed.

(**Teacher Note:** Density equals mass divided by volume. The density of water is 1 g/cc. If an object's density is greater than 1 g/cc, it sinks in water; if its density is less than 1 g/cc, it floats in water.)

(Adapted from Benedis-Grab, 2006)

Challenge

Will ice sink or float? Try it. What do you suppose its density is?

Literature Connections

Discovering Density by Jaqueline Barber, Marion E. Buegler, Laura Lowell, and Carolyn Willard (GEMS/Lawrence Hall of Science, 1988) is an activity guide that enables students to explore the concept of density.

Galileo Galilei by Mike Goldsmith (Raintree Steck-Vaughn, 2001) is a short biography of Galileo that includes information on density.

Continued on next page

Who Killed Olive Soufflé? By Margaret Benoit (Learning Triangle, 1997) is a murder mystery chapter book that shows the detective using the principle of density to help solve the crime.

3.19 CONSTRUCTING YOUR IDEAS

An Activity for Interpreting Data

Now it's your turn. Write a short activity that can be used to help children develop the skill of interpreting data. Specify grade level, and be sure the activity is appropriate to the children in the age/grade you specify. Cite a process-oriented objective for your lesson; this objective will read something like: "The student will interpret data gathered from an investigation of the effect of _____ on _____." Then, get together in small groups, and do the activities each member of the group has prepared.

DEFINING OPERATIONALLY

As noted previously, accurate communication is of paramount importance in science. Consequently, it often is necessary to define things in terms of something that everyone will understand.

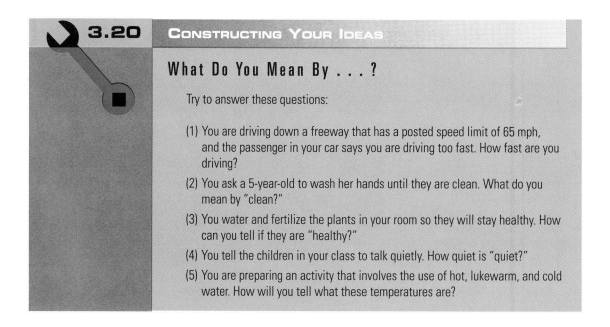

3.20 CONSTRUCTING YOUR IDEAS

What Do You Mean By . . . ?

Try to answer these questions:

(1) You are driving down a freeway that has a posted speed limit of 65 mph, and the passenger in your car says you are driving too fast. How fast are you driving?

(2) You ask a 5-year-old to wash her hands until they are clean. What do you mean by "clean?"

(3) You water and fertilize the plants in your room so they will stay healthy. How can you tell if they are "healthy?"

(4) You tell the children in your class to talk quietly. How quiet is "quiet?"

(5) You are preparing an activity that involves the use of hot, lukewarm, and cold water. How will you tell what these temperatures are?

In much of our daily activity, we come across phenomena that seem to require definitions. "Fast," "clean," "healthy," "quiet," "lukewarm" can all mean different things to different people. They also can mean different things to the same people at different times. In scientific investigations, it is critically important that all involved have the same understandings of the same things.

Defining a variable that cannot be measured or seen easily in terms that everyone understands in the same way is called *defining operationally*. Defining operationally involves finding equivalent ways of measuring something indirectly that cannot be conveniently measured directly. For example, in the pendulum activity, we found it necessary to measure the period of the pendulum in terms of the number of swings per 15 seconds, because we could not measure the time of one swing conveniently. It was difficult to measure this quantity directly, and so we had to find an indirect way of measuring it. The measurement we devised had to be equivalent to the measurement we were replacing it with, but it did not have to give the same measurement.

You have used operational definitions in many of the activities presented in this chapter. In "A Case of Moon Watching," students defined the direction the moon faces in terms of the perpendicular bisector of an imaginary line connecting the cusps. Operational definitions were used extensively in devising classification systems. In "Graphing Plant Growth" (In the Schools 3.8), children measured plant growth in terms of number of squares on graph paper. The strength of an electromagnet was defined in terms of the number of paper clips it would pick up (Constructing Science in the Classroom 3.41).

Have you done a "Sink-or-Float" activity with children? In most such activities, we ask children to predict whether objects will sink or float in water, after which they try each object to check the predictions. (See, for example, Constructing Science in the Classroom 3.24.) When children actually try their predictions, it is quickly found that they have to devise operational definitions of "sink" and "float." In many cases, the item stays submerged so that 100% is below the surface of the water, yet it does not go all the way to the bottom. Does this item sink? Does it float? We need to define these terms. In addition, most items that float do so with varying amounts of the object below the surface of the water. What is meant by "float?" Can an object be said to "float" if *any part* of it remains above the surface of the water? It is essential that you and the children work together to develop meaningful operational definitions when they become necessary.

As indicated, operational definitions are used to define variables or phenomena that cannot be measured directly. If an occurrence can be measured directly, there is no need for an operational definition, because the occurrence can be defined in terms of standard units of measurement. We would not need to define the length of a desktop in operational terms,

NSES Teaching Standard A. Inquiry-Based Program
NSES Program Standard B. Relevant, Inquiry-Based, and Connected with Other Subjects
NSES Content Standard A. Science as Inquiry: Abilities Necessary To Do Scientific Inquiry

for example, because we can measure it with a ruler or in terms of number of pennies or paper clips. Similarly, we would not need to define the weight of a person in operational terms, because the person can stand on a scale and get the "real" weight. The depth of the "moon craters" (Constructing Your Ideas 3.17) can be measured with a ruler. Outdoor temperature is measured directly with a thermometer (In the Schools 3.12). The time that it takes to run the length of the playground can be measured directly with a stopwatch or with a watch that has a sweeping second hand (In the Schools 3.15).

Take a few minutes and look through the activities you have done thus far. Which of them required operational definitions? Chances are you will find that you employed operational definitions in many of these activities, beginning as early in your inquires as observing rocks, in which you undoubtedly had to tell what you meant by "smooth" or "rough" and even what you meant by colors such as "gray" or "brown."

The purpose of operational definitions is to provide consistency and accuracy in scientific investigations.

Activities that can be used to help children develop the process of defining operationally are shown in Constructing Science in the Classroom 3.45 and 3.46.

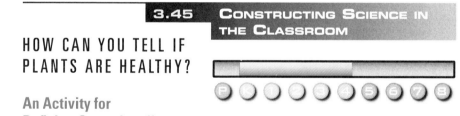

3.45 CONSTRUCTING SCIENCE IN THE CLASSROOM

HOW CAN YOU TELL IF PLANTS ARE HEALTHY?

An Activity for Defining Operationally

NSES Content Standard C. Life Science: The Characteristics of Organisms

Objective

The student will define *plant health* in operational terms.

Use the seedlings that grew well in Constructing Science in the Classroom 3.34, or obtain flower seedlings from a local nursery. Ask children to identify which of the plants are "healthy." Also, ask them to describe their reasons for identifying these plants as healthy. Responses might include "color of leaves," "thickness of stem," "number of leaves," and so on. Ask them to describe how they would measure each of these qualities so that they could tell which plants are healthiest. They are defining *plant health* in operational terms. Let the plants grow, and have children use their own definitions of plant health to decide which plants are the healthiest. Children may choose to revise their definitions of plant health once they see the sprouts.

Literature Connections

The Giant Carrot by Jan Peck (Dial, 1998). Little Isabelle's family plants and carefully tends to a carrot seed ... with wondrous results (adapted from the Russian folktale *The Turnip*).

Continued on next page

The Berenstain Bears Grow-It: Mother Nature Has Such a Green Thumb by Stan and Jan Berenstain (Random House, 1996). Brother and sister plant seeds, cuttings, and tubers. Plant science activities are suggested.

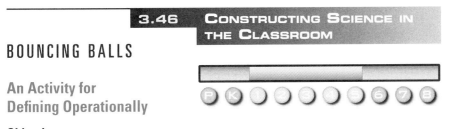

3.46   CONSTRUCTING SCIENCE IN THE CLASSROOM

BOUNCING BALLS

**An Activity for
Defining Operationally**

Objective

The student will define *bouncy ball* in operational terms.

Provide children with an assortment of different kinds of balls, such as a baseball, a softball, a ping-pong ball, a "superball," a tennis ball, a basketball, a soccer ball, a volleyball, and other balls used in sports. Children select one ball at a time and then drop it from a given height. This height can be determined by the children and can include children standing on chairs or tables to obtain greater heights from which to drop the balls. After each ball is dropped (not thrown), children look to see whether it bounces, and if it does, they measure how high it bounces (see Figure 3.29).

Ask children to devise a definition for "bouncy ball" based on their investigations and observations. Ask them to check out other balls and other situations to see if their definition maintains itself.

Literature Connection

Stop That Ball! by Mike McClintock (Random House, 1989) tells of a boy who encounters madcap adventures as he tries to retrieve his runaway bouncing ball. The text is written in rhyming prose.

NSES Content Standard B. Physical Science: Position and Motion of Objects

How high will the ball bounce?

FIGURE 3.29

3.21   **CONSTRUCTING YOUR IDEAS**

An Activity for Defining Operationally

Now it's your turn. Write a short activity that can be used to help children develop the skill of defining operationally. Specify grade level, and be sure the activity is appropriate to the children in the age/grade you specify. Cite a process-oriented objective for your lesson; this objective will read something like: "The student will define _____ in operational terms." Then, get together in small groups, and do the activities each member of the group has prepared.

EXPERIMENTING

Experimenting is the scientific process in which the investigator explores the effect that a change in one variable has on the change in a different, interacting variable. For example, the investigator may choose to explore the effect of changing the temperature of the air inside a balloon on the change of the balloon's diameter. Or, the investigator may wish to examine the effect of changing the amount of yeast put into bread on how high the bread rises. We have suggested several experiments in this chapter. One dealt with factors that influence how fast a pendulum swings. Another dealt with factors that influence how fast a toy truck rolls down a board.

Experimenting is different from formulating hypotheses. A hypothesis is a guess about what might happen if you were to do something. One variable is identified, and its effect on a different interacting variable is hypothesized. No methodical attempt is made to examine the *effect* of changing one variable on a possible change in the other variable. For example, a hypothesis might suggest that if I eat too much, I might gain weight. A corresponding experiment would investigate the relationship (if any) between the *amount* I eat and the *amount* of weight I gain. When experimenting, the investigator makes careful plans to explore *the effect of changing one variable on the change in the other, interacting variable.* The variable the investigator is changing is termed the **independent variable,** because it doesn't depend on anything except what the investigator does. The variable whose value is changed because of a change in the independent variable is termed the **dependent variable,** because it depends on the independent variable.

In experimenting, investigators ask questions about something they have observed or have wondered about. The question frequently takes the form of "I wonder why _____?" or "I wonder what would happen to _____ if I changed _____?" Often, but not always, this question is cast in the form of a hypothesis. Variables are identified, and those that are not being investigated but that may contribute to the outcome of the experiment are controlled. If necessary or desirable, the variables to be investigated may be expressed in operational terms. An experimental plan is developed that includes the procedure, the nature of the observations needed, and the data to be collected. The experiment is carried out, and the data is obtained. Modifications often are desirable, and these become part of a modified plan. After the investigation has been carried out and the data and observations have been recorded, the results are analyzed in terms of the original question or hypothesis. Conclusions are made accordingly, and the results of the investigation are communicated to classmates or other individuals for their reactions.

You will recall that science is skeptical. Thus, interaction among children about the conclusions they make and their reasons for making their conclusions represents the essence of the scientific enterprise. Investigators try to convince colleagues that their theories are correct while the colleagues probe with penetrating questions, some of which the investigator may not have thought of. Note that the design and execution of an original experiment is located at the *creating* level of the revised Bloom's taxonomy (see Chapter 5). The child becomes the scientist.

NSES Content Standard G. History and Nature of Science: Nature of Science

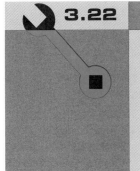

3.22   CONSTRUCTING YOUR IDEAS

NSES Content Standard B. Physical Science: Motions and Forces

Falling Parachutes

Try this experiment. What factors influence the rate of descent of a parachute? An exploratory activity involving parachutes was suggested in Chapter 2 (In the Schools 2.5). Turned into an experiment, the investigation will allow you to put together all the processes. As a group and class activity, design the experiment, obtain the data needed to answer the question, and formulate your conclusions. Share your conclusions and the rationale for your conclusions with the class.

Additional experiments appropriate for children in elementary grades are suggested in Constructing Science in the Classroom 3.47–3.49.

AN INVESTIGATION OF MAGNETISM

An Experiment

NSES Content
Standard B. Physical
Science: Magnetism

Objective

The student will devise and execute an experiment to show the ability of magnetism to penetrate different materials.

Ask "Do magnets attract through different kinds of materials?" Children design and execute an experiment to answer this question. They decide how to tell if the magnet attracts something (like a paper clip), and they decide what materials to try (like paper, cardboard, plastic, aluminum foil, overhead projector transparency sheets, sand, and water). They assemble the materials and execute the experiment. The data collected is qualitative. In other words, the magnet either does or does not attract the paper clip. From the data, children make their conclusions.

This activity can take a quantitative approach by varying the thicknesses of the materials. For example, children investigate how many paper clips a magnet will attract through 1 sheet of paper, 10 sheets of paper, 20 sheets of paper, and so on. When children have collected the data, they then prepare histograms to show the data in graphic form.

Literature Connection

Junior Science: Magnets by Terry Jennings (Gloucester Press, 1990) describes activities children can do to investigate magnetism.

 See the video clip "Are Coins Magnetic?" on the companion DVD.

ELECTRICAL CONDUCTION

An Experiment

NSES Content
Standard B. Physical
Science: Electricity

Objective

The student will design and execute an experiment to investigate the effects of various materials on the conduction of electricity.

Children are given batteries, wire, bulbs, sockets, and a variety of materials, such as paper, nails, paper clips, wood, lemon juice, water, salt, and so on. The children design an experiment to investigate the relationship between nature of the material and the conduction of electricity. An apparatus can be set up as shown in Figure 3.30.

Continued on next page

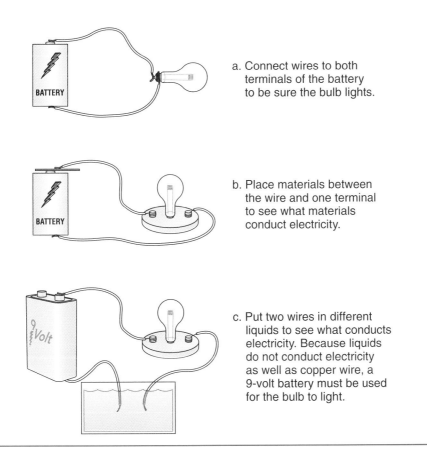

a. Connect wires to both terminals of the battery to be sure the bulb lights.

b. Place materials between the wire and one terminal to see what materials conduct electricity.

c. Put two wires in different liquids to see what conducts electricity. Because liquids do not conduct electricity as well as copper wire, a 9-volt battery must be used for the bulb to light.

FIGURE 3.30

Literature Connections

Dear Mr. Henshaw by Beverly Cleary (Demco Media, 1983). Ten-year-old Leigh is troubled by his parents' divorce and being the new kid in school. In one segment of the story, Leigh earns the respect of his peers when he solves the problem of his lunch box thief by experimenting with batteries and circuits. His battery-powered burglar alarm deters the thief.

The Magic School Bus and the Electric Field Trip by Joanna Cole (Scholastic, 1997) helps children follow the flow of electricity through power lines and explore how electric current lights up light bulbs, heats toasters, and runs electric motors.

NEWTON'S THIRD LAW

An Experiment

Objective

NSES Content
Standard B. Physical
Science: Motions and
Forces

The student will design and execute an experiment to investigate the effect of the force of air coming out of an inflated balloon on how far the balloon moves.

First, blow up a balloon, and let it go. Ask students to observe what happens.

Then, blow up a balloon partway. Pinch its end shut with a binder clip, and tape a piece of drinking straw on its side about halfway between its ends. String a fairly long piece of nylon string through the straw. Measure the circumference of the balloon with a string around its girth. Ask two students to stretch the string and hold it tightly. Release the binder clip and measure how far the balloon goes on the string. Students should repeat this three times and average the results. They should try this for several degrees of inflation of the same balloon, and they should build a data table, such as the one shown below, to record their data. Graphing their data will help them form conclusions.

Balloon Data Table

Circumference	Distance

Students infer the relative amounts of force of the air coming out of the balloon from its inflated circumference. The relationship between inflated size and force is not exact, but it is approximately proportional.

Students should try this activity using variations of several of the controlled variables, such as using different kinds of balloons, different sizes and shapes of balloons, and the like.

Literature Connections

Objects in Motion: Principles of Classical Mechanics by Paul Fleisher (Lerner Publications, 2002) presents many motion-related scientific principles together with experiments children can use to test them.

Continued on next page

Rocket! How a Toy Launches the Space Age by Richard Maurer (Crown Publishers, 1995) describes the history of rockets, from science-fiction speculations through the trials of Goddard and other rocket scientists.

The U.S. Space Camp Book of Rockets by Ann Baird (Morrow Junior Books, 1994) follows a group of Space Camp trainees as they tour the Rocket and Space Museum in Huntsville, Alabama.

Isaac Newton by Katheleen Krull (Viking, 2006) is a biography of Isaac Newton that describes several of his major theories.

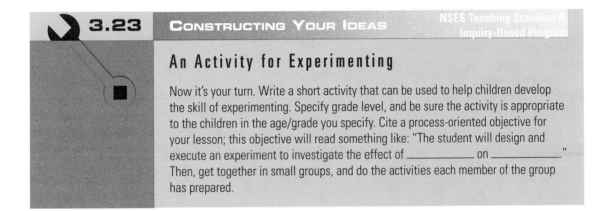

3.23   CONSTRUCTING YOUR IDEAS   NSES Teaching Standard A. Inquiry-Based Program

An Activity for Experimenting

Now it's your turn. Write a short activity that can be used to help children develop the skill of experimenting. Specify grade level, and be sure the activity is appropriate to the children in the age/grade you specify. Cite a process-oriented objective for your lesson; this objective will read something like: "The student will design and execute an experiment to investigate the effect of _____ on _____." Then, get together in small groups, and do the activities each member of the group has prepared.

CONSTRUCTING MODELS

You constructed a model when you investigated crater formation on the moon using a container filled with flour. Models are concrete representations of things or phenomena that we cannot readily see. Some good examples of models are the model of the atom (see Figure 2.1), the model of the cross-section of the earth (see Figure 3.31), and models of sound waves (see Figure 3.32). In these cases, models have been constructed to enable us to visualize what we cannot see. No one has seen the inside of an atom, the inside of the earth, or a sound wave. Yet, the atom behaves in certain ways, the earth behaves in certain ways, and sound waves behave in certain ways—ways that permit scientists to devise replicas that represent what they *ought* to look like to behave the way they do.

You constructed—or at least you thought about constructing—a model of the Mystery Box in Chapter 1 (Constructing Your Ideas 1.7). In this case, your model was a box identical to the Mystery Box, with things put into it and exchanged and moved around until your model behaved the way the Mystery Box behaved. Although the model box was not the same thing as the Mystery Box, the two behaved the same way, and you

NSES Teaching Standard A. Inquiry-Based Program
NSES Program Standard B. Relevant, Inquiry-Based, and Connected with Other Subjects
NSES Content Standard A. Science as Inquiry: Abilities Necessary To Do Scientific Inquiry

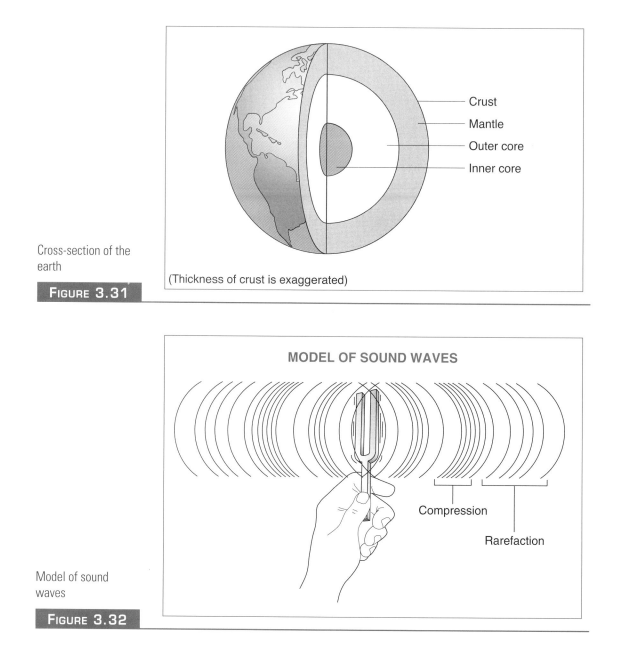

Cross-section of the
earth

MODEL OF SOUND WAVES

Compression

Rarefaction

Model of sound
waves

were reasonably confident that your model box was the same as (or very close to) the Mystery Box.

Constructing models in the scientific sense is different from building model airplanes or from the models that appear in fashion magazines. Model airplanes and model boats are intended to reduce the size of something we can already see to a size that is manageable to work with. Models in fashion magazines demonstrate what some item of clothing or makeup or a hairdo would look like on you *if* you looked like the model. The intent of these kinds of models is not to explain a phenomenon; rather, it is to replicate (in the case of model airplanes) or to advertise (in the case of fashion modeling).

Acher, Arcà, and Sanmarti (2007) showed that children as young as 7 and 8 years old can successfully construct models, and they concluded that "it is important to encourage the modeling process from the earliest school ages" (p. 415). One of the earliest ways children get involved in constructing scientific models is to observe some models that have already been developed. Several good examples come from the world of the solar system.

3.25   IN THE SCHOOLS   NSES Content Standard D. Earth and Space Science: Earth in the Solar System

Temperatures of the Planets

An early elementary teacher brought in nine bags containing costumes representing various climates: (1) dark sunglasses, fan, and sun visor; (2) dark sunglasses and fan; (3) dark sunglasses; (4) light sunglasses; (5) jacket; (6) jacket and gloves; (7) jacket, gloves, and cap; (8) jacket, gloves, cap, and scarf; and (9) jacket, gloves, cap, scarf, and earmuffs. The teacher distributed the costumes to children, who put them on and then lined up and moved around a large paper "sun" in accordance with the costumes they were wearing. Discussion questions included: "How does your distance from the sun affect how hot or cold you are?" "How big does the sun look from different positions?" "If you represented the planets, which would be the coldest?" "The hottest?" "Which planet would you like to live on?" "Why?" Then, the teacher passed out name tags for the planets, and the children wore them as they moved around the sun. These children were building a model of the solar system.

Literature Connection
Journey to the Planets (3rd ed.) by Patricia Lauber (Crown, 1990) describes prominent features of planets in our solar system and includes photos and information gathered by the *Voyager* explorations.

www   A direct link to NASA Web sites where children can find more information about the planets is available on the Student Book Companion Web Site.

How big is the sun? Constructing Science in the Classroom 3.50 shows an activity in which children can construct a model that compares the size of the earth with the size of the sun. The sun's diameter is 108 times the earth's diameter—it takes 108 earths to cross the sun. This is a model of something we cannot see for ourselves.

| 3.50 | CONSTRUCTING SCIENCE IN THE CLASSROOM |

HOW BIG IS THE SUN?

A Model-Building Activity

NSES Content Standard D. Earth and Space Science: Earth in the Solar System

Objective

The student will construct a model comparing the diameter of the earth with the diameter of the sun.

This activity shows a size comparison between the earth and the sun. The earth is approximately 8,000 miles in diameter, and the sun is approximately 865,000 miles in diameter. Thus, the diameter of the sun is about 108 times the diameter of the earth. This means that 108 earths could fit across the surface of the sun if they were flat.

Cut a circular "sun" that is 2 feet 3 inches in diameter, and laminate it. Use 1/4-inch, stick-on dots (available from office supply stores) to represent the earth. Have children stick the dots on in a straight line (diameter) across the center of the sun (see Figure 3.33). It will take 108 dots to extend all the way across.

This activity fosters development of the scientific processes of observing, measuring, and inferring as well as model building.

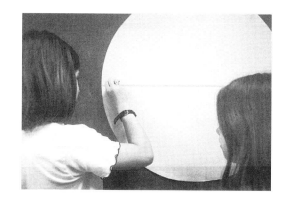

Constructing a model of the sun's diameter

FIGURE 3.33

Directions for constructing a model of the solar system that shows the true relationships among the distances of the planets from the sun are given in Constructing Science in the Classroom 3.51.

MODEL OF THE SOLAR SYSTEM

3.51   CONSTRUCTING SCIENCE IN THE CLASSROOM

An Activity for Constructing Models

Objective
The student will construct a model showing the relative distances of the planets from the sun.

Materials
Meter stick, 15 meters of 4-inch adding machine tape, a pencil, and a piece of yellow paper approximately 20 cm square

   This activity will give an idea of the actual distances of the planets from the sun.

   First, refer to the chart below. This chart gives the actual distances of each planet from the sun in units of 10 million kilometers and a proportionately scaled distance of each planet from the sun. The chart also provides actual and proportionately scaled diameters of each planet. Data for Pluto are included even though it recently has been reclassified as a dwarf planet instead of a planet (see Chapter 1), because whether its current classification will remain is uncertain. (Note that the scale for distance is different from the scale for diameter.)

NSES Content Standard D. Earth and Space Science: Earth in the Solar System

Planet	Actual Average Distance from Sun (in 10 million km)	Scaled Distance from Outer "Edge" of Sun	Actual Diameter (in km)	Scaled Diameter (Mars = 1.0 mm and Sun = 20 cm)
Mercury	5.8	12 cm	4,900	0.7 mm
Venus	11	22 cm	12,000	1.7 mm
Earth	15	30 cm	12,800	1.8 mm
Mars	23	46 cm	6,800	1.0 mm
Jupiter	78	156 cm	140,000	20.0 mm
Saturn	140	280 cm	120,000	17.0 mm
Uranus	290	580 cm	47,000	6.7 mm
Neptune	450	900 cm	50,000	7.1 mm
Pluto	590	1180 cm	1,500	0.2 mm

Continued on next page

A direct link to a blog that shows illustrations of the planets and dramatically illustrates the differences in their sizes is available on the Student Book Companion Web Site.

Cut out a circle 20 cm in diameter from the yellow paper to represent, the sun and fasten it to one edge of the adding machine tape.

Measure from the outer edge of the circle representing the sun to find the positions of each of the planets. Measure the distances given in the column labeled "Scaled Distance from 'Outer Edge' of Sun." Note that the distances given are *from the sun* and *not* from the preceding planet. Subtraction is necessary to find the distance from the preceding planet.

Draw in the planets at their locations, using circles of the diameters given in the "Scaled Diameter" column to show relative sizes of the planets. Note that the diameters of the planets are given in a different scale than their relative distances from the sun.

Literature Connection

The Magic School Bus Lost in the Solar System by Joanna Cole (Scholastic, 1990) takes children through in the solar system, with a stop at each of the planets.

Additional model-building activities are shown in Constructing Science in the Classroom 3.52–3.54.

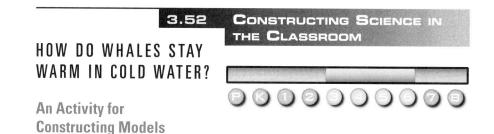

3.52   CONSTRUCTING SCIENCE IN THE CLASSROOM

HOW DO WHALES STAY WARM IN COLD WATER?

An Activity for Constructing Models

NSES Content Standard C. Life Science: Organisms and Environments

Objective

The student will develop a model showing the relationship between the fat on an animal's body and the animal's ability to survive in cold water.

Materials

Plastic bags, masking tape, shortening, and containers of ice water

Give children small plastic bags to secure over one of their hands with tape. Set up buckets of ice water around the room. Children place their "gloved" hand in the ice water while their partner records how long it takes before the hand gets too cold to keep in the ice water. Next, they immerse the gloved hand in another bag with shortening in it, squeezing the shortening around the gloved hand until the hand is fairly uniformly covered. They place the hand in the ice water, and their partner again records the time it takes for the hand to get too cold to stay in the ice water. The children are constructing a model of how whales are protected from cold.

Continued on next page

Literature Connections

Whales by Gail Gibbons (Holiday House, 1991) includes information about different kinds of whales and how they breathe, swim, stay warm, and bear young.

I Wonder If I'll See a Whale by Frances Ward Weller (Philomel, 1991) tells of a young girl who observes whales and their interactions with their environment.

Whales! Strange and Wonderful by Laurence P. Pringle (Boyds Mills Press, 2003) is an excellent and beautifully illustrated source of information about whales for young readers.

A MODEL OF RADIOACTIVE DECAY

3.53   CONSTRUCTING SCIENCE IN THE CLASSROOM

An Activity for Constructing Models

Objective

The student will construct a model of radioactive decay.

The **half-life** of a radioactive substance is the length of time it takes for half of that material to disintegrate into a nonradioactive material. Obtain a shoebox with a cover, and put a dot on the inside of one end of the shoebox. Put 100 pinto beans in the box, cover it, and shake it for 10 seconds. Remove and count all beans whose black eye is pointing toward the dot. (Students may find it necessary to define "toward the dot" in operational terms.) Repeat until all beans have been removed from the box. Students should record their data in a data table similar to the one below.

NSES Content Standard B. Physical Science: Transfer of Energy

Shake Number	Number of Beans Removed	Number of Beans Remaining

Have students construct a graph from their data. From the graph, they can infer the "half-life" of the pinto beans. (The "half-life" of the pinto beans would be expressed as the number of shakes it takes for half the beans to be removed from the box.)

Continued on next page

Challenge

Students can actually see radioactivity using a **cloud chamber.** Cloud chambers are available from science suppliers, or you can make your own using a Petri dish with a cover and some black blotting paper. In addition, you will need a source of radioactivity, a bright flashlight, some denatured or rubbing alcohol, and a cake of dry ice. *Safety note*: Dry ice is very cold and can damage skin quickly. You should handle it yourself using thick gloves; students should not handle it and should be cautioned about its hazards. The radioactive source can be a piece of old orange Fiesta ware, a lantern mantle, or a source purchased from a science supply company. All are safe to use.

    Cut the black blotter to fit the bottom of the Petri dish, place the Petri dish on the cake of dry ice, put the radioactive source on the blotter, and add a little alcohol. Shine the flashlight horizontally across the Petri dish, and look down at the black blotter paper. You will see vapor trails caused by the emission of particles from the radioactive material. (You may have to darken the room.) Most will be alpha particles (leaving short, thick trails), but occasionally, you can see **beta particles** (electrons that leave long, thin trails) and **gamma rays** (uncharged particles that leave twisting and circular trails).

    For complete directions, access the "How-To" tips about cloud chambers from the American Nuclear Society.

Literature Connection

Marie Curie and Radioactivity by Connie Colwell Miller (Capstone Press, 2007) is a novel that highlights the achievements of Marie Curie in the field of radioactivity.

A direct link to the "How-To" tips about cloud chambers from the American Nuclear Society is available on the Student Book Companion Web Site. This organization also has available additional information and activities on radioactivity suitable for children and an educational publication, *ReActions.*

3.54   **CONSTRUCTING SCIENCE IN THE CLASSROOM**

WHAT IS ACID RAIN?

An Activity for Constructing Models

Objective

The student will construct a model that can be used to investigate the effects of acid rain.

    Provide students with vials of red and blue litmus paper or pH paper and a clean beaker that has been rinsed using distilled water. Students place the beakers outdoors in an open area to capture rain. They test the rain with the litmus or pH paper to determine its acidity.

    Next, mix about half a cup of vinegar with a gallon of purified water. Students test this weak mixture with the litmus or pH paper and compare its acidity with that of the rain water. They add some pieces of limestone and let them set in this very dilute acid mixture overnight. They compare what the rocks look like the next day with what they looked like before they put them in the liquid. Students should try the same thing with other rocks, different kinds of soils, and different kinds and strengths of acidic liquids, always starting with a fresh batch of the liquid each time they add a new material to it.

NSES Content Standard F. Science in Personal and Social Perspectives: Population, Resources, and Environments

Continued on next page

How does this model represent the effects of acid rain? How close is it to the actual effects of acid rain?

Literature Connections

Acid Rain by Louise Petheram (Bridgestone Books, 2003) is a nonfiction book that discusses acid rain, its causes, and its effects.

Janice Vancleave's Ecology for Every Kid: Easy Activities that Make Learning Science Fun by Janice Vancleave (Wiley, 1996) is a book of experiments and activities children can do to explore principles of ecology.

One of the difficulties involved in building models is that the actual spatial relationships often are of such gigantic proportions that it becomes necessary to compress the space into something manageable for the model. As a result, models often are distorted to fit into the space available, such as a page in a book. The model of the solar system presented in Constructing Science in the Classroom 3.51 is an accurate representation, but it will not fit on the page of a book and probably will have to be displayed in the school hall—because it is more than 12 meters long. This is an inconvenient model, but it is realistic.

Another model that frequently is presented erroneously is the model of the thickness of the atmosphere. The correct model is shown in Figure 3.34. You will notice that when we use actual measurements of the thickness of the various layers of the atmosphere and construct them proportionately, the earth's atmosphere turns out to be very thin—much thinner than people normally assume, both because of the apparently huge depth of the atmosphere and because of the models we have been exposed to previously in textbooks. Difficult as it is to envision the thickness of the earth's atmosphere in the way this model presents it, the model is proportionately correct. We need only look at a photograph of the planet earth taken from outer space to verify this model (see Figure 3.35).

Models are extremely powerful tools. They present concrete and visual representations that make lasting impressions. Therefore, it is vitally important to present models that correctly represent what they are portraying. It is far more difficult to replace an erroneous model with the correct one than it is to provide the correct one in the first place. Check your own feelings about the models of the solar system and the earth's atmosphere presented above to confirm how difficult it is to replace a preconceived model with a new one.

To foster the skill of model building, children should be encouraged to build their own representations to explain phenomena they observe. Models are not required for everything, of course. For example, there would be no point in constructing a model of the toy truck rolling down the plank, because we can see the real thing. Similarly, it would not be necessary

NSES Content Standard D. Earth and Space Science: Structure of the Earth System

THICKNESS OF EARTH'S ATMOSPHERE

The atmosphere is thought of as consisting of several layers. These layers do not have definite separations, but intermingle with one another at their interfaces.

Table of Thicknesses of Layers of Earth's Atmosphere

EXOSPHERE Beginning of interplanetary space	250–625 miles (400–1000 km)
THERMOSPHERE Contains very few molecules	50–250 miles (80–400 km)

MESOSPHERE
    Contains electrically charged particles (ions) formed by
    collision of cosmic rays with air molecules. Ozone is
    found in lower levels of mesosphere and upper levels
    of stratosphere.
	30–50 miles
	(50–80 km)

STRATOSPHERE	16–30 miles (25–50 km)
TROPOSPHERE Contains the weather	0–16 miles (0–25 km)

To show the relationship of the thickness of the earth's atmosphere to the diameter of the earth, use the following proportional equation:

$$\frac{\text{Atmospheric thickness}}{\text{Earth's diameter}} = \frac{1000 \text{ km}}{12{,}800 \text{ km}}$$

If we convert this to meters, the relationship is 1000 meters : 12,800 meters.

Dividing by 100, the relationship becomes 10 meters : 128 meters or 10 cm : 128 cm.

This gives us the proportion for the earth's atmosphere as 10 cm above the earth's surface if the earth is represented by a circle 128 cm (or 1.28 m) in diameter.
Proportions are as follows in the layers of the atmosphere (given an earth 1.28 m in diameter):

Top of exosphere	10 cm
Top of thermosphere	4 cm
Top of mesosphere	.8 cm (8 mm)
Top of stratosphere	.5 cm (5 mm)
Top of troposphere	.25 cm (2.5 mm)

Cut off a strip of adding machine tape about 2½ meters long. Place a dot at the center of the strip. This represents the center of the earth. Measure out from the dot 64 centimeters in each direction and draw lines at the 64-cm marks. This represents the diameter of the earth. Now, draw lines at the proportional distances given above *from the surface of the earth* and label the atmospheric layers accordingly. The result is an accurate model of the thickness of the earth's atmosphere.

 FIGURE 3.34

The earth showing the atmosphere as seen from space (Courtesy NASA/JPL-Caltech)

FIGURE 3.35

to construct a model of the pendulum; again, we can see the real thing. However, the moon crater activity is itself a model, because our investigation closely parallels the conditions found on the moon. Because the rocks caused craters in the flour in a manner similar to what is observed on the moon, the container of flour and rocks represents a good model for the formation of craters on the moon.

Finally, let us look at an activity that involves making a model of the earth's surface. Do you remember using globes that show geographical relief? They show the Himalaya Mountains and other mountain ranges, and some of the large plateaus, in raised relief from the surface of the globe. This is a good model for children, showing them that there is substantial relief on the earth. Is it accurate? Here is some information.

NSES Content Standard D. Earth and Space Science: Structure of the Earth System

> ### DATA ABOUT RELIEF OF THE EARTH'S SURFACE
>
> Height of tallest mountain (Mt. Everest): 29,035 feet (8,850 m)*
> Depth of deepest trench (Marianas Trench): 36,198 feet (11,033 m)
> Maximum total relief of earth: 65,233 feet (19,833 m)
> Diameter of earth: 7,926 miles = 41,849,280 feet (12,755,600 m)
>
> *Measured in 1999 using sophisticated satellite-based technology and accepted by the National Geographic Society and government agencies.

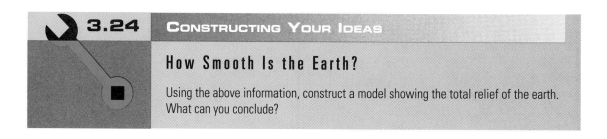

3.24   CONSTRUCTING YOUR IDEAS

How Smooth Is the Earth?

Using the above information, construct a model showing the total relief of the earth. What can you conclude?

3.25   CONSTRUCTING YOUR IDEAS   NSES Teaching Standard A, Inquiry-Based Program

An Activity for Constructing Models

Now it's your turn. Write a short activity that can be used to help children develop the skill of constructing models. Specify grade level, and be sure the activity is appropriate to the children in the age/grade you specify. Cite a process-oriented objective for your lesson; this objective will read something like: "The student will construct a model to show _____ in an investigation of _____." Then, get together in small groups, and do the activities each member of the group has prepared.

THE PROCESS-ORIENTED OBJECTIVE

NSES Teaching Standard A. Inquiry-Based Program

In the preface to his book *Preparing Instructional Objectives,* Mager (1984) relates a fable of a seahorse who cantered out to seek his fortune. After buying an eel's flipper and a sponge's jet-propelled scooter to help speed him on his way, he accepts the offer of a shortcut through a shark's mouth. He zooms into the interior of the shark, never to be heard from again. "The moral of this fable," writes Mager, "is that if you're not sure where you're going, you're liable to end up someplace else" (p. v).

For each of the processes, you have been asked to sketch an activity that could be used by children to investigate that process and gain skill in its use. You also have been asked to write a process-oriented objective in each case. Simply put, the process-oriented objective is an ordinary learning objective in which the verb is a process skill. "The student will observe _____." "The student will classify _____." "The student will predict _____." The process-oriented objective serves the same purpose as the instructional objective described by Mager (1984); it is "a description of a performance you want learners to be able to exhibit before you consider them competent" (p. 1). The process-oriented objective enables teachers and children to focus on the development of one or more process skills rather than on content as the main outcome of the lesson.

A process-oriented objective might be the following: "The student will *process objective* develop a hypothesis to explain the formation of craters in mud during a rainstorm." The objective focuses attention on hypothesis development. Contrast this with a more traditional objective: "The student will explain *— behavioral objective* why craters form in mud during a rainstorm." In this case, the focus is on content. In the former objective, students are to form a hypothesis; in the latter, students are to learn what someone else has discovered and then explain it. It is strongly encouraged that process-oriented objectives be written for science lessons to ensure that children focus on the ✳ processes.

If children are to learn to do science the way scientists do, if they are to do their own thinking, if they are to take charge of their own learning, then they must be encouraged in every possible way. The use of the process-oriented focus in science education turns the spotlight away from learning what others have discovered and places it on the children and on what and how they are investigating.

Conclusion

The process skills, both basic and integrated, are the core of doing science. Children use the processes to recognize problems, ask questions, formulate hypotheses, identify variables, and reach conclusions. They verify these conclusions and use them as starting points for further investigations. Through using the processes to inquire into science, children learn skills that help them think and reason while they are discovering scientific concepts. Crawford (1998) contrasts the process approach to doing science with the traditional step-by-step scientific method that teachers require their students to memorize and follow in all investigations. She writes, "[T]eaching our students to follow a set number and order of steps reinforces a misconception of the nature of scientific work, and sets up contradictions between school science and the real world ... When we guide our students in constructing appropriate questions, in meticulously collecting data, and then in grappling with that data, students construct their understanding of scientific ways of thinking" (p. 52). Through using the process skills, children do science the way scientists do science and begin to acquire scientific literacy.

CHAPTER 3

Additional Questions for Discussion

1. Develop an activity that includes all 12 processes. Identify each process, and show how each is experienced by children in the successful completion of the activity.

2. There is a certain sentiment in opposition to the use of behavioral objectives (with performance, conditions, and criteria) in lesson and unit planning. Contrast the process objective with the behavioral objective, and describe advantages and disadvantages of using process objectives in planning elementary science lessons and units.

3.   The Internet has many elementary science activities. Browse the Internet for activities that might be suitable for the grade level(s) you plan to teach, and share the Web sites and brief summaries of each activity you find with others in your class. Be sure the activities are process-oriented, have plenty of room for children to investigate on their own, and help children learn how to *do* science rather than teaching children *about* science.

Internet Activities

Many references the Internet deal with the food pyramid as it relates to children's nutrition and elementary education;

the moon, its composition, its surface, and its exploration; and other topics discussed in this chapter. Use the search engines to find additional information about these topics.

In searching for process-oriented activities that are suitable for the grade level(s) you plan to teach, try such keywords as "elementary science activities," "elementary science," and "science activities." Evaluate each activity on the basis of how well it fosters development of skills in the processes and how well it helps children to learn how to *do* science.

Notes

1. The activity described in "A Case of Moon Watching" was drawn from Duckworth (1986).

2. The complete Piagetian development assessment tasks are given in Appendix A of Charlesworth and Lind (2007).

3. See Appendix A in Charlesworth and Lind (2007).

4. Comets are named after the people who discover them. Halley's comet is named in honor of Edmund Halley, who calculated its orbit in the late 1600s and successfully predicted its return in 1758. It was last in the earth's vicinity in 1985, and it returns every 76 years.

5. Actually, we cannot calculate the speed of a pendulum, because it is constantly speeding up and slowing down. This is why pendulum investigations center on the period of the swing (the time to complete one cycle). The word *speed* is used here to simplify the problem.

CHAPTER ···· 4
CONSTRUCTIVISM IN ELEMENTARY SCIENCE EDUCATION

The single most important factor influencing learning is what the learner already knows.

David Ausubel, in D. P. Ausubel, J. D. Novak, and H. Hanesian, *Educational Psychology: A Cognitive View,* 2nd ed. (New York: Holt, Rinehart and Winston, 1978), p. iv

In the first three chapters, you explored many activities; in each, you developed your own understanding of the concept involved. For example, you developed your own understanding of how different variables influence the rate of swing of pendulums, and you formulated your own ideas about the origin of lunar craters. You also formulated your own ideas about the nature of science, what it means to be scientifically literate, and how scientists do science. You developed your own perception of the goals and objectives of the elementary science program. You investigated the processes of science and came to your own understanding about the nature of the processes, their importance to elementary science education, and how they can be taught by you and learned by children.

You constructed your understandings about each of these notions in ways that make sense to you.

Jean Piaget, seeking an answer to the perennial philosophical question "How do we come to know what we know?" concluded that knowledge cannot be transmitted intact from one person to another; people must construct their own knowledge and their

own understandings. Learning does not occur by transmitting information from the teacher or the textbook (or the video or the demonstration) to the child's brain. Instead, each child constructs his or her own meaning by combining prior information with new information such that the new knowledge provides personal meaning to the child (Cobern, 1993).

The notion that people build their own knowledge and their own representations of knowledge from their own experience and thought is called **constructivism.** Each activity that has been suggested thus far (and, indeed, this book itself) is constructivist in orientation. It is the basic premise of this book that learning in science occurs best when approached from a constructivist point of view.

BATTERIES AND ELECTRICITY

Once, I was asked to teach a lesson on electricity for a fifth-grade class. Equipment available consisted of several shoe boxes, each containing 1.5-volt batteries, a few pieces of wire, a few bulb holders, some 1.5-volt lightbulbs, a knife switch or two, and a 1.5-volt electric motor. The children in the class came from a wide background of pirior experiences with electricity. Some had studied electricity previously in school. Some had never studied it. Others had been exposed to textual material on electricity but never experimented with it. I asked the children to divide themselves into small groups, and I gave a box of materials to each group. Because of the wide range of prior experiences, I provided very simple directions: "Using the materials in the box, figure something out you didn't know before" (see Figure 4.1).

NSES Teaching Standard B. Guiding and Facilitating Learning
NSES Content Standard B. Physical Science: Electricity

Investigating batteries and bulbs: Does the number of batteries affect how brightly the light burns?

FIGURE 4.1

Some children connected a piece of wire to the bottom and the top of the battery and felt the wire get hot. It was the first time they had been given the opportunity to try things out with electricity. Other children overcame their fears of electricity by trying a variety of different connections, none of which hurt them or gave them a shock. Still others lit the bulbs, and some found that it did not matter which way the wires were connected to the batteries—the bulbs lit anyhow. Others set up elaborate series circuits and parallel circuits, discovering elementary principles of circuitry. One group fashioned a paper propeller and attached it to the motor, making an electric fan.

Each person learned something he or she had not known before; each person added to his or her store of information about electricity. And each child did it by constructing his or her own conceptualization about electricity, whether the conceptualization was basic or advanced. Children connected what they were able to make happen during that class with what they already knew; children developed their understanding of electricity. They shared their discoveries with each other, often arriving at new ways of conceptualizing their own information as a result of these interactions. They made connections to previously learned information in ways that were unique and meaningful to them.

CONSTRUCTIVISM

NSES Professional Development Standard B. Integrating Knowledge of Science, Learning, Pedagogy, and Students
NSES Program Standard B. Relevant, Inquiry-Based, and Connected with Other Subjects

For centuries, philosophers have debated the question of what constitutes *reality*. The traditional **epistemological** paradigm holds an *objective* view of reality: reality exists outside the individual, is discovered, and is communicated to learners by language or some other representation—"Teaching is telling."

An opposing view holds that individuals construct their own *subjective* reality—reality is that which has been constructed by the individual from his or her own observations, reflections, and logical thought. This reality must be built by each individual for himself or herself.

The constructivist view of learning is grounded in the notion of subjective reality. Far from being a contemporary paradigm, constructivism's basic ideas were proposed as long ago as 1710 by Giambattista Vico. His notions about the nature of reality included the following:

1. "Epistemic agents [people who know] can know nothing but the cognitive structures they themselves have put together."

2. "God alone can know the *real* world, because He knows how and of what He has created it."

3. "In contrast, the human knower can know only what the human knower has constructed." (vonGlasersfeld, 1989)

vonGlasersfeld, one of today's foremost scholars of constructivism, says that once a teacher abandons the notion that knowledge is a "commodity" transferable to children, that notion must be replaced with an attempt to discover what actually goes on in children's minds as they learn. He wrote:

> As long as the educator's objective was the generation of more or less specific behaviors in the student, the educator saw no need to ask what, if anything, might be going on in the student's head. Whenever the student could be got to 'emit' the desired behaviors in the situations with which they had been associated, the instructional process was deemed successful. The student did not have to *see* why the particular actions led to a result that was considered 'correct,' nor did the educator have to worry about how the student achieved it; what mattered was the 'performance,' i.e., that he or she was able to produce such a result.
>
> If, in contrast, the objective is to lead the children or students to some form of *understanding,* the teacher must have some notion of how they think. That is to say, teachers must try to infer, from what they can observe, what the students' concepts are and how they operate with them. Only on the basis of some such hypothesis can teachers devise ways and means to orient, direct, or modify the students' mental operating. (vonGlasersfeld, 1991, p. 22)

The constructivist believes that each learner must construct meaning for himself or herself—that the only learning that can take place is that which is connected to the individual's already-existing knowledge, experiences, or conceptualizations. What children learn is not a copy of what they observe in their surroundings but, rather, the result of their own thinking and processing.

In Chapter 1, you explored the notion that the same event can be interpreted differently by different people according to their prior experiences. Because no two people internalize the same experiences in the same way, it follows that information *imparted* by the teacher is not necessarily *learned.* Therefore, it is incumbent on teachers to learn how each child is constructing information and then to help the child attach new experiences in ways that are both meaningful and convincing to him or her. As Caine, Caine, and McClintic (2002) write, all natural learning "is constructivist, seeking to construct personal meaning in response to the world . . . The challenge for educators, then, is to link what we want to teach to what really matters to students . . ." (p. 70).

Constructivism suggests that "as we experience something new we internalize it through our past experience or knowledge constructs we have previously established" (Crowther, 1997, p. 3). In the constructivist approach, the primary job of the teacher is to enable children to find and make their own connections that result in valid, internalized meanings unique to each child. The teacher does this by asking questions to see how children may have previously constructed information related to the topic. The teacher leads the children through exploratory activities that enable them to investigate on their own and come to their own conclusions as to what is happening. The teacher interacts with each child to see *how* he or she is constructing the new information and helps children formulate sound conclusions by aiding each child in reconstructing the information in ways that are both valid and meaningful *to that child*. As Penner (2001) argues, "learning activities must begin by considering the role of students' current knowledge, how knowledge is constructed, and the role of the activity in building knowledge" (p. 3).

A direct link to the ACT Web site is available on the Student Book Companion Web Site.

▶ The Association for Constructivist Teaching (ACT) is a professional education organization devoted to the dissemination of effective constructivist education practices and the understanding of Piaget's constructivism as a scientific theory that explains how human beings construct knowledge. The ACT publishes an online journal, *The Constructivist*, that includes material about theoretical constructs of constructivism and a variety of classroom applications.

Prior Beliefs

NSES Content Standard B. Physical Science: Position and Motion of Objects
NSES Teaching Standard B. Guiding and Facilitating Learning

Children begin their formal study of science with ideas already in place about the natural world.[1] Some of these ideas are congruent with currently accepted scientific understandings. But some are not.

For example, children "know" that a baseball will fall faster than a marble, because a baseball is bigger and heavier. Although this preconceived notion is not supported by precise investigation, it is believable to the children and makes sense to them as a result of their limited experience with the phenomenon. Because it makes sense to them, it is difficult to change their beliefs simply by telling them otherwise. Children have to *experience* for themselves occurrences that contradict their currently held beliefs. Children are not going to understand that a baseball and a marble fall at the same rate simply by being told. In fact, many college-level preservice teachers believe the two balls do not fall at the same rate. In my classes, I have stood on a table to let a baseball and a marble drop from the same height onto a floor that is not carpeted so students could hear the sounds made in unison, demonstrating that the balls hit the floor at the same time. Only after several repeated attempts (often done by the students themselves) did these college seniors begin to successfully reconstruct their prior conception. Yet, it is likely they were exposed to this phenomenon somewhere along the line. If so, they probably memorized the correct answer for the test but retained reservations about the truth of the teacher's answer, because it was not reconciled with their own beliefs.

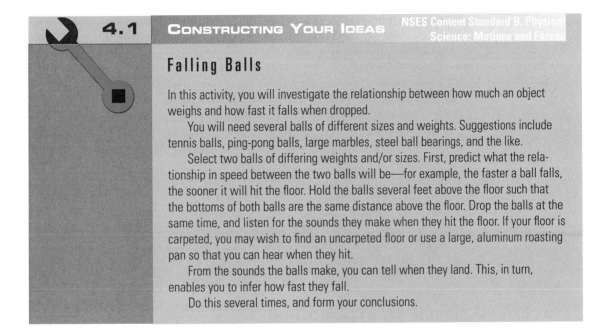

4.1   CONSTRUCTING YOUR IDEAS   NSES Content Standard B. Physical Science: Motions and Forces

Falling Balls

In this activity, you will investigate the relationship between how much an object weighs and how fast it falls when dropped.

You will need several balls of different sizes and weights. Suggestions include tennis balls, ping-pong balls, large marbles, steel ball bearings, and the like.

Select two balls of differing weights and/or sizes. First, predict what the relationship in speed between the two balls will be—for example, the faster a ball falls, the sooner it will hit the floor. Hold the balls several feet above the floor such that the bottoms of both balls are the same distance above the floor. Drop the balls at the same time, and listen for the sounds they make when they hit the floor. If your floor is carpeted, you may wish to find an uncarpeted floor or use a large, aluminum roasting pan so that you can hear when they hit.

From the sounds the balls make, you can tell when they land. This, in turn, enables you to infer how fast they fall.

Do this several times, and form your conclusions.

Conceptual Change

For conceptual change to occur, children must become dissatisfied with their existing conception. This can occur when their existing conception, which is believable on the surface, fails to explain some new observation satisfactorily. For example, the belief that heavy balls fall faster than light balls does not account for the baseball and the marble hitting the floor at the same time when dropped from the same height. Another way people can become dissatisfied with their existing conception is if it fails to predict similar occurrences accurately. For example, the conceptualization that the speed of a pendulum ought to depend on the weight of the bob is not supported by experimental evidence. A third way people can become dissatisfied with an existing conceptualization is if they learn or hear of contrary information from other people, such as their teacher or from other sources.

NSES Teaching Standard B. Guiding and Facilitating Learning
NSES Program Standard B. Relevant, Inquiry-Based, and Connected with Other Subjects

When experimental evidence fails to provide support for a prior conception, people begin to question the validity of the conceptualization. They become aware of conflict between what they *thought* was true and what they *observe* for themselves. Magic tricks and special effects in movies are good examples of this phenomenon. We hold fast to the notion that it is impossible for certain things to happen, such as a human body levitating, a man flying on his own power, or dinosaurs attacking people. When we see these things happen, we strive to resolve the conflict between what we observe and our notion that they *cannot* happen by suggesting plausible explanations such as "It's done with mirrors" or "It's done with a computer."

Discrepant events (surprising or unusual happenings) are used by constructivist teachers to spark children's curiosity about the validity of their prior beliefs. The "floating coffin" (see Figure 4.2) presents a good example of a discrepant event. It can be purchased at novelty shops and consists of two round bars of steel in a frame. One of the bars (the *coffin*) floats above the other. How can that be? Our experience tells us that steel bars do not float in air. Our experience also tells us there must be a reasonable explanation for what we observe. As we work to reconcile the difference between what we believe and what we see, we become satisfied that magnetism could explain this discrepant event.

 For videos that show some discrepant events, see the video clips titled "Defying Gravity," "Do Crayons Sink? Or Float?" and "The Pitch of Sound" on the companion DVD.

Cognitive Disequilibration

NSES Teaching Standard B. Guiding and Facilitating Learning NSES Program Standard B. Relevant, Inquiry-Based, and Connected with Other Subjects

One's dissatisfaction with what actually *is* happening as contrasted with what *ought* to happen is called, in Piagetian terms, *cognitive disequilibration* or, sometimes, *cognitive dissonance*. Disequilibration begs a solution.

The top steel rod floats freely above the bottom steel rod. How can that be?

The floating coffin

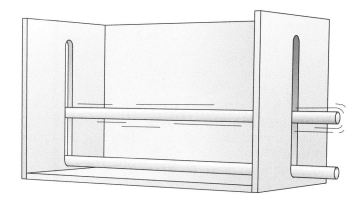

FIGURE 4.2

The constructivist teacher seeks to induce **cognitive disequilibration** by setting up situations that encourage children to question their existing beliefs and ask what is going on. Children attempt to make predictions about the situation based on prior understandings. When these predictions do not work, the children question their prior beliefs. This brings the existing beliefs to the surface, giving the teacher access to what is in the children's minds and, thus, the opportunity to help the children reconstruct their beliefs in valid ways that include the new information and make sense to them.

4.1   IN THE SCHOOLS   NSES Content Standard A: Science as Inquiry: Abilities Necessary To Do Scientific Inquiry

Dancing Raisins

A good example of an activity that challenges children's prior beliefs is making raisins dance. First, ask children if they think raisins sink or float. After they have predicted, put a few in a glass of water so that children can see them sink. Now, fill a plastic jar about three-quarters full of water and mix in about half a cup of white vinegar. Put a handful of raisins in the jar; they sink to the bottom. Then, add a tablespoon of baking soda and watch the raisins rise and sink. Ask children why they think the raisins are "dancing." Alternatively, fill the plastic jar with club soda or another carbonated beverage; the same thing will happen. (**Teacher Note:** The reason is that some of the carbon dioxide gas generated by the reaction between the baking soda and vinegar, or present in the carbonated beverage, becomes lodged in the crevices of the raisins, making them light enough to rise to the surface. When they reach the surface, the gas escapes, and they sink.)

Literature Connections

A Wizard of Earthsea by Ursula Le Guin (Parnassus, 1968) is a fantasy about a novice student wizard who struggles with opposing forces of good and evil within himself.

Elephant by Judy Allen (Candlewick Press, 1993). Receiving an ivory necklace made by her ancestors leaves Hannah uncomfortable as she attempts to reconcile her feelings and values that are different from her ancestors' beliefs.

To aid children in their reconstruction of previously acquired beliefs, the teacher may encourage the children to investigate on their own, or the teacher may introduce minimal understanding of the conceptualization as generally agreed on by the scientific community. The result is that the child is compelled to relate the new phenomenon, new ideas, and new experiences and observations to existing knowledge in ways that are most appropriate *to the child*.

It is a fundamental principle of the constructivist approach to learning that cognitive disequilibration is a necessary precursor of learning—that learning will not take place unless explanations are sought. If our existing understandings could explain everything, there would be no need for further understanding. As Dennett (1991) writes, "[T]he only work that the brain must do is whatever it takes to *assuage epistemic hunger*—to satisfy curiosity in all its forms. If [a person] is passive or incurious about topic *x*, then no material about topic *x* needs to be prepared. (Where it doesn't itch, don't scratch.)" (p. 16).

Validity of Self-Constructed Conceptualizations

NSES Teaching Standard B. Guiding and Facilitating Learning
NSES Professional Development Standard B. Integrating Knowledge of Science, Learning, Pedagogy, and Students
NSES Program Standard B. Relevant, Inquiry-Based, and Connected with Other Subjects

If a new conceptualization constructed by the child appears to be more plausible than the prior notion, it may be accepted by the child as a tentative replacement for the prior notion. For lasting acceptance, three factors must be achieved (see Figure 4.3).

1. The new conceptualization must have **explanatory power.** It must provide a plausible explanation for *each* occurrence of the phenomenon. For example, prior to investigating what is and what is not magnetic, children may believe that American coins are magnetic. They will need to try pennies, nickels, dimes, quarters, half-dollars, and maybe even silver- and gold-colored dollars to internalize a reconception that these coins are not magnetic. See the video clip "Are Coins Magnetic?" on the companion DVD.

2. The new conceptualization must have **predictive power.** It must accurately predict what will happen in new and as-yet-untried occurrences of the phenomenon. For example, the new conceptualization that coins are not magnetic must predict accurately that even foreign coins are not attracted to magnets. See the video clip "Are Coins Magnetic?" on the companion DVD for the interaction of magnets with coins from many countries.

3. The new conceptualization must utilize the input of others. Children discuss their ideas with each other in small groups, providing their own input and listening to others as they formulate their own notions. They refine and revise their ideas as they hear other people (including their teacher) critique their ideas and ask penetrating questions the child may not have thought of, offer suggestions, share information and their own experiences, and help students confront contradictions in their own thinking processes. Students seek additional information not only from peers and teachers but also from parents, friends, other people, and many sources, such as the Internet, books, videos, movies, and the like. In our coin example, if someone else in

the group or class has encountered a coin that is magnetic, the child will somehow have to deal with this information in forming the new conceptualization or explain the unanticipated occurrence in some manner. Be sure to view the video clip "Are Coins Magnetic?" on the companion DVD.

We must encourage children to share their conclusions and to demonstrate that the results of their investigation have both predictive and explanatory power and have used the input of others. Having children work in groups helps to promote this critical sharing. Different people investigate the same question in different ways, and when they share their information, the strengths and weaknesses of each person's thinking become apparent. The collective thinking of a group is more likely to be valid than the isolated thinking of any one individual. "Although children construct understandings for themselves—personal meaning—it does not occur in isolation of others" (Shepardson, 1997, p. 873).

If all three factors have been met (plausible explanation, accurate prediction, and input from other sources), the conceptualization is very likely to be valid. At least it is held valid until a new experience induces a new cognitive disequilibration and the conceptualization must be revised or refined again to accommodate the new information.

In this constructivist approach to science education, "learning is an active process that is student-centered . . . *[W]ith the teacher's help,* learners select and transform information, construct hypotheses, and make decisions" (Chrenka, 2001, p. 694).

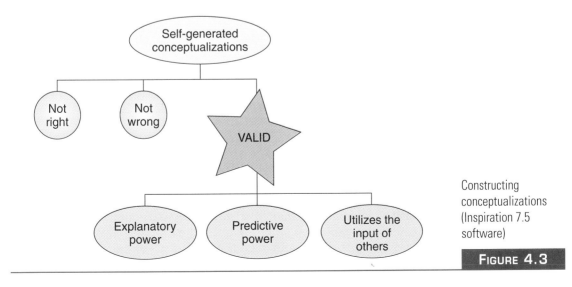

Constructing conceptualizations (Inspiration 7.5 software)

FIGURE 4.3

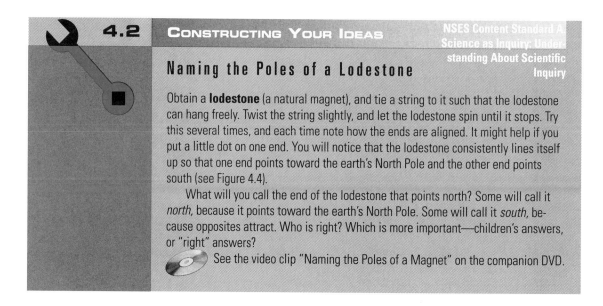

4.2   CONSTRUCTING YOUR IDEAS

NSES Content Standard A: Science as Inquiry: Understanding About Scientific Inquiry

Naming the Poles of a Lodestone

Obtain a **lodestone** (a natural magnet), and tie a string to it such that the lodestone can hang freely. Twist the string slightly, and let the lodestone spin until it stops. Try this several times, and each time note how the ends are aligned. It might help if you put a little dot on one end. You will notice that the lodestone consistently lines itself up so that one end points toward the earth's North Pole and the other end points south (see Figure 4.4).

What will you call the end of the lodestone that points north? Some will call it *north*, because it points toward the earth's North Pole. Some will call it *south*, because opposites attract. Who is right? Which is more important—children's answers, or "right" answers?

See the video clip "Naming the Poles of a Magnet" on the companion DVD.

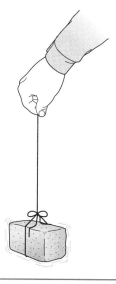

What should you call the ends of the lodestone?

FIGURE 4.4

Zahorik (1997) suggests that teachers should "help students negotiate meaning" by extending activities with discussions in which children compare their constructions with the experts' constructions to "gain insights into both and begin to reconceptualize their constructions in the direction of those of the experts" (p. 32). Yore, Anderson, and Shymansky (2005) argue that simply doing activities in elementary school science (even in a constructivist manner) does not necessarily lead to student learning—that teachers need to know scientific content so they can guide student explorations. The advantage of this approach is that children become aware of currently accepted scientific theory and see how their work parallels the work of the scientists. However, the disadvantage is that this practice may trivialize children's own work, minimize the importance of their self-constructed conceptualizations, and ultimately, confirm their suspicions that the *real* goal of learning is to acquire correct answers—answers the teacher knew all along. (See *Who Owns the Knowledge?* in Chapter 5.)

You will have to wrestle with the question of how much "expert" science to introduce into a lesson. In so doing, weigh the importance of children gaining confidence in their own abilities to construct sound and valid conceptualizations against the importance of children learning currently accepted principles of science.

INQUIRY

Cognitive disequilibration results from other factors in addition to teacher intervention; often, children get curious about some phenomenon as a result of a chance observation, a casual remark, or simply wondering about something. In the constructivist classroom, the teacher facilitates children in their personal investigations of these questions. The teacher asks, "How would you find out?" and encourages the children to explore possible ways of answering their questions. Because the children do it themselves, they are able to construct the answers to their questions in ways that make sense to them; discussions with the teacher and with classmates help to confirm validity or show where additional exploration is needed. Chapter 5 is devoted to the inquiry method of teaching.

NSES Teaching Standard A. Inquiry-Based Program

Constructivism and Science Learning

The learning of science is a process of construction and reconstruction of previously held personal theories. It is a process of continually refining existing knowledge and constructing concepts in intricate organized networks that are unique to each child and that provide explanatory and predictive power and have used input from outside sources—at least until the next observation that produces disequilibration.

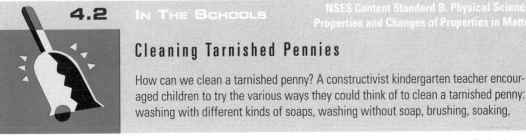

4.2   IN THE SCHOOLS

NSES Content Standard B. Physical Science: Properties and Changes of Properties in Matter

Cleaning Tarnished Pennies

How can we clean a tarnished penny? A constructivist kindergarten teacher encouraged children to try the various ways they could think of to clean a tarnished penny: washing with different kinds of soaps, washing without soap, brushing, soaking,

Continued on next page

and so on. Of course, none of these methods worked, so the teacher introduced such unexpected options as soaking the penny in vinegar, rubbing a lemon on it, soaking it in hot sauce, and soaking it in a mixture of vinegar and salt. She invited the children to try these new methods. The penny became bright and shiny!

Literature Connection
Water Magic by Phyllis Adams, Carole Mitchener, and Virginia Johnson (Modern Curriculum Press, 1987). Two young children question their dad about how objects appear to be different in water and how a tarnished penny can sparkle after placing it in a glass of water and vinegar.

In addition to experience in the processes of observation, communication, and prediction, what do kindergarten children get out of this activity? A fundamental scientific concept is at work here—the notion of the physical change versus the chemical change. Without realizing it, children are beginning to construct the underpinnings of this concept—they are beginning to notice that soaking the penny in certain liquids can produce a change. "How can this be?" they wonder. They do not completely understand, but they are now alert to other occurrences that produce changes similar to that produced by soaking a penny in vinegar. A cognitive dis-

Cleaning a tarnished penny

FIGURE 4.5

equilibration has entered their minds, and they begin trying to resolve it. They are constructing their own understanding of the phenomenon.

4.3   IN THE SCHOOLS

NSES Unifying Concepts and Principles: Constancy, Change, and Measurement

Examining Snowflakes

Do all snowflakes look alike? In a fourth-grade class, the teacher set a 10-power binocular microscope and some pieces of black construction paper outdoors on a cold and snowy day. After about 15 minutes, the paper was cold enough that snowflakes landing on it did not melt. Children captured the snowflakes on the black paper and examined them with the naked eye, with magnifying glasses, and under the microscope, drawing what they saw. Children began to construct the idea that every snowflake is at least slightly different from every other snowflake.

(**Teacher Note:** It is commonly believed that no two snowflakes are alike. This conception was disproved in 1988 when Nancy Knight, a meteorologist at the National Center for Atmospheric Research, discovered two identical snowflakes (Funk, 2004, p. 62).)

Literature Connection
Snowflake Bentley by Jacqueline Briggs Martin (Houghton Mifflin, 1998) is a richly illustrated, true story about Wilson Bentley from Vermont, who spent his life studying and photographing snowflakes.

In this activity, children began to construct notions about the infinite variation within the orderliness of nature in addition to the possibility that no two snowflakes are identical.

PIAGET, THE CONSTRUCTIVIST

Jean Piaget (1896–1980) was a constructivist (vonGlasersfeld, 1991). He is perhaps best remembered by education students for his stages of cognitive development. In his later years, however, he lamented the singular focus given to his stage theory. Piaget felt that his work on accommodation and assimilation, and especially the resulting **cognitive equilibration,** was far more important than the stages.

Piaget viewed knowledge as a *process* rather than a *state:* Knowledge is a relationship between the knower and the known in which the knower constructs his or her own representations of what is known. "Knowledge is not a copy of reality. To know an object, to know an event, is not simply to look at it and make a mental copy or image of it. To know an object is to act on it" (Piaget, 1964, 2003, p. S-8). Children's knowledge changes

NSES Professional Development Standard B. Integrating Knowledge of Science, Learning, Pedagogy, and Students NSES Professional Development Standard A. Learning Content Through Inquiry as their cognitive systems develop and as their experiences are filtered through increasingly mature ways of thinking and of constructing representations of knowledge.

Mechanism of Constructing Knowledge

Piaget viewed the mind as a collection of cognitive structures he called *schemata* (singular, *schema*). **Schemata** are opened, enlarged, divided, and connected in response to the influx of information into a person's mind. Two fundamental processes are at work in this mental activity—**assimilation** and **accommodation.** As we go through life, we record new experiences into existing schemata, which get bigger. Taking in new information and fitting it into existing schemata is called *assimilation.* However, there comes a time when either the existing schemata are too filled with information to warrant enlargement or there are no existing schemata appropriate for certain new pieces of information. In these cases, new schemata are opened. Brand-new schemata can be opened to accommodate exposure to experiences and observations that are new to the individual, or an existing schema can be split into two or more to accommodate a wider range of experience. The opening of new schemata or splitting of existing schemata into new ones is called *accommodation.* The human mind develops through assimilation and accommodation of new information into one or more schemata. (See Figure 4.6.)

The schemata are linked to each other in ways that are unique to the individual, representing the unique experiences of the individual and the unique connections the individual has made between and among those experiences. In a sense, schema theory is similar to computer files. Each file is labeled with its appropriate content. You might have separate files for addresses, finances, personal correspondence, business letters, term papers, and so on. You might need to open a new file for personal correspondence if the existing one became too full. If you were assigned to write lesson plans, you might open a new file entitled "lesson plans" if you did not already have one. You would assimilate new material when

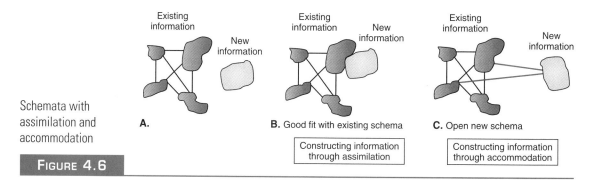

Existing information
New information

A.

Existing information
New information

B. Good fit with existing schema

Constructing information through assimilation

Existing information
New information

C. Open new schema

Constructing information through accommodation

Schemata with assimilation and accommodation

FIGURE 4.6

possible, and you would accommodate overloads of new categories with new files. You, alone, would know the rationale for opening the new files, and you, alone, would know how the new ones connect with the old ones. Your system would be unique to you!

The crux of Piaget's theory of cognitive development is the drive for achievement of *equilibration*—a state of mental equilibrium. An example may help to clarify the equilibration concept. Suppose you are taking a course in human **physiology** and are given hundreds of new terms to memorize and dozens of intricate processes to understand. Suppose, furthermore, you had never studied the human body in detail. All this new information about physiology comes at you, and you can't make heads or tails of it. What do you do with it? Well, because you have to know it at least until the exams are over, you store it in a mental file called "human physiology." This file (or schema) has no connection whatever with information that currently exists in your mind; it simply is there as mental storage. As the course progresses, you add information, expand the physiology schema, split it to create new ones, and try to make sense of the material when it is compared to itself, but you are not able to relate it to anything you have ever experienced. You are developing a whole set of schemata that is unrelated to anything else in your mind. This is disconcerting, and you feel a necessity (often not accomplished) to make some sort of connection to something you already know. You feel a drive to achieve equilibration.

As another example, suppose you are studying a course in elementary science methods. Some of the experiences you encounter in the course make immediate sense; these experiences have been assimilated into existing schemata that deal with the same ideas and cause the schemata to expand. This might be the case with the idea of doing hands-on activities with children. You may already have the understanding that hands-on activities are a meaningful way for getting children involved in science, and the new experiences reinforce and expand your understandings. However, some of the experiences may be new to you, and you either work to assimilate them into existing schemata or open new schemata that connect to existing schemata as you make sense out of this new material. This may occur when you are thinking about implementing technology in early childhood science activities. You may have some technological background in appropriate schemata, but you might never have thought about ways that technology could be used in early childhood science programs. You either assimilate the new information about technology into your schemata dealing with hands-on science or your schemata dealing with technology, or you create a new schema combining the two and linked to both. These new schemata are connected in ways that are unique to your method of thinking and your prior experiences.

In both cases, you are achieving equilibration relative to connecting the new experiences of this course with your prior experiences.

The same is true of children's thinking. To learn something new, they must be able to connect it to something they already know. They must construct personal meaning of the new material, either by assimilating it into existing schemata or by accommodating it through forming new schemata that are connected to existing ones. In the constructivist approach to learning, children are encouraged to make meaningful connections to previously existing information so the situation of having to construct schemata in isolation, as in the physiology example, will not occur. Exposure to new experiences often causes the phenomenon of cognitive disequilibration that we discussed earlier in this chapter. Cognitive disequilibration signifies that the new experience does not readily fit into any other previous experience the child may have had; the new experience cannot be assimilated into existing schemata (as the concept of *bear* could be assimilated into the schema dealing with *animals*). Therefore, to make sense out of the new experience, the child must either enlarge an existing schema to assimilate the novel experience or open a new schema that somehow is connected with existing schemata. In this manner, new information is constructed in terms of understandings that evolve and are reformulated in response to lack of fit between new experiences and previous understandings. vonGlasersfeld (1989) explained the phenomenon as follows:

> The learning theory that emerges from Piaget's work can be summarized by saying that cognitive change and learning take place when a scheme, instead of producing the expected result, leads to perturbation, and perturbation, in turn, leads to accommodation that establishes a new equilibrium. As a result, the human mind is a complex network of schemata which are intricately connected to each other in patterns completely unique to the individual (p. 128).

Because the development of schemata begins as soon as the mind is capable of processing stimuli, it is plain to see that it is to a child's advantage to experience the richest and most widely varied stimuli possible. Head Start and other preschool programs are designed to do precisely this. Elementary school science experiences should include the widest breadth of experiences possible to provide a rich experiential base for children as they process their disequilibrations through assimilation and accommodation.

Brain Research and Construction of Knowledge

NSES Professional Development Standard B. Integrating Knowledge of Science, Learning, Pedagogy, and Students NSES Professional Development Standard A. Learning Content Through Inquiry

One of the "hot topics" in education at the beginning of the 21st century is brain research. Much literature about brain research is available, and the research dealing with the physiology of the brain seems to support the ideas of constructivism. A few examples follow.

Constructivism holds that new information must be attached to information already existing in a person's mind for learning to occur. Brain research explains this: "If the brain can retrieve stored information that is similar to new information, it is more likely to make sense of the new information. This leads to increased understanding and retention" (Westwater & Wolfe, 2000, p. 50).

In addition, brain research shows that "[t]he brain changes physiologically as a result of experience. An individual's environment determines to a large extent the functioning ability of his or her brain. The brain can change its structure and function in response to external experiences . . . To maximize the brain's capacity to grow connections, teachers must provide an environment that is challenging yet nurturing. *The brain wants to learn*" (Caulfield, Kidd, & Kocher, 2000, p. 62; italics added). Zull (2004) describes the brain as being plastic—being molded and reshaped by growth, disappearance, and rearrangement of the brain's neurons in response to experiences throughout life. Current thinking suggests that when people sleep, the brain has a chance to move things to long-term memory and make connections with existing thoughts (Bodies Exhibition, 2006).

The Society for Neuroscience (2002) reports "there is much support for the idea that memory involves a persistent change in the relationship between **neurons**" and that the "stability of long-term memory is conferred by structural modifications within neurons that change the strength and number of **synapses**" (p. 18). Dr. Eric Kandel, a corecipient of the 2000 Nobel Prize in Medicine, has shown that learning produces changes in behavior by adjusting the synapses between the nerve cells in the brain. The human brain has at least 100 billion neurons and at least 100 trillion synapses. Kendal showed that short-term memory involves changes in synapse strength, and for long-term memory, new synapses are created (Office of External Affairs, Health Sciences Division, 2002; Wade, 2000). Restak (2003) writes, "[T]he brain never loses the power to transform itself on the basis of experience . . . [Y]our brain is different today than it was yesterday. This difference results from the effect on your brain of yesterday's and today's experiences as well as the thoughts and feelings you've entertained over the past 24 hours" (pp. 7–8).

Researchers have found that "students learn better when teachers used a constructivist approach that involved teaching science in a variety of ways . . . [T]his instructional approach may be more useful in enhancing conceptual growth than the traditional use of worksheets and note-taking" (Holloway, 2000, p. 85). Research also has shown that students develop a deeper understanding of science concepts when their prior knowledge is considered so that they integrate new knowledge (Barrow, 2006). Willis (2007), a neurologist, says that current evidence about brain physiology is highly supportive of teaching strategies that focus on meaning and personal understanding, and classroom environments that are conducive to learning, highly challenging, and safe.

The research on brain physiology is beginning to show what happens in the brain during memory formation, retrieval, and rearrangement (see, for example, Kalat, 2007). Although it may take decades for full understanding to be achieved, the progress being made in our understanding of the neurological basis for cognition and learning has serious implications for educators. This is a topic worth following.

VYGOTSKY, THE SOCIAL CONSTRUCTIVIST

NSES Professional Development Standard B. Integrating Knowledge of Science, Learning, Pedagogy, and Students NSES Professional Development Standard A. Learning Content Through Inquiry

In contrast to Piaget, who believed that learning is an individual, internal act that depends on the learner's cognitive development, Lev Vygotsky (1896–1934) saw learning as being dependent on social and cultural factors. According to Vygotsky, students construct knowledge through social interactions with each other (Santrock, 2004).

Both Vygotsky and Piaget were constructivists. The primary difference is that Vygotsky emphasized the social nature of learning and Piaget emphasized the individual nature, although he also said that equilibration arises from contact with the ideas of others (DeVries, 2006). Vygotsky was a social constructivist who believed that learners can and should use the input of others as they formulate their constructions and not rely solely on themselves. In Vygotskian theory:

* Learning is a social and collaborative activity.

* Learners must utilize the input of others.

* These "others" include peers, parents, friends, and many other people and sources of information, such as the Internet, books, videos, and movies.

* The teacher is the facilitator.

Vygotsky described a **Zone of Proximal Development** (ZPD), which is the region of activity that learners can navigate with aid, including, but not limited to, people (Vygotsky, 1934, 1986, cited in Ash & Levitt, 2003, p. 26; Vygotsky, 1978). The lower level of the ZPD represents tasks the learner can do independently. The upper level represents tasks that can be completed only with assistance. The ZPD represents the difference between a learner's capacity to solve problems on his or her own and the learner's capacity to solve them with assistance (Schütz, 2002). (See Figure 4.7.) The ZPD varies according to culture, experience, and innate ability.

According to Vygotsky, the teacher's role is to provide much support during children's early stages of investigating a problem or situation and then to diminish support as children are able to take on increasing responsibility for their own inquiries in a **scaffolding** strategy. The scaffolding is gradual, with the teacher carefully regulating adult interaction within each child's zone until the child can work independently (Ash & Levitt, 2003).

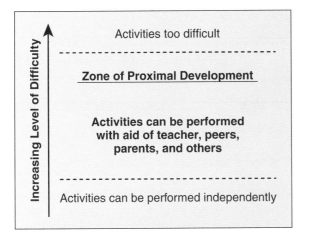

Zone of Proximal
Development (ZPD)

FIGURE 4.7

The result is a kind of inquiry that Tharp and Gallimore (1988) termed "assisted discovery" (cited in Slavin, 1997, p. 48).

Children's construction of knowledge, then, is complete when they use their own resources together with input from others.

CHARACTERISTICS OF CONSTRUCTIVIST TEACHING

Brooks and Brooks (1999) identify twelve descriptors of constructivist teaching; these provide a good summary of where our thinking has been taking us. Constructivist teachers:

NSES Program
Standard B. Relevant,
Inquiry-Based, and
Connected with Other
Subjects
NSES Teaching
Standard A. Inquiry-
Based Program

1. Encourage and accept student autonomy and initiative.

2. Use raw data and primary information sources with manipulative, interactive, and physical materials.

3. Use cognitive terminology, such as "classify," "analyze," "predict," and "create."

4. Allow student responses to drive lessons, shift instructional strategies, and alter content.

5. Inquire about students' understandings of concepts before sharing their own understandings about the concepts.

6. Encourage students to engage in dialogue, both with the teacher and with one another.

7. Encourage student inquiry by asking thoughtful, open-ended questions and encouraging students to ask questions of each other.

8. Seek elaboration of students' initial responses.

9. Engage students in experiences that might engender contradictions to their initial hypotheses and then encourage discussion.

10. Allow wait time after posing a question.

11. Provide time for students to construct relationships and create metaphors.

12. Nurture students' natural curiosity through frequent use of the learning cycle model.

These descriptors are appropriate for any constructivist classroom, including constructivist elementary science classes. They are based on the theories of Piaget and Vygotsky. You should check yourself relative to these descriptors. How well do they describe you? How well do they describe the kind of teaching you envision?

STAGES OF COGNITIVE DEVELOPMENT

NSES Professional
Development
Standard B. Integrating
Knowledge of Science,
Learning, Pedagogy, and
Students

Piaget suggested four stages of cognitive development commencing with birth: the sensorimotor stage, the preoperational stage, the concrete operational stage, and the formal operational stage (see Figure 4.8). Although he later expressed dissatisfaction with having proposed specific ages to accompany the stages, he believed that all people progress through the same four stages in the same unvaried sequence.

Each stage represents a more advanced capability for cognitive processing than the previous stage. Much has been written about the characteristics of each stage, so they will not be discussed in detail here. However, it is essential that the elementary science teacher understand the intellectual capabilities and limitations of children at the various stages.

Sensorimotor Stage

The child's intellectual endeavors in the **sensorimotor stage** consist of the senses interacting with the child's environment. It is crucial to the intellectual development of children that they be given the opportunity to act on the environment in unrestricted (but safe) ways to start opening up and building their schemata. Such activities as walking unaided up and down stairs, working puzzles with large pieces, playing with push toys, exploring the house and the yard, and going for rides with the family contribute to the development of a rich network of schemata.

Preoperational Stage

The **preoperational stage** of intellectual development characterizes children from preschool through first or second grade. The child's world

Stage	Characteristics	Ways to Foster Development
SENSORIMOTOR	Thought based on sensory input	Opportunity to act on environment
PREOPERATIONAL	Increased use of symbolism and language Limited logic Egocentric Perspective	Language and symbol use
CONCRETE OPERATIONAL	Must see—feel—touch—smell—hear to "know" Thinking is reversible Some classification Some conservation	Hands-on experiences
FORMAL OPERATIONAL	Abstract reasoning	Abstractions in the form of problems, hypothesis, probabilities, correlations, proportions Formal reasoning skills

The cognitive development stages of Piaget

FIGURE 4.8

becomes reshaped by developing the realm of mental representation: "intentionally manipulating symbols" (Salkind, 1985, p. 201). Language is developed, and the child begins to use the abstractions of language to communicate thought. The "beginning of language, of the symbolic function, and therefore of thought, or representation" (Piaget, 1964, 2003, p. S9) occurs during this stage.

Preoperational children are **egocentric** in perspective. Logical thought is not widely available to preoperational children; everything is based on what they see. They cannot assume a perspective that is different from their own. For example, they cannot imagine what someone in a different position would see. Thus, the elementary science teacher asks the preoperational child what HE or SHE sees, NOT what he or she thinks someone else would see. We ask the question "What do you see under this magnifying glass?" not "What do you suppose Mark sees under his magnifying glass?" We ask, "Why did you group the buttons the way you did?" not "Why do you suppose Janie grouped the buttons the way she did?"

Preoperational children cannot reverse operations. They can learn that 2 plus 4 equals 6. However, they cannot yet make the reverse logical inference that if you take 4 from 6 you get what's left (2), or that if you take 2 from 6 you get 4. They can find their way on an illustrated map from the school to the firehouse, but they cannot retrace their steps backward without instruction to get from the firehouse to the school. Elementary science educators must be careful not to expect operation-reversal capabilities from preoperational children. For example, a kindergarten teacher may introduce an activity in which children add heat to ice cubes and observe that the ice cubes melt; however, preoperational children normally would not infer from that activity that taking heat away (or, as they would put it, "adding cold") would produce the opposite effect. Or, a first-grade teacher may have the children do an activity to demonstrate that exercise increases one's rate of breathing. The preoperational children would not intuitively reason that resting will reduce the breathing rate; they have to try it for themselves.

Preoperational children cannot comprehend conservation of quantity or mass or volume. This was discussed in Chapter 3 in the section on measurement.

It is worthwhile to note that to a certain extent, adults also operate in a preoperational mode. To test this, go to a store that sells aquariums, and ask to see several 20-gallon tanks. It requires a terrific imagination to believe that all the tanks you are shown—which vary in shape from long and narrow to short and wide, pentagonal, circular, and spherical—have the same capacity. Adults also experience difficulty in reversing, as evidenced by our need to turn the map upside down when driving south.

Concrete Operational Stage

The primary characteristic of the **concrete operational stage** is that the individual must see, hear, feel, touch, smell, taste, or in some other way, use the senses to *know*. Concrete operational children cannot think abstractly, and they do not wonder about abstract concepts. "They operate on objects and not yet on verbally expressed hypotheses" (Piaget, 1964, 2003, p. S9). They are busy learning skills and how to manipulate things they can experience firsthand. Studies show that many children are concrete-bound through the middle grades; indeed, many adults never get out of this stage. Remember that a cognitive stage represents the capability of a level of intellectual development; it does not represent the accomplishment of that level.

The thinking process of concrete operational children can be reversed; they can think backward and reconstruct the original situation. For example, they can think about what would happen if a certain variable had *not* been changed the way it had been.

4.4   IN THE SCHOOLS

NSES Content Standard B. Physical Science: Properties and Changes of Properties in Matter

Solutions and Crystals

A good example that helps children understand reversibility of operations involves experimentation with **solutions** and **crystals.** Children add heat to a solution to enable more of a **solute** (the solid material) to dissolve in the **solvent** (the liquid part). The more the heat, the more solute will dissolve. Concrete operational children are able to infer what will happen to the solution if heat is taken away (cooled). The solute that dissolved because of the heating will **precipitate** out of the solution when it cools. In fact, the excess solute precipitates in the form of crystals, and the slower this happens, the larger the crystals will become. (See Constructing Science in the Classroom 4.1 for details of how to make crystals and ways of inquiring into crystal formation.)

4.5   IN THE SCHOOLS

NSES Content Standard B. Physical Science: Motions and Forces

Balancing

In a fourth-grade class, children were experimenting with the relationship between the weight of objects and their distance from the fulcrum on a balance (see Figure 4.9). Concrete operational children are able to predict what might happen when weights are moved without necessarily having to *do* it first; they then confirm their predictions by testing them (see Constructing Science in the Classroom 5.2 for suggested investigations involving levers).

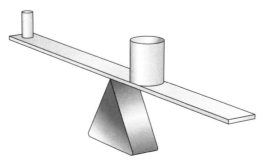

Balancing on a beam

FIGURE 4.9

NSES Professional Development Standard B. Integrating Knowledge of Science, Learning, Pedagogy, and Students

The classification capabilities of concrete operational children are extensive (refer to Chapter 3). They can create hierarchies and can understand relationships within classes, such as plants and animals, and relationships to the class itself, although they are not yet ready to devise complex hierarchical interrelationships and complex classification systems.

Concrete operational individuals can comprehend conservation of quantity, mass, and volume, although conservation of volume occurs toward the end of the concrete operational stage. For example, concrete operational children understand that the amount of solute dissolved in a solution is the same before and after mixing it with the solvent.

Concrete operational individuals have the ability to form hypotheses, including the ability to define the term, and they can verbalize hypotheses concerning the relationships between two variables. They have the ability to develop experimental conditions that test the validity of hypotheses, including identifying conspicuous variables and devising means for controlling all identified variables except one. However, in contrast to formal operational individuals, concrete operational people have difficulty discovering less evident variables. For example, they might have difficulty suggesting the effect of air resistance on freely falling objects. (If a light ball and a heavy ball are dropped at the same time, air resistance may slow the light ball's rate of descent, causing the heavy ball to hit the floor before the light ball. Concrete operational children may reason that the heavier ball falls faster because it is heavier; the possible interference by the air may not occur to them.) They often have difficulty with testing hypotheses about phenomena when their preconceived theories are strong; in these situations, they tend either to ignore or to distort data that contradict their preconceived beliefs. Part of the potential difficulty with the "light ball–heavy ball" experiment may be a result of prior beliefs. The pendulum activity suggested in Chapter 3 is a good example of the opportunity to distort or ignore data; if one believes, for example, that the height of the drop influences the rate of swing, then one may selectively record data to prove that hypothesis correct.

The following activities capitalize on the abilities of children in the concrete operational stage of cognitive development.

4.6   IN THE SCHOOLS

NSES Content Standard B. Physical Science: Heat Energy

Effect of Salt on the Length of Time It Takes to Heat Water

In a fifth-grade class, children gathered data to show the effect of adding salt to water on how long it takes the water to heat. They placed beakers containing mea-

Continued on next page

sured amounts of water on hot plates and then added different amounts of salt to the water. They used thermometers to record the temperature of the water at given intervals. If an individual believes the salt will cause the water to take less time to heat to a certain temperature, he or she will tend to record those data that support this hypothesis, omit the data that refute it, and interpret fractional parts of data in favor of this hypothesis. (**Teacher Note:** Adding salt to water increases the length of time it takes the water to heat and raises its boiling point to well above 100° Celsius.)

Literature Connection

A Wrinkle in Time by Madeleine L'Engle (Dell, 1962) begins in the Murry household, where many science experiments are performed using ingredients found in the cupboards.

4.1	**CONSTRUCTING SCIENCE IN THE CLASSROOM**

GROWING COPPER SULFATE CRYSTALS AND SUGAR CRYSTALS

NSES Content Standard B. Physical Science: Properties and Changes of Properties in Matter

Crystal growing provides an excellent vehicle through which children can hypothesize and experiment. Questions that might be asked include the following:

1. How big can crystals grow?
2. Do crystals of some materials grow bigger than others?
3. Can crystals be grown from all materials?
4. What effect does heat have on the rate of crystal growth?
5. What effect does rate of evaporation have on the rate of crystal growth?

To grow crystals, you need to have a **saturated** solution of some material* and let the liquid evaporate; as the liquid evaporates, the dissolved material is left behind in the form of crystals. Different substances require different treatments for most effective crystal formation. Below are "recipes" for growing sugar crystals and copper sulfate crystals. *Safety note:* Sugar is edible, but copper sulfate is poisonous. Do *not* store sugar and copper sulfate near each other. Caution children *not* to taste the copper sulfate—or the sugar, either. Instruct children to wash their hands thoroughly if they touch it.

*In a *saturated* solution, the maximum amount of solid has been dissolved in the liquid that *can* be dissolved without changing the temperature. Normally, the higher the temperature of the liquid, the more solid that can be dissolved.

Continued on next page

Sugar Crystals (Rock Candy)

Home-grown sugar crystals are called rock candy. Well-defined sugar crystals are difficult to grow, because sugar tends to become candy-like and noncrystalline when it is dissolved in water, heated, and then cooled.

Method 1: Formation on a String

Dissolve 2½ cups of sugar in 1 cup of water, heating the mixture until the sugar is dissolved. Let the mixture cool. Then, pour the syrup into a glass into which you have previously suspended a weighted string. Let the water evaporate. Rock candy will form on the string in a day or two.

Method 2: Formation Without String

Dissolve 2½ cups of sugar in 1 cup of water, heating the mixture until the sugar is dissolved. Let the mixture cool. Pour the syrup into a shallow, wide-mouthed container. Cover tightly with aluminum foil or plastic wrap, and poke three small holes in the covering with a pencil. Let the contents set without disturbing it for 6 weeks or so. Large, well-defined crystals will form on the bottom of the container.

If desired, you can pour off the fluid, remove the crystals, and put them in a warm, dry place to dry.

(In both methods, you can add food coloring to the solution to obtain colored crystals of rock candy.)

Inquiry Questions to Investigate

If you poke more holes in the wrapping, make the holes bigger, or leave off the wrapping, what happens to the size of the crystals and to the rate at which they form?

What happens if you put the container in a warmer place? A cooler place? (**Teacher Note:** The principle is that the more slowly the liquid evaporates, the larger the crystals grow.)

Copper Sulfate Crystals

Below are the directions for preparing a solution of copper sulfate. When the solution is left to evaporate, the copper sulfate crystallizes into beautiful, deep blue crystals in the shape of parallelograms. The more slowly the liquid evaporates, the larger the crystals grow.

1. Heat 300 ml of tap water to about 100°F (38°C)—about the temperature of a baby's bottle.

2. Stir in 175 g of powdered copper sulfate (cupric sulfate, or $CuSO_4 \cdot 5H_2O$). Most of it will dissolve, but a layer of undissolved copper sulfate will remain on the bottom of the container.

3. Let the solution cool, preferably overnight. The copper sulfate that cannot remain dissolved in the solution as it cools will precipitate out; thus, you will have a completely *saturated* solution at the temperature of the room.

4. Carefully **decant** (pour) the cool solution into a clean jar, filling it to about one-third or one-fourth full; be careful that no undissolved residue gets included. Leave the leftover solution (including the undissolved residue) in the original jar; this jar should be covered and sealed tightly. This will be the stock solution.

Continued on next page

Copper sulfate crystals grown in a science classroom—from left to right: 3 months, 1 month, 2 weeks, 6 days, 1 day

FIGURE 4.10

5. Put a piece of paper or plastic wrap over the top of the second jar, and fasten it with a rubber band. Poke two or three small holes into the paper with a pencil. Let it set overnight. Tiny crystals will form on the bottom of the jar because some of the water will evaporate.

6. Decant the solution from the second jar into a third container. Look at the crystals left in the bottom of the second jar. Select one well-formed baby crystal, and put it in the bottom of the third container, put the paper with the holes in it on that container, and let it set overnight. Pour the extra liquid and solid material into the stock solution jar.

7. The next day, use a pair of plastic or stainless-steel tweezers to remove the crystal. Wipe it clean, and put it back into the jar.

8. Keep doing this as long as you want. Each day or two, remove the growing crystal, wipe it clean, and return it to the jar. Add more solution from the stock solution as needed. Remove unwanted crystals as they form, and add them to the stock. Figure 4.10 shows crystals of copper sulfate after different periods of growth.

Inquiry Questions to Investigate
Does the rate of evaporation affect the rate of growth of the crystals? Does the temperature of the solution affect the amount of copper sulfate that will dissolve in the water?

Concrete operational individuals are capable of understanding the relationship between time and the length of a line to construct meaningful time lines.

NSES Content Standard D. Earth and Space
Science: Earth's History

4.7   IN THE SCHOOLS

A Geologic Time Line

A time line showing the entire period of geologic time from the formation of the earth to the present can be drawn on a length of adding machine tape about 10 feet long. The period of time that represents human inhabitation of the earth is less than 1 mm in length. Concrete operational children not only can construct such a time line, they can internalize the relative brevity of human life on earth (as well as the relative lengths of other major events in the history of the earth). Data generally accepted by the scientific community that can be used for a basic time line is shown in Figure 4.11.

NSES Professional
Development
Standard B. Integrating
Knowledge of Science,
Learning, Pedagogy, and
Students
NSES Program
Standard C. Coordinated
with Mathematics

Concrete operational children have the capability of understanding elementary probabilities, ratios, proportions, and variations, and they can calculate, for example, the ratio between number of boys and girls in the class, the lengths of lines represented by given periods of time, and the ratios involved in constructing scaled models of the sun and the solar system. (See Constructing Science in the Classroom 3.50 and 3.51.) These sorts of mental manipulations can take place in the mind of the concrete operational child, but the thinking must be fostered through actual manipulation of actual materials.

Questions posed for investigation often result from everyday observations.

NSES Content Standard A: Science as Inquiry:
Understanding About Scientific Inquiry

4.8   IN THE SCHOOLS

Investigating Laundry

Ernst vonGlasersfeld and Jack Lochhead tell of a teacher whose seventh-grade class investigated the problem of why underwear seems to get turned inside out in the dryer. The problem arose from ordinary observations and became the focus of a year-long study. Children devised experimental procedures to test hypotheses they proposed. They counted numbers of right-side-out and inside-out underwear after each different kind of experimental treatment, and they calculated the probabilities and the deviations from expected probabilities. They even wrote to relatives in Europe asking them to replicate the experiments to see if continent made a difference. This was a constructivist project, process in orientation, that utilized the full intellectual potential of the concrete operational child.

Eon	Era	Period	Epoch	Beginning (Years ago)	Life-forms	Landforms
P H A N E R O Z O I C	C E N O Z O I C	QUATERNARY	Recent (Holocene)	10,000	Modern man	
			Pleistocene (Ice Age)	2 Million	Rise of *Australopithecus*	
		TERTIARY	Pliocene	5 Million	Rise of hominids	
			Miocene	24 Million		Himalaya Mtns.
			Oligocene	37 Million		India and Asia
			Eocene	58 Million	Rise of horses	
			Paleocene	66 Million	Rise of primates	
	M E S O Z O I C	Cretaceous		144 Million	Extinction of dinosaurs Rise of flowering plants	Alps and Rockies
		Jurassic		208 Million	Rise of birds	Pangea fragments start to drift
		Triassic		245 Million	Rise of mammals Rise of dinosaurs	Pangea breakup; Atlantic Ocean
	P A L E O Z O I C	Permian		286 Million	Rise of reptiles	Pangea together; Appalachian Mtns.
		Carboniferous	Pennsylvanian	320 Million		
			Mississippian	360 Million		
		Devonian		408 Million	Rise of amphibians, insects, seed plants, trees	
		Silurian		438 Million	Rise of land plants	
		Ordovician		505 Million	Rise of fish and vertebrates	
		Cambrian		570 Million	Trilobites Shells Mollusks Brachiopods Echinoderms	
P R E C A M B R I A N		Proterozoic		2.5 Billion	Multicellular soft-body organisms Algae "Jellyfish" "Worm tubes"	Latest start of plate movement
		Archean		3.8 Billion	Bacteria Cells without nuclei	Crust development
		Origin of earth		4.6 Billion		

Geologic time scale

FIGURE 4.11

Formal Operational Stage

NSES Professional Development Standard B. Integrating Knowledge of Science, Learning, Pedagogy, and Students

The primary difference between the concrete operational and the formal operational stages is that in the **formal operational stage,** people have the ability to think and reason abstractly without requiring concrete examples. They are not bound by the present, and they are not bound by the concrete. "They can reason on hypotheses, and not only on objects" (Piaget, 1964, 2003, p. S9). Many children in elementary grades are capable of some degree of formal operational thought.

In Piagetian theory, formal operations is the ultimate achievement in human intellectual development. One must have progressed through the preceding three stages to arrive at a developmental stage that permits internal abstract thinking. However, mere arrival at this stage does not imply that the individual is employing formal operational thinking. These powers of thought must be developed. Tekkaya and Yenilmez (2006) studied 117 eighth-grade students who were studying plants and photosynthesis. They found that students with well-developed higher-order thinking skills exhibited greater understanding of the principles than those whose higher-order thinking skills were less well developed. They concluded that teachers should provide students with models, simulations, diagrams, and analogies to help make abstract concepts understandable; should pose problems and present questions and conflicting situations to encourage students to analyze their own thinking; and should use inquiry-oriented teaching strategies that help students relate new information to old information. It is worth noting that although this study was done with eighth-grade students, similar instructional techniques employed in lower grades help students who are ready move from concrete to abstract thinking.

Lawson (1978) identified five aspects of formal operations (abstract thinking): proportional reasoning, isolation and control of variables, probabilistic reasoning, correlational reasoning, and combinatorial reasoning.

Proportional reasoning is used in comparing the relationships between variables, such as distance and mass in balancing weights on a beam (see In The Schools 4.5) or the colors of M&M's® (see In the Schools 4.9).

4.9   IN THE SCHOOLS

NSES Unifying Concepts and Processes: Evidence, Models, and Explanation
NSES Program Standard C. Coordinated with Mathematics

Proportions of M&M® Colors

A teacher passed out bags of M&M's (plain milk chocolate candy) to groups in a fifth-grade class and asked them to count the numbers of each color and then calculate the percentage of each. The percentages calculated by each group of students were compared, and a class average was computed. These percentages were then used to

Continued on next page

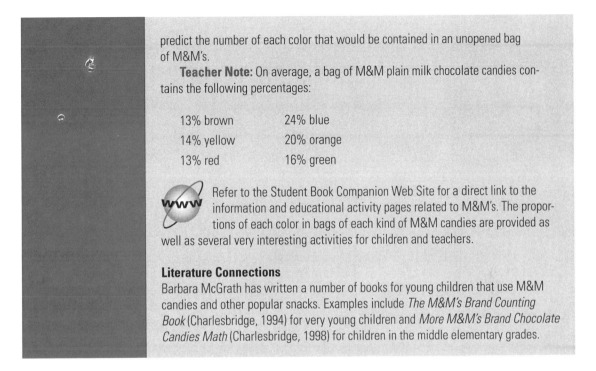

predict the number of each color that would be contained in an unopened bag of M&M's.

Teacher Note: On average, a bag of M&M plain milk chocolate candies contains the following percentages:

13% brown	24% blue
14% yellow	20% orange
13% red	16% green

Refer to the Student Book Companion Web Site for a direct link to the information and educational activity pages related to M&M's. The proportions of each color in bags of each kind of M&M candies are provided as well as several very interesting activities for children and teachers.

Literature Connections

Barbara McGrath has written a number of books for young children that use M&M candies and other popular snacks. Examples include *The M&M's Brand Counting Book* (Charlesbridge, 1994) for very young children and *More M&M's Brand Chocolate Candies Math* (Charlesbridge, 1998) for children in the middle elementary grades.

Isolation and control of variables refers to the ability to identify the variables that bear on a given hypothesis, to distinguish those that are to be manipulated from those that must be held constant, and to devise ways to ensure that the result of the experiment is caused by the manipulated variable and not by something else. The pendulum investigation in Chapter 3 is a good example of an activity that requires isolation and control of variables.

4.10   IN THE SCHOOLS

NSES Content Standard C. Life Science: Organisms and Environments
NSES Program Standard C. Coordinated with Mathematics

What Keeps Plants Healthy?

Kuhn and Brannock (1977) describe a plant problem that requires isolation and control of variables. Four plants were displayed on a table. Two of these plants appeared healthy; the other two were obviously in poor condition. Next to the plants were glasses of water, plant food, and bottles of leaf lotion as follows:

Healthy Plant 1: Large glass of water, light-colored plant food

Healthy Plant 2: Small glass of water, light-colored plant food, bottle of leaf lotion

Continued on next page

Nonhealthy Plant 1: Large glass of water, dark-colored plant food, bottle of leaf lotion

Nonhealthy Plant 2: Small glass of water, dark-colored plant food

The teacher explained that she had cared for each plant with weekly doses of those materials displayed next to it. She then asked the children what she ought to use in caring for her plants in the future.

To solve this problem, children must isolate the four variables—plant health, amount of water, type of plant food, and use of leaf lotion—and infer which is (are) operative. (**Teacher Note:** In this case, only the type of plant food seemed to operate on the health of the plants.) As an extension of this isolation of variables activity, children should be encouraged to develop their own experimental procedures.

Probabilistic reasoning includes such phenomena as coin tosses, lottery chances, and the like. Environmental studies often include estimating the probability of given occurrences (for example, the probability of camouflaged insects being discovered).

4.11   IN THE SCHOOLS

NSES Program Standard C. Coordinated with Mathematics
NSES Content Standard C. Life Science: Populations and Ecosystems

Camouflage

A natural camouflage activity that fosters development of probabilistic reasoning involves counting the number of colored toothpicks that can be picked up in a given period of time from a measured area of grass. The teacher measures several adjacent, 1-meter squares of grass in the schoolyard and outlines them with string. Teams of children work together at each square. One child is designated "It," and this child turns away so as not to see while another child scatters a given number of toothpicks of various colors throughout the measured square. (For example, the toothpicks may include 10 each of white, red, blue, green, and orange that you either purchase or make by coloring plain wooden toothpicks with food coloring.) At a signal, "It" turns around and gathers as many toothpicks as possible in, say, 10 seconds. The team then counts the number of each color and records the results. After each member of the team has had a chance to be "It," the data from the entire team and, ultimately, from the entire class are combined. The results indicate the probability of a given color of toothpick being selected. This principle carries over to insect camouflage and other natural protection phenomena.

Continued on next page

Literature Connections

Jumanji by Chris Van Allsburg (Houghton Mifflin, 1981) is the wild adventure of two children who are trapped playing a board game that comes to life. The only way to save themselves from a volcanic eruption is to roll a pair of sixes with the dice. What are the odds that they can succeed?

The Magic School Bus: Butterfly and the Bog Beast by Nancy Krulik and Joanna Cole (Scholastic, 1996) is a book about how butterflies use camouflage for survival.

Correlational reasoning, by definition, is the extent to which changes in one variable are associated with changes in another variable. Correlation does not imply causation; correlation is simply congruence in change. For example, there may be a correlation between grade point average (GPA) in college and amount of study, and there may be a correlation between people's vocabulary and the quality of their term papers. Correlations for variables that increase or decrease together are *positive* correlations. However, if one variable increases while the other variable decreases, the correlation between the two is *negative.* The relationship between exercise and stress is negative; to a point, the greater the exercise, the lower the stress. If no relationship exists between two variables, such as the relationship between amount of money in people's pockets and their heights, the correlation is *zero.*

Much scientific experimentation seeks to establish the presence and degree of correlation between two variables. Although one cannot establish a cause and effect from correlation alone, a consistently high positive or negative correlation between two variables suggests the possibility of a cause-and-effect relationship that warrants further investigation. For example, in the inside-out underwear investigation (see In The Schools 4.8), if it were to be shown that a higher incidence of inside-out underwear existed in the southern hemisphere compared with the northern hemisphere (all other variables being equal), one might want to investigate possible cause-and-effect reasons.

Graphs of the three kinds of correlations are shown in Figure 4.12. Figure 4.12(a) shows a positive correlation between average daily hours of study and the student's GPA. Figure 4.12(b) shows a negative correlation between the number of beers consumed the night before the exam and the student's grade on the exam; Figure 4.12(c) shows no correlation between the height of people and their GPAs.

Combinatorial reasoning refers to the statistics of permutations (how many ways one can arrange a given number of items in sequence) and combinations (how many ways one can arrange a given number of items in certain predetermined combinations). Combinatorial reasoning is used

NSES Professional Development Standard B. Integrating Knowledge of Science, Learning, Pedagogy, and Students
NSES Program Standard C. Coordinated with Mathematics

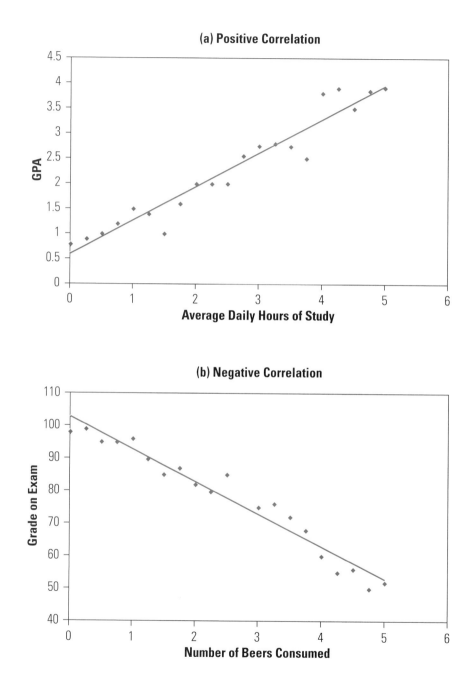

(a) Positive Correlation

(b) Negative Correlation

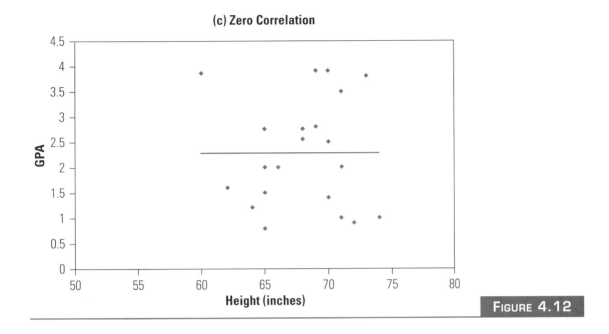

FIGURE 4.12

in establishing the number of different causal effects that are possible from interactions of more than one variable.

Stage Overlapping

According to Piagetian stage theory, individuals go through all the cognitive development stages in order. However, people function, to some extent, in all stages, including those that precede and follow the stage they are currently in. For instance, children in the concrete operational stage also function to a certain extent at the sensorimotor stage and at the preoperational stage. It is important to note that the ages and grades that Piaget originally identified with his stages of development are flexible, and children once thought to be solely in the preoperational stage may well have the intellectual capacity to function to a certain extent in the concrete operational stage. Many individuals in the concrete operational stage can and do function in formal operational ways; these individuals have been stimulated through challenging situations to use increasingly abstract and complex forms of thought. Conversely, many college students function at the concrete operational stage, never having been required to perform successfully at the formal operational level. One of the goals of science education is the development of higher-order thinking skills, and the alert teacher will ensure that children are challenged to think for themselves.

NSES Professional Development Standard B. Integrating Knowledge of Science, Learning, Pedagogy, and Students

DINOSAURS AND THE SOLAR SYSTEM

NSES Professional Development Standard B. Integrating Knowledge of Science, Learning, Pedagogy, and Students NSES context Standard D. Earth and Space Science: Earth's History

Many schools encourage the study of dinosaurs and the study of the solar system in kindergarten and first grade, when most children are still in the preoperational stage of cognitive development. Can preoperational children comprehend these concepts? Legions of stories tell of children coming home with descriptions of dinosaurs. "How big were they?" asks Mother. "This big," replies the child, holding her thumb and forefinger as far apart as they will go. The child is representing the size of the toy dinosaur she saw in school.

Preoperational children typically do not have the mental capability to abstract from a model to an actual size in proportional terms. That is to say, given a toy model of a dinosaur, the preoperational child cannot visualize it to be 100 or 1,000 times larger in real life. Preoperational children must *experience* life-size replicas of dinosaurs. Providing for this is not difficult.

4.12   IN THE SCHOOLS   NSES Content Standard D. Earth and Space Science: Earth's History

Size of the Dinosaurs

How big were the dinosaurs? Obtain the dimensions of several dinosaurs. Sketch them on large sheets of butcher paper, and cut them out. You will probably have to use the gymnasium or the cafeteria to have enough room, and you will have to mount the finished product on the gymnasium or cafeteria wall.

Then, read *The Dinosaur's New Clothes* by Diane Goode (The Blue Sky Press, 1999), the story of a vain, fashion-conscious emperor who is a Tyrannosaurus Rex and whose court also is composed of dinosaurs.

4.13   IN THE SCHOOLS   NSES Content Standard D. Earth and Space Science: Earth's History

Length of the Dinosaurs

How long were the dinosaurs? Have the children obtain essential information about dinosaurs of their choice and record this information in a booklet about their dinosaur. They may cut out a small model of their dinosaur to show its overall shape. In the hall, the teacher lays out a long strip of wide adding machine tape that has been marked into 1-foot segments. Each child, in turn, places his or her dinosaur cutout

Continued on next page

on the adding machine strip at the foot marker that represents how long the animal was. Or, children lay down on the adding machine strip, head to toe, until the entire length of the dinosaur has been filled with children. Then, they count how many children it takes to make one of each kind of dinosaur.

In these activities, the children see the *actual* sizes of dinosaurs. In addition, their concrete operational skills are being developed through comparison and through observation of actual dimensions. Perhaps the best way for children to see how big the dinosaurs were is to take them to a museum that exhibits reconstructed dinosaur skeletons (see Chapter 9).

Many excellent pieces of children's literature dealing with dinosaurs are available:

An Alphabet of Dinosaurs by Peter Dodson (Scholastic, 1995) is a book of information about familiar and newly discovered dinosaurs, focusing on the way these creatures lived.

The Dinosaur Who Lived in My Back Yard by B. G. Hennessy (Puffin Books, 1988) compares sizes of dinosaurs to things that children are familiar with. ("By the time he was 5, he was as big as our car.")

Janice VanCleave's Dinosaurs for Every Kid by Janice VanCleave (John Wiley & Sons, 1994) contains a wealth of information and activities for learning about dinosaurs.

Dinosaur World by Michael Dahl (Picture Window Books, 2004) is a series of six books suitable for children in kindergarten through fourth grade. Each provides illustrations and information about a different type of dinosaur. Each offers understandable size comparisons and answers "Where?" and "When?" questions. The titles are *Winged and Toothless, Three-Horn, T-Rex, Swift Thief, Long-Neck,* and *Bony Back.*

The Magic School Bus in the Time of the Dinosaurs by Joanna Cole (Scholastic, 1994). Children explore the age of dinosaurs and the many life forms that thrived during that time. A geologic time scale shows the relative period involved.

Oxford First Book of Dinosaurs by Barbara Taylor (Oxford University Press, 2001) is a well-illustrated reference book that describes the habitats, eating habits, and life cycles of major groupings of dinosaurs.

New Dinos: The Latest Finds! The Coolest Dinosaur Discoveries! by Shelley Tanaka (Atheneum Books for Young Readers, 2003) is a beautifully illustrated book that describes some of the newly discovered dinosaurs and what paleontologists have learned about dinosaurs in recent years.

 Direct links to several interesting Web sites dealing with dinosaurs are provided on the Student Book Companion Web Site.

NSES Professional Development Standard B. Integrating Knowledge of Science, Learning, Pedagogy, and Students
NSES Context
Standard D. Earth and Space Science: Objects in the Sky

How appropriate is studying the earth, the planets, and interplanetary space in the early elementary grades? The preoperational child can compare distances and sizes relative to each other, but cannot be expected to relate a scaled model of the solar system to the actual solar system. The "Temperatures of the Planets" activity (In the Schools 3.25) is a good example of this phenomenon. In this activity, children are asked to discover the relationship between how hot something gets and how close it is to the source of heat. They also are asked to extend their thinking along these lines to the solar system. Most preoperational children will understand the relationship and will be able to extend their thinking to the solar system, but they will not be able to visualize the distances involved in the solar system. The *only* way the planetary system can be represented is through models, and preoperational children cannot visualize the relationship between a model of something they cannot see and the real thing. A model of the planetary system is, to the preoperational child, relatively meaningless. The solution for cases of not being able to represent something in its true dimensions is to leave it out of the early childhood curriculum. There is plenty of time to study these topics as the child develops greater ability to reason abstractly. This is not to say that all studies of astronomy should be omitted from the early childhood science program; many topics are appropriate for investigation by preoperational children, such as phases of the moon, constellations, stars, planets, comets, and other celestial objects that can be viewed through a telescope or can be shown in picture form. What ought *not* to be introduced to preoperational children is material that requires intellectual skills they do not yet have, such as the skill of proportionality in model representation. Perhaps the biggest contribution that the study of the solar system can make to the intellectual development of the preoperational child is in the arena of imagination. The activities on the following pages use the magic of the moon, planets, and space to stimulate imagination and develop creativity.

4.14 In The Schools

NSES Content Standard D. Earth and Space Science: Objects in the Sky

Let's Make a Constellation

Give children six or eight gold or silver stars and a sheet of black paper. Have them arrange the stars in the shape of a constellation without connecting the stars with lines. Then, have other children guess what constellation it is. Finally, the child who

Continued on next page

made the constellation can reveal what it was supposed to represent and, if desired, connect the stars (see Figure 4.13).

To help children understand actual constellations, trace a set of constellations on a piece of white paper, and poke holes in the stars with a pin—small holes for dim stars and larger holes for bright stars. Project them on a screen using an overhead projector (see Figure 4.14).

Literature Connections

Sky Songs by Myra Cohn Livingston (Holiday House, 1984) is a collection of poetry about the beautiful and mysterious changes in the sky that occur from day to night and as a result of weather conditions. The acrylic paintings are bold and lively.

Star Climbing by Lou Francher (Laura Geringer Books, 2006) is a story of a little boy who imagines being on a nighttime journey across the sky where he can run and dance with the constellations.

Once Upon a Starry Night: A Book of Constellation Stories by Jacqueline Mitton and Christina Balit (National Geographic, 2003) presents Greek myths and facts about well-known constellations.

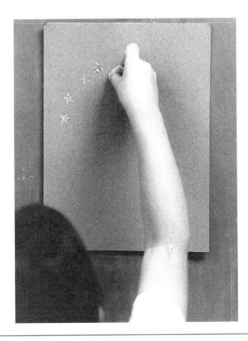

Constructing
constellations

FIGURE 4.13

Isn't this the Big
Dipper?

Exploring
constellations

FIGURE 4.14

NSES Content
Standard D. Earth and
Space Science: Objects
in the Sky

4.2   CONSTRUCTING SCIENCE IN THE CLASSROOM

HOW TO HOLD
A STARGAZING SESSION

When to Hold It
Season: Best viewing is late fall
or early winter.

   Time: After dark. Allow about 1 hour after sunset for the sky to get dark. Then, allow 20 minutes for eyes to get used to the dark. Try to avoid holding it when the full moon is high in the sky. Set an alternate date in case the sky is cloudy. Allow about an hour.

Where to Hold It
Some place dark—away from street lights—and away from buildings and tall trees. An open park or the schoolyard where the personnel will turn off the lights are ideal places. However, be sure that trees and building walls do not get in the way of viewing the lower portion of the sky. *Scope it out first!*

What to Bring
Binoculars, monoculars, telescopes
Star maps and star charts
Flashlights—cover them with red cellophane (two or three layers of red cellophane from

Continued on next page

cheese wrapping is fine); this avoids people being blinded by the lights.
Warm clothing (It gets cold out there at night!)

What to Look for

Moon: If the moon is out, you can see craters and other features very well through binoculars. Also, children can speculate on the cause of the moon's current phase—have them try to visualize where the sun just set.

Planets: Check local papers or science periodicals for listings of which planets are visible. Show children how to find this information for themselves. Planets most likely to be seen are Mars, Jupiter, and Saturn. (You can see Venus in the early morning.) You can see the moons around Jupiter with binoculars; there may be two, three, or four moons lined up around the planet. The rings of Saturn are visible with low-powered telescopes. How can you tell a planet from a star? (1) Planets are brighter than the stars in the area. (2) Planets tend to "glow" rather than "twinkle." (3) Planets are on an imaginary line that connects the position of the moon with the position where the sun set (called the **ecliptic**).

Stars: Observe differences in stars—differences in brightness and differences in color (white, blue-white, blue, yellow, green, and red).

Constellations in the Northern Sky:
- *Big Dipper* (forms part of *Ursa Major*)—This is an open cluster of five stars. *Mizar* (second star in the handle) is a double star; you can see two stars instead of one if you look slightly *away* from the star. The two stars in the front of the bowl of the *Big Dipper* point toward the *North Star.*
- *Little Dipper* (forms most of *Ursa Minor*)—The star at the tip of its handle is the *North Star* (also called *Polaris*).
- *Cassiopeia,* the Ethiopian Queen, is shaped like a *W.*
- *Cepheus,* the Ethiopian King, is shaped like a hat.

Prominent Late Autumn and Early Winter Constellations:
- *Orion,* the Hunter, is a very prominent constellation. Look for three bright stars lined up in a row and somewhat inclined to the horizon. These are *Orion's belt.* One of the shoulders is a red star named *Betelgeuse* (pronounced *beetlejuice*) and is a red giant. Orion contains the *Great Nebula of Orion,* a cloud of gas in the process of coming together to form new stars. It appears as the middle star in *Orion's sword,* but this middle star isn't a star at all—it is the nebula. The nebula is dramatic to look at with binoculars or a small telescope.
- *Canis Major* (Big Dog) follows Orion around the sky and contains *Sirius,* the brightest star in the sky.

Other Constellations Visible during Each Season in the Northern Hemisphere:

Autumn	*Andromeda,* Daughter of Cephus and Cassiopeia	*Saggita,* the Arrow
	Pegasus, the Winged Horse	*Cygnus,* the Swan
		Pisces, the Fish

Continued on next page

Winter	*Aries*, the Ram	*Auriga*, the Charioteer
	Perseus, Son of Zeus	*Taurus*, the Bull
	Triangulum, the Triangle	
Spring	*Cancer*, the Crab	*Leo*, the Lion
	Virgo, the Virgin	
Summer	*Boötes*, the Herdsman	*Corona Borealis*, the Northern Crown
	Hercules, the strong man of the Heavens	*Lyra*, the Harp
	Ophiuchus, the Serpent Hunter	*Scorpius*, the Scorpion
	Serpens Caput, the Serpent's Head	*Serpens Cauda*, the Serpent's Tail

 All constellations in the sky are listed on a very thorough Web site that can be accessed through a direct link on the Student Book Companion Web Site. Descriptions, major characteristics, prominent features, and the mythological basis for each constellation are provided on direct internal links.

The best months to view prominent constellations in the Northern Hemisphere can be found at the Washburn (Wisconsin) Observatory Web site. See the Student Book Companion Web Site for a direct link.

Literature Connections

The Night of the Stars by Douglas Gutiérrez and María Oliver (Kane Miller, 1988). A Native American man did not like the darkness of night, so he stood on the mountaintop and poked a hole into the dark sky. He continued poking holes until little sparks of light were visible, creating the beginning of our stars and moon.

Boat Ride with Lillian Two Blossom by Patricia Polacco (Philomel Books, 1988). A Native American woman takes two children on a boat ride in the sky. She explains how the appearance of the sky changes because of magical spirits.

Marcella and the Moon by Laura Jan Coats (Macmillan, 1986). Marcella paints the moon as it goes through its phases.

Conclusion

There is an "emerging consensus among psychologists, science educators, philosophers of science, and others that learners (including scientists) must construct and reconstruct their own meanings about how the world works" (Good, Wandersee, & St. Julien, 1993, p. 74). Yager (1993) wrote that "constructivist teaching is now offered by many as a way of reforming science education. Basic to this view of learning is the idea that each learner must construct meaning for him- or herself" (p. 146). Teachers of elementary science must encourage children to construct their own meanings of scientific concepts, develop their own understandings of the uses and nature of the processes, and apply science to their lives in ways that are meaningful to them, the children. Teachers of elementary science also must understand the intellectual limitations and advantages available to children as they progress through the stages of cognitive development. Combining intellectual capability with individual construction will ensure a meaningful science program—one that will meet the goals and objectives of science education.

In an address to the Holmes Group in 1987, Judith Lanier, then dean of the College of Education at Michigan State University, said:

> Competent teachers jump into the heads of their students to see how they are constructing information . . . Competent teachers combine content knowledge with a flexible and creative mind, constructing and reconstructing subject matter in multiple ways as they teach the children. They get inside the children's heads. They listen to them. They remain alert to *students'* interpretations and the ways *they* are making sense.

This is the essence of constructivism.

<small>CHAPTER **4**</small>

Additional Questions for Discussion

1. Discuss the significance of the quotation that opens this chapter: "The most important factor influencing learning is what the learner already knows."

2. Discuss ways in which your prior beliefs have influenced what you learned or were unable to learn.

3. In Chapter 1, the point was made that our beliefs about science and about teaching science, together with our metaphoric perspective of teaching, exert a strong influence on how we approach teaching elementary science. Discuss this proposition in terms of constructivist theory.

Internet Activities

Many references on the Internet deal with constructivism in education and the other topics discussed in this chapter, such as dinosaurs, astronomy, crystals, and the like. Use the search engines to find additional information about these topics. Compare this information with the investigations you have made in this chapter.

Look up brain-based learning and brain physiology research on the Internet to find the results of current brain research and their implications for education.

Note

1. I am indebted to Dr. Russell Yeany, former dean of the College of Education, University of Georgia, Athens, for summary material presented at a symposium on constructivist teaching of science, Georgia Academy of Science annual meeting, April 1993.

CHAPTER········5
INQUIRY

He who wishes to teach us a truth should not tell it to us, but simply suggest it with a brief gesture, a gesture which starts an ideal trajectory in the air along which we glide until we find ourselves at the feet of the new truth.

José Ortega y Gasset, "Preliminary Meditation," *Meditations on Quixote* (New York: Norton, 1961) (Original work published 1914)

In the first four chapters, you explored a number of concepts related to teaching science to young children. You examined the concept of scientific products versus scientific processes as the primary goal of elementary science education, and you considered the proposition that there is very little in the way of scientific facts, concepts, theories, and laws that *all* elementary children must know. You considered using those products of science that are of interest and relevance to children as vehicles for teaching the processes. You explored the suggestion that it is better for children to understand *how* science is done than it is for children to know the results of what has been done by others—that it is better for children to *do* science and be able to pose and investigate their own questions than it is to verify the results that have been concluded by others.

You also examined the constructivist view of learning, which suggests that children learn only by constructing their own conceptualizations—that they must make their own meaningful connections between what they already know and the new information they encounter. You considered the notion that the responsibility of the teacher is that of a facilitator of learning rather than an imparter of information. Now, the question arises of how to accomplish these goals.

In this chapter, you will construct your understanding of the *process-oriented guided inquiry* methodology of science teaching. You will examine a continuum of teaching strategies based on the relative amounts of student and teacher centeredness. You will focus on the process-oriented inquiry approach to science teaching, which enables children to learn how to *do* science rather than learning *about* science. You will investigate a lesson plan format that is appropriate for process-oriented inquiry lessons, and you will practice using this lesson plan format by teaching each other in the form of microteaching. Finally, you will explore ways to tell whether learning is taking place.

THE EXPOSITORY-DISCOVERY CONTINUUM

Many teaching methodologies have been described by various educators. Competent teachers develop an ever-expanding repertoire of teaching techniques that they can draw on as they make decisions about which techniques are most appropriate for the situation at hand. These methodological decisions are based on the nature of the material to be studied; the personality of the teacher; the age, capabilities, interests, and prior experiences of the children; and many other factors. No *single* method meets the needs of *all* children.

Teaching methodologies can be arranged on the basis of the relative amounts of teacher and learner contribution to the learning situation. Consider the continuum shown in Figure 5.1.

This continuum represents a succession of teaching methodologies from a hypothetical, totally teacher-dominated, **expository** methodology on the left to a hypothetical, totally student-dominated, **free discovery** methodology on the right. Any given lesson can be located somewhere on this continuum, depending on the relative degree of expository and discovery activities that are included.

At the left end of the continuum (no political analogy implied) is the expository methodology. Expository teaching is centered on the teacher as the controller of the class and the imparter of knowledge. The teacher does the work, and the student, who may or may not be engaged in the learning, is supposed to absorb the information. The most characteristic activity of the expository methodology is the lecture.

At the right end of the continuum is the free discovery methodology. Free discovery is characterized by children exploring subjects of their own interest in ways that are most comfortable to them. The teacher is the facilitator, and students are engaged in a variety of activities, such as investigating, experimenting, reading, writing, discussing, and other ways of exploring.

Somewhere near the center of the continuum, about halfway between the expository and the free discovery modes, is a broad band representing the **guided inquiry** methodology. In guided inquiry, teachers facilitate

Expository–free discovery continuum of teaching methodologies

EXPOSITORY	GUIDED INQUIRY	FREE DISCOVERY
(Teacher-Directed)		(Learner-Directed)

FIGURE 5.1

children in their investigations of teacher-established topics in ways that are comfortable for the children and that also stimulate children to ask and investigate additional questions suggested by the original explorations.

Expository Methodology

Expository teaching is teacher-dominated. The teacher decides what is to be taught. The teacher lectures, provides notes, shows videos, explains charts, solves sample problems, shows material on the Internet, provides PowerPoint presentations, demonstrates laboratory exercises, reads stories, and so on. All these activities focus on the teacher. What the teacher says is what is to be learned; the teacher is the source and the owner of the knowledge. The students may or may not be involved cognitively, and the teacher has no way of knowing except to stop and ask children to summarize as they would when reading a story—and even then, the understandings internalized by the children may not be apparent.

NSES Teaching Standard B. Guiding and Facilitating Learning NSES Professional Development Standard B. Integrating Knowledge of Science, Learning, Pedagogy, and Students

The expository methodology has its place in science education. You may need to present new information to the entire class as background for upcoming studies. You may desire to demonstrate an activity before setting children to work on their own. When giving directions, you will need to have the attention of all the children. You will need the attention of the whole class when you list specific safety precautions, cite rules for field trips, or give directions. Explanations of certain scientific concepts, such as nuclear energy, atomic theory, and cellular structure, may be handled best in an expository mode with the whole class. Certain scientific procedures, such as working with certain chemicals or using expensive equipment, also are best illustrated through demonstration. Lesson summaries and closures often are best accomplished in an expository mode. Other advantages of expository teaching include efficient dissemination of information, uniformity of presentation, and clear development of the topic.

However, expository teaching has serious disadvantages, including the uncertain degree of attention of the children, lack of tailoring the lesson to the needs of each child, inability of children to follow the flow of the lesson at the same pace, and potential lack of relevance of the material to children's lives. Jerome Bruner has argued that expository teaching has "two major weaknesses: (1) It makes the learner passive, and (2) the knowledge presented is inert" (Eggen & Kauchak, 1994, p. 411). He cited several additional disadvantages to expository teaching, including the following:

1. Expository teaching leads to overdependence on the teacher.

2. Children learn only what the teacher presents.

3. Expository teaching results in reduced ability to use the material and the thinking processes outside the classroom.

Free Discovery Methodology

NSES Teaching
Standard A. Inquiry-
Based Program
NSES Professional De-
velopment Standard B.
Integrating Knowledge
of Science, Learning,
Pedagogy, and Students

The free discovery methodology is located at the extreme right of the expository–free discovery continuum. The activity entitled "Batteries and Electricity" described at the beginning of Chapter 4 is a free discovery activity. The following activity is described to help you gain a better idea of what free discovery is like.

NSES Content
Standard D. Earth
and Space Science:
Structure of the Earth
System
NSES Professional
Development
Standard A. Learning
Content Through Inquiry

SAND

In this activity, students have samples of sand from three different locations in the Kingdom of Saudi Arabia (see Figure 5.2). One sample came from the far reaches of the Rub' al Khali (or Empty Quarter). The Rub' al Khali occupies the southcentral portion of the Arabian Peninsula; nearly the size of Texas, it is the largest continuous expanse of sand in the world (Lebkicher, Rentz, & Steineke, 1960, p. 275). Sand mountains in the Rub' al Khali are several hundred meters high, rising out of salt flats that are nearly at sea level. The temperatures in the Rub' al Khali soar to over 140°F in the daytime in summer and sink to as low as 25°F at night in winter (Nawwab, Speers, & Hoye, 1980, pp. 114, 240).

The sand from the Rub' al Khali is very fine, like the sand in hourglass egg timers, and is reddish orange in color, like rust or ground cinnamon. This sand is uniform in consistency.

The second kind of sand is ordinary beach sand that comes from the dunes near the beaches on the Arabian Gulf. The dunes were formed from the accumulation of windblown sand. This sand is yellowish white in color, contains a few impurities, and is much coarser than the Rub' al Khali sand, with grains two to three times larger.

The third kind of sand comes from a region near the Arabian Gulf called Al-Uqair. This region is thought to include the remains of the ancient city of Gerrah, described by Strabo and other ancient Greeks as being at the crossroads of ancient trade in Arabia and containing buildings whose "doors, walls, and roofs are variegated with inlaid ivory, gold, silver, and precious stones" (Bibby, 1970, p. 318). Geoffrey Bibby, a Danish archaeologist, concentrated his exploratory efforts for several seasons on locating and identifying this ancient city, and he came to the conclusion that circumstantial evidence at Al-Uqair (coupled with the lack of evidence at other sites) indicated that this site may, indeed, be the ruins of the ancient city. Nothing remains at the site except assemblages of potsherds and ancient irrigation ditches. The sand that comes from this area is a little deeper yellow than the beach sand and contains very fine, dark-gray flecks that, curiously, always remain at the top

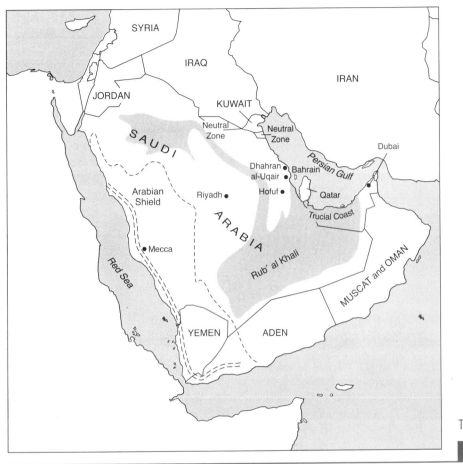

The Arabian Peninsula

FIGURE 5.2

of the sand no matter how thoroughly one tries to stir them in. Its grains are uniform and about the same size as the beach sand.

In a free discovery activity, groups of elementary science methods students are asked to explore samples of each of the three kinds of sand in any way they wish. After 15 to 20 minutes, during which time I have circulated and asked questions to help people focus their inquiries, groups are asked to share what they found out. Descriptions of the sand samples are among the first discoveries shared: color, texture, grain size, impurities, and so on. Then groups get into deeper questions, such as "Why is the red sand red?" "Why does the beach sand look like it has been bleached?" "What are those dark flecks mixed in with the Gerrah sand?"

Finally, I pose the question "If you had sufficient funds, time, and equipment at your disposal, what would your next step in your investigation be?" Some say they would like to subject the sands to chemical analyses to find their origins and the reason for the different colors. Others would like to have large sandboxes of each of the three kinds to see what it is like to walk on it and to try to find out why camels can walk on sand so easily. Others want to study the history of the ancient town of Gerrah. One group wanted to investigate what it must have been like to have lived in the time Gerrah was inhabited. For these students, the concept of sand sparked an interest in the integrated studies of social studies and the Middle East. Still others wanted to study the geology of the region and correlate it with the origins of the sand. Once in a while, a group has the courage to say their next step would involve anything *except* sand!

This is an example of a free discovery activity. The only factor keeping it from the extreme right side of the continuum is the fact that the general topic (sand) was suggested by the teacher.

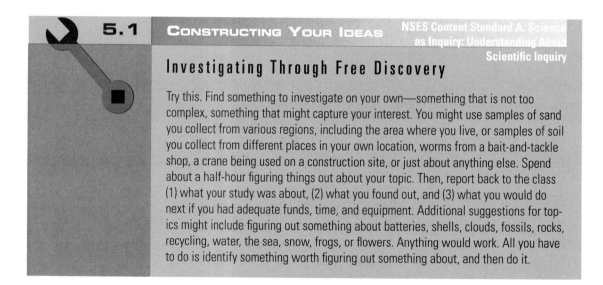

5.1   **CONSTRUCTING YOUR IDEAS**   NSES Content Standard A: Science as Inquiry: Understanding About Scientific Inquiry

Investigating Through Free Discovery

Try this. Find something to investigate on your own—something that is not too complex, something that might capture your interest. You might use samples of sand you collect from various regions, including the area where you live, or samples of soil you collect from different places in your own location, worms from a bait-and-tackle shop, a crane being used on a construction site, or just about anything else. Spend about a half-hour figuring things out about your topic. Then, report back to the class (1) what your study was about, (2) what you found out, and (3) what you would do next if you had adequate funds, time, and equipment. Additional suggestions for topics might include figuring out something about batteries, shells, clouds, fossils, rocks, recycling, water, the sea, snow, frogs, or flowers. Anything would work. All you have to do is identify something worth figuring out something about, and then do it.

REACTIONS TO FREE DISCOVERY

Reflect on how you felt about doing this activity. Did it leave you excited? Interested? Disinterested? Empowered? Free? Frustrated? Confused? Directionless?

Discuss your feelings as a class.

In free discovery, children decide what is important for them to learn. They set up their individual and unique learning activities to explore the topics they have chosen; they devise and explore their own inquiry situations; and they go to the reference books, the Internet, other electronic and digital resources, magazines, peers, parents, friends, and other sources of information to see what has been learned before. The teacher acts as a resource and coinquirer. The students are deeply involved cognitively.

Bruner (1965) urged involving students as active inquirers in the material they are learning. In discovery, children inquire into scientific phenomena, figuring things out for themselves. This, according to Bruner, is the route to meaningful learning. "Mastery of the fundamental ideas of a field involves not only the grasping of general principles, but also the development of an attitude toward learning and inquiry, toward guessing and hunches, toward the possibility of solving problems on one's own" (p. 20).

The primary advantages of the free discovery teaching methodology include the facilitation of the constructivist paradigm, the cognitive engagement of all children (for they will not be studying something that does not interest them), the opportunity for children to develop process skills, and the meaningfulness of the material learned.

Free discovery also has disadvantages. Chief among the criticisms are that discovery learning does not provide enough structure, can lead to frustration in the beginning as children wean themselves from dependence on the teacher, reduces the teacher's control of content, and requires additional materials and equipment. However, Dean and Kuhn (2007) found that whereas direct instruction may be capable of producing high levels of achievement, the achievement results are not sustained for more than 12 weeks and that discovery-based instruction produces longer-lasting results. Free discovery also may present management problems; when this methodology is used, it is possible for each child in the classroom to be studying something different at the same time. You may have felt some of these disadvantages yourself as you were doing a free discovery activity. Chapter 14 is devoted to a discussion of implementing the free discovery methodology in elementary school science.

Guided Inquiry Methodology

The guided inquiry methodology is located at the middle of the continuum. Guided inquiry combines the teacher focus of the expository methodology with the child focus of the free discovery methodology. In guided inquiry, the teacher selects the topic and sets the direction. The children ask questions that, in turn, set new directions. The teacher suggests open-ended activities that the children pursue to find out what they are able to, inquire into what they don't understand, and develop their own conclusions as they construct their own conceptualizations. The children check

NSES Teaching Standard B. Guiding and Facilitating Learning NSES Professional Development Standard B. Integrating Knowledge of Science, Learning, Pedagogy, and Students NSES Program Standard B. Relevant, Inquiry-Based, and Connected with Other Subjects their conclusions to see if they have explanatory and predictive power and whether they have used all the input from others that is available. If so, they discuss them with one another and with the teacher to confirm validity. If validity cannot be confirmed, they embark on further investigation to develop revised conclusions and reconstructed conceptualizations. Children's investigations include hands-on explorations and such resources as reference materials, textbooks, other print material, videos, CD-ROMs, the Internet, other electronic and digital resources, professional people, and other resources that will help them investigate the challenge thoroughly. The activities suggested in this text are developed in the constructivist guided inquiry methodology.

Guided inquiry involves learning by doing. The teacher serves as guide (not director), resource person, and coinquirer. The teacher selects the topic, introduces the unit and the lessons, and provides structure for the investigations. The teacher develops the initial activity. The teacher asks questions and helps the students in their *own* endeavors, *not* the teacher's endeavors. The teacher *listens*—seeking to understand what the student is saying. The teacher probes by asking more questions, some of which are leading questions and some of which are intended to help the teacher find out the children's thinking. The classroom is hands-on and laboratory in focus, and it typically features small groups of children working together. Students work to construct meanings and discover concepts that are new to them.

Avila (1998), a first-grade teacher, says that the most successful learning is the learning that results from what the children themselves decide to investigate. She writes, "Educators have to wait until the children's questions . . . tell the teacher what the students need to know and learn," and she notes that these questions often come "while the students are 'messing around' with stuff" (p. 14). Everett and Moyer (2007) suggest that teachers "inquirize" their teaching by turning demonstrations into inquiry activities using the 5E learning cycle model:

Explore whether the activity addresses a question that can be investigated.

Engage students by having them actually do the activity and formulate their conclusions.

Explain using small-group and whole-class discussions of student observations and conclusions together with teacher input.

Extend and apply the principles to other situations.

Evaluate through performance assessments.

In the beginning of a lesson, the teacher may provide a high degree of guidance, but as the lesson proceeds, the teacher works toward reducing the teacher-centered focus and increasing the student-centered focus.

The teacher provides both opportunity and fun, radiating the enthusiasm of a coinquirer.

The guided inquiry teaching methodology encourages children to construct their own conceptualizations while exposing them to the content suggested for their grade or level. It allows children to pursue given topics in depth and to ask and investigate their own questions. Studies have shown that students who are taught science in a hands-on, inquiry-based manner during elementary school develop such lifelong science literacy skills as independent thinking, critical thinking, and problem solving (Colburn, 2004; Science Emphasized, 2004). Guided inquiry provides enough structure to eliminate the feeling of "wandering" that children may get in free discovery approaches. Children are given the parameters in which to *start* their inquiries and such necessary constraints as time, group size, materials, and so on. The class is manageable, and the content of the curriculum is covered. Guided inquiry uses an inquiry constructivist approach in which science content is used as a vehicle for mastery of the processes. (See Chapter 13 for a discussion of the role of content curriculum in constructivist inquiry science).

Problem-based learning (PBL) has become a very popular teaching methodology and can be viewed as a form of guided inquiry. In problem-based learning, the teacher (often in conjunction with the students) selects a problem to be studied. The problem can be developed by the teacher to incorporate as much of the required curriculum as possible, or it can be suggested by the students without consideration of the prescribed curriculum. Problem-based learning provides students with real-life problems that form the basis and directions of their explorations. Problems might include studying and recommending how the school cafeteria can support better nutrition, studying body systems in order to recommend procedures for reducing accidents on the playground, developing museum-style exhibits of local Native American cultural artifacts, and studying and recommending safe ways of disposing of toxic waste (DeRoche, 2006). In the problem-based learning methodology, the teacher finds out what the students already know and what they want to learn before developing the problem statement. Individuals or groups of students present their findings to the class, and their achievement is assessed authentically.

Direct links to several university-based PBL Web sites are available on the Student Book Companion Web Site.

In the constructivist approach to learning, the teacher plays an integral role in fostering children's investigations. In response to a concern that teachers feel they might become invisible in a constructivist environment, Chrenka (2001) discusses the essential role of the teacher in constructivist learning. She writes, "Constructivism suggests that teachers need to help students become active inquirers, who, when they fail to find the meaning they seek, do not give up hope, but conclude that they have not looked in the right place. It is the teacher's job to help students see that there are an infinite number of 'right places'" (p. 695).

Despite all its advantages, the guided inquiry methodology also has disadvantages. Pierce (2001) suggests several:

- Inquiry may take more time than is allowed for science.
- When children develop their own questions, the questions do not necessarily relate to the required curriculum.
- Teachers may be uncomfortable responding to all questions posed by children.
- Teachers may feel unprepared to help children with difficult questions because of their perceived lack of background knowledge.
- Teachers may be more comfortable with greater classroom structure than the freedom suggested by open-ended inquiry.

Hayes (2002) found that inquiry teaching made the students in his pre-service elementary science methods class "ill at ease with taking themselves out of an authoritarian role in the classroom and working towards a position that afforded them an opportunity to work with students and develop their interests" (p. 161). He identified three major areas of concern:

1. Letting go
2. Going with students' interests
3. Asking the right questions

Education students (and, for that matter, all college students) have become accustomed to expository methods of instruction. Many students have not participated in a constructivist, inquiry-based classroom—or even seen it modeled—so they tend to teach in the way that they were taught (Alesandrini & Larson, 2002; Pringle, 2006). Therefore, education students need to move a little at a time from their beliefs in the merits of expository teaching to developing an understanding of the merits of guided inquiry teaching. This must be done slowly to give time to reconstruct prior conceptualizations about science teaching. Only by testing the waters and finding them safe will they build the trust that is prerequisite to successful constructivist approaches to teaching and learning science.

The same is true of children in the elementary and middle school grades. They may not be familiar with working and learning within the constructivist approach, and they may need to move slowly from expository to inquiry types of activities. Starting children out with a few activities that are between expository and guided inquiry in approach will help provide the children the practice needed to be successful at inquiry approaches and will gain their trust. The teacher initially sets up the situations and the problems. Later, the students set up their own problem situations. In the beginning, the teacher provides a high degree of structure, but as the class proceeds, the teacher is able to reduce the structure in the activities. (See Chapter 9 for suggestions on developing a safe classroom environment for guided inquiry.) Ultimately, the teacher poses a question or problem and then starts the exploration and questioning technique, letting the children decide the direction of the inquiry. The numerous activities presented in this book give you and the children the opportunity to move safely toward the guided inquiry area of the continuum.

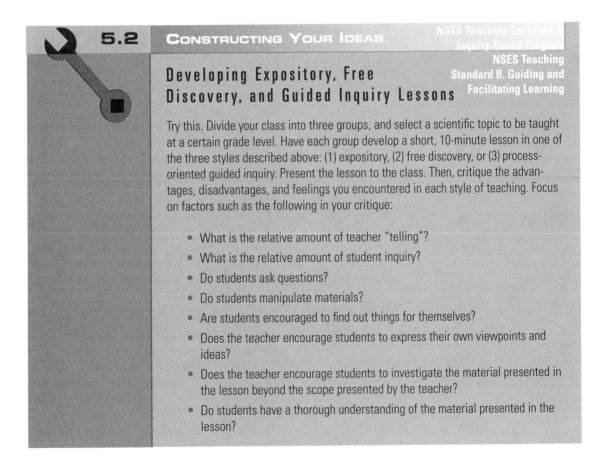

5.2   CONSTRUCTING YOUR IDEAS

NSES Teaching Standard A. Inquiry-Based Program

NSES Teaching Standard B. Guiding and Facilitating Learning

Developing Expository, Free Discovery, and Guided Inquiry Lessons

Try this. Divide your class into three groups, and select a scientific topic to be taught at a certain grade level. Have each group develop a short, 10-minute lesson in one of the three styles described above: (1) expository, (2) free discovery, or (3) process-oriented guided inquiry. Present the lesson to the class. Then, critique the advantages, disadvantages, and feelings you encountered in each style of teaching. Focus on factors such as the following in your critique:

- What is the relative amount of teacher "telling"?
- What is the relative amount of student inquiry?
- Do students ask questions?
- Do students manipulate materials?
- Are students encouraged to find out things for themselves?
- Does the teacher encourage students to express their own viewpoints and ideas?
- Does the teacher encourage students to investigate the material presented in the lesson beyond the scope presented by the teacher?
- Do students have a thorough understanding of the material presented in the lesson?

Process-Oriented Inquiry

Guided inquiry uses an inquiry-based, constructivist approach in which science content is used as a vehicle for mastery of the processes of science. Thus, this methodology can be termed the **process-oriented inquiry**

NSES Teaching
Standard B. Guiding and
Facilitating Learning
NSES Professional De-
velopment Standard B.
Integrating Knowledge
of Science, Learning,
Pedagogy, and Students
NSES Program
Standard B. Relevant,
Inquiry-Based, and
Connected with Other
Subjects

methodology. In process-oriented inquiry, the teacher focuses on helping children gain skill in one or more processes of science by using scientific concepts in guided inquiry experiences. This methodology "involves combining the use of science processes with knowledge of science content in an effort to develop new science knowledge" (Misiti, 2001, p. 38). However, we understand (as shown in Chapter 2) that "often the greatest value of testing a hypothesis is the potential for finding a factor that does *not* cause an expected change to occur" (Misiti, 2001, p. 39; italics added).

As science teachers, our goal is "to expose children to the scientific processes and to the thrill of discovery" (Bollman, Rodgers, & Mauller, 2001, p. 686). The process-oriented inquiry methodology enables teachers to achieve this goal, thereby teaching children how to do science.

Ausubel's Instructional Model

NSES Professional De-
velopment Standard B.
Integrating Knowledge
of Science, Learning,
Pedagogy, and Students

Ausubel (1968) said that for learning to be meaningful and, therefore, lasting, it must fit in with previous information taught in the class. Thus, in all instructional methodologies, the teacher must link new information with the previously taught information such that children are able to make the proper connections. Ausubel specified three stages of instruction to ensure the proper connections: (1) advance organizer, (2) progressive differentiation, and (3) integrative reconciliation.

The Ausubelian stages often are associated with expository learning. However, for any lesson to be effective, regardless of methodological orientation, it must have an advance organizer, be logically sequenced, possess appropriate content, and encourage children to make valid connections to the material previously taught.

Stage 1: Advance Organizer

Learning is facilitated when students are supplied with an appropriate frame of reference so new information can be related to information the students already possess. Ausubel called this frame of reference the **advance organizer.** Before starting a lesson of any sort (whether it is a new unit or a new lesson in an ongoing unit), the teacher must provide an advance organizer. The advance organizer serves to introduce children to the new unit or to briefly review prior material when continuing an ongoing unit. It provides an overview, shows the children what to expect, and summarizes all aspects of the unit or the lesson in advance. It sets the stage. It provides focus and direction, and it captures children's interest.

A typical advance organizer for a new unit might include an initial interest-provoking activity or discrepant event followed by a general discussion of what the unit entails, the unit's goals and objectives, and how children will get involved. For a new lesson in an ongoing unit, a typical advance organizer would remind children of previous material and would show how the current lesson is connected to prior information.

As I observe student teachers, one of the most prevalent weaknesses I see is the lack of advance organizers. The student teacher often starts a lesson as though the children already know what that lesson is all about. This is natural, because the teacher has been planning and thinking about this lesson for a long time. But, of course, the children do not know what it is all about, so the teacher has to introduce it. Advance organizers do not have to take very long; they can be as short as a few seconds: "You remember that yesterday we measured the temperature of glasses of water as they sat in the room. Well, today we are going to add ice to the water and see what happens to the temperature." The advance organizer can be a chart or a concept map portraying the scope of the unit; the teacher can refer to this visual portrayal at the beginning of each lesson, reminding children of earlier lessons and showing them how the new lesson fits in with the whole. (See Chapter 12 for ways of using concept maps as advance organizers.)

THE KALEIDOSCOPE

A student teacher assigned to a sixth-grade class wrote *kaleidoscope* on the board and asked the children to pronounce the word. Without comment on the correctness of their pronunciations, she proceeded to pass out inexpensive toy kaleidoscopes to pairs of children and asked them to look through them and record words that described what they saw. She wrote the responses of all pairs of children on chart paper in the front of the room. Children recorded words like "diamonds," "shapes," "triangles," "brilliant," "jewels," and "crystals." Next, she read aloud the poem "Kaleidoscope," from *Small Poems Again* by Valerie Worth (Farrar, Straus & Giroux, 1986), to show that the poem contains many of the same words they had written on their charts and to show the relevance of poetry to daily observations. Although this was an advance organizer for a unit on poetry, it would be ideal to introduce a unit on light, mirrors, and images.

Stage 2: Progressive Differentiation

Having set the tone of the lesson or the unit in the advance organizer, the next consideration is to isolate each item of information or skill so that it can be connected with previously learned information. This stage is called **progressive differentiation.** The key to effective progressive differentiation is to be sure that the lesson moves in a logical manner, making certain that all concepts necessary for understanding are included. The material is progressively differentiated.

Properly differentiated lessons flow smoothly. However, when material is not progressively differentiated properly, confusion and misunderstanding may result. This may occur when the teacher is giving directions for an activity and inadvertently leaves out a key component. For example, the teacher might be explaining to the class how to construct paper turkeys. She shows children how to attach paper feathers to a cutout turkey but forgets to tell the children to cut out the feathers. This results in confusion and the necessity of stopping the class to provide the missing directions. Techniques that help prevent this problem include advance practice, putting yourself in the shoes of the children in your class, and if necessary, preparing and referring to 3" × 5" note cards listing all components of the directions (or the lesson).

Often, the reason why lessons fail is that some necessary component is left out (Okey & Gagné, 1970). Proper attention to the progressive differentiation stage of Ausubel's model in developing lesson plans will help to prevent lesson failure because critical material has been omitted. Concept mapping is of great assistance in ensuring proper progressive differentiation of lessons (see Chapter 12).

Stage 3: Integrative Reconciliation

Having set the stage, and having progressed from the most general to the most specific in a manner that encourages children to make meaningful connections, the teacher now must be sure that the children have constructed the material effectively. To do this, the teacher helps each child reconcile the new material with previously taught material and with the child's own experiential bank. This stage is called **integrative reconciliation.** Integrative reconciliation helps children understand similarities and differences among components of the lesson or the unit. This stage also alerts the teacher to inconsistencies in children's thinking processes, enabling her to help the children reconcile these discrepancies.

NSES Teaching Standard B. Guiding and Facilitating Learning
NSES Teaching Standard F. Participating in Program Planning
NSES Professional Development Standard B. Integrating Knowledge of Science, Learning, Pedagogy, and Students

The Expository-Discovery Continuum Revisited

By now, you have discovered that lessons do not easily fit a precise location on the expository–free discovery continuum. All lessons require a certain amount of expository treatment: Directions have to be given, introductions and advance organizers have to be provided, large group discussions may be needed, and lessons have to be concluded. A certain amount of free discovery also is inherent in lessons where children are asked to formulate their own questions and develop their own procedures for obtaining and validating their own conclusions. It should not be difficult, however, to assess the relative amounts of expository, guided inquiry, and free discovery methodologies used in the lesson and, from this reflection and assessment, place a lesson on the continuum. It is to be expected that the beginning elementary science teacher will have many lessons to the left of center and that as experience and confidence are gained, the lessons will move slowly toward the right, until almost all the lessons of the experienced teacher center on the guided inquiry band.

The National Research Council (NRC) (2000) lists five essential features of classroom inquiry (p. 29):

1. Learner engages in scientifically oriented questions.

2. Learner gives priority to *evidence* in responding to questions.

3. Learner formulates *explanations* from evidence.

4. Learner connects explanations to scientific knowledge.

5. Learner communicates and justifies explanations.

The NRC expanded each essential feature into a continuum that shows variations of how the feature is seen in classrooms ranging from a high amount of teacher direction (on the right) to a high degree of learner self-direction (on the left). (Note that this orientation is in the opposite direction of the orientation shown on the expository-free discovery continuum.) This very important chart is shown in Figure 5.3. The chart suggests that children's conclusions and explanations should be based on evidence; this is part and parcel of the nature of science (see Chapter 2). The evidence must be supplied and can take any of a number of forms, including talking and writing, repetition of the activity, and drawings. Even students in the early elementary grades can and should be required to provide the evidence that supports their explanations (Folsom et al, 2007).

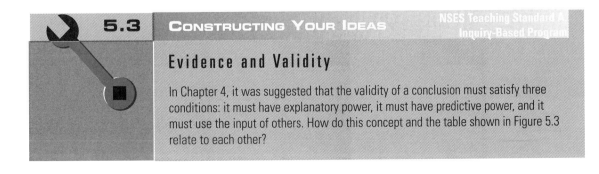

5.3 **CONSTRUCTING YOUR IDEAS**

NSES Teaching Standard A, Inquiry-Based Program

Evidence and Validity

In Chapter 4, it was suggested that the validity of a conclusion must satisfy three conditions: it must have explanatory power, it must have predictive power, and it must use the input of others. How do this concept and the table shown in Figure 5.3 relate to each other?

Essential Features of Classroom Inquiry and Their Variations

Essential Feature	Variations			
More ←——————— Amount of Learner Self-Direction ———————→ Less Less ←——————— Amount of Direction from Teacher or Material ———————→ More				
1. **Learner engages in scientifically oriented questions**	Learner poses a question	Learner selects among questions, poses new questions	Learner sharpens or clarifies question provided by teacher, materials, or other source	Learner engages in question provided by teacher, materials, or other sources
2. **Learner gives priority to** *evidence* **in responding to questions**	Learner determines what constitutes evidence and collects it	Learner directed to collect certain data	Learner given data and asked to analyze	Learner given data and told how to analyze
3. **Learner formulates** *explanations* **from evidence**	Learner formulates explanation after summarizing evidence	Learner guided in process of formulating explanations from evidence	Learner given possible ways to use evidence to formulate explanations	Learner provided with evidence
4. **Learner connects explanations to scientific knowledge**	Learner independently examines other resources and forms links to explanations	Learner directed toward areas and sources of scientific knowledge	Learner given possible connections	
5. **Learner communicates and justifies explanations**	Learner forms reasonable and logical argument to communicate explanations	Learner coached in development of communication	Learner provided broad guidelines to sharpen communication	Learner given steps and procedures for communication

Essential features of classroom inquiry and their variations

FIGURE 5.3

Figure 5.4 summarizes the characteristics of constructivist teaching and inquiry. It provides descriptors of constructivist teaching using the guided inquiry methodology. You investigated some of these descriptors when you critiqued the lessons you prepared in expository, free discovery, and guided inquiry styles in Constructing Your Ideas 5.2. You also saw some of these in Chapter 4 and in Figure 5.3. During the early stages of your lesson preparation and delivery, especially in your field experiences, you should use this list to check your own teaching.

Inquiry Works

Inquiry works (Bransford, Brown, & Cocking, 1999). The National Science Teachers Association (2004) urges all teachers from preschool through high school to embrace and use inquiry as "the centerpiece of the science classroom" (p. 1).

NSES Program Standard B: Relevant, Inquiry-Based, and Connected with Other Subjects

However, teachers seem reluctant to practice this proven approach. Researchers are beginning to investigate why this is so. In a study of college science professors, Brown *et al.* (2006) found that the professors rec-

---

DESCRIPTORS OF PERFORMANCE

1. Adequate planning; process-oriented goals
2. Relates lesson to processes more than products
3. Planning shows logical development of processes and concepts
4. Provides for hands-on learning: students handle materials
5. Asks open-ended, inquiry-oriented questions
6. Encourages children to ask questions
7. Encourages children to initiate ideas
8. Encourages children to investigate their own questions and ideas
9. Uses children's questions and responses to develop topic
10. Encourages the use of many sources of information, including printed material, multimedia, and people
11. Avoids supplying answers or explanations
12. Encourages children to suggest causes for what they observe
13. Encourages children to discuss and challenge each other's conceptualizations
14. Encourages children to reflect
15. Responds to individual needs
16. Relates topics to children's lives

Overall Location of Lesson on Expository / Free Discovery Continuum:

X——X——X——X——X——X——X——X——X——X——X
Expository   Guided Inquiry   Free Discovery

Descriptors of constructivist guided inquiry teaching performance

FIGURE 5.4

ognized both the benefits and the constraints of inquiry-based instruction but did not employ inquiry because they thought "inquiry" implied that the class was totally student-driven, with little or no input from the professors. Schwarz and Guekwerere (2006) found that modeling guided inquiry in elementary and middle school science methods classes resulted in the preservice teachers moving away from the familiar didactic instructional methodology to inquiry approaches.

I hope this textbook and the course in which you are using it is giving you confidence to teach science in a constructivist, exploratory, inquiry manner. You are learning in this manner, so you should be well equipped to teach this way.

5.4 CONSTRUCTING YOUR IDEAS   NSES Professional Development Standard C. Lifelong Learning

Philosophy and Metaphor Revisited

Compare the thoughts you now have about teaching science with the philosophy you wrote and the metaphor you chose in Chapter 1. What are the similarities? What are the differences?

TEACHER VOICE

In this age of high-stakes testing, tight standards, and science core curriculum, is it possible for teachers to implement constructivism? As educators, we know that the most meaningful learning takes place when students are interested in specific topics, make inquiries about them, or initiate learning experiences themselves. I am a fifth-grade teacher in a Title I school with a high rate of poverty, a high level of free and reduced lunches, and an extremely low level of parental involvement in school and their children's schoolwork. To address constructivist learning, I set my students on a course of action that was to enable all students to have individual, meaningful learning experiences in science—a student-oriented science fair held in my classroom. The science fair dealt with questions the students posed—not what the parents wanted. It was limited to my class. It was focused on the processes of science, not outcomes.

To find the time to implement this in my classroom when I hardly had enough time to teach everything that is required as it is, I had to let go of control of the students' learning. I put the students in the driver seats of their learning, and they worked on this project with minimal guidance from me. They were essentially on their own as they explored and investigated. This was especially true because they could expect to get little or no help at home.

It required four to five half-hour class periods for them to get their projects started. During these class periods, I taught the scientific processes using student-centered science activities. Then, I had students formulate the questions they would like to learn more about. This part took the longest, because students previously never had been given the opportunity to truly decide what they want to learn more about. There was a wide variety of questions, but I met with each student individually to develop a question he or she could realistically inquire about. While meeting with individual students, the rest of the class was meeting in groups and brainstorming questions that interested them. After all the students had developed their questions, I devoted two more class periods to helping them work out the mechanics of the science activities they planned to carry out as they sought answers to their questions. They completed the actual project work at home. I provided guidance in the mornings or during downtimes throughout the day for students who requested additional help.

The students were very creative in the questions they sought to answer; examples included the following:

1. Does a mouse go after piece of cheese it can smell? Or one it can see?

2. Which liquid discolors teeth the most?

3. Which brand of toy car is the fastest: Dollar Store® Brand? Hot Wheels®? Or Motor Max®?

4. Which sense is stronger: taste or smell?

5. Does air pressure affect the bounce of a basketball?

During the time the students were working on their own, many came to me to ask questions about their projects. I never had to remind them to continue working on their project. They knew what they had to do, and they did it. Each day, at least one student brought up the science project in class with such comments as "Guess what happened last night?" Or, "Guess what I tried because I heard you say that?" I really enjoyed hearing my students give these types of statements, and they allowed more "teachable moments" than I could have dreamed of. Their dedication and inquiries were truly amazing and really motivating to me as a teacher.

After the projects were completed, my students were so excited about what they had done they wanted to share their presentations with the whole school. I organized an in-class science fair and invited all the other students in second through fifth grades to visit. It was then that I realized my ultimate teachable moment. I told my students they had done just about everything themselves, and they could do science on their own whenever and wherever they wanted to. They could use me for guidance but, ultimately, they are the scientists with the questions they are investigating.

The most difficult aspect I encountered in this project for me as a teacher was releasing control of the students. I had to rely on the students actually doing their projects on their own. I should have felt more at ease because, of course they are going to work on their projects because they chose their topics themselves. I was truly impressed with my students' creativity and ingenuity in carrying out their in-class science fair projects.

Peter Manson

Fifth-Grade Teacher
Brown Elementary School
Cobb County School System
Marietta, Georgia

THE GUIDED INQUIRY LESSON PLAN

NSES Teaching Standard A. Inquiry-Based Program
NSES Professional Development Standard B. Integrating Knowledge of Science, Learning, Pedagogy, and Students

All well-developed lessons require planning, and the process-oriented inquiry methodology is no exception. Lesson plans guide the teacher in introducing and developing the lesson and provide some well-reasoned questions and initial direction. Good lesson planning helps the teacher focus on the objectives and intended outcomes of the lesson. Indeed, process-oriented inquiry lessons require extensive planning, because the teacher must anticipate as-yet unknown questions, contingencies, and paths of exploration that might emerge as each child works to develop his or her own personal constructions.

Figure 5.5 shows a recommended format for process-oriented inquiry lesson planning.

It is essential that you develop a lesson plan for each lesson you teach, using the lesson plan format shown in Figure 5.5 or one similar to it. One may argue that the process-oriented inquiry methodology encourages children to follow directions suggested by their own interests and, thus, it is impossible to write plans for every conceivable inquiry, including those that haven't even been thought of. However, the statement "All roads lead to Rome" comes to mind. In guided inquiry, children begin at a common starting point, and they work to develop self-constructed understandings

LESSON PLAN FORMAT FOR PROCESS-ORIENTED GUIDED-INQUIRY ELEMENTARY SCIENCE LESSONS

1. Targeted age or grade level
2. Scientific processes addressed
3. Science topic addressed

4. Process-oriented objective
5. What I want children to discover
6. Description of introductory activity and initial discussion

7. Materials needed

8. Description of activities
9. Typical discussion questions
10. How children will be encouraged to investigate on their own in the classroom

11. Expected conclusions

12. Assessment

13. Applications to real-life situations

---

1. Self-explanatory

2. One or more of the processes of science that serve as the focus of the lesson

3. The science topic that will be used as the vehicle for exploring the processes on which the lesson focuses. Appropriate content standard(s) from *National Science Education Standards*, state and local standards, or objectives prescribed by the school district should be referenced.

4. One or more objectives written according to the process-oriented guidelines provided in Chapter 3

5. The scientific information children should be able to articulate as a result of the lesson

6. Details about how you will introduce the lesson. This should contain the Ausubelian advance organizer as well as details concerning a demonstration or other interest-focusing activity, the initial discussion, the directions, and safety and management considerations appropriate for the lesson.

7. A list of equipment, materials, and available print, multimedia, electronic communications, and people resources together with materials needed for extensions and variations of the activity you anticipate children will want to explore. The list of materials is an integral part of the lesson plan; it enables you to assemble all necessary materials each time you do the lesson without having to search through the entire lesson plan to figure out what you will need.

8. Details of what the children will do to explore the concept and what you will do to help them in their explorations

9. Typical questions you will ask of groups to stimulate their thinking toward the objective

10. What children might do to continue the investigation in greater depth, exploring additional variations and related topics, and keeping the explorations going as they investigate the phenomenon fully. These continued explorations can be part of the current lesson, can be held over for the next class session, or could occur in a science learning center.

11. The goals and objectives you want the children to achieve and some conclusions you anticipate they might formulate as a result of their investigations

12. The way(s) you will use to find what children have learned as a result of this lesson

13. Answer to the question, "So what?" Many times, well-meaning teachers ask children to do activities that have little or no application to their daily lives. If an activity or lesson cannot be applied to children's daily lives, the lesson lacks meaning. Thus, this section of the lesson plan ensures meaningfulness of the lesson to the children.

FIGURE 5.5

of common concepts. Individuals may take different paths, but in guided inquiry, they start and end at the same place.

You will investigate methods of assessment (lesson plan item 12) in Chapter 8.

Many school districts prescribe specific curricula and content objectives for their elementary science programs. You should use these guidelines to decide on the content you will use as the vehicle for the inquiry activities. Coupling the required content with one or more processes enables you to arrive at the process-oriented objective. For example, if the third-grade curriculum calls for the study of simple machines, you may want to approach the study of levers (a simple machine) through the process of formulating and testing hypotheses. In this case, the process-oriented objective might be "The student will formulate and test hypotheses concerning the relationship between the distance an object is located from the fulcrum in different kinds of levers and the effort needed to move the weight." In this way, children learn both process and content.

Carefully prepared lesson plans help keep the focus on the objectives—or, if you will, the destination—while concurrently enabling you to follow the thought processes and various inquiry routes of the children. Two lesson plans developed according to the preceding guidelines are shown in Constructing Science in the Classroom 5.1 and 5.2.

5.1 **CONSTRUCTING SCIENCE IN THE CLASSROOM**

SPACE SNACKS

Process-Oriented Guided Inquiry Science Lesson Plan

NSES Content Standard F. Science in Personal and Social Perspectives: Science and Technology in Local Challenges

1. *Targeted age or grade level:* Preschool to grade 2

2. *Scientific processes addressed:* Observing, measuring, inferring

3. *Science topic addressed:* Science and technology (National Science Education Content Standard F. Science in Personal and Social Perspectives: Science and Technology in Local Challenges)

4. *Process-oriented objective:* The student will observe and measure crumbs resulting from eating snacks and will infer characteristics most appropriate for food to be eaten in space.

5. *What I want children to discover:* Children should discover that some snacks result in more crumbs than others and that the most appropriate foods for eating in space are those with the fewest crumbs and least waste.

6. *Description of introductory activity and initial discussion:*

   a. Show a short video that portrays the gravity-free environment of a spaceship.

Continued on next page

b. Pose the question "What do you suppose astronauts eat in space?"

c. Would they eat cookies? Why do you think so? Ask the same questions about crackers, apples, bananas, and potato chips. Use children's responses and input to extend the conversation.

d. Pose another question: "What would happen to the crumbs if astronauts were to eat a cracker?"

7. *Materials needed:*

Snack foods (cookies, crackers, potato chips, marshmallows, and M&M's®)

White paper napkins

8. *Description of activities:* First, find out if anyone is allergic to any of the snack foods being offered. If someone is allergic, ask that child to omit that food from the activity and to observe what others find out instead. Provide each child with one of each kind of snack. Children take a small bite of one snack over a white napkin. They use a different napkin for each snack, put the remainder of the snack piece on the napkin, and then put it to one side while they taste each snack. They then examine each napkin and make a judgment as to the quantity of crumbs that fell. If desired, they can develop a system for measuring the amount of crumbs left behind, such as estimating the number of crumbs, counting them, comparing their sizes, or arranging the napkins in order of which ones have the most crumbs so that children can identify the "crumbiness" of each snack. The specific method used by children will emerge during the lesson. Finally, children infer which of these snacks is/are best for space travel and provide reasons for their responses.

9. *Typical discussion questions:*

- Which snacks made the most crumbs?
- Which snacks made the fewest crumbs?
- Which snacks would you recommend that astronauts take with them to space? Why?
- What other foods could astronauts eat?
- What foods should astronauts *not* take with them? Why?
- Which snacks would make it uncomfortable in your bed if you were to eat them in bed?

10. *How children will be encouraged to investigate on their own in the classroom:* Napkins will be available, and children will be encouraged to make assessments of the "crumbiness" of different snacks they eat at school.

11. *Expected conclusions:* The potato chip will produce the most crumbs, followed by the cracker, the cookie, the M&M's®, and the marshmallow.

12. *Assessment:* I will assess children's achievement in this lesson by observing the ways they measure the "crumbiness" of each snack and by listening to the evidence they use to make their inferences.

Continued on next page

13. *Applications to real-life situations:* Some foods produce more crumbs than others. Whereas we, on earth, don't have to worry about crumbs floating in our air, we do have to be careful of making messes.

(This lesson is adapted from a presentation made at the National Science Teachers Association Southeast Conference in 1996 by Ms. Julie Stacy, a graduate student in education at Kennesaw State University.)

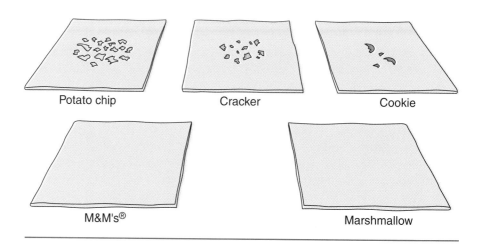

Potato chip   Cracker   Cookie

M&M's®   Marshmallow

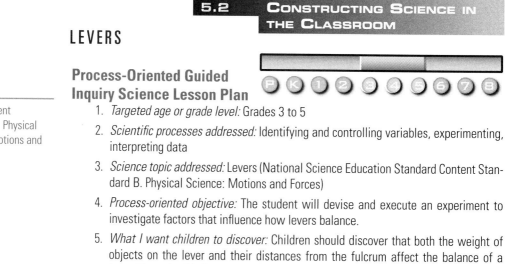

5.2 **CONSTRUCTING SCIENCE IN THE CLASSROOM**

LEVERS

Process-Oriented Guided Inquiry Science Lesson Plan

P K 1 2 3 4 5 6 7 8

NSES Content Standard B. Physical Science: Motions and Forces

1. *Targeted age or grade level:* Grades 3 to 5

2. *Scientific processes addressed:* Identifying and controlling variables, experimenting, interpreting data

3. *Science topic addressed:* Levers (National Science Education Standard Content Standard B. Physical Science: Motions and Forces)

4. *Process-oriented objective:* The student will devise and execute an experiment to investigate factors that influence how levers balance.

5. *What I want children to discover:* Children should discover that both the weight of objects on the lever and their distances from the fulcrum affect the balance of a lever. They should discover that the greater the weight, the shorter the distance it

Continued on next page

needs to be from the fulcrum, and that the less the weight, the further from the fulcrum it needs to be to achieve balance.

6. *Description of introductory activity and initial discussion:*

   a. I will introduce children to the concept of simple machines and the names of five simple machines (inclined plane, wheel and axle, lever, pulley, and wedge). We will discuss, as a class, how we use these machines in everyday life.

   b. I will reinforce this discussion through the book *The Mighty Lever,* an InfoTrek™ Leveled Reader (ETA/Cuisinaire, 2000), which is a nonfiction book about what levers are, what they are used for, and where we can find them being used. Then, I will read the beginning of *Levers* by Caroline Rush (Raintree Steck-Vaughn, 1996), which introduces the concept of the lever and suggests activities that children can do to explore them. I will also show children the book *Levers* by Sally Walker and Roseann Feldman (Lerner, 2001) which can be used as a resource in their investigations.

   c. We will discuss how children can balance on teeter-totters. If it is not raining, we will go outside to the playground and fool around with different children balancing on the teeter-totters.

   d. Finally, I will provide a demonstration of the lever activity we will be doing in groups in the class. I will also introduce the term *fulcrum.*

7. *Materials needed:*

   a. Cereal boxes

   b. 10–20 pennies per group

   c. Scotch® tape

   d. Plastic 12-inch ruler

   e. Data sheet (see "Data Sheet for Levers Experiment" at the end of this lesson)

   f. Wedge-shaped wooden block (alternative to cereal boxes)

   g. Books:

   > *The Mighty Lever,* an InfoTrek™ Leveled Reader (ETA/Cuisinaire, 2000)
   >
   > *Levers* by Caroline Rush (Raintree Steck-Vaughn, 1996)
   >
   > *Levers* by Sally Walker and Roseann Feldman (Lerner, 2001)

8. *Description of activities:*

   a. Cut part of a folded edge of a cereal box, and bend it in the shape of a triangle to make a wedge. Secure this to the desk with Scotch tape. (Use a wedge-shaped wooden block as an alternative.)

   b. Place the ruler on the wedge until it balances.

   c. Record the inch mark where the ruler balances, or use a second ruler to measure the distances from the fulcrum.

   d. Place one penny at a certain distance on the ruler one side of the fulcrum. Place a second penny on the ruler on the other side of the fulcrum, moving it back and

Continued on next page

forth until the ruler is level. On the data sheet, record the distances of both pennies (measuring from the centers of the pennies to the fulcrum).

   e. Try different distances from the fulcrum, recording the number of pennies and their distances on the data sheet.

   f. Try different numbers of pennies, stacked on top of each other, recording number of pennies and distances.

   g. Try changing the location of the fulcrum.

   h. Try balancing other things, such as pencils, stones, and the like.

9. *Typical discussion questions:*

   a. How far away from the fulcrum are the pennies on each side when there is only one penny on each side?

   b. How far away from the fulcrum are the pennies on each side when there is more than one penny on each side?

   c. Could you weigh a stone using the lever?

   d. How can the lever help us move things?

10. *How children will be encouraged to investigate on their own in the classroom:* I will put rulers, wedges, coins, stones, and other things in the science center for children to use as they continue their explorations.

11. *Expected conclusions:* Children should discover that there is a relationship between weight and distance as levers are balanced.

Data Sheet for Levers Experiment

Mark where the pennies are, and mark the measured distance (D) between the *center* of the pennies (or pile of pennies) and the fulcrum.

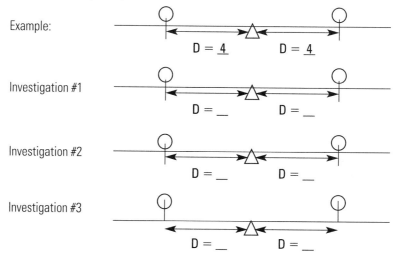

Continued on next page

12. *Assessment:* Observe experimental process; assess completeness of data tables and validity of data interpretations.

13. *Applications to real-life situations:* Balancing is seen in teeter-totters, double-pan balances, and many other common items. Levers are used to help us do work and can be found in many applications around the home, construction sites, and other places.

Microteaching

Microteaching involves presenting a short lesson to a small group of colleagues. Microteaching is "a technique that affords both beginning and advanced opportunities to *plan* and *practice* a wide array of new instructional strategies" (Orlich et al., 1990, p. 169). The *micro* in microteaching can refer to the lesson, which is considerably reduced in scope and length, and to the student peers, who typically are few in number.

Much has been written about the value of microteaching in preparing preservice teachers. Detractors argue that the technique is not sufficiently similar to actual classroom teaching to be valuable. However, research shows that microteaching is "an effective way to have students in methods classes plan, teach, and evaluate a lesson presented to a small group of their peers" (Pauline, 1993, p. 9). Students consistently report that microteaching is a valuable component of their methods experiences. Kilic and Cakan (2007) showed that when preservice teachers taught a science topic to their peers, the peer assessment scores of the teaching correlated significantly with the instructor assessment scores (albeit considerably higher) and met the test of reliability.

The constructivist paradigm of education and the process-oriented inquiry methodology for teaching elementary science are relatively new to education students. Thus, you should try out the methodology among yourselves. You already have done some peer microteaching when you availed yourselves of the opportunities to teach microlessons centered on the processes of science in Chapter 3 and when you taught lessons using different methodologies in Constructing Your Ideas 5.2. Microteaching that uses the process-oriented inquiry methodology should involve teaching a short lesson of about 15 minutes in duration to a small group of 8 to 10 peers. The teaching student prepares the lesson in accordance with the lesson plan format shown in Figure 5.5 and has all the materials available. The teaching student teaches the lesson to the group, which takes the intellectual role (but not the behavioral characteristics) of children of the age and grade for which the lesson is appropriate. At the end, the peers critique the lesson. Because nondirected peer critique is difficult and, often, is less than candid, use the descriptors in Figure 5.4 for

NSES Teaching Standard B. Guiding and Facilitating Learning
NSES Teaching Standard C. Assessing Teaching and Learning
NSES Professional Development Standard B. Integrating Knowledge of Science, Learning, Pedagogy, and Students

the critique. Ultimately, the lesson can be located at some point on the expository–free discovery continuum. Some guided inquiry activities are more teacher-guided than open, and they are located toward the left end of the continuum. Some are more open than guided, and they are located to the right of center.

In addition to peer critique, you should videotape your lesson so that you can critique yourself. Studies show that videotaping is extremely valuable in helping teachers refine their techniques.

The personal critique of the microteaching of the lesson on levers detailed in Constructing Science in the Classroom 5.2 is shown in Constructing Science in the Classroom 5.3.

5.3   **CONSTRUCTING SCIENCE IN THE CLASSROOM**

CRITIQUE OF MICROTEACHING LESSON ON LEVERS

NSES Teaching Standard C. Assessing Teaching and Learning

The "students" enjoyed the books on levers. However, they had difficulty, forming fulcrums out of the cereal boxes. Next time, I would use wedge-shaped blocks of wood. (I have included this option in the final lesson plan.) The students really got into balancing different numbers of pennies at different distances from the fulcrum. They were eager to try different things later on in the science center. I believe that the students were able to come to the conclusions about how weight and distance affect balancing levers on their own as a result of doing the experimenting in this lesson. Their data seemed complete given the time restrictions on this lesson, and their interpretation of the data seemed valid.

I had difficulty completing the lesson in the time allotted, and I believe I rushed the students instead of giving them time to explore.

My peers said they enjoyed the lesson. They felt it was truly guided inquiry in nature, even though I had to rush.

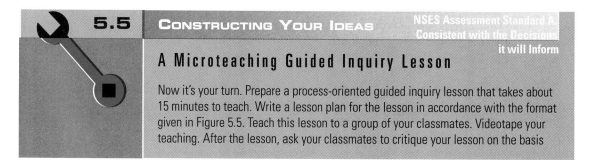

5.5   **CONSTRUCTING YOUR IDEAS**   NSES Assessment Standard A. Consistent with the Decisions it will Inform

A Microteaching Guided Inquiry Lesson

Now it's your turn. Prepare a process-oriented guided inquiry lesson that takes about 15 minutes to teach. Write a lesson plan for the lesson in accordance with the format given in Figure 5.5. Teach this lesson to a group of your classmates. Videotape your teaching. After the lesson, ask your classmates to critique your lesson on the basis

Continued on next page

of the inquiry descriptors presented in Figure 5.4, and ask them to assess where on the expository–free discovery continuum your lesson would be placed *as you taught it.* Then, in private, watch the videotape, and reflect on your recorded performance, the feedback from your group, and your own awareness of what went on during the lesson. From your reflections, develop an honest critique of your lesson. (Remember that a critique contains strengths as well as areas that need additional work.) Finally, rewrite the lesson plan to reflect changes you would make as a result of the critique.

IS LEARNING TAKING PLACE?

The primary goal of all education is for children to learn. Unfortunately, many well-intentioned learning activities do not necessarily produce this result. In this section, we will investigate the question of whether learning is taking place.

NSES Professional Development Standard B. Integrating Knowledge of Science, Learning, Pedagogy, and Students

Is Hands-On Minds-On?

We often hear the phrase "hands-on, minds-on." Is it true that hands-on activities ensure that minds are "on"—that learning is taking place? The National Science Teachers Association (2007) recommends that preschool, elementary, and middle school students should have multiple opportunities every week to participate in hands-on exploratory science activities.

Let us set up a "hands-on, minds-on" grid (see Figure 5.6). *Hands-on* is the degree of manipulation of materials and equipment and can refer to virtual manipulation as well as to the use of physical materials (Klahr, Triona, & Williams, 2007); *minds-on* is the degree of cognitive engagement. For purposes of the grid, *hands-on* is divided into high and low levels of manipulation, and *minds-on* is divided into high and low levels of cognitive engagement. Four cells result.[1]

		LEVEL OF COGNITIVE ENGAGEMENT	
		HIGH	LOW
LEVEL OF MANIPULATION	HIGH	Hands-on Minds-on	Hands-on Minds-off
	LOW	Hands-off Minds-on	Hands-off Minds-off

Hands-on, minds-on grid

FIGURE 5.6

As you can see from the top row of the grid, *hands-on* can be associated with either *minds-on* or *minds-off*. A high level of manipulation does not necessarily produce a high level of cognitive engagement, as can be the case in driving to school or in executing certain "cookbook" laboratory activities. Many traditional science activities require the student to verify what someone else has discovered. Although these activities are hands-on, students can accomplish their goals by following directions without the need for much in the way of real thinking. An example of this is the food test activity described in Chapter 1.

Conversely, looking down the first column, you can see that *minds-on* can be associated with either *hands-on* or *hands-off*. A high level of manipulation is not necessary to produce a high level of cognitive engagement. *Hands-off* could produce *minds-on,* as is the case when children are totally engaged in a fascinating story or video or when the teacher is presenting a captivating demonstration.

Because the idea of education is for learning to occur, we must be certain that children have the highest possible degree of cognitive engagement. Hands-on activities must produce "minds-on" for this to occur. The guided inquiry methodology promotes "minds-on" through "hands-on."

Deductive versus Inductive Teaching Styles

NSES Professional Development Standard B. Integrating Knowledge of Science, Learning, Pedagogy, and Students

Teaching styles can be inductive or deductive (see Figure 5.7). **Inductive teaching** proceeds from the most specific to the most general. For example, children might go outdoors to look for insects but encounter difficulties in observing different kinds of insects against the backgrounds of their natural habitats; this could lead them to form a generalization about camouflage. **Deductive teaching** is the other way around, proceeding from the most general to the most specific. For example, in deductive teaching, the teacher might move from the general concept of living things through the more specific concept of animals to specific varieties of animals as examples of living things.

This book is written largely in an inductive manner. That is to say, specific details are presented for each situation or phenomenon, and you are encouraged to explore the various details before coming to your own conclusion. Any conclusions suggested in this book are presented after the specific instances have been examined.

The activities suggested in this book also are inductive in nature. They are designed for the learner first to explore individual cases and then to form generalizations. For example, during the snowflake activity, in which children capture snowflakes on a piece of cold black paper and observe them with magnifying glasses and a microscope, children are asked to observe several snowflakes before they make conclusions about the variety of snowflake shapes (In The Schools 4.3). In the pendulum activity suggested in Chapter 3 (Constructing Your Ideas 3.14), you were asked to list and explore many variables before coming to a conclusion.

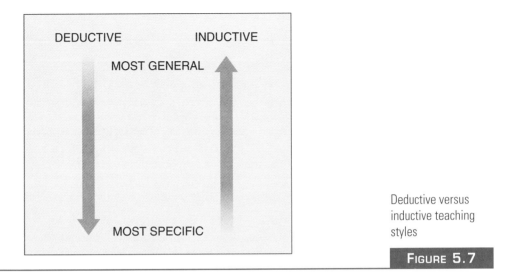

Deductive versus
inductive teaching
styles

FIGURE 5.7

Who Owns the Knowledge?

Kamii (1984) observed that "teachers do not often encourage children to think autonomously. Instead, they frequently use sanctions to prod children to give 'correct' answers . . . As early as first grade, many children have learned to distrust their own thinking. Children who are thus discouraged from thinking autonomously will construct less knowledge than children who are mentally active and confident" (p. 413).

It is obvious that we must teach in a way that fosters children's thinking and, thus, their ownership of the knowledge they construct. You investigated children's ownership of knowledge in Chapter 1. In The Schools 5.1 describes an activity that shows a way of fostering their ownership of knowledge.

NSES Professional Development Standard B. Integrating Knowledge of Science, Learning, Pedagogy, and Students

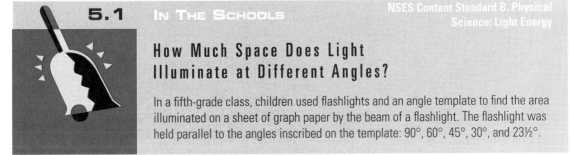

5.1   IN THE SCHOOLS

NSES Content Standard B. Physical Science: Light Energy

How Much Space Does Light Illuminate at Different Angles?

In a fifth-grade class, children used flashlights and an angle template to find the area illuminated on a sheet of graph paper by the beam of a flashlight. The flashlight was held parallel to the angles inscribed on the template: 90°, 60°, 45°, 30°, and 23½°.

Continued on next page

Children traced the area of illumination at each angle with different-colored pens and counted the number of squares. They found that the greater the angle from the vertical, the greater the area of illumination (see Figure 5.8). They also found that as the area of illumination increased, the intensity of the light over that area decreased. Applied to the revolution of the earth around the sun, this phenomenon explains the causes of seasons. As the angle of the earth's axis changes relative to its plane of revolution, any given latitude receives its solar energy at different angles from the sun, resulting in different intensities of solar radiation.

 The template used for this investigation is available on the Student Book Companion Web Site.

Literature Connection

The Greenhouse Effect by Rebecca Johnson (Learner, 1990) is a nonfiction book that presents a balanced approach to this sometimes-controversial topic.

How much space does light illuminate at different angles?

FIGURE 5.8

A DIFFERENT KIND OF BLOOM

Benjamin Bloom (Bloom et al., 1956) developed the taxonomy of the cognitive domain that all education students have studied. In 2001, a group of cognitive psychologists led by Lorin Anderson (a student of Bloom's) updated the taxonomy to make it more relevant to the 21st century. Several revisions were made:

1. The six cognitive categories were changed from noun form to verb form.

2. The *knowledge* category was renamed *remembering*.

3. The *comprehension* category was renamed *understanding*.

4. The *synthesis* category was renamed *creating*.

5. The hierarchical order of the two last categories was reversed so that *evaluating* comes before *creating* rather than being the final category.

The two versions of Bloom's taxonomy of the cognitive domain are shown in abbreviated form in Figure 5.9 (Forehand, 2005; Cruz, n.d.; Schultz, n.d.)

NSES Teaching Standard E. Developing Learners Who Reflect Intellectual Rigor and Attitudes Conducive to Science Learning
NSES Professional Development Standard B. Integrating Knowledge of Science, Learning, Pedagogy, and Students

---

BLOOM'S TAXONOMY OF THE COGNITIVE DOMAIN

I. KNOWLEDGE (old)—REMEMBERING (new)
Recall of facts and specific information
Characterized by recognizing, memorizing, remembering

II. COMPREHENSION (old)—UNDERSTANDING (new)
Transforming information; explaining information or concepts
Characterized by interpreting, translating, describing in one's own words

III. APPLICATION (old)—APPLYING (new)
Using information to solve new problems
Characterized by solving problems

IV. ANALYSIS (old)—ANALYZING (new)
Separating the whole of an idea into its component parts
Characterized by subdividing, taking apart thoughts and problems

V. (new hierarchy) EVALUATION (old)—EVALUATING (new)
Defending concepts or ideas
Suggesting well-reasoned decisions on debatable topics
Characterized by resolving differences of opinion

VI. (new hierarchy) SYNTHESIS (old)—CREATING (new)
Combining elements to create new and unique entities
Characterized by creating something new to the individual

Bloom's taxonomy of the cognitive domain

FIGURE 5.9

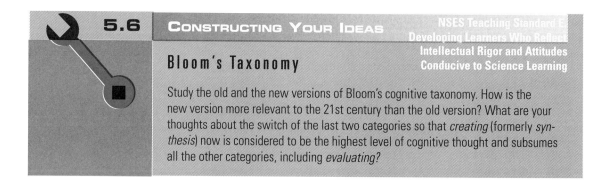

5.6   CONSTRUCTING YOUR IDEAS

Bloom's Taxonomy

Study the old and the new versions of Bloom's cognitive taxonomy. How is the new version more relevant to the 21st century than the old version? What are your thoughts about the switch of the last two categories so that *creating* (formerly *synthesis*) now is considered to be the highest level of cognitive thought and subsumes all the other categories, including *evaluating*?

How do we foster thinking at the higher levels? If we want children to think at higher levels, we must ask higher-level questions. If we want children to develop thinking ability above the levels of recall, knowledge, and comprehension, we must tell them our expectation. We tell children what we expect in several ways. We tell them through the language we use in our objectives by selecting verbs that focus on higher levels of Bloom's taxonomy, higher-order thinking skills, and processes of science rather than on recall of knowledge. For example, the following objective suggests the expectation of higher-level thinking: "The student will devise and execute an experiment to investigate the effect of sunlight on plant growth." On the other hand, the following objective suggests the expectation of lower-level thinking: "The student will name three factors required for plant growth."

We also tell children our expectation for higher levels of thinking through the questions we ask. You began exploring approaches to questioning in Chapter 1. Questioning is an extremely important teaching strategy with potential for stimulating student thinking, gaining understanding of what children are thinking, providing clarification, arousing curiosity, stimulating interest, and motivating students to seek new information. Questions asked by teachers also reflect the depth of thinking that teachers expect of their students. If the nature of the questions involves recall, children will get the idea that recall of factual information is the most important aspect of their learning. On the other hand, if the questions are directed at analyzing, evaluating, and creating, students will get the idea that their thinking must be at these levels. Open-ended questions encourage a greater diversity of responses and depth of thinking than closed questions for which there are a limited number of acceptable responses. Teachers who ask the right kinds of questions "kindle fires of critical thinking to create problem solvers" (Caram & Davis, 2005, p. 20).

The question is often asked whether young children can deal with the higher levels of learning in science. Following are examples of questions about plant growth that can be asked of very young children. These questions encompass the full spectrum of Bloom's taxonomy.

1. Name the parts of a plant. (*remembering*)

2. What part of the plant is this? (teacher points to the stem). How do you know? (*understanding*)

3. What are the leaves on this plant? (Teacher shows a plant children have not studied, such as an evergreen.) (*applying*)

4. If a plant were to lose all its roots, would it be able to live? (*analyzing*)

5. From our experiment, did we show that plants need food, light, and water to live? (*evaluating*)

6a. Suppose you lived on a faraway planet. Draw a plant that would grow on that planet. (*creating*)

6b. What do plants need to live? How would you prove that? (*creating*)

If we want our children to think at higher levels, we must provide wait time. In Chapter 1, you were asked to play a game with remembering-level questioning (Constructing Your Ideas 1.8). In that activity, you recognized that students require a much longer time to formulate their answers to a higher-level question than to a lower-level one. Wait time must be provided for children to organize their thoughts. It has been estimated that it takes five times longer for children to respond to a higher-level question than to a lower-level question. This naturally means that the teacher will be able to ask only one-fifth the number of questions. In her seminal article on wait time in elementary science education, Rowe (1974, 2003) reported that "Teachers allowed students to think an 'average' time of only one second to start an answer to a question. If a response did not commence within one second, teachers usually repeated the question or called on others to respond" (p. S22). She showed that when mean wait times are increased to between 3 and 5 seconds (achieved through teacher training), many students' variables are changed for the better; these variables include the following:

1. Length of student response increases.

2. Number of unsolicited but appropriate responses increases.

3. Failures to respond decrease.

4. Confidence increases.

5. Number of speculative responses increases.

6. Student–student comparisons of information increases.

7. Number of evidence-based responses increases.

8. Number of student-generated questions increases.

Furthermore, "Teachers who have learned to use silence report that children who do not ordinarily say much start talking and usually have exciting ideas" (Rowe, 1996, p. 36).

Teachers want to fill silence in a classroom with talking; silence is awkward and is considered wasteful. Quite to the contrary, silence provides the opportunity for children to formulate their thoughts and construct their responses to challenging questions. Practice waiting for children to respond to questions; after asking a question, count *at least* 5 seconds to yourself before you say anything else.

Other suggestions for fostering higher-order thinking in the classroom include demonstrating that you value all student responses and engaging children in interactions both among themselves and with the teacher.

Shulman (1989) has posited a seventh taxonomic level unique to teachers. To understand this level, we must recognize that Bloom's taxonomic system deals with the *individual* (in this case, the individual teacher). The *individual* is able to (1) remember knowledge, (2) understand it, (3) apply it to new situations, (4) analyze situations involving it, (5) evaluate new situations using it relative to some standard suggested by the student or someone else, and (6) create new material using it. However, teachers not only must be able to work by themselves within all six levels of the taxonomy as they prepare and teach their lessons, but they must be able to know how each of their children is constructing his or her own unique knowledge, understanding, application, analysis, evaluation, and creation of the information. No longer is the taxonomy limited to the individual; with teachers, it is expanded to include the children as well as the teacher. In other words, teachers not only know for themselves the information being taught but also know how the children are constructing it. Teachers must have a vicarious understanding of all six levels of processing for each of the children in their classes. This is most assuredly a level above the most advanced level for individual intellectual development. Shulman has dubbed this very empowering concept the *pedagogical* level.

For a person to be able to think at higher levels, that individual must possess the basic information necessary to do the thinking with. He or she must know the facts, must understand them, and must be able to apply them to different and unique situations. Having that ability with a certain collection of facts, the person can then proceed to analyze, evaluate, and create with them. This thinking must be fostered in the elementary science classroom through stimulating activities, higher-level questioning, and listening to children to understand how they are thinking and constructing information so the teacher can help them in their pursuit of learning.

Conclusion

This chapter has dealt with the process-oriented guided inquiry methodology, which is the agent of constructivist science teaching and is thought to be the most appropriate way of teaching science to elementary children. You have examined the methodology from a number of perspectives, including contrasting it with expository and free discovery methodologies, contrasting inductive and deductive learning, considering the taxonomy of cognitive learning outcomes, and focusing on the primary outcome of ownership of knowledge. The rest is up to you as you construct your own understanding of the methodology.

CHAPTER 5

Additional Questions for Discussion

1. Contrast the expository, guided inquiry, and free discovery methodologies of teaching elementary science with respect to (a) amount of learning likely to occur and (b) amount of prescribed science content likely to be learned.

2. Explain how the guided inquiry methodology fosters the development of scientific

processes and promotes children's constructions and validations of their own conceptualizations.

Internet Activities

Use the Internet to find additional information on discovery learning, inquiry learning, and other instructional methodologies. What does the current trend in education seem to be? Evaluate the arguments given for each of the methodologies described. How is modern pedagogy being applied in non-school settings? Also, find additional information on the revised Bloom's taxonomy of the cognitive domain.

Note

1. I am indebted to Dr. Mike Hale, formerly professor of mathematics and educational technology at the University of Georgia, Athens, for the ideas involved in the hands-on, minds-on grid.

CHAPTER 6

SCIENCE EDUCATION FOR STUDENTS WITH DIVERSE PERSPECTIVES

My father taught me in the wise way which unfolds what lies in the child's nature, as a flower blooms, rather than crammed it, like a Strasburg goose, with more than it could digest.

Louisa May Alcott (1831–1888), in Ednah D. Cheney (Ed.). *Louisa May Alcott: Here Live, Letters, and Journals.* Roberts Brothers, 1889, p. 29.

Children come to our schools with tremendously diverse backgrounds and genetics, bringing their unique capabilities, strengths and limitations, likes and dislikes, cultural environments, and experiential backgrounds with them to their classes. The goal of education in general—and of science education in particular—is that all children learn regardless of their differences. In previous chapters, we have suggested the notion that no two people are alike, that no two people perceive, internalize, process, and construct information the same way. We have suggested that inquiry teaching is the means by which all children are able to construct processes, products, and attitudes of science in unique and valid ways that result in meaningful and lasting learning.

Children are different in multitudinous ways, some of which can be identified and described and some of which cannot. Certain of these differences have been shown to have pronounced influences on achievement and understanding science.

In this chapter, you will investigate differences in the ways children learn, how these differences affect science achievement, and how you can accommodate these differences to maximize the science learning of *all* children. You will refine the inquiry methodology to accommodate these special needs, and you will consider the notion that the process-oriented inquiry methodology of science instruction enables teachers to teach science successfully to *all* children.

SOME DIFFERENCES IN THE WAYS CHILDREN LEARN

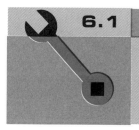

6.1   CONSTRUCTING YOUR IDEAS   NSES Program Standard E. Provides Equal Opportunities for All Students

Listing Individual Differences

Try this. In groups, list as many individual differences among children as you can think of in one minute. Consolidate all the lists into one.

How many different items did you list? Students in classes like yours have listed socioeconomic status, cultural background, facility with the English language, intelligence in each of several areas of intelligence, physical talents and limitations, emotional well-being, prior experiences, home environments, and many more. Indeed, it is safe to observe that there are very few areas of people's lives in which they are not decidedly different from other people.

Let us consider some characteristics that are common to all students, occur in varying degrees in different people, and are directly associated with achievement in science.

NSES Professional Development Standard B. Integrating Knowledge of Science, Learning, Pedagogy, and Students
NSES Program Standard E. Provides Equal Opportunities for All Students

LEARNING MODALITIES

People learn more—and retain it longer—when they learn in a manner that is comfortable to them. A style of learning that is comfortable for one individual, however, may be uncomfortable for someone else. To demonstrate this in a physical sense, do the following activity.

6.2   CONSTRUCTING YOUR IDEAS   NSES Professional Development Standard B. Integrating Knowledge of Science, Learning, Pedagogy, and Students

Which Way Do You Fold Your Hands?

Sit with your body relaxed and your hands folded in your lap or on your desk. Now, unfold your hands and refold them the other way—so the other thumb is on top.

One way was much more comfortable than the other, wasn't it? Yet, about half the class experienced comfort in one of the two ways of folding hands, and the other half experienced comfort in the other way. The same can be done for crossing legs, folding arms, and choosing which ear you bring the telephone to. These are personal preferences. Similarly, people have strong personal preferences in the way they learn.

Visual, Auditory, and Tactile/Kinesthetic Learning Modalities

People take in and process information in three fundamental ways termed modalities: **visual, auditory,** and **tactile/kinesthetic.** Visual learners learn best by seeing; auditory learners learn best by hearing; and tactile/kinesthetic learners learn best by touching, feeling, and moving. For each individual, one of these learning modalities is stronger than the other two, although the other modalities also are functional.

An individual's predominant learning **modality** is as comfortable to that individual as right- or left-handedness. It has been shown that people function primarily in one of the three modalities as they learn. The younger the children, the more likely they are to learn best through the tactile or kinesthetic modalities; fewer than 12 percent of elementary-age children are auditory learners and fewer than 40 percent are visual learners (Dunn, 2001). The older children become, the more their auditory and visual modalities develop. Thus, early childhood teachers should engage children in manipulating real materials as much as possible. It also has been shown that achievement is fostered by being taught in a compatible modality (Dunn, 1988; Ebeling, 2000). Teachers need to understand the way people think in each of the modalities to be better prepared to provide meaningful science experiences in all three modalities. But, you must be careful not to stereotype certain learning styles as being associated with particular cultural groups; all cultural groups have accommodated all the learning styles for thousands of years (McKinley, 2007).

Because people learn and process information in different modalities, and because is not always possible to tell which modality is the strongest for each child in a given classroom, it follows that we must teach in such a manner that all the modalities are accommodated. This is not difficult to accomplish.

Visual Learners

Visual learners learn best by using visual stimuli—by seeing what they are to learn. Thus, visual learners remember pictures, graphs, charts, and illustrations. They remember where on a page a certain passage of text or a certain illustration occurs. They remember locations, positions, and visual observations. Activities utilizing the strengths of the visual learner might include observing and classifying pictures showing different seasons, diagramming sound waves, drawing series and parallel circuit **schematics,** describing characteristics of rocks and minerals, and setting up bulletin boards or displays that show the results of experiments with plants.

The following is an activity intended primarily to support visual learners. Other learning modalities also are included. Can you tell where?

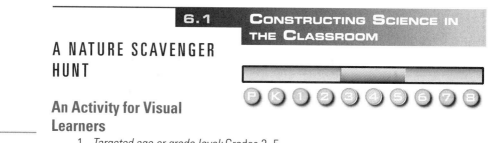

A NATURE SCAVENGER HUNT

An Activity for Visual Learners

NSES Content
Standard C. Life
Science: Populations
and Ecosystems

1. *Targeted age or grade level:* Grades 3–5

2. *Scientific process addressed:* Observing

3. *Science topic addressed:* Ecology

4. *Process-oriented objective:* The student will observe things found in nature.

5. *What I want children to discover:* Children should discover that there are many different things in outdoor natural locations.

6. *Description of introductory activity and initial discussion:* Put photographs and posters of natural habitats around the room. Ask children to describe what they see. Tell children they will be going on a nature hike around the school building to observe things in their natural setting. Children should look for items like flowers, seeds, seedpods, birds' nests, different kinds of leaves, animals, insects, and other things. Have them keep a log and draw pictures to record their observations. Discuss the importance of not disturbing the natural environment. **Safety note:** Caution children not to touch insects. Describe or show pictures of poison ivy, poison oak, and other poisonous plants in your area they might encounter, and instruct the children not to touch them.

   Share the books *Birds Build Nests* by Yvonne Winer and *All About Frogs* by Jim Arnosky. *Birds Build Nests* is a nonfiction picture book that shows varied habitats in which different bird species build their unique nests. *All About Frogs* provides factual information about frogs and their environments and contains many colorful and detailed illustrations.

7. *Materials needed:*

   Book: *All About Frogs* by Jim Arnosky (Scholastic, 2002)

   Book: *Birds Build Nests* by Yvonne Winer (Charlesbridge, 2002)

   Posters and/or photographs of natural habitats

   Pictures of poison ivy, poison oak, and other local poisonous plants

   Paper

Continued on next page

Pencils

Notebooks or clipboards

8. *Description of activities:* Bring children outdoors to observe natural areas. Children record and/or draw what they see. The teacher facilitates the excursion, interacting with the children, pointing out things the children may not have noticed, assembling the children to see things others have seen, and providing help as needed.

9. *Typical discussion questions:*

Can you name that (items seen by children)?

Where is it located?

What else is near it?

Why do you suppose these things are together?

What are the similarities (of things seen)?

What are differences (among groups of similar things, such as insects and leaves)?

10. *How children will be encouraged to investigate on their own in the classroom:* It may not be possible for children to go outdoors at will to continue their observations; however, they can continue to make observations while on the playground and at other times when they are outdoors. Children also can be encouraged to make similar observations elsewhere, such as at home, at recreational parks, and other places they frequent, and to compare these observations with those made during this activity.

11. *Expected conclusions:* Children should come to the conclusion that there are many different plants and animals in the outdoors and that they all contribute to the health of the area.

12. *Assessment:* Assessment will be based on the completeness and accuracy of the logs the children keep.

13. *Applications to real-life situations:* The assemblage of plants and animals in a given location is an **ecosystem.** Everything in an ecosystem is needed for it to survive. Great care must be taken when disturbing an ecosystem to be sure it survives. This includes making a garden, removing trees, paving new roads, and performing other actions that involve natural settings.

Auditory Learners

Auditory learners learn best by using sound stimuli—by hearing what they are to learn. They remember the voice of the person who explained something. They remember the tone of voice of the teacher and of the members of their group. They remember what they heard during activities. Activities utilizing the strengths of the auditory learner might include experimenting with sound, presenting his or her group's classifications system to the class, writing rap or hip hop songs that set explanations of concepts to music, engaging in creative writing activities about the sounds of weather, and investigating how animal sounds aid in their adaptation to their environments.

The following is an activity intended primarily to support auditory learners. Other learning modalities also are included. Can you tell where?

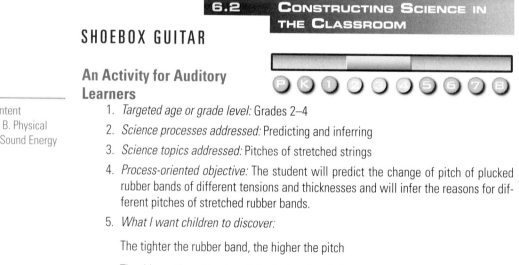

| 6.2 | CONSTRUCTING SCIENCE IN THE CLASSROOM |

SHOEBOX GUITAR

An Activity for Auditory Learners

NSES Content Standard B. Physical Science: Sound Energy

1. *Targeted age or grade level:* Grades 2–4

2. *Science processes addressed:* Predicting and inferring

3. *Science topics addressed:* Pitches of stretched strings

4. *Process-oriented objective:* The student will predict the change of pitch of plucked rubber bands of different tensions and thicknesses and will infer the reasons for different pitches of stretched rubber bands.

5. *What I want children to discover:*

   The tighter the rubber band, the higher the pitch

   The thinner the rubber band, the higher the pitch

6. *Description of introductory activity and initial discussion:* First, discuss behavior and safety rules, especially the proper use of rubber bands. Then, give rubber bands to groups of children, and ask them to stretch one of them and pluck it so they can hear the sound it makes. Show them a shoebox guitar you have made in advance. Tell them they will use the shoebox guitar to magnify the sounds of plucked rubber bands so they can hear them. Using the shoebox guitar, they will inquire into the effects that tension and thickness have on the pitch of the sound. Finally, they will arrange the shoebox guitar so they can play a tune.

7. *Materials needed:*

   Long rubber bands with several different thicknesses

   Shoeboxes with covers

   Cardboard "bridges" fashioned out of empty cereal boxes

   Glue

Continued on next page

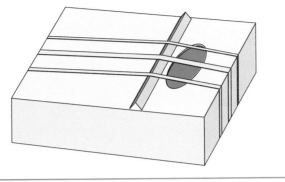

A shoebox guitar

FIGURE 6.1

8. *Description of activities:* First, children make a shoebox guitar patterned after the one you made previously. Children cut a hole in the top of the shoebox near one end. They fold a panel of an empty cereal box into the shape of a wedge that is as long as the width of the shoebox. This "bridge" should be glued to the surface of the shoebox that has the hole, just slightly forward of the hole on the long side. They then string three or four rubber bands, some thick and some thin, lengthwise over the shoebox and bridge (see Figure 6.1). They pluck the rubber bands, and compare the pitches they make. They also change the tension of different rubber bands at different places, pluck them, and compare their pitches.

9. *Typical discussion questions:*

    What is the sound like when you pluck the thin rubber bands?

    What is the sound like when you pluck the thick rubber bands?

    What happens to the pitch when you increase the tension on the long part? On the short part? On the part where you are plucking? On the part where you are not plucking?

    Can you arrange the rubber bands so you can play a tune?

10. *How children will be encouraged to investigate on their own in the classroom:* Children can try different rubber bands, try adding rubber bands to the shoebox guitar, and try using wires, string, and other things that vibrate when they are plucked. Children can try larger and smaller shoeboxes, and they can try different designs. In addition, they should be encouraged to alter the lengths of the rubber bands by stopping the vibrating part with their fingers, thus investigating the effect of length on pitch.

11. *Expected conclusions:*

    Tighter rubber bands produce higher pitches.

    Thinner rubber bands produce higher pitches.

    Some may find that the longer the rubber band, the lower the pitch it produces.

Continued on next page

12. *Assessment:* Assessment will be based on validity of predictions, inferences made about the relationships between pitch and string length and pitch and string thickness, and the appropriateness of inferred reasons.

13. *Applications to real-life situations:* This is the same principle used in guitars, violins, other stringed instruments, and pianos.

Tactile/Kinesthetic Learners

Tactile/kinesthetic learners learn best by using feeling stimuli—by feeling and manipulating materials involved in what they are to learn. Tactile learners focus on the feel of objects, and kinesthetic learners focus on movement. Tactile/kinesthetic learners remember the weight of an object hefted in their hand, the roughness of a rock, and the smoothness of polished wood. They remember the thrill of discovery. Activities utilizing the strengths of the tactile/kinesthetic learner might include investigating force, motion, and balancing; classifying objects by texture; presenting a pantomime about the planets in the solar system; constructing JELL-O® models of cells; and preparing interactive bulletin boards or charts about the topic being studied. Note that new educational computer devices are emerging that add the sense of touch to the visual sense in the use of computers; they can be used to increase tactile experiences while students are using the computer (Jones et al., 2006).

The following activity is intended primarily to support tactile learners. Other learning modalities are included. Can you tell where?

A direct link to a Web site that advertises and explains software and devices that add the sense of touch to the digital world is available on the Student Book Companion Web Site.

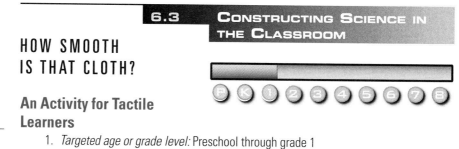

6.3   CONSTRUCTING SCIENCE IN THE CLASSROOM

HOW SMOOTH IS THAT CLOTH?

An Activity for Tactile Learners

NSES Content Standard A. Science as Inquiry: Abilities Necessary To Do Scientific Inquiry

1. *Targeted age or grade level:* Preschool through grade 1

2. *Scientific processes addressed:* Observing and inferring

3. *Science topic addressed:* Properties of materials

4. *Process-oriented objective:* The student will observe the textures of different fabrics and infer what unseen fabrics are from their textures.

5. *What I want children to discover:* Cloth and other things have many different textures that can be observed by feeling them.

Continued on next page

6. *Description of introductory activity and initial discussion:* First, read the books *Feely Bugs: To Touch and Feel* by David A. Carter and *I Touch* by Rachel Isadora. Both books are formatted as touch-and-feel books with which children can interact as they become familiar with the concept of feeling different textures. Pass around squares of different kinds of sandpaper, corrugated paper, colored paper, and regular paper. Ask children to feel them and compare how they feel.

7. *Materials needed:*

   Book: *Feely Bugs: To Touch and Feel* by David A. Carter (Simon & Shuster Children's, 1995)

   Book: *I Touch* by Rachel Isadora (Greenwillow Books, 1991)

   Several pairs of 3-inch squares of several different fabrics, such as silk, flannel, felt, lace, corduroy, burlap, imitation fur, imitation leather, oil cloth, etc.

   Three-inch squares of sandpaper, corrugated paper, colored paper, and regular paper

8. *Description of activities:* Put one set of the cloth squares in a small paper bag. Give the other set to children to feel. After they have acquired familiarity with the pieces of cloth, select one piece, and ask a child to find its matching sample in the bag by feeling. Put it back in the bag, and do the same thing with other children and different samples.

9. *Typical discussion questions:*

   What does each piece of cloth feel like?

   Can you find two or three pieces that feel about the same?

   If you close your eyes, do they feel the same as they do with your eyes open?

   (After selecting a matching piece from the bag) Why did you choose that one?

10. *How children will be encouraged to investigate on their own in the classroom:* Put the "feely" books, pieces of cloth, and other items with different textures, including the different kinds of paper, in a science center for children to continue their explorations. As they are doing routine work in the classroom, encourage them to feel the textures of things they come in contact with. Encourage them to come up with words to describe each texture, such as "rough," "smooth," "bumpy," and the like.

11. *Expected conclusions:* Children will be able to differentiate among different textures. They should be able to match similar textures. Some will be able to identify textures with appropriate words.

12. *Assessment:* Assessment will be based on number of cloth squares of the same texture that children are able to match.

13. *Applications to real-life situations:* We feel our way in the dark partly by recognizing textures. We sand wood to make it smooth. Roads often are made rough to help prevent cars from skidding.

The following is an activity intended primarily to support kinesthetic learners. Other learning modalities also are included. Can you tell where?

6.4	CONSTRUCTING SCIENCE IN THE CLASSROOM

SIMPLE MACHINES

An Activity for Kinesthetic Learners

NSES Content Standard B. Physical Science: Position and Motion of Objects

1. *Targeted age or grade level:* Grades 2–5

2. *Scientific processes addressed:* Observing and inferring

3. *Science topic addressed:* Simple machines

4. *Process-oriented objective:* The student will observe several different kinds of simple machines and infer the simple machines that make up complex machines.

5. *What I want children to discover:*

   There are six simple machines—lever, inclined plane, wedge, screw, pulley, and wheel and axle.

   Complex machines normally contain several simple machines that work together.

   Simple machines are used to change the direction of forces and to magnify forces.

6. *Description of introductory activity and initial discussion:* Read *The Berenstain Bears' Science Fair* by Jan and Stan Berenstain. Point out the lever, the wedge, and the wheel and axle as they occur in the book. Set up an inclined plane, and let a toy car run down it to show the inclined plane. Show a bolt with its matching nut, and a pulley as examples of machines. Ask children to think of examples for the uses of each of these simple machines.

7. *Materials needed:*

   Book: *The Berenstain Bears' Science Fair* by Jan and Stan Berenstain (Random House, 1977)

   Book: *Click, Rumble, Roar: Poems About Machines* by Lee Bennett Hopkins (Crowell, 1987)

   Several small pieces of board to use as ramps

   Toy cars

   Several bolts with matching nuts

   Several pulleys

   Several wooden and metal wedges

Continued on next page

Several wheel and axle sets (from broken toys and the like)

Crowbar

Hammer

Bottle opener

Posters, pictures, or drawings of a crane, eggbeater, scooter, bicycle, and other complex machines that are made of simple machines

8. *Description of activities:*

Divide the simple machine materials into boxes or bags such that each group gets a representative sample. Ask children to select or assemble each simple machine, observe it, and infer what kind it is. After completing the set of materials they were given, children can exchange boxes to identify the simple machines in the other boxes.

Provide pictures of complex machines, and ask children to identify the simple machines in them.

Read appropriate poems from *Click, Rumble, Roar: Poems About Machines* by Lee Bennett Hopkins. This is a collection of 18 poems about such complex machines as car washers, bulldozers, tractors, garbage trucks, escalators, and helicopters.

9. *Typical discussion questions:*

Why did you identify each simple machine as you did?

What do these simple machines do for us?

Try out some of the machines to see what they do.

Do they make work easier?

Do they help change direction so you can push instead of pull?

Which is easier, anyway—to push or to pull?

Where can you see these simple machines in everyday life?

What simple machines are in the complex machines?

How do all these simple machines work together?

10. *How children will be encouraged to investigate on their own in the classroom:* As a culminating and extension activity, ask groups of children to "make a machine that does something" out of scrap material found at school and around the house. The device should include simple machines that the children can point out.

11. *Expected conclusions:* Children should be able to identify each of the six simple machines both individually and in complex machines. They should come to the understanding that simple machines both change force to make it easier for us to move things, and change the direction of force so we can accomplish our tasks more easily.

Continued on next page

12. *Assessment:* Assessment will be based on the validity of children's inferences about which simple machines make up complex machines and the advantages of each simple machine.

13. *Applications to real-life situations:* Many mechanical devices such as those explored in this lesson are made of simple machines.

All learning modalities should be combined in each lesson to the extent possible by ensuring that appropriate stimuli are present. For example, an exploratory lesson on rocks and minerals involves looking (VISUAL STIMULUS), feeling (TACTILE STIMULUS), hefting (KINESTHETIC STIMULUS), and listening to discoveries, discussions, and explanations (AUDITORY STIMULUS). In the "Mystery Box" activity suggested in Chapter 1, some students focused their inquiry on what the box must look like on the inside (VISUAL MODALITY), some focused on the sounds made by the objects inside the box (AUDITORY MODALITY), and some focused on the feel of the magnet when it contacted the magnetic objects inside the box (KINESTHETIC MODALITY). Children in elementary grades tend to know the ways they learn most easily, so it is not necessary to check every child for modality preference. However, the Learning Styles Inventory (Dunn et al., 1975, 1979, 1981, 1985, 1989) can be used with children in third grade or higher.

The process-oriented inquiry methodology is the most appropriate vehicle for the accommodation of all three learning modalities, because children are able to pursue their explorations in the learning styles that are most comfortable to them. Traditional methodologies emphasize having children *look* and *listen*. In inquiry, children also can *do*.

 Direct links to several Web sites dealing with learning modalities are available on the Student Book Companion Web site.

6.3 **CONSTRUCTING YOUR IDEAS**

NSES Teaching Standard A Inquiry-Based Program

Activity That Includes the Three Learning Modalities

Now it's your turn. Select a process-oriented inquiry investigation, and write an activity that includes each learning modality, identifying each.

NSES Professional Development Standard B. Integrating Knowledge of Science, Learning, Pedagogy, and Students NSES Program Standard E. Provides Equal Opportunities for All Students

LOCUS OF CONTROL

Locus of control is a trait concerned with "whether people attribute responsibility for their own failure or success to internal factors or to external factors" (Slavin, 1997, p. 355). Individuals have either a predominantly internal locus of control or a predominantly external locus of control (see Figure 6.2). People with an *internal* locus of control believe their successes or failures result largely from their own abilities and efforts—their

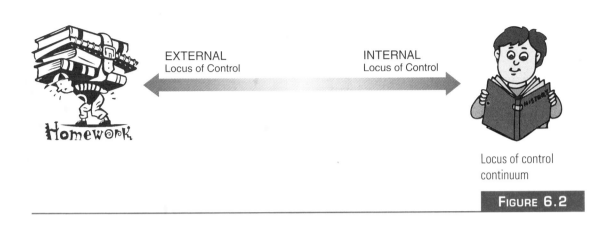

EXTERNAL
Locus of Control

INTERNAL
Locus of Control

Locus of control
continuum

FIGURE 6.2

behavior, persistence, inquisitiveness, and intelligence. People with an *external* locus of control believe their successes or failures are caused largely by external factors—luck, other people's actions, or the difficulty of the situation—they often exhibit "learned helplessness." People with a strong internal locus of control tend to be successful and happy in life whereas people with a strong external locus of control tend not to do well and to be chronically unhappy (Meyerhoff, 2004). Locus of control also relates to motivation. People with a strong internal locus of control are motivated internally, whereas people with a strong external locus of control rely on external stimulation for their motivation.

Like many other factors in education, locus of control can be thought of as a continuum, with external locus of control on one end and internal locus of control on the other.

The attributes discussed above represent extreme ends of the continuum. The point where an individual's locus of control lies on the continuum varies with circumstances. Most of the time, an individual is somewhere between the two extremes, perceiving both external and internal factors as influencing the situation at hand. Nonetheless, one tends to be the dominant factor.

The presence of an internal locus of control is a powerful predictor of academic achievement (Brookover et al., 1979), and it has been shown to have a positive relationship to the amount of voluntary investigation that children seek and to their willingness to make predictions (Rowe, 1978). Children with an internal locus of control believe they can influence the outcomes of investigations and, thus, are motivated to make predictions and test them through experimentation. Children with an internal locus of control demonstrate significantly higher achievement than children with an external locus of control, in part because children who believe that their success or failure results from their own efforts work hard to achieve success (when suitably motivated).

Children with an external locus of control, however, believe that they have little or no control over their performance or achievement. They attribute whatever success or failure they experience to outside factors, so they fail to see any point in trying. They are reluctant to expose themselves to the risk of failing to make accurate predictions, and they lack the internal motivation needed to pursue investigations on their own. They are likely to think, "What's the use; I can't do anything about it anyhow!"

People with a predominantly external locus of control can develop a more internal locus of control if the change is properly fostered. Fostering an enhanced internal locus of control involves encouraging children to become aware of the influence they can exert on various situations and the outcomes that occur as a direct result of their actions. Helping children discover that their efforts affect the results of an activity can aid them in developing a more internal locus of control. To facilitate this, teachers must provide activities that children can manipulate and must engage them in dialogue intended to help children see their roles. Teachers can ask "no risk" questions in which all responses are equally valid. For example, all children should be able to respond to the question "What do you know about plants?" In this way, children begin to internalize that they already possess some relevant information that can be of use to the class. Teachers also can encourage children who are hesitant to write or verbalize to draw pictures of the outcomes of their investigations (Rowe, 1978; Tomlinson, 2001).

Figure 6.3 contains suggested teaching strategies that can be used to foster the development of a more internal locus of control.

CLASSROOM STRATEGIES THAT FOSTER THE DEVELOPMENT OF AN INTERNAL LOCUS OF CONTROL

1. Encourage children to evaluate the outcomes of investigations.
2. Encourage children to suggest ways of changing variables.
3. Encourage children to suggest additional ways of investigating a given phenomenon.
4. Encourage children to suggest topics for investigation and to set their own goals.
5. Ask "no risk" questions.
6. Encourage speculation by asking questions.
7. Teach children to ask questions.
8. Use enough wait time in questioning to allow children to formulate well-thought-out responses.
9. Encourage children to evaluate their own progress.
10. Encourage children to use alternative ways such as drawing to present the results of their investigations.

FIGURE 6.3

Continued on next page

CLASSROOM STRATEGIES THAT FOSTER THE DEVELOPMENT OF AN INTERNAL LOCUS OF CONTROL

11. Encourage cooperative inquiry, and change cooperative groups when no longer functioning.
12. When possible, assign older children, parents, another teacher, or a paraprofessional to help with the inquiries.
13. Provide opportunities for children to revisit and revise their work.

FIGURE 6.3

Any activity described in this book can facilitate the development of a stronger internal locus of control when the teacher explicitly shows children the influence they, themselves, have in their investigations.

NSES Teaching Standard A. Inquiry-Based Program

6.1   IN THE SCHOOLS

NSES Professional Development Standard B. Integrating Knowledge of Science, Learning, Pedagogy, and Students
NSES Content Standard B. Physical Science: Heat Energy

Activity on Diffusion to Help Foster an Internal Locus of Control

In the activity on **diffusion** of food coloring in Constructing Science in the Classroom 3.37, children are asked to compare rates of diffusion in cold water and in warm water. To help children see that they can influence the results of this activity, ask them to decide for themselves how hot and how cold the water should be, and ask them to measure the rates of diffusion. Then show the children that they were the ones who manipulated the temperature variable and that they were able to influence the rate of diffusion by what they did. Ask what else the children can do to change the rate of diffusion, and ask them to try out their ideas, again reinforcing that the children are in control of the investigation.

In the process-oriented inquiry methodology, children develop their own investigations to answer questions that they themselves raised in response to observations they made. Children take charge of their own investigations and, thus, of their own learning. We referred to ownership of knowledge in Chapter 1 and Chapter 5. Children who increase ownership of their knowledge develop a more powerful internal locus of control.

 Direct links to three self-tests you can use to find your locus of control are available on the Student Book Companion Web Site.

FIELD DEPENDENCE/FIELD INDEPENDENCE

NSES Professional Development Standard B. Integrating Knowledge of Science, Learning, Pedagogy, and Students
NSES Program Standard E. Provides Equal Opportunities for All Students

Field independence is the ability to recognize camouflaged information easily.

You probably have seen the "hidden pictures" puzzles in publications like *Highlights for Children.* There may be, for example, a picture of a house with several common objects hidden in the drawing. The field-independent child is able to spot the objects in the picture quickly, much to the consternation of the field-dependent child (or adult) who sees the roof, the windows, the door, the chimney, and little else. The field-independent person has the ability to ignore the surrounding camouflaging field, whereas the field-dependent person is less able to do so.

A hidden pictures drawing is shown in Figure 6.4.

Another example comes from quiz shows, such as *Jeopardy!* Many questions include related but nonessential information. The field-independent person is able to separate what is important from what is not important and bore directly to the core of the question. For example, what is superfluous in the following question?

A direct link to *Highlights,* a very useful Web site developed and maintained by *Highlights for Children,* is available on the Student Book Companion Web Site. A direct link to an additional Web site with hidden picture puzzles is available on the Student Book Companion Web Site.

> What is the name of the world's longest river flowing from north to south in an African country known for two of the Seven Wonders of the Ancient World?

Field dependent people have difficulty extracting essential information from complex situations and tend to rely on external factors to achieve solutions to problems. In contrast, field-independent people tend to rely on their own internal frames of reference.

Studies have shown that persons who are field dependent exhibit lower levels of achievement in science and reduced acquisition of formal reasoning skills compared with people who are field independent (Lawson, 1985; Hall, 2000). Thus, it is desirable to encourage field-dependent children to operate in a more field-independent manner.

The methods used to foster a more field-independent manner of thinking primarily involve helping children focus on key patterns and issues. This can be fostered through process-oriented inquiry. Careful observation helps field-dependent children learn to spot characteristics closely associated with the background which they might otherwise overlook. For example, field-dependent children may become so engrossed in examining the wholeness of a rock sample that they do not see the texture, the layering, or the variegations in color. Teachers can help such children with their observations by asking questions that lead to discoveries of the unobserved properties. The observation sheet suggested in Figure 3.1 would be an appropriate aid for field-dependent children in their observation of rocks and minerals. Classification also often requires the identification of properties that may have been overlooked. Teachers can help

In this big picture, find the seal, hat, shoe, slice of pie, sewing needle, screwdriver, book, lollipop, ladder, baseball bat, ice-cream cone, lamp, pennant, letters B and E, and number 4.

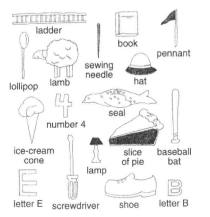

ladder

book

pennant

sewing needle

hat

lollipop

lamb

seal

number 4

ice-cream cone

slice of pie

baseball bat

lamp

letter E

screwdriver

shoe

letter B

FIGURE 6.4

STRATEGIES FOR FOSTERING FIELD INDEPENDENCE

- Emphasize development of the process skills, especially observing, classifying, isolating variables, and defining operationally.
- Utilize the process-oriented inquiry instructional methodology.
- Employ constructivist teaching techniques.
- Play games involving "Twenty Questions" and other incremental clues.
- Work puzzles.
- Play challenging board games.
- Provide overviews of lessons.
- Encourage work on computers.
- Provide concept maps so children can see how each segment of a lesson fits in with the whole (see Chapter 12)

FIGURE 6.5

field-dependent children by encouraging them to develop alternate systems of classification, thereby helping them focus their attention on several attributes concurrently.

When children engage in process-oriented investigations during which they try to figure out what caused what, they have to isolate the variables. Often, variables are camouflaged by other factors, and field-dependent children may encounter difficulties in isolating them. Helping field-dependent children seek and tease out the component variables helps them work in a more field-independent manner. For example, suppose your class is investigating the effect of weather on mood. Many weather variables exist—type of weather, temperature, amount of sunshine, barometric pressure, precipitation, cloud types, and so on—and they all seem to be rolled up into one variable called "weather." There also are many component variables that make up a person's mood. Children must isolate and identify the particular variables they are investigating.

Defining operationally involves deciding how to measure variables. Teachers can help field dependent children find equivalent ways to measure variables that are difficult to measure such as rate of plant growth, or that cannot be measured directly such as plant health.

Encouraging children to develop the ability to think in a field-independent manner is essential in paving the way for them to develop formal operational skills. This should be done in the elementary science classroom as early as possible. Specific suggestions are provided in Figure 6.5.

NSES Professional Development Standard B. Integrating Knowledge of Science, Learning, Pedagogy, and Students NSES Program Standard E. Provides Equal Opportunities for All Students

MULTIPLE INTELLIGENCES

Intelligence is defined as "the ability to learn or understand or to deal with new or trying situations" (Merriam-Webster, 2003). Human intelligence typically is measured by an individual's linguistic, mathematical, and to a lesser extent, spatial abilities as demonstrated on IQ tests.

Gardner (1983, 1995) has argued that contrary to this traditional conception of intelligence, humans have at least eight distinct intelligences: spatial, bodily-kinesthetic, musical, linguistic, logical-mathematical, interpersonal, intrapersonal, and naturalistic (see Figure 6.6). He also is investigating whether a spiritual or existential intelligence may satisfy his criteria for individual intelligences (Gardner, 2003).

The eight intelligences of Gardner's theory can be described as follows:

1. *Spatial:* the ability to perceive the visual-spatial world accurately and represent this world internally in one's mind. Well developed in architects, artists, sculptors, cartographers, anatomists, and scouts.

2. *Bodily-Kinesthetic:* the ability to use one's body or body parts such as hands and fingers to solve problems and express ideas. Well developed in athletes, dancers, actors, and mimes.

3. *Musical:* the ability to think in music, hear music almost continuously, and recognize, remember, and transform musical patterns. Well developed in musical performers, people who love to play musical instruments or sing, and people who enjoy listening to music.

4. *Linguistic:* the ability to use language effectively, either in oral or written form, to express ideas to others. Well developed in writers, poets, storytellers, lawyers, editors, journalists, and (hopefully) college textbook authors.

5. *Logical-Mathematical:* the ability to use numbers and operations mathematically and to reason logically. Well developed in mathematicians, accountants, statisticians, scientists, and computer programmers.

6. *Interpersonal:* the ability to understand other people, to interpret their verbal and nonverbal behavior correctly, and to exhibit sensitivity to their moods and feelings. Well developed in teachers, clergy, salespeople, and politicians.

7. *Intrapersonal:* the ability to understand oneself, know who oneself is, know one's own strengths and limitations, and act in accordance with this self-knowledge. Well developed in philosophers, psychologists, theologians, spiritual leaders, writers, and others who exhibit self-discipline and personal authenticity.

8. *Naturalistic:* the ability to discriminate among living things and exhibit sensitivity to one's natural surroundings. Well developed in botanists, zoologists, ecologists, explorers, farmers, and hunters.

Gardner's identification of different intelligences has brought about his **theory of multiple intelligences,** a theory which has become part

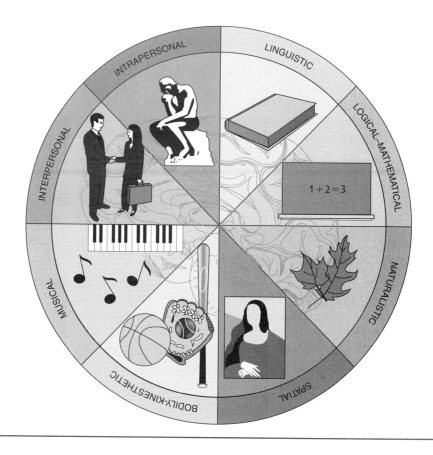

The eight basic intelligences identified by Howard Gardner

FIGURE 6.6

NSES Teaching Standard B. Guiding and Facilitating Learning NSES Professional Development Standard B. Integrating Knowledge of Science, Learning, Pedagogy, and Students NSES Program Standard E. Provides Equal Opportunities for All Students

of the way educators and other people view the world (Multiple Intelligences, 2005). Gardner's theory of multiple intelligences has been linked to increased achievement, especially for students with learning disabilities (Multiple Intelligences Theory, 2003). He believes all humans have all the intelligences; however, the strength in each intelligence area varies from person to person. The goal of the teacher is to develop a repertoire of learning activities and approaches that capitalize on each of the eight intelligences to "help students use their combination of intelligences to be successful in school [and] to help them learn whatever it is they want to learn as well as what the teachers and society believe they have to learn" (Checkley, 1997, p. 10). Gardner cautions against "going on the bandwagon" in an effort to include all eight intelligences in every lesson. The crux of the theory is that there is more than one way to learn, and teachers should make these ways available to their students by using the approaches associated with each of the intelligences. The idea is not to teach every subject in eight different ways; the idea is not even to ensure that every child develops every intelligence. The best use teachers can make of their understanding of Gardner's theory of multiple intelligences is to help them identify and respond to children's needs.

The theory of multiple intelligences is different from the concept of learning modalities. An *intelligence* is an aptitude for learning, whereas a *learning modality* is an orientation for approaching learning tasks. For example, a person could have a strong musical intelligence accompanied by an auditory learning style; other students could also have a strong musical intelligence but learn best visually or kinesthetically.

Figure 6.7 lists some strategies that can be used to help children with strength in each of the eight intelligences learn how to do science.

The following shows ways of utilizing approaches associated with each of the eight intelligences in a unit on dinosaurs and is presented to illustrate how each intelligence can be accommodated in the science classroom.

A direct link to an excellent multiple intelligences Web site developed and maintained by the Illinois Department of Education is available on the Student Book Companion Web Site. Direct links to Web-based, self-scoring self-tests of multiple intelligences for adults, youth, and children are available on the Student Book Companion Web Site.

6.2   IN THE SCHOOLS   NSES Content Standard D, Earth and Space Science: Earth's History

Dinosaurs Unit Utilizing the Eight Multiple Intelligences

A first-grade teacher introduced a unit on dinosaurs by reading the book *Digging Up Dinosaurs* by Aliki (Crowell, 1981) (PRIMARY INTELLIGENCE: LINGUISTIC). A large group activity followed in which children dug up dinosaur models that had been buried previously in pans of sand and matched each dinosaur model with its line drawing on a handout (PRIMARY INTELLIGENCE: LOGICAL-MATHEMATICAL). Children concluded the day's activity by learning the song "My Name is Stegosaurus" (PRIMARY INTELLIGENCE: MUSICAL). Pairs of children researched specific dinosaurs they had been assigned and made booklets for their dinosaurs in which they recorded pertinent facts, such as length, height, weight, food preference, and habitat (PRIMARY INTELLIGENCES: LINGUISTIC AND INTERPERSONAL). They then measured the actual length of their dinosaurs on a long sheet of butcher paper laid out on the gym floor (PRIMARY INTELLIGENCE: SPATIAL) and laid down, head-to-toe on the paper to count how many children it takes to equal the length of each dinosaur (PRIMARY INTELLIGENCE: BODILY-KINESTHETIC). They read the book *The Dinosaur Who Lived in My Back Yard* by B. G. Hennessy (Puffin, 1988) (PRIMARY INTELLIGENCE: LINGUISTIC) and discussed what they would do if the dinosaur they had researched suddenly were to appear in the schoolyard (PRIMARY INTELLIGENCES: NATURALISTIC AND INTRAPERSONAL).

STRATEGIES FOR FOSTERING SCIENTIFIC INQUIRY UTILIZING THE EIGHT INTELLIGENCES

SPATIAL	• Draw maps • Make models • Draw pictures
BODILY-KINESTHETIC	• Dance • Pantomime • Play-act phenomena such as order of planets from sun, orbits of planets and moons, movement of clock hands
MUSICAL	• Sing songs • Learn tunes • Write tunes and rap songs • Play classical music in background
LINGUISTIC	• Read • Write • Send e-mail • Search the Internet • Write poetry, news reports, fiction stories • Write for the class or school newspaper
LOGICAL-MATHEMATICAL	• Search the Internet • Argue points successfully • Draw and/or interpret concept maps • Draw graphs • Interpret graphs • Express conclusions in mathematical formats
INTERPERSONAL	• Lead discussions • Participate in discussions • Ask clarifying questions • Participate in cooperative groups
INTRAPERSONAL	• Lead discussions • Organize games • Direct activities • Engage in self-reflection
NATURALISTIC	• Classify according to natural surroundings • Find origins • Collect objects from nature • Label and mount specimens from nature

Strategies for fostering scientific inquiry utilizing the eight intelligences

FIGURE 6.7

I believe in my students. From Day One, I tell my classes that I believe every single person can learn, although some students may not learn as fast as others, and, for others, learning may come more easily. Regardless of how the students learn, I try to empower them to believe that they can learn; that they may not learn the same way as the other people at their table, but they *can* learn.

After introducing the idea of constructivism to my students, I encourage them to think of ways they can be responsible for their learning. Students typically create a diverse list, ranging from not giving up on hard questions to studying for tests. I then pose the question "How do you learn best?" After students spend time reflecting about this question in their journals, they share their responses, first with their peers at their tables and then in a large group. As students share, I often hear things like "I'm good at math" or "I work best in a quiet place." Others may say "I like working in groups" or "I really like to read."

Some students can easily identify their strengths while others find it more difficult to describe how they learn best. To examine this further, I introduce the "Eight Smarts," Howard Gardner's theory of multiple intelligences. Students begin by guessing what they think their areas of strength and weakness are so they can get to know their "smarts."

Once students' intelligences have been identified, our next step involves brainstorming lists of activities students could do in school that relate to their areas of intelligence. This activity can be challenging because students can become so focused on the obvious activities they don't look beyond. For example, students whose strength is the bodily-kinesthetic intelligence may immediately think of sports; but they often overlook creating models or acting out a concept as a skit which also are bodily-kinesthetic activities. The end results of the students' thinking are eight "Smarts Posters" that list the ideas and activities students have generated that relate to each strength.

The students' different learning styles receive considerable attention throughout the year. My goal is to help students view their unique learning styles in a positive way. When students work in groups, I often ask them to think about what strengths they can bring to the group, because different individuals will be able to share different abilities and perspectives. We revisit Howard Gardner's ideas frequently enough that students are able to make decisions and explain their own learning styles using the language of multiple intelligences.

Because styles of learning aren't the only ways students differ, I also encourage them to share their prior knowledge and experiences about topics we are studying. We begin each new unit with one or two goals related to a central concept. Once the outcomes have been established, students begin by sharing what they already know about the idea. Right away I get a feel for where students are in their understanding based on previous educational and personal experiences. Some bring a wealth of knowledge to a topic, while others know very little. I let students know that both are okay. I try to emphasize that it is what happens next as they work to find answers to unanswered questions that matters. I ask students to think about what they know, write questions, and to write "I wonder" statements about what they want to know about our central concept.

Once we have questions to explore, students begin planning their learning process. I frequently use a contract system. I offer two kinds of contracts. At the beginning of the year, all students work to find answers to the same question(s). With this type of contract, students take responsibility for their learning by being in control of the learning process. The contracts ask students to make choices about how they will work (alone or with a group), how they will learn new information (reading books, doing Internet research, interviewing someone, watching videos, and so on), how they will present their new knowledge (poster, skit, PowerPoint®, and so on), and how often they will check in with me to show their progress. Later in the school year, I use the second type of contract which adds the freedom for students to pursue questions related to our central theme they are interested in. With contracts, the knowledge that students have about their intelligences is important, because in the planning process, they are able to select projects and methods of learning that connect with their "smarts." I meet with students or groups once they have decided on their contracts, and we discuss the expectations and plan before making the contract official with our signatures.

On a typical day in my classroom, you would find students doing a variety of different activities at the same time, all working toward an understanding of the same central concept. Some students may be sitting at their desks reading and doing research while others may be working to put together a poster. Small groups might be meeting with me to discuss their progress and ask questions. At other times, students are taking on the role of teacher and sharing their ideas with the rest of the class. It's a busy place, but the benefits are invaluable. When students are put in charge of building their knowledge and given the ability to make decisions, profound learning happens!

Lisa A. Johnson

Upper School Teacher
Chippewa Falls School District
Chippewa Falls, Wisconsin

TEACHERS' LEARNING STYLES

Just as children have their own unique styles of learning, teachers also have their own personal learning styles. As adults, teachers have developed their styles more completely than children, and have had the opportunity to strengthen those areas in which they have perceived weaknesses. For example, many adults with a dominant visual learning modality have been able to strengthen the auditory area. Many who have experienced difficulty in tasks and activities that field-independent individuals find less challenging have strengthened their field-independent thinking skills (even though they may not be aware of doing so) by working puzzles, figuring out computer programs, playing challenging board games, and so on.

Teachers tend to teach in their dominant learning styles. As Ebeling (2000) writes, "Our own learning style often becomes our most comfortable teaching style" (p. 247). This is advantageous for children with the same learning style as the teacher's but is disadvantageous for children with opposing learning styles. Dunn (1990) says that to foster student achievement, teachers should teach in styles compatible with those of the children in their classes. She writes, "Students can learn almost any subject matter when they are taught with methods and approaches responsive to their learning style strengths; those same students fail when they are taught in an instructional style dissonant with their strengths" (p. 18). Thus, it is incumbent on teachers to know their most comfortable learning styles so they can (1) utilize the strengths associated with them in their teaching and (2) make overt efforts to teach in their less dominant styles so all children can have an equal advantage.

Many factors bear on the abilities of children to learn, and the learning styles discussed in this chapter represent selected examples. Good teachers are aware of the learning that is taking place with their students and constantly search for ways to optimize learning on the part of all children in their classroom.

NSES Teaching Standard B. Guiding and Facilitating Learning
NSES Professional Development Standard B. Integrating Knowledge of Science, Learning, Pedagogy, and Students
NSES Program Standard E. Provides Equal Opportunities for All Students

Conclusion

Children bring to the classroom many ways of learning that affect science achievement. Effective teachers provide strategies that accommodate the needs of students with visual, auditory, and tactile/kinesthetic learning modalities and with each of the eight multiple intelligences. They provide strategies to foster an internal locus of control and field independence. Constructivist process-oriented inquiry enables teachers to accommodate these learning differences.

CHAPTER 6

Additional Questions for Discussion

1. How can you accommodate the many learning differences in one classroom?

2. How important is it to know what the learning styles of each child are?

3. For each of the learning differences explored in this chapter, list accommodating instructional strategies that specifically relate to process-oriented inquiry.

Internet Activites

Use the Internet to find current information on applications of the theory of multiple intelligences in the elementary science classroom and on the other topics explored in this chapter.

CHAPTER 7

SCIENCE EDUCATION FOR STUDENTS WITH LEARNING DIFFERENCES

The most universal quality is diversity.

Michel Eyquem de Montaigne, "Of the Resemblance of Children to Their Fathers," *Essays* (New York: G. P. Putnam's Sons, 1907) (Original work published c. 1580–1588)

All students have unique perspectives, ways of learning, and abilities. And each student can learn regardless of individual differences. We have suggested that constructivist inquiry teaching and learning is the means by which *all* children can be successful in science learning.

The National Research Council (NRC), author of the *National Science Education Standards,* based its work on the premise that all students can—and should—learn science. The NRC's guiding principle of equity reflects the position that "all students regardless of age, sex, cultural or ethnic background, disabilities, aspirations, or interest and motivation in science should have the opportunity to obtain high levels of scientific literacy" (National Research Council, 1996, p. 20). The October 1993 working paper set the tone:

> We emphatically reject the current situation in science education where members of populations defined by race, ethnicity, economic status, gender, physical or intellectual capacity are discouraged from pursuing science and excluded from opportunities to learn science . . . [T]he commitment to Science for

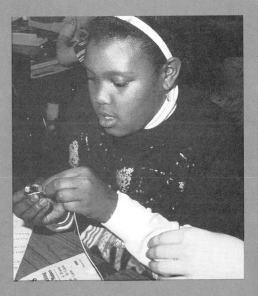

All implies inclusion not only of those who traditionally have received encouragement and opportunity to pursue science, but of women and girls, all racial and ethnic groups, students with disabilities, and those with limited English proficiency. Further, it implies attention to various styles of learning and differing sources of motivation. Every person must be brought into and given access to the ongoing conversation of science. (National Research Council, 1993, p. 7)

Constructivism says that all children learn in different ways. Inquiry provides the means.

In this chapter, you will consider special needs of diverse learners. You will investigate ways of teaching science to boys and girls, students with disabilities, students who are gifted and talented, English language learners, and students from diverse cultural backgrounds to promote maximum science learning on the part of *all* students.

GENDER BIAS

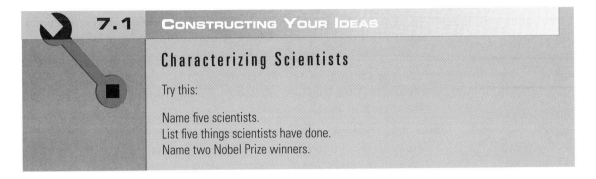

7.1   CONSTRUCTING YOUR IDEAS

Characterizing Scientists

Try this:

Name five scientists.
List five things scientists have done.
Name two Nobel Prize winners.

Were your responses predominantly focused on males? Were they predominantly focused on females? Or, were they equal in focus? If your responses were predominantly male or female, you might want to examine your own belief system about science and gender.

Numerous studies show that women and minorities "are far from having the same opportunities in science education as white men" (Bianchini, Cavazos, & Helms, 2000, p. 516). For example, from kindergarten onward, boys have greater access than girls to science materials and more opportunities to manipulate these materials; and by third grade, 51% of boys—but only 37% of girls—have used microscopes (Bianchini, Cavazos, & Helms, 2000). During the past few decades, efforts to improve science education for girls have produced some positive effects. Girls are now as likely as boys to be enrolled in advanced science courses in high schools; gender differences in science achievement as measured by international tests have decreased; and about as many college women as men major in science (Brickhouse, 2001). However, women still earn fewer college degrees in science and mathematics than men (Zeldin & Pajares, 2000), and in 2004, only about 20 percent of undergraduate degrees in engineering and related fields were awarded to women (Women in Engineering, 2006).

If we are serious about including girls in science, more work needs to be done.

A feminist pedagogy aimed at making science more attractive to girls and women is one of the initiatives geared toward increasing attention to the inclusion of girls in science (see e.g., Kahle, 1985, 1990). Central to the feminist pedagogy is teachers valuing girls' experiences, voices, and ways of knowing about science as well as their interests and concerns, thereby helping to empower them in their science learning (Capobianco, 2007).

NSES Professional Development Standard B. Integrating Knowledge of Science, Learning, Pedagogy, and Students NSES Program Standard E. Provides Equal Opportunities for All Students

Try drawing a scientist. Directions can be found on a university Web site that is linked from the Student Book Companion Web Site. Score your drawing using a rubric found on a Web site also linked from the Student Book Companion Web Site.

Several additional initiatives have been undertaken recently to promote the success of girls in science:

- "Girls in Science" is a program at the San Diego Zoo in which women scientists at the zoo function as role models and describe their work to girls in the middle grades (McLaughlin, 2005).

- *Sally Ride Science* is a company dedicated to empowering girls to explore science that was started by Sally K. Ride, the first American woman astronaut (Ride, 2005).

- In 2006, the federal government relaxed the 30-year-old sex discrimination laws, thereby allowing public school districts to create single-sex schools and classes (if enrollment is voluntary) (Schemo, 2006). Since then, a number of school districts have developed same-sex classrooms to accommodate the unique developmental characteristics of boys and girls and, hopefully, to narrow the gender achievement gap in science.

- A new science and mathematics residential school for girls is scheduled to open in 2009 at new North Carolina Research campus; this institution will accept only girls and will offer them a unique opportunity to interact with female research scientists (Getting women, 2007).

- It has been shown that having women science teachers in middle school increases the likelihood that girls will view science as useful for the future, thus suggesting that school districts redouble their efforts to employ women science teachers (Gorman, 2006).

 Direct links to the San Diego Zoo Girls in Science Web site and the *Sally Ride Science* Web page are available on the Student Book Companion Web Site.

Nonetheless, despite these efforts, teachers who believe that science belongs in the realm of males exhibit behaviors and teaching strategies that lead to science avoidance and negative attitudes toward science on the part of females (Becker, 1989). This sends the message that science is best undertaken by boys and men. If girls are to be given the same opportunities to learn science as boys, teachers must do everything possible to dispel the notion that science is for males. This means involving girls as often as boys as helpers in demonstrations and as laboratory assistants. It means recognizing the in-class and out-of-class science achievements of girls as much as boys. It means talking about female scientists as much as male scientists.[1] And, above all, it means examining your own beliefs to reveal any science gender bias you may have. In Chapter 1, the point was made that one's beliefs affect one's behavior. Teachers who believe that science is more appropriate for boys than for girls tend to convey that belief in their classroom interactions. Only by recognizing your biases can you begin to change the way you act and, ultimately, the way you believe.

 Names and contributions of women who have won the Nobel Prize in the sciences are shown in an addendum on the Student Book companion Web Site.

Science taught from a constructivist perspective—in which teachers seek to help children connect new material to their prior experiences and make the new material relevant to children's lives—fosters science learning on the part of all children, including girls. Some specific strategies for teaching in a gender-neutral manner are suggested in Figure 7.1.

STRATEGIES TO HELP AVOID GENDER BIAS IN ELEMENTARY SCIENCE EDUCATION

1. Call on girls as often as boys.
2. Give girls as much wait time as boys (at least 3–4 seconds).
3. Be sure you call on *all* students instead of only volunteers to ensure that girls and boys have equal opportunities to contribute to class discussions
4. Watch group dynamics to ensure girls are not given stereotypical roles, such as secretary or recorder, and that they are as active in investigations as boys.
5. Rotate group roles so girls have opportunities to function as team leaders.
6. Consider having same-gender groups so girls are active in all roles.
7. Engage girls as much as boys in actual hands-on classroom experiences.
8. Honor the perspectives girls bring to scientific inquiries.
9. Relate science concepts to real-life experiences that are meaningful to both girls and boys.
10. Be aware of your own gender biases and take steps to ensure they do not influence either your classroom management or instruction.
11. Give attention to the subject of women in science.
12. Bring women scientists and upper-level women science teachers into the classroom to talk about their careers.
13. Arrange a "career day" and include women who have careers in science.
14. Provide lists of famous scientists that include as many women as possible.
15. Refer to scientists as "he or she."

FIGURE 7.1

SCIENCE EDUCATION FOR CHILDREN WITH DISABILITIES

As we have seen, one of the primary goals of science education is that *all* students should have the opportunity to obtain high levels of science literacy. Thus, it is essential for teachers to make appropriate adaptations so that every student, including those with disabilities or special needs, has an equal opportunity to become involved in learning science.

In the 2002–2003 academic year, the most recent year for which data is available, 13.7 percent of the U.S. school population age 3–21 received

NSES Professional Development Standard B. Integrating Knowledge of Science, Learning, Pedagogy, and Students NSES Program Standard E. Provides Equal Opportunities for All Students special education services; of these, one-third had physical disabilities and two-thirds had cognitive or social/personal disabilities (National Center for Education Statistics, 2005a).

The Individuals with Disabilities Education Act (IDEA), passed into law in 1990, amended in 1997 and reauthorized in 2004, stipulates that all children with disabilities are to be provided a free and appropriate public education in the least restrictive environment. The law extends to many different types of disabilities, including physical, cognitive, and social/personal. Best practice and the new IDEA mandate that children with disabilities be educated to the greatest extent possible in general education classrooms. This means that children with disabilities are entitled to be educated in general classroom settings to the extent possible given the child's disability, and it calls for inclusive classrooms that involve full-time placement of children with disabilities in a regular class.

Many teachers harbor anxiety over the inclusionary classroom, concerned about how to teach science to students with disabilities together with all the other students in the classroom and, perhaps hoping that a specially assigned inclusion teacher will do the job for them. Recognizing this apprehension, McGinnis and Stefanich (2007) urge regular teachers to teach science to *all* the students in their classes rather than assigning this job to special education teachers, because the special education teachers may not have the expertise that regular teachers have in teaching science. They note that many students are labeled as "students with disabilities" because of their performance or limitations in areas other than science, but that they are capable of high performance in science. Teachers need to recognize this phenomenon and the all-too-common stereotyping of students with disabilities and special needs. They must respond to the unique science learning needs of each student, regardless of label. Of course, it is not reasonable to expect that every teacher has complete knowledge of all accommodations, technologies, and resources available to assist students with disabilities. But all teachers can be expected to be aware of the resources that will help them foster optimal science learning for every student—and to seek them (Stefanich, 2005).

Inclusion often refers to students with identified disabilities, but it is much more than that. To Friend and Pope (2005) and Sailor and Roger (2005), the term *inclusion* is not limited to students with disabilities but, rather, applies to the entire class based on the belief that *all* students— gifted, average, disabled, and those who struggle for any reason—should be fully included in the class. Inclusion should center on the education of *all* children, not just a few "special education" children.

▶ I once supervised a student teacher in a middle-grades science classroom who was teaching a unit on landforms. She had developed several inquiry stations, including a stream table, photos of rock formations, maps, rock specimens to be observed with a geologic microscope, and a library assignment. Groups of students rotated to different stations each day and did the activities requested at the station. Each group was totally engaged in the activities at each station—exploring, trying different things, discussing, recording their findings, and drawing illustrations. There were about 20 students in the class.

During my regular observation one day, I noticed that there were many more students in the class than had been there before—probably 30 altogether. As usual, the students were totally engaged in the activities at each station—exploring, trying different things, discussing, recording their findings, and drawing illustrations. And, as usual, there were no behavior problems, for students were far too busy with their exploratory work to do unacceptable things. At the end of the class, a teacher whom I had not met before came to me and asked if I had noticed there were more students than usual in the class. I was somewhat surprised, because I had assumed that completion of the library assignment had accounted for the extra students. I said, "Yes." The teacher said that these students comprised her behavior disorder class and that once a week, they come to this science class for enrichment.

Not once had I observed a single distraction or irregularity. These students, labeled as students with disabilities, functioned extraordinarily well in the science hands-on atmosphere and were indistinguishable from the regular students.

Strategies for Teaching Students with Disabilities

As with other unique characteristics of students, a few basic principles can help teachers teach science to children with disabilities. The first is the process-oriented inquiry methodology. This methodology embodies those factors that are necessary for teaching all children, including those with disabilities. These factors include (1) concrete, hands-on learning experiences; (2) reduced need for reading and writing skills; (3) involvement in group interactions and group activities; (4) providing for individual differences; and (5) encouraging areas of interest and inquisitiveness (Caseau & Norman, 1997).

Research has shown that inquiry is a successful method for teaching students with disabilities. Brown (2006) showed that elementary science that focused on inquiry resulted in marked improvement in science achievement on the part of both students with special needs and regular students. McCarthy (2005) found that middle school students with serious emotional disturbances who studied science using a hands-on program performed significantly better than the comparison students in a traditional, textbook-oriented program. Lynch, et al (2007) observed students in inclusionary eighth-grade classrooms as they studied a unit on chemistry and found that both students with disabilities and regular students who used the guided inquiry approach exhibited significantly better achievement than those in the comparison group who did not use that approach.

NSES Teaching Standard A. Inquiry-Based Program
NSES Professional Development Standard B. Integrating Knowledge of Science, Learning, Pedagogy, and Students
NSES Program Standard E. Providing Equal Opportunities for All Students

Another strategy that has been shown to be effective with students with disabilities is the Science–Technology–Society (STS) curriculum model (Caseau & Norman, 1997). In this model, teachers develop studies around problems and issues of interest to the children. Children have a high degree of input into lesson planning and take ownership of the material they develop because of its relevance to the topic under study (see Chapter 10).

Several specific accommodations shown to improve the science learning of all students, including those with disabilities, are shown in Figure 7.2 (McGinnis & Stefanich, 2007; Science for students, 2007; Special Education, 2005).

SPECIFIC ACCOMMODATIONS FOR ADAPTING SCIENCE INSTRUCTION FOR CHILDREN WITH DISABILITIES

1. Prepare materials to be explicit, specific, and delivered in small bites.
2. Ensure that children have previously achieved the skills and understandings they need.
3. Demonstrate procedures while giving directions.
4. Develop written or pictorial cue cards for directions and display them in the proper order.
5. Modify reading levels to meet the capabilities of the children.
6. Use large print.
7. Use graphic organizers.
8. Identify and define any vocabulary words that may come up.
9. Provide consistent feedback.
10. Allow students to improve and resubmit assignments.
11. Encourage children to demonstrate their competencies through various means.
12. Modify assessments so students with disabilities can demonstrate their understanding and achievement.
13. Modify equipment and materials to be sure all children can use them.
14. Provide assistive and adaptive technology resources.
15. Enlarge aisles and areas of movement to accommodate all children.

FIGURE 7.2

NSES Teaching Standard D. Providing Time, Space, and Resources
NSES Program Standard D. Appropriate with Sufficient Resources

Materials and Equipment for Students with Disabilities

In some cases, instructional materials need to be adapted to meet the needs of students with disabilities. Some adaptations are inexpensive or free, such as putting rubber expanders on pencils to make them easier to hold, making a variety of pictures and drawings available to assist in conceptual understanding, putting up signs to help students with vision impairments, providing clipboards to serve as tilting desktops, providing "sensory" stories, and the like (Leatherman, 2006). Other adaptations are expensive such as ergonomic technology workstations, wheelchairs, slant boards, angled writing surfaces, automatic page turners, computer screen readers, and a whole range of assistive and adaptive technological hardware and software (see Figure 7.3).

 Direct links to West Virginia University Web sites that contain science inclusion classroom strategies for persons with disabilities are available on the Student Book Companion Web Site.

If all this sounds familiar, it should. The research on teaching science to children with disabilities suggests using learning strategies that center on open-ended, inquiry-oriented, problem-solving investigations that are challenging to children and require their cognitive engagement. The learning experiences should be tailored to meet the needs of each individual child, including those with disabilities. This is the essence of the

Video magnifier
(Courtesy Enable Mart)

Page turner
(Courtesy The Assistive Technology Training Online Project, University of Baffalo School of Public Health and Health Professions)

Alternate keyboard
(Courtesy The Assistive Technology Training Online Project, University of Baffalo School of Public Health and Health Professions)

Braille notetaker
(Courtesy Sighted Electronics Inc.)

Big keys
(Courtesy Enable Mart)

Adaptive and assistive technological devices

 FIGURE 7.3

process-oriented inquiry method of instruction. From the constructivist viewpoint, teaching children with disabilities is seen as a special case of teaching all children rather than as a special problem requiring a special methodology.

Above all, it is the attitude of the teacher that encourages children with special needs to succeed in science. As indicated in Chapter 2, one of the major goals of science education is the achievement of scientific literacy by *all* citizens. *All* children have the capability of learning science, and *all* children can participate successfully in doing science. As McCann (1998) writes, "[P]erhaps the most critical aspect of involving disabled students in the classroom is that teachers realize the significance of their attitudes and expectations toward students with special needs. *Such students must know that science is for them, too*" (p. 4; italics added).

Science Education for Students Who Are Gifted and Talented

NSES Professional Development Standard B. Integrating Knowledge of Science, Learning, Pedagogy, and Students NSES Program Standard E. Providing Equal Opportunities for All Students

There are at least two factors to consider in programs for students who are gifted and talented: how to identify children who are gifted and talented, and how to facilitate their education.

The federal government (U.S. Department of Education, 1993, p. 8) describes students who are gifted and talented as follows:

- Children and youth with outstanding talent perform or show the potential for performing at remarkably high levels of accomplishment when compared with others of their age, experience, or environment.

- These children and youth exhibit high performance capability in intellectual, creative, and/or artistic areas, possess an unusual leadership capacity, or excel in specific academic fields. They require services or activities not ordinarily provided by the schools.

- Outstanding talents are present in children and youth from all cultural groups, across all economic strata, and in all areas of human endeavor.

The most common method of identifying children who fall into the category of "gifted" is the use of tests. But, the identification of students who are gifted and talented in science focuses more on observable performance in specific activities (McGinnis & Stefanich, 2007), and teachers should use these observations rather than the results of detached testing in identifying talented children and in planning science lessons for them. (See the inquiry descriptors in Chapter 5 and methods of authentic assessment in Chapter 8.)

Depending on state and local policies, special programs may be offered to children who are identified as gifted and talented. These programs may be offered at special times on special days and in special classrooms. Or, they may occur in regular classrooms in inclusionary models similar to those used for integrating children with exceptional needs. When gifted and talented students are included in the regular classroom, the teacher should form groups of those who are gifted in the area of science in order to provide exceptional considerations to children with similar high abilities.

It is a premise of this book that *all* children can learn—and that they will learn as much science as they are able to through the constructivist, process-oriented inquiry approach. Children will start any given investigation with their own prior conceptions and understandings, and they will progress as far and as wide as they are able. In this sense, children who are gifted and talented are seen as a special case of teaching all children rather than as a special problem requiring a special methodology. The process-oriented inquiry method of science instruction is the most appropriate and challenging way of helping children whose giftedness lies in the realm of science.

Nonetheless, there are several principles that good teachers employ when working with children who are gifted and talented in science. These techniques are shown in Figure 7.4.

SOME STRATEGIES FOR TEACHING CHILDREN WHO ARE GIFTED AND TALENTED IN ELEMENTARY SCIENCE

1. Allow students to demonstrate and get credit for previous mastery of concepts.
2. Provide faster pacing of new material.
3. Incorporate students' passionate interests into their independent studies and build inquiry lessons based on their interests.
4. Facilitate sophisticated research investigations.
5. Allow deeper and more penetrating probes into inquiries.
6. Encourage cross-disciplinary and interdisciplinary aspects to the inquiries.
7. Encourage a focus on contemporary, real-world issues.
8. Encourage independent excursions into unknown and unfamiliar areas of inquiry.
9. Help children figure out how they can continue their investigations and inquiries outside of class.
10. Allow children to work independently or with others who are focusing on similar areas of inquiry, and allow large blocks of time for them to work on their inquiries.

(Adapted in part from Winebrenner & Devlin, 2001)

FIGURE 7.4

Science Education for English Language Learners

NSES Professional Development Standard B. Integrating Knowledge of Science, Learning, Pedagogy, and Students NSES Program Standard E. Providing Equal Opportunities for All Students

English language learners (ELLs) are students whose first language is not English and who either lack proficiency or have only a beginning-level proficiency in English (Center for Research on Education, Diversity, and Excellence, 2002); they are non–English speaking students. English language learners are the fastest-growing group of students in the United States; between 1992 and 2002, the ELL population grew by 95 percent while the total school enrollment increased by only 12 percent (Genesee, Lindholm-Leary, & Christian, 2005). During the 2002–2003 academic year, more than 5 million school-age students were identified as ELLs, representing more than 10 percent of the total public school population. These students spoke more than 400 languages, and 80 percent of these were native Spanish speakers (Genesee, Lindholm-Leary, & Christian, 2005).

It is essential that teachers give attention to ways of teaching ELL students to make science available to this rapidly growing segment of the student population. These students normally are assigned to regular classrooms and are just as capable of achieving in science as any other student; indeed, many have been well-educated in their native language. The only difference is that they have an English language deficiency. Many teachers believe that ELLs must acquire English proficiency before learning subject matter; however, this approach almost always leads to ELLs falling behind their English-speaking peers (Lee, 2005). Teachers must teach ELLs the subject matter being discussed using ELL accommodations as appropriate. In fact, it has been shown that when teachers employ ELL practices in their science teaching, not only do ELLs learn science, they also learn a great deal of English as well (Fathman & Crowther, 2006; Lee & Avalos, 2003).

Teaching science to children for whom English is a second language is complex. Not only must teachers help ELLs develop facility in the scientific processes and methods of inquiry, they also must help these children do so in a language with which their familiarity ranges from none to some. In addition, because of the difficulties in communicating, teachers cannot be sure whether the problems that ELL children may be having with science represent low science achievement or limited facility in English. Many good teachers are baffled when faced with a child who obviously brings intelligence, experiences, and skills to the classroom but has difficulty demonstrating these because of language difficulties (Rice, Pappamihiel, & Lake, 2004).

Given this predicament, it is tempting for teachers to view ELL students as low achievers, and this may lead to a tendency to "water down" the science program to accommodate these children. Verplaestse (1998) found that teachers often do not pose achievement-enhancing higher-level questions to ELL children; instead, they engage them in a "benevolent conspiracy" intended to save them from embarrassment but, in so doing, deprive them of valuable learning opportunities (Rice, Pappamihiel, & Lake, 2004, p. 121). In addition, Brown and Bentley (2004), found that when the teachers in their study were teaching elementary science, they tended to avoid interacting with ELLs and failed to adjust their instruction to meet the needs of ELLs. The instruction must not be a "watered down" science curriculum that limits ELLs to learning terms and vocabulary and memorizing key concepts. Nor should English Language Learners receive instruction that simply calls for lower levels of thinking (Rice, Pappamihiel, & Lake, 2004). However, these actions happen all too often. In short, "[s]cience instruction typically has failed to help ELLs learn science in ways that are meaningful and relevant to them" (Lee, 2005, p. 504). This business of watering down the curriculum and instruction and ignoring the ELL students is "simply an indefensible solution," writes Gersten, et. al (1998, p. 70), for this practice denies ELL children "access to quality instruction, and, ultimately, academic opportunity" (ibid., p. 70).

In an effort to accommodate English language-minority children, teachers often wonder if they should study foreign languages so they can communicate with the children in their own languages. It is good for teachers to learn a foreign language so they can help students in their native language as well as gain an understanding of the mechanical and cultural elements of foreign language discourse. (Based on the demographics shown above, it would seem that the most useful second language for English-speaking teachers to study would be Spanish.) However, it is a virtual impossibility for teachers to become conversant in all the languages they might encounter in the classroom. Indeed, in one elementary school where I have done quite a bit of work, ELL students come from more than 40 different countries and speak more than 40 different native languages—and many of these children had no previous acquaintance with English. In a study reported by Gersten et. al (1998), only 2 percent of the teachers in exemplary programs in which **ESOL** (English for Speakers of Other Languages) students were enrolled communicated in both English and some other language, and fewer than 1 percent spoke mostly in a non-English language.

If you are bilingual or have facility in a foreign language, by all means you should use it. The Association for Supervision and Curriculum Development (2003) suggests the following:

- Teach the students in English for half the day and in Spanish for the other half—without duplicating the material. This plan uses native English– and Spanish-speaking teachers, and students learn in both English and their native language.

- Connect new terms with children's native languages. Some teachers keep a running vocabulary list in English on the board with translations into the native language of each student in their class.

Instructional Strategies for ELL Students

As we have indicated, ELL students are just as capable as anyone else of achieving in science; their primary difficulty is with language. Consequently, it is necessary to employ instructional strategies that help ELLs compensate for their language difficulty when teaching science. Below are strategies from the research findings that have been shown to be successful in helping ELL students learn science (Gersten, 1998; Hansen, 2006; Lee, 2005; Lee & Luyks, 2007; Rice, Pappamihiel, & Lake, 2004):

- Use hands-on inquiry-based science instruction. Research consistently shows that inquiry investigations by ELL students provide the highest levels of achievement.

- Focus on the scientific processes of observing, classifying, measuring, predicting, and inferring. Nonnative speakers of English will find fewer difficulties with expressing themselves in activities that focus on these basic processes than in activities that are more complex. Be sure to incorporate the process of communicating in all science investigations, and remember that people can communicate effectively in a variety of ways (see Chapter 3).

- Use cooperative learning strategies in which *all* students, including ELL children, participate, explore, discuss the concepts, discuss how to do the activity, carry out the activity, and formulate the conclusion. Structure the groups to require participation by every student.

- Provide a low-anxiety environment that encourages and supports the risk-taking that will be encountered by language-minority children. This environment must be supportive and trusting so that the children are not afraid of speaking out or taking risks.

- Analyze the language requirements of your lesson, and decide which words are essential and which are likely to produce confusion. For example, the word "force" may be essential in a lesson dealing with force and motion, but it has several meanings, such as "power," "energy," "compelling," "pushing," "influencing," and "strength." These meanings may need to be sorted out for English language-minority students.

- Use concept mapping and other methods of cognitive charting to help language-minority children focus on lesson development and to provide alternative forms of assessment (see Chapter 12). Make extensive use of children's literature that is understandable to ELL students to augment the science program (see Chapter 10). Include multicultural literature not only to help the development of English but also to help break down any cultural boundaries that may exist between language-minority children and other children and their teachers.

- Value and respect the experiences that ELL students bring to the classroom, and encourage them to share home-country experiences that relate to the concepts being studied.

- Consider extending your science program to include children's families and the community. Hammond (2001) describes a project in which families of language-minority children teamed with their children's science teachers to develop and implement programs that were meaningful to the families as well as the children.

- Develop the same positive attitudes toward language-minority children that you have for *all* children—namely, that they, along with all other children, can learn and can aspire to your high expectations.

Materials for Use with ELL Students

It is important to use linguistically and culturally appropriate materials when teaching science to ELLs. Some existing science programs offer Spanish-language components. For example, the *Full Option Science Series (FOSS)* has developed student sheets, assessment pages, and science stories in Spanish for use with Spanish-speaking elementary students. Materials are being prepared for use with other programs, and new materials are being tested. It is worth your while to keep up with the progress being made in this area.

The National Science Teachers Association has published a practical guide for teaching science to English Language Learners in kindergarten through high school titled *Science for English Language Learners: K-12 Classroom Strategies,* edited by A. K. Fathman and D. T. Crowther. The guide has many strategies and even a chapter devoted to activities developed with ELL students in mind. In addition, NSTA is preparing other materials to help science teachers work successfully with ELLs. These will be announced on the NSTA Web site and in NSTA publications as they become available.

NSES Teaching Standard D. Providing Time, Space, and Resources
NSES Program Standard D. Appropriate with Sufficient Resources

 A direct link to the home page of the *Full Option Science Series* Web site is available on the Student Book Companion Web Site.

In addition to materials, activities need to be adapted so ELL students can participate fully and successfully. Three activities with adaptations for ELL students are shown below. Can you tell what the adaptations are?

7.1   IN THE SCHOOLS

NSES Content Standard F. Science in Personal and Social Perspectives: Science and Technology in Local Challenges

Oil Spill Cleanup

A fourth-grade class was discussing pollution, and the topic of oil spills came up. The teacher asked the students to explore different ways of cleaning up an oil spill. She provided the following materials for each group:

Aluminum dish	Piece of nylon netting
Water	Piece of nylon stocking
Motor oil	Piece of Styrofoam
Cotton balls	Piece of cardboard
Spoon	Piece of string
Eyedropper	Straw
Liquid detergent	

Students poured about an inch of water into the dish and added a few drops of motor oil (which they counted) onto the surface. They used the materials one by one to clean up the oil spill, using a stopwatch or clock with a second hand to measure how long it took to clean up the spill. The students found they had to come up with an operational definition of "clean water" that would apply to all trials, so they started over with a clean bowl of water and added the same number of drops of motor oil for each material.

Students plotted the amount of time each material took to clean the spill on a bar chart. The class compared the charts each group had developed and made their conclusions.

Literature Connections

Oil Spills by Jillian Powell (Bridgestone Books, 2003) is an illustrated book that describes several kinds of oil spills and solutions for averting serious pollution problems. Activities students can do are suggested.

After the Spill: The Exxon Valdez Disaster, Then and Now by Sandra Markle (Walker and Co, 1999) examines the impact of the 1989 Exxon Valdez oil spill on the environment and describes the steps taken to minimize the damage and prevent a recurrence.

7.2

Plant Cells

A middle grades teacher wanted the students in her classes to observe plant cells. She obtained a few sprigs of *elodea* (or other thin-leafed seaweed plant) from a store that sells aquarium supplies. The students broke off the tip of a new yellow-green leaf, put it on a slide, and put a cover slip over it. Using an eyedropper, they placed a drop of tincture of iodine next to the cover slip so that it was "sucked" under the cover slip and stained the piece of leaf.

The teacher also provided an onion. Students carefully peeled off the outer layer and lifted the very thin skin that covered the next layer. They peeled off a small piece of this onion skin, placed it flat on a slide, and put a cover slip over it. They stained the onion skin with tincture of iodine as they did with the *elodea* leaf tip.

The students observed the slides under a microscope and compared what they saw with drawings of plant cells that highlighted the cell wall, nucleus, chloroplasts, and cytoplasm. They also compared what they saw with drawings that showed mitotic division of the cells.

The students drew diagrams of the cells they saw under the microscope and labeled their main parts.

Literature Connections

Plant Cells: The Building Blocks of Plants by Darlene R. Stille (Compass Point Books, 2006) contains illustrated descriptions of plant cells, their structure, and their function.

Plant Cells and Tissues by Nicholas Stephens (Chelsea House Publishers, 2006) is an illustrated reference book on plant cells, their structure and function, how they join to form tissues, and how they reproduce.

 Direct links to several Web sites with diagrams of plant cells are available on the Student Book Companion Web Site.

7.3

Animal Cells

A middle grades teacher wanted the students to observe living animal cells. He decided to have them observe single-celled animals called **protozoans.** He collected some foul-smelling water from a dank swamp in a jar and put some leaves and other

Continued on next page

vegetative debris in with it, resulting in a **hay infusion.** He covered the jar and left it in a warm, dark place for several days.

When the teacher brought out the hay infusion, the students squeezed the air out of an eyedropper, carefully put its nozzle in the infusion beneath or close to the debris, and sucked a few drops of the liquid into the eyedropper. They ejected a drop or two (complete with debris) onto a slide and covered them with a cover slip. They examined the slide under a microscope and moved it around until they saw something moving. They moved the slide to keep up with the moving organism, remembering to move it in the opposite direction from where the organism was moving.

Students compared what they saw with drawings and photographs of protozoans and drew diagrams of what they saw.

Literature Connections

Animal Cells: Smallest Units of Life by Darlene R. Stille (Compass Point Books, 2006) is a reference book on the structure and function of animal cells.

Cells by Alvin Silverstein, Virginia Silverstein, and Laura Silverstein Nunn (Twenty-First Century Books, 2002) is a detailed presentation of the structure and function of different kinds of cells; the book compares animal and plant cells.

 Direct links to several Web sites that have diagrams and photographs of animal cells are available on the Student Book Companion Web Site.

Assessment Strategies for ELL Students

NSES Professional Development Standard B. Integrating Knowledge of Science, Learning, Pedagogy, and Students NSES Program Standard E. Provides Equal Opportunities for All Students NSES Assessment Standard D. Fair Assessments

In assessing what the ELL student has accomplished in science, it is important to distinguish science knowledge from English language proficiency. Shaw (1997) found that the best techniques for assessing science proficiency without language interference are performance assessments and those assessments that use graphs, calculations, data tables, equations, and overall summary questions. Some specific considerations for assessing the science proficiency of ELL students are given below (Lee, 2005; Rice, Pappamihiel, & Lake, 2004; Shaw, 1997):

1. Be sure there is no cultural or linguistic bias.

2. Be sure you are assessing the science objective(s) and not the language.

3. Use non–language based assessments.

4. Use performance assessments.

5. Use graphics, numbers, and symbols rather that written scenarios.

Families

It is imperative that teachers provide abundant opportunities for family members to be involved in their children's education. Several strategies are suggested in Chapter 9. When family members are nonspeakers of English, teachers should make adaptations such as providing written material in the family's native language (using translators if needed) and having liaisons present at conferences who can translate. Of particular note are the evening education programs offered to non–English speaking family members by some schools.

TEACHER VOICE

In my twenty years of teaching, I have learned that the most important factors in a classroom are the teacher's attitude and beliefs. Most of my career has been spent in inner-city schools with high poverty rates, where the majority of children are learning to speak English as their second language. I see all my students as learners who are capable of growth if I engage them in motivating activities, value their backgrounds, and allow them to be accountable for their own learning. I believe these children, like all children, are eager learners and bring the gift of diversity to a school. Their ideas, cultures, and varied backgrounds share a richness with the classroom that becomes particularly evident during science investigations. My job is to inspire, motivate, and tap into their natural curiosity.

In the last few years, while teaching fourth grade, my classes have engaged in the study of animals, their habitats, and their adaptations. Many students from the Sudan and rural Mexico have encountered animals and habitats that other students and I have only seen on television or in books. As we engage in inquiries, these students have the ability to ask rich, higher-level questions because of their background knowledge. The challenge comes in the communication and exchange of ideas, hypotheses, and findings. I allow my students to communicate with each other in their native tongues and write in their native languages until they are more comfortable using English. As they begin writing in English, I support them by offering carefully chosen feedback aimed at addressing English language acquisition. I am mindful of my own speech as I communicate with them and assess their understanding by watching them as they explore and experiment. I post science vocabulary in English on a word-wall, and I use the words over and over. I read aloud daily from books that support the science content and vocabulary. I particularly like using Big Books as they have large pictures and manageable chunks of text. The books I choose stimulate student conversations and questions that can be developed into investigations. They offer visual support for students with limited English and help their understandings of vocabulary, concepts, and ideas.

From the beginning of the school year, the students and I create a classroom environment that is safe for every student and accepting of differences. Children will model their teacher. If they see that I treat all students with respect, they will also be respectful. If I show that I am comfortable around children who speak little or no English, they will be comfortable. If I persevere in trying to understand what a second-language learner is communicating, they will also try to listen and understand. The beauty of teaching science using inquiry or other student-centered methods is that children have multiple opportunities to interact and communicate. This allows more vocabulary development in a nonthreatening, student-to-student atmosphere. I believe it is important to accept all student responses and probe for clarification when necessary. Avoiding judgment of their responses encourages free dialogue in which children can question and support each other in learning. Listening to them talk, I can identify alternate conceptions and design investigations, choose books, and provide other activities that address student needs.

English language learners, like other children, benefit from having a real-life or field experience at the start of a unit. Children build their backgrounds and have a "hook" on which to build their understanding of a given concept. A few years ago, at the beginning of a unit on wetlands, I took my students to a local shorebird refuge. One of my students was a "newcomer"—a child who was in his first year of school in the United States. He was quiet by nature, and I had trouble seeing his progress because he said and wrote very little in any language. Within minutes of disembarking from the bus, I heard him call my name loudly and say in beautiful English, "A snake, a snake! It went in the water! It's a garter snake!" This experience provided me with the assurance that he was, indeed, learning. I was so proud of him I couldn't contain my excitement. From that moment on, his confidence continued to grow as well as his ability to demonstrate his learning. From that moment on, my confidence grew as a teacher, and I was sure that my constructivist teaching style was effective with second language learners.

Machelle Dahl

Fourth-grade teacher
Escalante Elementary School
Salt Lake City, Utah

MULTICULTURAL FACTORS

This book is about teaching from a constructivist approach, utilizing the process-oriented inquiry methodology to facilitate the science education of all children, each of whom is uniquely different from each other in multiple ways. Race, ethnicity, and culture are included among these differences. Thus, from a constructivist perspective, multiculturalism can be considered a special case of individual learning needs.

The population of nonwhite ethnic groups in the United States is growing rapidly, and American schools are becoming increasingly multicultural. In 2003, the most recent year for which data is available, the enrollment in U.S. public schools was 66.1 percent white, 16.6 percent black, 12.7 percent Hispanic, 3.6 percent Asian/Pacific Islander, and 1.1 percent Native American/Alaskan Native (National Center for Education Statistics, 2005b). The U.S. Census Bureau predicts that by the year 2010, as many as one of every 10 children in the United States will be foreign-born (Franklin, 2001a). Furthermore, it has been predicted that by the year 2025, the proportion of students of color will increase to approximately 50 percent of the student population (McFalls & Cobb-Roberts, 2001).

It has never been acceptable to ignore a small segment of the population in school; however, what used to be small segments are rapidly becoming large. This rapid change in cultural and racial demographics requires a closer look at the potentially serious cultural dichotomy between teacher and student and a careful look at ways of teaching science in the most meaningful way for these students and making multicultural classrooms responsive to the needs of all children.

Ethnic and cultural factors exert powerful influences on the way children learn. Children of different cultures have constructed culture-based information in different ways and, thus, bring different perceptions and understandings to the classroom. From the constructivist perspective, it is clear that children's differing cultural backgrounds have led to differing prior experiences. Elementary science teachers often assume that students already have some understanding of scientific inquiry when they come to school. But, the understandings of scientific inquiry are not the same in all cultures, and they are not necessarily the same as the science taught in schools. For example, cultural norms may emphasize teachers as being authoritative sources of knowledge, and children may not be encouraged to question the teacher's knowledge in ways consistent with the Western tradition of scientific inquiry (see Chapter 2) (Lee, 2005).

Furthermore, culture and language cannot be separated; teachers should be aware of the cultural values that English language learners bring to the classroom.

Many educational techniques can be applied to foster science achievement by minorities. Basu and Barton (2007) found three factors that foster minority students developing interest in science: (1) Science experiences

NSES Professional Development Standard B. Integrating Knowledge of Science, Learning, Pedagogy, and Students NSES Program Standard E. Provides Equal Opportunities for All Students connect with their future visions; (2) learning environments support the social relationships they value; and (3) science activities connect with students' views of the purpose of science. The National Science Teachers Association (2000) suggests six tenets to be followed in teaching science to students from a variety of cultures. They are as follows:

- Schools are to provide science education programs that nurture all children academically, physically, and in development of a positive self-concept.

- Children from all cultures are to have equitable access to quality science education experiences that enhance success and provide the knowledge and opportunities required for them to become successful participants in our democratic society.

- Curricular content must incorporate the contributions of many cultures to our knowledge of science.

- Science teachers are knowledgeable about and use culturally related ways of learning and instructional practices.

- Science teachers have the responsibility to involve culturally diverse children in science, technology, and engineering career opportunities.

- Instructional strategies selected for use with all children must recognize and respect differences that students bring based on their cultures.

There are at least three aspects to multicultural considerations: (1) attitude, (2) teaching methodology, and (3) curriculum.

Attitude in Multicultural Education

NSES Professional Development Standard B. Integrating Knowledge of Science, Learning, Pedagogy, and Students NSES Program Standard E. Provides Equal Opportunities for All Students

Nothing inherent in culture itself, or in other forms of human diversity, creates pedagogical problems. . . . It is that attitude of the educator toward diversity that creates problems in the education setting. When educators do not notice diversity, when they give negative notice, or when they lose the opportunity to give positive notice of the natural diversity that is always there, they create a bogus reality for teaching and learning. (Hilliard, 1994)

Teachers' attitudes toward diversity exert powerful influences over curriculum and lesson development, instructional methodology, teacher–child interactions, and interactions with colleagues, parents, and the community. Teachers must acquire general cultural sensitivity. To do so, first examine your own cultural, ethnic, and racial beliefs to disclose to yourself any bias you might have. With this information, you will be able to change the way you act and then the way you believe. By resolving any concerns you have about multicultural classroom settings, you will be able to make your classroom a warm and receptive environment for all children.

Meyer and Rhoades (2006) suggest several ways teachers can use to help transform their attitudes about multicultural education. They include the following:

• Engage in discussions of cultural topics not considered "safe" with members of a different culture.

• Exchange values and beliefs with people from other cultures.

• Read biographies of people from other cultures.

• Correspond with a culturally different pen pal.

• Undergo cultural immersion experiences through traveling, tutoring, visiting, and the like.

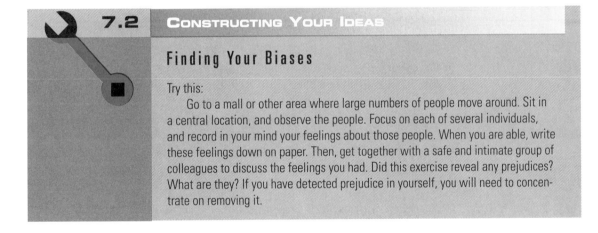

7.2 **CONSTRUCTING YOUR IDEAS**

Finding Your Biases

Try this:
Go to a mall or other area where large numbers of people move around. Sit in a central location, and observe the people. Focus on each of several individuals, and record in your mind your feelings about those people. When you are able, write these feelings down on paper. Then, get together with a safe and intimate group of colleagues to discuss the feelings you had. Did this exercise reveal any prejudices? What are they? If you have detected prejudice in yourself, you will need to concentrate on removing it.

Multicultural Instructional Methodology

In a multicultural approach to learning, teachers use a variety of teaching styles consistent with the learning styles of the cultural and ethnic groups represented in their classrooms. This principle is not different from the principle of accommodating the wide variety of learning styles or the needs of English language learners. Different racial, ethnic, and cultural groups may have different prevalent learning styles, and competent teachers provide for these learning styles as well as for other special learning

NSES Teaching Standard B. Guiding and Facilitating Learning
NSES Program Standard E. Provides Equal Opportunities for All Students

needs in multicultural settings. When students are not from the primary cultural tradition of the classroom, teachers need to make the student's cultural norms explicit and visible so that students learn to cross any cultural barriers there might be between their home and school. Lee (2005) refers to this as "culturally congruent" instruction.

Several studies have validated the use of the constructivist approach for science teaching in multicultural classrooms. Cuevas et. al (2005) found that elementary students from multicultural backgrounds who explored science in an inquiry manner showed significant increases in their ability to conduct inquiry and employ the processes of science. This increase occurred regardless of their grade, previous achievement level, gender, socioeconomic status, home language, or English proficiency. Upadhyay (2006) investigated elementary science instruction in urban schools with high ethnic minority populations. He found that elementary science teachers who utilized the experiences of their students as primary funds of knowledge in the classroom helped linguistically and culturally diverse learners learn science meaningfully. Lee et. al (2006) found that elementary students from multicultural backgrounds who executed a semistructured inquiry science activity showed gains in inquiry abilities, with students from non-mainstreamed and less privileged backgrounds showing greater gains than their more privileged counterparts.

One teacher reported that she uses virtual field trips and multicultural PowerPoint presentations to reach children of different linguistic and cultural backgrounds and found these strategies to be "quite effective."

NSES Professional Development Standard B. Integrating Knowledge of Science, Learning, Pedagogy, and Students NSES Program Standard E. Provides Equal Opportunities for All Students

All cultural groups display all learning styles; however, some are especially associated with individual cultural groups. A few generalizations are given below for African Americans, Hispanics, Asians, and Native Americans (Cushner, McClelland, & Safford, 1992; Deyhle & Swisher, 1997; Franklin, 2001a; National Council for the Social Studies, 1992; Padilla, 2005; Starnes, 2006; Willis, 1993).

- African-American students may learn best when cooperative teaching techniques and collaborative hands-on approaches are used. They tend to be field dependent in learning style.

- Hispanic students tend to learn best when they have a personal relationship with the teacher and can interact with peers in cooperative learning groups. They prize collaboration, cooperation, and teamwork. The work of the group is more important than the work of an individual, and family is very important.

- In Asian cultures, learning often is "circular" rather than "linear," and students learn through active discussion. They often rely on teachers as the source of knowledge and are reluctant to question this knowledge or the teacher's authority.

- Native American children are raised to be careful observers and thoughtful listeners, and they tend to be better at processing visual information than verbal information. They often learn by observing and imitating the actions of parents, elders, and older siblings, and they often are uncomfortable with "individual public performance" such as recitation and being asked to respond to teacher-generated questions. In Native American cultures, learning tends to be greatest when the deductive method of teaching is employed, allowing students to look at a whole concept before focusing on the details.

Characteristics of effective multicultural teaching are essentially the same as the general characteristics of constructivist inquiry teaching (see Figure 5.4). They include:

- Encouraging children to share their experiences with each other

- Providing activities that meet the needs of individual children

- Ensuring that lessons and units are relevant to children's lives

- Using hands-on activities

- Encouraging children to verbalize their reasoning processes

- Guiding children in how to ask questions

- Providing concrete analogies

- Helping children connect new information to information they already possess

Multicultural Curriculum

In a multicultural approach to learning, teachers not only employ teaching strategies congruent with the learning styles of the children, but they also include content areas representative of other cultural and ethnic groups. It is clear that multiculturalism does not mean the occasional inclusion of material on notable people and significant events from minority ethnic and racial groups, such as what often happens during Black History Month. Rather, multiculturalism involves the continuous inclusion of material from other cultures.

Teachers should have a collection of literature from many cultures in the classroom or available in the media center for use in conjunction with science lessons. The list in Figure 7.5 shows just a few of the many fine pieces of multicultural literature that support process-oriented inquiry science.

www West Virginia University has developed a comprehensive Web site that suggests many multicultural science classroom strategies for African Americans, Hispanic Americans, and Native Americans. A direct link to this Web site is available on the Student Book Companion Web Site.

NSES Teaching Standard F. Participating in Program Planning
NSES Program Standard E. Equal Opportunities for All Students
NSES Professional Development Standard D. Coherent and Integrated Programs

SELECTED EXAMPLES OF PROCESS-ORIENTED MULTICULTURAL CHILDREN'S LITERATURE

Great Black Heroes: Five Brave Explorers by W. Hudson (Scholastic, 1995) includes a biography of Mae Jemison, the first African-American woman to explore space. (Fourth to sixth grades: occupations)

How the Sun Was Brought Back to the Sky by Mirra Ginsburg (Macmillan, 1975) is a Slovenian folktale about how animals restored the sun to its original brilliance after it had been hidden behind the clouds. (Kindergarten: observing; astronomy; fantasy)

Ming Lo Moves the Mountain by Arnold Lobel (Greenwillow Books, 1982) is an Oriental folktale of a couple whose house was being destroyed by rocks falling from the mountain. A sage advised them to move the mountain; instead, they moved their house. (Second to third grades: observing; communicating; relativity)

Stone Soup: An Old Tale by Marcia Brown (Charles Scribner's Sons, 1975) is an old Irish tale of the successful efforts of hungry soldiers to get the villagers to contribute ingredients for a hearty soup so it would not have to be made of stones. (First to third grades: inferring; communicating; rocks and minerals)

The Turnip by Pierr Morgan (Philomel Books, 1990) is an old Russian folktale of many people working together who are unable to pull a giant turnip from the ground, but when a field mouse helps, it is pulled successfully. (First to third grades: communicating; predicting; inferring)

Mufarro's Beautiful Daughters: An African Tale by John Steptoe (Lothrop, 1987) is a story about two beautiful young women, one of whom the king must choose for his wife. One is selfish and spoiled and seeks to be certain that her sister is not chosen. (Kindergarten to third grade: observing; predicting; inferring)

The Egyptian Cinderella by Shirley Climo (Thomas Y. Crowell, 1989) is an Egyptian version of *Cinderella* in which the Pharaoh is seeking his queen. (Kindergarten to third grade: observing; predicting; inferring)

Yeh-Shen: A Cinderella Story from China by Al-ling Louie (Penguin Putnam Books for Young Readers, 1982) presents the Chinese version of *Cinderella,* which is almost a thousand years older than its European counterpart. In this story, Yeh-Shen earns her wishes through kindness to a magic fish instead of a fairy godmother. (Kindergarten to third grade: observing; predicting; inferring)

Literature and the Child (6th edition) by Lee Galda and Bernice Cullinan (Wadsworth, 2006) has an extensive section in which culturally diverse literature is described.

FIGURE 7.5

An excellent way of incorporating a multicultural perspective is to utilize an **ethnocentric curriculum,** wherein units and lessons revolve around facts, problems, and issues of ethnic significance.

An Afrocentric issue, for example, might center on finding ways to solve the problem of who really discovered America. Several lines of

NSES Teaching Standard B, Guiding and Facilitating Learning

7.3 | **CONSTRUCTING YOUR IDEAS**

Multicultural Literature

Multicultural literature is extremely important in fostering understanding and achievement by all cultures. Use the Internet, your college or university library, your local public library, and other sources to find both fiction and nonfiction multicultural literature that you could use with the students in the grade level you would like to teach. For each, list the title, author(s), publisher, date of publication, genre (fiction or nonfiction), and a brief summary.

Keep this list and add to it as you find additional appropriate pieces of literature.

---

evidence suggest that Africans arrived in the New World before Columbus. Columbus reported the presence of people with African features when he arrived. Archaeologists in Central and South America have excavated stone heads of men of African descent dating from 800 to 700 B.C. African folklore tells of Abubakari, the African king of Mali, who set out in the year 1311 to sail the Atlantic and reached the New World by following the strong African-Atlantic oceanic current (see Figure 7.6). Various additional archaeological data, historical correlational data between Africa and Central and South America, and ethnographic data support the notion that Africans may have settled the New World before Columbus (Van Sertima, 1976). The possible areas of scientific inquiry centering on this theme are numerous and include oceanography, archaeology, geology, human biology, and meteorology. The processes of science and employment of logical thinking skills can be taught using this case as a basis for study.

Cotton indigenous to Africa is grown in Central and South America. Very interesting experiments have been executed in modern laboratories to test the theory that these varieties of cotton entered the New World as seeds that floated on the Atlantic Ocean and were carried across by the oceanic currents. These experiments centered on the effects of ocean water over varying amounts of time on the germination capability of the seeds. Similar experiments can be designed using locally available seeds to replicate the cottonseed experiments.

An example from ancient Egypt shows the struggle that humans have had in giving up well-established concepts, such as the geocentric nature of the universe. The scarab (see Figure 7.7), sacred to ancient Egyptians and amply illustrated in the treasures from the tomb of King Tutankhamun, was thought to be the agent that pushed the sun around the sky in the daytime. Everyone knew, of course, how the sun gets from one side of the earth to the other at night: There was a huge boat manned by the

NSES Professional Development Standard B. Integrating Knowledge of Science, Learning, Pedagogy, and Students

NSES Content Standard C. Life Science: Reproduction and Heredity

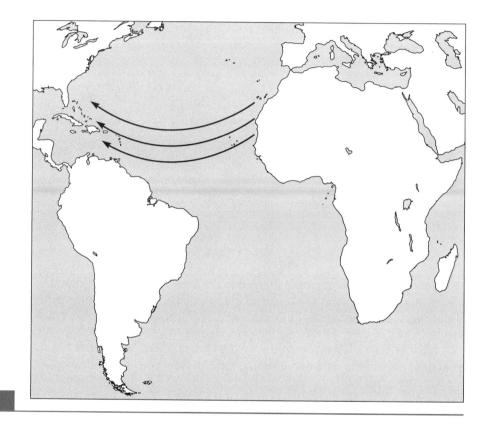

North Equatorial
Current between
Africa and Central
America

FIGURE 7.6

NSES Content
Standard G. History
and Nature of Science:
Nature of Science

gods, who put the sun in the boat when it set and rowed it to the other side across the huge lake that lies under the earth. But, how did the sun move in the daytime? There is a beetle called the dung beetle, or scarab, that is indigenous to desert environments. This beetle lays its eggs in the nearly spherical droppings of camels and rolls the dung ball around the sandy floor of the desert all day long (breaking down the animal waste into fertilizer (Berger, 2006)). If this happens on earth, why shouldn't it also happen in the sky? So the explanation emerged: A giant scarab in the sky rolls the sun across the sky just as the dung beetle rolls dung balls. Thus, the scarab became sacred, and is found depicted in many Egyptian tombs and on many items of jewelry. This event, African in nature, is ideal for promoting discussion on the nature of science, the lengths to which we will go in order to support preconceived notions, our willingness to use mystification and deification when rational explanations cannot be found, and the difficulties we encounter when we try to change conceptual bases. The behavior of dung beetles also is ideal to stimulate discussions on ecology, adaptation, specialization, reproduction, and preservation of species.

And, of course, there is the perennial question of how the pyramids of Giza were built, with the solutions centering on the principles of simple machines.

Native Americans have developed a scientific outlook that is "based on observation of the natural world coupled with direct experimentation in the natural setting" (Kawagley, Norris-Tull, & Norris-Tull, 1998, p. 140). The most effective way to teach Native American children is to infuse their culturally based knowledge and scientific outlook into the curriculum. For example, the Yupiaq design specific items of fishing gear for each species of fish in their unique habitats. To do this, they must have detailed knowledge about the behavior and migration patterns of the fish, the tidal patterns of the waters, and the patterns of river flow. These natural phenomena could become the subject of an integrated study wherein children investigate wildlife habits, the geology and alteration of natural habitats, and ecological interactions between the two. The study could center on an exploration of how the fishing gear invented long ago fills the local need.

Kawagley, Norris-Tull, and Norris-Tull (1998) report an experiment that children designed to investigate the effectiveness of various substances in removing hair from caribou hides. This activity enabled children to combine their own culturally based knowledge with the experimental

 Direct links to Web sites that discuss theories how the pyramids of Giza were built are available on the Student Book Companion Web Site.

NSES Content Standard F. Science in Personal and Social Perspectives: Science and Technology in Local Challenges
NSES Program Standard E. Provides Equal Opportunities for All Students

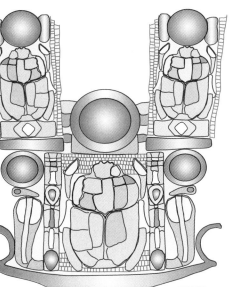

Drawing of scarabs from King Tutankhamun's jewelry

FIGURE 7.7

techniques inherent in process-oriented inquiry, resulting in a hands-on investigation that focused on a problem relevant to the children's lives.

Although culturally diverse topics are included in the education of all children, in an elementary classroom with high numbers of individuals representing particular cultures, a science curriculum that is grounded in self-referencing ethnocentricity increases the opportunities children have to use relevant prior experiences to make the science investigations meaningful. The ethnocentric occurrence becomes the starting point for the exploration of concepts—the event that provokes children to ask, "Why?" "How did that work?" "How could they do that?" "How does that relate to what we know today?" The chosen event becomes the base on which learning experiences are constructed that lead to achievement of the desired objectives.

Teachers must consider cultural and ethnic differences when planning instruction. Instructional programs must be structured to reflect the cultures and learning styles of students from the diverse cultural and ethnic groups in the classroom. Most important, we must "stop seeing cultural differences as developmental disturbances and . . . allow competence to be expressed in many different ways. Our thinking about the education of . . . minority children needs to begin not from an assumption of deficiency but from a recognition of cultural competence" (Bowman, 1994, p. 221).

Conclusion

Children exhibit many learning styles and capabilities, and they bring the heritage and prior experiences of many cultures to the classroom. Elementary science teachers must examine their own cultural literacy and biases and work toward eliminating any negative or intolerant biases. They must design and deliver instruction that achieves the maximum possible congruity with the learning styles, abilities, and cultural factors of the children. Only in this way will all children be able to construct meaning successfully.

CHAPTER 7

Additional Questions for Discussion

1. Hilliard (1994) has written, "When educators do not notice diversity, when they give negative notice, or when they lose the opportunity to give positive notice of the natural diversity that is always there, they create a bogus reality for teaching and learning." Discuss the implications of this statement for the elementary science classroom.

2. How does teaching in an inquiry-oriented constructivist manner promote optimum learning by all children regardless of their differences?

3. For each of the learner differences discussed in this chapter, list some accommodating instructional strategies that specifically relate to process-oriented inquiry.

Internet Activities

Use the Internet to find current information on ways of helping English language learners and children with disabilities and special needs develop process skills and learn how to do science and information on ways of implementing the principles of multicultural education in the elementary science classroom.

Use the Internet to locate information on any culture you might find in your elementary science classroom. Use this background to help you tailor your teaching so it uses the heritages from those cultures.

Note

1. The Association for Women in Science (AWIS) promotes opportunities for women in science.

Regional chapters throughout the United States sponsor a variety of programs aimed at promoting girls and women in science; many maintain lists of women scientists who are willing to speak at elementary schools. For more information, contact the AWIS, 1200 New York Avenue NW, Suite 650, Washington, DC 20005.

A direct link to the AWIS Web site is available on the Student Book Companion Web Site.

CHAPTER···8
ASSESSMENT

It ain't over till it's over.

Yogi Berra, *The Yogi Book: "I Really Didn't Say Everything I Said"* (New York: Workman Publishing, 1998), p. 121

The primary goal of assessment in education is to obtain and interpret information about student attainment—what children know and what they can do. To accomplish this, the assessment information that is obtained must reflect the goals and objectives of the curriculum and must represent student achievement fully, completely, and accurately.

A second and equally important goal of assessment is the evaluation of teacher performance and the program itself.

It is well known that assessment sends clear messages to children about what is valued in the classroom and, thus, what must be done to get good grades. In elementary science, children must be sent the message that the important outcomes of their work are facility and progress in the processes of science and in inquiry—that science is a process and not merely a collection of facts. Sometimes teachers succumb to the notion of teaching what is tested rather than testing what is taught. Because acquisition of factual information is relatively easy to test, tests of factual information tend to dominate, and teachers teach facts so children will do well on the factual tests. This tendency must be replaced with the notion of testing what we teach rather than teaching what we test.

American education is undergoing a paradigm shift in assessment. Testing in traditional pencil-and-paper formats is yielding to more authentic methods such as interviews, observations, portfolios, performance assessment, and human judgment. Furthermore, rather than assessment being limited to specific occasions scheduled at the end of lessons, units, or school terms, it is becoming an integral part of learning, woven directly into the instruction. This new paradigm enables teachers to gather the maximum possible information about the achievement and progress of each child.

In opposition to this shift to more authentic methods of assessment, great emphasis is being placed on "high-stakes" standardized testing, especially in response to the *No Child Left Behind Act* and its high-stakes requirement for annual standardized testing (see Chapter 2). These tests are exerting tremendous influences over the curriculum, the method of instruction, the amount of time spent on science, and methods of assessing children's achievement.

In this chapter, you will consider ways in which process-oriented inquiry science teachers can assess the learning of their students. Several authentic assessment models are offered. You will look at the question of process versus content as the focus of various assessment plans is considered, and you will examine the role of standardized tests in elementary science. You also will look at the pros and cons of high-stakes testing as it relates to elementary science education. Thus, you will be able to construct your own assessment program to meet the needs of both children and educational constituencies.

In the quality elementary science program, teacher performance and the science program itself also must be assessed. To this end, you will consider ways to reflect on the success of the work you do in the classroom and the program you develop.

As is the case throughout this text, no formulas are offered. Rather, you are encouraged to construct your own valid conceptualizations about assessing student progress and achievement in elementary science as you begin developing assessment systems congruent with your conceptualization of constructivism and process-oriented inquiry science teaching in the elementary grades.

AUTHENTIC ASSESSMENT

There are three sides to the education triangle: what to teach, how to teach it, and how to measure the results. Most of the attention in science education has focused on the first two sides—what to teach (curriculum), and how to teach it (methodology). The assessment side has been less prominent.

Because teachers have received limited guidance on developing assessment systems, many have relied on textbook tests and standardized achievement tests for much of their elementary science assessment program. These tests—the only assessment instruments that are readily available—have driven the curriculum, with the result that teachers have taught what is to be tested and the concept of the test-driven curriculum has been reinforced. Furthermore, similar to the notion that teachers tend to teach the way they were taught, teachers tend to test the way they were tested—largely through paper-and-pencil tests. In addition, the *No Child Left Behind* legislation seems to reinforce the concept of the test-driven curriculum by requiring annual testing in reading and mathematics and, by the 2007–2008 academic year, science as well. Unfortunately, these typical science tests generally are not "consistent with current science education goals" (Smith, Ryan, & Kuhs, 1993, p. 8).

NSES Assessment Standard A. Consistent with the Decisions it will Inform
NSES Teaching Standard C. Assessing Teaching and Learning

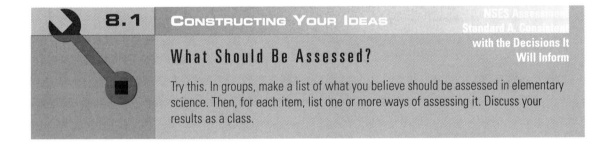

8.1   **CONSTRUCTING YOUR IDEAS**

NSES Assessment Standard A. Consistent with the Decisions It Will Inform

What Should Be Assessed?

Try this. In groups, make a list of what you believe should be assessed in elementary science. Then, for each item, list one or more ways of assessing it. Discuss your results as a class.

There is a principle that underlies all assessment: Teachers must assess what children are supposed to learn. Assessment in science must be congruent with the goals of science education and must "mirror what we value most" (Eisenkraft, 2001, p.2). Everyone is familiar with the incongruities that often are encountered between objectives and assessment. For example, there was a teacher who assessed her children's facility in addition and subtraction by presenting complex story problems. When children failed the test, she attributed the poor performance to their not knowing addition and subtraction facts. Then there was a teacher who assigned the children inquiry investigations about the behavior of mealworms under various circumstances and then gave a test on the external anatomy of the worms.

If children are supposed to accomplish a certain objective, they must be assessed on their achievement of that objective and not on something else. For example, if we want children to learn to classify, we must assess their ability to classify, not their ability to reproduce classification systems devised by someone else. The objectives of elementary science are process and inquiry in orientation. Thus, the focus of the elementary science assessment program must be on student attainment in process and inquiry—areas that are difficult to assess using paper-and-pencil tests.

Assessment must provide the best possible picture of what children know and how they think. Traditional paper-and-pencil tests do not always provide clear indications of what children have achieved. Typical multiple-choice and short-answer tests may do a reasonably good job of assessing acquisition of content, but content is not the focus of the elementary science program. This dilemma has provided the impetus for shifting to alternative forms of assessment that are congruent with the goals of science education and that enable teachers to find out what the children *really* know.

The notion of assessing what children *really* know in the areas of the program they are being taught is termed **authentic assessment.**

NSES Assessment
Standard D. Fair Assessments
NSES Teaching
Standard C. Assessing
Teaching and Learning

The national science organizations support the shift to authentic assessment. The National Science Teachers Association says that science assessments should assess the following curriculum areas (National Science Teachers Association, 2001):

- Understanding of science content and process knowledge and skills

- Ability to think critically and solve problems

- Capability of designing scientific experiments, analyzing data, and drawing conclusions

- Capacity to see and articulate relationships between science topics and real-world issues

- Skills for using mathematics as a tool for science learning

The *National Science Education Standards* describes assessment as a range of strategies involving the collection and interpretation of educational data (National Research Council, 1996, p. 76). In its companion volume devoted to inquiry in science education, the National Research Council (2000) says that "[a]ssessment in inquiry-based classrooms . . . asks what each student knows and understands, what is fuzzy or missing, and what students can do with what they know" (p. 75). Appleton (2007) observes from the elementary science education literature of the past decade that "[a]ssessment tasks *must* be authentic—that is, they should relate to the real world of the student in a meaningful way" [italics added] (p. 508).

WHAT IS ASSESSED IN ELEMENTARY SCIENCE EDUCATION?

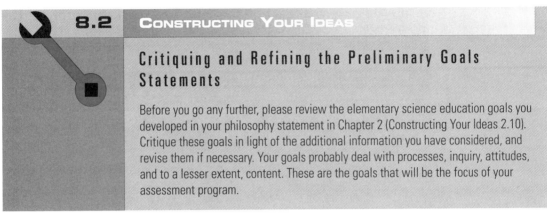

8.2   **CONSTRUCTING YOUR IDEAS**

Critiquing and Refining the Preliminary Goals Statements

Before you go any further, please review the elementary science education goals you developed in your philosophy statement in Chapter 2 (Constructing Your Ideas 2.10). Critique these goals in light of the additional information you have considered, and revise them if necessary. Your goals probably deal with processes, inquiry, attitudes, and to a lesser extent, content. These are the goals that will be the focus of your assessment program.

In this chapter, you will consider the question of what children can do to show they have accomplished these goals.

Assessment of Process Skills

A primary goal of elementary science is for children to acquire facility in the process skills. Assessment of the process skills involves determining how well children have mastered them. How can a teacher tell how well children have mastered a process skill? It is helpful to identify things the children can be expected to do if they truly understand the process. For example, a second-grade teacher could reasonably infer that children have mastered the skill of classifying if they sort things into two or more mutually exclusive groups and include one or more subgroups for each. If the children are working with leaves, they might come up with a group of elongated leaves and a group of leaves that look like hands with fingers. Then, they might subdivide each group into several subgroups and give descriptive names to each main group and subgroup that show how the characteristics of the leaves in each group are different from the characteristics of the leaves in any other group.

The actions children take that demonstrate they understand the processes they are working on are called **indicators.** Indicators are performances children do that help the teacher gauge mastery.

Some of the indicators that can show children's progress in the process skills are shown in Figure 8.1. These indicators represent a few of the things that children in kindergarten through grade eight should be able to do to demonstrate competence in each process. They are listed somewhat hierarchically for each process, from less advanced to more advanced. The extent to which children actually can demonstrate proficiency in a

NSES Assessment Standard B. Assess Achievement and Opportunity to Learn Science
NSES Assessment Standard A. Consistent with the Decisions It Will Inform
NSES Assessment Standard B. Assess Achievement and Opportunity to Learn Science
NSES Teaching Standard C. Assessing Teaching and Learning

process depends on many factors. These factors include at least grade, age, and individual differences among the children as well as the context and circumstances in which the skill is being investigated. For example, children in lower grades generally can be expected to exhibit proficiency in fewer advanced indicators than children in upper grades.

SOME INDICATORS OF PROFICIENCY IN THE PROCESSES

Observing
Identifies objects
Uses more than one sense
Uses all appropriate senses
Identifies the senses used
Uses observation equipment such as magnifying glasses correctly
Describes properties accurately
Provides qualitative observations either verbally or pictorially
Provides quantitative observations
Describes changes in objects

Classifying
Identifies major properties by which objects can be sorted
Identifies properties similar to all objects in a collection
Sorts accurately into two groups
Sorts accurately in multiple ways
Forms subgroups
Establishes own sorting criteria
Provides sound rationale for classifications
Develops complex classification systems

Communicating
Identifies objects and events accurately
Describes objects and events accurately
Provides descriptions such that others can identify unknown objects
Formulates reasonable and logical arguments to justify explanations and
    conclusions
Transmits information to others accurately in oral and written formats
Verbalizes thinking

Measuring
Selects appropriate type of measurement (length, volume, weight, and the like)
Selects appropriate units of measurement
Uses measurement instruments properly
Applies measurement techniques appropriately

FIGURE 8.1

Continued on next page

SOME INDICATORS OF PROFICIENCY IN THE PROCESSES

Uses standard and nonstandard units
Uses measurements as evidence
Uses measurements to help explain conclusions

Predicting
Forms patterns
Extends patterns
Performs simple predictions
Applies the process of prediction in appropriate situations
Exhibits sound logic in verbalizing reasons for predictions
Suggests tests to check for accuracy of predictions
Predicts by interpolation of data
Predicts by extrapolation of data

Inferring
Describes relationships among objects and events observed
Uses all appropriate information in making inferences
Makes inferences based on evidence
Does not use nonexistent information
Separates appropriate from nonessential information
Exhibits sound reasoning in verbalizing inferences
Applies the process of inference in appropriate situations
Interprets graphs, tables, and other experimental data

Identifying and Controlling Variables
Identifies factors that might affect the outcome of an experiment
Identifies factors that will not affect the outcome of an experiment
Identifies variables that can be manipulated and those that can be controlled
Shows ways of keeping controlled variables constant
Shows ways of changing manipulated variables such that useful data can be
    obtained.

Formulating Hypotheses
Constructs a hypothesis when given a problem or question
Formulates own hypothesis from own problem
Suggests several plausible hypotheses to explain observed situations
Develops ways of testing hypotheses
Systematically tests all hypotheses concerning observed situations by collecting
    data and analyzing evidence
Formulates tentative conclusions based on evidence from hypothesis testing

Interpreting Data
Identifies data needed and how to measure it
Plans for the collection of both qualitative and quantitative data

Continued on next page

FIGURE 8.1

SOME INDICATORS OF PROFICIENCY IN THE PROCESSES

Collects data that is usable as evidence
Constructs data tables
Constructs and interprets graphs
Makes valid interpretations of data

Defining Operationally
Tells whether a variable can be measured conveniently
Recognizes the need for an operational definition in given situations
Decides how to measure the variable in operational terms
Verbalizes congruence between operational definition and the variable to be
measured

Experimenting
Follows directions for an experiment
Develops alternative ways to investigate a question
Manipulates materials
Performs trial-and-error investigations
Identifies testable questions
Designs own investigative procedure
Formulates valid conclusions based on evidence

Constructing Models
Differentiates between model and real thing
Identifies appropriate needs for models
Interprets models in terms of the real thing
Develops own accurate and appropriate models

FIGURE 8.1

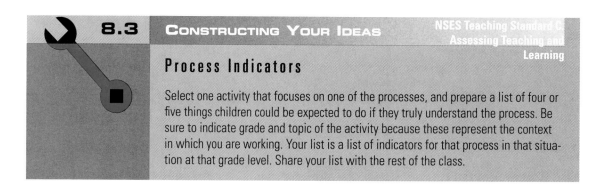

8.3 **CONSTRUCTING YOUR IDEAS** NSES Teaching Standard C:
Assessing Teaching and
Learning

Process Indicators

Select one activity that focuses on one of the processes, and prepare a list of four or five things children could be expected to do if they truly understand the process. Be sure to indicate grade and topic of the activity because these represent the context in which you are working. Your list is a list of indicators for that process in that situation at that grade level. Share your list with the rest of the class.

Teachers should prepare checklists of indicators that show proficiency in the processes at the grade level being taught and compare children's actual proficiencies with the indicators. You may prepare indicators as specific as assessing children's competence in one process during one lesson or as general as assessing children's competence in several processes during a unit of study or at the end of a term or a marking period. Lists constructed by teachers for use in their own classrooms reflect their own situations and the needs of their children. The indicators shown in Figure 8.1 are shown only as a guide to help you get started in developing your own indicators.

Observation

Teacher observation is an excellent technique for assessing children's mastery of the processes. Combined with formal or semistructured interviewing (discussed below), observation can yield much information about children's achievement and progress in the process skills. Observation can be informal or structured.

Informal observation occurs as the teacher watches children do activities while circulating among groups. Informal observation gives the teacher a general idea about what the children are doing, whether they are on the right track, whether they are exploring the processes they are supposed to be exploring, and whether they are sequencing operations in a logical and appropriate manner.

Structured observations can be set up in several ways. Most commonly, teachers prepare a list of specific behaviors indicative of achievement of the objective or objectives, such as the indicator lists explored in Figure 8.1, and, as they circulate throughout their classroom, check off those behaviors they see exhibited by each child.

For **qualitative assessment,** the teacher checks off the indicators on the list as the child demonstrates them. When all indicators are checked off, the child is considered to have achieved mastery of the process at that age and grade level.

For **quantitative assessment** that can be used in grade calculations, the teacher assigns numerical values of, say, 1 to 4 for each indicator and calculates the sum or the average. The average of the averages for all indicator lists would be the total process score of the child.

The checklist system of assessment is subjective in that the teacher makes a personal judgment about proficiency in each process. However, it is objective in that each process is broken into several indicators that can be assessed and evaluated quantitatively.

Practical Assessments

Another way of using structured observations is to give a "practical test." This is similar to the "lab tests" you may have taken in your science courses. These are performance-based assessment activities that can be used to test children's proficiency in the process skills. The technique

A station where children demonstrate proficiency in the skill of observation

FIGURE 8.2

may involve setting up several stations like the one shown in Figure 8.2, each of which requires the children to perform one or more activities that indicate proficiency in a process skill. Children rotate from station to station, either individually or in groups, and perform the required activities. Figure 8.3 shows an example of a practical process skill assessment for early elementary children. The test assesses skills appropriate for children in the early elementary grades and is derived from the general list of indicators given in Figure 8.1. Of course, teachers must design their own hands-on practical assessment tasks to reflect their expectations of the children and the activities done in class.

SAMPLE PRACTICAL PROCESS SKILL ASSESSMENT FOR EARLY ELEMENTARY CHILDREN

Station 1: Three or four different vegetables
Activity: Describe the characteristics of each. Tell what senses you used.
Process skill assessed: Observing

Station 2: A collection of 10–15 seeds
Activity: Group the seeds into two groups and name each group.
Process skill assessed: Classifying

Station 3: An object in a paper bag
Activity: Describe the object to a partner, without naming it, such that the partner can identify it correctly.
Process skill assessed: Communicating

Station 4: A wooden block and a ruler
Activity: Measure the length of the block.
Process skill assessed: Measuring

Station 5: A tub of water with several objects beside it
Activity: Predict whether each object will sink or float.
Process skill assessed: Predicting

Station 6: Three opaque canisters with different things in them
Activity: Tell what's in the canisters.
Process skill assessed: Inferring

Station 7: Two glass soda bottles, each filled to a different level with water; a wooden stick
Activity: Tell which will make the higher sound when hit with the stick.
Process skill assessed: Predicting

Station 8: Three different rocks
Activity: Describe the characteristics of each rock. Tell the similarities and differences among them.
Process skill assessed: Observing

Station 9: A collection of 10–12 shells
Activity: Group the shells and name each group.
Process skill assessed: Classifying

Station 10: Two wooden blocks and a two-pan balance
Activity: Tell which is heavier; tell how you know.
Process skill assessed: Measuring

Station 11: Picture of an outdoor scene with long shadows
Activity: Tell where the sun is.
Process skill assessed: Inferring

FIGURE 8.3

SCORING SYSTEM FOR PRACTICAL PROCESS SKILLS ASSESSMENT SHOWN IN FIGURE 8.3

Score	Criterion
1	Not seen
2	Performed satisfactorily
3	Performed well
4	Performed in an outstanding and advanced manner

Station	Process Skill	Score
1	Observing	_____
2	Classifying	_____
3	Communicating	_____
4	Measuring	_____
5	Predicting	_____
6	Inferring	_____
7	Predicting	_____
8	Observing	_____
9	Classifying	_____
10	Measuring	_____
11	Inferring	_____
	TOTAL	_____
	Divided by maximum total of 44 = PERCENTAGE	======

FIGURE 8.4

In the lower elementary grades, the teacher records each child's response to the task; in the upper elementary grades, a sheet may be provided on which children record their responses. Children's performance on each task can be scored on the basis of 1 to 4, where 1 means the skill was not seen, 2 means it was done satisfactorily, 3 means it was done well, and 4 means it was done in an outstanding and advanced manner (see Figure 8.4). An example of this system that includes reasons for each score is provided in Figure 8.5.

A variation of the practical assessment uses the "unknown." Given suitable material and equipment, students are asked to apply the processes to determine the nature or composition of something unknown. For example, Townsend and Bunton (2006) use a "sick aquarium" assessment in which students use indicator chemicals they have not seen before to test whether a water sample is an acid or a base.

SAMPLE OF SCORING FOR A CHILD DOING PRACTICAL PROCESS SKILL ASSESSMENT SHOWN IN FIGURE 8.3

Station	Process	Score	Reason for Score
1	Observing	2	Child did not use sense of smell.
2	Classifying	4	Child formed two mutually exclusive groups.
3	Communicating	1	Child was able only to identify object, not describe it.
4	Measuring	3	Child measured whole units; did not round increments to nearest whole.
5	Predicting	4	Child made accurate predictions and tested each.
6	Inferring	2	Child used limited investigation.
7	Predicting	4	Child made accurate predictions and tested each.
8	Observing	3	Child described properties; did not tell similarities and differences.
9	Classifying	3	Child formed only two groups, but they were mutually exclusive.
10	Measuring	4	Child operated balance properly.
11	Inferring	2	Child said "sun is in the sky;" did not give location.
	TOTAL SCORE	32	
	PERCENTAGE	$32 \div 44 = \underline{\underline{73\%}}$	

FIGURE 8.5

The hands-on activities method of assessment has several advantages. You can see what the children can do under relatively controlled and constant conditions, and you can obtain quantitative data comparable for all the children in your class. Children's performance on the activities is representative of their proficiency in the process skills. The cultural bias and the emphasis on verbal skills often inherent in other assessment methods are reduced, and different learning styles and intelligences can be accommodated. The disadvantage is that the atmosphere can be "test-like," and children may bring the anxieties and fears to this situation that they bring to any testing situation.

Assessment of Inquiry

A second major goal in elementary science education is proficiency in inquiry. Inquiry implies a penchant for investigating, curiosity, a personal necessity to resolve cognitive disequilibrations, and the desire to pursue questions to satisfactory solutions. The *National Science Education Standards* says that inquiry "refers to the activities of students in which they develop knowledge and understanding of scientific ideas, as well as an understanding of how scientists study the natural world" (National Research Council, 1996, p. 23.) In process-oriented inquiry science, the teacher suggests open-ended activities. Children pursue these activities to construct initial understandings and inquire in greater depth into what they do not understand readily. They investigate additional questions suggested by their explorations and develop their own tentative conclusions. They discuss their conclusions with one another and with the teacher to confirm validity or to plan further investigations to achieve revised conclusions. The role of the teacher is to develop the rationale, goals, and objectives for the lesson or unit; prepare the initial activity; have additional activities available; ask questions; help children ask their own questions; and especially, *listen* to gain understanding of what the children are saying. Inquiry is the agent of constructivist teaching.

Children's facility with inquiry is a major component of their achievement in science. Thus, assessment of children's inquiry skills is an integral component of the elementary science assessment program.

As we showed in Chapter 5, the National Research Council identified five essential features of classroom inquiry. These five features capture the essence of inquiry and show how students can validate their conceptualizations through inquiry (National Research Council, 2000, p. 29). They are repeated below:

1. Learner engages in scientifically oriented questions.

2. Learner gives priority to *evidence* in responding to questions.

3. Learner formulates *explanations* from evidence.

4. Learner connects explanations to scientific knowledge.

5. Learner communicates and justifies explanations.

A number of specific indicators represent student facility in inquiry. Some are shown in Figure 8.6. The actual indicators that teachers use depend on the grade, age, and individual differences among the children as well as the context, circumstances, and depth of the inquiry activities. Teachers or teams or schools must develop their own list of indicators that reflects their particular program and the expectations of their particular children. The student indicators provided in Figure 8.6 will help you get started.

SOME INDICATORS OF STUDENT PROFICIENCY IN INQUIRY

- Selects and applies processes appropriately
- Asks appropriate questions about phenomena under investigation
- Initiates own ideas for investigation
- Investigates own questions and ideas
- Uses a variety of information sources, including printed material, multimedia, and people
- Relates investigations to prior experiences
- Collects qualitative and quantitative data that is usable as evidence
- Suggests causes for what is observed based on evidence
- Explains thinking process in a rational and logical way
- Presents ideas and conceptualizations to others for their input
- Discusses and challenges the ideas and conceptualizations of others
- Analyzes conclusions and reformulates them in light of new evidence, new experiences, and input from others
- Subjects conclusions to tests of explanatory power and predictive power
- Formulates reasonable and logical arguments based on evidence to justify conclusions
- Seeks opportunities to continue explorations
- Exhibits realistic self-appraisal
- Relates learning to out-of-school situations

FIGURE 8.6

The inquiry indicator checklists are used in the same way as the process checklist—through informal and structured observations. In a qualitative approach, the list can be used as a guide for an overall, subjective assessment of the child's inquiry. In a quantitative approach, each indicator can be rated on a 1 to 4 basis (1 = not seen; 2 = performed satisfactorily; 3 = performed well; and 4 = performed in an outstanding and advanced manner), with the average equaling the inquiry grade.

An example of the use of all the indicators on the inquiry checklist of Figure 8.6 is shown in Figure 8.7.

The results of the process and inquiry indicator checklists can be coupled with other assessment methods to enable the teacher to arrive at an authentic assessment of the child's progress and achievement in science. Once again, it is best if you get together with your team members and develop your own lists of indicators that you tailor to meet the needs of the children in your classes. You should field test the checklists by analyzing children's responses and performances and, especially, by asking children to share their thoughts and perceptions of the assessment activity.

INQUIRY CHECKLIST REPORT

Score	Criterion
1	Not seen
2	Performed satisfactorily
3	Performed well
4	Performed in an outstanding and advanced manner

1. Selects and applies processes appropriately   _____
2. Asks appropriate questions about phenomena under investigation   _____
3. Initiates own ideas for investigation   _____
4. Investigates own questions and ideas   _____
5. Utilizes a variety of information sources, including printed material, multimedia, and people   _____
6. Relates investigations to prior experiences   _____
7. Collects qualitative and quantitative data that is usable as evidence   _____
8. Suggests causes for what is observed based on evidence   _____
9. Explains thinking process in a rational and logical way   _____
10. Presents ideas and conceptualizations to others for their input   _____
11. Discusses and challenges the ideas and conceptualizations of others   _____
12. Analyzes conclusions and reformulates them in light of new evidence, new experiences, and input from others   _____
13. Subjects conclusions to tests of explanatory power and predictive power   _____
14. Formulates reasonable and logical arguments based on evidence to justify conclusions   _____
15. Seeks opportunities to continue explorations   _____
16. Exhibits realistic self-appraisal   _____
17. Relates learning to out-of-school situations   _____

TOTAL _____

PERCENTAGE (Total ÷ 68) _____

FIGURE 8.7

NSES Assessment Standard A. Consistent with the Decisions It Will Inform
NSES Assessment Standard B. Assess Achievement and Opportunity to Learn Science
NSES Teaching Standard C. Assessing Teaching and Learning

Assessment of Attitude

A third major goal of elementary science education is the development of positive attitudes toward science and scientists. Positive attitudes revolve around valuing scientific reasoning, scientific accomplishments, and the benefits to society of advancing science and technology. To a certain extent, attitudinal factors are incorporated in the inquiry indicator list. Factors such as collaboration, reflection, curiosity, search for evidence, use of evidence, and extension of learning to out-of-school situations are

SOME INDICATORS OF POSITIVE ATTITUDES TOWARD SCIENCE

- Uses extra time for science investigations
- Talks about science being fun and interesting
- Verbalizes curiosity
- Extends science to out-of-school situations
- Voluntarily participates in out-of-school science activities
- Visits museums, planetariums, aquariums, botanical gardens, and other science-oriented public attractions
- Inquires into scientific occupations and careers
- Seeks additional work in science
- Volunteers to assist in the setup and cleanup of science activities
- Takes an active role in maintaining the science center and live plants and animals in the classroom
- Chooses science-oriented television programs to watch
- Seeks science-oriented informational Web sites on the Internet
- Chooses science-oriented computer-based media such as CD ROMs
- Participates in Invention Conventions, Science Olympiads, and science fairs

FIGURE 8.8

included as inquiry indicators that represent positive attitudes toward science. There also are additional indicators that reflect children's attitudes toward science, some of which are shown in Figure 8.8. Of course, the exact nature of the list will depend on your unique situation, the availability of science-oriented resources in the community, the characteristics of your class, and the needs and prior attitudes of the children. You are certain to observe additional indicators of positive science attitudes. Be sure to add these to the list so you maintain as complete a list of attitudinal indicators as possible.

Attitudinal questionnaires also can provide a means of assessing children's feelings about science. Figure 8.9 shows an informal survey designed to assess children's attitudes about their science program; it was adapted from an attitudinal questionnaire developed for fourth-, fifth-, and sixth-grade children in one school district. You may want to have children complete a survey like this at the beginning of the school year and again toward the end to see if there is any change in attitude as a result of your teaching.

Assessment of Content

The emphasis in this text is process-oriented inquiry where children construct their own conceptualizations. Scientific facts, concepts, theories,

NSES Assessment Standard A. Consistent with the Decisions It Will Inform
NSES Assessment Standard B. Assess Achievement and Opportunity to Learn Science
NSES Teaching Standard C. Assessing Teaching and Learning

SCIENCE CLASS ATTITUDE SURVEY

Directions to student: Please answer each of the following items as honestly as possible.

1. Do you wish you had more time for science in school?
   A. Yes　　　B. No　　　C. I don't know
2. Do you have fun in science class?
   A. Yes　　　B. No　　　C. I don't know
3. Is your science class interesting?
   A. Yes　　　B. No　　　C. I don't know
4. Is your science class exciting?
   A. Yes　　　B. No　　　C. I don't know
5. Do you feel comfortable in your science class?
   A. Yes　　　B. No　　　C. I don't know
6. Do you feel successful in science?
   A. Yes　　　B. No　　　C. I don't know
7. Does your science class make you feel curious?
   A. Yes　　　B. No　　　C. I don't know
8. Does your teacher ask you questions about science?
   A. Yes　　　B. No　　　C. I don't know
9. Do you like to ask questions about science?
   A. Yes　　　B. No　　　C. I don't know
10. Do you like keeping a science portfolio?
    A. Yes　　　B. No　　　C. I don't know
11. Are the things you learn in science useful to you when you are not in school?
    A. Yes　　　B. No　　　C. I don't know
12. Do you think that knowing a lot about science will help you in the future?
    A. Yes　　　B. No　　　C. I don't know
13. Do you feel that the science you study is generally useful to you?
    A. Yes　　　B. No　　　C. I don't know
14. Do you think that being a scientist would be fun?
    A. Yes　　　B. No　　　C. I don't know
15. Do you think that being a scientist would make you feel important?
    A. Yes　　　B. No　　　C. I don't know

Courtesy: Larry Small, Science/Health Coordinator, School District 54, Schaumburg, IL 60194

FIGURE 8.9

and laws are used as vehicles for inquiry and process skill development, and are constructed by children through their process-oriented inquiries.

Because the emphasis is on *doing* science rather than on *learning about* science, it is obvious that the assessment should deal with how children *do* science rather than with the science they learn *about*. Nevertheless, there is a certain public sentiment favoring the acquisition of science content by children. Educators are accountable to the public, so you most likely will need to assess student achievement in scientific content in addition to processes and inquiry. Furthermore, as we indicated earlier, *No Child Left Behind* requires testing in science by the 2007–2008 academic year.

One of the basic understandings in the process-oriented inquiry approach to elementary science is that children will learn the content selected to be the vehicles through which the processes are mastered, will learn it more thoroughly, and will retain it longer than they would using other methodologies, because children are constructing their own meaning. Roberts (2006/2007) writes that in guided inquiry, "teachers can give students the freedom to discover through exploration, yet guide the search so that students can't help but bump into the target knowledge" (p. 68). If you believe this, then student acquisition of content should pose no particular concern. In situations where content assessment is required, there generally is a listing of content that children are expected to acquire. Use this content as the vehicles for process attainment and for the basis of inquiry investigations. However, bear in mind that in inquiry, it is desirable to let children explore in directions their own thinking takes them. To restrict the content used for process and inquiry vehicles is to limit the explorations of children.

Using the content required by the district as the basis for the process and inquiry activities enables children to learn both content and process. For example, if the district requires that kindergarten children learn about magnets, you can use magnets and magnetism as the vehicle through which children observe, classify, communicate, measure, predict, and infer. You can develop inquiry activities that use magnets and magnetism. If necessary or desirable, you may choose to give occasional content-oriented tests to demonstrate content achievement. Tests provided by textbook publishers normally contain suggestions for content-oriented tests.

Assessment of content achievement should be considered simply another aspect of the total assessment program rather than its focus. The focus is on processes and inquiry and on how well children are learning how to *do* science.

ADDITIONAL AUTHENTIC ASSESSMENT TECHNIQUES

In the constructivist methodology, children construct their own valid meanings. In assessing what children have learned and how they think, it is necessary to discover the meanings children have constructed. Paper-and-pencil tests are inadequate for accomplishing this goal.

NSES Assessment
Standard D. Fair
Assessments

We have already suggested several authentic methods of assessing process skills and inquiry. Several additional alternative forms of assessment enable teachers to probe deeper into children's thinking than is possible using traditional methods of assessment.

Interviewing

NSES Assessment Standard C. Data Matched to Resulting Decisions and Actions NSES Assessment Standard D. Fair Assessments

In keeping with the constructivist view, one of the best ways to find out how much children have learned and how well they understand what they have learned is to ask them about it. Open-ended and partially structured interviews with individual children accomplish this goal and are truly authentic ways of obtaining information about children's achievement and their thinking (Seda, 1991, p. 24).

The open-ended interview is a free-flowing conversation between teacher and child in which the teacher asks questions relating to the objectives of the lessons and follows up on the child's responses. The teacher probes, asks additional questions, and in general, attempts to discover how the child has arrived at the responses given. Duckworth (1987) offers these examples (p. 97):

"What do you mean?"

"How did you do that?"

"How does that fit in with what she just said?"

"Could you give me an example?"

"How did you figure that?"

The open-ended interview is, perhaps, the ideal way to "jump into the heads of students to see how they are constructing information," as Lanier (1987) said. The primary advantage of the open-ended interview technique is that, given enough time, the teacher ultimately can gain a greater depth of understanding about what the children are thinking. It takes time, however, and time usually is a constraint. Furthermore, the teacher's understandings are subjective in nature and cannot easily be translated into marks.

In the partially structured interview, the teacher prepares the questions and the guidelines for the interview to be certain that the same questions are asked of all children. The line of questioning was somewhat predetermined as the lesson plans were developed (Item 9, "Typical Discussion Questions," of the lesson plan format suggested in Figure 5.5). While asking the questions, the teacher engages the children in discussion and probes their responses to understand what the children are thinking. In addition, children's thinking is clarified and taken a step further because of the interchange.

This method provides an opportunity for children to talk and for teachers to listen, but because the questions are predetermined, the conversation does not reach as deeply into children's thinking as the open-ended interview. The opportunity for children to explain something that is not on the list of questions is limited.

Good teachers conduct open-ended and partially structured interviews continually as their students work on their investigations. They move from group to group asking salient questions about what the children observed, what they concluded, and why they concluded it. The interview should become a routine part of the assessment program in elementary science education. It is only by asking children questions and listening to their responses—by probing until the *teacher* understands what the *children* understand—that the teacher will know what the children know and how they think.

Notes of informal interviews can be made throughout the day. In addition, at the end of an activity, experiment, or area of inquiry, the teacher should engage the children (individually or in groups) in discussions of what they did, what they concluded, what their conclusions were based on, what they learned, and what their thought processes were. Such discussions provide a great deal of information concerning student achievement and how children have constructed ideas and concepts.

Throughout this text, questioning has been suggested as one of the best ways teachers can jump into children's heads to see how they are constructing information. The *think-aloud* is another questioning technique that aids the teacher in informal assessment. Children are asked to think out loud—to describe their thinking as they do activities, make decisions in an experiment, or work through problems. In this manner, the teacher can obtain information about how the child is constructing meaning. We engage in think-alouds when we talk out loud to ourselves about the next move in a game of chess or discuss unit planning with members of our team.

The directions for employing the think-aloud technique are simple: The teacher asks the child to talk his or her way through the situation and follows up with open-ended questions as necessary about why the child did this or that. Indirect questions are used so as not to suggest "correct" responses to the children. Examples of such questioning are:

"Tell me what you are thinking."

"Talk me through this."

"Can you tell us more?"

"Why?"

"And, so . . ." (asking the child to end the comment)

Think-alouds have been shown to foster teacher understanding of children's thinking in reading (Wade, 1990), and they are excellent tools to assess children's understanding of science. In addition, think-alouds help children clarify their own thinking.

Note that the primary purpose of oral assessment techniques is to listen to the children so you can find out what they are thinking, *not* to find out if they are right or wrong. Remember the concept of "no wrong answers." Sometimes children put information together in invalid ways, and oral assessment gives the teacher the opportunity to help correct the problem. And sometimes the children's thinking is, in fact, valid but something the teacher never thought of. Oral assessment gives the teacher the opportunity to help the child assume ownership.

Science Journals and Science Notebooks

NSES Assessment Standard C. Data Matched to Resulting Decisions and Actions NSES Assessment Standard D. Fair Assessments

Many teachers ask their students to keep journals, in which they record a variety of information, some of which is assigned (such as weather information and information on special events or happenings) and some of which is unassigned (such as spontaneous reflections). Children's science journals can contain a plethora of information about their activities, their experiments, questions they have asked, answers they have found, their feelings, and their reflections. The kinds of entries children make in their science journals can include at least the following:

- Observations
- Descriptions of experimental procedures
- Informal experiment reports
- Formal experiment reports
- Narratives
- Fictional stories
- Drawings

- Illustrations
- Charts
- Concept maps
- Other graphic organizers
- Data tables
- Lists of evidence obtained during inquiries

Children in all grades can keep science journals. Entries can be as simple as marking the results of a prediction activity, such as sink-or-float, on a teacher-prepared data sheet and stapling it into the journal. They can be more open, such as writing "What I learned about ————." Or they can be fairly extensive descriptions of an investigation in which children cite what they did, how they did it, what the evidence was, and what they concluded and why.

Science journals help children shape their understandings of science inquiries and phenomena. They can help teachers become aware of ways in which children's prior experiences influence their understandings and ways in which children are constructing new information (Shepardson &

Britsch, 2001). They also can serve as a dialogue between the child and the teacher. Read the entries regularly, and write comments back to the children. Act on the concerns they share. Help children confront contradictions in their thinking process. Help them find meaningful ways to construct information as the need is revealed in their journals.

Journals can be formal, with the teacher prescribing what children are to enter. They can be informal, with collections of children's thoughts. Or they can include both teacher-directed entries and entries the children add spontaneously. It is well to involve the children in the decision about what to include in the science journal if you choose to have them keep one.

Several examples of ways teachers use science journals and science notebooks follow:

- Steenson (2006) requires each student in her middle grades science classes to keep a "learning log." Each page in the log is divided into two columns. Students take standard notes in one column and write about their understanding of the importance and significance of the subject in the other column. The logs are turned in every day, and the teacher reads and responds to the material, making suggestions for deeper inquiry and how to find more information.

- Gilbert and Kotelman (2005) use the science notebook as a place where students record their observations, notes, thoughts, and drawings about science investigations. They use the student work to help them differentiate their teaching to meet the needs of their students.

- Klentschy (2005) requires students to include questions, problems, and purpose of inquiries; predictions; plans and projected ways of organizing data; observations and claims based on data and evidence; conclusions; and reflections in their science notebooks.

- Chesbro (2006) requires students in his middle grades science classes to keep notebooks with "input information" (class notes, laboratory and demonstration data, notes taken from reading, and the like) on one side of two opposing pages and "student output" (concept maps, written summaries, tables and graphs, flow charts, pictures and drawings, and so on) on the opposite page. The notebooks are assessed, and the assessment makes up between 15 and 20 percent of the marking period grade.

 A direct link to a Web site on using science notebooks developed and maintained by the Tucson, Arizona, Unified School District is available on the Student Book Companion Web Site.

Examples of science journal entries are shown in Figure 8.10.

Portfolios

A portfolio is "a container of evidence of someone's knowledge, skills, and dispositions" (Lawrenz, 1991, p. 15). The purpose of the portfolio drives

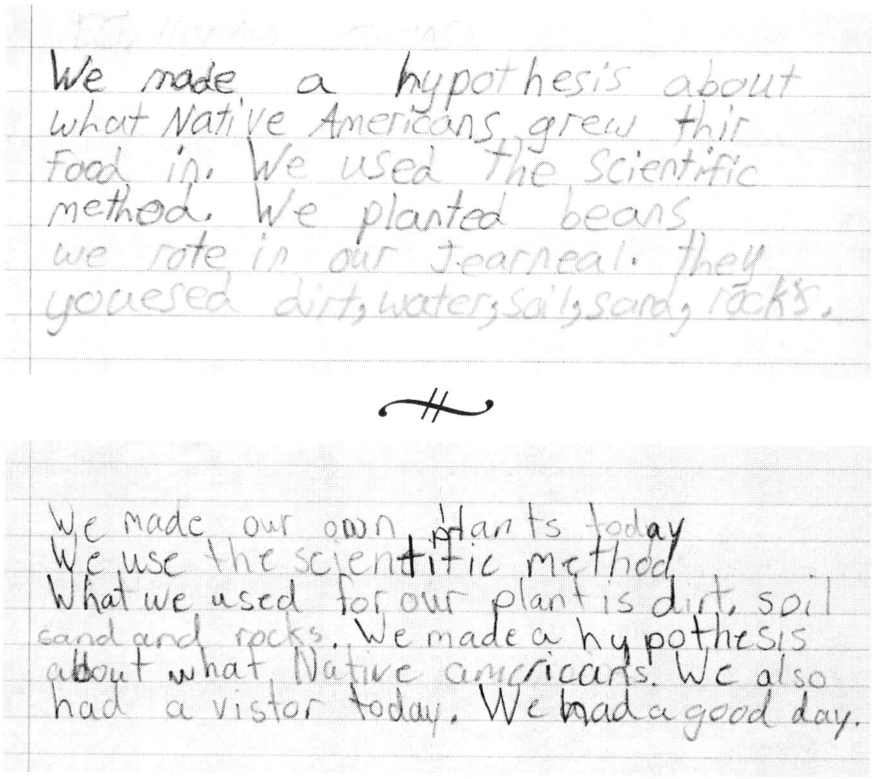
We made a hypothesis about what Native Americans grew thir Food in. We used the Scientific method. We planted beans we rote in our Jearneal. they youesed dirt, water, soil, sand, rocks.

We made our own plants today We use the scientific method What we used for our plant is dirt, soil sand and rocks. We made a hypothesis about what Native americans. We also had a vistor today. We had a good day.

Entries in science journals

FIGURE 8.10

the content in it. Its purpose may be to showcase students' best products, to show that students have achieved the expectations, or to communicate with parents what the student is learning and how well he or she is doing (Niguidula, 2005).

The chief purposes of portfolio assessment are

NSES Assessment Standard C. Data Matched to Resulting Decisions and Actions
NSES Assessment Standard D. Fair Assessments
NSES Assessment Standard E. Sound Interpretations

1. To enable the teacher to assess the *whole* child rather than just the child's test scores
2. To encourage children to reflect on their own work and engage in self-assessment rather than relying solely on test scores for their personal views of their accomplishments
3. To foster increased communication between teacher and student, teacher and parent, and teacher and other professionals in the school concerning the child's achievement, progress, and growth
4. To enable the teacher to evaluate the instructional program

Portfolios have many advantages over tests. Unlike tests, which show achievement at a particular point in time, a portfolio provides evidence about a child's progress over a period of time, up to the entire school year. Tests assess factual knowledge and information largely at the lower taxonomic levels, whereas a portfolio provides evidence of a child's overall understandings, including the higher taxonomic levels. Tests contain selected items about what the *teacher* wants children to know; the portfolio provides complete evidence of what the child has accomplished. Tests limit communication, but the portfolio is a collaborative communication effort between teacher and child.

In assessing achievement through portfolios, *all* facets of a child's progress and growth can be considered. Through the portfolio, a picture of the whole child emerges, including attitudes, interests, ideas, learning styles, strengths of different intelligences, and cognitive development as well as skill with the processes, facility in inquiry, acquisition of content, and attitude.

The portfolio system of assessment must be designed carefully before it is implemented so that the end product is manageable and provides the needed information. Elements of design include the purpose and uses of the portfolio, how it will be assessed, how it will be used in establishing course marks, how often it will be reviewed, the nature of the evidence that goes into the portfolio, who determines which evidence should be included, how much evidence will be included, the physical nature of the portfolio, and where it will be kept (Popham, 2005).

Recording experimental data for inclusion in portfolio

FIGURE 8.11

Evidence of achievement appropriate for elementary science portfolios may include the following:

- Summaries of activities
- Experiment write-ups with hypothesis, method, data, evidence, and conclusion
- The student's own version of an experiment
- Raw data and measurements made during investigations
- Lists of observations made in activities
- Classification systems devised
- Charts and graphs
- Individual and group reports

- Written classwork and homework assignments
- Tests
- Evidence of out-of-class science activities (for example, Scout work, museum visits, planetarium visits, aquarium visits)
- Evidence of the child's recognition and application of science in daily life
- Anecdotal records
- Checklists
- Results of observation and practical tests

Children may present evidence in any of the following forms:

- Written material
- Videotapes
- Audiotapes
- Photographs
- Computer printouts
- Drawings, diagrams, and other artwork
- PowerPoint® presentations

- Web pages
- Other computer applications
- Concept maps
- Other graphic organizers
- Any other form children decide would show their accomplishments fairly and completely

Because the primary purpose of portfolio assessment is to understand the whole child and how he or she is constructing information, you should consider having children include reflections, "portfolio paragraphs," or "memos to portfolios." These allow children to communicate their feelings and understandings in a nonthreatening way. Of course, you must be sure to respond to them. Also, consider including notes you have made of informal observations and conferences in the portfolio, which, for younger children, would include records of discussions and interviews you held with them about their science work.

The question of who determines what goes into the portfolio is answered from a collaborative perspective. The constructivist viewpoint suggests that the children themselves have the best idea of what is in their heads and are best able to decide how to portray this. Thus, children need to help decide what to include. In the lower elementary grades, children need assistance in making these decisions; teachers should ask why the child wants to include something and can encourage children to include items of particular significance. In the upper elementary grades, children are given more freedom in making their selections. Children should write (or communicate in some other way) the reason they selected what they did so that the teacher will know what to look for. As an example, a child may want to include a creative writing story about dinosaurs, because it shows he knows the names of many dinosaurs or, for a different child, because it shows she has a good grasp of the ecosystems in which dinosaurs lived. The teacher will review the evidence differently, depending on the reason for its inclusion.

It is a good idea to solicit the input of parents because the portfolios ultimately go to them. Parents can help in deciding what is most helpful and meaningful to them as they help their children. This practice has the added advantage that the parents know what to look for and praise when the portfolio comes home.

The teacher may require the inclusion of certain items that are indicative of student achievement and progress or that will enable grades to be determined fairly and efficiently. Teachers should explain why they have chosen the items they require to be included in the portfolio.

Should only the *best* work be included? This depends on the purpose of the portfolio. It may be desirable to include examples of less excellent work to demonstrate growth. It also may be desirable to include early drafts of experimental work and investigations to show development of thinking and increased sophistication in applying process skills. Each item should have a date on it so that progress over time can be shown.

What does a portfolio look like? The product should be carefully planned. What you do *not* want is a huge folder filled with a potpourri of children's work that you have to sift through and try to make sense of when the time period ends. Experienced portfolio users suggest having a "working" portfolio and a "permanent" portfolio (Lambdin & Walker, 1994. The working portfolio is an accordion-style folder easily accessible to children into which they drop items they may eventually want to include in the permanent portfolio. Much of this material will be discarded or taken home as children select what is most representative of their efforts and their thinking for inclusion in the permanent portfolio.

The permanent portfolio also is an accordion-style folder, but of a different color and kept in a secure place. It includes specific items that the child, parents, and teacher have jointly agreed will make up the portfolio. Each item the child includes in the portfolio should be dated and labeled—and the reason for its inclusion written—so that the teacher will know what to look for.

To be effective as assessment tools, the portfolios must receive continual attention and must be accessible to the children. The whole idea is for the permanent portfolio eventually to contain the best possible evidence of each child's science work. Do not wait until the end of the marking period and then have everyone—including yourself—hustle to create gradable portfolios. Have children keep them up-to-date on a daily basis as they grow, improve, and achieve.

Older children should include a table of contents, a paragraph describing the contents and what the items show, and a self-evaluation paragraph.

How many items should be in the permanent portfolio? That depends on many factors, not the least of which is the time you have available. Most users of portfolios urge limiting the number of items to the minimum necessary to get a complete picture; many suggest that five or six carefully selected items often are sufficient for assessing a child's progress during a grading period. (These, of course, are in addition to the items the teacher chooses to include.)

Many teachers find it desirable to assess the quality of the portfolios. Because the portfolio includes the products the child feels are most indicative of his or her best work, keenest interests, and most pronounced progress, you should assess this portion of the portfolio relative to the evidence presented. Use such criteria as the following:

1. *Selection.* Did the child select examples that show what he or she wanted to show? Are the examples indicative of the child's best thinking and best work? Do the examples show progress and growth?

2. *Reflection.* Are the explanations logical? Do they show what they were intended to show? Do the child's evidence and explanations showcase strengths and exhibit progress in weaker areas? Overall, does the child indicate an accurate grasp of the quality of his or her work? Does the evidence show that the child understands what is going on? Does it show that the child has worked effectively to gain understanding in weaker areas?

3. *Mechanics.* Is there a table of contents? Are all exhibits properly dated, labeled, and explained? Has the agreed-on format been followed?

You can assess the child's portfolio on a scale of 1 to 3 for each criterion and assign an overall mark of *excellent, satisfactory,* or *needs improvement.*

The records the teacher keeps are likely to be more objective in nature, including such items as:

- Process skill assessments

- Inquiry assessments

- Content assessments

- Interview notes

- Observation notes

- Results of hands-on process skill activity tests

- Completed checklists

- Test scores

- Activity evaluations

- Homework and classwork grades

These records should be compared with the children's selections to establish a complete picture. For example, if a child's daily grades are low, the portfolio may demonstrate excellence in achieving the objectives even though the grades may not have reflected it. Term grades can be derived from the combination of the child's and the teacher's contributions. For upper elementary children, teacher–student collaborations can be invoked to establish how the portfolio will be assessed. In addition, some schools may have schoolwide evaluation guidelines for portfolio assessment.

The portfolio system of assessment provides the opportunity for information to be presented that best shows each child's abilities and understandings.

Assessment Techniques that Support Learner Differences

In Chapters 6 and 7, you explored a number of individual differences that affect children's performance in science. Different people have different ways of learning. Teaching to individuals' strengths is important for their achievement; assessing their achievement through their strengths is equally important. Therefore, different individuals must be assessed in different ways so they are comfortable with the assessment process and can produce their best work. For example, it would yield false assessment data if an auditory learner were taught in an auditory manner and then required to take a written test to demonstrate achievement. Similarly, it would yield questionable assessment data to require a child with a strong and highly developed bodily kinesthetic intelligence to demonstrate understanding by writing or singing songs (unless the child also had strong musical intelligence). This student's "comfort zone" might be in the realm

NSES Assessment Standard D. Fair Assessments

of pantomime, acting, dancing, or gesturing rather than music. Indeed, it might be a good idea to team this child with one who has highly developed musical intelligence to develop a musical show that enables both to demonstrate their understandings. In addition, you must be careful to select assessments that allow all students to express their understandings equally well. For example, children who have difficulty expressing their understandings in writing (but not in their speech) may underperform on written assessment tasks when compared with more proficient writers even though their understandings may be similar (Appleton, 2007). Assessment must be customized to learning style.

Several customized assessment suggestions are offered in Figure 8.12.

Science assessment of children with cultural differences poses a particular challenge. As we have seen, the cultural background of children

ASSESSMENT TECHNIQUES CUSTOMIZED TO LEARNING STYLES

- Devise a "visual essay," such as a collage, poster, slide presentation, overhead transparency, or PowerPoint® presentation, depicting main ideas (*visual learner*)
- Tape record responses (*auditory learner*)
- Prepare a scrapbook or collection of articles, pictures, and other artifacts to portray main ideas (*kinesthetic learner*)
- Illustrate concepts with diagrams or concept maps (*strong spatial intelligence*)
- Act out understandings in pantomime fashion (*strong bodily kinesthetic intelligence*)
- Write a musical theme or a rap song that deals with the concept (*strong musical intelligence*)
- Write a play or a skit (*strong linguistic intelligence*)
- Develop simple principles that summarize the main ideas (*strong logical-mathematical intelligence*)
- Lead a discussion on the main ideas (*strong interpersonal intelligence*)
- Show how the concept can be (or is) used in one's personal life (*strong intrapersonal intelligence*)
- Show how the concepts fit in with the natural order of the environment (*strong naturalistic intelligence*)
- Devise a game to challenge others on their understandings, thereby demonstrating their own understandings (*field-dependent learners*)
- Encourage both boys and girls to portray their understandings in comfortable ways (*gender differences*)
- Draw or represent their inquiries in concept map form (*English-language learners*)
- Explain their inquiries to peers and the teacher (*students with learning disabilities*)
- Construct models that show their conclusions and conceptualizations (*students who are gifted and talented*)

FIGURE 8.12

influences their prior experiences and knowledge. The children build on these prior understandings as they construct and reconstruct their new understandings. These cultural influences must be considered in the assessment process, because the cultural backgrounds of the children influence the ways in which they interpret the material presented in assessments and the ways in which they respond (Solano-Flores & Nelson-Barber, 2001). Thus, assessments must be constructed with sensitivity to any cultural bias that might be present and must be interpreted in light of the cultural and social understandings children bring. As you can tell, the authentic assessment methods suggested in this chapter allow maximum teacher understanding of children's achievement in science, regardless of cultural background.

The same thing is true for English language learners. They may understand the science they are exploring but not be able to demonstrate their understandings verbally because of insufficient vocabulary. Authentic assessment strategies help teachers get beyond the language barrier so they can assess what the children truly understand.

REPORT CARDS

One of the functions of the assessment process is to formulate marks to be communicated to parents and shared with other professionals in the school using report cards, progress reports, conferences, or other communication devices. The most authentic reporting system is one that consists of narratives and/or parent conferences. In this case, the data collected from checklists, observations, interviews, and portfolios provide everything needed for reporting progress, together with backup documents and data.

As you doubtless have inferred, the establishment of marks is artificial, because marks cannot represent the totality of what a child has achieved. Furthermore, they do not always represent the same criteria across the country, within a school, or even from subject to subject with the same teacher. As desirable as it would be to replace quantitative marking systems with narrative progress reports, marks are inherent in the accountability system of education.

Thus, the question arises of how to translate the assessment data into marks. Indeed, the type of assessment data you collect is a direct function of the way the data will be used to establish report card marks. If the marking system is broad (such as E for *excellent,* S for *satisfactory,* and N for *needs improvement*), you will need less quantitative data than you will if the marking system is quantitative (A, B, C, D, and F, or percentages).

For quantitative marking systems, the first task is to establish the factors that go into the mark and the percentage or weight of each factor. *All* factors that go into determination of the mark for science should deal

NSES Assessment Standard A. Consistent with the Decisions It Will Inform

NSES Assessment Standard C. Data Matched to Resulting Decisions and Actions

NSES Assessment Standard D. Fair Assessments

with science achievement, not such factors as behavior or performance in other areas such as reading, writing, spelling, and mathematics—except as they play significant roles in the science program.

Factors to be considered when calculating the science mark could include the following:

- Interviews—children can be assigned grades for the project or activity or area of inquiry based partly on the interview and partly on their actual execution of the activity

- Scores on process checklists and/or practical tests

- Scores on inquiry checklists

- Scores on tests of content

- Scores on portfolio assessments

- Extra activities that exhibit positive or improving science attitudes

- Quizzes, unit tests, major tests, and final exams

- Homework

- Classwork

- Projects, reports, and presentations—in grading major activities, such as reports and presentations, you might consider basing half the grade on the planning, preparation, execution, and completion of the activity and half on the child's understandings as revealed through interviews

- Participation

Journals and notebooks should *not* be used for grading if they are considered private documents shared between teacher and child.

The final mark should be calculated in accordance with a weighted system that has been pre-established and, especially in the case of upper elementary grades, shared with the children. Either the point system or the percentage system can be employed.

A typical plan for establishing marks might look like this:

▶ Process skill achievement   30%
▶ Inquiry achievement   30%
▶ Portfolio   20%
▶ Other activities   20%

You will notice there is no provision for content achievement. Considering its secondary place in the scheme of elementary science education, the content achievement factor—if it is included in the marking system at all—should be small. However, in today's climate of standardized tests and high-stakes accountability, you may find it necessary and desirable to include a percentage for content achievement.

Clymer and Wiliam (2006/2007) describe a science reporting system they use in the middle grades that provides a fairly accurate indication of student achievement. The teacher assesses each student's performance on each of several tasks and content understandings in a unit of study. The assessments are based on a three-level scale, where Green represents *Mastery* and is worth 2 points; Yellow represents *Developing* and is worth 1 point; and Red represents *Beginning* or *Below Basic* and is worth 0 points. The final grade is obtained by adding the scores of each element in the unit and comparing the sum with the total perfect score (all Green designations). The percentage provides the grade (see Figure 8.13).

Many states and individual school districts work to establish criteria for report cards. Often this work is done in committees composed of teachers, administrators, and parents. You can bring an authentic assessment perspective to such committee work.

Key: Green = 2 points Yellow = 1 point Red = 0 points										
Student	Use of Equipment	Measuring	Predicting	Forming and Testing Hypothesis	Forming and Validating Conclusions	Inquiry Skills	Content Understanding	Total Score	Total Maximum Score	Percentage
Candis	1	2	1	2	2	2	2	12	14	85.7%
Harold	2	2	1	1	2	2	2	12	14	85.7%
James	1	2	2	1	2	2	2	12	14	85.7%
Joey	1	2	1	0	2	2	2	10	14	71.4%
Josh	0	2	1	0	2	2	2	9	14	64.3%
Katie	1	1	2	1	2	1	1	9	14	64.3%
Liz	2	2	2	1	2	1	2	12	14	85.7%
Shannon	2	2	2	2	2	1	2	13	14	92.9%

Color-Coded Recording of Task Accomplishments (Microsoft Excel) (Adapted from Clymer & Wiliam, 2006–2007)

FIGURE 8.13

Marks are difficult to assign in process-oriented inquiry science, because it is difficult to establish measurable criteria that can be administered uniformly with all children. However, the suggestions provided in this chapter for quantifying assessment information and preparing marks should help you grade your students both fairly and consistently. Above all, your report cards should be positive, reflect progress of individual children, and communicate individual success to both children and their parents. Ultimately, the report card represents your "philosophy of teaching for maximum individual growth" (Tomlinson, 2001, p. 15).

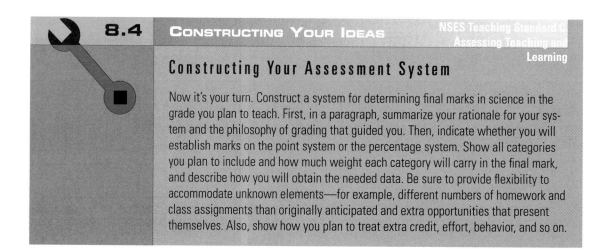

8.4 **CONSTRUCTING YOUR IDEAS**

NSES Teaching Standard C. Assessing Teaching and Learning

Constructing Your Assessment System

Now it's your turn. Construct a system for determining final marks in science in the grade you plan to teach. First, in a paragraph, summarize your rationale for your system and the philosophy of grading that guided you. Then, indicate whether you will establish marks on the point system or the percentage system. Show all categories you plan to include and how much weight each category will carry in the final mark, and describe how you will obtain the needed data. Be sure to provide flexibility to accommodate unknown elements—for example, different numbers of homework and class assignments than originally anticipated and extra opportunities that present themselves. Also, show how you plan to treat extra credit, effort, behavior, and so on.

HIGH-STAKES TESTING AND THE STANDARDIZED ACHIEVEMENT TEST

NSES Assessment Standard A. Consistent with the Decisions It Will Inform

School districts often require specific content preparation for specific standardized achievement tests, the results of which are used to highlight areas of strength and diagnose specific weaknesses. However, the standardized percentile ranks, grade equivalents, and stanines that are reported often overshadow the diagnostic potential of the tests and frequently are used to compare individual children or groups of children (such as classes, schools, or school districts) with each other and with national norms.

National and International Standardized Science Achievement Tests

Certain standardized tests are administered to assess the state of scientific knowledge among America's youth, to assess the progress of the nation's students in science, and to compare America's children with children of other nations. Science scores of the fourth graders tested for the Nation's Report Card (see Chapter 2) were higher in 2005 than in previous years, with 36 percent of the students achieving the *Basic* level, 26 percent achieving the *Proficient* level, and 3 percent achieving the *Advanced* level (National Center for Education Statistics, 2006). Science scores of fourth graders on the Third International Mathematics and Science Study (TIMSS) tests have been consistently high compared with those in other countries, and science scores of eighth graders have increased through the three administrations of the test given thus far (see Chapter 2).

A new international assessment program measures the capabilities of 15-year-old students in reading literacy, mathematics literacy, and science literacy every three years. Known as PISA (Programme for International Student Assessment), the program was implemented in 2000. A different subject is assessed in depth during each test administration, although the other two subjects also are assessed but not in as much depth. The year for in-depth science assessment was 2006, and results will be available in 2008 (Bybee et al., 2005). During the 2003 administration of PISA, American 15-year-olds scored slightly below the international average on the not-in-depth science test, with 14 countries having average scores statistically higher than the U.S. average and 6 countries having average scores statistically lower than the U.S. average (Schmidt, 2005).

 Direct links to the complete 2005 National Assessment of Educational Progress science report; a Boston College Web site from which you can access the full reports of all the TIMSS administrations; and a U.S. Government Web site with details of PISA are available on the Student Book Companion Web Site.

Much rhetoric is devoted to the notion that because tests often drive instruction, it is necessary to change the tests if there is to be permanent change in instruction. This is especially true in the area of science education where tests must be revised to focus on processes and inquiry skills—quite different from content, much more difficult to assess objectively, and extremely difficult to norm on a national basis. Then, too, there is the constructivist notion that children often understand scientific content in forms that are different from those presumed by the question writers and, therefore, cannot demonstrate their understandings on machine-graded standardized tests. As Plitt (2004) writes, "Student achievement can be demonstrated through standardized test scores or through information gathered by teachers in their work with students in the classroom. We have neglected the value of the latter by relying almost solely on test scores" (pp. 745–746). Some standardized tests are beginning to include open-ended and constructed response items wherein children write their own answers instead of selecting one of the predetermined choices. Professional assessors compare children's responses with standard rubrics and assign points that reflect how well the children's responses parallel the requirements of the rubric. However, whereas these items measure achievement more authentically than typical multiple-choice items, they are more expensive, costing 80 times as much as multiple-choice items to prepare, standardize, and grade (Lawrenz et al., 2000).

High-Stakes Testing

The focus on standardized tests has been exacerbated by the testing requirement of the *No Child Left Behind Act of 2001.* The basic provisions of this legislation are summarized in Chapter 2. Among these are the requirements for challenging state standards and annual testing for all students, normally tests that are standardized and objective in nature. Although the current focus has been on reading and mathematics, testing in science is scheduled to begin in 2007. Children's scores on the state- and federal-mandated standardized tests are used not only to measure achievement but also to assess teachers, principals, the curriculum, and even the schools themselves. Teachers' salary increases are linked to children's performance on the tests, as are administrator salaries and school funding. In some cases, teachers may or may not be rehired for the next year, depending on how children perform on the standardized tests. Moreover, in certain grades, children must obtain minimum scores on the standardized tests to be promoted to the next grade. In addition, schools that fail to make "adequate yearly progress" for two years in a row can be "reconstituted" and must provide the option for their students to attend other schools. Testing programs that involve high stakes such as these are termed **high-stakes testing.**

8.5   **CONSTRUCTING YOUR IDEAS**   NSES Assessment Standard C
Data Matched to Resulting Decisions and Actions

Your State's Standardized Testing Requirements

Use the Internet and other sources to find the requirement for testing in your state that meets the requirements of *No Child Left Behind.* In particular, find the details of the science testing required in your state.

The educational literature is bursting with articles that both criticize and defend high-stakes testing. For example, Kohn (2001) writes, "The intellectual life is being squeezed out of our schools as they are transformed into what are essentially giant test-prep centers. The situation is most egregious, and the damage most pronounced, where high stakes are attached to the tests . . ." (p. 350). An outspoken critic of *No Child Left Behind,* Kohn (2004) wrote, "Making schools resemble businesses [in accountability] often results in a kind of pedagogy that's . . . reactionary, turning back the clock on the few changes that have managed to infiltrate and improve classrooms" (p. 570). He is so opposed to the high-stakes testing inherent in the Act that he also wrote, "Ultimately, we must decide whether we will obediently play our assigned role in helping to punish children and teachers" (ibid., p. 576). Thomas Sergiovanni, an authority on educational leadership and school administration, says "If the superintendent tells [the principal] that your job is on the line because of test scores, then you don't care about constructivism—you work to get the test scores up" (quoted in Allen, 2003, p. 1). He adds that "fretting about numbers won't necessarily cultivate a positive school culture that's focused on raising the achievement of all students" (ibid., p. 1). Amrein and Berliner (2003) found that in 18 states that use high-stakes testing, student motivation decreased, a greater proportion of students left school early, and student achievement failed to improve after implementation of the state-mandated high-stakes tests. They suggest abandoning high-stakes policies and substituting more formative testing programs that can uncover reforms which will make a difference for the students. Jones & Ongtooguk (2002) fear that the current high-stakes standardized achievement tests will "consign even more Alaska Native students to an unpromising future" (p. 500), but they also acknowledge that the tests may offer a means of counteracting a long history of low standards in the state of Alaska.

Lederman & Burnstein (2006) observe that standardized tests are not always reliable measures of student achievement and that they cannot account for nonschool factors, such as culture, race, home environment, poverty level, disabilities, and English-language proficiency. Yet, under the *No Child Left Behind* mandates, these single end-of-year tests are the primary measures of student achievement and of school success or failure. The authors suggest using formative assessments embedded within the instruction together with summative assessments to determine what students know and to assess the schools.

Needless to say, with the stakes so high, teachers are very concerned about their students' performances on the standardized tests. In a recent large study of new elementary teachers, Certo (2006) found that the greatest concern of these new teachers dealt with standardized test pressure and preparation and that this concern overshadowed all other predictable areas of concern—even classroom discipline.

On the other hand, Franklin (2001) writes that schools can use standardized tests "as an opportunity for thoughtful curriculum restructuring, [although] some schools are actually teaching the test itself as the curriculum" (p. 1). Hamilton & Stecher (2004) urge educators to use *No Child Left Behind* and its prescribed testing regimen to increase the effectiveness of education and improve instruction. In an article that examines alternatives to the current objective standardized achievement tests, Yeh (2001) writes, "If one accepts the premise that tests drive curriculum and instruction, perhaps the easiest way to reform instruction and improve educational quality is to construct better tests" (p. 16). He says that tests which combine both open-ended and forced-choice items could be used to assess critical thinking in a practical, cost-effective way.

Because the stakes of standardized testing are so high, elementary science teachers may find themselves concentrating on teaching the facts that are likely to be on the tests rather than on teaching children how to do science, how to inquire, and how to formulate their own valid conclusions to problems and questions that they, themselves, come up with. Jorgenson and Vanosdall (2002) say, "Ironically, even as inquiry methods and science resource centers stand poised to reinvigorate K–12 science education in America, the national movement emphasizing . . . instruction as measured by high-stakes standardized tests, threatens to suppress the effort to make truly revolutionary progress in science education" (p. 602).

Many suggestions teachers can use to solve the high-stakes testing problem are found in the literature. Some include the following:

- Incorporate the concepts to be covered on the tests into the regular curriculum.

- Identify material on the test that crosses subject lines, and include these in all classes so children are exposed to them often.

- Develop curriculum time lines so all required material is covered before the tests are given.

- Identify the concepts on the test that lend themselves well to inquiry, and use these as the basis for process-oriented inquiry lessons.

- Limit the time spent on presenting factual material that is on the test.

You also should assist children in developing their test-taking skills, such as how to fill in chosen responses, how to eliminate unlikely responses in multiple-choice questions, how to use other test items to help in answering more difficult items, and how to manage time. Having children take one or two practice tests in the same format as the standardized test helps both you and them identify test-taking difficulties that need attention. Helping children develop sound test-taking skills helps to ensure that test results reflect competence in subject matter and not lack of test-taking skills. For young children, try the book *Hooray for Diffendoofer Day!* by Dr. Seuss, Jack Prelutsky, and Lane Smith (Random House, 1998). In this book, the children in Diffendoofer love their school and their wacky teachers but are told they must do well on the upcoming test. Their teachers work with the children to help them relax and show them they already know plenty of information and so should have no fear of the test.

A word of caution is in order. Although a compromise solution to the standardized test dilemma has been suggested, this in no way is meant to imply that the process-oriented inquiry teaching methodology should become secondary to preparation for achievement tests. It is far better to teach in the style and methodology known to be effective while concurrently working for the replacement of content-oriented standardized tests with tests that measure what is taught.

Haladyna, Haas, & Allison (1998) remind us we must recognize that "the public continues to support [standardized] testing because it perceives that test scores are valid indicators of children's learning" (p. 264). They suggest that because this is the case, we must at least take steps to "ensure that the test results are responsibly interpreted and used" (p. 264).

Reauthorization of No Child Left Behind

The *No Child Left Behind Act of 2001* is to be considered for reauthorization in 2007 by Congress. In an address delivered at the National School Boards Association conference in January 2007, Senator Edward Kennedy, chairman of the U.S. Senate Health, Education, Labor, and Pensions Committee, outlined four major proposed changes to the law. They are: (1) make needed resources available, (2) find more effective ways to measure progress and goals, (3) look for creative ideas to meet the goals for turning around struggling schools, and (4) renew commitment to teacher quality (Kennedy, 2007a). The Committee's plans include hosting a series of round-table discussions to hear from experts, educational leaders, and others who know what is and what is not working in schools and classrooms and it plans to use the information from these discussions to propose "necessary changes to improve and strengthen the Act, and ensure its effectiveness for students, parents, and teachers" (Kennedy, 2007b).

 You can read the executive summaries of the progress of the re-authorization of *No Child Left Behind* on the U.S. Department of Education Web site; a direct link is provided on the Student Book Companion Web Site.

As this book goes to press, the outcome of the discussions is not known. We urge you to find information on the reauthorized law and use this information in your discussions about accountability and assessment.

ASSESSMENT OF THE ELEMENTARY SCIENCE TEACHER AND PROGRAM

In his seminal article on knowledge and teaching, Shulman (1987) suggests six aspects to pedagogical reasoning:

NSES Assessment Standard E. Sound Interpretations
NSES Teaching Standard C. Assessing Teaching and Learning

1. *Comprehension* of the material to be taught

2. *Transformation* of the material into forms that meet the needs of the children

3. *Instruction* of the material in the classroom

4. *Evaluation* of children's understandings and one's own performance

5. *Reflection* on one's own performance and that of the class

6. *New comprehensions* of the material, the children, and one's teaching

This is a cyclical model in which the new comprehensions (step 6) become the new original comprehensions (step 1) as the cycle begins again.

Competent teachers continually evaluate their understandings, their performance, and their teaching effectiveness while they are teaching in the classroom. Competent teachers engage in reflection (alone or with other professionals), looking backward to capture the strengths of previous work and identify areas that need improvement. Competent teachers also reflect on whether the curriculum is appropriate for the children in their classes and reflect on their own changing attitudes toward science and science teaching.

Introspective reflection is supported in the literature (see, for example, Danielson, 1996; Sparks-Langer & Colton, 1991) and is a powerful vehicle for enabling teachers to recreate science lessons that are meaningful to children and that better accommodate the individual differences and the varying prior constructions that children bring to the class. Introspective reflection also enables teachers to check their own skill in urging children to inquire, to come up with their own ideas, and to develop their own plans to investigate their own ideas.

Teachers should keep their own reflective journals. Journals, portfolios, learning cohorts, and attendance at professional seminars all assist the teacher with introspective reflection. You commenced this practice of self-appraisal when you critiqued your microteaching lessons. You are urged to continue this vital process of reflection throughout your teaching careers to reconcile your actions with your beliefs; your teaching practices with your education; and the outcomes of your teaching with your intents. The indicators of constructivist approaches and inquiry teaching provided in this chapter and in Figure 5.4 are suggestions you may wish to use to aid in your reflection and self-assessment process.

Bodzin & Beerer (2003) have developed a rubric that elementary science teachers can use to help them "understand how they implement the essential features of inquiry [as stated by the National Research Council] into their classroom instruction" (p. 42). This rubric is reproduced in Figure 8.14 and may help you focus your reflections about your teaching.

No lesson, unit, or school term is complete until you, the teacher, have examined the class's response and your own performance and have reflected on both to construct for yourself increasingly accurate understandings of your effectiveness as a teacher.

SCIENCE TEACHER INQUIRY RUBRIC (STIR)

Learner-Centered ←					→ Teacher-Centered
Learners are engaged by scientifically oriented questions.					
Teacher provides an opportunity for learners to engage with a scientifically oriented question.	Learner is prompted to formulate own questions or hypotheses to be tested.	Teacher suggests topic areas or provides samples to help learners formulate own questions or hypotheses.	Teacher offers learners lists of questions or hypotheses from which to select.	Teacher provides learners with specific states (or implied) questions or hypotheses to be investigated.	No evidence observed.
Learners give priority to evidence, which allows them to develop and evaluate explanations that address scientifically oriented questions.					
Teacher engages learners in planning investigations to gather evidence in response to questions.	Learners develop procedures and protocols to independently plan and conduct a full investigation.	Teacher encourages learners to plan and conduct a full investigation, providing support and scaffolding with making decisions.	Teacher provides guidelines for learners to plan and conduct part of an investigation. Some choices are made by the learners.	Teacher provides the procedures and protocols for the students to conduct the investigation.	No evidence observed

Science teacher inquiry rubric (Reproduced with permission from Bodzin & Beerer (2003), courtesy of the *Journal of Elementary Science Education*)

FIGURE 8.14

Teacher helps learners give priority to evidence which allows them to draw conclusions and/or develop and evaluate explanations that address scientifically oriented questions.	Learners determine what constitutes evidence and develop procedures and protocols for gathering and analyzing relevant data (as appropriate).	Teacher directs learners to collect certain data or only provides portion of needed data. Often provides protocols for data collection.	Teacher provides data and asks learners to analyze.	Teacher provides data and gives specific direction on how data is to be analyzed.	No evidence observed.
Learners formulate explanations and conclusions from evidence to address scientifically oriented questions.					
Learners formulate conclusions and/or explanations from evidence to address scientifically oriented questions.	Learners are prompted to analyze evidence (often in-the form of-data) and formulate their-own conclusions/ explanations.	Teacher prompts learners to think about how analyzed evidence leads to conclusions/ explanations, but does not cite specific evidence.	Teacher directs learners' attention (often through questions) to specific pieces of analyzed evidence (often in the form of data) to draw conclusions and/or formulate explanations.	Teacher directs learners' attention (often through questions) to specific pieces of analyzed evidence (often in the form of data) to lead learners to-predetermined correct conclusions/ explanations (verification).	No evidence observed.

FIGURE 8.14

Learners evaluate the explanations in light of alternative explanations, particularly those reflecting scientific understanding.					
Learners evaluate their conclusions and/or explanations in light of alternative conclusions/ explanations, particularly those reflecting scientific understanding.	Learner is prompted to examine other resources and make connections and/or explanations independently.	Teacher provides resources to relevant scientific knowledge that may help identify conclusions and/or explanations. Teachers may or may not direct learners to examine these resources, however.	Teacher does not provide resources to relevant scientific knowledge to help learners formulate alternative conclusions and/or explanations. Instead, the teacher identifies related scientific knowledge that could lead to such alternatives, or suggests possible connections to such alternatives.	Teacher explicitly states specific connections to alternative conclusions and/or explanations, but does not provide resources.	No evidence observed.
Learners communicate and justify their proposed explanations.					
Learners communicate and justify their proposed conclusions and/or explanations.	Learners specify content and layout to be used to communicate and justify their conclusions and explanations.	Teacher talks about how to improve communication, but does not suggest content or layout.	Teacher provides possible content to include and/or layout that might be used.	Teacher specifies content and/or layout to be used.	No evidence observed.

FIGURE 8.14

TEACHER VOICE

Assessment can be one of the most difficult aspects of teaching science. As you discovered in this chapter, assessment can and should take many forms in your classroom. Unfortunately, many of us experienced science as a series of facts to be learned and tested, not as a process of investigating the world around us. As a new teacher, it is especially important not to fall into the trap of simply using standard paper-and-pencil assessments as the sole means of evaluating student achievement. It is undoubtedly much more time-efficient to use these types of assessment, but the loss of learning opportunities to your students and yourself is immeasurable.

Perhaps the most important thing to remember about assessment is that it should be a daily activity in science class. Whether it is using questioning to explore the students' lines of thinking or a formal lab exercise, assessment must become second nature to you as a teacher. I think that my most valuable form of assessment is the daily questioning I use to see how my students are comprehending the topic of study. Student responses to my questions allow me to adjust my instruction to fit their needs. Their responses also help me to see where their thinking needs to be redirected. All of this information enables me to design my instruction to help them build a sound foundation of scientific knowledge.

There are three main considerations to providing authentic assessment in the classroom: time, materials and space, and the quality of the assessments themselves.

It takes time to teach and assess science well. If your goal as a teacher is to have students really understand the scientific ideas you are teaching, then you have to be flexible in your timing. As a beginning teacher, I used to get very frustrated when an assessment activity took longer to complete than I thought it should. However, I soon realized that the students were learning the material much more thoroughly and deeply than if we had rushed. Another thing I realized was that a well-designed assessment activity could assess many areas of learning. Once I learned to deconstruct a lab activity and really determine all of the tasks that were being accomplished, I realized that I could easily assess several process skills in one activity.

A second consideration that can greatly affect your ability to assess students is the space and material you have at your disposal. Engaging students in authentic assessment takes more than pencils and paper. It takes supplies. Fortunately, there is a plethora of science investigations that use inexpensive materials and equipment. However, you will have to be an advocate in your school to make sure that money is available for the needed supplies. Space can also be a problem. Some activities and their assessment may require a large space, such as the gym or lunchroom. You will probably have limited space to keep materials for ongoing investigations in your classroom whether you are a self-contained teacher or teach science all day long. You will undoubtedly make a mess in your classroom, so make friends with the custodian! You will learn how to overcome these problems as you gain experience in the classroom.

The third consideration in assessment is building a repertoire of effective assessment tools. You probably will have science textbooks in your classroom. Often, these contain activities that are related to the topic being studied. While textbooks have improved a great deal, I have found that they tend to contain rather simple activities that really do not engage students in higher thinking. However, they can be a place to start if you are stuck on what to do. My two favorite resources are other teachers and journals such as *Science and Children,* a publication of the National Science Teachers Association. Finding an experienced teacher to serve as your science mentor is probably the most crucial thing you can do as a beginning teacher. I am fortunate to have several teachers I can contact when I am stumped on how to present or assess a concept. I have also found many wonderful assessment activities in professional journals. These activities have already been field-tested and meet the *National Science Education Standards.*

As you may have realized, it takes work to teach science well. However, the reward of seeing that your students really "get" the concepts they are learning about makes all of your work worthwhile.

Liz Ward

Fourth-Grade Science and Fifth-Grade Science and Mathematics Teacher
St. Vincent's Cathedral School
Bedford, Texas

Conclusion

In this chapter, you have considered multiple aspects of the question of assessment, and you have begun to design your own authentic assessment programs that are congruent with your conceptualizations of process-oriented inquiry science teaching. You have explored the nature, advantages, and disadvantages of a number of methods of assessment. You have tackled the issue of how to turn assessment indicators into course marks, and you have explored ways of helping children succeed on standardized tests while concurrently preserving the integrity of your constructivist teaching. Your conceptualizations of assessment will become more solidified with time and experience. However, you must continue to search for new ideas and better ways for assessment that truly indicate what children have gained in their science education.

CHAPTER 8

Additional Questions for Discussion

1. Contrast traditional assessment methods with authentic assessment methods relative to advantages and disadvantages.

2. How can a teacher justify giving class grades when using authentic assessment and constructivist teaching and learning methodologies?

3. How can a teacher use discovery, inquiry-based, constructivist teaching strategies while concurrently meeting the requirements of high-stakes testing?

Internet Activities

Use the Internet to find updated material on the work of the National Assessment of Educational Progress (*The Nation's Report Card*) and the international mathematics and science assessment programs.

Use the Internet to find articles on high-stakes testing. In your search, include articles by John Merrow and Alfie Kohn, two authors who have written extensively about this topic. Using the ideas you gain from your reading, develop a plan for meeting high-stakes testing requirements while concurrently preserving your constructivist teaching methodology. Share your plan with the class, and then refine your own plans based on the input of others.

Use the Internet to find additional information on assessment and measurement of achievement. Compare the information you find with the conceptualizations you have constructed in this chapter.

Use the Internet to find current information on the status of the reauthorization of the *No Child Left Behind.*

CHAPTER 9

THE ELEMENTARY SCIENCE CLASSROOM

"The time has come," the Walrus said, "To talk of many things."

Lewis Carroll, *The Walrus and the Carpenter* (Berkeley, CA: Archetype Press, 1938), st. II

You have been constructing your own conceptualization about how and what to teach in the elementary science program, how to assess children's growth and achievement, and how to assess your own performance. This chapter is devoted to practical suggestions for implementing your constructivist, process-oriented inquiry science program in your elementary classroom.

NSES Teaching Standard E. Developing Learners Who Reflect Intellectual Rigor and Attitudes Conducive to Science Learning
NSES Professional Development Standard B. Integrating Knowledge of Science, Learning, Pedagogy, and Students

TRUST

Many researchers have come to the conclusion that the trust students have in their teachers is established during the early grades. It is redundant of the awesome array of literature on the subject to say that the relationship between teacher and child frequently is based on the teacher being the repository of knowledge; that the child is required to absorb the knowledge the teacher imparts and demonstrate this possession through tests of one form or another; that the teacher has the "right" answers, and it is the job of the child to figure out what they are. Even when the teacher doesn't seem to have the right answers, it is assumed that correct answers exist. The impression is given that in discussions, in activities, and in all other types of science class events, the goal of the child is to obtain or achieve the "right" answers or the "right" conclusions. This has been the case since the earliest grades, and children are extremely adept, through a huge variety of subtle actions, at figuring out and supplying the correct responses. In addition, grades are omnipotent, and no one wants to take the chance of getting a bad grade. So children play the game, which often consists largely of figuring out what the teacher considers to be the correct responses.

It is no wonder that children are suspicious when a teacher encourages them to investigate their own conclusions and form their own unique constructions of information. The *trust* factor is missing.

What can we constructivist teachers do about this situation? First, we must act to develop trust with our students. Recall your explorations in Chapter 1, in which you investigated the concept of "no right answers—no wrong answers," ways that an individual's perception can color his or her responses, ways of fostering children's ownership of knowledge, and the importance of personal beliefs in shaping excellence in teaching. We need to become authentic human beings in our classrooms, complete with good days and bad days, right, wrong and missing information, and strengths as well as weaknesses. Do we really believe that the thinking of children is important? Do we really believe children are interested in learning what is meaningful to them? Do we really believe children can behave with integrity, both socially and academically? If so, we need to let our beliefs show.

Do we have that penchant so necessary to investigate unfamiliar territory? If so, we need to show we have it by participating actively in the investigations of our students, helping them formulate their own questions and come to their own conclusions. We need to let them know that we also are still learning and discovering—that we are, and always will be, students.

Do we really believe that children are capable of investigating situations on their own? Do we really believe they have brains and are capable of using them? If so, we need to let our students know that we believe it.

The development of this trust in young children "depends greatly on children's sense that they are understood, respected, and accepted. The disposition to trust teachers—a disposition that may set a pattern for all subsequent responses to school—can be strengthened or undermined during the early years of school" (Katz, 1994, p. 201).

We do all this not by *talking* about it but by *acting* on our beliefs. We present ourselves as co-inquirers, as honest and sincere and dependable individuals, as concerned leaders of children. We demonstrate our genuine concern for children as cognitive beings through *all* our actions, both verbal and nonverbal. We treat children like people, and we do this all the time. In short, we demonstrate throughout the day that children are important—as individuals, as social beings, and as inquirers.

We must start slowly in encouraging children to explore in a constructivist mode; we must remember that change comes slowly and that some discouragement is apt to occur. Because children are accustomed to expository methods, we need to move them a little at a time toward constructivist learning and guided inquiry. Only when children find that the inquiry method of doing science is safe will the trust that is prerequisite to successful constructivist approaches to teaching and learning science be built.

I suggest you start children out with two or three activities that are somewhere between expository and guided inquiry in nature, because it is critical to get children thinking for themselves and to demonstrate that we truly regard their own constructions of information as valuable as our own. Constructing Science in the Classroom 9.1 to 9.4 show somewhat structured inquiry-oriented science activities children can do to get started on developing confidence in their own thought processes and developing trust that their thoughts are valuable to the teacher.

9.1   CONSTRUCTING SCIENCE IN THE CLASSROOM

HOW DOES WATER AFFECT DIFFERENT MATERIALS?

Objective
The student will predict the effect of water on various materials.

NSES Content Standard B. Physical Science: Properties and Changes of Properties in Matter

Materials
Cups of water and samples of sugar, salt, baking soda, pepper, flour, rice, oil, vinegar, paper clips, cardboard, chips, noodles, macaroni, and the like. It also may be a good idea to have

Continued on next page

a data sheet available for children to record their predictions and their observations of what happens to the material in water.

For each item, children predict what happens to it when water is added. Then, they add the water, observe what happens, and record their observations. Discuss the processes of prediction, observation (before and after), and classification.

Literature Connection

Water: Simple Experiments for Young Scientists by Larry White (Millbrook Press, 1996) is a book of simple and fun experiments that illustrate scientific principles relating to air, energy, gravity, and water.

9.2   **CONSTRUCTING SCIENCE IN THE CLASSROOM**

HOW CAN YOU TELL THAT AIR TAKES UP SPACE?

Objective

The student will infer why paper in the bottom of a transparent glass remains dry when the glass is inverted and submerged into a pail of water.

P K 1 2 3 4 5 6 7 8

NSES Content Standards B. Physical Science: Properties of Objects and Materials

Materials

Transparent plastic cup, paper towel, pail partly filled with water

The children wad up a paper towel and stuff it into the bottom of the transparent plastic cup. Then they turn the cup upside down and submerge it into the pail of water.

Ask the children to explain what they observe. Ask them how the result of this activity (the paper towel remains dry) can lead them to the conclusion that air takes up space.

Now, ask children to devise variations on this activity, such as trying other materials in the cup and in the pail, using different temperatures of water, and so on. The main reason for this is to encourage children to come up with their own ideas.

Literature Connections

Hot-Air Henry by Mary Calhoun (Mulberry Books, 1981) Henry the cat takes a solo flight in a hot-air balloon.

Gilberto and the Wind by Marie Hall Ets (Viking, 1963) Gilberto has many adventures with the wind, his constant companion.

Super-Sized Science Projects with Volume: How Much Space Does it Take Up? by Robert Gardner (Enslow, 2003) is a book of experiments and reference material on the concept of volume, including a section on the topic of air taking up space.

9.3   **CONSTRUCTING SCIENCE IN THE CLASSROOM**

EVAPORATION

Objective

The student will predict what will happen to water sprayed onto a surface after setting for a short time and will predict the effect of moving air on evaporation.

NSES Content Standard B. Physical Science: Heat Energy

Materials

Mini-chalkboards or other smooth surface, water, spray bottles

Ask children to predict what would happen if they were to spray the chalkboard with the water bottle. "Where do you think the water would go?" Allow children to take turns spraying small amounts of water on the chalkboard. Have the children observe what happens and record their findings. Have the class discuss reasons for the happening.

Next, children predict which hand will dry faster if sprayed with water: one that is held still, or one that is waved in the air. Then, they do the activity and compare their results with their predictions. As before, discuss results, inferences, and reasons with the class.

Literature Connections

A Drop of Water: A Book of Science and Wonder by Walter Wick (Scholastic, 1997) focuses on the physical properties of water and the changes that water undergoes through evaporation and condensation. It has magnificent photographs, including close-ups of a falling water drop and a snowflake. Activities for children are suggested.

The Water Cycle by Rebecca Olien (Capstone Press 2005) is a nonfiction book about many concepts and interesting facts about liquid, solid, and gaseous water.

9.4   **CONSTRUCTING SCIENCE IN THE CLASSROOM**

GATHERING WEATHER DATA

Objective

The student will observe and record several types of weather data each day.

NSES Content Standard D. Earth and Space Science: Structure of the Earth System

Several kinds of weather data can be observed and recorded by children each day. These observations include (1) temperature, (2) barometric pressure, (3) wind speed, (4) rainfall, and

Continued on next page

(5) type of cloud cover. Using a data collection sheet similar to the one suggested at the end of this activity, children record weather information each day and plot graphs of the data to interpret.

Temperature should be taken at the same time each day in a shady spot. Pressure can be read from a barometer. Wind speed requires an **anemometer** (wind speed gauge), which can be homemade or purchased from science supply firms. Rainfall requires a rain gauge, which also can be homemade or purchased from science supply firms. Type of cloud cover requires comparing clouds with charts that name the types of clouds and indicate the type of weather with which they normally are associated. Show children how to read weather charts in newspapers so they can compare their data with that reported officially. Many meteorologists from local television stations are willing to discuss weather forecasting with elementary school children; it is an excellent idea to make use of these resource people.

Literature Connections

The Cloud Book by Tomie De Paola (Holiday House, 1975) describes specific clouds and the weather that comes from them.

What Does the Cloud Say? by Nancy White Carlstrom (Eerdmans Books for Young Readers, 2001) shows different seasons and accompanying weather changes through the eyes of a child.

The Man Who Named the Clouds by Julie Hannah and Joan Holub (A. Whitman, 2006) is a biography of Luke Howard, who studied clouds, catalogued them together with the weather patterns they predicted, and provided the names we use today.

Once Upon a Cloud by Rob D. Walker (Blue Sky Press, 2005) is a whimsical story with rhyming text that asks what clouds are made of and where they came from.

Homemade Anemometer (see Figure 9.1)

1. Cut two 16-inch pieces of thin wooden strips, cross them at their centers at right angles to each other, and glue them together. Drill a hole through both pieces of wood at the center large enough for the end of a plastic medicine dropper to fit through snugly.

2. Glue a very small paper cup on the end of each of the four wooden vanes, making sure all cups face the same direction. Paint one cup a different color.

3. Construct a base of two pieces of wood. Use electrical tape to attach a long nail to one side of the support.

4. Place the medicine dropper of the wooden vane apparatus over the nail, and adjust the whole thing so the apparatus spins freely.

5. To measure wind speed, count the number of turns the anemometer makes in one minute; the colored cup helps keep track of the rotations. To convert the number of turns per minute to wind speed, count the number of turns it makes per minute in a wind of known speed as reported by an area weather station. Divide this number by the speed of the wind to find the number of turns the anemometer makes per mph of wind speed.

Continued on next page

The Weather Channel has a multitude of resources about almost every aspect of weather, including material for teachers, students, and parents. A direct link to the Web site is provided on the Student Book Companion Web Site.

CHART OF DAILY WEATHER OBSERVATIONS

Date and Time	Temperature	Pressure	Wind Speed	Rainfall	Type of Cloud Cover

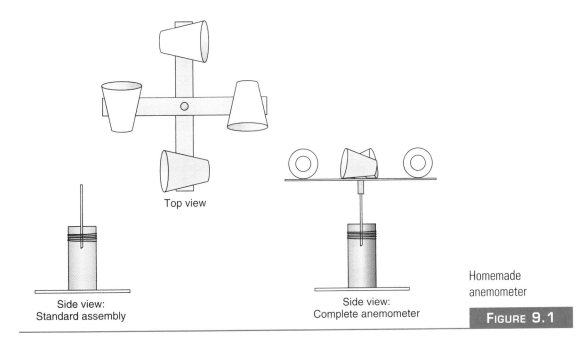

Top view

Side view:
Standard assembly

Side view:
Complete anemometer

Homemade
anemometer

FIGURE 9.1

Homemade Rain Gauge

A rain gauge is a vessel that collects rainwater. The depth of the water in the vessel after it rains is equal to the amount of rainfall. Use a coffee can, cat food can, or other straight-sided container. Put it outdoors so it can collect the rain as the rain falls. Use a ruler to measure

Continued on next page

The number of turns the anemometer makes in one minute tells wind speed

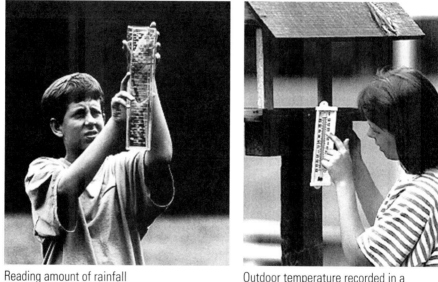

Gathering weather data

Reading amount of rainfall

Outdoor temperature recorded in a shady place

FIGURE 9.2

the depth of the water. The depth equals the number of inches of rain. (Be sure to empty the vessel after each time the rainfall is measured.)

STRATEGIES FOR SUCCESSFUL SCIENCE ACTIVITIES

NSES Teaching Standard A. Inquiry-Based Program
NSES Teaching Standard B. Guiding and Facilitating Learning

Science activities in the constructivist elementary classroom involve children devising and executing their own investigations to answer their own questions that arise from observations they make. Nonetheless, it is prudent for teachers to exercise some measures to ensure that the activities achieve maximum productivity with minimum disruption. Some factors you may wish to keep in mind include the following:

TO THE STUDENT

1. There's no such thing as "it didn't work."

2. There's no such thing as a dumb question.

3. There are no wrong answers.

4. Question everything!

TO THE TEACHER

1. Try it yourself first.

2. Discuss the activity in class before the children start work.

3. Demonstrate the activity in class first if necessary.

4. Show connections to prior lessons.

5. Be very specific and very structured if necessary.

6. Be sure your directions are clear and complete. Practice giving the directions ahead of time, and use notes on 3" × 5" cards if you are afraid you might forget something, or write the directions on an overhead transparency or a PowerPoint slide that you project for children to refer to during the activity.

7. Have all materials ready, counted out, and packaged so that all the materials needed by each group are together.

8. *Do not* pass materials out until you have completed all introductory work and have given the directions. Children will start to fool with the materials as soon as they get them—no matter what you say to the contrary.

SAFETY IN THE ELEMENTARY SCIENCE CLASSROOM

It is of paramount importance that elementary science teachers take appropriate safety precautions. As teacher and role model, you are expected to display good safety habits at all times and set sound safety expectations for the children. Before you assign children to work on any activity, it is absolutely essential that you discuss safety precautions with them and that you assure yourself they understand the precautions. You should

NSES Program Standard D. Appropriate with Sufficient Resources

include needed safety precautions in your lesson plans, and you should be on the lookout for unsafe practices as the children explore. (Safety precautions that need to be observed with the activities described in this text are highlighted with the safety icon.)

It is a good idea to discuss science safety in general terms with children at the beginning of the school year. Focus on the following:

1. Cooperation between you and the children and among each other on safety matters ensures that they will act in a safe manner.

2. Orderly behavior reduces the likelihood of accidents.

3. Listening for your voice as they do their activities enables them to hear additional instructions.

4. Common sense must be invoked at all times when dealing with science activities.

In The Schools 9.1 presents a fun, multiple-choice Science Activities Safety Inventory that children in the upper elementary and middle grades can complete as an introduction to the discussion on safety. The inventory is intended to facilitate the safety discussion by highlighting frequently encountered safety and behavior problems as well as providing "correct" choices for various laboratory situations. Included in the discussion should be a thorough review of all safety features available in your classroom, such as a sink, running water, location of fire extinguisher, locations of exits, location of trash cans, and so on.

A Science Activities Safety Contract is shown in In The Schools 9.2. This contract, adapted from National Science Teachers Association materials, is intended to impress upon children the importance of following instructions for science activities. Experience has shown that asking children to sign a contract such as this reinforces the importance of following safety and behavior rules. It also demonstrates that the teacher has stressed safety, thereby providing a degree of legal protection. After the teacher makes a copy for school records, children should include it in their portfolio or science journal.

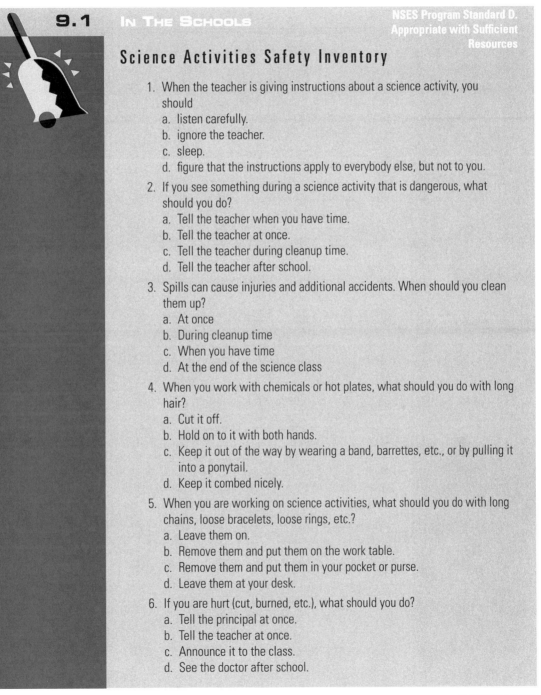

NSES Program Standard D.
Appropriate with Sufficient
Resources

9.1   IN THE SCHOOLS

Science Activities Safety Inventory

1. When the teacher is giving instructions about a science activity, you should
   a. listen carefully.
   b. ignore the teacher.
   c. sleep.
   d. figure that the instructions apply to everybody else, but not to you.

2. If you see something during a science activity that is dangerous, what should you do?
   a. Tell the teacher when you have time.
   b. Tell the teacher at once.
   c. Tell the teacher during cleanup time.
   d. Tell the teacher after school.

3. Spills can cause injuries and additional accidents. When should you clean them up?
   a. At once
   b. During cleanup time
   c. When you have time
   d. At the end of the science class

4. When you work with chemicals or hot plates, what should you do with long hair?
   a. Cut it off.
   b. Hold on to it with both hands.
   c. Keep it out of the way by wearing a band, barrettes, etc., or by pulling it into a ponytail.
   d. Keep it combed nicely.

5. When you are working on science activities, what should you do with long chains, loose bracelets, loose rings, etc.?
   a. Leave them on.
   b. Remove them and put them on the work table.
   c. Remove them and put them in your pocket or purse.
   d. Leave them at your desk.

6. If you are hurt (cut, burned, etc.), what should you do?
   a. Tell the principal at once.
   b. Tell the teacher at once.
   c. Announce it to the class.
   d. See the doctor after school.

Continued on next page

7. If you think there is something wrong with a piece of equipment you are using, you should stop, turn it off (if necessary), and
   a. tell your best friend.
   b. tell the teacher.
   c. tell another student.
   d. tell the custodian.

8. If you accidentally break a piece of equipment, you should
   a. tell the teacher at once.
   b. clean it up with your hands.
   c. hide it so no one finds out.
   d. blame someone else.

9. How do you move around the room during science time?
   a. Run
   b. Skip
   c. Hop
   d. Walk

10. Helping clean up after a science activity is the job of
    a. new students.
    b. old students.
    c. each student.
    d. the teacher.

11. When you use science equipment and/or chemicals, you should give the activity all of your
    a. interest.
    b. attention.
    c. effort.
    d. interest, attention, and effort.

12. Chemicals, small parts, and glassware are *not* to be
    a. treated with respect and care.
    b. put into your mouth.
    c. used properly.
    d. stored properly.

13. To prevent accidents during science activities involving equipment or chemicals, you should
    a. use shortcuts.
    b. follow your teacher's directions.
    c. hurry ahead of the other students.
    d. ask someone else to do the work.

Continued on next page

14. Playing instead of working, or bothering other people during science activities, is
    a. always against the rules.
    b. all right.
    c. not dangerous.
    d. okay after you have finished your project.

15. If you see a fire in a piece of apparatus you are using during a science activity, what should you do?
    a. Throw water on it.
    b. Grab your stuff and run.
    c. Tell your teacher immediately.
    d. Open a window.

16. In case of fire during a science activity, notify the teacher at once, and then
    a. follow the teacher's directions.
    b. open the windows.
    c. yell.
    d. run.

17. Before you touch an electrical switch, plug, or outlet,
    a. your hands must be dry.
    b. your hands must be clean.
    c. you should ask the custodian.
    d. you should check with the nurse.

18. How should you remove an electrical plug from the outlet?
    a. Pull on the plug.
    b. Pull on the cord.
    c. Pull on the appliance it is connected to.
    d. Get your teacher to do it.

19. Why must you wear eye protection during science activities?
    a. To protect your eyes
    b. To prevent nearsightedness
    c. To prevent farsightedness
    d. To look cool

20. You should wear eye protection during science activities even though you wear regular glasses or contact lenses.
    a. True
    b. False

21. Cabinet drawers and doors that are left open cause a hazard. You should
    a. walk around them.
    b. close them.
    c. leave them alone.
    d. wait for the teacher to close them.

Continued on next page

22. If chemicals get on your skin or your clothes, what should you do?
    a. Wash at once with vinegar.
    b. Soak the clothes or your skin with milk.
    c. Wash with soap.
    d. Run plenty of water onto the area.

23. Disturbing other students while they are working on science activities is
    a. helpful.
    b. welcome by the teacher.
    c. dangerous.
    d. the quickest way to do a job.

24. Materials and equipment that are already set up for a science activity when you arrive should be left where they are.
    a. True
    b. False

25. Who gets out the materials and equipment for science activities?
    a. The teacher
    b. The laboratory assistant
    c. Either the teacher or the lab assistant
    d. The principal

Suggested "Correct" Responses

1. a	10. c	18. a
2. b	11. d	19. a
3. a	12. b	20. a
4. c	13. b	21. b
5. c	14. a	22. d
6. b	15. c	23. c
7. b	16. a	24. a
8. a	17. a	25. c
9. d		

(Adapted from materials provided by the National Science Teachers Association.)

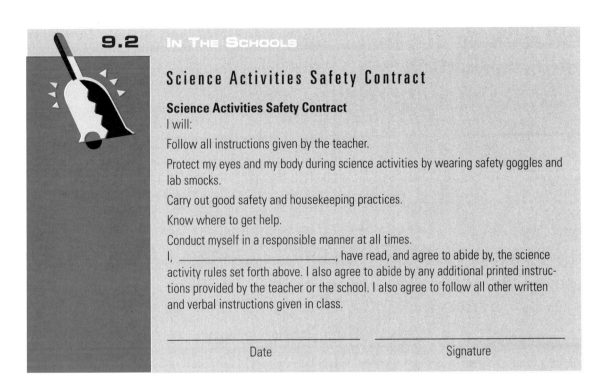

9.2   IN THE SCHOOLS

Science Activities Safety Contract

Science Activities Safety Contract
I will:

Follow all instructions given by the teacher.

Protect my eyes and my body during science activities by wearing safety goggles and lab smocks.

Carry out good safety and housekeeping practices.

Know where to get help.

Conduct myself in a responsible manner at all times.

I, _____, have read, and agree to abide by, the science activity rules set forth above. I also agree to abide by any additional printed instructions provided by the teacher or the school. I also agree to follow all other written and verbal instructions given in class.

_____   _____
Date   Signature

Children should wear safety goggles during all science activities, especially those with any potential for liquids or solids accidentally getting into a person's eyes. This includes activities involving water, chemicals, rocks, and minerals. As a matter of fact, children should wear their goggles for every science activity, and you, the teacher, should wear them as well (see Figure 9.3).

Children wear safety glasses while cracking open **geodes** (Courtesy Delta Education, P.O. Box 3000, Nashua, NH 03061-3000, Tel. 800-442-5444)

FIGURE 9.3

Ask children to bring old, long-sleeved shirts to use as laboratory coats. As with the goggles, it is a good idea to have children wear their smocks for every science activity.

Use plastic instead of glass. Clear plastic containers are available that do everything glass can do—except shatter.

Tell children *never* to taste or eat *anything* unless you specifically tell them otherwise.

Chemicals must be treated with respect. You will not be using dangerous chemicals in elementary science. All activities suggested in this book use materials that are safe for children to handle and that can be stored without special consideration. Nonetheless, the materials you do use must be handled and stored safely. Factors include the following:

1. The strongest acid you will use is vinegar, which is a dilute acetic acid. You should not use any acids stronger than vinegar in the elementary grades.

2. The Occupational Safety and Health Administration (OSHA) has established the degrees of hazard of all chemicals to inform consumers of the best way to store them. Five categories are normally identified:
   a. General
   b. Corrosive
   c. Flammable
   d. Oxidizer
   e. Poisonous

   When considering whether chemicals are safe, look in science supply catalogs for the OSHA rating. If the chemical is rated as "general," it is safe to use in the elementary school classroom and can be stored anywhere. Do not use chemicals with any of the other four ratings. It is a good idea to check with a science supervisor or an upper grades science teacher if you are in doubt.

3. Most rocks and minerals are safe; however, a few fall into the *poisonous* category. These include galena (lead sulfide), cinnabar (mercury sulfide), asbestos, and arsenopyrite, realgar, and orpiment (all minerals of arsenic). Do not include these in your mineral collections. If they are already present, dispose of them. Put the specimen in a paper or plastic bag, and alert the building custodian to this disposal need. Any college geology department or state geological society will be able to assist you in collecting rock and mineral specimens and provide advice about minerals that are possibly toxic or harmful.

4. *Do not use dry ice.* This is solid carbon dioxide and has a temperature of nearly 100 degrees below zero Fahrenheit. It can cause severe frostbite on contact with skin.

A thorough treatment of safety in the elementary science classroom can be found in the book *Safety is Elementary: The New Standard for Safety in the Elementary Science Classroom* by Roy, Markow, & Kaufman (Laboratory Safety Institute, 2001). The book contains *A* to *Z* safety topics; a safety checklist; directions for caring for animals in the classroom; lists of common chemicals available in grocery, drug, and hardware stores; descriptions of poisonous plants; and other safety topics appropriate for elementary science education. A thorough treatment of safety in middle school science is provided in the National Science Teachers Association publication *Inquiring Safely: A Guide for Middle School Teachers* by Terry Kwan and Juliana V. Texley (2003, NSTA Press).

EQUIPMENT AND MATERIALS

To the extent possible, you should use equipment and materials available from familiar sources, such as grocery stores, hardware stores, and drugstores. These materials are safe, inexpensive and easy to obtain; can be duplicated for independent storage of materials for different activities; and can be acquired by children who are interested in doing science at home. It is a good idea to reserve a separate storage area for science equipment and materials. Many teachers put the nonexpendable materials for an activity in a small, appropriately labeled box that is not to be touched except when children are doing that activity. This may mean duplicating some materials, but the time saved from not having to hunt, assemble, and replace materials every time you have children do that activity is worth the minor extra expense. Shoe boxes make excellent storage containers for the materials for individual activities, as do the inexpensive plastic boxes and containers available in many stores. Be sure to label containers of materials that are available for children's use, and show the children where these materials are so they can get them themselves.

Occasionally, you may want to order science equipment from a science supply company. Because most items are available in many varieties, it is strongly recommended that you check with someone who is knowledgeable about science materials and equipment before purchasing. For example, there are dozens of kinds of thermometers, plastic laboratory ware, and microscopes. It is better to check with someone knowledgeable about what you are proposing to order than to purchase something you cannot use.

ANIMALS AND PLANTS IN THE CLASSROOM

Living organisms are valuable additions to the classroom. The National Science Teachers Association issued a position statement in 2005 that

NSES Teaching Standard D. Providing Time, Space, and Resources
NSES Program Standard D. Appropriate with Sufficient Resources

NSES Teaching
Standard B. Guiding and
Facilitating Learning
NSES Teaching
Standard D. Provid-
ing Time, Space, and
Resources
NSES Program
Standard D. Appropri-
ate with Sufficient
Resources

supports including live animals as part of the K–12 science program to foster students' interaction with live organisms, thereby fostering achievement
in science (National Science Teachers Association, 2005). Animals are "the
touchstone to real-life experiences . . . and they tend to stimulate curiosity,
motivate students, and foster learning" (Roy, 2004, p. 10). Studying animals in the classroom enables children to develop skills of observation, a
sense of stewardship, and an appreciation for the interrelationships and
complexities of life (National Science Teachers Association 1991).

You should consider having one or two class pets in your classroom
(see Figure 9.4). Class pets provide a way of teaching children responsibility as well as how to take care of animals humanely. Animals commonly
found as classroom pets include the following:

Goldfish	Lizards
Birds	Chameleons
Gerbils	Iguanas
Hamsters	Tropical fish
Guinea pigs	Rabbits
Salamanders	Crickets

A bunny in the
classroom (Elizabeth
Crews)

FIGURE 9.4

All living organisms should be properly cared for and treated humanely, responsibly, and ethically. Pet stores and local and school libraries can provide material on how to care for the animals in your classroom. As the teacher, you are expected to be knowledgeable about the proper care of the animals. Children should take a certain amount of the responsibility (depending on their age) for feeding and watering the animals, cleaning the cages, and doing other chores that have to be done. Be sure the living space for the animal is large enough and, to the extent possible, replicates its natural environment, and be sure to make adequate provisions for weekend and vacation care of the animals. Pet stores normally have personnel who can give you advice on the proper care of your classroom pets. Include a lesson on the humane treatment of animals.

Federal regulations prohibit experimenting with vertebrate animals. All experimentation should be done with invertebrate animals, such as worms, insects, and bugs. This means that fish, hamsters, and lizards should not be subjected to experimental procedures. For example, federal regulations would not permit an activity in which children add ice cubes to a jar containing goldfish to see how the goldfish react.

Plants can be grown in the classroom, and children can observe their characteristics and measure their rates of growth. Terrariums (containers with small plants, ferns, and mosses planted in a shallow layer of soil and pebbles) can be started by the children and maintained throughout the school year (see Figures 9.5a and b).

 Many Web sites are devoted to the care of animals in the classroom. See the Student Book Companion Web Site for direct links to several of these sites.

 Details for building and maintaining terrariums can be found on the Internet; a direct link to the horticultural Web site maintained by the University of Columbia–Missouri is available on the Student Book Companion Web Site.

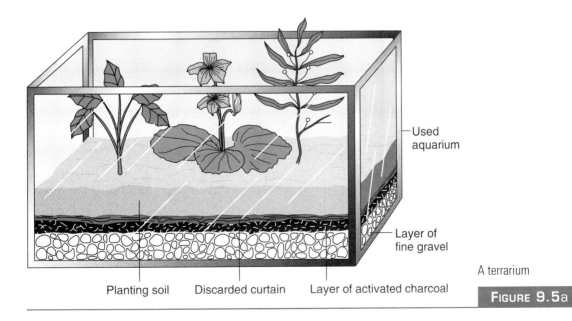

Used aquarium

Layer of fine gravel

Planting soil   Discarded curtain   Layer of activated charcoal

A terrarium

FIGURE 9.5a

Watering the classroom terrarium

FIGURE 9.5b

FAMILY INVOLVEMENT

NSES Teaching
Standard D. Provid-
ing Time, Space, and
Resources
NSES Program
Standard D. Appropri-
ate with Sufficient
Resources

It has been shown that strengthening the involvement of parents in the education of their children fosters increases in student achievement (Allen, 2005). Family involvement strategies in science can include communicating, volunteering, home-based inquiries, helping children make decisions, science nights, workshops, donating materials, chaperoning field trips, and many other creative ideas.

With the increasing emphasis on family involvement, parents, guardians, and caretakers are becoming increasingly comfortable working with the schools toward common goals for their children. Many family members, despite busy work schedules, are able to donate an hour or two each week or two to school activities. Parents and other family members can serve as lab assistants during science, and they can be enlisted to help set up the classroom for science activities. Family involvement can be encouraged by writing a weekly science newsletter that includes descriptions of the current emphasis in science and suggests home activities to accompany an "experiment of the week." Families can be asked to donate materials required for science activities. They may be willing to serve on committees to determine criteria for portfolios or to help establish guidelines for authentic systems of reporting children's achievement and progress. If they cannot come to school during the day because of work schedules, they may be able to participate in a "Family Science Festival" (see below).

Thier (2003) suggests encouraging families to "take part in science activities infused with literacy" (p. 1). Such activities might include organizing discovery activities in natural habitats, such as meadows, wooded areas, or beaches, and keeping a science journal at home in which the children describe what they did, reflect on what they observed, list questions they might have, and even write stories.

Many Internet sites are devoted to science inquiries that children and their parents can do together at home. Among these is a collection of activities and science activity Web links produced and maintained by the American Association for the Advancement of Science (AAAS). The work of the AAAS has been a major force in the field of science education (see Chapter 2). The Exploratorium in San Francisco also provides many online activities for children and their families; it was conceived by nuclear physicist Frank Oppenheimer of the Manhattan Project.

Another way to involve families in science is to prepare family science activity modules to be taken home by children and returned within a few days. These modules consist of inexpensive materials, a book, and clear and simple directions for one or more activities that the child and his or her family can do together at home. Take-home science modules are particularly successful in homes where family members may be hesitant to come to school for various reasons such as limited proficiency in the English language. A sample take-home science module is shown in Figure 9.6.

The National Science Teachers Association (1994) has published a position statement, *Parent Involvement in Science Education,* in which it affirms that "parents play an essential role in the success of students in schools. Parents who encourage the daily use of science concepts and process skills enhance their child's ability to learn the skills necessary for success" (p. 5).

There are many ways of sparking family interest in your science program. Invite family members to the classroom for a "Family Science Festival" evening of science activities in which you explain the science program and involve them as co-inquirers with their children in several science investigations; this way, they will be doing science the way their children do science in the classroom and will be better prepared to encourage their children to do science-related activities at home. Lundeen (2005) suggests that teachers use discrepant events to help students and their families begin some scientific explorations. Individual students demonstrate a particular discrepant event and engage the families in inquiries similar to those they use in their science classes. They present the activity to all the families in attendance, who rotate to several discrepant event stations during the evening, each manned by a different student. Salinas (2005) uses the "Scientist of the Day" program with her first-grade students. Children do science activities with their families at home and get them ready for presentation to the class when it is their turn to be "Scientist of the Day." Students describe or demonstrate the activity to the class and explain why it did or did not have the expected outcomes.

Direct links to the AAAS and San Francisco Exploratorium Web sites are provided on the Student Book Companion Web Site.

The U.S. Department of Education maintains Web sites with information on the "Partnership for Family Involvement in Education" program and other materials on parent and family involvement in education. The Student Book Companion Web Site has direct links to these sites.

FREEZING WATER
A Take-Home Science Module

Processes fostered: Measuring, formulating, and testing hypotheses

In this activity, children explore factors involved in water freezing.

Materials provided in kit: Six plastic cups
Magic marker
Curious George Goes to an Ice Cream Shop by
Margaret and H.A. Rey (Houghton Mifflin, 1989)

Materials to be provided at home: Water
Salt
Sugar
Cola with sugar
Diet drink
Other liquids

Directions: Fill the cup about ⅔ full with water. Hold the cup level, and mark the level of the water with the magic marker. Put the cup in the freezer keeping it level. Check the state of the water in the cup every 20 minutes or so until it is completely frozen. What happens to the water? Compare the level of the water in the cup with the level when it turns to ice. How long did it take to freeze completely?

Try other variations such as those suggested below. Be sure you fill the cup to the same mark as the original water experiment each time so that you will have the same volume.

• Add a few tablespoons of salt to a cup of water, and see how long it takes to freeze.

• Add a different amount of salt to a cup of water to see how long it takes to freeze.

• Do the same things with sugar.

• Open a bottle or can of regular soda with sugar, pour some into a cup, and see how long it takes to freeze.

• Do the same thing with diet soda.

• Do the same thing with fruit juices or drink mixes. Fill the cup about ⅔ full with the liquid, add a Popsicle® stick, and freeze it. (Children can eat their lesson.)

• Try other variations that you and your child can think of.

At some point, read the book *Curious George Goes to an Ice Cream Shop* with your child.

FIGURE 9.6

Continued on next page

Explanation for adults: When water freezes, tiny crystals of ice form. The crystals of ice arrange themselves in a complex pattern in which individual crystals are linked to each other at their edges. This takes up more room than the water molecules; thus water expands when it freezes.

OPTIONAL DATA TABLE
How Long it Took to Freeze Different Liquids

Liquid	How Long It Took to Freeze
Water	
Water with _____ spoons of salt	
Water with _____ spoons of salt	
Water with _____ spoons of sugar	
Water with _____ spoons of sugar	
Regular soda	
Diet soda	
(Other)	

Evaluation by Family

When did you do this activity with your child? _____

Do you feel this activity was meaningful to you and your child? _____

_____

Were the directions easy to follow? _____

Do you have any suggestions for how we can improve this activity? _____

_____

What did you and your child learn from this take-home kit? _____

_____

Please suggest other science topics you would like to have us put in a take-home

kit. _____

FIGURE 9.6

CLASSROOM ORGANIZATION

NSES Teaching Standard D. Providing Time, Space, and Resources
NSES Program Standard D. Appropriate with Sufficient Resources

The modern elementary classroom typically is furnished with movable desks to accommodate a variety of classroom arrangements. Most teachers place the desks in groupings of four to six with children facing each other. Because constructivist science is facilitated by children working in groups, this cluster-type arrangement is ideal. From time to time, you may want to rearrange the desks so all children are facing the front during substantial periods of large-group instruction. Occasionally, it may be desirable to rearrange the desks to provide for individual work or to clear a large floor space. The constructivist classroom has "maximum flexibility of space and movement" and "can accommodate individual, small group, and large group learning experiences each day at varying levels of difficulty" (Wood, 1990, p. i).

The science center takes many forms. It may simply be a desk or a table located at one side of the room where you and the children place ongoing projects to facilitate continuing investigation. It may be a cabinet with a work surface and storage space where many of the science activities are performed, although this limits the number of children who can work on science at any one time. Terrariums, aquariums, and animal cages can be located wherever convenient in the room. You may want to reserve a desk or table somewhere in the room for interesting "try this" activities that will not be done with the class. Although laboratory facilities that include gas and water seldom are required in elementary classrooms, some teachers have at their disposal counter space with plumbing that can be used for science investigations. Portable laboratory tables suitable for elementary school children are available through educational science supply firms and can be shared among several classrooms. Regardless of how you allocate space, the science center should be easily accessible to all children. It should contain equipment and materials that children can use to continue investigations started in class or to pursue investigations they themselves have developed. Then you can suggest to children that they use their free time in the science center.

Be sure to consider the special needs of children with handicaps—wider aisles, freedom to move around the classroom, special desks and tabletops, access to materials and equipment, access to technologies, and other needs (see Chapter 7).

NSES Teaching Standard D. Providing Time, Space, and Resources
NSES Professional Development Standard B. Integrating Knowledge of Science, Learning, Pedagogy, and Students

COOPERATIVE TEACHING AND COOPERATIVE LEARNING

Cooperative *teaching* refers to a teaching strategy in which individual teachers assume the responsibility for instruction in a subject or area of their expertise. Cooperative *learning* is a teaching strategy in which students are grouped together and work as a group to help each other learn.

Several models of cooperative teaching are appropriate for elementary science education. One model suggests that in a teaching team, one or two teachers who have particular interest and expertise in science assume responsibility for all the science education of the children in the team. In another model, subject specialists are responsible for teaching their subject to all children in a grade level. These models have the advantage that science is taught by instructors with knowledge and expertise; however, curriculum integration is difficult to achieve.

In a third model, all teachers for the grade level cooperate in the teaching of science by rotating the responsibility for lessons in a jointly planned unit. One teacher assumes responsibility for a certain lesson and sets up all the needed materials. Each class rotates into that teacher's room for their science lesson during the day. A different teacher assumes responsibility for the next lesson, and so on. Rotating assignments provides coordination of lessons across the curriculum in all sections of the grade level; enables teachers to provide increased depth because they do not have to do everything; and provides different viewpoints to stimulate children's thinking. This system also saves teachers valuable preparation time, because they only have to prepare certain lessons out of the total prepared by the team.

It has been established that cooperative learning fosters achievement. Achievement in science is no exception. Indeed, in the constructivist approach, children must discuss their thinking and their conclusions with one another to establish validity. Discussing their thoughts among themselves often leads to new insights and new ways of constructing concepts that increase meaningfulness.

The traditional system of cooperative learning calls for division of labor wherein one child is responsible for performing the activity and the others are assigned such roles as materials manager, recorder, and communicator. We suggest you think carefully about this model, because the emphasis in constructivist learning is that all children should do all the activities and formulate their own ideas as a result of having done them. Each child must do the activities; each child must record observations; and each child must feel free to interact with the teacher. Only by becoming totally involved in the entire process of doing science will children develop the process and inquiry skills needed to construct sound conceptualizations. Thus, children should work in unstructured groups during their science activities. Groups should include most knowledgeable and least knowledgeable children. You also might consider forming same-gender groups (see the section on gender bias in Chapter 7).

In a large-group activity, first-grade children discuss the results of their seed-sprouting activity.

FIGURE 9.7

TIME MANAGEMENT

NSES Teaching Standard D. Providing Time, Space, and Resources
NSES Program Standard D. Appropriate with Sufficient Resources

Science in the elementary classroom can be scheduled in several ways. One is to hold it daily for short periods of time. This has the advantage of daily contact with science but the serious disadvantage that there probably will not be enough time during any one session for children to get deeply involved in their inquiries. Another way to schedule science is to hold it two or three times weekly for longer periods of time. This has the advantage of providing enough time for children to complete their explorations. A third way is to adjust your classroom schedules from week to week to provide the time needed for science lessons. Yet another way is available to teachers who use integrated and interdisciplinary approaches; by their very nature, interdisciplinary approaches require allocation of the time needed for children to do their scientific explorations and investigations in conjunction with the overarching topic under study.

There is no rule that can be invoked to guide the teacher in the scheduling of science. The important consideration is to be flexible in scheduling. The elementary school daily schedule may be predetermined by the administration, and science in the elementary schools often is allocated less time in the daily schedule than is desirable or necessary to permit children to inquire openly. You should work with the daily schedule in flexible ways to provide blocks of time that meet the needs of the children and the program objectives.

Local science enrichment programs, preparation for state and national Science Olympiad Fun Days and competitions, science fairs, invention conventions, and other science-oriented extracurricular activities normally are held after school to provide supervised time for children to explore areas of inquiry.

In science education, time management also includes preparation time. This is likely to be substantial for process-oriented inquiry lessons. Not only do the lessons have to be planned, but the materials and equipment have to be assembled and organized such that the materials can be easily passed out to children when the time comes. In addition, multiple centers and/or inquiry follow-up areas often have to be set up. You may be able to use the services of parent volunteers to help in setting up your classroom. In the upper elementary grades, you may choose to appoint student laboratory assistants, who can save you a great deal of time in setting up for science activities. You could select the lab assistant on the basis of interest, achievement, or other appropriate criteria. Lab assistants can be given the responsibility for setting up before science activities, obtaining additional materials as needed during the activities, and cleaning up afterward. Teach them where things are, and show them what they are supposed to do. Some teachers elect to have several lab assistants at the same time (in case one is absent). Some teachers rotate the lab assistant position throughout the school year so that everyone gets to be lab assistant at least once. It may be possible to invite older children to serve as lab assistants in classes of younger children; such service strengthens their understanding of science and helps the younger children in the same way that cooperative learning groups aid all participants.

CLASSROOM MANAGEMENT

Professor Herbert Kliebard of the University of Wisconsin has observed that good teaching often is perceived as keeping good classroom order (Kliebard, 1989). So teachers teach in ways that ensure good order—recitation, teacher-dominated questions and answers, worksheets, choral reading, and the like. Teaching in discovery and inquiry modes runs the risk of disorder, and only the most courageous teachers are willing to take that risk.

In a constructivist approach to science teaching, the order kept in the classroom is of a different type than Kliebard was talking about. Children talk with each other; they try out different things; they argue; they pursue their positions; and they often seem to be "off-task." I get disturbed when I hear the phrase "on-task," because in the constructivist approach to science education, every child conceivably could need to pursue a given problem or situation from a different angle. Therefore, they may be seen as being off-task by observers who believe children should be doing essentially the same thing at the same time. *On-task* in a constructivist science classroom means that children are pursuing their investigations in ways that are meaningful to them. These ways may range from a slight

NSES Teaching Standard A. Inquiry-Based Program
NSES Teaching Standard D. Providing Time, Space, and Resources
NSES Program Standard D. Appropriate with Sufficient Resources

divergence from the main task to a radical departure from the primary activity when children pursue something that will help them construct their own meanings of the situation. Children who are interested in what they are doing *are* on-task! Therefore, classroom management is different from setting down rules and requiring obedience.

The primary rule in a constructivist classroom is that every child has the right to learn and the teacher has the right to facilitate this learning. This is an extremely open rule, because it precludes the use of regulatory rules and prescribed punishment for given infractions of rules. However, children are accustomed to having rules to follow, and when we let them have too much freedom, we fear they will take advantage of the situation and that bedlam will erupt. Therefore, I offer a few suggestions for successful management in a constructivist science classroom.

MANAGEMENT STRATEGIES IN THE CONSTRUCTIVIST SCIENCE CLASSROOM

1. No matter how committed we are to constructivist teaching and learning, we all use the expository mode in our classes to some extent. Rules of behavior appropriate for expository settings should be enforced.

2. Teachers should move slowly from the expository mode to which children have become accustomed toward guided-inquiry approaches.

3. As children are introduced to more inquiry-oriented activities, the teacher should demonstrate the activity before turning it over to the children. While demonstrating it, the teacher should explain ways in which children can explore on their own. During this demonstration, the teacher should discuss behavior expectations and, especially, the safety precautions to be taken during the activity.

4. While children are working on their own activities, a high degree of interaction exists between teacher and individuals and small groups. (This is exhausting and demanding!) Opportunities continually exist for private encouragement of students to exhibit appropriate behavior and for private correction of inappropriate behavior.

5. Let your building administrators know what you are doing, what your goals are, and what to look for in your classroom. This will keep them informed and may help you achieve your goals through their input (which you have solicited). Invite your build-

ing administrators to your class when you are doing an activity. Support for the child-centered constructivist approach to teaching and learning must come from within the school; inviting family members, colleagues, and administrators to your classroom to observe children at work helps secure the needed support.

In a constructivist classroom, behavior management problems are minimal, because (1) children aren't bored, (2) children are treated with dignity, (3) children's explorations and constructions are valued, (4) children have a say about what they do during the science class, (5) children are building positive self-concepts while they are performing the activities, and (6) children have power to work out their own activities in the way they see as best.

If children want to "play" instead of work, you may wish to use a quasi-contractual approach in which child and teacher are equal contributors. A plan of study is agreed on that includes the activities the child will do, a method of reporting daily progress (such as a log or a journal), the method of evaluation, and a time table. As long as the child is working within the parameters of the agreed-on plan of study, there should be no need for concern about the child not devoting all attention to science.

Teachers also might profit from using the principle of self-referencing behavior management: "You are doing a great job today . . . much less fooling around than yesterday." This is to be contrasted with rule-referencing behavior management: "You broke the rule, and now you have to pay the price." Constructivist teachers effectively eliminate the reward–punishment system of classroom management.

Teachers also might profit from the 1-2-3 method of correcting undesirable actions: (1) name the individual; (2) state the specific action to be stopped; (3) state the reason why. ("James, stop talking out of turn; children cannot hear what others are saying.") Say this quietly and in close proximity to the offending child so as not to call widespread attention to the child or the problem. This encourages self-referencing behavior, eliminates confusion and ambiguities, and treats each individual with dignity. Others have written that treating children with dignity is key to successful classroom management. I have found this to be true.

If we want to teach in a constructivist mode, we must recognize that we ourselves also are constructing information out of our own experiences. The only way we can change our discipline road map is to try a different approach, begin developing different teacher–child interactions, and evaluate the results. Success in these new interactions will aid in our cognitive and physical construction of the more complete constructivist classroom. Changing our expectations that children conform to a set of rules, and changing our conceptualization of how children solve problems and construct their own information are good first steps. Most important, we must change the outlook that effective teaching is synonymous with good order in the classroom.

▶ "'Do you think you can maintain discipline?' asked the Superintendent. 'Of course I can,' replied Stuart. 'I'll make the work interesting and the discipline will take care of itself.'"
E. B. White, *Stuart Little* (New York: Harper Trophy, 1945), Cp. XII "The Schoolroom"

TEACHER VOICE

Having taught all subjects in a sixth-grade, self-contained classroom for many years, I recently began teaching sixth-grade science in a depart-mentalized situation. My school is a Title I school, and my classroom is in a trailer. Little in the way of science materials and equipment is available to us. When I told the other teachers that I planned to teach in a constructivist mode and did not plan on using "the book" except as a reference tool, I received reactions that ranged from admiration to comments such as "You're crazy!" I believe many "experienced" teach-ers are afraid that if you are not always center-stage telling the students what to do, your classroom will be chaotic and not a place where learn-ing is going on.

I have learned several things that are invaluable for making sure my constructivist classroom provides the optimum learning environment for each student. Foremost among these is the need for order. My class-room may not look orderly to a new person who walks in my door and sees 24 students at tables all talking together, but it is.

When my students come into my classroom at the beginning of the year, the first thing we talk about is classroom procedures. I have them sitting at tables, with four students at a table. When we do an activity or lab, all students have "jobs" for which they are responsible. Although some do not agree that this is the best practice, I use the cooperative learning system of assigning four specific jobs so that I have (1) the "primary investigator" who is the person in charge; (2) the "reporter-recorder" who writes down information or reports back to the whole group; (3) the "materials manager" who gets materials from me or the table; and (4) the "maintenance director" who is in charge of making sure everything gets put back and is cleaned up. By assigning these jobs for every activity, I always have a person from each group who is responsible for doing a particular task when needed. The jobs are changed for every activity so that every student gets to do every job at one time or another. It takes a few minutes at the beginning of the class to assign jobs, but this procedure saves time in the long run and also distributes the responsibilities throughout the group instead of always having the same person "take charge." To deal with the possibility that a student may not be capable of doing certain tasks, I suggest that they get help doing their jobs so they can be successful.

Another procedure that is very important in maintaining order in my classroom is being able to get the students' attention right away without having to raise my voice or keep calling out to them to quiet down and listen. I use a bell signal which indicates that the students should stop talking immediately and look up at me. The reason could be to "turn down the volume" or to get ready to clean up, or it could be because I want to clarify or add to a procedure, discuss a concept, or answer a question that is coming up for many groups at the same time. For the most part, the students are very responsive to this signal. Some teachers use other variations, such as raising the hand or saying something like "If you can hear me, clap once." This system also seems to eliminate some of the negative atmosphere that telling students to "be quiet" can create.

My students have assigned seats and tables, but this is mainly because of the need to take attendance since I have four different science classes each day. In other situations, I have allowed students to sit wherever they like as long as they work well with their groups. Occasionally, I have even varied the seating arrangement on a daily basis. I have found, though, that most students like knowing where they belong and like to sit in the same place each day.

I practice the procedures I want students to follow every day for as long as it takes them to learn them satisfactorily. This may take a lot of time during the first week or two of school, but after that it is second nature and makes the daily routine much less stressful since you, as the teacher, are not constantly directing it. Once the procedures have been established and students know when, where, and how to move around the room, we begin doing activities and labs. A very important component of a successful lab or activity is to be sure you have the supplies for each group organized and ready for the "materials manager" to pick up. The time it takes to do this ahead of class is well spent as it eliminates the distractions and wasted class time that will surely result if you don't have the materials assembled for each group.

To teach in a classroom of involved and actively learning students can be the most physically tiring teaching job there is! You must be as involved as the students are to keep them going. This means that in my classroom I walk around constantly. I am observing, listening, answering questions, asking students to share their thoughts, helping students clarify their thinking, redirecting behaviors, and learning from the students themselves in many cases. The days are never boring. I would not teach any other way!

Jean Stevens

Sixth-Grade Science Teacher
James Arthur Intermediate School
Kennedale, Texas

OUTDOOR CLASSROOMS

NSES Teaching Standard D. Providing Time, Space, and Resources
NSES Program Standard B. Relevant, Inquiry-Based, and Connected with Other Subjects

Outdoor classrooms are excellent ways to extend science beyond school walls. Outdoor classrooms can be as simple as designated areas of the school campus where children can observe grass growing through the cement and can do measurement activities. An example of an outdoor activity is shown in Constructing Science in the Classroom 9.5.

9.5   CONSTRUCTING SCIENCE IN THE CLASSROOM

SIDEWALK ECOLOGY

An Outdoor Learning Center Activity

Objective

NSES Content Standard C. Life Science: Organisms and Environments

The student will observe living things in the environment of a sidewalk.

Take the children outdoors and ask them what they can see in general area near the sidewalk. They may see grass and other plants poking up through the sidewalk cracks. Ask why plants grow like this and what this shows about how plants grow and what they need to grow. The children may see ants. Ask them to observe the ants carefully. Do all ants follow the same path? How do the ants know what path to follow? Are any of the ants carrying anything? What? What is it for? What do they use to carry things? Are there any groups of ants helping each other carry something? Why is more than one ant needed to carry it? Are there any anthills nearby? How do the ants go in and out of their hill?

Ask similar questions about other insects and other living things that children may notice.

Can children see the edges of the sidewalk? If so, maybe they can see what the sidewalk is made of. Is there evidence of erosion near the sidewalk? If so, ask children what they think might have caused the erosion.

Continued on next page

Back in the classroom, have books with pictures of living things seen on the excursion available for children to explore.

Safety Note: Do not let children touch any insects or get so close to them that they crawl onto the children. Children may be allergic to insects, and many ants, especially fire ants, can and do bite. Also, be on the lookout for bees, wasps, and hornets. If you see them, *quietly* coax the children to a different area.

Children examine a school sidewalk

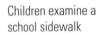

FIGURE 9.8

Literature Connections

Plantzilla by Jerdine Nolen (Harcourt, 2002) is the story of a third-grade boy who cares for a plant named *Plantzilla* that becomes more human as the summer progresses.

Mud Matters by Jennifer Owings Dewey (Marshall Cavendish Corporation, 1998) features rich descriptions of mud taken from the recollections of the author's own childhood and describes its use for childhood games, pottery making, and Native American rituals.

Butterfly Count by Sneed B. Collard, III (Holiday House, 2002). Amy and her mother look for a very special kind of butterfly while attending the annual Fourth of July Butterfly Count gathering at a prairie restoration site. The book includes factual information about butterflies, how to attract them, and how to watch them.

Many schools have gardens available for instructional purposes. Studies show that school gardening programs foster increased science achievement and that gardening is equally effective at teaching science for both boys and girls (Shapiro, 2006). You can solicit the help of family members, local businesses, and others who are interested to help you plan and build a garden. Be sure to involve students in all stages, and be sure to assign responsibilities for upkeep when school is not in session. You can ask local Master Gardners for their help and guidance in starting and maintaining a school garden. See the video "Outdoor Gardening" on the companion DVD.

Outdoor classrooms can be simple, or they can be as complex as outdoor learning facilities complete with nature trails, butterfly and hummingbird gardens, vegetable gardens, and amphitheaters. When planning an outdoor learning center, be sure to establish goals and objectives for its use, and be sure to involve all interested faculty and administrators. Soliciting the involvement of family members, the parent–teacher organization, and local businesses may aid in your planning and, often, in financing the project.

Paraprofessionals, family members, personnel from local businesses, and preservice teachers may be willing to assist in other ways. Such help can range from assisting children in performing their activities and preparing the needed materials to helping plan special facilities, giving special presentations, and providing financial assistance.

You can access an interactive map that enables you to find Master Gardeners in your area through a direct link on the student book companion Web site. The National Gardening Association maintains a Web site devoted to tips and ideas for teachers and a registry of school gardens with a description and location of each. You can access this site through a direct link on the Student Book Companion Web Site.

Tending the garden in the outdoor learning center (Elizabeth Crews)

FIGURE 9.9

SCIENCE OUTSIDE THE CLASSROOM

The classroom is only one of many places where children can learn science. As noted above, an outdoor classroom gives children the opportunity to observe and study natural phenomena firsthand. In addition, there are many nontraditional settings where science learning can be enhanced, such as museums, aquariums, planetariums, and science and technology centers. Furthermore, field trips taken away from the school setting can open channels of learning not otherwise available. For example, in a study of 700 third- and fourth-grade children studying forestry, Morell (2003) found that children who participated in field trips to a hands-on workshop on wood, forestry, and forest products acquired more knowledge about that topic and retained it longer than children who did not go on the field trip. Field trips also can have a positive effect on children's attitudes about science (Jarvis & Pell, 2005).

NSES Teaching Standard E. Developing Learners Who Reflect Intellectual Rigor and Attitudes Conducive to Science Learning
NSES Program Standard B. Relevant, Inquiry-Based, and Connected with Other Subjects

Field Trips

There are many places beyond the school and its grounds where children can observe and explore science. These nontraditional settings include ponds, farms, plant nurseries, grocery stores, hardware stores, banks, zoos, aquariums, botanical gardens, museums, and a host of other places where science abounds. By venturing into the community and into nature through field trips, teachers and children reap the benefits of authentic learning, and children become actively engaged in their own learning by interacting with the world around them.

NSES Program Standard B. Relevant, Inquiry-Based, and Connected with Other Subjects

Field trips require planning, and in the constructivist classroom, much of this planning is done in conjunction with the children. In planning a field

Catching insects on a field trip (Elizabeth Crews)

FIGURE 9.10

trip, the first step, of course, is to decide where to go. (See Figure 9.11 for a summary of the elements of planning and going on field trips.) A field trip possibility can be suggested by the teacher to supplement the topic under study, or it can arise from children's own ideas as they pursue their investigations, although Kisiel (2005) found that teachers feel strongly that field trips must connect to the classroom curriculum. Once the decision to take the field trip has been finalized, you should take the trip yourself to work out logistics. Obtain the necessary permissions from the field trip site, determine entrance fees, and list specific activities available for children to pursue at the site. Determine how long the trip will take, scout out lunch and rest room facilities, and plan what kind of clothing children will need to wear. Also, scout out features that are likely to engage children's interest along the way.

Then, back at school, establish the date, the method of funding, the mode of transportation, and the number of chaperones needed. (A ratio of one chaperone for every four or five children is suggested for elementary education field trips.)

Once all this is done, describe the trip and its features and opportunities to the children, and engage them in a discussion of what they would like to learn and would like to do during the trip. Plan the details in conjunction with the children. Keep a running list of trip objectives proposed by the children for use in helping them stay focused during the trip and for use in the post-trip discussion. Using the children's input, write a letter to their parents explaining the trip, the goals of the trip, and what the children will do. Attach the permission blank required by the school.

Because there may be one or more children who, for one reason or another, will not be able to go on the trip, plan equally interesting activities for them to do while the rest of the class is away.

On the day of the trip, remind children about the learning objectives and goals they decided on earlier. Establish behavior expectations and discuss safety regulations. During the trip, interact with the children as you would during a classroom science inquiry activity. Help them crystallize their questions and thoughts. Help them figure out answers to their questions in an inquiry manner. Point out interesting features seen during the trip that the children may have missed. In general, act as a facilitator for their personal constructions of new ideas.

When the trip is over, ask children to identify the most important or significant things they learned on the trip. Suggest follow-up activities as appropriate, based on the demonstrated interests of the children, questions that remain unanswered, and concepts that remain unexplained.

Figure 9.12 shows a variety of field trip sites together with some of the learning opportunities available at each. The list is provided to give you some ideas. You are sure to be able to refine the list to reflect available

(text continued on page 422)

ELEMENTS OF PLANNING AND GOING ON FIELD TRIPS

What to Do	Source
1. Decide where to go	Teacher and children
2. Take the trip in advance	Teacher
• Establish route	Teacher
• Obtain site permission	Site representative
• Find out entrance fees	Site representative
• List available activities	Site representative and teacher
• Determine time for trip	Teacher
• Find lunch facilities	Teacher
• Find rest room facilities	Teacher
• Determine clothing requirements	Teacher
3. Establish date of trip	Teacher and administration
4. Arrange transportation	Teacher and administration
5. Determine cost	Teacher
6. Establish funding	Teacher and administration
7. Arrange chaperones	Teacher and parents
8. Discuss trip with children	Teacher and children
• Ask what children would like to learn and record their responses	Teacher and children
• Ask what children would like to do and record their responses	Teacher and children
9. Write parent letter	Teacher and children
10. Secure parent permission	Teacher and parents
11. Plan for children unable to go on trip	Teacher
12. Collect money	Teacher
13. Plan for medical emergencies	Teacher
14. Provide first aid kit	Teacher
15. Establish behavior expectations	Teacher and chaperones
16. Establish groups for each chaperone	Teacher and chaperones
17. Reconfirm with the site	Teacher and site representative
18. Go on trip	Teacher, children, chaperones
• Facilitate inquiries	Teacher and chaperones
• Point out interesting features	Teacher and chaperones
• Help children focus on their goals	Teacher and chaperones
19. Hold post-trip discussion	Teacher and children
• Ask most significant thing each child learned	Teacher and children
• Arrange for follow-up activities as appropriate	Teacher and children

Figure 9.11

SOME SCIENCE-FOCUSED FIELD TRIPS AND THEIR LEARNING OPPORTUNITIES

Destination	Some Learning Opportunities
Pond	Observe plants and animals, plant and animal habitats, and ecosystems. Collect insects. Collect leaves.
Lake shore	Observe plants and animals, plant and animal habitats, shoreline features, and sand and rocks. Identify water sports.
Ocean beach	Observe plants and animals, plant and animal habitats, and shoreline features. Observe intertidal area, effects of tides, waves and wave motion. Observe dunes and dune shapes. Watch crabs. Collect shells.
Desert	Observe plants and animals, desert ecology, kinds of sand, and sand dunes and dune shapes. Identify adaptations of plants and animals to desert environment. Infer dune movement. Observe windblown sand.
Grocery store	Study organization of merchandise. Observe methods of refrigeration. Observe food preparation. Identify methods of ensuring food safety. Identify uses of technology. Observe what individual workers do.
Hardware store	Study organization of merchandise. Identify uses of different kinds of hardware. Observe materials and supplies found in hardware stores. Identify uses of technology. Observe what individual workers do. (Note that some hardware stores have project-building events for children.)
Bank	Observe security systems. Observe money handling and money sorting. Identify uses of technology. Observe what individual workers do.
Zoo	Many activities are available. Check with educational coordinator. Children also may be able to see what animal scientists do.
Aquarium	Many activities are available. Check with the educational coordinator. Children also may be able to see what marine biologists do.
Botanical Gardens	Observe plants, plant varieties, and exotic plants. Observe plant care. Observe ways in which different plants grow. Observe what plant scientists do.

FIGURE 9.12

Continued on next page

Planetarium	Observe images of constellations, the sun, the moon, stars, planets, comets, and eclipses. Observe apparent movement of the night sky. Observe apparent movement of the daytime sky. Identify uses of technology. Children also may be able to interact with scientists.
Dairy farm	Observe cows. Identify the food that cows eat. Observe milking machines and milk storage facilities. Trace the dairy process from cows feeding to milk storage and shipment. Observe sanitation, cleanliness, and cleanliness tests.
Commercial diary	Observe dairy product processing, manufacturing, and packaging. Identify kinds of dairy products. Observe pasteurization. Identify methods of ensuring food safety and cleanliness. Observe what individual workers do.
Ice cream plant	Identify ingredients and the sources of ingredients. Identify flavors. Observe manufacturing and preparation techniques.
Plant nurseries	Observe plant varieties. Observe plant germination, growth, and care. Identify best plants for the local area and regions in local yards where plants grow best. Compare outside and inside plants. Observe what individual workers do.
Vegetable garden	Observe plants. Identify parts of plants eaten. Observe how vegetables grow. Observe planting, cultivating, caring, and harvesting.
Flower garden	Observe plants and flowers and how the different flowers are grown. Observe planting, cultivating, and caring.
Farm	Observe plants and animals, care of animals, how vegetables are grown, cultivated, cared for, harvested, and prepared for selling. Observe farming equipment. Identify uses of technology.
Television station	Observe equipment. Interact with personalities. Observe broadcast booths. Identify responsibilities of director, cameraperson, producer, and others. Identify uses of computers. Observe use of blue backgrounds for superimposed computer images. Interact with different specialists.
Radio station	Observe equipment. Interact with personalities. Observe broadcast booths. Identify responsibilities of director, cameraperson, producer, and others. Identify uses of computers. Interact with different specialists.

Continued on next page

FIGURE 9.12

Weather station	Observe instruments and identify what they tell. Identify responsibilities of meteorologists. Identify uses of technology. Observe method used for forecasting. Observe production of weather maps. Identify severe weather warnings and the role of the U.S. Weather Service.
State and national parks	Many activities are available. Check with educational coordinator. Children may be able to interact with different specialists.
Symphony or band rehearsal or concert	Identify instruments of the orchestra and band and the sounds they make. Identify characteristics of sound: pitch, volume, and quality.
Fisherman's wharf	Observe whole fish. Identify kinds of fish. Smell the odors. Observe fishermen unloading the catch. Identify ways seafood is preserved and how seafood is distributed to markets.

FIGURE 9.12

facilities in your local area. The learning opportunities are related to science and are suggested to help you facilitate children's discussions of what they would like to accomplish. Of course, each teacher will tailor the trips planned to meet the local situations and the needs of the children in the class.

Nontraditional Science Settings

NSES Program Standard B. Relevant, Inquiry-Based, and Connected with Other Subjects

A direct link to the American Association of Museums and the Association of Children's Museums is available on the Student Book Companion Web site.

Museums are particularly attractive destinations for field trips. There are some 17,500 museums across the United States (American Association of Museums, n.d.). They focus on all kinds of topics, and they include all types, sizes, budgets, and rural as well as urban geographic locations. More than 300 museums have been designed specifically for children and youth (Association of Children's Museums, 2007). Many of these employ science educators who are skilled at leading children through the museum and, often, at engaging them in inquiries (Tran, 2006), although the teacher needs to contextualize children's experiences based on the purpose of the trip and the overall classroom goals (Tel & Morag, 2007).

The meaningful displays and interactive exhibits found in museums provide rich opportunities for discovery learning. A good example is the San Francisco Exploratorium mentioned earlier. You can get a good idea of their exhibits from their Web site. Children can give their attention to exhibits that interest them. Museums provide concrete learning experiences, and they facilitate inquiry by providing examples of principles the children have investigated previously. In fact, Bamberger and Tal (2007) found that the free choices available to students in informal science learning settings allow a variety of learning opportunities without the teacher having to direct the students.

Museums also provide the opportunities to investigate discrepant events (see Chapter 4). An example of such a discrepant event is the exhibit of two concave reflectors that look like satellite dishes facing each other at opposite ends of a hall some 100 feet long. A child whispers into one of the dishes and another child, listening inside the other dish, can hear the whisper clearly. This gives rise to the question of why the sound can be heard so clearly across such a large distance. Children are encouraged to explore a variety of reasons for the phenomenon, eventually discovering that the concave surfaces focus the sound, thereby concentrating it.

Visits to museums and other informal science attractions also help provide positive attitudes about science. Teachers are encouraged to let children find their own areas of interest in trips to these facilities and explore them as they see fit. This is the constructivist approach to museum visits. There is much to be learned in museums, and much to be experienced. Taking advantage of these resources is a *must* in quality elementary science education.

Yet, museums do not have to be housed in special buildings. The schoolyard, children's backyards, and local parks are living museums. Children can observe animals and plants, describe the habits of the animals, and infer the elements of the ecosystems they find. What do the animals eat? How do they get their food? How do they keep warm? Why are they here instead of someplace else? Daily or weekly visits to the same

See the Student Book Companion Web Site for a direct link to the Exploratorium Web site. You can obtain additional information about educational opportunities available at museums and download a summary publication and a case study workbook of museum education entitled *True Needs, True Partners* from the Institute of Library and Museum Services Web site. A direct link is provided on the Student Book Companion Web Site.

Experiencing dinosaurs in a museum (Elizabeth Crews)

FIGURE 9.13

Backyard science

FIGURE 9.14

sites enable children to observe and chart changes. The school building itself is filled with phenomena worthy of observation and study such as pipes, water pressure, heating and ventilation systems, and so on.

9.1   CONSTRUCTING YOUR IDEAS

Local Science Attractions

Make a list of science-centered attractions that are available in your local area. Include museums, aquariums, interactive scientific exhibits, and the like. Make it a point to visit each of these attractions, and form your own opinion as to the suitability of each for the science learning of students in the grade level you plan to teach.

REVISITING YOUR METAPHOR

In Chapter 1, you were asked to decide on a metaphor for elementary science teaching. Now is the time to examine your metaphor to see if it accurately portrays your beliefs about elementary science teaching.

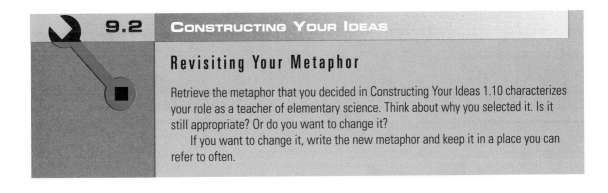

9.2   **CONSTRUCTING YOUR IDEAS**

Revisiting Your Metaphor

Retrieve the metaphor that you decided in Constructing Your Ideas 1.10 characterizes your role as a teacher of elementary science. Think about why you selected it. Is it still appropriate? Or do you want to change it?

If you want to change it, write the new metaphor and keep it in a place you can refer to often.

A few quotations seem apropos as we conclude Part I:

▶ "Discovery consists of seeing what everybody has seen and thinking what nobody has thought."
Albert Szent-Grorgi von Nagyrapott, from J. I. Good (Ed.), *The Scientist Speculates: An Anthology of Partly-Baked Ideas* (London: Heinemann, 1962).

▶ "Every great advance in science has issued from a new audacity of imagination."
John Dewey, *The Quest for Certainty* (Carbondale, IL: Southern Illinois University Press, 1929), Chap. 11.

▶ "The whole of science is nothing more than a refinement of everyday thinking."
Albert Einstein, *Out of My Later Years* (New York: Philosophical Library, 1950).

Conclusion

The effective elementary science teacher focuses on teaching children as much as teaching science, leading children to their development of process and inquiry skills and to a deep belief that they can do science and that the science they do is valuable. The effective elementary science teacher varies instructional methodologies and curriculum to meet the needs of all children in the class. The effective elementary science teacher encourages children to construct their own conceptualizations and provides ownership of knowledge and thinking to the children. The effective elementary science teacher includes nontraditional science learning settings and field trips to provide valuable and relevant hands-on learning experiences. The effective elementary science teacher *listens* to children.

CHAPTER 9

Additional Questions for Discussion

1. Describe ways of securing support from the school district and community for a constructivist, process-oriented inquiry science program.

2. Describe how a constructivist teacher might start a process-oriented inquiry science program in a class of children who have

not previously undertaken their own investigations.

Internet Activities

The Internet contains much material on weather, weather forecasting, and weather instruments. You can help children answer their questions through the use of this resource.

Use the Internet to find information on the care of various pets you might have in your classroom and on how to build and maintain classroom terrariums.

Use the Internet to find additional information on outdoor education and nontraditional science learning venues, such as museums and exhibits, to expand your repertoire of learning experiences that can take place in these settings.

PART 2 BEYOND THE SCIENCE CLASSROOM

CHAPTER···· 10
READING, WRITING, AND INTERDISCIPLINARY APPROACHES

The sole substitute for an experience which we have not ourselves lived through is art and literature.

Alexander Isayevich Solzhenitsyn, Nobel lecture, 1972

The means by which we live have outdistanced the ends for which we live. Our scientific power has outrun our spiritual power. We have guided missiles and misguided men.

Martin Luther King, Jr., *The Strength to Love* (Cleveland, OH: Fount Books, 1963), p. 73

Having constructed solid notions about the methodology that is most effective in elementary science education, you are now ready to consider additional topics that contribute to program excellence.

No subject can be studied in isolation. This includes science, an interdisciplinary study that is inextricably intertwined with technology and social issues, requires mathematics for the interpretation of data, and requires language for communication of findings and discoveries.

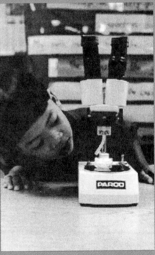

Mary P. Martin

Even the traditional boundaries within science itself—the life sciences, physical sciences, and earth and space sciences—erode in the face of their mutual interdependence.

One cannot study, for example, the nature of life (a life science topic) without also studying the chemical makeup of living things (a physical science topic) and the relationship of living things to the environment (an earth science topic). Nor can one discuss the weathering and erosion of landforms (an earth science topic) without also discussing the contributions of living organisms to the erosion process (a life science topic) and the laws of motion, inertia, and friction that cause the breakup of rocky material (all physical science topics).

In this chapter, you will extend your conceptualization of the process-oriented inquiry science teaching methodology by considering the role of reading, writing, and literature; models of interdisciplinary study; and the Science–Technology–Society approach. In each, you will examine advantages, disadvantages, and arguments both for and against as you deepen your views of the quality elementary science program.

READING, WRITING, AND LITERATURE

Science without language is like a ship without a compass. Reading is critical to discovering what others have learned, and writing is critical for children to communicate what they have discovered.

Literature enhances the study of science in a variety of ways. Many activities suggested in this book refer to one or more *literature connections*. Some are fiction and some are nonfiction. What is the best way to use these materials? That depends on the nature of the activity, the nature of the piece of literature, the objectives for the activity, and your personally constructed vision of quality elementary science education. The overriding principle is that literature is used to *enhance* children's inquiries and promote their own thinking and not used as a substitute for actual inquiry.

NSES Teaching Standard A. Inquiry-Based Program
NSES Program Standard B. Relevant, Inquiry-Based, and Connected with Other Subjects
NSES Professional Development Standard D. Coherent and Integrated Programs

10.1   CONSTRUCTING YOUR IDEAS

NSES Program Standard B. Relevant, Inquiry-Based, and Connected with Other Subjects

Two Bad Ants

Obtain a copy of *Two Bad Ants* by Chris Van Allsburg (Houghton Mifflin, 1988), and ask someone in your class to read it aloud.

Did you notice that several processes of science can be fostered with this book? Many opportunities exist for children to infer, as illustrated in the following questions:

- What are the crystals? What makes you think so? How could you be sure?

- What is the "boiling brown lake?" What makes you think so? How could you be sure?

Opportunities also exist for children to predict, as illustrated in the following questions:

- What do you suppose will happen to the ants after they fall asleep amidst the crystals? Why do you think so?

- What do you suppose will happen to the ants after they fall into the "boiling brown lake?" Why do you think so?

- Do you suppose the ants will go back to their homes? Do you think they *want* to go back home? Why?

The process of careful observation of the illustrations is a necessary precursor for making inferences and predictions.

Let us consider the question of what the crystals are. To gain additional information, children can examine regular sugar crystals with magnifying glasses or a low-power microscope, observing their shapes carefully and comparing the shape of the real sugar crystals with the shape of the crystals depicted in the book (see Figure 10.1). Children will notice that the real sugar is box-like in shape, whereas the crystals in the book's illustrations are shaped somewhat like a soccer ball. This seems to contradict the idea that the crystals in the story are sugar. Making a list of evidence, children find there are several reasons for believing that the crystals are sugar: (1) they are sweet, (2) the Queen likes them, and (3) they are in a bowl labeled ".... GAR." The preponderance of evidence in the book suggests that the crystals are sugar. The only thing wrong is the shape of the crystals. This may prompt one to wonder, "Do *all* crystals of sugar look the same?"

10.1   IN THE SCHOOLS

NSES Content Standard B. Physical Science: Properties and Changes of Properties in Matter

Growing Sugar Crystals

To investigate the question of what the crystals are in *Two Bad Ants,* children can grow their own sugar crystals in the form of rock candy. (See the crystal-making activities in Constructing Science in the Classroom 4.1.) Comparing the shape of the homemade crystals with the shape of the crystals of granulated sugar, the children are prepared to form the tentative generalization that sugar crystals always are box-like in shape.

Why, then, are they depicted as a different shape in the story? What would the pictures look like if the crystals were box-like in shape? Children can draw a number of box-shaped crystals and overlay their drawing on the illustration to see the effect. What does this tell us about how illustrations capture a reader's attention?

This book also is an ideal introduction to inquiries involving crystal solutions and crystal formation as suggested in the crystal-making activities (see In the Schools 4.4 and Constructing Science in the Classroom 4.1). Such questions as the following can be investigated:

- Are all crystals of a certain substance the same shape?

- How can you make large crystals?

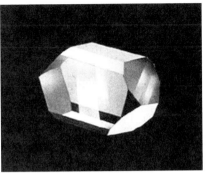

Sugar crystals seen through a 20-power microscope projected onto a TV screen using a small video camera

Single sugar crystal (Courtesy The Sugar Association, Inc., 1101 15th Street N.W., Suite 600, Washington, DC 20005)

Crystals of sugar

FIGURE 10.1

- What is the relationship between temperature and the amount of a solid that will dissolve in water?

- What is the relationship between the rate of evaporation of the solvent (the liquid into which the material is being dissolved) and the size of the crystals?

INTEGRATING CHILDREN'S LITERATURE AND SCIENCE

The activity with *Two Bad Ants* illustrates how children's literature can be used for continued process development and as an introduction to science inquiry activities. Children's literature can be integrated into science in a variety of ways. Following are ideas and suggestions from actual lessons and units. These are but a few examples; you are encouraged to devise your own.

Introducing Lessons

Literature can be used as an introduction to a lesson—to establish interest, to promote questioning, to present an area of inquiry, or to provide introductory information. *Two Bad Ants* was used to promote questioning that led to an inquiry into the characteristics of crystals and crystal formation. The poem *Kaleidoscope,* used in the advance organizer described in Chapter 5, provided a bridge from actual observations of kaleidoscopic images to poetic descriptions. *Jack and the Beanstalk,* as told by L. B.

NSES Teaching Standard A. Inquiry-Based Program
NSES Program Standard B. Relevant, Inquiry-Based, and Connected with Other Subjects
NSES Professional Development Standard D. Coherent and Integrated Program

Cauley (Putnam, 1983), is useful to introduce inquiries on plants, requirements for plant growth, and conditions that would promote the tallest and most rapid growth of bean plants.

The poem "What's in the Sack?" in *Where the Sidewalk Ends* by Shel Silverstein (Harper & Row, 1974) can be used as an introduction to the activity "What's in the Bag?" (Constructing Science in the Classroom 3.2). After reading this poem, the teacher asks children to guess what's in the man's sack, asks for their reasons for each guess, and then has the children do the activity.

Popcorn! by Elaine Landau (Charlesbridge, 2003) is a nonfiction book of facts and amazing anecdotes about one of the world's most popular and healthful snacks. This book can be used to introduce a number of process-oriented activities such as those shown below:

- Measure the time that elapses before the first kernel pops. Use different brands of popcorn to see whether there is a difference among brands.
  Processes: communicating, measuring, predicting, interpreting data

- Describe how popcorn looks, feels, smells, tastes, and sounds when you drop it before and after popping.
  Processes: observing, communicating

- Compare the volume of popcorn before and after popping.
  Processes: measuring, predicting, interpreting data

- Find whether unpopped and popped corn sinks or floats in water.
  Processes: observing, communicating, predicting

- Predict and measure how far kernels pop out of an uncovered pan.
  Processes: predicting, measuring

- Compare the weight of popcorn before and after popping.
  Processes: measuring, predicting, interpreting data

Miss Rumphius by Barbara Cooney (Viking Press, 1982) is the story of a lady who has followed her grandfather's wish to make the world a more beautiful place but, instead, becomes too ill to tend to the flowerbed she has planted. The following spring, she finds that the wind and the birds have done a magnificent job of reseeding the land and bringing color to the hills. This book can be used to introduce questions about seed **dispersion, propagation,** growth requirements, and elements of ecosystems, and is appropriate for fostering development of the affective domain.

Agatha's Feather Bed: Not Just Another Wild Goose Story by Carmen Agra Deedy (Peachtree, 1994) can be used as a springboard for inquiries into natural resources and their uses. The story focuses on Agatha who has purchased a feather bed, and on the plight of the naked geese whose feathers were used to stuff the bed. Agatha solves the dilemma by making coats for the geese out of her hair. This delightful story is filled with puns, word play, and illustrations of various natural materials used to make common products.

The Last Basselope: One Ferocious Story by Berkley Breathed (Little, Brown, 1992) can be used to introduce the concept of endangered and extinct species. The story is about an expedition to find the last remaining Basselope, a fictitious animal. Members of the party use the processes of observation, inference, and prediction as their search leads them along a trail made by the creature.

Adopted by an Owl: The True Story of Jackson, the Owl by Gijsbert and Robbyn Smith Van Frankenduyzen (Sleeping Bear Press, 2001) is a true story about a great horned owl named Jackson who chose his adopted human family over his natural instincts to live in the wild and is a good introduction to wildlife and ecosystems.

Brother Eagle, Sister Sky: A Message from Chief Seattle by Susan Jeffers (NAL/Dutton, 1993) tells the story of an Indian chief who is required by white men to sell his land. The chief wonders how one can sell air and wind, but he requests that the purchasers "preserve the land and air and the rivers for your children's children and love it as we have loved it." This book can be used as an introduction to a study of how environmental changes can cause animal species to become extinct. The teacher provides bird and insect nests so children can discover the materials that go into making the nests. The teacher asks, "Why do animals make their nests the way they do?" "Where do the materials come from?" "What would happen if these resources were destroyed?" "What kinds of things do people do to hinder animals from building their nests?" "What kinds of things can people do to help keep animals from becoming extinct?"

A River Ran Wild by Lynne Cherry (Harcourt, 1992) describes a community of Native Americans who are helping to restore a river ecosystem. This book can be used as the spark for a unit on river ecology and ecosystems.

The Sun, the Wind, and the Rain by Lisa W. Peters (Henry Holt, 1988) is the story of a girl who builds a sand mountain on a beach and compares it to a mountain she sees in the distance. The story describes the rapid reshaping of the sand mountain by rain and wind, the same forces that took eons of time to reshape the real mountain. The story can be used to set the stage for children's inquiries into weathering of the earth's surface structures by water and wind. A complete lesson using this story as the introduction is shown in Constructing Science in the Classroom 10.1.

NSES Content
Standard D. Earth and
Space Science: Changes
in Earth and Sky

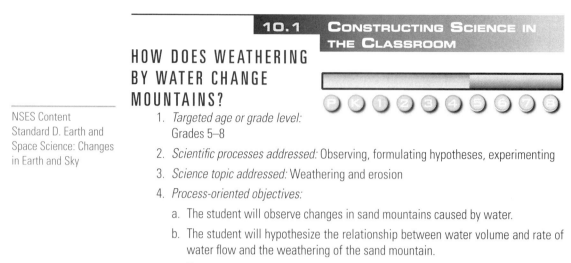

10.1   CONSTRUCTING SCIENCE IN THE CLASSROOM

HOW DOES WEATHERING BY WATER CHANGE MOUNTAINS?

1. *Targeted age or grade level:* Grades 5–8

2. *Scientific processes addressed:* Observing, formulating hypotheses, experimenting

3. *Science topic addressed:* Weathering and erosion

4. *Process-oriented objectives:*

   a. The student will observe changes in sand mountains caused by water.

   b. The student will hypothesize the relationship between water volume and rate of water flow and the weathering of the sand mountain.

   c. The student will experiment to discover the relationship between water volume and rate of water flow and the rate of weathering of the sand mountain.

5. *What I want children to discover:* The mountains on the earth's surface are constantly being changed by water.

6. *Description of introductory activity and initial discussion:* Read the story *The Sun, the Wind, and the Rain* by Lisa Westberg Peters. Ask questions such as, "Why does the sand mountain wear down?" "Why does the real mountain wear down?" "Do you suppose the same forces cause both?"

7. *Materials needed: The Sun, the Wind, and the Rain* by Lisa Westberg Peters; chart paper; markers; sand; large, solid, plastic storage bins; sticks; pebbles; buckets; shovels; watering cans (one with fine holes and one with large holes); water

8. *Description of activities:* Working in pairs or small groups, children build a sand mountain in their plastic storage bins, complete with sticks to represent trees and pebbles to represent animals, just like Elizabeth did in the story. Next, children decide who will be the rain pourer and who will be the recorder. The rain pourer slowly pours two cups of water from the fine-holed watering can onto one side of the mountain to represent gentle rain. The recorder records the results. Children compare their results with what they see in the book. Next, the rain pourer pours two cups of water from the large-holed watering can onto the other side of the mountain, representing a heavy rainfall. Again, the recorder records the results, and children compare their results with what they see in the book. Each group records its data on a central chart, and the whole class discusses the patterns seen between force of the water poured and the amount of weathering that each side of the mountain received. The next step is to vary the *amount* of water.

9. *Typical discussion questions:*

   • What happens to the sand mountain when you sprinkle water on it lightly? What happens when you pour water on it more heavily? Why is there a difference?

Continued on next page

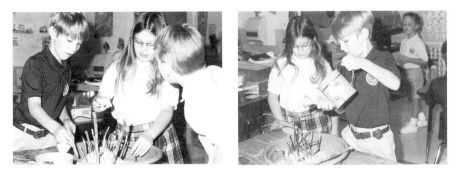

Investigating forces that cause erosion

FIGURE 10.2

- Do you suppose the same thing happens to the rocks that make up mountains? Why?
- Does the volume of water have anything to do with how fast the sand mountain wears away? How about the force of the water?

10. *How children will be encouraged to investigate on their own in the classroom:* Children will be asked to vary the volume of water, the force of the water, the structure of the sand mountain, and anything else they can think of that might influence how fast the sand mountain weathers.

11. *Expected conclusions:* Children will probably conclude that the rate of weathering of the sand mountain depends on the force of the water and the volume of water poured on it. They may or may not see the relationship between the sand mountain and real mountains, because the weathering of real mountains proceeds too slowly to be discernable to children.

12. *Assessment:* Assess validity of children's answers to the above questions based on the evidence they see from the experiment.

13. *Applications to real-life situations:* Weathering occurs all around us: garden soils, lawns, beaches, overhanging rock structures, and so on. Heavy rainstorms and hurricanes can cause mudslides and extreme damage. Encourage children to bring in newspaper and magazine articles and pictures dealing with hurricanes, tornadoes, severe thunderstorms, mudslides, and other severe weather occurrences that cause weathering.

Additional Literature Connections:

McCrephy's Field by Christopher and Lynne Myers (Houghton Mifflin, 1991). Joe McCrephy abandons his Ohio farm to begin a new venture with his brother in Wyoming. The story details the changes that occur in the farm and the land over the next 50 years.

Hurricane Force: Tracking America's Killer Storms by Joseph B. Treaster (Kingfisher, 2007) is a photoessay that describes hurricane disasters in the United States.

Sedimentary Rocks by Melissa Stewart (Heinemann, 2002) describes how sedimentary rocks are created from the erosion of landforms.

Analyzing Conclusions

Children's literature can be used to compare the conclusions children have formed as a result of their investigations with the science presented in the book. Science in literature often is exaggerated and inaccurate (see the investigation into crystal shapes in In The Schools 10.1). Comparing their conclusions with similar phenomena described in literature stimulates children to ask who is right as they compare their conclusions with those presented in the book. Many children accept what is written as fact, and through this type of comparison, they begin to question the accuracy of the written word. On the other hand, seeing the same conclusions they derived being discussed in a book helps empower children to gain new ownership of their knowledge and thought processes.

10.2   IN THE SCHOOLS

NSES Content Standard B. Physical
Science: Light Energy
NSES Program Standard B. Relevant,
Inquiry-Based, and Connected with
Other Subjects

Investigating Mixing Colors

In a kindergarten class, the teacher provides tubes of red, yellow, and blue cake icing. Children squeeze a little of each color on a paper plate and mix the colors with toothpicks. They observe the resulting colors and record them on a chart. The teacher then reads *Mouse Paint* by Ellen Stoll Walsh (Harcourt Brace, 1989), a story about mice who walk into red, yellow, and blue paint. As they walk from color to color, they mix the paints, forming new colors. This story, read after children perform their own investigations, may help them validate their conclusions or may stimulate them to pursue further investigations if their conclusions are not congruent with those presented in the story.

My Five Senses by Aliki (Demco Media, 1985) can be used after children have investigated the sense of touch using such activities as "What's in the Sock?" (see Constructing Science in the Classroom 3.1).

From Seed to Plant by Gail Gibbons (Holiday, 1991) explains how seeds grow into plants and illustrates the parts of both seeds and plants. It can be used after children explore the nature of seeds to verify their findings (see Constructing Science in the Classroom 3.3). Children first observe the outside of lima bean seeds and discuss how they look and feel. Then they guess what they will find on the inside of the seeds and compare their guesses with precut seeds. After children open the seeds, they compare their observations with those depicted in the book. Children then plant their seeds and compare the growth with the descriptions and illustrations in the book to provide verification of their conclusions. They may choose to plant whole seeds or halves. They may choose to remove parts of the seed to investigate whether the part will grow by itself, without the rest of the seed.

Providing Factual Information

Children's literature may be used to provide factual information about many topics.

Digging Up Dinosaurs by Aliki (Crowell, 1988) explains how scientists uncover, preserve, and study fossilized dinosaur bones. It can be used to help children understand the reconstruction of dinosaur skeletons seen in museums.

10.3   IN THE SCHOOLS

NSES Content Standard C. Life Science: Life Cycles of Organisms
NSES Program Standard B. Relevant, Inquiry-Based, and Connected with Other Subjects

Investigating the Metamorphosis of Caterpillars

The Very Hungry Caterpillar by Eric Carle (Philomel, 1987) describes a caterpillar's preparation for metamorphosis into a beautiful butterfly. Children collect caterpillars and put them in jars or a terrarium to see for themselves. The book will help children decide what to put in the jars for caterpillar food and will help them make predictions as to what will happen with their own caterpillars. Children record their predictions, make daily observations, and record what happens. The book provides factual material against which children can compare their discoveries. See this chapter's *Teacher Voice* for a real-world example using monarch butterfly observation and celebration in the classroom.

The Ocean Alphabet Book by Jerry Pallotta (Charlesbridge Publishers, 1986) contains factual information about many kinds of animals and plants in the ocean. *The Bird Alphabet Book,* also by Pallotta (Charlesbridge Publishers, 1989), contains a wealth of factual information about birds. For example, "Y is for Yellow-Bellied Sapsucker. The Yellow-Bellied Sapsucker is a woodpecker that got its name because it drinks sap out of its favorite trees. It has a tongue with a brush-like tip." Pallotta has written

44 well-researched alphabet books that deal with topics in science and mathematics.

Beaks! by Robin Brickman (Charlesbridge, 2002) is a nonfiction book about the variety of bird beaks and their uses.

Oceans: The Vast, Mysterious Deep by David L. Harrison (Boyds Mills, 2003) is a nonfiction book that explains how oceans were formed, how water is recycled, and what the ocean floor looks like.

The Very Busy Spider by Eric Carle (Philomel, 1985) can introduce very young children to the characteristics of spiders and help children verify characteristics they have observed. *The Lady and the Spider* by Faith Mc-Nulty (Harper & Row, 1986), a story of a spider that has made its home in a head of lettuce, provides brief general descriptions of the spider; the main idea of the story is that *all* life is valuable. *A First Look at Spiders* by Millicent E. Selsam (Walker, 1983) classifies spiders according to several characteristics, including eyes, leg positions, webs, jaws, size, and habitat. The book is an excellent guide for field studies of spiders. Note that wildlife experts in the local area often are willing to provide assistance to teachers and children in identifying wildlife and discussing their habitats.

Safety note: All spiders can bite, and people exhibit differing sensitivities to spider bites. Certain species, such as the black widow spider and the brown recluse spider are very poisonous. Therefore, caution children not to touch or handle spiders.

The teacher reads *Stellaluna* by Jannell Cannon (Harcourt Brace, 1993) after children have investigated the differences between birds and mammals and have compared their findings. The story is about a mother fruit bat (a mammal) who is attacked by an owl and drops her baby. The baby, Stellaluna, has to live with a family of birds to survive. The story looks at the differences and similarities between the bat, a specific mammal, and birds.

The Forces Be with You! by Tom Johnston (Gareth Stevens, 1988) contains detailed information about the forces of inertia, friction, and gravity presented as cartoon captions of children demonstrating and talking about these principles.

Providing Practical Examples

Literature can provide practical examples of investigations that children are pursuing. For instance, *Thunder Cake* by Patricia Polacco (Philomel, 1990) is a story about a little girl who fears the sound of thunder. Her grandmother shows her how to estimate the distance of a storm by counting the seconds between the lightning flash and the thunder crash and how to calm her fears by making a "thunder cake." Factual material about thunderstorms is blended with the process of measurement. The recipe for "thunder cake" is presented in the book. The story can be used in conjunction with inquiries into the difference between the speed of light and the speed of sound. (A complete lesson using this story is shown in Constructing Science in the Classroom 10.2.)

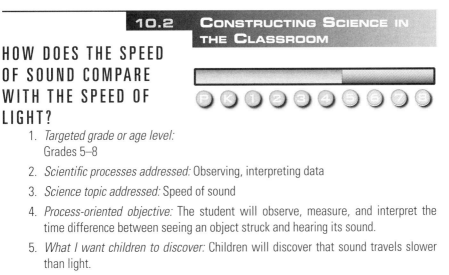

10.2   CONSTRUCTING SCIENCE IN THE CLASSROOM

HOW DOES THE SPEED OF SOUND COMPARE WITH THE SPEED OF LIGHT?

NSES Content Standard B. Physical Science: Sound Energy and Light Energy

1. *Targeted grade or age level:* Grades 5–8

2. *Scientific processes addressed:* Observing, interpreting data

3. *Science topic addressed:* Speed of sound

4. *Process-oriented objective:* The student will observe, measure, and interpret the time difference between seeing an object struck and hearing its sound.

5. *What I want children to discover:* Children will discover that sound travels slower than light.

6. *Description of introductory activity and initial discussion:* Ask children if they have observed that there often is a time delay between seeing lightning and hearing the thunderclap in a thunderstorm. Engage children in a discussion of what this tells us about how far away the lightning is and how fast sound travels compared with light.

7. *Materials needed:* Hollow pail such as a garbage pail or garbage can cover; wooden mallet or bat; *Thunder Cake* by Patricia Polacco (Philomel, 1990)

8. *Description of activities:* Take children outdoors to the playground or some other fairly large area. Divide the class into two groups, and place one group at each end of the field. One child hits the garbage pail with the mallet or the bat (or makes some other loud sound that children at the other end of the field can both see and hear). Children observe that sound travels slower than light. Read the story *Thunder Cake* by Patricia Polacco (Philomel, 1990) to show how this activity enables a person to calculate how far away thunderstorms are.

9. *Typical discussion questions:*
   - Does the loudness of the sound change its speed?
   - The speed of sound is approximately 1,088 feet per second (740 miles per hour) at normal temperatures. Why is the speed of sound specified "at normal temperatures?" What do you suppose happens to the speed of sound if the air is warmer? Cooler? What happens to the speed of sound if the air pressure is higher? Lower? How would we find out?
   - How can you use the speed of sound to calculate distances?

Continued on next page

The Weather Channel provides much information on severe weather phenomena and safety precautions. The Student Book Companion Web Site has direct links to educational materials and weather explanations from The Weather Channel.

10. *How children will be encouraged to investigate on their own in the classroom:* Children will be encouraged to try the same activity when the air is warmer and cooler and when the barometric pressure is higher and lower. They can collect newspaper and magazine articles and pictures on thunderstorms.

11. *Expected conclusions:* Children should conclude that sound travels slower than light.

12. *Assessment:* Check the measured time of the sound and the calculated difference between when children see the mallet hit the pail and when they hear the sound. Check the validity of interpretation based on experimental data.

13. *Applications to real-life situations:* The distance of a thunderstorm can be calculated from the time difference between seeing the lightning and hearing the thunder—the smaller the difference, the closer the storm. (**Teacher Note:** A thunderstorm is 1 mile away for every 5 seconds of delay between seeing the lightning and hearing the thunder. Thus, if there is a 15-second delay between lightning and thunder, the storm is 3 miles away.)

Safety note: Be sure to review the safety procedures to be taken in severe thunderstorms.

In another example, literature can help children understand chemical reactions.

10.4   IN THE SCHOOLS

NSES Content Standard B. Physical Science: Properties and Changes of Properties in Matter
NSES Program Standard B. Relevant, Inquiry-Based, and Connected with Other Subjects

Investigating the Reaction of Materials with Vinegar

In a fourth-grade class, groups of children were provided with pieces of limestone, marble, sandstone, and shale; some baking soda, baking powder, sugar, and salt; a plastic plate; and some vinegar. They were asked to predict which of the materials would fizz when vinegar was dropped on them and then try each material one at a time and record their results. (The limestone, marble, baking soda, and baking powder all fizz in the presence of vinegar.) To show practical examples of this phenomenon, the teacher read *The Magic School Bus Gets Baked in a Cake: A Book About Kitchen Chemistry* by Joanna Cole (Scholastic, 1995). This book is based on an episode from the animated TV series that portrays children exploring the chemistry involved in baking, especially the production of gas from baking soda mixed with vinegar.

Continued on next page

Additional Literature Connections

States of Matter (Delta Science Reader, 2003) is a nonfiction book about solids, liquids, gases, physical changes, and chemical changes.

Acids and Bases by Rebecca L. Johnson (National Geographic Society, 2004) is a nonfiction book about acids and bases, where they are found, what they are, and how they are used.

Developing Process Skills

Children's literature can be an integral component of a science lesson designed to help children develop process skills.

10.5   IN THE SCHOOLS

NSES Content Standard D. Earth and Space Science: Objects in the Sky
NSES Program Standard B. Relevant, Inquiry-Based, and Connected with Other Subjects

Daytime Sky Watching

In a lesson on observing, children go outside, observe the sky, and write down what they see in as much detail as possible. While they are still outside, the teacher reads *The Sky* by Arlane Dewey (Green Tiger Press, 1993), pausing after each page to ask the children to compare what they observed with what was described on that page. The lesson culminates in a creative writing activity, such as haiku or other poetry. The discussion can be carried into a multicultural dimension by discussing the symbolism, significance, and explanations that different cultures have for what can be seen—and not seen—in the sky.

Safety note: Never allow children to look directly at the sun. The lens in the human eye acts as a magnifying glass, concentrating the sun's rays on the retina and burning it, much as a magnifying glass can be focused to burn a leaf. However, the retina does not contain nerves that are sensitive to pain, so people cannot feel the burn. Because children want to look at the sun, it is necessary to provide them with an alternative to looking at it directly. A pinhole camera apparatus will work *providing that people do not look at the sun through the pinhole but, instead, focus the sun through the pinhole onto a piece of paper.* Perhaps the best way is to focus the sun through binoculars onto a piece of paper. Hold the binoculars such that the wide (objective) lens is facing the sun and the eyepiece is aimed toward a piece of white paper. DO NOT LOOK AT THE SUN THROUGH THE EYEPIECE! Move it around until you get the sun's image focused onto the paper. The binoculars will not become hot because they reflect all the sun's energy through mirrors or prisms from the objective lens to the eyepiece (see Figure 10.3).

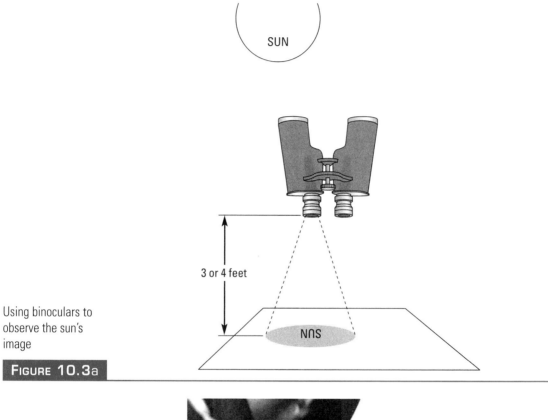

3 or 4 feet

SUN

Using binoculars to observe the sun's image

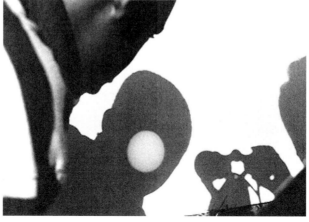

Using binoculars to project the image of the sun onto a shadow on a white poster board

Mysteries provide an excellent source of practice in the processes of observing, predicting, classifying, inferring, communicating, measuring, and formulating hypotheses. The book *Encyclopedia Brown Takes the Cake!* by Donald J. Sobol and Glenn Andrews (Scholastic, 1984) contains several short mysteries that readers must solve throughout the story by using scientific processes as they read.

Another mystery, *The Million Dollar Potato* by Louis Phillips (Simon & Schuster, 1991), tells the story of a little boy who inherits a million dollars on the condition that he spend it in 24 hours. Children participate in solving the mystery as they read the book. *The Westing Game* by Ellen Raskin (Dutton, 1978) is a murder mystery that can be solved before the end of the book. In *Science Mini Mysteries* by Sandra Markle (Atheneum, 1988), the author uses the unique format of a short-story mystery that the reader must solve using the scientific processes. Procedures and materials necessary for the experiments are listed.

The Mystery of the Stranger in the Barn by True Kelley (Dodd, Mead, 1986) is a good story to demonstrate the difference between evidence and inference. Items seem to be disappearing from a barn, but a hat was left behind. Is there a mysterious stranger hiding in the barn?

Providing Vicarious Experiences

Literature can be used to provide experiences the children would not otherwise be able to have when they are needed for a lesson. For example, several pieces of children's literature can be used to provide mental experiences for kindergarten children exploring rain. In *Bringing the Rain to Kapiti Plain* by Verna Aardema (Dial, 1981), children can see that clouds are the source of rain. In the rhythmic book *Listen to the Rain* by Bill Martin, Jr. and John Archenbault (Henry Holt, 1988), children can "hear" different sounds that rain makes through the poet's use of alliteration.

Providing Interdisciplinary Bridges

Children's literature can lead children from activities in science into activities associated with other areas. For example, *Out and About* by Shirley Hughes (Lothrop, Lee & Shepard, 1988) is a compilation of poetry about various weather occurrences. The poems can be read after children's exploration of such phenomena as rainbows and wind and inspire children to compose their own poetry or other creative writing or artistic expressions.

Shaping Students' Perceptions About Science

Children's literature can change students' perceptions about science and scientists. Farland (2006) showed that students in elementary grades who read nonfiction textual material on the work of individual scientists demonstrated a broad understanding of science and the activities scientists do.

Selecting Children's Literature

There is a plethora of children's literature available from which you can select both fiction and nonfiction. We have listed only a few of the many fine pieces. Some reliable sources of fiction and nonfiction children's literature include the following:

- *Book Links* is a magazine dedicated to connecting books, libraries, and classrooms. Published by the American Library Association, this magazine features descriptions of quality children's books.

- The Children's Book Council, an organization dedicated to encouraging literacy and the use and enjoyment of children's books, lists and reviews new pieces of children's literature each week on their Web site.

- The National Science Teachers Association publishes a list of outstanding children's science trade books (nonfiction books dealing with scientific information) each year. These books are intended for kindergarten thorough eighth grade. The list is compiled in conjunction with the Children's Book Council and includes all fields of science. Each book is referenced to the appropriate *National Science Education Standards.* Books in Spanish also are listed.

- *Science and Children* and *Science Scope,* both of which are publications of the National Science Teachers Association, contain lists of newly published fiction and nonfiction children's books dealing with science. The books listed in *Science and Children* are intended for elementary grades, and the books listed in *Science Scope* are intended for middle grades.

- Each issue of *Childhood Education,* the journal of the Association for Childhood Education International (ACEI), includes listings of children's books suitable for elementary grades.

- The ACEI publishes *Bibliography of Books for Children,* which is revised every three years.

- Many public libraries have extensive collections of children's literature—both fiction and nonfiction.

In deciding what to use in your classes, you may wish to apply the criteria listed in Figure 10.4. Be careful that the books have potential for scientific inquiry and that they do not center only on factual material.

Direct links to *Book Links,* the Children's Book Council homepage, the NSTA children's literature sites, and other sources of children's literature are provided on the Student Book Companion Web Site.

CRITERIA FOR SELECTING CHILDREN'S LITERATURE FOR USE IN SCIENCE CLASSES

1. Does the book foster development of processes?
2. Does the book provide an opportunity for children to ask and answer their own questions?
3. Does the book encourage children to think for themselves?
4. Is the science topic addressed in ways that are appropriate to the lesson?
5. Is the content based on sound scientific principles? Is it accurate?
6. Does the book distinguish between fact and fiction?
7. Are the illustrations clear and accurate? Do they accomplish the purpose you have in mind?
8. Is the book written at the level of your students?
9. Is there a multicultural component? Is it free from stereotyping?
10. Is the book free from gender bias?
11. Does the book show the close association between science and other disciplines?
12. Does the book present a positive attitude toward science and technology?

FIGURE 10.4

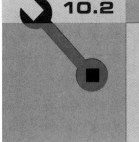

10.2 **CONSTRUCTING YOUR IDEAS** NSES Program Standard B. Relevant, Inquiry-Based, and Connected with Other Subjects

Using Literature in Elementary Science

Now it's your turn. Briefly describe one way literature can be incorporated into elementary science education. Then, to illustrate, sketch out one process-oriented inquiry science activity, the specific literature you would use to accompany it, and how you would use it.

SCIENCE TEXTBOOKS

Many school districts provide a basic textbook series for the study of science. The temptation is to let the text determine the science program. There are several reasons for this. Elementary teachers may feel unprepared to teach science and want the guidance provided by the textbook. Teachers may prefer to have a structured program of the sort provided by textbooks. Teachers may look to texts for instructional resources, avenues of questioning and discussion, and directions for demonstrations and children's activities (Armbruster, 1993). In fact, the *Washington Post* reported that more than 90 percent of science teachers use textbooks and

NSES Teaching Standard A. Inquiry-Based Program
NSES Teaching Standard F. Participating in Program Planning
NSES Program Standard B. Relevant, Inquiry-Based, and Connected with Other Subjects
NSES Program Standard E. Equal Opportunities for All Students

that 59 percent of science teachers say that textbooks have a major influence on their teaching (Strauss, 2003).

In the extreme, some teachers may limit their science program to the textbook. Their typical lesson begins with the children reading out of the text. The teacher then may do a demonstration, show a video, or hold a question-and-answer discussion in an effort to get children involved and to increase meaningfulness. Occasionally the children may participate in an activity. The text then is used to close the lesson, and the questions at the end of the section serve as classwork or homework. It should be obvious that such use of the text replaces inquiry with knowledge acquisition and verification activities—children read about science instead of doing science. They do not have the opportunity to make and test predictions and to verify their conclusions, because the investigations are written in the text. They do not have the opportunity to develop facility in the processes of science. The text provides all the needed information, and children are discouraged from "actively making meaningful connections to their existing knowledge" (Ulerick, 1989). This is the antithesis of constructivism.

Textbooks, by their very nature, ignore the individual needs of individual children and assume that all children have the same prior knowledge. Given this characterization of science textbooks, constructivists have reacted with an inclination to throw away the texts. However, textbooks have several advantages:

1. Textbooks are excellent sources of information for children.

2. Teacher's guides are excellent resources for teachers.

3. A textbook series provides scope and sequence to ensure continuity from grade to grade and consistency within grade levels.

4. Topics included in textbooks generally are appropriate for the age level/grade of the children.

5. Topics in textbooks are developed thoroughly, with prerequisite information introduced in proper sequence.

Constructivist Uses of Elementary Science Textbooks

Much as we constructivists like to espouse getting rid of textbooks in elementary science, it is incumbent on us to see how we can use them to good advantage. The premise of constructivist learning is that children discover new concepts for themselves and internalize these concepts by constructing valid connections to prior information. To foster this, it may be desirable to have several copies of several different texts available in the classroom to aid children in their investigations.

Textbooks can serve well in the validation role. The elementary science textbook typically provides discussions and explanations of scientific concepts, followed by activities children can do to verify the textual material. For a constructivist approach, the teacher can use the text in reverse—having the children do the activities first and then using the text for validation (Barnam, 1992). Fello, Paquette, and Jalongo (2006/2007) suggest having children first draw their representations of a scientific concept, such as layers in a rain forest, and describe their drawings before reading about the concept in a textbook. For example, a recent edition of a third-grade textbook contains a section on friction. Friction is defined, several examples are cited, and ways of reducing friction are listed. The constructivist teacher wishing to use this text might first ask children to make and describe drawings that show their current understanding of friction and then engage them in an exploratory activity concerning friction. Such an activity is shown in Constructing Science in the Classroom 10.3. After children have done the activity, they can read in the text to validate what they have discovered. Furthermore, the text may spark additional questions children may wish to investigate on their own.

Textbooks also may be used for information that is required in the curriculum but which does not lend itself well to inquiry. If content coverage is an issue in your school, you might consider dividing the topics to be studied into two categories—those that can be mastered through inquiry, and those that do not lend themselves to hands-on inquiry methods (see Chapter 13). The textbook is an excellent resource for studying those topics that cannot be explored directly by children. Examples might include learning the names of the planets, learning the names of cloud types, learning how nuclear reactors work, and studying plate tectonics.

Textbooks also provide assistance in the area of career explorations. Many texts describe the nature of various careers in science and what scientists do in those careers. Textbooks also frequently include biographies of famous scientists.

10.3 **CONSTRUCTING SCIENCE IN THE CLASSROOM**

AN INVESTIGATION INTO FRICTION

1. *Targeted age or grade level:* Grades 3–5

2. *Scientific processes addressed:* Observing, measuring, predicting, inferring

3. *Science topic addressed:* Friction

4. *Process-oriented objectives:*

NSES Content Standard B. Physical Science: Motions and Forces

Continued on next page

a. The student will observe the effect of various surfaces on the force necessary to move a solid object.

b. The student will predict the relative force required to move a solid object across different surfaces.

c. The student will measure and compare the forces required to move a solid object across various surfaces.

d. The student will infer reasons for the differing forces required to move a solid object across different surfaces.

5. *What I want children to discover:* Children will discover the concept of friction and the effects of various surfaces on friction.

6. *Description of introductory activity and initial discussion:* Put a book on a smooth surface, such as a tile floor or a smooth tabletop, and give it a sharp push. Observe how far it goes. Then, put the book on a carpet, and do the same thing, again observing how far it goes. Ask questions such as "Why does the book go farther on the smooth surface?" "Does the nature of the surface have anything to do with how far the book goes?" "How could we find out?"

7. *Materials needed:* Book, pieces of wood with hooks in one end, waxed paper, coarse sandpaper, fine sandpaper, piece of carpet, piece of plywood, wooden dowels or round pencils, spring balance or equivalent*

8. *Description of activities:* Provide the materials to each group, and ask them to predict the effect that each surface will have on the amount of force necessary to move the block of wood across it. Children hook the spring balance into the hook in the piece of wood and, holding the spring balance parallel to the surface, drag the block of wood along each of the various surfaces available. They feel the amount of force it takes to move the block of wood and record the reading from the scale. (If the block of wood is light, children may weigh it down with a book; just be sure the weight is the same for all trials.)

9. *Typical discussion questions:*

- Which material takes the most force to move the block? The least force?
- Why does it take different amounts of force to move the block across different kinds of materials?
- How can you reduce the force needed to move the block?
- What other materials would you like to try?

10. *How children will be encouraged to investigate on their own in the classroom:* Children can reproduce the same activity using different surfaces. They can use oil, wax, and soap. They can vary the bottom surface of the block. They can use wooden dowels or rollers to compare rolling friction with sliding friction. Children may observe that it takes more force to get the block started than it takes to keep the block going once it is in motion. (This is because of inertia—see Newton's first law of motion.)

Continued on next page

11. *Expected conclusions:* I expect children will conclude that the smoother the surface, the less force is required to keep the block moving. They will form conceptual understanding of friction, but they may not use the proper terminology.

12. *Assessment:* Check comparisons between predicted and actual forces required with different surfaces; check that children's inferences are valid relative to the experimental data they collected.

13. *Applications to real-life situations:* Friction is present whenever two surfaces are in contact with each other. It is desirable to reduce friction to reduce the force that it takes to move something. Wheels, rollers, oiled surfaces, polished surfaces, and so on are desirable energy-saving aids.

*A rubber band spring scale can substitute for the spring balance. See the following illustration.

RUBBER BAND SCALE

Tape a rubber band to the zero end of a ruler. Attach an opened paper clip to the other end of the rubber band to act as a hook. Use the hook to pull objects. Observe how far the rubber band is stretched. The amount of stretch is an indication of the force needed to move the object.

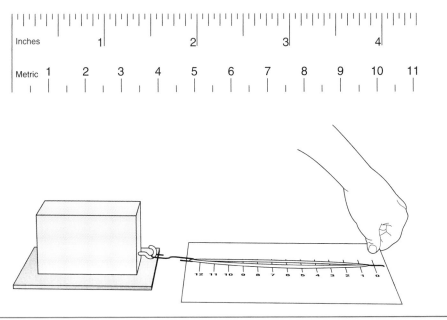

Rubber band scale (©Idea Factory, Inc, 1988. Reprinted with permission)

Commercially Available Hands-On Materials

In response to the desire of teachers to implement hands-on science programs, many publishers are providing materials designed to foster hands-on science. Assuming that these materials are selected with the input of the teachers who will use them, that teachers understand them, and that teachers are given both time and resources to implement them, they are excellent classroom materials. Several hands-on investigative elementary science programs are described in Figure 10.5.

SELECTED ELEMENTARY SCIENCE MATERIALS THAT USE CONSTRUCTIVIST APPROACHES

AIMS (Activities for Integrating Mathematics and Science) uses a hands-on, inquiry-oriented approach that integrates mathematics, science, and other disciplines. AIMS materials include 20 to 30 hands-on, inquiry-based activities for each of the three major science disciplines in each grade level, K–9. AIMS also has available complete laboratory kits, manipulatives, equipment, data organizers and charts, a newsletter, and a magazine showing new activities and evaluation results. The activities are inquiry in orientation and constructivist in nature. Some Spanish language materials are available. The AIMS activities are probably the best inquiry-oriented constructivist activities that have been developed for science education in recent years.

GEMS (Great Explorations in Math and Science) is a major resource for inquiry-oriented elementary science programs. This program was developed by the Lawrence Hall of Science at the University of California–Berkeley. GEMS has published more than 70 teacher's guides and handbooks on hands-on science inquiry topics ranging from astronomy to bubbles and elephants and their young. Most units focus on integration of math and science and are aligned with national and state standards. Complete materials kits are available for many of the activities. A companion program entitled *PEACHES* provides hands-on, inquiry-oriented science units suitable for preschool through first grade. Both programs provide teacher workshops, newsletters, and continuous updates.

FOSS (Full Option Science System), developed at the Lawrence Hall of Science under a grant from the National Science Foundation, is a science program for grades K–8 that is process oriented and guided inquiry in nature. Activities are designed to match children's cognitive abilities at their different levels of development. Teacher guides, equipment kits, CD ROMs, and videos are available in kit form from Delta Education. Many materials are available in Spanish

ESS (Elementary Science Study) is among the original discovery approaches to elementary science education. Its developers came from both the scientific and

FIGURE 10.5

Continued on next page

the teaching fields. Units detailed in teacher's guides are designed to help children develop the fundamental skills necessary for organized scientific thought. More than 40 units deal with common scientific phenomena, from ant farms to "whistles and strings." Each unit suggests many open-ended, hands-on, inquiry-oriented activities that children can investigate as they form and validate personal conceptualizations of the phenomena. Equipment kits and teacher guides are available from Delta Education.

Insights is a hands-on, inquiry-based elementary science curriculum designed to meet the needs of all children in grades K–6. Specifically addressing urban children, the program integrates science with language arts and mathematics in a Science–Technology–Society setting. Seventeen 6- to 8-week modules are available, each including a comprehensive teacher's guide and a set of materials. The program was developed by the Education Development Center in Newton, Massachusetts, and is available from Education Development Center.

 See the Student Book Companion Web Site for direct links to the Web sites for these materials.

FIGURE 10.5

Review of Science Curriculum Materials

It is critically important that teachers become involved in the selection of materials they will use in their classrooms. Many teachers serve on textbook adoption committees. The chart in Figure 10.6 is offered as a generic aid to the textbook review process. Of course, each school district develops its own textbook review form to meet its unique needs; the form in Figure 10.6 suggests important elements that are supportive of a constructivist approach to science. It is particularly important that the curriculum materials selected for implementation be aligned with the *National Science Education Standards.*

There are pros and cons to using textbooks in elementary science; textbooks can serve many different functions. As always, you have to make up your own mind.

SCIENCE TEXTBOOK REVIEW FORM

TITLE _____

AUTHOR(S) _____

PUBLISHER _____

COPYRIGHT DATE _____ LEVEL(S) _____

Rate each of the following from 1 (lowest) to 10 (highest)

_____ Aligned with *National Science Education Standards*
_____ Process-oriented
_____ Fosters inquiry
_____ Suggests inquiry activities

_____ Inductive in presentation
_____ Encourages children to explore on their own
_____ Suggests extended activities
_____ Suggests remedial activities
_____ Contains appropriate content
_____ Content accurate
_____ Illustrations clear and accurate
_____ Reading level appropriate
_____ Treats men and women in science equally
_____ Contains multicultural component without stereotyping
_____ Reflects interdisciplinary approaches
_____ Interdisciplinary problems are relevant and issue oriented
_____ Suggests literature connections
_____ Special treatment for children with special needs
_____ Contains information on scientific careers
_____ Includes technology
_____ Attractive
_____ Material well organized
_____ Ancillary materials available
_____ Physical characteristics of student texts
_____ Cost value
_____ Teacher's Edition contains activities and resources
_____ Teacher's Edition rich in supplemental materials

======== Total Points

Comments _____
_____
_____

Overall recommendation: Strongly recommend   _____
                          Recommend   _____
                          Questionable   _____
                          Do not recommend   _____

Reviewer's name _____ Date _____

FIGURE 10.6

The Role of Reading and Writing in Elementary Science

There are opposing views on incorporating reading and writing in the elementary science program. A growing body of research affirms that language is essential for effective science learning (Douglas et al., 2006; Miller, 2006, Teale et al., 2007)—that nonverbal methods of communication are not enough. In addition, research shows that skills in reading and reading comprehension can be improved when the reading material focuses on direct experience and offers the opportunity to engage learners, as is the case with reading in science.

On the other hand, Crawford (2005) argues that reliance on reading and writing rather than making other forms of communication available results in "an unequal distribution of opportunity to demonstrate knowledge and understanding that privileges some students while alienating others" (p. 139). She urges including multiple ways of displaying knowledge, including oral and visual as well as written.

Most assuredly, reading and writing skills are essential areas of development for children. On the other hand, through process-oriented inquiry, science is one area that can be investigated successfully by children independent of reading and writing. This gives rise to questions about the role of reading, writing, and literature in quality science education and the extent to which reading and writing should be an integral part of the science program.

One argument suggests that reading and writing should have a *limited* role in elementary science. Some children learn to read and write faster than others, some have greater facility than others, and some enjoy reading and writing more than others. Science is a field that can be studied *without* having to read or write. Children who experience difficulty with language can succeed in science by doing activities, experimenting, engaging logic, and discussing with others. For example, children can classify shells without having to read about their characteristics; their success can be assessed by talking with them about their classification system rather than through a written description. It is entirely possible to experiment successfully with the effects of different surfaces on the force needed to move a block of wood without reading about the concept of friction or writing one's findings.

However, children's success in the arena of science can serve as a catalyst to develop the self-confidence needed for more successful language experiences. The most powerful reading strategy teachers can implement is to enable children to develop for themselves meaningful purposes for reading. Science can generate purposes for reading and writing through children's own desire to pursue interesting areas of science inquiry in greater depth. Children will develop a desire to read to obtain background or explanatory information, to find out what has already been discovered,

NSES Teaching Standard A. Inquiry-Based Program
NSES Program Standard B. Relevant, Inquiry-Based, and Connected with Other Subjects
NSES Professional Development Standard D. Coherent and Integrated Programs

to challenge their ideas with new viewpoints, and to confirm or validate their conclusions.

An argument in favor of emphasizing reading and writing in science suggests that reading and writing must be an integral part of *every* aspect of the elementary curriculum, including science. All children are capable of recording their observations by picture or by writing statements in journals. Children's literature and writing activities can enhance science learning by improving vocabulary, refining auditory and visual skills, and fostering creativity. A good example of this (discussed earlier in this chapter) is writing poetry in conjunction with reading the poems on weather in *Out and About* by Shirley Hughes (Lothrop, Lee & Shepard, 1988). Reading and doing science also foster development of process skills, such as observing, formulating hypotheses, inferring, predicting, and interpreting data. Reading requires children to engage prior knowledge. "Because of the reciprocal relationship between science and reading, teaching them together can be mutually beneficial" (Armbruster, 1993, p. 347). Reading and writing also may stimulate greater interest in science on the part of children who are not interested in science. Furthermore, "[w]riting makes thinking visible" (Miller & Calfee, 2004, p. 20) and allows teachers to access children's constructions.

Whatever the textual material chosen for use in the classroom, good teachers adapt it to meet the needs of the students by emphasizing certain passages, using the text to stimulate individual inquiries, capitalizing on students' backgrounds, and using other adaptations commonly used in curriculum planning (Davis, 2006).

Many strategies for incorporating reading and writing in the elementary school science education program have been suggested (Akerson & Young, 2005; Collins, 2006; Fulton & Campbell, 2004; Glynn & Muth, 1994; Hapgood & Palinscar, 2006/2007; Heuser, 2005; Mintz & Calhoun, 2004; Robertson & Mahlin, 2005; Jablon, 2006). These strategies are summarized in Figure 10.7.

The National Science Teachers Association has published *Linking Science & Literacy in the K–8 Classroom,* edited by Rowena Douglas, Michael P. Klentschy, and Karen Worth (NSTA Press, 2006). This book contains theoretical discussions, case studies, and numerous practical suggestions for implementing reading and writing education within the context of science teaching. The book is divided into six sections: (1) scientific inquiry, (2) oral discourse, (3) writing, (4) reading, (5) culture, and (6) implementation issues. Regardless of your thoughts about requiring reading and writing in conjunction with science education, it is imperative that students learn to be literate. I urge every elementary and middle grades science teacher to use the material in this book as an integral part of the science program.

As you have seen, there is ambivalence toward reading and writing in science education that is bolstered by powerful arguments on each side.

SOME STRATEGIES FOR INCORPORATING READING AND WRITING IN ELEMENTARY SCIENCE EDUCATION

Sources of Reading Appropriate for Science
- Children's literature dealing with science topics
- Children's nonfiction books on a variety of topics
- A variety of different textbooks
- Magazines such as *Highlights for Children, Ladybug, ChickaDEE, Your Big Backyard, National Geographic Explorer, Owl, Kids Discover, Ranger Rick, Zoobooks, Odyssey,* and others that contain scientific and science-related materials
- Internet sites
- Newspaper stories about new developments in science and technology
- Nonfiction books on a variety of topics
- A variety of different textbooks to compare explanations and discussions
- Biographies of scientists, especially those from groups traditionally underrepresented in science
- Science fiction works, such as those by Isaac Asimov and Arthur C. Clarke

Writing Activities Appropriate for Science
- Observations and experimental data
- Science journals, notebooks, or diaries in which children describe their participation in science activities and reflect on their experiences
- Class books on science topics
- Individual books on science topics
- Daily class newspaper on current science events
- Drawings and graphs, with appropriate labeling of content items
- Questions about explorations
- Descriptions of exploration procedures
- PowerPoint® presentations
- Web pages
- Essays in which students describe their understanding of complex science concepts in depth
- Field trip notes in which children record their observations and reactions
- Documentation of activities and how they were set up
- Lab logs in which children record their observations, hypotheses, methods, findings, interpretations, and especially, their mistakes
- Student-authored books
- E-mails to scientists

FIGURE 10.7

You will have to decide for yourself the extent to which reading and writing will be incorporated in your science program. We do not take sides on this issue. However, we stress once again that children must learn science by *doing* science, not by reading *about* science.

INTERDISCIPLINARY APPROACHES

NSES Teaching Standard A. Inquiry-Based Program
NSES Teaching Standard F. Participating in Program Planning
NSES Program Standard B. Relevant, Inquiry-Based, and Connected with Other Subjects
NSES Professional Development Standard D. Coherent and Integrated Programs

The prevailing approach to curriculum in elementary schools involves separating learning into discrete components of individual subjects, each with its own time slot, its own textbook, and its own program of study. This fractionalized approach to learning sends the powerful message to children that each subject has its own domain and is independent of the others.

Hurd (1991) wrote:

> The reform movement of the 1990s calls for an integration of school subjects: a conceptual convergence of the natural sciences, mathematics, and technology with the social and behavioral sciences and the humanities into a coherent whole. A unity of knowledge will make it possible for students to take learning from different fields of study and use it to view human problems in their fullness from several perspectives (p. 35).

There is a paradigm shift from this discipline-centered, compartmentalized approach to an integrated, holistic approach to learning that provides children with the opportunity to confront problems that require multiple and overlapping solutions and to apply their knowledge to real-life situations. This emerging paradigm is known as *interdisciplinarianism*. In the preceding section, you explored one example: ways of including reading and writing within the science program. Research has shown that as a result of interdisciplinary studies, students exhibit increased positive attitudes toward science, are more highly motivated, and show improvement in their problem-solving skills (Czerniak, 2007).

Interdisciplinarianism involves including more than one discipline in an area of study. It is an approach that "consciously applies methodology and language from more than one discipline to a central theme, issue, problem, topic, or experience" (Jacobs, 1989, p. 8). Interdisciplinary studies can be approached in at least two ways—multidisciplinarianism and integration. The multidisciplinary approach involves identifying a central theme and establishing what each individual subject can contribute to the theme (Beane, 1997). For example, the theme may be dinosaurs (or apples, the environment, transportation, or any of a number of other themes). Teachers arrange each subject so that it relates to the theme, but teach each subject separately. This is very similar to the "daisy model" discussed below.

The other way of approaching interdisciplinary studies is through **integrated curriculum.** The integrated approach organizes curriculum around "significant problems and issues without regard for subject-area boundaries" (Beane, 1997, p. *xi*). The organizing themes are drawn from actual life experiences and are developed by both the teacher and the children. In the integrated approach, children study and learn what they need to learn in order to construct their understandings of the topic being investigated. This is done without reference to individual disciplines. This is similar to the "rose model" discussed below.

As we have observed previously, no subject can be studied in isolation. To attempt to do so is futile—it simply cannot be done. For example, it is impossible to teach science without some use of language. Mathematics is essential for obtaining measurements, calculating data trends, constructing graphs, and interpreting experimental results. Social studies provides the essential link between the idealism of science and its usefulness to society; indeed, science derives its meaning in large measure from social contexts.

McBee (2000) argues that interdisciplinary approaches make the material meaningful, interesting, and relevant, all of which are "'essential preconditions' for building motivation" (p. 258). The revised Standards for Science Teacher Preparation (National Science Teachers Association, 2003) says that "[a]t the elementary level, in particular, the sciences should be interwoven to develop interdisciplinary perspectives" (Standard A-2, p. 7). Conn (2004) writes that all students need to make informed decisions as citizens about crucial science issues, such as the environment, energy, and financial and ethical concerns. She says that "we must transform traditional science teaching into meaningful science learning in every grade—by nurturing students' need to know" (p. 30) through interdisciplinary approaches such as project or case-study strategies.

Interdisciplinary learning is the natural way people learn. People constantly cross disciplines in their daily life. For example, to run for political office, one needs to have positions on many issues (social studies, science, economics, political science), manage campaign finances (mathematics), tabulate the number of votes required (mathematics), put together speeches and slogans (communications and language arts), choreograph campaign appearances (drama and physical education), refine political strategies (political science), choose thematic and background music (music), know the constituency one represents (social studies), and so on. Police officers use many disciplines in the course of their work. They read reports of escaped convicts, write tickets and incident reports, use the scientific processes in searching for clues to mysteries and in inferring solutions, calculate how much over the speed limit the targeted vehicle has gone. They use physical education skills to keep in shape and they use art skills when they draw diagrams of accidents. They must be well versed in the law, sociology, emergency medicine, and many other fields. Teachers integrate into their daily work such areas as psychology, sociology, mathematics, economics, nutrition, safety, communication, drama,

music, and the scientific method of discovery—all in addition to their instructional responsibilities.

A few examples of interdisciplinary teaching and learning are given
below.

- In a third- and fourth-grade class, the teacher combined bird songs
  (music) with the scientific processes of observing and describing
  bird sounds, classifying bird sounds, and inferring what is going
  on from bird sounds (disagreement, fighting, courtship, show of
  strength, and the like) (Silverman, Coffman, & Younker, 2007).

- A study of art paintings used the process skills of observing, communicating observations, inferring what is portrayed in the painting,
  and predicting what might happen next (Rommel-Esham, 2005).

- An elementary grades study of **biomes** included life science, earth
  science, geography, and art (Gooden, 2005).

- Students in an elementary school wrote and published an illustrated
  guide to the ferns found on the school's nature trail. The project
  involved careful observation, classification, accurately-made drawings of the ferns, and reading and writing, thus integrating at least
  science, art, and language arts (Siry & Buchinski, 2005).

- Early elementary children went on an interdisciplinary field trip to
  the produce section of a grocery store, where they observed the
  various kinds of produce, classified them in their own ways, drew
  pictures of items that were not familiar to them, and researched
  where in the world the various items of produce come from
  (Wolfinger, 2005).

Two Interdisciplinary Models

The multidisciplinary approach to interdisciplinarianism can be shown
with a *daisy model.* In the daisy model, the major area of study is represented by the center of the flower, and the other areas of study are represented by the petals of the daisy (see Figure 10.8). Each subject retains
its own distinctive characteristics and is readily identified by teacher and
children alike. For example, let us suppose the topic of friction is to be
used as the main focus of study. Mathematics can be included through
calculating speed from distance and time; reading can be incorporated
with books that explain friction; writing can be incorporated by having
children write their views about what a frictionless world would be like;
music can be incorporated by having children can learn songs about runaway bicycles; and physical education can be incorporated by having
children run on surfaces with varying degrees of slipperiness. In this ap-

THE DAISY MODEL
Main subject is in the
center; other subjects
are attached as petals.

THE ROSE MODEL
All subjects are
intertwined.

Models of two
approaches to
interdisciplinary
studies

FIGURE 10.8

proach, each subject is treated independently, although it is related to the central topic. Mathematics is still taught as mathematics, reading is still taught as reading, and writing is still taught as writing. The primary difference between this approach and the discipline-centered approach is the thematic nature of the material. The mathematics instruction uses friction for the problems; reading and writing focus on friction for their subjects.

The daisy model is different in approach from curriculum integration. In the daisy model, teachers focus on individual disciplines, whereas in curriculum integration, the lines of subject demarcation cease to exist. Nonetheless, it is a good beginning to your development of interdisciplinary classes. You can start by combining one other content area with science as you did when you investigated ways of including literature with science. With experience, you can tackle true curriculum integration.

The integrated curriculum approach can be shown with a *rose model*. In this model, the subject areas lose their distinctive subject matter delineations (see Figure 10.8). In the rose, all the petals are closely intertwined—unlike the daisy, where each petal is separate and distinctly visible. In the rose, one sees the whole flower without regard to individual petals; in the daisy, one sees each petal. In the rose model, learning focuses on a particular problem or situation that is meaningful and of interest to children, and the children study whatever is necessary to bring about personal understanding.

Charting plant growth

A first-grade child records the results of a plant growth investigation in chart form, integrating mathematics principles with science.

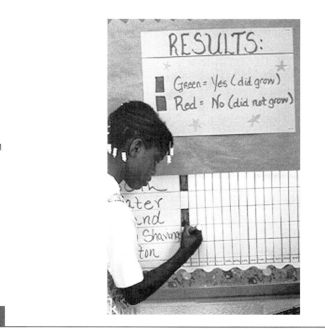

FIGURE 10.9

The class might study, for example, the impact of soft drinks on society. To do this, they would have to consider many concepts, including the differences among brands of soft drinks, the ways that marketing trends and needs are assessed, profit and loss, and many other factors involving sociology, politics, science, finance, and so on. Children bring in newspaper advertisements on different kinds of soft drinks. They conduct class surveys and graph the results to see which soft drink is most popular. The study is put together in such a way that the children study each of the subject areas normally included in the curriculum, but without the isolation of each discipline.

The account below of a student teacher whose second-grade class produced a video about their school is a good example of the rose model of integrated studies.

THE VIDEO

I once supervised a student teacher who was assigned to second grade. This teacher had previously studied the communications field, and had mastered the technique of producing documentary videos. When the principal learned this, she asked the student teacher to engage the class in producing a 10-minute video about their school to be used to familiarize new faculty, staff, and parents with the school. The student teacher discussed the project with his class, and together they decided on the contents of the video. He divided the children into several groups, each with responsibility for one or more distinct phases of the video. In groups, children drew the storyboards and wrote the script for each segment. The student teacher taught the children how to operate the camcorder, and the children shot the video footage. When this was done, the children refined the script and read it into a tape recorder. The only thing the student teacher did by himself was to combine the script with the video footage and edit the production.

During the course of this project, which lasted several weeks, the student teacher lamented that although he was perfectly willing to engage the children in this project, and although he was certain they were having a lot of fun, he was becoming increasingly frustrated over the time spent where "no teaching was going on." He felt the prescribed curriculum had been set aside during this production and that he was not fulfilling his responsibilities as a teacher because he had not covered the topics required for this period of time. I suggested that he list the topics that were supposed to be covered and indicate those that the children had learned through the video project. He did so and returned the list to me, dumbfounded that the children had in fact covered more of the prescribed curriculum than they would have if he had taught it in the traditional manner. The production of the video had enabled the children to learn more than they otherwise would have learned.

This student teacher was engaging in a totally integrated rose model approach to learning. In addition, the children were involved in all aspects of Bloom's cognitive taxonomy, from remembering factual material (for example, describing what is in the school) to analyzing the strands that should be depicted on the video, evaluating the video and its component parts, and creating the video itself.

TEACHER VOICE

What continues to bring me, a 28-year veteran teacher, back to my first-grade classroom in Pelham, Massachusetts each fall with ever increasing excitement and enthusiasm? Monarch butterflies! About 20 years ago, in the beginning of the school year, a little girl brought a monarch butterfly chrysalis to school for "show and tell." It looked like a bejeweled gem, ringed in gold, and fit for a king. When she told me it would turn into a butterfly, I laughed and asked her to stop teasing me. She insisted that it stay in our classroom, and to my amazement, two weeks later we watched it split open to reveal a monarch butterfly.

The class was captivated and so was I, and for the next 20 years, I learned as much as I could about monarch butterflies and worked hard to make them the focus of our fall curriculum. But, was I addressing the three *R*'s of writing, reading, and arithmetic? Was I meeting district, state, and federal standards? How could I justify spending so much of our time looking at monarch butterflies? The answers were to be found in using an interdisciplinary approach to curriculum.

My students read about butterflies, write about butterflies, and count butterflies. Each fall, I empty our school library of every bug book on the shelves and bring them into my classroom, and because this monarch butterfly unit is now a published science unit in our district, our librarian adds to the school collection each year. Over the years, I have accumulated a classroom collection of butterfly and insect books at various reading levels along with accompanying big books for guided reading lessons. I have been careful to include titles with simple texts as well as more challenging ones for advanced readers. We practice word-attack skills and reading strategies using our insect books, and we continually add high-frequency first-grade words taken from these books to our "Word Wall." Every Friday afternoon, we invite the sixth-grade class to listen to first graders read the books they have mastered and to read the more difficult books aloud to them. With only 125 children in our small rural school, this is easy to coordinate. "Reading Buddies" has grown to include "Writing Buddies" (for writing stories) and going on field trips together. Our favorite "Buddy" trip is to a local butterfly conservatory. I have also established a larger network of community "Reading Buddies" which includes parents and senior citizens who come into my classroom to listen to children read.

One of the best ways for children to focus their monarch butterfly observations is through detailed drawings and written journal entries, which we share as a class. Good scientists communicate their findings, and so do we. I created a "Butterfly Journal" for each child that includes paper for drawing and writing, simple stories about butterflies, insect facts, insect coloring pages, and some butterfly math pages as well. We create shared-writing "Big Books" that are kept on display for children to read to themselves. Students make stick puppets and use them to perform dramatic readings of their own new big books.

Counting is critical to the development of number sense, and we spend time counting our caterpillars, both the real ones and the ones I have put in their Butterfly Journals. We count and record the number of days it takes for the caterpillars to grow before becoming chrysalises, and we count the number of days until their metamorphoses are complete. I have integrated this counting routine into my daily morning meeting when we record the numbers on a large class calendar. Sorting and classifying differences among butterflies, moths, and other insects provides both science and math experiences as does the study of butterfly wing symmetry. The children enjoy applying paint to one side of a pair of paper wings and folding it up to transfer their design to the other side.

When the chrysalises open, we hold a "release" party and parade. This event includes wearing symmetry masks with party blower proboscises, butterfly-shaped snacks, nectar sipped through proboscis straws, and a song that ends with "It's time to let our Monarchs go; they're flying south to Mexico." Parents and the local press are invited to join in the celebration and to help communicate the importance of this natural wonder to our community. The butterflies are tagged with identification stickers from the University of Kansas which is studying the migration route of the Olympic flyers that can float more than 2,000 miles to their wintering site high in the Sierra Madre Mountains of Central Mexico. The people of Mexico celebrate their arrival with a holiday called "The Day of the Dead," and some believe that the butterflies represent the returning souls of their ancestors. First graders study this holiday along with other cultural information about Mexico. At our morning meeting, we learn to recite the date and take attendance in Spanish. Our Spanish lives on throughout the year, but the monarch butterflies eventually die after they return to the southern United States the next spring and lay their eggs. It will be their offspring that return north to the fresh milkweed fields where the young caterpillars feed and where my young first graders again collect caterpillars.

Paul Lipman

First-Grade Teacher
Pelham School
Pehlam, Massachusetts

Science, Technology, and Society

One of the greatest difficulties with developing elementary science programs seems to be the belief that there is essential information found in curriculum guides and texts that teachers must cover. The applications suggested often are artificial and have limited relevance to children's lives. An alternative is to provide situations and problems for study that are real to the children—situations and problems that children encounter in their daily lives. For example, studying how a mountain bicycle is designed for

NSES Program Standard B. Relevant, Inquiry-Based, and Connected with Other Subjects
NSES Program Standard C. Coordinated with Mathematics
NSES Professional Development Standard D. Coherent and Integrated Programs

its specific function might be more real to fifth- and sixth-grade children than studying the principles of simple machines.

Science–Technology–Society (STS) is a project-centered approach to science education that embodies curriculum integration as shown in the rose model. STS involves teaching and learning science in the context of human experience. The experiences selected for investigation are identified by the children, who are "full partners in planning and carrying out their own science lessons" (Yager, 1994, p. 34).

In the STS approach, children identify problems, questions, or unknowns, and they participate in deciding what they need to know and do as they research answers and explanations. STS projects can involve any problem that children care to investigate. Problems can be global (energy resources, global warming, population explosion, poverty), national (health care, childhood obesity, land use, endangered species), local (waste disposal, recycling, traffic patterns), or personal (science fiction, stopped-up toilets, mountain bicycles, power failures at home). STS projects center around real-world issues that children bring up. Local problems such as recycling, trash removal, and pollution control often are used as the basis for STS projects. Projects may begin with a situation at school, such as cleaning up a playground and keeping it clean. Teacher and children collaborate in deciding what should be studied, how to proceed, and how children will get involved. Many new questions and problems are encountered along the way that suggest new inquiries and new avenues of investigation. Teacher and children are coinquirers into investigations that are inquiry oriented.

STS is grounded in the constructivist learning model. Research shows that STS approaches result in achievement levels comparable to those seen with conventional teaching, but also result in improvement in attitudes to science and reduced gender differences in science attitudes (Bennett, Lubben, & Hogarth, 2007). Children come to understand the concepts and processes because they are useful to the children, can be applied to their own lives, and surface from their daily living situations. Children learn through their involvement with real-world problems and issues.

STS gives children an understanding of what science and technology are and the role they play in our lives. In addition, science anxiety is reduced because in the STS approach, children are studying familiar phenomena.

The incorporation of children's literature into the science program is one of the easiest ways to embark on an STS approach and, as we have seen, can begin as early as kindergarten. The book *Mike Mulligan and His Steam Shovel* by Virginia Lee Burton (Houghton Mifflin, 1939) presents the problem of people having to adapt to rapidly changing science and technology. In the story, an old-fashioned steam shovel becomes outdated by more modern equipment. This problem of adapting to technological change can be explored by children from a variety of viewpoints, including the nature of simple machines and compound machines; building novel machines, providing directions for their operation, and citing reasons why people should buy them; competing for the highest ratings of novel machines, and exploring the societal issues of equipment aging and obsolescence. Children will develop their own questions, problems, and avenues of exploration.

Many topics are appropriate for STS studies. Energy is a major concern in today's world. An STS project centering on energy can take many directions—history of energy use; energy resources; comparisons of energy uses between the United States and other countries; supply, demand, and cost factors; consumption and consumers; efficiency of different energy sources; **fossil fuel** issues; newly developed energy resources; and conservation of energy. Children can evaluate energy consumption at the personal, family, school, and community levels.

Environmental and population issues also are of major concern. STS problems can center on how to live in a constantly changing environment, how to improve personal lifestyles to exert positive influences on environmental factors, the role of government in environmental protection, and so on. The same is true of global warming, childhood obesity, and other contemporary science-related issues.

Waste management is an issue that directly impacts children's lives. Recycling, conservation, and landfill problems are appropriate STS topics. As an introductory activity, children can collect trash for a day, put it in a paper bag, and bury it in the schoolyard. If this is done at the beginning of the school year, it can be dug up every two or three months to see what is happening. Variations on this activity abound, and children are sure to come up with their own.

A listing of some topics that can be used for STS investigations is shown in Figure 10.10.

Personal Bias in STS Projects

To what extent should teachers introduce their personal biases when a class is pursuing a project? We all have personal—and, sometimes, emotional—feelings about many of the STS topics children bring up, from issues of population explosion to conservation, recycling, and preservation of endangered species. A major goal of education is for children to learn to think for themselves. This means children must come to their own informed conclusions based on their own evaluation and validation of evidence.

There are many reasons for teachers to encourage children to come to their own conclusions. One involves promoting children's ownership of their own thinking. When teachers allow their personal biases to set the direction of an investigation, children are denied the opportunity to

SOME TOPICS THAT CAN BE USED FOR STS INVESTIGATIONS	
Acid rain	Newsworthy happenings (including current newspaper articles dealing with science)
Air pollution	
Childhood obesity	Oil spills
Computers in the workplace	Overpopulation
Conservation	Ozone depletion
Drunk driving	The rain forest
Endangered species	Recycling
Electronic communications	Robotics
Energy and renewable energy resources	Seatbelt laws
Food	Space exploration
Global warming	Substance abuse
Hazardous waste disposal	Water pollution
Health	Weather
The Internet	Work
Leisure	
Medical issues	

(Adapted, in part, from M. O. Thirunarayanan, 1998)

FIGURE 10.10

think freely for themselves. For example, a teacher may slant a study of recycling such that children get the idea that they are supposed to come up with supportive evidence. In an open investigation, children would be asked to consider both positive and negative factors influencing recycling and come to their *own* decisions on whether recycling is useful. There is a story of a teacher who tried to get her second-grade children to embrace the principles of recycling. She asked all children to come to class with descriptions of how their parents recycle materials. Several of the children's parents did not recycle and, in fact, thought recycling a waste of time. This put the children in the untenable position of choosing between parents and teacher.

Another reason involves the potential for children to slant data to support a given position. It is incumbent on us as teachers to require children to interpret data objectively and to search for hidden variables. For example, the notion that recycling is good is based, in part, on conservation of energy resources. Recycling efforts often involve curbside waste management programs that require more collection trucks, which mean more fuel consumption and increased air pollution. Some recycling programs require considerable resources just to transport the materials to the recycling plants. These factors are part of the overall situation and should be considered by children as they study recycling.

STS represents an ultimate amalgamation of constructivism, science, and integrated investigations. It is to be hoped that all elementary science teachers will explore STS possibilities for their own classes.

Conclusion

To be scientifically literate, people must know how to *do* science. And they must know how science and all other areas of study are interrelated. Studying science in isolation is impossible. Identifying science as a separate intellectual endeavor sends the message that science is elite, difficult, and esoteric.

There are many ways of integrating science and the rest of the curriculum. Integrating literature (both fiction and nonfiction) with science helps provide relevance for the studies to children's lives, and literature opens avenues of inquiry that include the thoughts of others. Other disciplines can be included as adjuncts to the science program to show interrelationships. Alternatively, the science program can center on a totally integrated investigation of topics of interest and value to children. The Science–Technology–Society approach allows children to study science in the context of the totality of human experience.

For maximum learning to occur, science must be integrated with all other disciplines and be approached as one of many aspects of understanding the complexities of the world and the people who inhabit it.

CHAPTER 10

Additional Questions for Discussion

1. Contrast the subject-centered approach to teaching science with the interdisciplinary and integrated approaches, relative to content exposure and meaningful learning.
2. What advice would you give to a person who claims that science can be taught adequately through a literature-centered approach?
3. How would you incorporate writing into your science program?

Internet Activities

Use the Internet to find information about current trends in interdisciplinary approaches to education, the role of reading and writing in science education, reading and writing across the curriculum, and current trends and applications of the Science–Technology–Society (STS) interdisciplinary approach.

Use the Internet to find current information on the topics suggested for STS treatment.

CHAPTER · · · · · · 11

TECHNOLOGY IN ELEMENTARY SCIENCE EDUCATION

Technology . . . the knack of so arranging the world that we don't have to experience it.

Max Frisch, *Homo Faber* (Frankfurt: Suhrkamp Verlag, 1957)

Man is still the most extraordinary computer of all.

John F. Kennedy (1963)

We live in an age of technology in which the children in our schools often know more about technology than their teachers do. Most teachers did not grow up with the technology that has become part of the everyday lives of today's children. Only during the last few years have talking on cellular phones, playing video games, and surfing the Internet become commonplace activities.

Nonetheless, education has used technology for many years. Films, videos, and filmstrips have become staple supplements to the curriculum. Models, charts, and displays continue to provide enrichment and depth to programs. Audiotapes continue to have uses in song and dance. We use overhead projectors to show transparencies, manipulatives, money, clocks, color tiles, pattern blocks, the spectrum of visible light, and even magnetic fields (by sprinkling iron filings onto a sheet of acetate that has been placed over a magnet on the projector glass). See the video "Where Are the Poles of a Refrigerator Magnet?" on the companion CD. Calculators continue to be used to help children in both mathematics and science.

Computers have been used in education since the late 1950s; the early focus was on computer-assisted instruction (CAI) involving tutorials, drill-and-practice formats, and the mechanics of computer **hardware** and programming techniques. The 1960s brought computers solidly into the field of education through computerized applications of programmed instruction.

However, it was the emergence of the personal computer during the mid-1970s and the Internet during the 1990s that has expanded the educational use of computers to include word processing, spreadsheets, databases, graphing programs, laboratory computer interfacing systems, presentation software, electronic mail, the Internet, and a multitude of increasingly sophisticated applications.

Computers can provide practice, create realistic simulations, gather experimental data previously impossible to obtain, process experimental data rapidly and accurately so valid conclusions can be reached, provide instant access to huge amounts of information, and enable children and their teachers to communicate with peers and experts throughout the world.

It is imperative that teachers become familiar with current technology so they can use it with their students. Many aspects of educational technology have been infused into the investigations you have already explored in this text. In this chapter, you will examine specific technological advances and ways they can be used in the classroom to foster the process-oriented inquiry elementary science program.

A Technology Inventory

What is your "ETQ" (educational technology quotient)? To find out, place an X on the blank that represents your level of proficiency in each of the following technologies commonly used in schools today. Then calculate your ETQ using the scoring guide below.

MY PROFICIENCY

TECHNOLOGY	I Don't Know the First Thing About It	I Can Use It Somewhat	I Can Use It Well	I Know It So Well I Can't Do Without It
Chalkboard	1	2	3	4
White board	1	2	3	4
Overhead projector	1	2	3	4
Typewriter	1	2	3	4
Film Camera	1	2	3	4
Tape recorder	1	2	3	4
CD player	1	2	3	4
Television	1	2	3	4
Video player	1	2	3	4
DVD player	1	2	3	4
Camcorder	1	2	3	4
Basic calculator	1	2	3	4
Word processing program	1	2	3	4
Database program	1	2	3	4
Spreadsheet program	1	2	3	4
Graphing program	1	2	3	4
Presentation software	1	2	3	4

Continued on next page

	I Don't Know the First Thing About It	I Can Use It Somewhat	I Can Use It Well	I Know It So Well I Can't Do Without It
Graphic organizer program	1	2	3	4
Video games	1	2	3	4
Computer games	1	2	3	4
Desktop publishing program	1	2	3	4
E-mail	1	2	3	4
The Internet	1	2	3	4
Making your own Web site	1	2	3	4
CD-ROMs	1	2	3	4
Subject-specific computer programs	1	2	3	4
Science laboratory probes	1	2	3	4
Digital camera	1	2	3	4
Digital scanner	1	2	3	4
Interactive Whiteboard	1	2	3	4

Scoring: Add your points and divide by 120. This is your ETQ, or educational technology quotient.

What did you score? A score of 85 is about average. If you scored in this range, you will want to improve the technologies you don't know very well (the 1s and 2s). The motivation for doing so will come from need. If you scored below 60, you should give serious consideration to improving your technological skills. If you scored 100 or above, you're practically home!

Many people think of technology only in terms of computers. But when the chalkboard was invented, it was considered revolutionary. Among other hurdles, teachers had to learn to write on one without making the eviscerating squeak so dreaded by students but so often heard. The overhead projector was first used for business applications to illustrate presentations. Its introduction to schools posed several challenges to teachers, including getting the knack of which way to put the transparency on the glass so the image is right-side up.

Yes, there is more to technology than computers. However, because computers and the Internet dominate conversations about educational technology, the focus of this chapter is on computer-based technology.

WHY USE ADVANCED TECHNOLOGY IN ELEMENTARY SCIENCE EDUCATION?

There are many reasons for using advanced technology in the constructivist elementary science program. These reasons range from the near universality of technology in today's society to technology's enormous potential for aiding children and teachers in their inquiries.

NSES Teaching Standard F. Participating in Program Planning
NSES Professional Development Standard C. Lifelong Learning

Widespread Use of Computer Technology

Nearly every American business, from banks and brokerage firms to warehouses and fast-food restaurants, requires some knowledge of computers. Nearly every manufacturing facility uses computers and computer-based technology. In 2004, more than three-fourths of American men and women said that they used computers, and more than 60 percent said they had access to the Internet (Brunner, 2007). These statistics suggest one reason for employing computers and advanced technology in our schools: *They are used everywhere.*

Familiarity with Advanced Technology

A second reason for using advanced technology in the elementary science classroom is that many children are accustomed to using it at home in the form of videos, television programs, digital cameras and camcorders, cell phones, computers, the Internet, video games, and computer games. The children in today's classrooms are, as Craig (1999) puts it, the "Net Generation" (p. 28). Prensky (2005/2006) uses the term "digital natives," referring to people who are "native speakers of technology, fluent in the digital language of computers, videogames, and the Internet" (p. 9), but laments that schools are operating as though they were still in the 20th century when the students are well settled in the 21st century.

Technological Access to Information

Third, in elementary science, technology can be used to gain access to amounts and types of information previously unavailable to children. For example, using **CD-ROM**s and the Internet, children can witness experimental procedures that are either too dangerous or too expensive for the classroom. They can see photographs and action scenes and hear explanations and information presentations on just about any topic of interest, from animal habitats to aviation, from plate tectonics and volcanoes to nuclear reactors. Entire encyclopedias are available on CD-ROMs, some of which are "talking" encyclopedias, complete with videos, from which children can obtain desired information in a matter of seconds. The Internet enables children and teachers to access huge amounts of specialized information on any topic from anywhere in the world.

Computer Support in Inquiry Investigations

NSES Teaching Standard A. Inquiry-Based Program
NSES Program Standard C. Coordinated with Mathematics

Fourth, technology in elementary science provides speed, accuracy, and convenience in inquiry investigations. Technology enables children to spend less time on data collection and mathematical manipulation and more time processing and interpreting experimental data, thus achieving greater accuracy in data collection, mathematical operations, and experimental results. Probes and sensors that accompany laboratory computer interfacing systems enable children to measure force, temperature, light intensity, barometric pressure, acidity, and even heart rate with a degree of accuracy, sensitivity, and speed not otherwise available. For example, temperature probes can be used to compare the small difference between air temperatures at the floor and the ceiling of the classroom. Motion sensors can be used to record the continuously increasing speed of a cart rolling down an inclined plane.

Spreadsheets can be programmed to do mathematical calculations on raw data entered by children to provide desired information. For example, children can enter the number of swings a pendulum makes in 15 seconds into a spreadsheet; by means of the equations programmed into the spreadsheet, they can calculate the average period.

Database programs can be used to store a variety of information that children (or the teacher) have researched on a topic; this information then can be sorted in different ways to help children answer their questions. For example, children who are investigating dinosaurs can research facts about a number of different dinosaurs. These facts are entered into a "dinosaur database," and commonalities among dinosaurs are searched, such as which dinosaurs were plant eaters, how many dinosaurs were less than 10 feet long, and where the most dinosaur bones have been found.

Graphing programs can be used to generate instant graphic portrayal of data collected by children, such as daily outdoor temperature or rate of plant growth, providing visual assistance in interpreting data.

Support of Learning Differences Through Technology

NSES Teaching Standard A. Inquiry-Based Program
NSES Professional Development Standard B. Integrating Knowledge of Science, Learning, Pedagogy, and Students

Fifth, advanced technology can be used to provide learning experiences suitable for individual needs of children. For the visual learner, the array of video material available is virtually unlimited, ranging from programs that air on commercial and public television channels to videos, DVDs, and CD ROMs prepared specifically for educational use on specialized topics, and videos and photographs available on the Internet. With the appropriate technology, it is possible for children to access information about chosen topics from a variety of sources and then produce their own video on that topic. Presentation software such as PowerPoint®, makes it possible for children (and teachers) to develop multimedia presentations. These presentations might include material extracted from the Internet, video and audio clips that the children themselves produced, photographs that children took with digital cameras, and text—all in the same presentation. In addition, children can develop their own classroom publications and can publish their investigations and accomplishments to Internet sites.

As described in Chapter 6, programs and computer devices are available that add the sense of touch to virtual images on computer screens, making it possible to touch and manipulate the virtual objects, thus helping kinesthetic learners.

Technology has been shown to provide a stimulus to foster the internal locus of control (Steinberg, 1989). Using suitable technologies, children are encouraged to pursue their own strategies for solving problems, thus demonstrating that they are in control of their own learning. Technology has been used to stimulate the field-independent mode of cognitive operations on the part of field-dependent children. Computer programs were created to increase children's ability to recognize differences in randomly shown paired shapes and pictures, decreasing their dependence on surrounding details for figure recognition and helping to foster higher levels of field independence and, ultimately, critical thinking (Collings, 1985). The operation of computer programs is itself an aid for developing a more field-independent style, because children must focus on the details of the programmed material rather than on the global aspects of the program. As shown earlier, the use of computers also can be an invaluable aid to children with learning disabilities, children with handicaps, and English language learners.

A direct link to a Web site that describes software and devices that add the sense of touch to computerized images is available on the Student Book Companion Web Site.

Use of Computer Technology by Scientists

Finally, perhaps the most compelling reason for using advanced technology in elementary science education is that *scientists use it.* One of the premises underlying elementary science education is that children should *do* science, not just read *about* science, and that children should do science the way scientists do science. This means using technology. The National Science Teachers Association (1999) adopted this posture in their position statement, "The Use of Computers in Science Education":

> Just as computers play a central role in developing and applying scientific knowledge, they can also facilitate the learning of science. It is, therefore, the

NSES Content Standard E. Science and Technology: Understanding About Science and Technology
NSES Teaching Standard A. Inquiry-Based Program
NSES Teaching Standard F. Participating in Program Planning

position of the National Science Teachers Association that computers should have a major role in the teaching and learning of science.

COMPUTERS IN THE ELEMENTARY SCIENCE CLASSROOM

NSES Teaching Standard F. Participating in Program Planning

The development of the personal computer and the rich array of educational **software** and related technologies now available have virtually transformed the use of technology in the classroom. In 2005, 100 percent of elementary schools in the United States had computers with access to the Internet (Wells & Lewis, 2006).

▶ The first general-purpose electronic computer was developed in 1946. Called ENIAC (Electronic Numerical Integrator and Calculator), it weighed 30 tons, had 18,000 vacuum tubes, and occupied 3,000 cubic feet of space. In 1949, the magazine *Popular Mechanics* predicted that computers would eventually weigh no more than 1½ tons (Hamilton, 1949). ENIAC was used largely for military operations and generally burned out one or more of its vacuum tubes every few minutes. Grace Hopper, a young naval officer, was one of the early computer operations experts. One day, while she was trying to find the cause of a problem, she discovered that a bug caught between two electrical terminals was preventing the flow of electricity. She solved the problem by removing the bug, giving rise to the term *debugging* for the act of looking for program errors. Hopper later became an admiral and was one of the American pioneers of computer use.

A TECHNOLOGY INQUIRY CONTINUUM

NSES Teaching Standard A. Inquiry-Based Program

You will recall that in Chapter 5, we suggested a methodology continuum ranging from teacher-centered expository methodologies to child-centered free discovery (see Figure 5.1). The position a particular lesson occupies on the continuum depends on the extent to which children are free to explore on their own.

A similar continuum can be constructed for the wide array of computer technology applications available (see Figure 11.1).

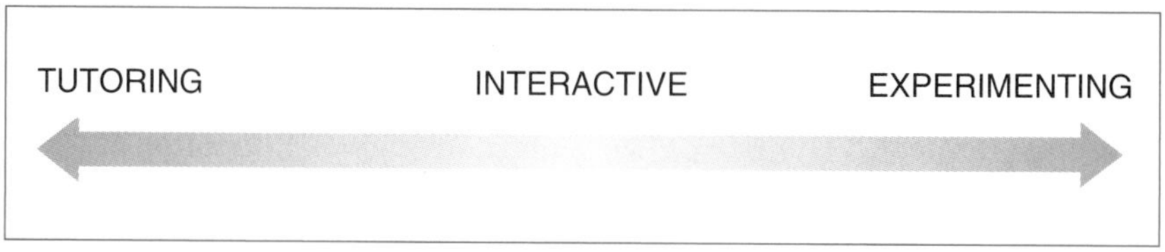

A technology continuum

TUTORING　　　INTERACTIVE　　　EXPERIMENTING

FIGURE 11.1

Tutoring applications are expository in nature. They dispense information. They teach something to the child. Tutoring applications include such programs as drill-and-practice, tutorials, course reviews, remediation, and testing.

Interactive applications are those that allow children to interact with the computer in some fashion, and include such applications as games, word processing programs, spreadsheet programs, database programs, graphing programs, simulations, graphic organizers, CD-ROMs, presentation software, e-mail, and the Internet.

Experimenting applications are those that allow children to use technology as an adjunct to their own experimental procedures. Laboratory computer interface systems permit data gathering that would not otherwise be possible, especially long-term data (such as overnight effects); short-term data (such as increase in speed of a cart rolling down an inclined plane); and hard-to-obtain data (such as air temperature differences between the floor and the ceiling). In laboratory computer interface systems, a probe or a sensor is used to collect data, and the computer to which it is connected (interfaced) displays and processes the data. In addition, many Internet applications encourage children to pursue their own inquires with the aid of Web-based resources such as communicating with scientists and interfacing with specific inquiries through using Web-Quests, the Apple Learning Interchange, and other online facilities.

TUTORING USES OF COMPUTERS

Tutoring programs are used as dispensers of information and testers of children's mastery of the information. Typically, a piece of information is presented on the screen, and the child is asked to key a response to a question about this information. The computer gives a "yes" or a "no" response. The "yes" response may be in the form of points awarded, or distances along an animated path, or height up a mountain, or some other system of portraying success. The "no" response normally refers the child to additional screens that "teach" the material, after which the child tries a similar question. The tutoring programs provide immediate positive reinforcement of children's responses. A good example of such programs are the tutorials that accompany many computer programs you might purchase. You may have used one yourself to help you master a word processing program.

Tutoring programs can be used as part of an advance organizer or introduction to a lesson or unit of study. They can be used as a follow-up on a topic the teacher has introduced or as a review of material. They can be used to reinforce concepts explored in class from different perspectives. They can be used to enable children to learn about something that has captured their interest or to cover material they missed because

NSES Teaching Standard B. Guiding and Facilitating Learning
NSES Teaching Standard D. Providing Time, Space, and Resources

of absence. Tutorials also are useful in helping teachers study scientific material.

Computerized tutoring has been shown to exert a small but positive effect on learning (Hancock & Betts, 1994). However, these programs are designed to lead the child to correct responses and, as such, clearly are expository in nature. There is no room in these programs for children to interact or to apply their own thinking. The computer "owns" the knowledge, and it is the job of the child to discover what this knowledge is (see Chapter 5).

See the Student Book Companion Web Site for direct links to some tutoring programs.

INTERACTIVE USES OF COMPUTERS

Interactive uses of computers permit children to use computers as tools to aid them in their inquiries. Although limited in scope by the material written into the programs, these applications allow some degree of mental manipulations directed by children.

NSES Teaching Standard B. Guiding and Facilitating Learning
NSES Teaching Standard D. Providing Time, Space, and Resources

Word Processing and Desktop Publishing Applications

Word processing programs are used for written reports, essays, descriptions, and the like. Features such as spell-check and grammar analysis permit attention to the substance of the material without having to worry unduly about mechanics. It has been shown that children who regularly use word processors for their writing exhibit higher quality and greater quantity of writing (Goldberg, Russell, & Cook, 2003). Children can use word processing programs to record experimental data; however, they cannot manipulate data using such programs.

Desktop publishing programs are word processing applications that allow children and teachers to put together such products as newsletters with a professional look and information pamphlets (see Figure 11.2). How better to show the community what is happening in your science class than to distribute a professional-looking periodic newsletter? Options are available for producing signs and banners, flash cards, calendars, and even your own big books. Children can make banners to advertise special classroom science events such as "Science Day" or to welcome guest speakers. They can make signs to label where various kinds of equipment are stored.

Spreadsheet, Database, and Graphing Applications

NSES Program Standard C. Coordinated with Mathematics

Spreadsheet programs are used to record quantitative data and to provide rapid and accurate calculations by using mathematical formulas to process the data. Figure 11.3 shows a spreadsheet used to calculate average

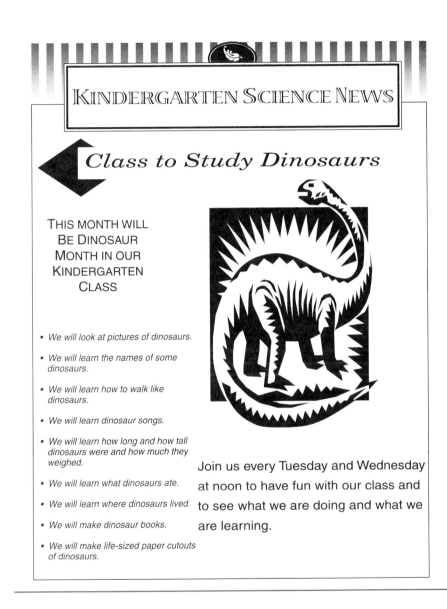

KINDERGARTEN SCIENCE NEWS

Class to Study Dinosaurs

THIS MONTH WILL
BE DINOSAUR
MONTH IN OUR
KINDERGARTEN
CLASS

- *We will look at pictures of dinosaurs.*

- *We will learn the names of some dinosaurs.*

- *We will learn how to walk like dinosaurs.*

- *We will learn dinosaur songs.*

- *We will learn how long and how tall dinosaurs were and how much they weighed.*

- *We will learn what dinosaurs ate.*

- *We will learn where dinosaurs lived.*

- *We will make dinosaur books.*

- *We will make life-sized paper cutouts of dinosaurs.*

Join us every Tuesday and Wednesday at noon to have fun with our class and to see what we are doing and what we are learning.

A science announcement prepared using desktop publishing (Microsoft Publisher® software)

FIGURE 11.2

period of a pendulum from raw data. (See Constructing Your Ideas 3.14 for a complete description of the pendulum investigation.) Children first input the number of washers they used, the length of the string, and the distance of the pull. They count the number of swings in 15 seconds for each of three trials, and enter the result in the appropriate blank after each trial. Each time a variable is changed, they enter the new values and the results of each of the three trials of swing counting. Formulas entered into the spreadsheet calculate the average of the three trials, the average number of swings per minute, and the average period of the pendulum (length

The Pendulum

A	B	C				Column G	Column H	Column I
No. Washers	String Length (cm)	Pull Dist (cm)	Swings in 15 sec			Avg Swings in 15 sec	Avg Swings per min	Average Period
			Trial #1	Trial #2	Trial #3			
3	30	10	12	12	13	12.33	49.33	1.22
4	30	10	12.5	11.5	12	12.00	48.00	1.25
4	30	10	12	12	12.5	12.17	48.67	1.23
5	30	10	13	11.5	12.5	12.33	49.33	1.22

Formulas	Column G Avg. Swings in 15 sec.	AVERAGE (D6:F6)
	Column H Avg. Swings per min.	G6*4
	Column I Average Period	1/((H6)/60)

Spreadsheet used for pendulum inquiry (Microsoft Excel® software)

FIGURE 11.3

of time for one swing). By using the spreadsheet, children can interpret the results of their explorations from accurately calculated averages. The spreadsheet and the calculation formulas are shown in Figure 11.3.

Spreadsheets can be used to calculate the rate of growth of each of several plants; children input periodic height measurements, and the spreadsheet is programmed to calculate averages. Spreadsheets have many other uses where calculations from raw data are needed to interpret experimental results. Spreadsheets aid children in their development of the processes of prediction, inference, and interpreting data.

Database programs enable users to search large amounts of information about particular topics in any of a number of categories. For example, commercial searchable online catalogs and fast-food nutrition facts are stored in databases that the user can access to retrieve specific information such as a listing of umbrellas available from a catalog or the nutritional value of a Big Mac. Online banking and bill paying are database applications, and search engines like Google are huge databases. Database programs are used to help children sort and analyze data about related phenomena. After entering many items of information about each of many examples of a set, children can sort the information in different ways to answer questions. For instance, one could develop a database of bird characteristics. Such characteristics as length, male–female resemblance, habitat, song, and nesting habits might be included. Each child might be assigned responsibility for researching the agreed-on information about one or two birds. This information is recorded in the labeled sections of each database cell, one cell per bird (see Figure 11.4). The information

DATABASE CELL

Name: Red-headed woodpecker
Length: 21–24 inches
Male-Female Res: Similar
Habitat: Groves
Song: Churr
Nest: Hollows in trees

Database cell
(Microsoft Works®
software)

FIGURE 11.4

BIRDS DATABASE IN TABULAR FORM

Name	Length (in.)	Male-Female Resemblance	Habitat	Song	Nest
Red-headed woodpecker	21–24	Similar	Groves	Churr	Hollows in trees
Bluebird	18	Sl. different	Open country	Musical	Natural cavities
Oriole	18–20	Similar	Open woods	Whistle	Lower tree branches
Starling	19–21	Similar	Cities	Whistles; clicks	Builds nest
Sparrow	15	Different	Cities	Chips	Builds nest
Nuthatch	11	Similar	Open pine woods	Twitter	Nests in cavities
Chickadee	11	Similar	Woods	Whistle	Nests in cavities
Cardinal	19–23	Different	Woodland edges	Whistle; chirp	Shrubbery
Titmouse	15	Similar	Woodlands	Whistle	Nests
Red-winged blackbird	18–24	Different	Marshes	Gurgle	Nests: Water shrubs
Robin	23–28	Different	Cities	Caroling	Lower tree branches

Database application: Microsoft Works® software

FIGURE 11.5

also can be presented in tabular form (see Figure 11.5). Once the information has been entered, children use the sorting function to discover similarities among birds, such as which birds are located in certain areas, birds in which the male and female look alike, and the most common nesting habits (see Figure 11.6).

NAMES OF BIRDS IN WHICH MALE AND FEMALE LOOK ALIKE

Name	Length (in.)	Habitat	Song	Nest
Red-headed woodpecker	21–24	Groves	Churr	Hollows in trees
Oriole	18–20	Open woods	Whistle	Lower tree branch
Starling	19–21	Cities	Whistles; clicks	Builds nest
Nuthatch	11	Open pine woods	Twitter	Nests in cavities
Chickadee	11	Woods	Whistle	Nests in cavities
Titmouse	15	Woodlands	Whistle	Nests

Names of birds in which male and female look alike (Microsoft Works® software)

FIGURE 11.6

Databases can be developed for just about any topic from dinosaurs to populations, from animals to planets. Many databases are available commercially and on the Internet, many of which can be used to help children in their inquiries. However, as Braun (2004) points out, "Students' learning reaches its highest stages when students actively participate in the design of the database, collect the data themselves, and then develop questions and probes for other classmates or adults" (pp. 71–72).

A good way to introduce children to the concept of databases is to have them write the data on cards and then sort the cards by common characteristics. For example, children record the information about each different kind of bird on a different card labeled with the name of the bird. The children flip through the cards to find similar characteristics, such as which birds live in cities. The electronic database is the next logical step, and has the advantage that it can manipulate large amounts of information quickly and can sort by numerical parameters, such as finding birds longer than 15 inches, between 15 and 20 inches long, or up to 18 inches long.

Graphing programs use the computer to construct any of a variety of graphs from data entered by children. Options for graph construction normally include line graphs, bar graphs, and pie graphs, drawn either to predetermined specifications or to the child's specifications. Graphing programs are extremely useful in helping children visualize the impact of their data and interpret the meaning of the data. A graphing program was used to portray the depths and diameters of simulated moon craters formed by dropping marbles from different heights (see Figure 3.25 and 3.26). Graphing programs can be used as early as kindergarten to chart plant growth, daily temperatures, times of sunrise and sunset, and the like, and some are so child-friendly that children can use them by themselves with little

Daily Noontime Temperatures

Date	Temperature (Degrees F)
6/21	74
6/22	74
6/23	82
6/24	81
6/25	91
6/26	86
6/27	84
6/28	82
6/29	78
6/30	78

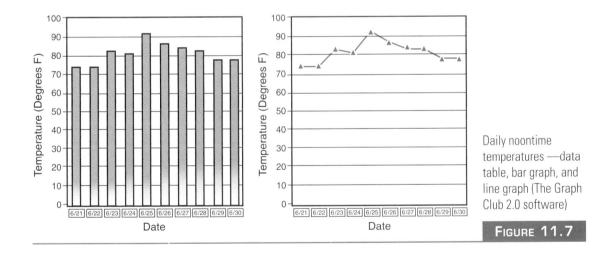

Daily noontime temperatures —data table, bar graph, and line graph (The Graph Club 2.0 software)

FIGURE 11.7

teacher input. Figure 11.7 shows the data table and resulting graph of a kindergarten activity involving measuring noontime temperatures.

Graphing programs can show percentages and frequencies (quantities) of non-numeric variables in the form of pie graphs and bar charts. These programs are appropriate for charting data that are partially qualitative, such as percentages of basic food groups consumed during a day, numbers of children with certain hair color or eye color, numbers of days with given weather conditions, and the like. Figure 11.8 shows two graphs

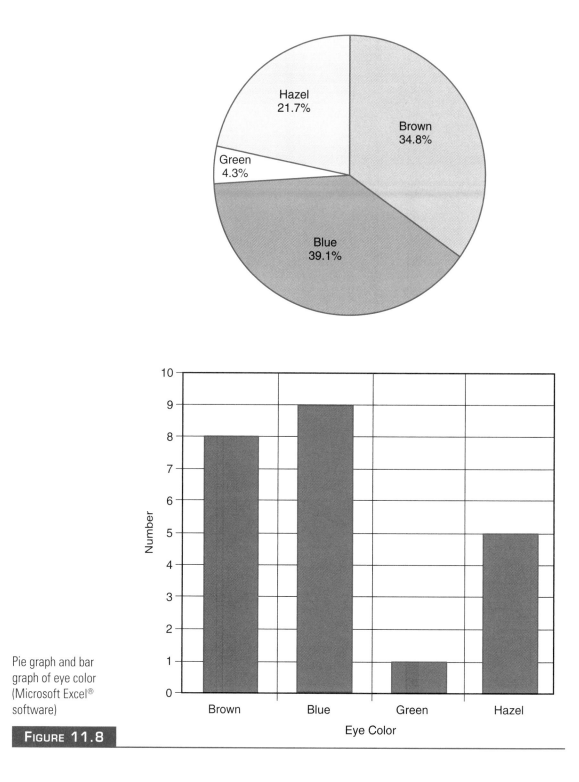

Pie graph and bar graph of eye color (Microsoft Excel® software)

FIGURE 11.8

that portray numbers of children in a third-grade class with brown, blue, green, and hazel eyes.

Presentation Applications

Presentation software such as PowerPoint® is used for creating presentations and can include headline slides, pictures, photographs, videos, graphs, and sound in addition to the text. The presentations often are used by teachers to present illustrated material. Presentations can be used by elementary science students to show what they did in their investigations and illustrate summary results. For example, Wang, Kedam, and Hertzog (2004) describe a project in which kindergarten and first-grade children prepared PowerPoint presentations (with the help of an adult) about their investigations into "Who Measures What in Our Neighborhood?" They found that this use of computer technology in the early childhood classroom helped children articulate their thinking and fostered personal reflections. Carter, Sumrall, and Curry (2006) implemented a project in grades 4, 5, and 6 in which students prepared PowerPoint presentations showing their use of photographs of the leaves and bark of trees (which they took with digital cameras) to identify the trees. Presentation software is very flexible, and its components can be manipulated to show topics succinctly and thoroughly. However, as Brown (2007) points out, teachers need to help children sharpen their thinking as they prepare PowerPoint presentations so they don't rely solely on the available templates.

Graphic Organizer Software

Graphic organizer software is used to depict pictorial or graphic organization of material. Graphic organizers, which include concept maps, webs, and the like, are powerful tools to help people organize information. Electronic graphic organizers include concept mapping programs, such as *Inspiration*® (for upper grades) and *Kidspiration*® (for lower grades); several other programs are available on the Internet. Graphic organizers help science students develop plans for their inquiries, show visually how they are fitting information together, and show how they reach their conclusions. Chapter 12 is devoted to concept mapping as an educational heuristic.

Simulations, Animations, and Games

Simulation programs enable the child to input a series of inquiries and actions for realistic or hypothetical problems and receive graphic information about the effect of the actions. For example, a program suitable for the upper elementary grades called *SimCity* invites children to inquire into urban environments. A city plan is presented and children are asked

Direct links to the *Sim-City* Web site home page from which you can access an online version and the Virtual Courseware Web sites are available on the Student Book Companion Web Site.

to respond to hypothetical community changes, such as sudden population changes, natural disasters, rush-hour traffic, and poor planning by suggesting redesigns of the city. Effects of their newly input designs are shown so children can see the results of their planning suggestions. Murray and Bartelmay (2005) describe a second-grade project in which children use Legos® and *Robolab*® (the Lego computer programming software) to create and operate their own motorized inventions of something that would solve a common problem. In the project, students use many process skills, including observing, inferring (what the various pieces are used for), predicting (what each piece does), classifying (sorting the pieces for later use), and the integrated processes (as they planned and tested their inventions). Waight and Abd-El-Khalid (2007) describe using a virtual pond and a heart-transplant simulation in sixth-grade science. The *Virtual Courseware* Web site offers a set of Web-based experiment simulation science activities emphasizing inquiry that can be used in middle grades (Limson, Wizlib, & Desharnius, 2007).

Simulation programs are used to train pilots and astronauts and to pose clinical problems for medical students. In elementary science education, simulation software often is used to explore concepts that require (1) expensive or hazardous materials or procedures (such as nuclear reactions and experiments involving strong acids or highly reactive chemicals); (2) levels of skill not yet attained by children (such as activities involving micromeasurement, vacuum treatment, or supercooling); or (3) more time than is possible in a classroom situation (such as population growth simulations). Computer-based simulations enable students to "see" and manipulate abstract concepts such as density and to model complex ideas such as predator–prey relationships.

Animation programs simulate processes such as acceleration, cell division, mountain formation, and wave motion. Programs range in content sophistication from simple (such as blood coursing through the body or the motion of particles in sound waves), to complex (such as forces acting on space vehicles). They enable children to see models of phenomena that otherwise cannot be seen and allow children to manipulate given variables to see what happens, thus encouraging children in their development of the process skill of making models.

A direct link to a Web site that shows animations of longitudinal and transverse waves is available on the Student Book Companion Web Site.

A direct link to the Web site that offers games based on the *Magic School Bus* titles is available on the Student Book Companion Web Site.

Games are interactive programs that offer both competition and the opportunity to learn. The competition may be with other players or with the computer. Many people believe that video games, generally used for entertainment only, can foster inquiry and higher-order thinking skills and should be adapted for educational purposes (Playing to Learn, 2006; Shaffer et al., 2005). For example, Dibley and Parish (2007) describe using a video game to help middle-grade students understand human body systems, how they work together, and how all animals maintain their balance of temperature. Many educational games are available on CD-ROMs and many are available on the Internet.

CD-ROM Information Base Applications

CD-ROM information bases enable children to isolate desired facts and other information through search-and-sort mechanisms. A CD-ROM is a compact disc that has the capability of storing huge amounts of information. The *ROM* in the term means "read-only memory," because you cannot add anything to the disc. A single CD has the capacity to store some 550,000 pages of print information; many are multimedia in nature and provide videos, sound, and pictures in addition to textual material. For example, illustrated encyclopedias, talking dictionaries, and maps with databases showing facts about major cities and geographic features are available on CD-ROM. The National Geographic Society has produced a number of CD-ROMs that contain facts, essays, color photos, maps, sounds, video clips, and games. Interactive CD-ROMs are available for many *Magic School Bus* titles. Normally, the CD-ROM has a menu built into the program, enabling children to quickly access the desired information by category.

CD-ROMs are available for multitudes of scientific topics and can take the form of databases, providers of multimedia information, simulation programs, or combinations. Although CD-ROMs cannot save children's work, they can provide exciting information presentations and interactive simulations.

A direct link to the National Geographic Society store where you can purchase their CD-ROMs, is available on the Student Book Companion Web Site.

EXPERIMENTING USES OF COMPUTERS

Microcomputer-Based Laboratories (MBLs) consist of computer-operated software with probes designed to collect data beyond the range normally available in the classroom. The probes extend observation capabilities by detecting very small differences in data (such as hundredths of a degree in temperature readings), and by recognizing sensory input to which humans are not sensitive (such as ultraviolet and infrared radiation and inaudible sounds). They can provide data points at very small intervals (such as the speed of a falling object at 1/100-second intervals), and they can record observations over very long periods of time (such as the temperature of the classroom every 10 minutes for 24 hours).

Accompanying the probes and sensors are programs that provide readouts of the data, graph the data according to the experimenter's specifications, and perform mathematical manipulations of the data to meet the experimenter's needs such as averaging trials and calculating acceleration from change in velocity.

Although children are limited in their investigations by the capacity of the program and the sensitivity of the probe or sensor, MBLs greatly expand the range of available inquiry. The use of MBLs supports the constructivist approach to elementary science teaching and learning.

NSES Teaching Standard A. Inquiry-Based Program

NSES Content
Standard B. Physical
Science: Heat Energy

MBLs are available for a wide variety of experimental purposes. The temperature probe is an electronic thermometer that detects and records temperatures from below freezing to above 100°Celsius. Temperatures can be read to the nearest tenth of a degree (or finer), and readings can be taken at any interval (long or short) over any period of time (long or short). For example, a child may wonder how fast warm water cools. Using the temperature probe provides data to answer the question. Figure 11.9 shows the raw data and the resulting graph of the temperatures for a cup of warm water left in a room for 10 minutes to which an ice cube was added after the first 2 minutes. Temperature readings were recorded every 30 seconds, and the result was graphed.

The temperature probe also can be used to record outdoor temperatures, monitor aquarium temperatures, and record the conversion of light energy to heat energy.

NSES Content
Standard D. Earth and
Space Science: Earth in
the Solar System

The light sensor is a **photoelectric cell** used to detect and record light intensity. Children experimenting with the effect of distance on intensity of illumination can use the light sensor to obtain measurements of the actual amount of light received from a light source as the distance is changed. The light sensor can be used to provide a visual portrayal of the effects of the tilt of the earth's axis on the amount of radiant energy received at

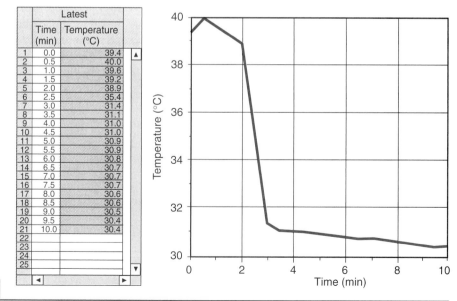

Graph and data table of changes in water temperature (GO! Temp™, version 1.2, Vernier Software)

FIGURE 11.9

	Latest	
	Time (min)	Temperature (°C)
1	0.0	39.4
2	0.5	40.0
3	1.0	39.6
4	1.5	39.2
5	2.0	38.9
6	2.5	35.4
7	3.0	31.4
8	3.5	31.1
9	4.0	31.0
10	4.5	31.0
11	5.0	30.9
12	5.5	30.9
13	6.0	30.8
14	6.5	30.7
15	7.0	30.7
16	7.5	30.7
17	8.0	30.6
18	8.5	30.6
19	9.0	30.5
20	9.5	30.4
21	10.0	30.4
22		
23		
24		
25		

Children shine a flashlight beam on a tilted balloon representing the earth to find the Tropic of Cancer

FIGURE 11.10

various latitudes on a globe. Using a flashlight to simulate the sun, children focus the light beam onto various latitudes of a globe or balloon that simulates the earth to investigate the tilt of the earth in its revolution about the sun and the effect of that tilt on the concentration of radiant energy (see Figure 11.10 and In The Schools 5.1).

Motion detectors allow children to gather data on the motion of objects. Similar to the automatic range finders on Polaroid® cameras, they send ultrasonic pulses at high frequency and record the time each pulse takes to make one round trip from the device to the moving object and back to the device. From the time for each round trip, the accompanying computer program can calculate distance, velocity, and acceleration of a moving object. The motion detector is ideal for measuring the rate of acceleration of a cart rolling down an inclined plane, rate of deceleration of an object rolled down a hall floor, or rate of acceleration of freely falling objects. The results can be displayed graphically, in terms of actual data and as reductions in velocity, acceleration, or distance.

Heart rate monitors are similar to those found on exercise equipment. The sensor clips to the ear or slips onto a finger or may be a belt worn round the waist or chest, and it measures pulse rate, which is recorded over time. This sensor is ideal to help children explore the effects of exercise and rest on heart rate (see In The Schools 2.4).

The pH sensor measures and records the acidic levels of liquids (see In The Schools 3.23).

These and other kinds of probes and sensors are available from science supply companies and can be installed in a matter of minutes by anyone familiar with computers (see Figure 11.11)

NSES Content Standard B. Physical Science: Motions and Forces

Temperature probe   Light sensor

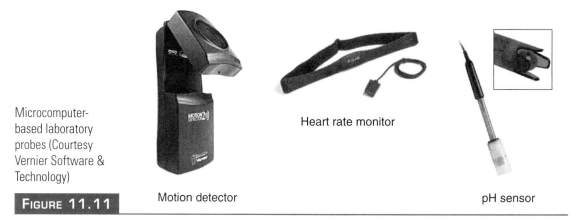

Microcomputer-
based laboratory
probes (Courtesy
Vernier Software &
Technology)

Heart rate monitor

Motion detector   pH sensor

FIGURE 11.11

EVALUATING COMPUTER SOFTWARE

NSES Teaching
Standard F. Participating
in Program Planning

As you have seen, there is a tremendous array of computer software available. Some programs are free. Some cost only the price of the disc plus postage. Some are expensive. Some require additional items of apparatus. As you also have seen, computer programs vary enormously in the degree of children's inquiry they can support.

Before investing in computer software for use by children, you need to know what you are getting. Does it foster inquiry? Is it user-friendly? Has it been debugged? Is the content appropriate? Can it be networked so that many children can use it simultaneously in a computer lab? Is it affordable?

A software evaluation profile is provided in Figure 11.12. The profile asks for "boilerplate" information above the double line; this information is obtainable from the manufacturer. The essence of the evaluation is contained in the items below the double line that require you to preview and rate the program. The suggested rating score system is subjective; the overall recommendation is the result of the entire review.

SOFTWARE EVALUATION PROFILE

Evaluator _____

Title and version _____

Subject area _____

Cost _____ Cost for site license/Number of sites _____

Grade Level		**Type**	
High school	_____	Informational	_____
Middle school	_____	Drill and practice	_____
Upper elementary	_____	Tutorial	_____
Lower elementary	_____	Game	_____
Kindergarten	_____	Simulation	_____
Preschool	_____	Lab assistance	_____
Teacher	_____	Lab activities	_____
		Teacher support	_____
		Organizational	_____
		Teacher utility	_____
		Other	_____

Amount of Effort/Supervision Required for Students to Learn Program

        Much   _____

        Some   _____

        Little   _____

Hardware Requirements

   Type of computer needed _____

   Hard drive capacity required _____

   CD drive needed? _____

   Other special hardware required _____

- -

Rating Scores (10 points each)		**OVERALL RECOMMENDATION**	
Documentation & instructions	_____	Strongly recommended	_____
General design	_____	Recommended	_____
Content	_____	Questionable	_____
Technical quality	_____	Not recommended	_____
Ease of program use	_____		
Ease of installation	_____		
TOTAL (60 MAX)	**_____**		

- -

COMMENTS _____

_____

_____

Software evaluation profile

FIGURE 11.12

NSES Teaching Standard F. Participating in Program Planning

Sources of Computer Software

There are so many sources of computer software that it is difficult to know what is available and which of these could be considered for the elementary science education program. Nonetheless, there are several reliable sources you will want to check regularly.

Many journals and magazines, such as *Educational Technology* and *Journal of Computers in Mathematics and Science Teaching,* contain software review columns; these will keep you apprised of new software and will aid in the evaluation process. *Technology and Children,* published by the International Technology Education Association (ITEA) is a journal devoted to technology education in elementary schools. *NSTA Reports,* published by the National Science Teachers Association, contains periodic listings of computer software that has been reviewed and assessed. Specialized journals such as *Science and Children, Science Scope,* and *Childhood Education* also contain reviews of software.

See the Student Book Companion Web Site for a direct link to the ITEA Web site.

▶ Tom Snyder Productions, a subsidiary of *Scholastic,* produces a large number of award-winning software titles for the main subject areas and for utility work. Many are used in this textbook. Examples include the following:

- *Inspiration*
- *Kidspiration*
- *The Graph Club*
- *Graph Master*
- *Science Court Explorations* (grades 2–4)
- *Science Court* (grades 4–6)
- *Science Seekers* (grades 5–8)

▶ Vernier Software & Technology produces a large number of award-winning microcomputer-based laboratory probes, hardware, and software. Many of their applications have been adapted for use in elementary schools, and all are user-friendly. Several have been used in this textbook. Examples include the following:

Direct links to the Tom Snyder Productions and Vernier Software and Technologies Web sites are available on the Student Book Companion Web Site.

- Barometer
- Dissolved Oxygen Probe
- Heart Rate Monitor
- Light Sensor
- Motion Detectors
- Oxygen Gas Sensor

- pH Sensor
- Relative Humidity Sensor
- Salinity Sensor
- Sound Level Meter
- Temperature Probes

Keep a running list of excellent software titles you come across and add to it as you find new software that will help you meet the science inquiry needs of the children in your class. In all cases, you should give special consideration to the degree to which a particular technology or technological application supports the process-oriented inquiry method of science instruction and the degree to which it enables children to explore on their own.

THE INTERNET

The development and growth of the Internet probably is the largest factor contributing to the explosive growth in accessibility to information that we are experiencing today. There are hundreds of billions of pages on the Internet, most of which are readily accessible using common search engines.

NSES Teaching Standard A. Inquiry-Based Program

The Internet is a complex network of electronic communications that loosely connects millions of information sites worldwide. It was developed in 1969 as a military application to ensure that communications would continue uninterrupted even if global conditions were to become catastrophic. The World Wide Web was developed in 1991 to permit the inclusion of links in local sites that can take the viewer to other related local and distant sites.

Each and every site has its own unique address that normally starts with http:// (which stands for *HyperText Transfer Protocol*). The address is called the URL (*Uniform Resource Locator*) and contains several elements separated by dots or forward slashes. The letters at the end of the site designate its affiliation. Common designations include *.edu* for an educational institution; *.gov* for a government site; *.com* for a commercial site; *.mil* for a military site; and *.org* for a site that is a non-commercial organization.

There are millions of Internet sites useful for elementary science education. Of course, much of this material is unsubstantiated, and you should look at sites with some degree of skepticism. It is a good idea to look for the source of information on Internet sites and to judge their value accordingly. For example, Web pages dealing with Gardner's theory of multiple intelligences that are developed and maintained by Harvard University are more likely to be authoritative than Web pages prepared by commercial developers of teacher materials.

Of particular interest to science teachers is *The Gateway to Educational Materials* (GEM) Web site, an initiative of the U.S. Department of Education. GEM provides access to thousands of educational resources, including lesson plans, curriculum units, research, professional guides, activities, tips for teachers, background information, and other education-related materials available on the Internet. When teachers connect to GEM, they are able to use the GEM database search facility instead of other Internet search engines to locate quality educational resources quickly and efficiently.

The National Science Teachers Association (1999) has developed a program called *SciLINKS®* in which science textbook publishers can elect to include Internet icons and codes in the margins at key subject areas that direct users to professionally selected Web sites which support the learning of the topic referenced. *SciLINKS* codes are included in the books NSTA publishes and in many of the articles that appear in their journals. To search for Internet information, students and teachers access the *SciLINKS* Web site and enter the code that guides them to several of the best Web sites on the Internet dealing with that topic. The Web site links are selected and maintained by teachers to ensure appropriateness and recency.

NSTA also offers a classroom resource called *SciGuide* to help science teachers integrate the Internet in their teaching. Each guide deals with a different topic and includes approximately 100 Internet resources. A recent *SciGuide* is the *Coral Ecosystem SciGuide* that helps teachers understand and teach about the fragile coral animal, coral reefs, and the coral reef ecosystem (NSTA and NOAA, 2006).

The National Science Digital Library was established in 2000 and includes more than 1½ million resources useful to science teachers, such as pictures, videos, audios, animations, software, datasets, journal articles, lesson plans, and many others. The quality of each item has been verified. It is free and it has a first-time user section where you can learn how to use it.

The Internet offers the full range of technological applications depicted in the continuum shown in Figure 11.1, from tutoring to interactive and experimenting uses. The Internet is the ideal classroom tool to support constructivist teaching and learning, and it is essential that teachers find ways to augment their curricula and instruction to incorporate this very important resource to help children learn.

 Direct links to the Web site sources cited in this section are available on the Student Book Companion Web Site.

▶ Because of the huge number of software and video titles available, and because different teachers will assess different titles from their own perspectives, very few titles are given in this text. In addition, multimedia materials come and go, and those that are considered excellent today may not be available in a year or two. You should develop the habit of keeping your own lists of multimedia titles and Internet addresses. Draw on the information your colleagues have found as well as what you, yourself, have found.

▶ Many Web sites useful for elementary science teachers are available on the Student Book Companion Web Site. They are "hot links," which means all you need to do is click on a link and you will automatically reach the desired Web site. The links are monitored regularly and are updated and augmented frequently so they are kept current. We have included links to a few of the more popular Web sites to whet your appetite. Try accessing them to see what you can find, and use these sites as springboards to investigate more sites.

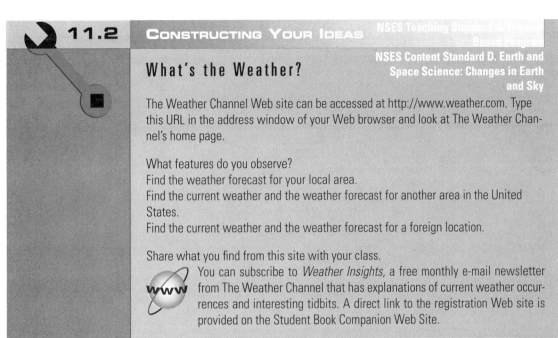

11.2   CONSTRUCTING YOUR IDEAS   NSES Teaching Standard A: Inquiry-Based Program

NSES Content Standard D: Earth and Space Science: Changes in Earth and Sky

What's the Weather?

The Weather Channel Web site can be accessed at http://www.weather.com. Type this URL in the address window of your Web browser and look at The Weather Channel's home page.

What features do you observe?
Find the weather forecast for your local area.
Find the current weather and the weather forecast for another area in the United States.
Find the current weather and the weather forecast for a foreign location.

Share what you find from this site with your class.

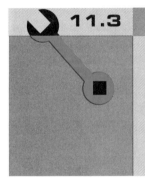

You can subscribe to *Weather Insights,* a free monthly e-mail newsletter from The Weather Channel that has explanations of current weather occurrences and interesting tidbits. A direct link to the registration Web site is provided on the Student Book Companion Web Site.

11.3   CONSTRUCTING YOUR IDEAS   NSES Teaching Standard A: Inquiry-Based Program

NSES Content Standard D: Earth and Space Science: Earth in the Solar System

Exploring NASA

The address for the home page of NASA is http://www.nasa.gov. Type this URL in the address window of your Web browser and look at the enormous array of information available for students and teachers that can be accessed through the NASA Web pages. Select one link and follow it through, link after link, page after page, and summarize what you find. Share your findings with your class.

11.4   CONSTRUCTING YOUR IDEAS   NSES Professional Development Standard C: Lifelong Learning

Surfing the Web for Science Sites

Use your Web browser to find Internet sites suitable for elementary science education. Type a few descriptive words in the search box such as "elementary science education," "elementary science activities," or "elementary science teaching." Or, you could enter specific topics, such as "weather," "dinosaurs," "gears," and the

Continued on next page

like, perhaps combined with limiting terms, such as "children," "elementary school," "activities," "elementary school activities," "teaching," "lesson plans," and so on.

Explore some of the promising sites that your search produced. When you come across a site you believe would be useful to yourself and other members of your class, write a one- or two-sentence summary of the site together with its URL and distribute it to other class members. Make a class list or booklet for use by all class members. If your class has its own Web page or uses an electronic bulletin board or message center, post your discoveries for others to access.

USING THE INTERNET IN THE ELEMENTARY SCIENCE CLASSROOM

NSES Teaching Standard A. Inquiry-Based Program
NSES Teaching Standard B. Guiding and Facilitating Learning
NSES Teaching Standard F. Participating in Program Planning

The question arises of how you can incorporate the Internet into your elementary science curriculum. Craig (1999) suggests asking children to create a list of topics relating to the subject matter being studied that they would like to learn about, with the top choices becoming the focus of class investigations. Those topics for which information is unavailable in libraries or through community resources then become the subjects for Internet browsing. Students explore the Internet either individually or in groups. Of course, children must first learn how to explore the Internet; the technology or media specialist in the school often meets that need, frequently in technology lab settings. Waight and Abd-El-Khalid (2007) observe that teachers tend to use technology like traditional methodologies and that they need to work toward using technologies to help their students learn. And Kuiper, Volman, and Terwel (2005); McNabb (2005/2006); and Cohen and Cowen (2007) note that children need to be taught how to navigate the previously unfamiliar hyperlinked text found on the Internet.

The federal government has worked to support the implementation of educational technologies in our schools. A major area of support has been the development of educational technology plans for the nation. The First National Educational Technology Plan was released in 1996. The second plan was released in 2000 to reflect the tremendous rate of growth in technology. The third National Education Technology Plan was released in 2005 and centers around seven action steps that will "help states and districts prepare today's students for the opportunities and challenges of tomorrow" (U.S. Department of Education, 2005, p. 1). The seven action steps are:

1. Strengthen leadership.

2. Consider innovative budgeting.

3. Improve teacher training.

4. Support e-learning and virtual schools.

5. Encourage broadband access.

6. Move toward digital content.

7. Integrate data systems.

A direct link to the third National Education Technology Plan is available on the Student Book Companion Web Site.

Not everyone believes that technology can be used to help educate our children. Oppenheimer (2003), an award-winning journalist and outspoken critic of educational technology, shows many examples in which technology either has failed to improve student learning or has failed to work. Consequently, he suggests that education would be better served by increasing attention to the real-life experiences rather than the virtual experiences of the students. However, Burns (2005/2006) urges that before we dismiss computers as an expensive fad, educators should ensure they are using computers to their maximum instructional potential in fostering student learning. And Friedman (2005) takes the position that the most important force of change in the late 20th and early 21st centuries has been the explosion of technology.

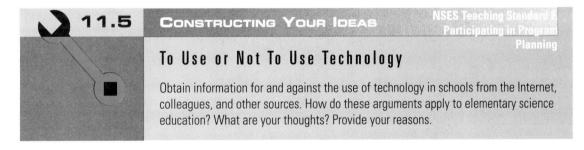

11.5   **CONSTRUCTING YOUR IDEAS**   NSES Teaching Standard F, Participating in Program Planning

To Use or Not To Use Technology

Obtain information for and against the use of technology in schools from the Internet, colleagues, and other sources. How do these arguments apply to elementary science education? What are your thoughts? Provide your reasons.

WebQuests

A WebQuest is a student-centered inquiry-oriented activity designed by teachers in which some or all of the information with which students interact comes from the Internet (Norton & Wiburg, 2003). It is a semidirected plan for students to use in independent investigations of topics that combines discovery learning, integrated approaches, and technology. A WebQuest is a tried-and-true format for investigating real-world problems using various available technologies. It includes the following basic components (Dodge, 1999):

1. An introduction that sets the stage for the inquiry

2. A basic task

3. A set of information sources including links to Internet sites, e-mail conferencing, searchable databases, computer programs, books, magazines, and other available resources

4. A description of the process the students should go through in accomplishing the task, broken into steps

5. Guidance on ways to organize the material

6. Conclusion that also includes ideas for further study

7. Evaluation through a rubric that is part of the WebQuest.

 Direct links to some highly rated WebQuests are provided on the Student Book Companion Web site. We also have provided a direct link to the WebQuest site at San Diego State University, its birthplace, where you can access teacher training materials and full information.

The WebQuest employs the guided inquiry method of instruction where the teacher's role is to get students started on an investigation and facilitate their continued inquiry in the directions their efforts and interests take them (see Chapter 5). Using WebQuests, students can investigate virtually any subject they would like to pursue as thoroughly as they would like. For example, they can analyze the effects of the space program, take a virtual trip to bird- or turtle-nesting sanctuaries, prepare a virtual zoo exhibit, investigate the destructive forces of tornadoes and hurricanes, simulate animal survival in a disappearing forest, and build a better mousetrap.

Many WebQuests dealing with a wide variety of topics have been prepared and are available on the Internet. These can be adopted intact or can be tailored to meet the needs of your class. Once you "get the hang" of WebQuests, you may want to develop your own and possibly post them on the Internet for others to use as well.

School and Class Web Sites

Many teachers develop their own class Web sites that contain information about their classes, homework postings and helps, notices of class activities, and examples of children's work. Numerous Internet sites provide step-by-step instructions for developing your own Web site. Some have templates you can use to simplify the process, and some allow you to post your self-prepared Web page free of charge. Many teachers have the children in their classes develop their own Internet sites to which they publish their work as a means of demonstrating their achievement. These sites normally are linked to the main class Web site.

Scientific Research

You and the children in your classes can use the Internet to participate in scientific research efforts. For example, bird migrations and animal habitats are tracked through several Internet sites.

- In *Journey North,* children forward their sightings of birds through the Internet to be included with the data. Periodic results are forwarded to all contributors to enable them to chart the migration habits of given species of birds.

- *Operation Ruby Throat* is an international, cross-disciplinary research initiative designed for K–12 teachers and their students in North and Central America. Students make observations of the ruby-throated hummingbird and input their observations into the Internet site. Data is exchanged among all participants via the Internet and is made available to practicing scientists who are studying the habitats of the birds and the effects of habitat disruption. The scientists provide input and guidance to the participating teachers and students during all phases of the project.

- Children can participate in the *Great Backyard Bird Count,* a scientific study of bird migration and habits, by counting birds in their school yard or their own backyards and inputting the data. Children also can participate in *Frogwatch USA,* a scientific study that gives students the opportunity to collect and input information about frogs to a national Web site, thus helping increase the information needed by scientists to develop means of protecting frogs and toads.

Direct links to the Web sites for these Internet research projects are available on the Student Book Companion Web Site.

In a project that was conducted by successive classes over many years, first- and second-graders investigated several factors about a local water habitat that appeared to be deteriorating. The teachers and students used word processors, spreadsheets, and presentation software to develop a Web site where they presented the results of their inquiries. They also prepared presentations for their City Parks commission, which approved funding to restore the habitat based on the work the classes did (Wiske, 2004).

Bringing the World Into the Classroom

Internet technology also permits teachers to bring the world into the classroom, such as in the following examples:

- *The JASON Project* is a science-based interdisciplinary curriculum in which children participate in multimedia virtual research expeditions. A different focus is provided each year. Although the project is designed for older children, those as young as third or fourth grade age have participated successfully with modifications in reading level requirements (JASON Project, 2001).

The Student Book Companion Web Site has direct links to the JASON Project Web Site and the NASA Web site.

- Children who are working on projects in their schools in the United States and desire information, experiment replication, or feedback from children elsewhere can make the request through e-mail or the Internet. For example, recall that in Chapter 4 (In The Schools 4.8), we told of a project wherein children wanted to find out why underwear turns inside out in the drier. One child wondered if the same thing would happen in Australia, because it is in the Southern Hemisphere. E-mail would enable the child to ask the question and enlist Australian children to pursue the same project.

- Children can communicate with astronauts in orbit via e-mail and closed-circuit television transmitted by satellite to ascertain the current status of experiments they themselves designed to be carried out in space. Indeed, children and their teachers are invited to prepare experiments to be carried out in space aboard NASA spacecraft. If accepted, the astronauts perform the experiment in space while communicating with the classes of children through closed-circuit television.

As you can tell, there are many ways to incorporate Internet technology into the curriculum. Owston (1997) reports, "When computers are introduced into classrooms, teachers inevitably report that they change their teaching style to allow students greater autonomy in their learning. They tend to shift their style of teaching from a didactic to a more project-based approach" (p. 30). The overriding questions about how to incorporate Internet technology into the curriculum are "Does this application help children *do* science?" and "Does this application help children assume ownership of their inquiries?"

Internet Safety

The Student Book Companion Web Site has direct links to the SafeKids.com Web site, an excellent source for specific information, tips, and sample contracts between parents and children that can be adapted for use in schools, and to the FBI Kids site that has safety tips for children using the Internet.

There is a very real concern over Internet safety. Filters are only partially effective in protecting children from pornography, stalkers, and other undesirable exposures. Craig (1999) provides guidelines for children's use of the Internet; these guidelines are presented in adapted form in Figure 11.13.

NETIQUETTE

- Obtain approval for your topic from your teacher before you use the Internet.
- Use *only* your topic selections in exploring the Internet resources.
- Check for correct spelling.
- Read the description of the search results *carefully* before you click on the site.
- When selecting a site, be sure the title is related to your topic.
- Skim and scan the site for information related to your topic.
- Take notes.
- Record the addresses (URLs) of useful sites.
- *Chat Rooms are OFF LIMITS!*
- *NEVER* give out your name or the name of your school or your teacher!

Rules for children exploring the Internet

FIGURE 11.13

Ultimately, it is the children's own behavior and sense of responsibility that determines Internet safety, and you need to talk with them about "do's" and "don't's."

E-MAIL

E-mail (The *E* stands for *electronic*) involves typing messages on a computer and sending them through designated telephone or Internet lines to recipients anywhere in the world. E-mail facilities normally accompany a subscription to an Internet service provider (ISP) and each subscriber has a unique address. To use e-mail, type the address of the intended recipient in the address box, type the message, and click *send.* The recipient will receive your message in a matter of seconds.

NSES Teaching Standard A. Inquiry-Based Science Program
NSES Teaching Standard F. Participating in Program Planning

VIDEO AND TELEVISION IN THE ELEMENTARY SCIENCE CLASSROOM

Many advances have been made in the field of video and television. Commercial and public television stations offer instructional videos that are telecast during regular school hours so schools can receive them and pipe them into appropriate classrooms. The Public Broadcasting System (PBS) regularly airs programs on science and nature. The Learning Channel airs programs on science topics suitable for children. The Weather Channel broadcasts daily 10-minute explanations of weather phenomena and offers documentary videos for use in schools (see Constructing Your Ideas 11.2). Most educational television material is copyright-cleared and free of commercials. Cable in the Classroom monitors and publicizes educational telecasts and also provides schedules of upcoming educational programs.

NSES Teaching Standard A. Inquiry-Based Science Program
NSES Teaching Standard F. Participating in Program Planning

TV PROGRAMS

Several TV programs are worth mentioning because of their applicability to elementary science education:

- *Curious George* taps the innate eagerness of children to learn how things work by example.

- *Go, Diego, Go!* provides scientifically accurate information about animals and their adaptations to their environments.

- *The Discovery Channel School* includes such programs as *Animal Planet, Discovery Health,* and *Travel Channel.* Teacher materials are available.

Direct links to the Web sites devoted to these programs and sources are available on the Student Book Companion Web Site.

- *Bill Nye the Science Guy* has been off the air since 1998, but classroom editions of the show are available.

- *PBS* offers teacher support material for science and mathematics.

One of the advances in educational technology has been video production by children (see *The Video* in Chapter 10). All it takes to help children make their own videos is a little know-how (or the assistance of the media specialist) and a desire to let children expand their horizons. Yerrick & Ross (2001) found that incorporating video production in elementary science education fostered children's understanding of how to do science as well as their organizational and writing skills, and that it served to "place children's voices and motivation for learning at the forefront of educational decisions" (p. 9).

A direct link to the Apple Learning Interchange Web site where many other useful links can also be accessed is available on the Student Book Companion Web Site.

To aid teachers and students in making their own videos, the Apple Computer Company has developed the Apple Learning Interchange, an Internet site that provides materials to help teachers in their teaching and their professional growth. A major section of the Web site is devoted to lesson ideas and help for developing videos on a variety of science topics.

INTERACTIVE WHITEBOARDS

An *interactive whiteboard* is an electronic whiteboard that interfaces with a computer (see Figure 11.14). The system includes a computer, a computer projector, the interactive whiteboard, and a cable that connects the whiteboard and the computer. The teacher projects the computer screen onto the interactive whiteboard and moves from behind the computer to the front of the room where virtually everything that is done on the computer can be done on the whiteboard. The primary differences are that with the interactive whiteboard, fingers and pens are used instead of the mouse, and teacher is in the front of the room instead of behind a computer in back. The interactive whiteboard allows the teacher to incorporate technology into group instruction rather than trying to arrange a whole class of students around one or two computers.

Teachers can do everything using the interactive whiteboard that they can do using a regular computer—perform manipulations, solve problems, graph data, explore Internet sites, interact with CD-ROMs, play games, explore simulations, and run any standard computer program. Work can be saved to the computer, and writing, diagrams, notes, and scribbles that people write on the board can be captured as a picture or a graphic by the computer with which it interfaces so it can be recalled or printed at a later time.

An interactive whiteboard (Used with permission of SMART Technologies ULC (www.smarttech .com). SMART Board, Notebook and the SMART logo are either registered trademarks or trademarks of SMART Technologies ULC.)

FIGURE 11.14

TECHNOLOGY FOR TEACHERS

Not only is technology advantageous for children's learning, it also is a tremendous help to teachers. Programs used primarily to help teachers do their administrative work sometimes are called *production* programs. These include word processing, spreadsheets, database programs, publishing programs, sign makers, banner makers, and other software teachers can use to help them in their work. You saw some of these applications earlier in this chapter.

Word processing programs make it possible for teachers to store, edit, and update written documents. Using the mail-merge feature available in most word processing programs, teachers can customize letters for individual recipients and generate individual mailing labels, eliminating the need to spend hours writing addresses by hand.

Spreadsheets significantly reduce the time teachers need to spend calculating grades, and they guarantee accuracy. In the spreadsheet, rows are labeled with children's names, and columns are used for the various numerical grades. The teacher writes simple formulas for grade calculations and enters these formulas in appropriate summary columns. As each set of grades is recorded, the computer automatically calculates averages; at the end of the marking period, the grades are ready for transfer to periodic reports. School districts sometimes provide gradesheet programs that interface with other student records. Many commercial "gradebook" programs are available; however, before investing in one, be sure that it meets the needs of your class.

Database programs are ideal for keeping track of student data. On a single database, you can record children's names, addresses, phone numbers, parents' names, the buses they take, medical problems, learning styles, interests, hobbies, and other pertinent information. You can sort to

NSES Professional Development Standard C. Lifelong Learning

obtain collective information such as names of children who take a certain bus, common medical problems, all children with the same first name, or children with similar learning styles, interests, or hobbies for purposes of group formation.

E-mail is an ideal and convenient form of communication. It is easier to use than conventional forms of communication and is a time-saver.

The Internet is an indispensable source of information, lesson plans, lesson helps, activity ideas, and a whole host of other needs.

Preparing tests using test-generating software saves huge amounts of time. Once the initial test is written, items can be added, deleted, or changed; the order of questions can be varied; certain items or categories of items can be selected; and entirely new tests—including several forms of the same test—can be generated from the original test. To adopt a con-structivist approach in computer-generated and computer-scored tests, invite children to explain their response to any item that was marked "incorrect" by the computer. In this way, you save time by eliminating the need to hand-grade the tests and by encouraging children to offer their individual explanations on an exception-only basis.

Many school districts have adopted computerized systems for one or more administrative tasks. These systems often are interfaced with the teacher's individual classroom systems.

TEACHER VOICE

When I walked into the Florence E. Smith School of Science, Math, and Technology in West Hartford, Connecticut, I had no idea how much I would learn about teaching science or how much technology I would learn to use. I was the first elementary science teacher in this one-of-a-kind position in my district. My duties were to set up and teach in a state-of-the-art science lab in this elementary magnet school. Each student in kindergarten through fifth grade was scheduled to have learning time in the lab every week. I only had very basic knowledge of technology when I first started; I could turn on a computer and handle basic word processing, but that was about it. The idea of using advanced technology to teach science was foreign to me, as was this idea of using the "constructivist" method to teach science. All my lessons in the beginning were teacher-directed activities, not student-directed experiments. Technology in my early days meant eyedroppers, hand lenses, and pencils. As I became more comfortable with my new position, I began to notice how my students learned best. All of the students, regardless of grade level, got excited when I brought them outside and they spotted a worm. We would bring it in, look at it with the hand lenses, ask questions, and construct hypotheses. Sometimes these questions led to experiments, and sometimes they didn't. It didn't matter because they were learning and loving it. I saw their excitement and started to take risks with more open-ended lessons where I wasn't sure of what the students might ask or what experiment we might end up doing. It was a little frightening at first, but it was also very interesting and fun for both my students and me. Little by little, I have become comfortable with this method of teaching. There hasn't been a boring moment in my classes since I began using the constructivist method. The use of advanced technology in my teaching came a little later.

It is entirely possible to teach very good, hands-on, inquiry-based lessons in science without using advanced technology. All that is needed are a few of the five senses and part of the brain. However, for every piece of technology added, another layer is added to the lessons, another chance is given for the students to discover information, and another opportunity exists for understanding. Technology is a tool. It is a tool that will stretch students' senses as when they are using hand lenses and microscopes, a tool that will give them information they need to progress as when they use CD-ROMs and access the Internet, and a tool for them to share and learn from others as when they use presentation software and video cameras.

I have found that as I incorporated each new piece of technology into the lab, it has brought a new level of inquiry with it. The flexible camera was the first piece of technology I attempted to use for teaching. It allows me to present what is under a microscope or on a table to the entire class via a TV monitor. I introduce protozoans, small microscopic animals that live in water, to the third grade as part of their food chains and food webs unit of study. The flexible camera allows me to show all the students what these little creatures are, and show them extraneous things like air bubbles that should not be confused with protozoans. The students can move forth with confidence that they are looking at the correct material, they can make observations and inferences about these creatures, and they can engage in thorough class discussions about them.

Computers have made it possible for students to see and do much more than is possible without one. For example, my students visit Mars on a CD-ROM as they collect information while planning the structure of a Mars rover they will craft from Legos®. They first test their Mars rover on a mock Mars obstacle course during a simulation. The information they collect helps them make decisions about what their rovers should include. Should it have four large tires or eight smaller ones? How tall should it be? They construct the rover and then attach it to an engine and infrared controllers. They use a small digital camera to see where it is going, and a notebook computer with software to send and receive information from the rover. Their rovers must navigate the obstacle course of sand and rock while sending pictures and receiving movement commands from the team of students. Using all this technology is great, but during the process, students also learn a valuable lesson: technology doesn't always work. It can be very frustrating to get technology to work correctly. It requires problem solving and patience. When it does work, it is exciting and opens their minds to new possibilities. I like to think they get a little taste of what the NASA scientists do when they send rovers to Mars.

The interactive whiteboard is by far the best technological addition I have made to my lab and has had the greatest impact on my inquiry-based, constructivist teaching. The applications I have found for it have been inspiring! Since I only have one computer in my room, gathering a class of 23 students around this single computer is nearly impossible. The interactive whiteboard allows me to project Web sites, pictures, and videos so all can see. I recently had an opportunity to see how that could work in a constructivist context. A first-grade class walked in for their weekly lab time after a story in the library. A voice popped up as they were getting seated and said, "Mrs. Bennett, moose don't have whiskers!" I questioned the student as to how he came up with that fact, and his response was, "We read a nonfiction book and looked up 'whiskers' in the index and it wasn't there." We had a short discussion about how everything can't be covered in every book, so perhaps it was just left out. Or maybe it was true. How could we find out? Someone suggested looking at a moose. Many retorted that doing such a thing wasn't possible here in West Hartford. I suggested that it might be possible and left them wondering how it could be accomplished as we went on with the scheduled lesson. Toward the end of their lab time, I brought up some pictures of moose from a website. I projected them on the interactive whiteboard. We scrutinized the pictures, trying to decide whether or not moose had whiskers. We discussed the purpose of whiskers on cats, mice, and dogs, and whether the same would apply to moose as well. The consensus was that moose don't have whiskers, or if they do they are too short to be seen or to be of much use. We promised each other that we would keep looking for the correct answer, but what a great conversation to have with six-year-olds, and it would not have happened in that manner without my computer and interactive whiteboard setup.

A similar situation occurred when the hurricanes hit Florida. I was easily able to pull up radar maps on the Internet and have discussions with fourth-grade students regarding the path, intensity, and size of these storms. It is wonderful to be able to have these teachable moments at the time of occurrence. This is when the investigations have the greatest impact on students, and when they can lead to some wonderfully meaningful demonstrations or experiments. In another example, my second graders were very curious and concerned about the tsunamis in Indonesia. They had many questions about what was going on and why the tsunamis happened. I took a few days to download some pictures and simulations, and I showed them before and after satellite pictures of some of the harder hit areas on the interactive whiteboard. The amount of debris alone in these pictures showed the power of water without its being traumatizing to these young children. We watched simulations of what tsunamis look like and how warning systems work. After using all that technology, we conducted a simple activity of making waves in a jar using blue-tinted water and mineral oil. The next class session was more technical; I set up a simulation in a baby pool with a plastic coffee can attached to a string in the water to simulate the upheaval of an earthquake, using sand for land. I knew the wave action would happen too quickly to really see, so I used my digital video camera to film several trials. Again, thanks to the interactive whiteboard, I was able to hook up the camera in minutes and show them what happened in slow motion. The level of understanding these seven- and eight-year-olds have about tsunamis and wave action has greatly increased because of the application of this technology.

The uses of an interactive whiteboard go beyond surfing Web sites. It has diagrams and pictures in the software that have been very useful to label or illustrate a point, and the graphing capability has been very valuable. The fifth grade studies ecosystems, and we spent part of our time looking at specific components of ecosystems. Recently, we played a game outdoors that simulated the effect of limiting factors on a herd of deer. When the game was done, we headed back to the lab where we entered the population data directly onto a line graph on the interactive whiteboard. We discussed the trends and generalizations in that format, and I saved the graph and printed it. I then photocopied the graph and handed it out during the next class when we extrapolated the population and looked deeper into its effect on the environment such as how the deer's population affects the population of predators. This discussion was much more constructivist in nature than it might have been because of the interactive whiteboard. Everyone was able to see, contribute, and go beyond what was done in the simulation because we could readily share or exchange the information.

These examples are only a small part of what is possible with the technology available today. It can be very overwhelming and frightening to try to think of ways to incorporate technology into your teaching, especially if you are unfamiliar with it. Take one thing at a time. I certainly did not start doing all of this all at once. It has taken several years and a lot of trial-and-error to get to where I am now. My next plan is to write a grant to add Palm Pilots and probes for gathering data such as temperature, speed, light intensity, and pH. I'm hoping that they will add a new dimension to my lessons just as the technology I have added has in the past. The great thing about technology is that it is always dynamic— there's always something new to discover and pass on to others.

Tracy Bennett

Elementary Science Teacher, Kindergarten Through Grade 5
Florence E. Smith School of Science, Math, and Technology
West Hartford, Connecticut

GETTING STARTED

NSES Professional
Development
Standard C. Lifelong
Learning

The array of technology available to support process-oriented inquiry science programs is dazzling. Terminology often seems indecipherable, choices are seemingly infinite, and hardware can be expensive. How do you get started?

If you already are familiar with computers and other technology, you may feel ready to jump right in and enrich your classes with a wide array of computer applications. However, if you are uncomfortable with technology, it is a good idea to start slowly.

Every teacher should know how to use at least a word processing program, a spreadsheet program, a graphing program, e-mail, and the Internet. Consider signing up for a computer course or two; many are offered at colleges and universities and at local school districts in the form of in-service training. Technology training also is available through federal- and state-sponsored programs. Courses range from entry level (starting with how to turn a computer on) to highly sophisticated training. The short time invested in becoming familiar with basic programs will save you countless hours in your professional role and enable you to use computer technology effectively in your classroom.

Chances are that you are being asked to do certain technology-based activities in this class. You may find that you must access an on-line syllabus, communicate with your instructor via e-mail, use an electronic bulletin board, develop a Web site, search the Internet, and make presentations using presentation software.

As you begin to incorporate technology in your classroom, try one or two applications that seem to have particular merit, such as using a word processing program to write letters and reports, using a spreadsheet to keep track of grades or attendance, using a program to create signs and banners, or searching the Internet to find ideas for a unit or lesson you are planning. Do not be dismayed by initial difficulties; we all experience them at first. Keep working with the programs you choose, and you will be amazed at how rapidly you achieve proficiency and you will be amazed at how much work and time you save.

Then try a scientific application, perhaps a tutoring program that presents a unit you are teaching. Children can run through this program as an additional activity or as a review activity. Many teachers allow children to include computer work in their free-time choices. Perhaps a game or two might be appropriate, or a program on some topic that is interesting to your children but that you will not be able to include in your curriculum.

When you decide it is time to use e-mail, the Internet, or an experimenting application, you may wish to demonstrate it to the children first using a computer projector or an interactive whiteboard if they are available, or by having children watch you at the computer before you have them do the activity themselves.

When the time comes for you to provide input into the district's or the school's budget, be prepared to discuss the virtues of technology; your voice and your expertise may help put your school on the cybernetic information highway. You can serve on your local school committee for software evaluation, and you can help develop the 5-year plan for technology in your school. You can request that your school subscribe to technology magazines.

As you progress in your quest to use modern technology in your classroom, your excitement will mount from day to day. Keep adding to your store of information, expertise, and software, and you will find you are helping your students open doors to inquiry never before available. With technology, there is no limit to children's inquiries.

NSES Teaching Standard F. Participating in Program Planning
NSES Program Standard F. Encourages, Supports, and Sustains Teachers

Conclusion

In this chapter, you have examined a variety of advances in educational technology from the constructivist point of view. A continuum suggesting levels of technology use was presented to help you decide which types of technology you might use in your science program. A hierarchy of uses ranges from tutoring and simulation applications through interactive uses such as word processing, spreadsheets, databases, graphing programs, e-mail, and the Internet, to experimenting uses represented by laboratory computer interfacing systems. Much available technology is preprogrammed to some degree, thus limiting student inquiry; however, many applications, especially the Internet, can aid children in conducting their own inquiries. As an elementary science educator, you must consider the extent to which a given program or application aids children in investigating their own questions.

One of the goals of learning technology is to become "technologically literate." Technology was once considered futuristic. The future is here, and advances in technology provide unlimited access to learning opportunities never even imagined. It is worth the effort it takes to become technologically current. It is essential that teachers use technology in the classroom to provide the richest education possible for our students.

CHAPTER 11

Additional Questions for Discussion

1. Max Frisch is quoted as having said that technology is "the knack of so arranging the world that we don't have to experience it." Discuss how today's educational technology applications can help children experience the world.

2. What advice would you give to an individual who claims that technology is too expensive to be included in schools—that children can learn just as well without it?

3. How can you use technology in your elementary science instruction to help children in their inquiries?

4. How can you use the Internet in your elementary science instruction to help children in their inquiries?

5. How can you use technology to help you as a teacher?

Internet Activities

Use the Internet to look up information about various dinosaurs. Then use this information to build a dinosaur database that can be used by elementary school children.

Use the Internet to find arguments both for and against using technology to support elementary school science education. Use the results of your own explorations into educational technology and the various positions you read about to develop your own position statement about educational technology and your rationale for this position.

CHAPTER 12
CONCEPT MAPPING IN ELEMENTARY SCIENCE

Natural science always involves three things: the sequence of phenomena on which the science is based; the abstract concepts which call these phenomena to mind; and the words in which the concepts are expressed.

Antoine Laurent Lavoisier, *Traité Elémentaire de Chimie* (Paris: Cuchet, 1789)

The concept map is an extremely valuable tool in constructivist science education. It fosters achievement, provides relevance of material, and enables teachers to see how children are constructing information.

A concept map is a graphic representation of the way a person relates given concepts. Concepts appear hierarchically on the map from the most inclusive at the top to the least inclusive at the bottom. Lines connecting the concepts and labeled with linking words indicate the relationships among the concepts. Analogous to geographic maps, which portray land features and connecting roads and highways, concept maps show arrangement and connections of knowledge.

Concept mapping is used as a planning, learning, and assessment aid at all levels of education, from kindergarten through college. This device has been shown to foster increased achievement in science and, thus, has become increasingly popular in the field of science education. In their review of concept map literature, Nesbit and Adesope (2006) found that the use of concept maps is consistently associated with increased knowledge retention and is more effective than studying text passages, lists, and outlines. Concept maps are included in many student science texts, teacher's editions, and reference materials.

The purpose of this chapter is to show what concept maps are, how the technique can be taught, and how concept maps can be used to enhance the effectiveness of your elementary science program. As is true throughout this text, you will construct your own notions about concept mapping, and ultimately, you will decide the extent to which you feel the device can be useful to you and the children in your classes.

EXPLORING CONCEPT MAPPING

This section contains three activities that will enable you to learn how to construct concept maps. Please do all three.

First, please do the following activity as a class to gain familiarity with what a concept map is.

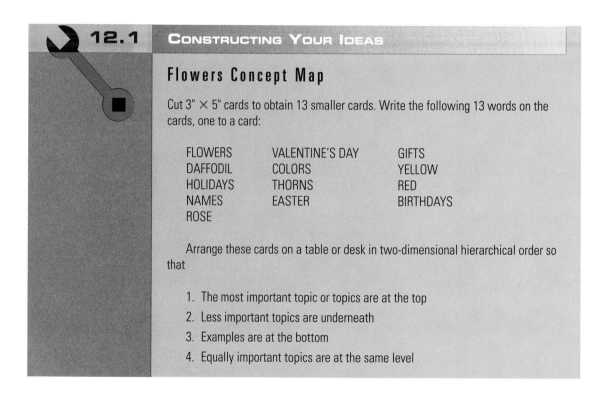

12.1   CONSTRUCTING YOUR IDEAS

Flowers Concept Map

Cut 3" × 5" cards to obtain 13 smaller cards. Write the following 13 words on the cards, one to a card:

FLOWERS	VALENTINE'S DAY	GIFTS
DAFFODIL	COLORS	YELLOW
HOLIDAYS	THORNS	RED
NAMES	EASTER	BIRTHDAYS
ROSE		

Arrange these cards on a table or desk in two-dimensional hierarchical order so that

1. The most important topic or topics are at the top
2. Less important topics are underneath
3. Examples are at the bottom
4. Equally important topics are at the same level

NSES Teaching Standard A. Inquiry-Based Program
NSES Professional Development Standard A. Learning Content Through Inquiry
NSES Program Standard B. Relevant, Inquiry-Based, and Connected with Other Subjects

It is very important that you do your *own* work in this exercise, because different students are very likely to come up with different arrays. There is no "correct" way of arranging these words, and there is no "incorrect" way. The way you arrange them represents the way *you* think about them.

▶ When you have completed your arrangement to your own satisfaction, copy the array you have made onto a sheet of blank paper, putting an oval or a circle around each word to separate it from the others as the cards were separated.

There are two reasons for committing your movable array to paper. One is to create something that will not blow around easily. The other is to encourage you to take ownership of your view of how these topics relate to each other.

Now, look at Figure 12.1. This is what *I* did with these words. Figure 12.1 is only one person's interpretation. This does not make it "right," nor does it make it "wrong." It simply makes it *mine.* Compare your array with the one shown in Figure 12.1. (Whereas you drew your concept map by hand, most of the concept map illustrations in this chapter have been done using *Inspiration*® software and its little cousin, *Kidspiration*®.) Is your array similar to the one shown in the figure? Does it have FLOWERS at the top? Perhaps yours looks more like one of those shown in Figure 12.2. Regardless of how you constructed your array, it is "right," because it represents the way you perceive the relationships.

▶ Take a minute or two and share your constructions with the rest of your class. Explain why you did what you did. A good way of doing this is to "talk your way" through the map.

For example, I could describe Figure 12.1 as follows:

Flowers have names, come in different colors, and are used as gifts. Names include "daffodil" and "rose," which has thorns. "Yellow" and "red" are examples of flower colors. Flowers are used as gifts on birthdays, Valentine's Day, holidays, and Easter.

During your sharing, take special note of the unique ways people visualized how these same 13 words relate to each other. Recall that constructivism suggests that people put notions together in ways that make sense to *them,* and that these ways are based on each person's prior

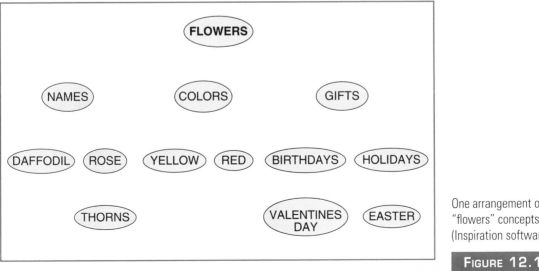

One arrangement of "flowers" concepts (Inspiration software)

FIGURE 12.1

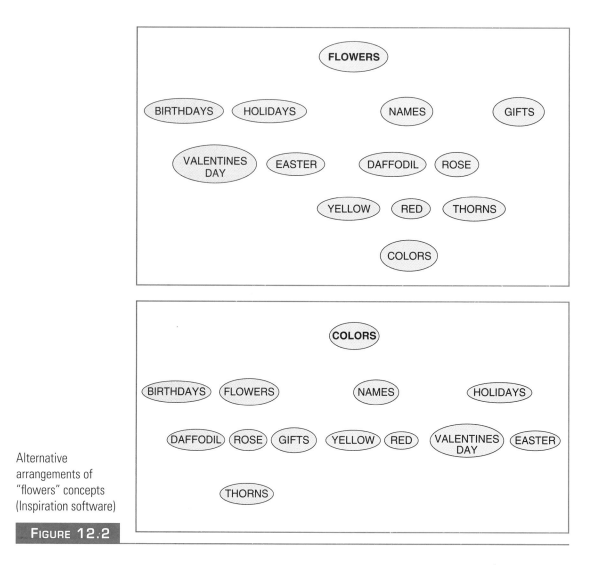

Alternative arrangements of "flowers" concepts (Inspiration software)

FIGURE 12.2

experiences. One of the values of concept mapping is that you can literally *see* how people perceive and construct information from the ways they arrange key words.

Each word in this exercise represents a *concept*. A concept is a word used to mean some kind of object, event, or condition. For example, the words *dog, grass,* and *chair* represent *object* concepts; the words *drive, sew,* and *hop* represent *event* concepts; and the words *hot, soft,* and *green* represent *condition* concepts. Concept words bring pictures to mind. Figure 12.3 provides an activity for you to tell the difference between words that represent concepts and words that do not.

The next step is to draw linking lines between the concepts on your diagram that relate to each other and to write one or two words on each

CONCEPTS

Which of these words represent concepts?

among	eating	loud
tree	air	truth
dog	swimming	group
soft	the	land
has	bright	shape
cat	when	thought
table	talking	question
metallic	may	color
yellow	be	deep
train	will	where

FIGURE 12.3

line to describe the relationship. These words are termed *linking words.* Linking words are words that show the relationship between two concepts. For example, the linking words are italicized in the following phrases:

Sky *is* blue

Vegetables *include* peas

Halloween *uses* pumpkins

Vegetables *for* health

Animals *such as* cows

Classified *by* color

Figure 12.4 contains an activity to help you gain familiarity in identifying linking words.

Concepts can be linked up, down, or sideways. If they are linked vertically or quasi-vertically, it is assumed the linking lines aim from the upper word to the lower word. Arrows may be used to show the direction of the relationship. In Figure 12.1, FLOWERS can be linked vertically with NAMES with the word *have.* DAFFODILS can be linked with YELLOW with the word *are.*

▶ Now, take a few minutes and add the lines with a linking word on each line.

Compare what you did with what I did as shown in Figure 12.5. This figure is the same as that shown in Figure 12.1, except that it also shows the relationships. Having done this, you now have completed your first concept map. Congratulations!

LINKING WORDS

Complete the following concept sentences with appropriate linking words.

1. Turkey _____ Thanksgiving.

2. Grass _____ green.

3. Fish _____ water.

4. Eagles _____ fly.

5. Dinner _____ dessert.

6. Student _____ teacher.

7. Birds _____ wings.

8. Music _____ loud.

9. Plants _____ tall.

10. Sun _____ moon.

11. Sun _____ energy.

12. Behavior _____ talking.

13. Window _____ square.

14. Teacher _____ questions.

15. Leading _____ group.

16. Triangle _____ shape.

17. Dogs _____ ducks.

18. Parents _____ children.

19. Clock _____ time.

20. Star _____ light.

(Adapted from E. C. Lucy and D. J. Martin. *Get Your Hands on Concept Mapping.* Workshop presented at Georgia Academy of Science annual meeting, Kennesaw, GA, April 29, 1994.)

FIGURE 12.4

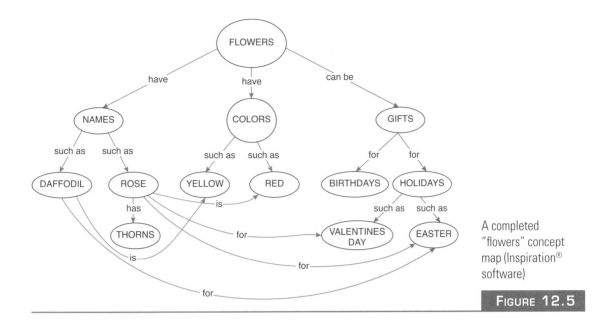

A completed "flowers" concept map (Inspiration® software)

FIGURE 12.5

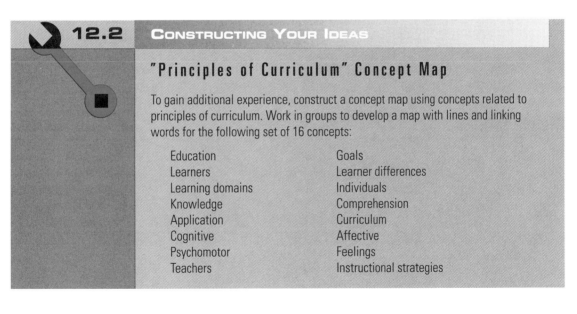

12.2   CONSTRUCTING YOUR IDEAS

"Principles of Curriculum" Concept Map

To gain additional experience, construct a concept map using concepts related to principles of curriculum. Work in groups to develop a map with lines and linking words for the following set of 16 concepts:

Education	Goals
Learners	Learner differences
Learning domains	Individuals
Knowledge	Comprehension
Application	Curriculum
Cognitive	Affective
Psychomotor	Feelings
Teachers	Instructional strategies

As an alternative, you may wish to create your own list of concepts. You can do this in different ways. (1) You can obtain a text on curriculum and extract key concepts from, say, the first chapter. (2) You can *brainstorm* the topic "Principles of Curriculum," write the concepts suggested by class members on the board, and create the concept map from them. However, it is suggested that fewer than 20 concepts be used for initial

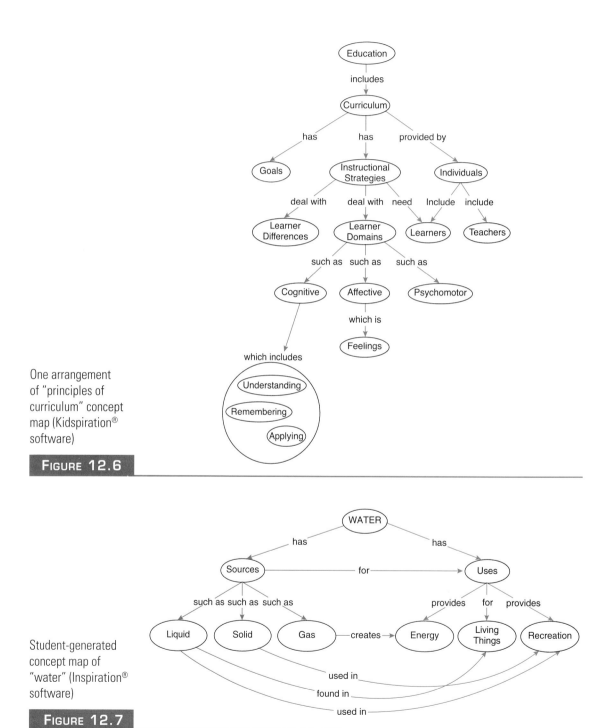

One arrangement of "principles of curriculum" concept map (Kidspiration® software)

FIGURE 12.6

Student-generated concept map of "water" (Inspiration® software)

FIGURE 12.7

concept mapping activities; that is why the above concept words have been limited to 16.

As you develop this concept map, be sure all members of your group agree with the way it is being constructed. One concept map using these terms is shown in Figure 12.6.

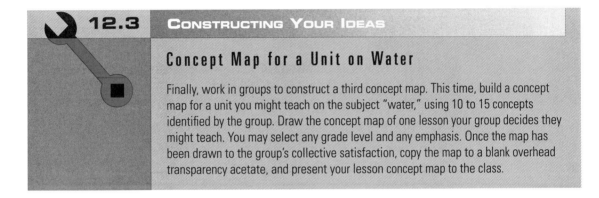

12.3 | CONSTRUCTING YOUR IDEAS

Concept Map for a Unit on Water

Finally, work in groups to construct a third concept map. This time, build a concept map for a unit you might teach on the subject "water," using 10 to 15 concepts identified by the group. Draw the concept map of one lesson your group decides they might teach. You may select any grade level and any emphasis. Once the map has been drawn to the group's collective satisfaction, copy the map to a blank overhead transparency acetate, and present your lesson concept map to the class.

Figure 12.7 shows the "water" concept map drawn by a group of students in one class.

CONCEPT MAPPING TECHNIQUE

You have now drawn and interpreted three concept maps. As you probably have observed, concept maps are different from outlining and flow charting in that concept maps show interconnectedness of concepts at similar hierarchical levels, whereas outlines and flow charts are linear, progressing from one point to another without showing linkage between branches. Concept maps differ from classification charts in that concept maps show interconnected relationships at all levels. They differ from semantic webbing in that concept maps show both hierarchical arrangement and meaningful interconnectedness.

The procedure for constructing concept maps involves first identifying the key concepts of the topic to be mapped, deciding their relative importance, and finally ranking them from most inclusive to most specific. The concepts are then arranged in hierarchical fashion with those that are at similar levels of inclusion aligned at approximately the same horizontal levels. The array flows in a tree-like form from the most inclusive concepts at the top through several levels of subordinate concepts, each increasing in specificity. Examples of the most specific concepts often appear at the bottom of each branch.

Although by now you probably have developed your own notions of how to construct concept maps, the following list may help clarify the technique or provide validity to the ideas you have already formulated.

1. Select a topic.

2. Pick out the main concept and generate a set of concepts associated with the main concept or topic.

3. Rank the concepts hierarchically, from most general (or most inclusive) to most specific (or least inclusive). Group the concepts that are related.

4. Draw the concept map with the concepts in ovals.

   • Most general concepts at the top

   • Intermediate concepts below

   • Most specific concepts at the bottom

   • More general concepts normally connected to two or more specific concepts

5. Draw the lines connecting the concepts.

6. Write in the words describing the relationships.

7. Draw in the linking lines.

8. Write in the linking words.

9. REVISE! REVISE! REVISE!

(Adapted from E. C. Lucy, Georgia State University, personal communication, February, 1990)

Uses of Concept Maps in Science Education

Concept maps have been used successfully in a wide variety of teaching and learning situations. Most commonly, teachers use them as aids for planning, instructing, reviewing, and assessing. Students use concept maps to help them organize material they are studying and to express the organization of their thoughts.

You have seen that concept maps provide visual representation of the way people relate given concepts. This is one of the primary benefits of using concept maps. Children's maps provide a vehicle by which we can look into their heads and see how *they* are constructing information.

Sometimes a concept map constructed by a child shows questionable thinking. For example, the FLOWERS concept map shown in Figure 12.8 contains indications of several possible areas of confusion. Try to find them. Although it may be that the child simply made errors in constructing the map, the presence of such anomalies in the product alerts the teacher to potential problems. The teacher can ask questions to see if there really is questionable thinking and, if so, can act to correct it. Sharing concept maps in small groups and comparing each other's portrayals also may alert children to their own uncertainties and discrepancies.

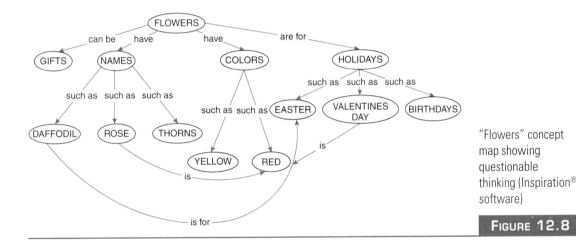

"Flowers" concept map showing questionable thinking (Inspiration® software)

FIGURE 12.8

Using Concept Maps for Lesson Planning

Tyler (1949) listed three major criteria to be met in lesson planning: (1) continuity, (2) sequencing, and (3) integration. Thirty-five years later, Novak and Gowin (1984) suggested using concept mapping to aid teachers in achieving these criteria. Concept maps suggest possible sequencing for lessons in the form of hierarchies of ideas that imply meaningful and valid sequences of lesson development. They show continuity within lessons by visually portraying the relationships between concepts. They show integration with their networks of cross-links.

Concept maps can help teachers organize their lessons. Suppose, for example, you had decided to teach your kindergarten children a lesson

NSES Program Standard A. Consistent Goals Across Grades

on flowers that involved names of flowers, colors of flowers, and how they can be used as gifts. (See Figure 12.5.) One way of organizing the lesson is to divide it into three parts corresponding to the three main sections of the map—one each on names, colors, and gifts. If this is done, however, the cross-relationships among the three parts are lost (except, perhaps, as examples or afterthoughts). Often, we teachers teach one of the branches of a topic, and then the next one, and then the next one, and so on sequentially, relating the parts to each other at the end of the unit, sometimes as an afterthought. The concept map shows that the interconnectedness of concepts throughout the entire scope of the topic is as important as those within each major section. Using the concept map as a basis for organizing the lesson, the teacher can ensure that the topic is treated in an integrated fashion.

A number of researchers have used concept mapping to help teachers develop elementary science curricula. They found that concept mapping results in more cohesive and integrated elementary science curricula (Starr & Krajcik, 1990) and provides teachers with guidance in showing the relationships among key ideas (Willerman & MacHarg, 1991). Martin (1994) reported that concept mapping helped preservice teachers develop lesson plans that exhibit continuity, are well-integrated, and are logically sequenced. Furthermore, although using concept maps to develop lesson plans required that students learn the concept mapping technique and expend extra effort and time, the device was well accepted and was used by many students in their full professional capacities.

The technique for using concept maps to develop lesson plans involves first developing a concept map of the main ideas to be included. Hierarchical and cross-linked relationships are shown. It is a good idea, once the initial map is drafted, to share it with peers where you must convincingly "talk your way" through the map. Peer review and critique are used to help revise the map. From this revised map, lesson plans are written that include properly scoped and logically sequenced learning objectives, teaching and learning activities for each objective, materials, and methods of assessment.

Instruction is linear in form, and concept maps are two-dimensional, showing interrelationships as well as hierarchies. Thus, the concept map can suggest a variety of integrated approaches and teaching sequences, and it can help the teacher tailor the material to the needs and interests of the children. Concept mapping (sometimes called curriculum mapping) can be used by teachers to chart curriculum that details the topics to be taught during a unit, a grading period, or even an entire school year (Willis, 2006). They can be used to identify gaps and duplications in the curriculum, and maps developed for different subjects can be combined in an interdisciplinary treatment.

Concept maps are extremely useful in developing a process-oriented elementary science curriculum. The technique is simple: Merely key one or more processes to the links. For example, in the FLOWERS concept map, you might key the process *observation* with the link between FLOW- ERS and COLORS. This suggests the following process-oriented objective: "The child will observe colors of flowers."

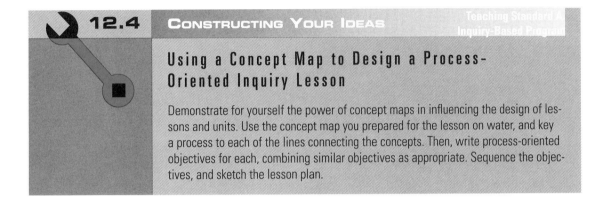

12.4 **CONSTRUCTING YOUR IDEAS**   Teaching Standard A Inquiry-Based Program

Using a Concept Map to Design a Process- Oriented Inquiry Lesson

Demonstrate for yourself the power of concept maps in influencing the design of les- sons and units. Use the concept map you prepared for the lesson on water, and key a process to each of the lines connecting the concepts. Then, write process-oriented objectives for each, combining similar objectives as appropriate. Sequence the objec- tives, and sketch the lesson plan.

Figure 12.9 shows a concept map for a unit on ecology with processes keyed to the links. Some of the resulting process-oriented objectives ex- tracted from the concept map are shown below the map.

Using Concept Maps in Instruction

Concept maps can be used in the actual instructional phase before, dur- ing, and after lessons and units. Concept maps can be used as advance organizers to set the stage for units on new material or for individual les- sons. As mentioned in Chapter 5, advance organizers for new units inform children of the basic scope and sequence of the material—what will be studied, and in what order. Advance organizers used at the beginning of individual lessons show children how the upcoming lesson relates to the main body of the study. Concept maps have been used successfully for this purpose. In one application, the teacher presents a concept map of the unit in conjunction with the introductory material and leaves the map posted in a prominent place so children can refer to it as they progress through the unit. In another application, the teacher gives each student a copy of the overall unit concept map, and children augment it as they progress through the lesson. Alternatively, augmentation of the intro- ductory concept map can be done by the class as a whole, with children building a map of the material studied that looks like a bowl of spaghetti

NSES Program Standard A. Consistent Goals Across Grades

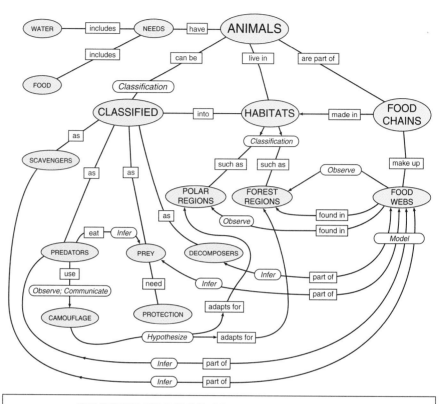

SELECTED PROCESS-ORIENTED OBJECTIVES

1. The student will infer predator–prey relationships between animals in polar and forest habitats.

2. The student will classify habitats into polar and forest.

3. The student will hypothesize how animals adapt to polar and forest environments.

4. The student will observe and communicate ways in which animals use camouflage in their environments.

5. The student will infer the animals that are predators, prey, decomposers, and scavengers in polar and forest habitats.

6. The student will create a model of food webs in polar and forest environments.

"Ecology" concept map showing processes keyed to links and selected process-oriented objectives derived from the map (Inspiration® software)

FIGURE 12.9

by the end of the unit. It makes perfect sense to the children, but not to outsiders.

In another introductory application, children build their own map of their ideas about what to study in a unit, and this map is used to guide the overall direction the unit takes. Concept maps used in middle school science give students an opportunity to think about connections among the science concepts being studied and the meanings of scientific terms, and enable them to better organize what they learn and to store and retrieve information more efficiently. Vanides et al. (2005) describe two ways of using concept maps in middle grades science: (1) teach students how to construct concept maps and then have them construct maps of the units being studied; and (2) teach students how to use concept maps, and use teacher-prepared maps to introduce the units, the concepts and terms, and their meanings and interrelationships.

In all these applications, the concept map helps children internalize the scope of the material and, more important, see the ways in which different aspects of the material connect to form an integrated whole.

Concept maps can be used for review. In one application, the teacher presents a concept map showing the scope and interrelationships of the material that has been included in a unit of study. In another application, the teacher uses the concept map prepared for the introduction for the review. Perhaps the most satisfactory application is for children to augment the introductory concept map as they progress through the unit and then help build a final concept map showing salient points and their interrelationships. If the class has kept up a running concept map, the end result (bowl of spaghetti) can serve as the review.

Using Concept Maps for Assessment

In Chapter 8, the position was taken that children should demonstrate their understandings and masteries in ways that are authentic and that are comfortable to them. Experience has shown that concept mapping is one such vehicle.

NSES Assessment Standard D. Fair Assessments

In the use of concept mapping for assessment, children are asked to construct a concept map showing the scope and interrelationships of key concepts of the study. The concepts may be provided to the children, or the children may be asked to provide their own concepts. On a one-to-one basis, the teacher asks the child to explain the map. This technique is similar to an interview except that the child has already gathered his or her thoughts about the material. Using this technique, the teacher can probe for deeper understandings and can obtain a true assessment of the child's understanding of the material. The results of the concept map interview can be used as the basis for future studies.

In another approach, children are asked to draw concept maps as their final activity in a unit; these maps are graded using rubrics for inclusion of key concepts, "correctness" of hierarchy, and inclusion of key cross-links—much as an essay exam would be graded. The completed concept map can be included in the child's science journal or portfolio. Bell (2007) reports that using concept maps for assessment appears to be reliable when the scoring rubric that is used is based on accuracy, level of explanation, and the complexity portrayed by the concept map.

Uses of Concept Maps by Children

NSES Unifying Concepts and Processes: Systems, Order, and Organization

Concept maps have been used by children at all grade levels, from pre-school and kindergarten onward (Gallenstein, 2005). Children have used them to illustrate main points in a piece of literature, to develop the plan for a piece of creative writing, to isolate variables for an experiment, to develop a plan for investigating a topic, and to write the report of an experimental procedure. Children use concept maps to keep track of where they have been, where they are now, and where they are going in a course of study.

Concept mapping has been shown to aid children with weak academic backgrounds in their understanding of new material (Snead & Snead, 2004; Stice & Alvarez, 1987). It has been proposed as an effective teaching and learning aid for children with learning disabilities (Crank & Bulgren, 1993), and it has been shown to assist field dependent students in science comprehension and achievement (Martin, 1991). Nesbit and Adesope (2006) found that teacher-constructed concept maps are especially useful for communication with students who have low verbal proficiency, including English language learners.

Of course, in order for children to use concept maps, they first must learn how to construct them. Children as young as kindergartners can be taught to construct concept maps; the technique is similar to that presented in the first section of this chapter. Have the children draw concept maps of familiar topics using four or five concepts, and gradually increase their complexity. Have children "talk their way" through their maps with each other, and provide both peer and teacher critique. Make it a class project to develop a continuous concept map that shows the progression of learning in a unit; this will show them the significance of concept mapping. It usually takes children several months of regular practice to learn to construct good concept maps. However, the time is well spent, and children are provided with a tool they can use for the rest of their lives.

Novak (1991), the developer of the concept map heuristic, writes:

> My experience has been that when students are required to construct their own personal concept maps for topics they are studying, they find new meanings in the subject and new ways to relate what they already know to the new things they are learning. In short, concept maps constructed by students help them to learn meaningfully. (p. 48)

TEACHER VOICE

A few years ago, I was conducting an action research project on the integration of technology in a constructivist sixth-grade science class. As part of the study, I gave my students two additional tools to use: the vocabulary of constructivist teaching and learning, and concept mapping. The vocabulary made it possible for the class and me to be collaborators as we discussed their learning, planned activities and strategies, and assessed how things were progressing. It also prompted a near-revolution in their reading class where they wanted to take responsibility for their own learning, have a voice in what they were reading, and "use constructivism too!" I was amazed that in addition to working on their reading skills, they learned to negotiate the teacher's guide and create their own lesson plans. They were empowered and in charge of their own learning, turning to me primarily for advice and materials. In discussions with those students when they were in high school, I learned they still had (and used) the tools to take control of their own learning, decide what they need in order to do their best in the class, and to understand how the class operates.

The other tool they still use is concept mapping. Concept maps and graphic organizers are tools used extensively by both teachers and students. At the beginning of the year, much modeling is required to walk students through the tasks that enable them to use graphic organizers and concept maps. To acquire these skills, we work together preparing a large concept map on the chalkboard that the students copy into their science logs.

As time progresses, students work in small groups and individually to organize their learning through concept maps. The concept maps can be used to check prior knowledge as a pretest, with students adding to the pretest concept map throughout the unit. The concept maps can be used to review for summative assessments. Sometimes, partially completed concept maps can be used for formative or summative assessment, with students completing the blank areas. For essay exams, students can use their concept maps to write organized responses. As students research topics such as the geologic history of the area in which they live, a concept map helps them organize their research and their information. A poster of their concept map is used to help present their findings to the rest of the class.

As a teacher, I use concept maps to plan units and activities. I start to plan a unit by selecting the big, enduring ideas I want students to learn. For each big idea, the students and I work together to develop a concept map that organizes the concepts and activities so they are meaningful for the students. When I work with my teaching partner or even my whole team on larger, integrated units or projects, concept maps help us focus on the big ideas and show us how individual pieces fit into the bigger picture.

As educators we are constantly using tools such as concept maps to work more efficiently and effectively. When we pass these tools onto our students we outfit them to take more responsibility for their own learning and arm them for success.

Karen Bejin

Sixth-Grade Teacher
DeLong Middle School
Eau Claire, Wisconsin

Conclusion

Concept mapping has been in use since the late 1970s and has been shown to have positive influences on children's learning, especially in the field of science. Advantages of using concept maps include increased meaning of cognitive material for both teachers and children, ownership of material by teachers and children, increased ability to integrate concepts, increased thoroughness and efficiency in lesson planning, increased capacity of teachers to meet children's individual needs in a variety of ways through understanding how children are constructing the material, and increased capacity of teachers to construct conceptual meaning in multiple ways for their students.

Concept mapping helps teachers understand the nature of the science topics they are teaching and helps them design and implement units of study that are meaningful, relevant, pedagogically sound, and interesting to children. There is merit in the use of concept mapping. You will have to decide the extent to which you feel this device is useful to you and the children in your classes.

CHAPTER 12

Additional Questions for Discussion

1. Describe how the use of concept mapping can help promote children's development of process skills and facility in inquiry investigations.
2. Contrast concept mapping with other diagrammatic techniques, such as outlines, flow charts, and semantic webbing with respect to the constructivist approach to teaching and learning.

Internet Activities

Use the Internet to find additional information about concept mapping and ways concept mapping is used in science education.

CHAPTER 13

THE ELEMENTARY SCIENCE EDUCATION PROFESSIONAL

And gladly wolde he lerne, and gladly teche.

Geoffrey Chaucer, *The Canterbury Tales* (San Marino, CA: Huntington Library Press, 1995), 1. 308 (Original work published c. 1387)

To teach is to learn twice over.

Joseph Joubert, *Pensées* (Paris: Union General D'Editions, 1966). (Original work published 1842)

As a teaching professional, you have tremendous opportunities to share successes, to contribute to discussions on open issues with other professionals, and to exert your professional influence on the direction education takes. You also have the responsibility for providing the best possible education for each individual child; for meeting the educational needs of the school, the community it serves, and the nation; and for keeping up with new curricular materials, new ideas about pedagogy, and current developments in the profession.

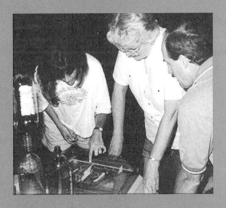

Penner (2001) writes:

> Science education in school typically focuses on accumulating facts and formulas. Scientific activity is often restricted to prepackaged experiments that are little more than demonstrations of the state of current scientific knowledge. The tacit goal in these experiments is to reproduce a known effect . . .
>
> Science education needs to move beyond the demonstration and so-called experiments that are characteristic of school science. This requires that researchers and educators

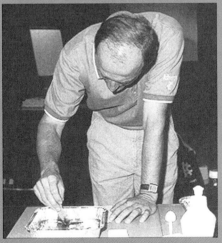

consider ways of engaging students that involve them in seeking to understand and explain natural phenomena. (p. 1)

The professional development of science teachers is a continuous, lifelong process that must be coherent, integrated, and non-administrative (National Research Council, 1996). Yager (2005) writes that professional development activities should focus not only on the study of science content but also on new ways of teaching and on plans for implementing these new ways which are put into practice for several years during which evidence is collected to determine their impact on students.

This chapter offers suggestions on how you can take advantage of the opportunity to influence education through making and justifying curriculum and methodology decisions, keeping up with new developments, and contributing to your personal professional growth and the growth of science education.

DECISIONS ABOUT METHODOLOGY

One of the most significant contributions you can make to your profession lies in the decisions you make about methodology and the manner in which you justify these decisions. In this text, many issues have been raised about elementary science teaching methodology, such as the following:

- Doing science versus learning about science

- Deciding on goals of elementary science education

- Instructing from a constructivist perspective versus imparting knowledge

- Teaching in an inquiry mode versus an expository mode

- Identifying and accommodating individual learner differences

- Assessing children's accomplishments authentically

- Developing integrated and interdisciplinary studies versus using a discipline-centered approach

- Including reading and writing in science

- Considering the influence of state and federal goals and state and district mandates

- Considering the role of standardized tests

- Keeping classroom order

- Using technology to help children with their inquiries

We have urged you to weigh all sides of each issue with an open mind and to formulate your own ideas concerning each issue.

NSES System Standard A. Policies Consistent Across All Standards with Adaptations to Local Circumstances
NSES System Standard G. Policies Intended To Achieve the Vision of Science Education Portrayed in the *Standards*

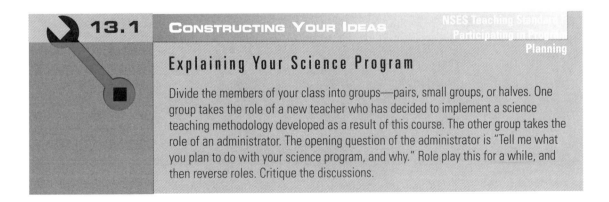

13.1   CONSTRUCTING YOUR IDEAS
NSES Teaching Standard
Participating in Program Planning

Explaining Your Science Program

Divide the members of your class into groups—pairs, small groups, or halves. One group takes the role of a new teacher who has decided to implement a science teaching methodology developed as a result of this course. The other group takes the role of an administrator. The opening question of the administrator is "Tell me what you plan to do with your science program, and why." Role play this for a while, and then reverse roles. Critique the discussions.

Did the teacher have a sound methodology in place? Was he or she able to justify it? Did the teacher cite experts in the field? Professional societies? Research? Was the teacher cognizant of opposing views? Was he or she sensitive to the needs of the local school and community? Had the teacher considered all aspects, both pro and con? Was the teacher thoroughly prepared and able to provide satisfactory answers to the "administrator's" questions?

This exercise enables you to refine the philosophy of science education you have been developing and state it in operational as well as theoretical terms, giving you a committed and firm foundation for the successful implementation of your elementary science program.

You now (or shortly will) have the opportunity to explain your methodological approach to colleagues, parents, administrators, concerned citizens, and other professionals. Every teacher should be able to explain and defend his or her methodological decisions based on personal constructions of the research and the various positions, arguments, and situations.

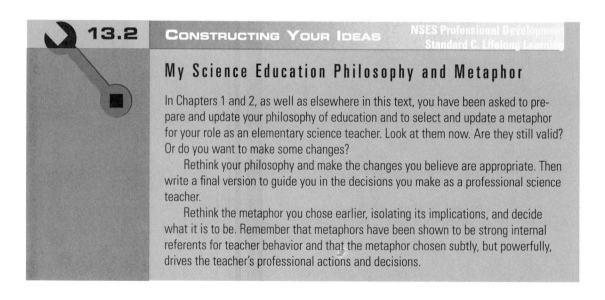

13.2   **CONSTRUCTING YOUR IDEAS**   NSES Professional Development Standard C. Lifelong Learning

My Science Education Philosophy and Metaphor

In Chapters 1 and 2, as well as elsewhere in this text, you have been asked to prepare and update your philosophy of education and to select and update a metaphor for your role as an elementary science teacher. Look at them now. Are they still valid? Or do you want to make some changes?

Rethink your philosophy and make the changes you believe are appropriate. Then write a final version to guide you in the decisions you make as a professional science teacher.

Rethink the metaphor you chose earlier, isolating its implications, and decide what it is to be. Remember that metaphors have been shown to be strong internal referents for teacher behavior and that the metaphor chosen subtly, but powerfully, drives the teacher's professional actions and decisions.

DECISIONS ABOUT CURRICULUM

As noted previously, there are three sides to the education triangle—what to teach, how to teach, and how to assess. This text is concerned primarily with how to teach and how to assess. However, there must be congruence between methodology and curriculum; thus, we have given attention to what to teach.

We have suggested it is better to teach the processes than the products of science. We have suggested that the products—in the form of facts, concepts, and theories—can be used as vehicles for process mastery—vehicles through which children learn to *do* science. We have suggested that integrated and interdisciplinary approaches are more representative of real-world situations than the compartmentalized approach in which science is taught separately and the three main branches of science are taught in isolation from each other.

Nowhere have we stipulated specific content to be taught. A fundamental premise of this text is that when children learn how to *do* science, they also are learning *about* science. They use scientific content as the vehicle for developing mastery in applying the scientific processes, and as they investigate science concepts through process-oriented inquiry, they also are constructing personal, valid, and firm conceptualizations about the science content being used as the vehicle.

This is the essence of constructivist science education.

Volumes have been written about the reform of science education; much of this material concerns the reform of science curriculum. The nation's leading science educators urge us to abandon product-oriented science programs in favor of process-oriented, inquiry, constructivist approaches that teach children how to do science and to use interdisciplinary approaches that are closely aligned with the way in which scientists do science and that capture children's interest and are meaningful to them.

Despite decades of persuasive argument and overwhelming agreement on the part of educators, many science programs remain content-oriented. This is caused, in part, by the role that standardized achievement tests have in driving the curriculum and by the administrative requirements that teachers cover a prescribed scope and sequence.

Today's elementary science teachers are faced with a curriculum dilemma characterized by the forces of constraint and dedication to teaching science products on the one hand and the relentless forces of science reform on the other.

Contemporary science education seeks to achieve three overarching goals:

1. Science as a process of inquiry and problem solving

2. Sufficient working knowledge of science to deal effectively with societal and technical issues

3. Preparation of the next generation of scientists

To accomplish these goals, contemporary science curriculum development is guided by several broad considerations:

1. Process is more important than content.

2. Discipline boundaries among the sciences are softened.

NSES System Standard A. Policies Consistent Across All Standards with Adaptations to Local Circumstances
NSES System Standard G. Policies Intended to Achieve the Vision of Science Education Portrayed in the *Standards*

3. Science is integrated with the rest of the curriculum.

4. Science is attached meaningfully to life.

5. Science content is based on fundamental scientific principles and concepts.

In your professional capacity as an early childhood teacher, however, you may be asked to cover certain science content. Because teaching prescribed science content seems to oppose our constructivist point of view, it is well to give consideration to this apparent dichotomy. How can you teach prescribed content and still maintain the constructivist approach? Many questions emerge that you will need to answer to your satisfaction. A few are suggested below; you are sure to be able to add more. Answers are suggested that may help you establish congruency between a requirement to cover certain prescribed content and the principles of constructivist science education.

1. Q: What content should I use?

A: If you are faced with an imposed curriculum or scope and sequence, you are required to use the content that is prescribed. But, you can separate this content into two categories: (1) the content that lends itself well to inquiry investigation, such as magnetism, animal camouflage, nature of rocks and minerals, and the like; and (2) the content that does not lend itself well to inquiry, such as names of planets, names of dinosaurs, nature of ecological principles, and the like. Spend as much as two-thirds of the time available for science on activities that lend themselves to inquiry and spend the remainder of the time available for science "imparting" the rest of the required information.

2. Q: How can I tell what content lends itself to inquiry as opposed to content that has to be imparted?

A: If children have requested or are truly interested in a topic, or if a topic involves manipulation of actual materials such as ice cubes, balls, rocks, toothpicks, and the like, then the topic can be approached from an inquiry perspective. However, if a topic involves learning something that children are not likely to be able to discover for themselves, such as relative temperatures of planets, living habits of dinosaurs, method by which batteries work, and the like, then the topic probably lends itself better to a didactic approach than an inquiry approach. But, even with these topics, a truly constructivist environment promotes individual broadening and deepening of inquiries.

3. Q: Where can I get the background for the science content I must use?

A: If your school requires the use of a text or other basic commercial material, the teacher's manual may include the basic background you will need. The Internet is an excellent source of information (see Chapter 11). The *Gateway to Educational Materials* (GEM) site, the *SciLINKS* and *SciGuide* programs of the National Science Teachers Association, and the National Science Digital Library are excellent online resources. The supplemental chapter that accompanies this textbook on the Web site provides brief overviews of the content normally taught in elementary science education.

 Direct links to the GEM, the *SciLINKS*, and the *SciGuide* home pages as well as the National Science Digital Library are available on the Student Book Companion Web Site. You can access the Supplemental Chapter, "Basic Concepts and Principles for the Elementary Science Program," through the Student Book Companion Web Site.

4. Q: How do I accommodate children's interests when the science content is prescribed?

A: Employ the project-centered rose model of teaching and learning (see Chapter 10). Focus the project on the required subject material, and engage children in a discussion of their questions about the topic. The questions chosen for investigation repre sent the common interests of the children in the class. If you are required to introduce concepts that may, in your opinion, be of questionable interest to the children in your class, develop bombastic introductions and dynamic lessons, and use all the interest-grabbing devices at your disposal to make the material as interesting and engaging as possible. Remember that material is interesting to children only to the extent that it involves their own activities and is applicable to their own lives and living situations.

5. Q: How close do I keep to a prescribed scope and sequence or curriculum?

A: This varies from school to school and from district to district. If you have latitude, use it judiciously. If you do not have latitude, follow the prescribed curriculum, alternating between inquiry and didactic styles of teaching and learning as appropriate to the prescribed content. (See Question 1 above.)

13.3   CONSTRUCTING YOUR IDEAS

NSES Teaching Standard
Participating in Program
Planning

Teaching the Content of Science

Now it's your turn to wrestle with the curriculum and content issues.

Continue the list of questions suggested above as appropriate for your individual situation. Write the questions, and for each, suggest answers and alternative solutions. Discuss each in your whole class setting, and record ideas you may not have thought of that are valid according to your current conceptualization of quality early childhood science education.

As a professional educator, you have the opportunity to participate in this continuing professional dialogue about the elementary science curriculum, to make informed decisions about what to teach in your elementary science program, and to contribute to the improvement of elementary science education. Ultimately, you will have to make the decisions about the content to be included in your science program. The constructions you have been making as a result of this text will help you make these very difficult—and sometimes controversial—decisions.

As Glasser (1992) said, "We should never forget that people, not curriculum, are the desired outcomes of schooling. What we want to develop are students who have the skills to become active contributors to society, who are enthusiastic about what they have learned, and who are aware of how learning can be of use to them in the future" (p. 694).

PROFESSIONAL DEVELOPMENT WORKSHOPS AND INSTITUTES

NSES Professional
Development
Standard C. Lifelong
Learning

Teachers can keep up with developments in science and science education through participating in science-oriented professional development workshops and institutes. Often, schools, school districts, colleges, universities, and professional science organizations offer inservice programs on various topics lasting from an hour or two to a week or two. These topics may range from an overview of a newly developed curriculum to in-depth, constructivist, process-oriented, inquiry-based explorations of a variety of science topics. The content- and methodology-based workshops generally encourage those attending to participate in the constructivist manner that you have become used to in this text. Summer institutes and other science professional development workshops often focus on science content—especially new and exciting topics that can be used in the classroom. Just as often, these workshops also focus on how to teach the topics explored in an inquiry manner. Workshop participants can earn credits for use in periodic certificate renewal requirements or for college graduate credit.

Professional development does not have to involve workshops, institutes, and other external programs. It can occur individually or within a school. Self-study and self-reflection, mentoring, structured collaboration, and coaching programs are alternatives carried out during the school year in the context of actual classroom practice (Bransfield, Holt, & Mastasi, 2007; Cokshi & Fernandez, 2005; Luft, 2007; Ruby, 2006; Samaras et al., 2005).

Finally, professional development can be accomplished technologically. For example, distance learning using live interactive television has been used successfully to help rural elementary teachers strengthen their understanding of science content (Annetta & Shymansky, 2006).

PROFESSIONAL ORGANIZATIONS

One of the responsibilities of teachers is to keep up with the times regarding both subject matter and pedagogy. Teachers of elementary grades are given an impossible task—they are expected to know about all subjects and to teach all things well. No one can possibly keep up with everything! So, in this age of specialization, it is suggested that you single out one area in which to focus your continued professional development. Choose an area that holds particular interest to you, and become an expert in it. Others will look to you for expertise in your area, and you will find yourself assuming a leadership role in that field.

The area may be subject-specific, such as mathematics, language arts, reading, music, science, physical education, social studies, and so on. Or it may focus more on specific methodologies such as teaching preschool children or teaching English language learners or children with special needs. You have the opportunity to assume an active role in the field where your interest lies. Join the professional societies, subscribe to their publications, submit manuscripts for publication, and attend their national, state, and regional meetings as participant and as presenter of the results of your work.

This section describes the professional organizations that elementary teachers who are interested in science might wish to consider.

The **National Science Teachers Association (NSTA)** is the largest science teachers' organization in the nation. Its purpose is to stimulate, improve, and coordinate science teaching and learning.

NSTA publishes four journals, all of which welcome teachers' classroom ideas and reports of teachers' action research. *Science and Children* is devoted to science teaching in preschool through middle school. Articles include descriptions of innovative projects and programs, descriptions of hands-on activities, reports of research in science education, informational pieces, and helpful hints. *Science Scope* focuses on the unique needs and characteristics of children in middle and junior high school; articles include ideas for laboratory activities and demonstrations and discussions of issues important to teachers of middle-level science. *The Science Teacher* focuses on high school science, and the *Journal of College Science Teaching* focuses on the teaching and learning of science in college.

In addition, NSTA publishes *NSTA Reports,* a bimonthly newsletter, which contains articles of current interest and importance to all science educators. NSTA holds an annual conference—attended by tens of thousands of teachers from all grade levels—at which thousands of presentations are made, many by classroom teachers presenting new and innovative classroom teaching ideas and the results of individual research projects. NSTA also holds several regional conferences each year.

Each state has one or more state science associations affiliated with NSTA that are concerned with helping classroom teachers at all levels

NSES Professional Development Standard C. Lifelong Learning
NSES System Standard A. Policies Consistent Across All Standards with Adaptations to Local Circumstances
NSES System Standard G. Policies Intended To Achieve the Vision of Science Education Portrayed in the *Standards*

improve their teaching of science and students' learning of science. Most state associations have annual meetings at which papers are presented and information and ideas exchanged in such areas as current education paradigms, issues in science education, classroom ideas, and results of action research projects.

The **National Association for Research in Science Teaching (NARST)** promotes scholarly research and discussion of issues in the field of science education. The association publishes the monthly *Journal of Research in Science Teaching,* which contains refereed articles on research activities seeking to impact science teaching practice. The articles are thoroughly researched and reviewed. NARST hosts an annual conference at which panel discussions, position papers, and research papers dealing with science education are presented.

The **Association for Science Teacher Education (ASTE)** focuses on research in science education teaching and learning and the application of research in the classroom. ASTE publishes three journals. *Science Education* contains descriptive articles and research reports dealing with curriculum, instruction, assessment, science teacher education, learning, current issues and trends, and international science education. The *Journal of Science Teacher Education* contains articles on methodology, instructional design, current science education issues, position statements, new ideas, and consolidated research findings as well as critical reviews of literature pertaining to professional development in science teaching. In addition, members of ASTE have the option of subscribing to the *Journal of Elementary Science Education.* All three journals publish results of action research. ASTE holds an annual meeting at which papers about new developments in science education are presented. Several regional associations are affiliated with ASTE, and each of these holds its own annual conference. These regional conferences provide excellent forums for classroom teachers to present the results of their action research.

The **Council for Elementary Science International (CESI)** is a professional organization for preschool through eighth-grade teachers who have responsibility for teaching science, and for preservice teachers who will become preschool through eighth-grade teachers. Its mission is to promote equity and excellence in science education. CESI is affiliated with NSTA and publishes the biannual *CESI Science* in which research and classroom activities are shared.

Each state has an **Academy of Science** that provides a forum for interaction among professors, students, and teachers on a variety of scientific topics; many have sections devoted to science education. The individual state academies of science normally are affiliated with the National Association of Academies of Science. Each state also has a Junior Academy of Science that promotes science with elementary, middle grade and secondary school students. Junior academies of science are affiliated with the American Junior Academy of Science. Both the National Association of Academies of Science and the American Junior Academy of Science are affiliated with the American Association for the Advancement of Science (AAAS).

The **School Science and Mathematics Association (SSMA)** is dedicated to improving instruction at all levels in and between science and mathematics. SSMA publishes the monthly *School Science and Mathematics* (October through May), which emphasizes issues, concerns, and lessons both within and between the disciplines of science and mathematics in the classroom. Members are encouraged to submit articles for publication.

The **Association for Constructivist Teaching (ACT)** is dedicated to fostering teacher development based on the principles of constructivist teaching. Its mission is to enhance the growth of all educators and students through identification and dissemination of constructivist teaching practices. Members include classroom teachers, students, administrators, college and university personnel, and others who are interested in the field of education. ACT publishes *The Constructivist* three times a year on the Internet and holds an annual conference on constructivist teaching and learning.

Regardless of your primary interests, it is imperative that you keep up to date in science education, science content, and constructivist methodology through active participation in professional organizations, conferences, and workshops, and through regular review of professional publications. There are literally dozens of additional science-oriented organizations, including some with a specialized focus such as the Sierra Club and the Audubon Society. Elementary science teachers desiring to get involved with science will not have a difficult time finding the organization that best suits their individual needs and interests.

Direct links to the Web sites for professional organizations discussed are provided on the Student Book Companion Web Site.

THE ELEMENTARY SCIENCE TEACHER AS RESEARCHER

Every teacher is a researcher. At a minimum, teachers reflect on lessons, assess the good points and the weak areas, and make changes to strengthen them. They revise the instruction to accommodate the changing needs of children. They reconstruct lessons to ensure that every child is successful. They develop assessment techniques that are authentic. They share successful teaching strategies with colleagues.

NSES System Standard G. Policies Intended to Achieve the Vision of Science Education Portrayed in the *Standards*

The time may come when teachers want to try out a new system, such as a different methodology or a different approach to curriculum. They often do this informally, comparing the results of two classes, or this year's class with last year's class. If the results seem to be better, the new system may be adopted.

Many times, however, the research done by teachers never leaves the classroom or the school. It is considered *experience,* not *research.* Yet these very ideas that have been tried and proven in individual teachers' classrooms can comprise a large portion of the research base. The ultimate goal of all effective research in science education is to improve classroom practice. How do children best learn science? What works? What doesn't work? How effective are various teaching techniques and new and innovative teaching strategies? Teachers can and should play a significant role in that research.

Much research is conceived, planned, controlled, executed, and analyzed by college- and university-based researchers. They use children in teachers' classrooms for their subjects, imposing experimental conditions and controls to ensure validity. They select the questions to be investigated, design the experimental method, and formulate conclusions from the application of statistical procedures to show the significance (or lack of significance) of outcomes with regard to the research hypothesis. The studies concern problems that teachers probably are not faced with in the first place, are published in journals that teachers probably do not read, using language and statistical manipulations that are unfamiliar to teachers, and suggest solutions that teachers probably would not find useful to implement.

There is little reason to do research in science education unless there is a payoff in the classroom. But this rarely happens. Teachers view most research findings as impractical, difficult to interpret, and rarely possible to implement. (Hurd, 1986)

One solution to the dilemma about irrelevant and meaningless science education research is for teachers to become involved in research.

There are many ways teachers can get involved in research. One way is to collaborate with university researchers, thus providing a teacher's views and input.

Another more powerful way is for teachers to do it themselves. The National Association for Research in Science Teaching has coined the phrase "Every teacher a researcher" (ETR) to demonstrate commitment to the notion that meaningful, relevant, and valid research can be done by teachers in their own classrooms.

Van Zee (1998) offers several "beliefs" concerning the science teacher as researcher:

- Prospective teachers can and should learn how to do research as they learn how to teach.

- Beginning teachers can and should conduct research in their own classrooms.

- Both beginning and experienced teachers should conduct research that documents and articulates positive aspects of their practices.

- University faculty should create opportunities for interaction among prospective, beginning, and experienced teachers so all can learn by sharing experiences and insights with each other.

- Teachers possess unique knowledge that should be articulated and contributed to development and application of new theories of teaching and learning in guiding reform efforts (pp. 246–247).

The research done by teachers researching their own classrooms is called *action research* or *applied research*. This type of research seeks to determine effectiveness of classroom practice. The term *action* comes from the idea that the teacher is a participant in the development of new knowledge: The study occurs while the teacher is teaching, and the teacher is part of the group under study. Action research is essential if changes in teaching practices are to occur, because action research is what determines the ultimate effectiveness of any proposed change in classroom practice.

In action research, you systematically inquire into the teaching practice in your classroom and document and share the results. The procedure involves five stages: (1) developing a specific problem or question, (2) reading other action research reports, (3) obtaining data, (4) forming conclusions, and (5) sharing the results.

1. The problem or question may be a simple statement of what you think will happen as a result of doing what you plan to do, such as "If I implement a hands-on approach, children should become more interested in science." Or it may be a statement of a problem, such as "I wonder what would happen if I took children outdoors every day to observe their natural surroundings?" The question may emerge when you notice a reaction to something being done in the classroom, such as "I notice that when I provide simple hands-on activities, children get very involved in their own inquiries."

2. You should read as much as you can about the subject to see what others have found out and how they proceeded with their inquiries.

3. To obtain data, you need to plan what kind of data you want to collect and how you will use it to form conclusions. Many objective tests are available to help you gather quantitative data, or you may wish to design your own tests. Attitude and interest surveys can be used. Videotaping, audiotaping, interviews, journals, observations, work samples, written records of formal discussions, and so on are all valid kinds of information that can be collected.

4. In forming your conclusions, you pore over all the information you obtained to see what makes sense. You have already planned how you are going to analyze the information; so now you do it. However, much new data that you never considered previously will present itself. Thus, it is entirely possible that you may find unexpected results. Sometimes these results are valid and become part of the analysis, and sometimes they suggest additional avenues of new research or ways of continuing the original research.

5. It is imperative that you share the results of your research with others. Share your work with focus groups at your school; publish your work in professional journals; present it at professional conferences.

Many references are available to help.

A caveat is in order. Research is different from trying out new ideas or new activities that are implemented primarily to lend spice and uniqueness to your class. New ideas, hints to the teacher, and the like describe new or unique ways of doing something already known to have an effect. For example, one might try out a new way of teaching the types of clouds and find that it "works" better than other ways. This would be an improvement in teaching clouds and should be published as such, but it is not research. In research, the goal is to establish some degree of cause and effect or to explain why something may have occurred—the understandings and insights that emerge from field work and subsequent analysis.

Once again: The basic goal of action research is the improvement of children's achievement. A research project is only valuable to the extent that it helps us improve our practice.

GRANTS

NSES System Standard D. Policies Supported with Resources

Direct links to a few Web sites where you can find information about grants recently funded and requests for proposals are provided on the Student Book Companion Web Site.

There is money out there for science education! You can get some of it for your science program in the form of grants. Grants can range in monetary value from $100 or less to as much as several million dollars, and they are available from governmental agencies, public foundations, private foundations, colleges and universities, large and small companies, and even parent–teacher associations.

Individual elementary science teachers should focus on smaller grants in the $100 to $1,000 range that will be used to purchase equipment, materials, and services to expand or enrich the science education program. Grants have been funded for constructing butterfly gardens, preparing planting areas, building outdoor amphitheaters and nature trails, purchasing basic calculators for children's use, purchasing software and texts for special projects, and the like. Grants probably will *not* be funded if they request money for snacks, giveaways, additional supplies normally provided by the school, materials and supplies traditionally supplied by the teacher, or uses that do not have definite and unique end products. To find sources of grant money, check the Internet, and ask your school administrator, school district personnel, local colleges and universities, and others "in the know."

The first rule of "grantsmanship" is to be sure that your proposed use of the grant money is consistent with the granting agency's purposes. Granting agencies normally stipulate the kinds of projects they will consider. For example, communications companies are interested in grant proposals dealing with technological advances. Medical foundations are more interested in awarding grants for medical research than they are in awarding grants for improving elementary science education. Similarly, you would not request funding to build an outdoor garden from a group dedicated to improving public television programming; instead, you would look for a grant source that offers money for projects that include outdoor gardening. It is not only permissible but also a good idea to contact the granting agency for examples of projects that have been funded in the past and how much the projects were awarded.

The second rule of grantsmanship is to make your proposal succinct, direct, and to the point. Follow the guidelines provided by the granting agency in writing the proposal. Supply *all* the information they require. In describing your proposal, be sure that it is very clear. Avoid the temptation to ramble or to assume the reviewers know what you are writing about. (Many of the reviewers come from the world of business and professional service, *not* from the world of education.) Be sure the words you write describe your project vividly. Ask a colleague or a friend who doesn't know anything about your situation or your idea to read your proposal to see if it is understandable. Accept their comments! This is not a time to defend either your pride or your writing. Successful grant proposals are clear to the reviewers on the first reading, and you want yours to be successful! Remember that the reviewers are completely in the dark about your situation and your project.

In developing the budget, be as detailed as you can be. The granting agency wants to know what the money will be used for, so show them precisely what you plan to buy and what services you plan to purchase. If a summary budget is all that is required, prepare a detailed budget and attach it as an appendix if at all possible. And, above all, check your arithmetic!

The third rule for preparing successful grants is to show how your proposed project will make a difference in the science education of the children in your class and how you are going to measure its effectiveness. For example, it is not enough to write that children will love their new science computer program. You must show how the proposed purchase is expected to improve their achievement in science.

The fourth rule of good grantsmanship is to persevere. If at first you don't succeed, try again. Very few proposers are awarded grants the first time they submit one. Refine your proposal the next time you submit it, or revise your proposal and submit it to a different granting agency. Contact the agency that rejected your first proposal, ask for feedback, and incorporate their feedback into your next proposal. Remember that if you believe your proposed project is a good one, there *are* granting agencies that also believe it is a good one and are willing to fund it—if they know what it's all about.

Gill (2007) offers the following suggestions for educators seeking grant funds:

1. Research the foundation or charity before you ask for money to ensure their funding goals match your proposal. Follow their guidelines in submitting your proposal.

2. Consider forming partnerships with outside agencies such as community groups or universities.

3. Think creatively and come up with projects that are unique.

4. Before you write your own, read other grant proposals, especially those that have been funded by the agency that will be considering yours.

5. Show that your proposed program is sustainable.

6. Think big.

There is money out there for projects that cannot be funded internally. This money is yours for the asking, but you have to ask through clearly written proposals.

EXCELLENCE IN SCIENCE TEACHING

NSES System Standard A. Policies Consistent Across All Standards with Adaptations to Local Circumstances

What constitutes excellence in elementary science teaching? Penick and Yager (1993) found several common characteristics:

1. Excellent science teachers give up on textbook-oriented science and develop their own programs that are relevant and responsive to the needs of children and the community. Programs are discovery in orientation and hands-on in nature.

2. Excellent elementary science programs focus more on process than on content. The teachers develop materials and kits and package them for easy distribution.

3. Excellent elementary science programs provide much in-service training and have strong support from the central and building administrations.

4. Excellent elementary science programs are considered to be in a continuous state of evolution.

Yager (1988) offers additional generalizations:

1. Effective teachers tend to reach out and to seek new ideas.

2. Increased preparation in science content is not a significant factor in differentiating between the most and the least effective science teachers.

3. Effective teachers elect to participate in several professional growth experiences per year, such as in-service programs and conferences.

Finally, standards for excellence in science teaching are provided in the *National Science Education Standards* (National Research Council, 1996). It is hoped that all science teachers will become familiar with these standards and will use them to guide development and implementation of their science programs.

Teaching science in the elementary grades is not difficult. Children love science, and successful teachers encourage them to wonder, to explore, and to construct their own meanings. Excellent elementary science teachers stimulate children to ask their own questions about phenomena that are meaningful and interesting to them, to develop their own methods of investigating these questions using the scientific processes, and to validate their conclusions through connections with their prior knowledge, the presence of explanatory and predictive power, and the use of input from other people and outside sources. Excellent elementary science teachers challenge children to do science the way scientists do science, using the world and all fields of knowledge as the arena for the development of scientific literacy. Excellent elementary science teachers involve *all* children in scientific inquiry regardless of gender, ethnicity, academic ability, or any other factor.

By using the constructivist approach suggested in this book, you can develop an elementary science program that meets the needs of all children, that provides them with a foundation for the academic challenges that lie ahead, and that prepares them for a lifetime of successful learning.

Conclusion

The professional educator makes decisions about curriculum and methodology based on sound pedagogical theory, research, and the standards of the professional societies. The professional educator is responsible for keeping up with new curricular materials, new ideas about pedagogy, and current developments in the profession. Many opportunities are provided by national, state, regional, and local science teachers associations for elementary science teachers to attend conferences where they can share their experiences and expertise with each other.

Research in science education is vital to establishing the best ways of teaching science and the most appropriate curricula. The professional educator is in a unique position to undertake action research projects and share the results of this research with the professional community through conference papers and publications. By engaging in such activities, the professional elementary science teacher engages in lifelong learning.

CHAPTER 12

Additional Questions for Discussion

1. Cite the current professional literature that supports the system of elementary science education you have constructed, and describe what each says.

2. Discuss the desirability of preservice teachers becoming involved with action research during their field experiences. Discuss the extent to which teachers can get involved with action research during their first 1 or 2 years of service.

3. Prepare a "pretend" grant request to a granting agency for a science project you would like to have the agency fund.

4. What attributes do *you* believe characterize an excellent elementary science teacher?

Internet Activities

Explore the Internet to find information on grants that are available and grants that have been funded. Focus on the specific needs that each grant meets. Also, use these resources to find information on professional development opportunities for science teachers.

PART 3 BACK TO THE FUTURE

CHAPTER····· 14

A MODEL OF TEACHING BY LISTENING

You will find something more in woods than in books. Trees and stones will teach you that which you can never learn from masters.

Saint Bernard, *Epistle 106*

I have seen the future, and it works.

Lincoln Steffens, letter to Marie Howe, 1919

In this text, you have constructed your own meaningful and valid conceptualizations of the elementary science program. In coming to these constructions, you have taken innumerable factors into account such as the process-oriented inquiry methodology, the amount and kind of science content used to teach the processes, methods of assessment, and the enormously wide differences among children in the classroom. It has been proposed that children learn best that which is meaningful to them; yet not all children consider the same topic meaningful at the same time. It has been suggested that children begin their understanding of science with preconceived notions and that they construct and reconstruct these ideas in increasingly sophisticated forms as they experience new phenomena. Yet each child comes to the class with a different set of preconceived notions and prior experiences. It will occur to the perceptive student that the ultimate in science education would po-

tentially be each child studying something different at the same time.

This chapter offers a model of teaching science so that it is maximally meaningful to all children: *a model of teaching by listening.*[1]

NSES Content
Standard E. Science and
Technology: Abilities of
Technological Design
NSES Teaching
Standard B. Guiding and
Facilitating Learning

A CONSTRUCTIVIST EXPLORATION OF MOTORS

I once had a group of four boys in eighth-grade science who, for several years, had been learning that they weren't very smart, that they couldn't succeed because they couldn't (or wouldn't) read, and that they needed constant watching because if they were left alone, even for a moment, they would cause trouble.

You can imagine that these boys really felt great about themselves. But in fact, they did! They were the most popular boys in school because of the things they did and got away with. They were highly creative. With the kinds of restrictions placed on them by family and school, it took a great deal of creative planning for them to successfully pull off some of the things they got by with.

But academically, they were a most unhappy lot.

One day, early in the school year, I talked with them, trying to find out what would motivate these boys in science. I reasoned they were not learning any science out of the textbooks anyway, so if we could find something they were interested in, they just might learn something.

They responded that they wanted to study motors. Not out of books, but from motors themselves.

They outlined their goals—what they wanted to learn. Their goals were fuzzy, but basically they wanted to find out how each part of the motor worked. Not only the pistons, but all the parts.

So we requisitioned an abandoned V-8 engine and secured it in the back of the science classroom. The boys brought in tools from home, and they started taking the thing apart. As each part came off, they examined it and tried to figure out how that part fit in with the whole engine, understanding that without each part, the engine would not work. They were successful for some time, but eventually the day came when they could not figure out what a certain part was for. I knew next to nothing about automotive mechanics and was unable to help, so they had to find out in a different way. They looked in the textbooks, but none had information about motors. So they borrowed automotive repair manuals to read about how the component worked and how it related to the rest of the motor. Reading??? For those boys???

They delighted in explaining the motor to onlookers, verbalizing what they had learned and teaching the onlookers something they might not otherwise have learned. They decided to write descriptions of how the parts operated. The descriptions were not lengthy, but they were accurate and concise.

There were no discipline problems—lots of noise, but no behavior problems. The boys were far too busy investigating the motor to be bothered with trying to get attention or create difficult situations for the teacher.

They pursued this project for some 3 months, and when it was over, at their request, an automotive mechanic quizzed them on their understanding of how motors work. They passed with flying colors (Martin, 1975).

THE NEED FOR A DIFFERENT MODEL

Consider this scenario. It is early in the spring, and the pollen in the air is profuse. Children are asking questions about what pollen is, what it looks like, and why it causes allergies to act up. So you decide to capitalize on the children's demonstrated interest and provide a lesson on pollen. You collect pollen from several different kinds of plants—pine trees, hardwood trees, flowering plants, and grass—and you set up a microscope so the children can examine the pollen. The idea is for children to observe what pollen looks like and to describe the subtle but definite differences among the various kinds of pollen. You also plan to extend this concept to air pollution in general; for the next lesson, you will have children paint a thin layer of clear petroleum jelly on 1-foot-square pieces of black paper that they will suspend outdoors in various locations. They will count the number of grains that stick to the paper after, say, one full day and use the data to formulate hypotheses about the relationship between location and concentration of impurities in the air.

During the pollen lesson, a child unexpectedly begins asking questions about frogs. It seems he has discovered that a pond near his house is home to many frogs, and he wonders how they got there, what they eat, how they reproduce, and so on.

NSES Teaching Standard A. Inquiry-Based Program

14.1   CONSTRUCTING YOUR IDEAS

How Can Teachers Accommodate the Interests of All Children?

What can you do about this situation? Before you go any further, discuss this as a class.

You can handle this situation in several ways:

1. You can tell the child to wait until the topic of frogs comes up.

2. You can tell the child that you will be happy to begin a study of frogs after the study of air pollution is complete.

3. You can suggest that the child spend his free time pursuing references on frogs.

4. You can try to integrate the subject of frogs with the current lesson.

However, none of these options encourages the child to pursue his own interest. Your responses seek to preserve the integrity of the lesson you have planned. They send the message that the lesson you have planned is more important than some quixotic interest the child happens to have at the moment. Your hope is that the child will pursue the investigations of pollen and air pollution you have planned, even though he seems to be more interested in frogs.

There is another solution. You could encourage the child to begin an independent study of frogs *instead* of continuing with the lesson you had planned. This, of course, means that you will have two lessons going on at the same time: one on pollen and air pollution for most of the children in the class, and one on frogs for one child.

14.2   CONSTRUCTING YOUR IDEAS

Reaction to Multiple Simultaneous Inquiries

What is your reaction to the solution presented above? Discuss this as a class.

All teachers are faced with these situations; most try to resolve the issue by developing the most interesting lessons they can to capture the full attention of the children. The question, however, remains in the back of the teacher's mind: Would children do better in science if they were studying what *really* interests them?

A MODEL OF TEACHING BY LISTENING

The model of teaching by listening addresses this very issue.

For many years, the science education research agenda has focused on how to provide *meaning* to science education. A significant indicator of meaning is *interest*. This is not new. Ausubel said that the most important factor influencing what a child learns is what he already knows

(Ausubel, Novak, & Hanesian, 1978). Scardamalia (1988) said at a Holmes Group seminar, "The way you start is by asking students what they want to know." Easley (1990) proposed that teachers *listen* rather than *talk* to students. He called this concept *teaching by listening,* and it is this term that provides the title for the model.

The model of science teaching by listening is predicated on the idea that topics of interest to children carry inherent meaning and that only the children themselves know what is interesting to them. Grace (1999) and Diffily (2001) suggest that children in elementary grades select their own curriculum. Teachers must *listen* to children to find out what is meaningful. Novak (1992) defined meaningful learning as the constructive integration of thinking, feeling, and acting, leading to human empowerment. *Meaningfulness* of science thus becomes child-centered and child-generated. It becomes relevant and nonimposed. Teachers listen not only to children's interests but also to what they are thinking, how they are constructing information, and how they are validating the conceptualizations they construct. Children talk first, and teachers facilitate as necessary.

The model is cyclical and involves four phases: (1) topic selection, (2) plan of action, (3) activity, and (4) evaluation (see Figure 14.1).

The model involves close and continual interaction between the teacher and groups of children investigating the same topic. Initially, a team is formed of the teacher and several children with similar interests. During the *topic selection* phase, this team establishes the specific topic to be studied based largely on interest expressed by the children.

Next, a *plan of action* is developed by the team; this plan details the specific activities to be pursued. Children's abilities and learning style preferences; the availability of materials, resources, and facilities; and the teacher's previous knowledge of the children and academic goals for the class influence the choice of activities. A timetable and methods of reporting progress and achievement are established during this phase.

During the *activity* phase, the teacher acts as facilitator of the children's learning. The children work in groups while the teacher observes and listens, offering helpful guidance and clarification as required. During this phase, much valuable information about process skill mastery, content acquisition, personal learning style, and other factors is obtained by both children and teacher to help guide the direction of current and future studies.

The *evaluation* phase completes the cycle and serves as the transition between the current study and the proposed new topic. New groups are formed, again based on interest, and a new cycle begins.

Topic Selection Phase

The first phase is the topic selection phase. To get started, an ad hoc team is formed that consists of the teacher and several children who have expressed similar interests. The teacher and the children meet to establish

NSES Program Standard A. Consistent Goals Across Grades
NSES Program Standard B. Relevant, Inquiry-Based, and Connected with Other Subjects
NSES Program Standard C. Coordinated with Mathematics
NSES Program Standard D. Appropriate with Sufficient Resources
NSES Program Standard E. Equal Opportunities for All Students
NSES Program Standard F. Encourages, Supports, and Sustains Teachers

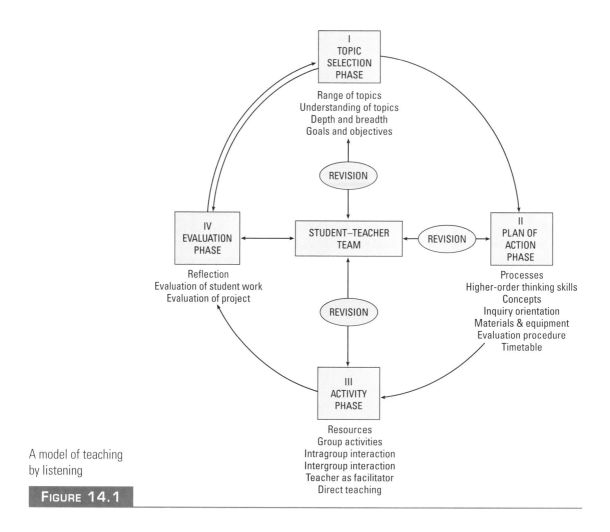

A model of teaching by listening

FIGURE 14.1

the specific topic. The teacher asks questions of the children, and the children ask questions of the teacher in a safe, interactive dynamic. This continues until both teacher and children have a clear understanding of what is to be studied. Topics can be selected from the full spectrum of science or interdisciplinary topics and can be treated in many different ways, from in-depth studies of single concepts to broad, "big picture" overviews of a large area.

For example, one child may express interest in studying frogs. As discussions proceed, it may emerge that the best way to achieve the child's goals is to study the external and internal anatomy of the frog. Or, perhaps the best way is to study the frog's interaction with its environment. Or, perhaps both are warranted. In addition, as other children overhear the discussions between the teacher and the child, they may want to get involved, thus enlarging the group.

In the case of the boys who studied engines, the topic of engines was the only interest they had. All four of them had the same interest, and all four of them worked as a team. Their topic began as a detailed study of a large area of inquiry—the way engines work.

The teacher with a new class possesses limited information about the children. However, as the children work, both child and teacher gain more and more insight into the educative process for that child. The teacher plays a critical role in helping children organize inquiry skills, process skills, higher-order thinking, and so on into their proposed studies.

Concurrent with topic selection is determination of one or more goals or objectives to be accomplished as a result of having studied the proposed topic. Indeed, when a group of children works on the same topic, the objectives often differ for each child in the group. But, they are always investigative, always inquiry-oriented, and always reflective of what the students are interested in studying by using "expressive outcomes" rather than formal objectives (Poetter, 2006). Membership of the group may change during this initial phase as the degree of congruency between the interests of individual children and the emerging topic of study becomes apparent.

Factors influencing selection of the topic to be studied include at least the following:

Child-Oriented Considerations

- Interest
- Meaningfulness of topic
- Abilities
- Developmental needs
- Social interaction needs
- Experience with group work
- Reading ability
- Personal factors: gender, age, intelligence, socioeconomic status, culture
- Home factors
- Attitudes

Academic Considerations

- Prior science experiences
- Prior science achievement
- Academic needs and goals: process skills and content
- Problem-solving needs
- Level of understanding
- Higher-order thinking skills
- Understanding of scientific values
- Academic outcomes: program goals, scientific and techno-logical literacy

Plan of Action Phase

The next phase of the model is the plan of action phase. Having established the topic to be studied and the goals or objectives of the study, the team formulates a plan of action that details the specific activities to be pursued. Children have their own ideas of what to do, and the teacher has specific ideas of what the children ought to do in the way of developing process skills, higher-order thinking, conceptual understandings, and so on. The activities might include reading, performing lab activities, doing computer work, viewing videos, looking for relevant information on the Internet, working with a WebQuest, building a Web site, and a whole host of other learning experiences. The specific activities are listed together with the resources to be used for each activity. The specific activities that are planned depend, to a large extent, on what material is available. A checklist of resources to be considered includes at least the following:

- Books
- Audiovisual materials such as charts, maps, drawings, models, videos, films, filmstrips
- Computers
- Computer-assisted instruction programs
- The Internet

- WebQuests
- Library materials
- Concept maps
- Laboratory materials and equipment
- Lectures and demonstrations on videotape and audiotape
- People

Various learning strategies are considered, such as the following:

- Independent study
- Group work
- Grouping by interest
- Cooperative learning
- Question-and-answer and discussion sessions in groups or with the teacher

- Teacher demonstrations
- Inquiry and guided discovery activities
- Whole-class activities

During this phase, the team decides how to evaluate the work and how the children will report their progress to the teacher. Reporting options include at least the following:

- Written and verbal reports
- Demonstrations
- Tapes
- Video productions
- Drawings
- Model construction
- Concept map development

- Construction of Web sites
- Poster presentations
- Class presentations
- PowerPoint® presentations
- Panel discussions
- Web publishing

A timetable for activities and completion also is established. It is important to note that this plan of action is not set in cement—it is the team's best approximation at the time. Revision is crucial to the success of the program.

Activity Phase

In the activity phase, children begin their investigations. In a well-designed classroom, children know where the resources are and assemble what they need: table space, materials, things they bring in from home, reference books, visuals, models, videos, computers with Internet access, computer programs, CD-ROMs, and so on.

The classroom is busy. One group is dissecting a frog, using models, lab manuals, and drawings to guide their work. Once they perfect the technique, they plan to demonstrate dissections for children in the lower grades. Another group of children is watching a video (using earphones) or a filmstrip on the human circulatory system, relating what they see and hear to what they read in texts in their efforts to understand how the human body functions. Still another group is drawing charts of observations of the night sky they made over the past two or three nights, checking their charts against the references. One group is dissecting a worm (it is their first dissection, so from time to time they seek guidance from the group dissecting the frog), and another group is investigating friction using inclined boards with various surfaces. Some children are taking notes. Some are writing in their journals. Some are drawing. Some have left the room to use other resources. Locations of activity may include the classroom, study carrels, the hallway, the media center, resource rooms, the playground, school grounds, and home.

The teacher is very busy, moving from group to group, listening to the children, asking questions, probing for understandings, and challenging new understandings. The room is noisy, but everyone soon gets used to the din as they focus on their own activities. Children are busy figuring out things for themselves.

Groups visit other groups, and individual children get ideas about what they do and do not want to do. Groups welcome these visits, because it gives them an opportunity to explain what they are doing and studying.

Revision is the key to this phase. The teacher understands the children better, and the children increase their awareness of themselves, each other, and the topics under study. As a result, the plan, the objectives, or even the topic itself may be revised to reflect this new and increased understanding.

For example, a group of children who decided to study the human circulatory system may find the topic is too specific and revise their topic to include the interaction of the circulatory system with other systems of the body. A group working on friction may find they do not understand how to isolate the variables in complex systems, so they decide to focus on a simpler inquiry such as the relationship between the degree of incline of a board and the time it takes for a cart to roll down the board. Once they gain familiarity with isolating variables, they will return to the friction investigations.

From time to time, a team forms a huddle and rethinks a topic or holds an evaluation session. Or a newly formed group may need to begin its topic selection and plan of action phases. Sometimes the teacher pulls the whole class together for an item of interest to all—a demonstration, a guest speaker, a contemporary event. Now and then, the teacher provides direct instruction for a group.

Evaluation Phase

The final phase in this cyclical model is the evaluation phase. When the investigation or project is complete, the children submit the agreed-on evaluation, and the team spends a few minutes reflecting on the just-completed topics: understandings, thinking, processes, concepts, strengths, areas for improvement, work habits, acceptance of responsibility, most effective activities, least effective activities, and so on.

Evaluation is a continual process. The teacher encourages the children to constantly evaluate themselves with respect to academic goals, inquiry skills, processes, thinking, learning styles, and so on.

At the conclusion of the project and its evaluation, the teacher prepares a formal assessment that documents the child's performance (1) relative to self (Were the objectives met? Were the developmental goals met? Were the time goals met?) and (2) relative to norms based on standardized test and criterion-referenced test results and to other national norms (science content, processes, concepts, understandings, and thinking and reasoning skills attained). In the post-project conference, children and the teacher discuss the children's overall performance, focusing primarily on mutually increased understanding of each child's academic needs, developmental needs, interests, abilities, and attitudes. A progress report is sent to parents (see Figure 14.2), and the information is recorded in a permanent file (see Figure 14.3) that forms a record of the child's progress and is forwarded to the science teacher in the next grade.

The Next Cycle

Many academic and developmental factors emerge as a result of a study, and these factors are taken into account when the next topic is planned. When the boys who investigated the workings of the V-8 engine had passed their "final exam," it was time for them to select the next topic. Recall that although they had never read for information in the past, they found it necessary to read to obtain enough information to answer their questions about the workings of the engine. This project helped those boys accomplish a heretofore impossible goal—to want to read for information. This desire to read for information became apparent as they selected their next topics. All four boys chose topics that required substantial reading, such as archaeology and astronomy. In my planning conferences with them, I explained that the topics they had selected would require a lot of reading. That was fine with them. They had always wanted to learn about these things.

Management

As this system progresses, the teacher builds a repertoire of projects undertaken by previous groups, maintained in the form of outlines that list activities done previously and materials available for the study. These are used to form the basis of similar studies for other groups interested in the same topic so the teacher does not have to start from scratch each time. It also may be possible to enlist the help of other teachers (especially if you are in a team-teaching situation), older children, family members, and community resources.

You should have experience in teaching science before you embark on this type of science program. And even then, it would be well to start the program slowly. You might want to limit the diversity of projects in your classroom to accommodate only those who are having difficulty with the material you are presenting. To scrap the class-oriented approach and move to this model in one fell swoop is folly. It takes time to prepare children to assume their responsibility, and it takes time for children to become adjusted to this way of doing business. Children need much modeling at first to show them how to make decisions and perform investigations with minimal help from the teacher, especially if they have grown accustomed to learning about science and doing science activities "by the numbers."

I found that having children make daily journal entries helps keep them focused on their project and reminds them each day where they had left

PROGRESS REPORT

Pupil _____   Date _____

Unit Studied _____   Time Period _____

PART I—COMPETITION WITH SELF

This part shows how well your child has been working and learning compared with ability as indicated by standardized test results and classroom performance.

During this time period, your child's success in fulfilling potential is rated as follows:

_____   Your child has been performing within ability range.
_____   Your child has been performing exceptionally well.
_____   Your child has been performing below ability range.

PART II—RELATIVE PERFORMANCE

This part reflects your child's achievement level in learning experiences compared with the achievement levels for the class as a whole.

At this date, your child's relative achievement is rated as follows:

_____   Above average
_____   Average
_____   Needs improvement

CONFERENCE NOTES

_____   I feel that a conference with you would be helpful. Parents are invited to initiate conferences at any time and may do so by calling the school office.

COMMENTS:

_____   _____
Teacher   Date

Teaching by listening progress report

FIGURE 14.2

CUMULATIVE RECORD

CUMULATIVE RECORD OF PROGRESS IN SCIENCE

Name _____   Year _____   Grade _____

Inferred academic ability _____ based on _____

Demonstrated interest in science _____

Standardized Test Results

Test						
National Score						

Time Period	Unit	Progress in Regard to Self[1]			Progress in Regard to Norm[2]			Comments and Conference Notes
		S	EX	BR	AB	AV	NI	

(1) S: Satisfactory progress
    EX: Exceptional progress
    BR: Below ability range

(2) AB: Above average
    AV: Average
    NI: Needs improvement

Teaching by listening cumulative record

FIGURE 14.3

off the day before so they do not have to ask the teacher every time. However, at first children need help in making journal entries. I also found that providing storage space for children helps them keep track of their materials; when the time for science is over, children merely slide their things into the designated area, knowing that everything will be there the next time they have science. Behavior management ceases to be a problem because all children are interested in what they are doing and they pursue their studies with a vigor and intensity seldom seen in traditional settings. However, it is impossible to insist on silence. The room is noisy—but creatively noisy.

CONCLUDING REMARKS

Children can only learn what is meaningful to them. Science has so many topics to choose from that every child can find topics that are meaningful. Yet science educators persist in covering certain prescribed content out of fear that if children are not exposed to every science topic in a systematic manner, their science education will be lacking, the U.S. science achievement report card will plummet, and we will register declines in international "scienceship."

For many years, leaders in education and business have urged defocusing from content-oriented science programs and, instead, working toward a science education that teaches "less so it can be taught better" (American Association for the Advancement of Science, 1989); that teaches science not as a body of knowledge but as a way of thinking (Sagan, 1989); that focuses on children rather than teachers (Glasser, 1990). Outcomes of science education are described today in terms of the "what" and "how" and "why" of scientific investigation rather than the accumulation of facts (Aldridge, 1989), and in terms of scientific literacy (Hurd, 1986). Ingenious instructional techniques designed to engage children more actively in the learning process are being advanced. Teachers are urged to take hard looks at the nature of learners and to use their findings to devise appropriate instructional strategies that teach all children how to do science and encourage all children to make choices about scientific values. Integration of science with other subject matter, innovative instructional practices, and unification of topics in science, technology, and society are among the contemporary goals for quality science education.

The literature abounds with descriptions of individual differences among learners: learning style, cognitive style, learning modality, intelligence, creativity, reasoning ability, special physical, cognitive, and language needs and on and on and on. No teacher can possibly know each and every individual difference that characterizes each and every individual child. However, teachers are expected to teach in ways that enable each individual child to learn maximally, given that child's unique learning style. Expository teaching methodologies, of necessity, are directed at the nonexistent middle-of-the-road child. Free discovery teaching may leave children so much in charge of their own learning process that they may fail to advance to their full potential or to meet specific objectives.

The model of teaching by listening is a child-focused science teaching strategy that takes into account scientific processes, scientific content, the myriad individual differences among children, and learning by doing. The basic assumption of the model is that if children are studying something that interests them, they are more likely to learn than if they are required to study something solely because the teacher said so. The certainty of each child learning *something* is preferable to the possibility of children *not* learning.

There are concerns with this model. Most frequently raised are concerns about children's freedom and the lack of methodical coverage of content. These concerns are more a matter of perception than reality. Children are not treated permissively. They have the freedom to choose, but they also have responsibility and accountability for their studies. Concerning content coverage, it has been my experience that children do, in fact, study the traditional amount of content. They may cover it in different ways—and it may take longer—but they do cover it.

Teaching in this manner is difficult. But, as Glasser (1990, p. 60) says, "Being an effective teacher may be the most difficult of all common jobs in our society."

> The true scientist never loses the faculty of amazement. It is the essence of his being. Hans Selye, *Newsweek,* March 31, 1958

Note

1. I am indebted to Dr. Edward C. Lucy, Professor of Science Education, Georgia State University, for guidance in preparing this chapter.

Appendix A
Activities Cross-Referenced to Basic Scientific Concepts and Principles

PHYSICAL SCIENCE CONCEPTS AND PRINCIPLES

FORCE AND MOTION

HEAT ENERGY AND STATES OF MATTER

SOUND ENERGY

LIGHT

ELECTRICITY AND MAGNETISM

MATTER AND CHEMICAL ENERGY

APPENDIX B
Listing of Children's Literature

Some titles are out of print but may be available in school or public libraries.

GLOSSARY

accommodation   Forming new schemata or splitting off new schemata from existing schemata to accommodate new information

advance organizer   The introductory frame of reference that precedes each lesson

anemometer   Wind speed gauge

anomalous   Deviating from accepted rules or ideas

assimilation   Enlarging schemata with new information

auditory   A style of learning in which the learner relies on hearing the information

authentic assessment   Assessment of what children *really* know

beta particle   An electron emitted from an atom

biome   A kind of ecological community, such as tropical rain forest, grassland, or desert

CD-ROM   (compact disc, read-only memory) A data disc on which audio and visual information is stored for access and playback

chromosomes   Rod-shaped structures in the nucleus of living cells that contain the genetic material for organisms

class inclusion   A classification system in which groupings are included as subordinates of a larger class

closed question   A question with a single answer (see *convergent question*)

cloud chamber   A device the enables people to see trails left by the emission of particles from radioactive materials

cognitive disequilibration   A state of mental uncertainty about the explanation of an occurrence

cognitive equilibration   A state of mental satisfaction

combinatorial reasoning   Finding ways that items can be arranged in sequence

concrete operational stage   A stage of cognitive development in which people think in terms of concrete objects

conservation   (in Piagetian theory) The ability of a person to recognize that the amount of material does not change when the shape of material changes

constructivism   The notion that people build their own knowledge and representations of new information from their own experience

convergent questions   A question with a single answer

correlational reasoning   Finding the extent to which changes in one variable are associated with changes in another variable

crystal   A solid of a regular shape that has a regularly repeating internal arrangement of atoms; formed by the solidification of a chemical compound

culture medium   A nutritional environment that promotes the growth of microorganisms, especially bacteria

database   A computer program in which either numeric or nonnumeric data are entered into rows and columns for calculation and manipulation

decant   Pouring off the top liquid without disturbing the lower layers

deductive teaching   A teaching style in which the content proceeds from the most general to the most specific

dendrochronology   The study of tree rings

density   Weight or mass divided by volume; expressed in terms of weight per unit of volume

dependent variable   The variable in an experiment for which the value may change because of a change in the interacting independent variable

diffusion   The even distribution of materials within each other

discrepant event   An event that is at variance with what is expected

dispersion   Scattering

displacement   A technique for measuring the volume of an irregularly shaped object by immersing it in a liquid and measuring the volume of liquid that it replaces

divergent question   A question that may have many equally valid answers

DNA   Deoxyribonucleic acid; the building block of genetic material

dwarf planet   A planet that is too small to attract other objects in its orbit and, thus, cannot "clear its neighborhood"

earwigs   Insects with many antennae and a pincer-like tail end

ecliptic   The great circle of the celestial sphere that is the apparent path of the sun among the stars

ecology   The study of the relationships among living things and their environments

ecosystem   A living community, including its environment

egocentric   Pertaining to one's self

electron   An atomic particle with a negative charge and a mass 1/1,837th the mass of a proton (almost zero mass)

English-language learner (ELL)   A person who is learning to read, write, and speak English

eon   One billion years

epistemology   The study of the nature and basis of knowledge

ESOL   Acronym for *English for Speakers of Other Languages*

ethnocentric curriculum   A curriculum approach in which topics relate to a particular ethnicity

explanatory power   The ability of a theory to satisfactorily explain an occurrence

expository   Conveying information

field dependence   A trait of people whereby they have difficulty recognizing camouflaged information

field independence   The ability of individuals to recognize camouflaged information easily

formal operational stage   A stage of cognitive development in Piagetian theory in which people think in abstract terms

fossil fuel   Fuel formed from living organisms that died millions of years ago (e.g., coal, oil, and gas)

free discovery   A methodology in which children are free to explore topics of their own interest under the facilitation of the teacher

friction   The force between two objects or materials that resists their relative motion

fusion   An atomic reaction in which nuclei combine to form heavier nuclei and release vast amounts of energy

gamma ray   High-energy radiation emitted by radioactive materials

genes   Specific sequences of DNA located on a chromosome that determines inherited traits

genetics   The study of inheritance and variation in living organisms

genome   The total genetic material of an organism

geode   A hollow rock that often is lined with crystals on the inside

geology   The study of the earth's history and life, especially as recorded in rocks

gradient   Rate of change

graphic organizer software   Computer programs used to develop pictorial organization of material

graphing program   A computer program used to generate graphs of data

guided inquiry   A methodology in which children investigate topics established by the teacher in their own ways

half-life   The time it takes for half a given quantity of radioactive material to decay

hardware   The physical components and apparatus of computers

hay infusion   A medium in which single-celled or very small animals can thrive made of stagnant water to which pieces of hay, dry leaves, and dry grass have been added

high-stakes testing   Standardized tests whose results determine children's promotions in school, teacher's evaluations, school funding, and other areas critical to education

hypothesis   A tentative assumption regarding the influence of one variable in a system on another variable in the system

igneous   A rock formed from magma

independent variable   The variable in an experiment that the investigator is changing

indicator   (for assessment) An item that is used to gauge or indicate children's achievement

inductive teaching   A teaching style in which the content proceeds from the most specific to the most general

integrated curriculum   A curriculum organized around themes, problems, and issues, without regard for subject-area boundaries

integrative reconciliation   A teaching strategy in which the teacher helps students to reconcile new information with their backgrounds, experiences, and prior knowledge

interdisciplinarianism   A curriculum design that includes more than one discipline in an area of study

interpolation   Estimating values between two known values

isolation and control of variables   The scientific process of identifying variables that bear on a hypothesis and keeping all variables constant except the one that is being experimented with

kinesthetic   A style of learning in which the learner relies on touching and feeling for information

kinetic   The state of being in motion

locus of control   The degree to which people attribute responsibility for success or failure to internal or external factors

lodestone   An iron ore mineral that is a natural magnet

metamorphic   A rock formed through radical changes (usually high temperatures and pressures) to previously existing rocks

metamorphosis   Change in the form of an animal during its life cycle

metaphor   A figure of speech suggesting an analogy

meteoroid   A meteor particle

modality   The manner in which people take in and process information

multidisciplinary   An approach to curriculum in which individual subjects and skills are related to a central theme

multiple intelligence theory   A theory that posits that humans have several intelligences of varying strengths

neuron   A nerve; a single, elongated cell that is the basic unit of the nervous system

neutron   An atomic particle with no charge and a mass of one atomic mass unit

nucleus   The positively charged central mass of an atom

opaque   Unable to transmit light or other radiant energy

open-ended question   A question that may have many equally valid answers (see *divergent question*)

paradigm   A pattern of concepts

parsimony   Economical use of means to an end

perception   One's mental image of what is experienced

period   The time required for a cycle to complete itself and begin the next cycle

petri dish   A shallow dish with a loose cover that is used in bacteriology work

pH   A measure of the degree to which a substance is an acid, a base, or neutral

photoelectric cell   A device that converts light energy into electric energy

physiology   The study of the functions and activities of living things

planet   A celestial body that is not a star, orbits around a star, is nearly spherical in shape, has "cleared the neighborhood" around its orbit, and is not a satellite

plate tectonics   The theory regarding crustal movement of the earth's continents and ocean basins

precipitate   An insoluble substance separated from a solution by a chemical or a physical change

predictive power   The ability of a theory to correctly predict an outcome

preoperational stage   An early stage of cognitive development in Piagetian theory applicable to children in the preschool and early school years

presentation software   Computer programs used for electronic presentations

probabilistic reasoning   Finding probabilities of events occurring

process-oriented inquiry   A methodology in which students explore concepts through the use of the scientific processes

progressive differentiation   A teaching strategy in which information is isolated so that it can be connected to information learned previously

propagation   Reproduction

proportional reasoning Comparing the relationships between variables

proton An atomic particle with a positive charge and a mass of one atomic mass unit

protozoan A single-celled animal

qualitative Description of attributes or characteristics of objects or events

qualitative assessment Assessment that is interpreted through nonnumeric data

quantitative Measurement of the quantity of attributes or characteristics of objects or events

quantitative assessment Assessment that is interpreted through numeric data

saturated A solution that contains the maximum solute possible under existing conditions

scaffolding Adjusting the amount of teacher or peer guidance to fit the current performance level of the student

schema (pl. *schemata*) A cognitive structure

schematic (in electricity) A drawing that shows the connection of wires, sources of power, and electrical devices included in the circuits

Science–Technology–Society (STS) A multidisciplinary, project-centered approach to science education

scientific literacy The knowledge and understanding of scientific concepts so that they can be used in personal decision making, participation in civic and cultural affairs, and economic productivity

sedimentary A rock formed from the consolidation and cementation of sediments, usually on the floors of lakes, seas, and oceans

sensorimotor stage The earliest stage of human cognitive development in Piagetian theory

small solar system bodies All objects other than planets and dwarf planets that revolve about a star

software Programs that are used by computers; software may be available on CD-ROMs or hard drives or may be downloaded from the Internet

solute A substance dissolved in a solution

solution A homogeneous mixture

solvent A substance that can dissolve something

spreadsheet A computer program in which numeric data are entered into rows and columns for calculation and manipulation

synapse The point at which a nerve impulse passes from one neuron to another

tactile Perceptible by touch

translucent Able to transmit diffused light or other radiant energy such that images are blurred

transparent Able to transmit light or other radiant energy such that images are seen clearly

turbidity The degree of opaqueness or muddiness of a substance

validity (in research) A conclusion correctly deduced from the evidence

variable An attribute of a system that influences how the system behaves

visual A style of learning in which the learner relies on seeing the information

word processing programs Computer programs used for writing and editing textual material

zone of proximal development (ZPD) The range of learning activities that are too difficult for children to master alone but that can be learned with guidance and assistance from teachers and peers

REFERENCES

References with the World Wide Web icon can be accessed directly from the Student Book Companion Web Site.

Aardema, V. (1981). *Bringing the rain to Kapiti Plain: A Nandi tale.* New York: Dial.

Acher, A., Arcà, M., & Sanmarti, N. (2007). Modeling as a teaching learning process for understanding materials: A case study in primary education. *Science Education, 91*(3), 398–418.

Adams, P., Mitchener, C., & Johnson, V. (1987). *Water magic.* Cleveland, OH: Modern Curriculum Press.

Adler, D. A., & Tobin, N. (1999). *How tall, how short, how far away?* New York: Holiday House.

Adler, J. (2006, November 6). Plotting Pluto's comeback: Some astronomers want to reclaim the status of planet for the distant ball of rock and ice. *Newsweek,* 60.

Akerson, V. L. (2005). "How should I know what scientists do? I am just a kid": Fourth-grade students' conceptions of nature of science. *Journal of Elementary Science Education, 17*(1), 1–11.

Akerson, V. L., & Young, T. A. (2005, November/December). Science in the "write" way. *Science and Children, 43*(3), 38–41.

Aldridge, B. G. (1989). *Essential changes in secondary school science: Scope, sequence, and coordination.* Washington, DC: National Science Teachers Association.

Alesandrini, K., & Larson, L. (2002). Teachers bridge to constructivism. *The Clearing House, 75*(3), 118–121.

Aliki. (1981). *Digging up dinosaurs.* New York: Crowell.

Aliki. (1985). *My five senses.* New York: Crowell.

Aliki. (1988). *Digging up dinosaurs.* New York: Crowell.

Aliki. (1989). *My five senses.* New York: Crowell.

Aliki. (1990). *My feet.* New York: Crowell.

Aliki. (1993). *Communication.* New York: Greenwillow Books.

Allen, J. (1990). *Mucky Moose.* New York: Macmillan.

Allen, J. (1993). *Elephant.* Cambridge, MA: Candlewick Press.

Allen, P. (1980). *Mr. Archimedes' bath.* Sydney: HarperCollins.

Allen, R. (2003). Building school culture in an age of accountability. *Education Update, 45*(7), 1–8.

Allen, R. (2005). New paradigms for parental involvement. *Education Update 47*(3), 3–4.

American Association for the Advancement of Science. (1989). *Project 2061: Science for all Americans.* Washington, DC: Author.

American Association for the Advancement of Science. (1994). *Benchmarks for science literacy: Project 2061.* New York: Oxford University Press.

American Association for the Advancement of Science. (1997). *Resources for science literacy.* New York: Oxford University Press.

American Association for the Advancement of Science. (1998). *Blueprints for reform.* New York: Oxford University Press.

American Association for the Advancement of Science. (2001a). *Atlas of science literacy* volume 1. Washington, DC: Author.

American Association for the Advancement of Science. (2001b). *Designs for science literacy.* New York: Oxford University Press.

American Association for the Advancement of Science. (2008). *Atlas of science literacy* volume 2. Washington, DC: Author.

 American Association of Museums. (n.d.). Museums FAQ.

Amrein, A. L., & Berliner, D. C. (2003). The effects of high-stakes testing on student motivation and learning. *Educational Leadership, 60*(5), 32–38.

Annetta, L. A., & Shymansky, J. A. (2006). Investigating science learning for rural elementary school teachers in a professional-development project through distance-learning strategies. *Journal of Research in Science Teaching, 43*(10), 1019–1039.

Anthony, J. A. (1997). *The dandelion seed.* Nevada City, CA: Dawn Publications.

Appleton, K. (2007). Elementary science teaching. In S. K. Abell & N. G. Lederman (Eds.), *Handbook of research on science education.* Mahwah, NJ: Lawrence Erlbaum Associates.

Armbruster, B. B. (1993). Reading to learn. *The Reading Teacher, 46*(4), 346–347.

Arnett, R. H., & Jacques, R. L., Jr. (1981l). *Simon and Schuster's guide to insects.* New York: Simon and Schuster.

Arnosky, J. (1983). *Secrets of a wildlife watcher.* New York: Lothrop, Lee & Shepard.

Arnosky, J. (1992). *Crinkleroot's guide to knowing the trees.* New York: Bradbury Press.

Arnosky, J. (2002). *All about frogs.* New York: Scholastic Press.

Ash, D., & Levitt, K. (2003). Working within the zone of proximal development: Formative assessment as professional development. *Journal of Science Teacher Education, 14*(1), 23–48.

 Association of Children's Museums. (2007). Stats and trends.

Association for Supervision and Curriculum Development. (2003). *Maximizing learning for English language learners* (CD and instructor's manual). Alexandria, VA: Author.

Ausubel, D. P. (1968). *Educational psychology: A cognitive view.* New York: Holt, Rinehart & Winston.

Ausubel, D. P., Novak, J. D., & Hanesian, H. (1978). *Educational psychology: A cognitive view* (2nd ed.). New York: Holt, Rinehart and Winston.

Avila, C. B. (1998). What the real experts say. *Science and Children, 35*(7), 14–17, 42.

Baird, A. (1994). *The U.S. Space Camp book of rockets.* New York: Morrow Junior Books.

Baker, K. (1990). *Who is the beast?* San Diego: Harcourt Brace Jovanovich.

Bamberger, Y., & Tal, T. (2007). Learning in a personal context: Levels of choice in a free choice learning environment in science and natural history museums. *Science Education, 91*(1), 75–95.

Barber, J., Buegler, M. E., & Willard, C. (1988). *Discovering density.* Berkeley, CA: CEMS/Lawrence Hall of Science.

Barman, C. R. (1992). An evaluation of the use of a technique designed to assist prospective elementary teachers use the learning cycle with science textbooks. *School Science and Mathematics, 92*(2), 59–63.

Barrow, L. H. (2006). A brief history of inquiry: From Dewey to standards. *Journal of Science Teacher Education, 17*(3), 265–278.

Bartlett, S. (2006). Pluto left out in the cold. *The Lancet, 368* (9538), 828–829.

Bash, B. (1989). *Desert giant: The world of the saguaro cactus.* San Francisco: Sierra Club/ Little, Brown.

Basu, S. J., & Barton, A. C. (2007). Developing a sustained interest in science among urban minority youth. *Journal of Research in Science Teaching, 44*(3), 466–489.

Baylor, B. (1974). *Everybody needs a rock.* New York: Aladdin.

Beane, J. A. (1997). *Curriculum integration: Designing the core of democratic education.* New York: Teachers College Press.

Becker, B. J. (1989). Gender and science achievement: A reanalysis of studies from two meta-analyses. *Journal of Research in Science Teaching, 26*(2), 141–169.

Bell, B. (2007). Classroom assessment of science learning. In S. K. Abell & N. G. Lederman (Eds.), *Handbook of research in science education.* Mahwah, NJ: Lawrence Erlbaum Associates.

Benedis-Grab, G. (2006). Sinking and floating. *Science Scope, 30*(2), 18–21.

Benner, B. (1996). *The plant that kept on growing.* Milwaukee, WI: Gareth Stevens Publishing.

Bennett, J., Lubben, F., & Hogarth, S. (2007). Bringing science to life: A synthesis of the research evidence on the effects of context-based STS approaches to science teaching. *Science Education, 91*(3), 347–370.

Benoit, O. (1997). *Who killed Olive Soufflé?* New York: Learning Triangle.

Berenstain, J., & Berenstain, S. (1977). *The Berenstain Bears' science fair.* New York: Random House.

Berenstain, S., & Berenstain, J. (1996). *The Berenstain Bears grow-it: Mother Nature has such a green thumb.* New York: Random House.

Berger, C. (2006, October/November). What are bugs worth? *National Wildlife, 44*(6), 37–43.

Berger, M. (1992). *All about seeds.* New York: Scholastic.

Berra, Y. (1998). *The Yogi book: "I really didn't say everything I said."* New York: Workman Publishing.

Bianchini, J. A., Cavazos, L. M., & Helms, J. V. (2000). From professional lives to inclusive practice: Science teachers and scientists' views of gender and ethnicity in science education. *Journal of Research in Science Teaching, 37*(6), 511–547.

Bibby, G. (1970). *Looking for Dilmun.* New York: Alfred A. Knopf.

Biological Sciences Curriculum Study (BSCS). (1989). *New designs for elementary school science and health: A comparative project of Biological sciences Curriculum Study (BSCS) and International Business Machines (IBM).* Dubuque, IA: Kendall Hunt.

Bloom, B. S., Englehart, M. D., Furst, E. J., Hill, W. H., & Krathwohl, D. R. (Eds.). (1956). *Taxonomy of educational objectives: The classification of educational goals. Handbook I: Cognitive domain.* New York: McKay.

Bodies, The Exhibition (2006).

Bodzin, A. M., & Beerer, K. M. (2003). Promoting inquiry-based science: The validation of the Science Teacher Inquiry Rubric (STIR). *Journal of Elementary Science Education, 15*(2), 39–49.

Bohr, N. (1958). In G. Holton & H. D. Roller (Eds.), *Foundations of modern physical science.* Reading, MA: Addison-Wesley.

Bollman, K. A., Rodgers, M. H., & Mauller, R. L. (2001). Jupiter quest: A path to scientific discovery. *Phi Delta Kappan, 82*(9), 683–686.

BouJaoudi, S. (2000). Conceptions of science teaching revealed by metaphors and by answers to open-ended questions. *Journal of Science Teacher Education, 11*(2), 173–186.

Bowman, B. T. (1994). The challenge of diversity. *Phi Delta Kappan, 76*(3), 218–224.

Bradley, F. M. (1988). *Air is all around you.* New York: Crowell.

Branley, F., & Vaughn, E. (1956). *Mickey's magnet.* New York: Scholastic.

Bransfield, P., Holt, P., & Mastasi, P. (2007). Coaching to build support for inquiry-based teaching. *Science Scope, 30*(5), 49–51.

Bransford, J. D., Brown, A. L., & Cocking, R. R. (Eds.) (1999). *How people learn: Brain, mind, experience, and school.* Washington, DC: National Academy Press.

Braun, J. A., Jr. (2004). Technology in the classroom: Tools for building stronger communities and better citizens. *Kappa Delta Pi Record, 40*(2), 69–73.

Breathed, B. (1992). *The last basselope: One ferocious story.* Boston: Little, Brown.

Brett, J. (1989). *The mitten: A Ukrainian folktale.* New York: G. P. Putnam.

Brickhouse, N. W. (2001). Embodying science: A feminist perspective on learning. *Journal of Research in Science Teaching, 38*(3), 282–295.

Brickman, R. (2002). *Beaks!* Watertown, MA: Charlesbridge.

 Britt, B. R. (2006). Scientists decide Pluto's no longer a planet. Pluto definition approved, but dissenters plan a counteroffensive. *MSNBC .com.*

Brookover, W., Beady, C., Flood, P., Schweister, J., & Wisenbaker, J. (1979*). School social systems and student achievement.* New York: Praeger.

Brooks, J. G., & Brooks, M. G. (1999). *In search of understanding: The case for constructivist classrooms.* Alexandria, VA: Association for Supervision and Curriculum Development.

Brown, C. L., & Bentley, M. (2004). ELLs: Children left behind in science class. *Academic Exchange Quarterly, 8*(3), 152–157.

Brown, J. (2002). *Journey into the desert.* New York: Oxford University Press.

Brown, K. (2006, Fall). The power of 'mental velcro': Learning that sticks. *Human Sciences Matters, NA Newsletter for Alumni and Friends of the College of Human Sciences, Iowa State University.* Ames, IA: Iowa State University College of Human Sciences.

Brown, M. (1975). *Stone soup: An old tale.* New York: Charles Scribner's Sons.

Brown, P. L., Abell, S. K., Demir, A., & Schmidt, F. J. (2006). College science teachers' views of classroom inquiry. *Science Education, 90*(5), 784–202.

Brown, V. (2007). The power of PowerPoint: Is it in the user or the program? *Childhood Education, 83*(4), 231–233.

Bruner, J. S. (1960). *The process of education.* Cambridge, MA: Harvard University Press.

Brunner, B. (Ed.). (2007). *Time almanac 2007 with Information Please.* Boston: Information Please.

Burningham, J. (1970). *Mr. Gumpy's outing.* New York: Henry Holt.

Burns, M. (2005/2006). Tools for the mind. *Educational Leadership, 63*(4), 48–53.

Burton, V. L. (1939). *Mike Mulligan and his steam shovel.* Boston: Houghton Mifflin.

Bush, G. W. (2004). The essential work of democracy. *Phi Delta Kappan, 86*(2), 114, 118–121.

Bybee, R. W., & Fuchs, B. (2006). Preparing 21st century workforce: A new reform in science and technology education. *Journal of Research in Science Teaching, 43*(4), 349–352.

Bybee, R. W., & Sund, R. B. (1982). *Piaget for educators* (2nd ed.). Columbus, OH: Charles E. Merrill.

Bybee, R. W., Kilpatrick, J., Lindquist, M., & Powell, J. C. (2005, Winter). PISA 2003: An introduction. *Natural Selection, the Journal of BSCS,* pp 4–7.

Caine, G., Caine, R. N., & McClintic, C. (2002). Guiding the innate constructivist. *Educational Leadership, 60*(1), 70–73.

Calhoun, M. (1981). *Hot-Air Henry.* New York: Mulberry Books.

Cannon, J. (1993). *Stellaluna.* San Diego, CA: Harcourt Brace.

Capobianco, B. M. (2007). Science teachers' attempts at integrating feminist pedagogy through collaborative action research. *Journal of Research in Science Teaching, 44*(1), 1–32.

Caram, C. A., & Davis, P. B., (2005). Inviting student engagement with questioning. *Phi Delta Kappa Record, 42*(1), 18–23.

Carle, E. (1985). *The very busy spider.* New York: Philomel.

Carle, E. (1987). *The very hungry caterpillar.* New York: Philomel.

Carle, E. (1991). *The tiny seed.* New York: Simon & Schuster.

Carroll, L. (1938). *The walrus and the carpenter.* Berkeley, CA: Archetype Press.

Carter, D. A. (1995). *Feely bugs: To touch and feel.* New York: Simon & Schuster Children's.

Carter, L. A., Sumrall, W. J., & Curry, K. M. (2006). Say cheese! Digital collections in the classroom. *Science and Children, 43*(8), 19–23.

Caseau, D., & Norman, K. (1997). Special education teachers use science–technology–society (STS) themes to teach science to students with learning disabilities. *Journal of Science Teacher Education, 8*(1), 55–68.

 Casey, M. (2007). 20 new ocean species found in Indonesia. ABC News Internet Ventures.

Cauley, L. B. (1983). *Jack and the beanstalk.* New York: Putnam.

Caulfield, J., Kidd, S., & Kocher, T. (2000). Brain-based instruction in action. *Educational Leadership, 58*(3), 62–65.

Cendrars, B. (1982). *Shadow.* (M. Brown, Trans.). New York: Charles Scribner's Sons.

Certo, J. L. (2006). Beginning teacher concerns in an accountability-based testing environment. *Journal of Research in Childhood Education, 20*(4), 331-349.

 Center for Research on Education, Diversity, & Excellence. (2002). Glossary.

Charlesworth, R., & Lind, K. K. (2003). *Math and science for young children* (4th ed.). Albany, NY: Delmar Learning.

Chaucer, G. (1995). *The Canterbury tales.* San Marino, CA: Huntington Library Press. (Original work published c. 1387)

Checkley, K. (1997). The first seven . . . and the eighth: A conversation with Howard Gardner. *Educational Leadership, 55*(1), 8–13.

Cheney, E. D. (Ed.). (1889). *Louisa May Alcott: Her Life, Letters, and Journals.* Boston: Brothers.

Cherry, L. (1992). *A river ran wild: An environmental history.* San Diego, CA: Harcourt.

Chesbro, R. (2006). Using interactive science notebooks for inquiry-based science. *Science Scope, 29*(7), 31–34.

Chokshi, S., & Fernandez, C. (2005). Reaping the systemic benefits of lesson study: Insights from the U.S. *Phi Delta Kappan, 86*(9), 674–680.

Chrenka L. (2001). Misconstructing constructivism. *Phi Delta Kappan, 82*(9), 694–695.

Cleary, B. (1983). *Dear Mr. Henshaw.* Madison, WI: Demco Media.

Climo, S. (1989). *The Egyptian Cinderella.* New York: Thomas Y. Crowell.

Clymer, J. B., & Wiliam, D. (2006/2007). Improving the way we grade. *Educational Leadership, 64*(4), 36–42.

Coats, L. J. (1986). *Marcella and the moon.* New York: Macmillan.

Cobb, V. (1981). *Lots of rot.* New York: Lippincott.

Cobern, W. W. (1993). Contextual constructivism: The impact of culture on the learning and teaching of science. In K. Tobin (Ed.), *The practice of constructivism in science education* (pp. 51–69). Hillsdale, NJ: Lawrence Erlbaum Associates.

Cobern, W. W., & Loving, C. C. (2002). Investigation of preservice elementary teachers' thinking about science. *Journal of Research in Science Teaching, 39*(10), 1016–1031.

Cohen, V. L., & Cowen, J. E. (2008). *Literacy for children in an information age.* Belmont, CA: Thomson Wadsworth.

Colburn, A. (2004). Inquiring scientists want to know. *Educational Leadership, 62*(1), 63–66.

Cole, J. (1987). *The magic school bus inside the earth.* New York: Scholastic Press.

Cole, J. (1990). *The magic school bus lost in the solar system.* New York: Scholastic Press.

Cole, J. (1994). *The magic school bus in the time of the dinosaurs.* New York: Scholastic.

Cole, J. (1995). *The magic school bus gets baked in a cake: A book about kitchen chemistry.* New York: Scholastic Press.

Cole, J. (1995). *The magic school bus in the haunted museum: A book about sound.* New York: Scholastic Press.

Cole, J. (1995). *The magic school bus plants seeds.* New York: Scholastic Press.

Cole, J. (1997). *The magic school bus and the electric field trip.* New York: Scholastic Press.

Collard, S. B., III. (2002). *Butterfly Count.* New York: Holiday House.

Collings, J. N. (1985). Scientific thinking through the development of formal operations: Training in the cognitive restructuring aspect of field-independence. *Research in Science & Technology Education, 3*(2), 145–152.

Collins, K. (2006). Notetaking skills can enhance science learning. *NSTA Reports, 18*(1), 15.

Combs, A. (1993, July 19). [Effectiveness of the helping professional]. From a lecture at Kennesaw State University, Kennesaw, GA.

Conn, K. (2004). The dangerous intersection project . . . and other scientific inquiries. *Educational Leadership, 61*(5), 30–32.

Cooney, B. (1982). *Miss Rumphius.* New York: Viking Press.

Costa, A., & Liebman, R. (1995). Process is as important as content. *Educational Leadership, 52*(6), 23–24.

Craig, D. V. (1999). Science and technology: A great combination. *Science and Children, 36*(4), 28–32.

Crank, J. N., & Bulgren, J. A. (1993). Visual depictions as information organizers for enhancing achievement of students with learning disabilities. *Learning Disabilities Research, 8*(3), 140–147.

Crawford, B. A. (1998). The scientific method—a fatal flaw. *Science Scope, 21*(7), 50–52.

Crawford, T. (2005). What counts as knowing: Constructing a communications repertoire for student demonstration of knowledge in science. *Journal of Research in Science Teaching, 42*(2), 139–165.

 Crowther, D. T. (1997). The constructivist zone: Editorial. *Electronic Journal of Science Education, 2*(2).

Crowther, D. T., Lederman, N. G., & Lederman, J. S. (2005). Understanding the true nature of science. *Science and Children, 43*(2), 50–52.

 Cruz, E. (n.d.). Bloom's revised taxonomy.

Cuevas, P., Lee, O., Hart, J., & Deaktor, R. (2005). Improving science inquiry with elementary students of diverse backgrounds. *Journal of Research in Science Teaching, 42*(3), 337–357.

Cushner, K., McClelland, A., & Safford, P. (1992). *Human diversity in education.* New York: McGraw-Hill.

Czerniak, C. M. (2007). Interdisciplinary science teaching. In S. K. Abell & N. G. Lederman (Eds.). *Handbook of Research on Science Education.* Mahwah, NJ: Lawrence Erlbaum Associates.

Dahl, M. (2004). *Bony back: The adventure of Stegosaurus.* Minneapolis, MN: Picture Window Books.

Dahl, M. (2004). *Dinosaur world.* Minneapolis, MN: Picture Window Books.

Dahl, M. (2004). *Long-neck: The adventure of Apatosaurus.* Minneapolis, MN: Picture Window Books.

Dahl, M. (2004). *Swift thief: The adventure of Velociraptor.* Minneapolis, MN: Picture Window Books.

Dahl, M. (2004). *Three-horn: The adventure of Triceratops.* Minneapolis, MN: Picture Window Books.

Dahl, M. (2004). *T-Rex: The adventure of Tyrannosaurus Rex.* Minneapolis: Picture Window Books.

Dahl, M. (2004). *Winged and toothless: The adventures of Ppteranodon.* Minneapolis, MN: Picture Window Books.

Danielson, C. (1996). *Enhancing professional practice: A framework for teaching.* Alexandria, VA: Association for Supervision and Curriculum Development.

 Darling-Hammond, L. (2000). Teacher quality and student achievement: A review of state policy evidence. *Educational Policy Analysis, 8*(1), 1–45

A day in the desert. (1994). St. Petersburg, FL: Willowisp.

de Montaigne, M. E. (1907). *Essays.* New York: G. P. Putnam's Sons. (Original work published c. 1580–1588.)

De Paola, T. (1975). *The cloud book.* New York: Holiday House.

Dean, D., Jr., & Kuhn, D. (2007). Direct instruction vs. discovery: The long view. *Science Education, 91*(3), 394–397.

DeBoer, G. E. (1991). *A history of ideas in science education: Implications for practice.* New York: Teachers College Press.

DeBoer, G. E. (2000). Scientific literacy: Another look at its historical and contemporary meanings and its relationship to science education. *Journal of Research in Science Teaching 37*(6), 582–601.

Deedy, C. A. (1994). *Agatha's feather bed: Not just another wild goose story.* Atlanta, GA: Peachtree.

Delta Science Reader. (2003). *States of matter.* Nashua, NH: Delta Education.

Delta Science Reader (2004). *Magnets.* Nashua, NH: Delta Education.

Delta Science Reader. (2004). *Sink or float?* Nashua, NH: Delta Education.

Dennett, D. C. (1991). *Consciousness explained.* Boston: Little, Brown.

DePaola, T. (1996). *Tony's bread: An Italian folktale.* New York: Putnam Juvenile.

DeRoche, S. J. K. (2006). An adventure in problem-based learning. *Phi Delta Kappan, 88*(9), 705–708.

 DeVries, R. (2006). Piaget's social theory. *The Constructivist, 17*(1).

Dewey, A. (1993). *The sky.* New York: Green Tiger Press.

Dewey, J. (1929). *The quest for certainty.* Carbondale, IL: Southern Illinois University Press.

Dewey, J. (1938). *Experience and education.* New York: Macmillan.

Dewey, J. O. (1998). *Mud matters: Stories from a mud lover.* Tarrytown, NY: Marshall Cavendish Corporation.

Deyhle, D., & Swisher, K. (1997). Research in American Indian and Alaska Native education: From assimilation to self-determination. In M. W. Apple (Ed.), *Review of research in education, 22,* 113–194. Washington, DC: American Educational Research Association.

Dibley, J., & Parish, J. (2007). Using video games to understand thermoregulation. *Science Scope, 30*(8), 32–35.

Diffily, D. (2001). Project reptile! When kindergarten students explore a topic of their own choosing, the result is good science learning. *Science and Children, 38*(7), 30–35.

Dodd, A. W. (1992). *Footprints and shadows.* New York: Simon & Schuster Books for Young Readers.

 Dodge, B. (1999). Original Webquest Template.

Dodson, P. (1995). *An alphabet of dinosaurs.* New York: Scholastic.

Dorros, A. (1991). *Follow the water from brook to ocean.* New York: HarperCollins.

Douglas, R., Klentschy, M. P., Worth, M., & Binder, M. (2006). *Linking science and literacy in the K-8 classroom.* Arlington, VA: NSTA Press.

Duckworth, E. (1986). Teaching as research. *Harvard Educational Review, 56*(4), 481–495.

Duckworth, E. (1987). *"The having of wonderful ideas" and other essays on teaching and learning.* New York: Teachers College Press.

Dunn, R. (1988). Teaching students through their perceptual strengths or preferences. *Journal of Reading, 31*(4), 304–308.

Dunn, R. (1990). Rita Dunn answers questions on learning styles. *Educational Leadership, 48*(2), 15–19.

Dunn, R. (2001). Learning style differences of nonconforming middle-school students. *NASSP Bulletin, 85*(626), 68–74.

Dunn, R., Dunn, K., & Price, G. E. (1975, 1979, 1981, 1985, 1989). *Learning style inventory.* Lawrence, KS: Price Systems.

Easley, J. (1990). Could we make a breakthrough for an at-risk nation? [Guest editorial] *Journal of Research in Science Teaching, 27*(7), 623–624.

Ebeling, D. G. (2000). Adapting your teaching to any learning style. *Phi Delta Kappan, 28*(3), 247–248.

Eggen, P., & Kauchak, D. (1994). *Educational psychology: Classroom connections.* New York: Merrill.

Einstein, A. (1950). *Out of my later years.* New York: Philosophical Library.

Einstein, A. (1954). *Ideas and opinions.* New York: Crown.

Eisenkraft, A. (2001). Testing, testing, 1 . . . 2 . . . 3 . . . *NSTA Reports! 12*(5), 2, 5.

Ellul, J. (1964). *The technological society.* New York: Vantage Books.

Emberly, E. (1994). *Ed Emberly's great thumbprint drawing book.* New York: Little, Brown.

 Engeler, E. (2007). 52 new species discovered on Borneo. ANC News Internet Ventures.

Ets, M. H. (1963). *Gilberto and the wind.* New York: Viking.

Evans, I. O. (1966). *Inventors of the world.* London: Frederick Warne.

Everett, S., & Moyer, R. (2007). "Inquirize" your teaching: A guide to turning favorite activities into inquiry lessons. *Science and Children, 44*(7), 54–57.

Farland, D. (2006). The effect of historical, nonfiction trade books on elementary students' perceptions of scientists. *Journal of Elementary Science Education, 18*(2), 31–47.

Fathman, A. K., & Crowther, D. T. (Eds.). (2006). *Science for English language learners: K-12 classroom strategies.* Arlington, VA: NSTA Press.

Faulkner, K. (2002). *The five senses.* New York: Scholastic/Cartwheel Books.

 Feldman, S. (2003). A commentary from President Feldman on the *No Child Left Behind Act.* American Federation of Teachers.

Fello, S. E., Paquette, K. R., & Jalongo, M. R. (2006/2007, Winter). Talking drawings: Improving intermediate students' comprehension of expository science text. *Childhood Education, 83(2),* 80–85.

Ferguson, B. (2004). *Teeth. Mankato,* MN: Benchmark Books.

Fleisher, P. (2002). *Objects in motion: Principles of classical mechanics.* Minneapolis, MN: Lerner Publications.

Folsom, J., Hunt, C., Schoenemann, A., & D'Amato, M. (2007). How do you know that? Guiding early elementary students to develop evidence-based explanations about animals. *Science and Children, 44(5),* 20–25.

Forehand, M. (2005). Bloom's taxonomy: Original and revised. In M. Orey (Ed.), *Emerging perspectives in learning, teaching, and technology.*

Francher, L. (2006). *Star climbing.* New York: Laura Geringer Books.

Franklin, J. (2001a). The diverse challenges of multiculturalism. *Education Update, 43*(2), 1–8.

Franklin, J. (2001b). Trying too hard? How accountability and testing are affecting constructivist teaching. *Educational Update, 43*(3), 1, 4–5, 8.

Franklin, J. (2006). NCLB a year before reauthorization. Squaring off on issues that will frame the debate. *Education Update, 48*(7), 1, 7–8.

Friedman, T. L. (2005). *The world is flat. A brief history of the twenty-first century.* New York: Farrar, Straus and Giroux.

Friend, M., & Pope, K. L. (2005). Creating schools in which all students can succeed. *Kappa Delta Pi Record, 41*(2), 56–61.

Frisch, M. (1957). *Homo Faber.* Frankfurt: Suhrkamp Verlag.

Fulton, L., & Campbell, B. (2004). Student-centered notebooks. *Science & Children, 42*(3), 26–29.

Funk, M. (2004, February). Don't be a carrier: Five misconceptions you (yes, you) have been known to spread. *Popular Science, 264*(2), 62.

Galda, L., & Cullinan, B. E. (2006). *Literature and the child* (6th ed.). Belmont, CA: Wadsworth Publishing.

Gallenstein, N. (2005). Never too young for a concept map. *Science and Children, 43*(1), 44–47.

Gardner, H. (1983). *Frames of mind: The theory of multiple intelligences.* New York: Basic Books.

Gardner, H. (1995). Reflections on multiple intelligences: Myths and messages. *Phi Delta Kappan, 77*(3), 202–203, 206–209.

 Gardner, H. (2003). Multiple intelligences after 20 years. Paper presented at the annual meeting of the American Educational Research Association, Chicago, IL, April 21, 2003.

Gardner, R. (2003). *Super-sized science projects with volume: How much space does it take up?* Berkeley Heights, NJ: Enslow Publishers.

Genesee, F., Lindholm-Leary, K., & Christian, D. (2005). English language learners in U.S. schools: An overview of research findings. *Journal of Education for Students Placed at Risk, 10*(4), 363–385.

Gersten, R. M. (1998). The double demands of teaching language-minority students. In R. M. Gersten & R. T. Jiménez (Eds.), *Promoting learning for culturally and linguistically diverse students: Classroom applications from contemporary research.* Belmont, CA: Wadsworth Publishing Company.

Gersten, R. M., Brengleman, S. U., Marks, S. U., Keating, T., & Baker, S. (1998). Recent research on effective instructional practice for content-area ESOL. In R. M. Gersten & R. T. Jiménez (Eds.), *Promoting learning for culturally and linguistically diverse students.* Belmont, CA: Wadsworth Publishing Company.

Getting to the core or science standards. (2007). *NSTA Reports, 18*(8), 1, 5.

Getting women into science: What works. (2007). *NSTA Reports, 18*(5), 19.

Getz, D. (1994). *The frozen man.* New York: Henry Holt.

Gibbons, G. (1991). *From seed to plant.* New York: Holiday House.

Gibbons, G. (1991). *Whales.* New York: Holiday House.

Gibbons, G. (1999). *The pumpkin book.* New York: Holiday House.

Gilbert, J., & Kotelman, M. (2005). Five good reasons to use science notebooks. *Science and Children, 43*(3), 28–32.

Gill, E. K. (2007). Courting grants: The enticement of grant money challenges for schools. *Education Update, 49*(3), 4–7.

Gingerich, O. (2006). The inside story of Pluto's demotion: How many planets are there in our solar system? It depends on what you mean by the word "planet." *Sky & Telescope, 112*(5), 34–39.

Ginsburg, M. (1975). *How the sun was brought back to the sky.* New York: Macmillan.

Glasser, W. (1990, February). The quality school. *Phi Delta Kappan,* 52–62.

Glasser, W. (1992, May). The quality school curriculum. *Phi Delta Kappan,* 690–694.

 GlaxoSmithKline and Human Genome Sciences announce initiation of phase 3 clinical trial of lymphostat-B(R) in systemic lupus erythematosus. (2007, February 13). *PipelineReview.com.*

Glynn, S. M., & Muth, K. D. (1994). Reading and writing to learn in science: Achieving scientific literacy. *Journal of Research in Science Teaching, 31*(9), 1057–1073.

Goldberg, A., Russell, M., & Cook, A. (2003). The effect of computers on student writing: A meta-analysis of studies from 1992 to 2002. *The Journal of Technology, Learning, and Assessment.*

Goldberg, M. F. (2004). The test mess. *Phi Delta Kappan, 85*(5), 361–366.

Goldsmith, M. (2001). *Galileo Galilei.* Austin, TX: Raintree Steck-Vaughn

 Gonzales, P. (2004). Highlights from the Trends in International Mathematics and Science Study (TIMSS) 2003. Washington, DC: National Center for Education Statistics.

Gonzales, P., Guzmán, J. C., Partelow, L., Pahlke, E., Jocelyn, L., Pauline, D., & R. F. (1993). Microteaching: An integral part of a science methods class. *Journal of Science Teacher Education,* 4(1), 9–17.

Good, I. J. (Ed.). (1962). *The scientist speculates: An anthology of partly-based ideas.* London: Heinemann.

Good, R. G., Wandersee, J. H., & St. Julien, J. (1993). Cautionary notes on the appeal of the new "Ism" (constructivism) in science education. In K. Tobin (Ed.), *The practice of constructivism in science education* (Chap. 5). Hillsdale, NJ: Lawrence Erlbaum Associates.

Goode, D. (1999). *The dinosaur's new clothes.* New York: The Blue Sky Press.

Gooden, K. (2005). Biome is where the art is. *Science and Children, 43*(1), 28–32.

Goor, R., & Goor, N. (1981). *Shadows here, there, and everywhere.* New York: Crowell.

Gordon, S. (2002). *Exercise.* New York: Children's Press.

 Gorman, L. (2006). Teachers and the gender gaps in student achievement. *National Bureau of Economic Research Digest.*

Grace, M. (1999). When students create their own curriculum. *Educational Leadership, 57*(3), 49–52.

Graham, J. B. (1994). *Splish, splash.* New York: Ticknor and Fields.

Greenblat, R. (1991). *Aunt Ippy's museum of junk.* New York: HarperCollins.

Greenburg, D., & Davis, J. E. (1998). *The misfortune cookie.* New York: Grossett & Dunlap.

Griswold, P. A. (2005). Relating academic data from the elementary grades to state test results in high school: Implications for school improvement through professional development. *Journal of Research in Childhood Education, 20*(2), 65–74.

Gutierrez, D., & Oliver, M. F. (1988). *The night of the stars.* Brooklyn, NY: Kane/Miller.

Haas, D. (1986). *The secret life of Dilly McBean.* New York: Bradbury Press.

Haladyna, T., Haas, N., & Allison, J. (1998). Continuing tensions in standardized testing. *Childhood Education, 74*(5), 262–273.

Hall, J. K. (2000. *Field dependence-independence and computer-based instruction in geography.* Doctoral Dissertation, Virginia Polytechnic Institute and State University, Blacksburg, VA, 2000.

Hamilton, A. (1949). Brains that click. *Popular Mechanics Magazine, 91*(3), 162–167, 256, 258.

Hamilton, L., & Stecher, B. (2004). Responding effectively to test-based accountability. *Phi Delta Kappan, 85*(8), 578–583.

Hammond, L. (2001). Note from California: An anthropological approach to urban science education for language minority families. *Journal of Research in Science Teaching, 38*(9), 983–999.

Hancock, V., & Betts, F. (1994). From the lagging to the leading edge. *Educational Leadership, 51*(7), 24–29.

Hannah, J., & Holub, J. (2006). *The man who named the clouds.* Morton Grove, IL: A. Whitman.

Hansen, L. (2006). Strategies for ELL success. *Science and Children, 43*(4), 22–25.

Hapgood, S., & Palinscar, A. (2006/2007). Where literacy and science intersect. *Educational Leadership, 64*(4), 56–60.

Harrison, D. L. (2003). *Oceans: The vast, mysterious deep.* Honesdale, PA: Boyds Mills Press.

 Harvard School of Public Health. (2002). Food pyramids: What should you really eat?

 Hawking, S. (1998, March 6). Science in the next millennium.

Hawking, S., & Mlodinow, L. (2005). *A briefer history of time.* New York: Bantam Dell.

Hayes, M. T. (2002). Elementary preservice teachers' struggle to define inquiry-based science teaching. *Journal of Science Teacher Education, 13*(2), 147–165.

Hennessy, B. G. (1988). *The dinosaur who lived in my back yard.* New York: Puffin Books.

Herbert, R. (2001). True or false? *New Scientist, 169*(2282), 52.

Heuser, D. (2005, November/December). Learning logs: Writing to learn, reading to assess. *Science and Children, 43*(3), 46–49.

Hilliard, A. G. (1994). Foreword to E. W. King, M. Chipman, & M. Cruz-Janzen, *Educating young children in a diverse society.* Boston, MA: Allyn and Bacon.

Hiscock, B. (1988). *The big rock.* New York: Atheneum.

Hoare, N. (2006). Scientists discover what makes us human. *Geographical, 78*(1), 8.

Hoban, T. (1978). *Is it red? Is it yellow? Is it blue? An adventure in color.* New York: Greenwillow Books.

Hoban, T. (1984). *Is it rough? Is it smooth? Is it shiny?* New York: Greenwillow Books.

Hoban, T. (1985). *Is it larger? Is it smaller?* New York: Greenwillow Books.

Hoban, T. (1990). *Shadows and reflections.* New York: Greenwillow Books.

Holliday, W. G., & Holliday, B. W. (2003). Why using international comparative math and science achievement data from TIMSS is not helpful. *The Educational Forum, 67*(3), 250–257.

Holloway, J. (2000). How does the brain learn science? *Educational Leadership, 58*(3), 85–86.

 Home computers and Internet use in the United States, August 2000. (2001). Washington, DC: U.S. Census Bureau.

Hopkins, L. B. (1987). *Click, rumble, roar: Poems about machines.* New York: Crowell.

Hudson, W. (1995). *Great Black heroes: Five brave explorers.* New York: Scholastic.

Hughes, S. (1988). *Out and about.* New York: Lothrop, Lee & Shepard.

Hughes, S. (1992). *The big Alfie out of doors storybook.* Boston: Lothrop.

 Human genome study breakthrough reported. (2007, February 5). *Science Daily.*

 Hurd, P. D. (1986). Issues linking research to science teaching. *ERIC Information Bulletin No. 1.* (ERIC Document No. ED271293)

Hurd, P. D. (1986, January). Perspectives for the reform of science education. *Phi Delta Kappan, 67,* 353–358.

Hurd, P. D. (1991). Why we must transform science education. *Educational Leadership, 49*(2), 33–35.

Hurd, P. D. (2002). Modernizing science education. *Journal of Research in Science Teaching. 39*(1), 3–9.

Hurst, C. O. (2001). *Rocks in his head.* New York: Greenwillow Books.

Hutchins, P. (1970). *Clocks and more clocks.* New York: Macmillan.

InfoTrek Leveled Readers. (2002). *The mighty lever.* Vernon Hills, IL: ETA/Cuisenaire (Under license from Nelson, a division of Thomson Canada, Ltd.).

International Human Genome Sequencing Consortium. (2001). Initial sequencing and analysis of the human genome. *Nature, 409*(6822), 860–921.

 International Society for Technology in Education. (2004). *Curriculum and content area standards: NETS for students.* Washington, DC: Author.

Isadora, R. (1991). *I touch.* Fairfield, NJ: Greenwillow Books.

Jablon, P. (P2006). Writing through inquiry. *Science Scope, 29*(7), 18-20.

Jacobs, H. H. (Ed.). (1989). *Interdisciplinary curriculum: Design and implementation.* Alexandria, VA: Association for Supervision and Curriculum Development.

Jarvis, T., & Pell, A. (2005). Factors influencing elementary school children's attitudes toward science before, during, and after a visit to the UK National Space Centre. *Journal of Research in Science Teaching, 42*(1), 53-83.

 JASON Project. (2001). Needham Heights, MA: JASON Foundation for Education.

Jeffers, S. (1993). *Brother Eagle, Sister Sky: A message from Chief Seattle.* New York: NAL/Dutton.

Jennings, J., & Rentner, D. S. (2006). Ten big effects of the No Child Left Behind Act on public schools. *Phi Delta Kappan, 88*(2), 110–113.

Jennings, T. (1990). *Junior science: Magnets.* New York: Gloucester Press.

Johnson, R. L. (1990). *The greenhouse effect.* Minneapolis, MN: Learner.

Johnson, R. L. (2004). *Acids and bases.* Washington, DC: National Geographic Society.

Johnston, T. (1988). *The forces be with you!* Milwaukee, WI: Gareth Stevens.

Jones, K., & Ongtooguk, P. (2002). Equity for Alaska natives: Can high-stakes testing bridge the chasm between ideals and realities? *Phi Delta Kappan, 83*(7), 499–505, 544.

Jones, M. G., Minogue, J., Tretter, T. R., Negishi, A., & Taylor, R. (2006). Haptic augmentation of science instruction: Does touch matter? *Science Education, 90*(1), 111–123.

 Jorgenson, O., & Vanosdell, R. (2002). The death of science? What we risk in our rush toward standardized testing and the three R's. *Phi Delta Kappan Online Article.*

Joubert, J. (1966). *Pensées.* Paris: Union General d'Editions. (Original work published 1842.)

Kahle, J. (1985). *Women in science.* Philadelphia: Falmer Press.

Kahle, J. (1990). Why girls don't know. In M. B. Rowe (Ed.), *What research says to science teachers* (pp. 55–67). Washington, DC: National Science Teachers Association.

Kalat, J. W. (2007). *Biological psychology.* Belmont, CA: Thomson Wadsworth.

Kamii, C. (1984, February). Autonomy: The aim of education envisioned by Piaget. *Phi Delta Kappan,* 410–415.

Karplus, R. (2000). Science teaching and the development of reasoning. *Journal of Research in Science Teaching, 40*(Supplement), S51–S57. (Originally published in *Journal of Research in Science Teaching, 14*(2) (1977), 169–175.)

Katz, L. G. (1994). Perspectives on the quality of early childhood programs. *Phi Delta Kappan, 76*(3), 200–205.

Kawagley, A. O., Norris-Tull, D., & Norris-Tull, R. A. (1998). The indigenous worldview of Yupiaq culture: Its scientific nature and relevance to the practice and teaching of science. *Journal of Research in Science Teaching, 35*(2), 133–144.

Kelley, T. (1986). *The mystery of the stranger in the barn.* New York: Dodd, Mead.

Kellis, M. (2006). Finding evolution's signatures: Comparing genomes of different animals, explains Manolis Kellis, allows scientists to decipher hidden elements in the human genome. *Technology Review, 109*(14), 28.

 Kennedy, E. M. (2007a). Kennedy outlines agenda for NCLB

reauthorization at National School Boards Association conference.

 Kennedy, E. M. (2007b). Senator Kennedy announces plans for reauthorization of the No Child Left Behind Act.

Kilic, G. B., & Cakan, M. (2007). Peer assessment of elementary science teaching skills. *Journal of Science Teacher Education, 18*(1), 91–107.

Kim, J. S., & Sunderman, G. L. (2005). Measuring academic proficiency under the No Child Left Behind Act: Implications for educational equity. *Educational Researcher, 34*(8), 3–13.

King, E. (1996). *The pumpkin patch.* East Rutherford, NJ: Viking Penguin.

King, M. L., Jr. (1963). *The strength to love.* Cleveland, OH: Fount Books.

Kisiel, J. (2005). Understanding elementary teacher motivations for science fieldtrips. *Science Education, 89*(6), 936–955.

Klahr, D., Triona, L. M., & Williams, C. (2007). Hands on what? The relative effectiveness of physical versus virtual materials in an engineering design project by middle school children. *Journal of Research in Science Teaching, 44*(1), 183–203.

Klentschy, M. (2005). Science notebook essentials. *Science and Children, 43*(3), 24–27.

Kliebard, H. (1989). Remarks made at the annual conference of the Holmes Group, Atlanta, GA.

Knapp. A. (1998). *The color of noodles.* Sarasota, FL: Sandpiper Press.

Kohn, A. (2000). *The case against standardized testing: Raising the scores, ruining the schools.* Portsmouth, NH: Heinemann.

Kohn, A. (2001). Fighting the tests: A practical guide to rescuing our schools. *Phi Delta Kappan, 82*(5), 349–357.

Kohn, A. (2004). Test today, privatize tomorrow: Using accountability to reform public schools to death. *Phi Delta Kappan, 85* (8), 569–577.

Kottke, J. (2000). *From seed to pumpkin.* Danbury, CT: Children's Press.

Kovalski, M. (1992). *Queen Nadine.* Custer, WA: Orca Book Publishers.

Krauss, R. (1945). *The carrot seed.* New York: Harper & Row.

Krulik, N. E., & Cole, J. (1996). *The magic school bus: Butterfly and the bog beast.* New York: Scholastic.

Krull, K. (2006). *Isaac Newton.* New York: Viking.

Kudlinski, K. (1991). *Animal tracks and traces.* New York: Franklin Watts.

Kuhn, D., & Brannock, J. (1977). Development of the isolation of variables scheme in experimental and "natural experiment" contexts. *Developmental Psychology, 13*(1), 9–14.

Kuhn, T. S. (1970). *The structure of scientific revolutions.* Chicago: University of Chicago Press.

Kuiper, E., Volman, M., & Terwel, J. (2005). The Web as an information resource in K-12 education: Strategies for supporting students in searching and processing information. *Review of Educational Research, 75*(3), 285–328.

Kwan, T., & Texley, J. V. (2003). *Inquiring safely: A guide for middle school.* Arlington, VA: NSTA Press.

L'Engle, M. (1962). *A wrinkle in time.* New York: Dell.

Lambdin, D. A., & Walker, V. L. (1994, February). Planning for classroom portfolio assessment. *Arithmetic Teacher,* 318–324.

Landau, E. (2003). *Popcorn!* Watertown, MA: Charlesbridge Publishing.

Landmark legislation has changed landscape of American education. (2007). *The Achiever, 6*(1), 1–2.

Lanier, J. (1987). From a tape recording of an address to the first Holmes Group conference.

Lauber, P. (1990). *Journey to the planets.* (3rd ed.). New York: Crown.

Lavoisier, A. L. (1789). *Traité elémentaire de chimie.* Paris: Cuchet.

Lawrenz, F. (1991). Authentic assessment. *Research Matters . . . To the Science Teacher.* National Association for Research in Science Teaching, June 1991, No. 26.

Lawrenz, F., Huffman, D., & Welch, W. (2000). Policy considerations based on a cost analysis of alternative test formats in large scale science assessments. *Journal of Research in Science Teaching, 37*(6), 615–626.

Lawson, A. E. (1978). The development and validation of a classroom test of formal reasoning. *Journal of Research in Science Teaching, 15*(1), 11–24.

Lawson, A. E. (1985). A review of research on formal reasoning and science teaching. *Journal of Research in Science Teaching, 19*(3), 233–248.

Le Guin, U. (1968). *A wizard of Earthsea.* Berkeley, CA: Parnassus Press.

Leatherman, J. M. (2006). Suggestions and resources for successful inclusion classrooms. *ACEI Focus on Inclusive Education, 4*(1), 1–5, 7.

Lebkicher, R., Rentz, G., & Steineke, M. (1960). *Aramco handbook.* Dhahran, Saudi Arabia: Arabian American Oil Company.

Lederman, L. M., & Burnstein, R. A. (2006). Alternative approaches to high-stakes testing. *Phi Delta Kappan, 87*(6), 429–432.

Lee, O. (2005). Science education with English language learners: Synthesis and Research Agenda. *Review of Educational Research, 75*(4), 491-530.

 Lee, O., & Avalos, M. (2003). Integrating science with English language development. *SEDL Letter, XV*(1).

Lee, O., & Luykx, A. (2007). Science education and student diversity: Race/ethnicity, language, culture, and socioeconomic status. In S. K. Abell & N. G. Lederman (Eds). *Handbook of Research on Science Education.* Mahwah, NJ: Lawrence Erlbaum Associates.

Lee, O., Baxton, C., Lewis, S., & LeRoy, K. (2006). Science inquiry and student diversity: Enhanced abilities and continuing difficulties after an instructional intervention. *Journal of Research in Science Teaching, 43*(7), 607–636.

Leedy, L. (1996). *The edible pyramid: Good eating every day.* New York: Holiday House.

Lessem, D. (1994). *Iceman.* New York: Crown.

Levine, S., & Johnstone, L. (2003). *Ultimate bubble book: Soapy science fun.* New York: Sterling Publishing Co.

Limson, M., Wizlib, C., & Desharnius, R. A. (2007). Using Web-based simulations to promote inquiry. *Science Scope, 30*(6), 36–42.

Linn, R. L., Baker, E. L., & Betebenner, D. W. (2002). Accountability systems: Implications of requirements of the No Child Left Behind Act of 2001. *Educational Researcher, 31*(6), 3–16.

Livingston, M. C. (1984). *Sky songs.* New York: Holiday House.

Lobel, A. (1982). *Ming Lo moves the mountain.* New York: Greenwillow Books.

Lord, J. V. (1987). *The giant jam sandwich.* Boston: Houghton Mifflin.

Louie, A. (1982). *Yeh-Shen: A Cinderella story from China.* East Rutherford, NJ: Penguin Putnam Books for Young Readers.

Lowery, L. F. (Ed.). (1997). *NSTA Pathways to the science standards* (Elementary School Ed.). Arlington, VA: National Science Teachers Association.

Lucy, E. C., & Martin, D. J. (1994, April 29). *Get your hands on concept mapping.* Workshop presented at the Georgia Academy of Science annual meeting, Kennesaw, GA.

Luft, J. (2007). Guest editorial. Minding the Gap: Needed research on beginning/newly qualified science teachers. *Journal of Research in Science Teaching, 44*(4), 532–537.

Lundeen, C. (2005). So you want to host a family science night? *Science and Children, 42*(8), 30–35.

Lynch, S., Taymans, J., Watson, W. A., Ochsendorf, R. J., Pyke, C., & Szeze, M. J. (2007). Effectiveness of a highly rated science curriculum for students with disabilities in general education classrooms. *Exceptional Children, 73*(2), 202–223.

Lyon, G. E. (1990). *Come a tide.* New York: Orchard Books.

Macaulay, D. (1990). *Black and white.* Boston: Houghton Mifflin.

Macfarlane, G. (1984). *Alexander Fleming: The man and the myth.* Cambridge, MA: Harvard University Press.

Machotka, H. (1992). *Breathtaking noses.* New York: Morrow Junior Books.

Maestro, B. (1994). *Why do leaves change color?* New York: HarperCollins Children's.

Maestro, B., & Maestro, G. (1990). *Temperature and you.* New York: Lodestar.

Mager, R. F. (1984). *Preparing instructional objectives* (rev. 2nd ed.). Belmont, CA: Davis S. Lake.

Markle, S. (1988). *Science mini mysteries.* New York: Atheneum.

Markle, S. (1993). *Outside and inside trees.* New York: Bradbury.

Markle, S. (1999). *After the spill: The Exxon Valdez disaster, then and now.* New York: Walker and Co.

Martin, B., Jr., & Archenbault, J. (1988). *Listen to the rain.* New York: Henry Holt.

Martin, D. J. (1975). Individualizing junior high science. *The Science Teacher, 42*(3).

Martin, D. J. (1991). *The effect of concept mapping on biology achievement of field dependent students.* Unpublished dissertation, Georgia State University.

Martin, D. J. (1994). Concept mapping as an aid to lesson planning: A longitudinal study. *Journal of Elementary Science Education, 6*(2), 11–30.

Martin, D. J., Jean-Sigur, R., & Schmidt, E. (2005). Process-oriented inquiry, a constructivist approach to early childhood science education: Teaching teachers to do science. *Journal of Elementary Science Education, 17*(2), 13–26.

Martin, J. B. (1998). *Snowflake Bentley.* Boston: Houghton Mifflin.

Mason, J. B., Degen, B., & Cole, J. (1997). *The magic school bus: Ups and downs.* New York: Scholastic Press.

Mathis, S. B. (1986). *The hundred penny box.* New York: Puffin Books.

Matkins, J. J., & Bell, R. L. (2007). Awakening the scientist inside: Global climate change and the nature of science in an elementary science methods course. *Journal of Science Teacher Education, 18*(2), 137–163.

Maurer, R. (1995). *Rocket! How a toy launched the space age.* New York: Crown Publishers.

Mayer, M. (1968). *There's a nightmare in my closet.* New York: Dial Press.

McBee, R. H. (2000). Why teachers integrate. *The Educational Forum, 64*(3), 254–259.

 McCann, W. S. (1998). Science classrooms for students with special needs. *ERIC Digest.* (ERIC Document No. ED433185)

McCarthy, C. B. (2005). Effects of thematic-based, hands-on science teaching versus a textbook approach for students with disabilities. *Journal of Research in Science Teaching, 42*(3), 245–263.

McClintock, M. (1989). *Stop that ball!* New York: Random House.

McDougall, J. (2002). *SunSprouts®: Snails and slugs.* Vernon Hills, IL: ETA/Cuisenaire.

McFalls, E. L., & Cobb-Roberts, D. (2001). Reducing resistance to diversity through cognitive dissonance instruction: Implications for teacher education. *Journal of Teacher Education, 52*(2), 164–172.

McGinnis, J. R., & Stefanich, G. P. (2007). Special needs and talents in science learning. In S. K. Abell & N. G. Lederman, (:2007). *Handbook of Research in Science Education.* Mahwah, NJ: Lawrence Erlbaum Associates.

McGrath, B. B. (1994). *The M&M's brand counting book.* Watertown, MA: Charlesbridge Publishing.

McGrath, B. B. (1998). *More M&M's brand chocolate candies math.* Watertown, MA: Charlesbridge Publishing.

McKinley. E. (2007). Post colonialism, indigenous students, and science education. In S. K. Abell & N. G. Lederman (Eds.). *Handbook of Research in Science Education.* Mahwah, NJ: Lawrence Ehrlbaum Associates.

McLaughlin, R. (2005). Girls in science. *Science Scope, 28*(7), 14–15.

McMillan, B. (1994). *Sense suspense: A guessing game for the five senses.* New York: Scholastic.

McNulty, F. (1986). *The lady and the spider.* New York: Harper & Row.

Meister, C. (2001). *I love rocks.* New York: Children's Press.

Merriam, E. (1991). *The wise woman and her secret.* New York: Simon & Schuster Books for Young Readers.

Merriam-Webster (2003). *Merriam-Webster's collegiate dictionary* (11th ed.). Springfield, MA: Author.

Meyer, C. F., & Rhoades, E. K. (2000, Winter). Multiculturalism: Beyond food, festival, folklore, and fashion. *Kappa Delta Pi Record, 42*(2), 82–87.

Meyerhoff, M. K. (2004). Locus of control (Perspectives on Parenting). *Pediatrics for Parents, 21*(10), 8–10.

Miller, C. C. (2007). *Marie Curie and radioactivity.* Mankato, MN: Capstone Press.

Miller, M. (2006). *Hurricane Katrina strikes the Gulf Coast: Disaster & survival.* Berkeley Heights, NJ: Enslow Publishers.

Miller, R. G. (2006). Unlocking reading comprehension with key science inquiry skills. *Science Scope, 30*(1), 30–33.

Miller, R. G., & Calfee, R. C. (2004). Making thinking visible. *Science & Children, 42*(3), 20–25.

Mintz, E., & Calhoun, J. (2004). Project notebook. *Science & Children, 42*(3), 30–34.

Misiti, F. L., Jr. (2001). Standardizing the language of inquiry. *Science and Children, 38*(5), 38–40.

Mitton, J., & Balit, C. (2003). *Once upon a starry night: A book of constellation stories.* Washington, DC: National Geographic.

Mohler, R. R. J. (2000). More space shuttle experiments take flight. *Science and Children, 38*(2), 39–43.

Morgan, P. (1990). *The turnip.* New York: Philomel Books.

Morrell, P. D. (2003). Cognitive impact of a grade school field trip. *Journal of Elementary Science Education, 15*(1), 27–34.

Morris, W. (1990). *Just listen.* New York: Atheneum.

Multiple intelligences: After twenty years. (2005). *Instructor, 114*(2), S2.

Multiple intelligences theory, multiple improvements. (2003). *Techniques, 78*(6), 10.

Munby, H. (1986). Metaphor in the thinking of teachers: An exploratory study. *Journal of Curriculum Studies, 18,* 197–209.

Murray, J., & Bartelmay, K. (2005). Inventors in the making. *Science and Children, 42*(4), 40–44.

Myers, C., & Myers, L. (1991). *McCrephy's field.* New York: Houghton Mifflin.

Myller, R. (1962). *How big is a foot?* New York: Atheneum.

 National Assessment of Educational Progress. (2006). *The nation's report card. Executive summary: Science results for grades 4, 8, and 12.*

 National Center for Education Statistics. (2005). *Reporting brief. NAEP 1999 trends in academic progress: Three decades of student performance.*

 National Center for Education Statistics. (2005a). Table 50 Children 3 through 12 years old served in federally supported programs for the disabled, by type of disability: School years 1976-1977 through 2003-2004. Washington, DC: Author.

 National Center for Education Statistics. (2005b). Digest of Education Statistics: 2005. Table 38. Percentage distribution of enrollment in public elementary and secondary schools, by race/ethnicity and state or jurisdiction: Fall 1993 and fall 2003. Washington, DC: Author.

 National Center for Education Statistics. (2006). *The nation's report card Science 2006.*

National Council for the Social Studies (NCSS) Task Force on Ethnic Studies Curriculum. (1992, September). Curriculum guidelines for multicultural education. *Social Education,* 274–292.

 National Education Association. (2004). 'No Child Left Behind' Act/ESA: The issue. National Education Association, Issues in Education.

National Research Council, National Commission on Science Education Standards and Assessment. (1993). *National science education standards: An enhanced sampler.* Washington, DC: National Science Education Standards.

National Research Council. (1996). *National science education standards.* Washington, DC: National Academy Press.

National Research Council. (2000). *Inquiry and the National Science Education Standards: A Guide for Teaching and Learning.* Washington, DC: National Academy Press.

National Science Board. (2006). *Science and engineering indicators, 2006.* Arlington, VA: National Science Foundation.

National Science Teachers Association. (1990). *Science teachers speak out: The NSTA lead paper on science and technology education for the 21st century.* Washington, DC: Author.

 National Science Teachers Association. (1991). Responsible Use of Organisms in Precollege Science. NSTA Background Paper.

 National Science Teachers Association. (1994, Oct./Nov.). Parent involvement in science education. NSTA Position Statement. *NSTA Reports!* Washington, DC: Author.

 National Science Teachers Association (1999). The use of computers in science education. NSTA Position Statement.

 National Science Teachers Association. (1999). Use of the metric system. NSTA Position statement.

 National Science Teachers Association (2000, July). The nature of science. NSTA Position Statement.

 National Science Teachers Association. (2000). Position Paper: Multicultural Science Education. Arlington, VA: Author.

 National Science Teachers Association. (2001). Assessment. NSTA Position Statement.

 National Science Teachers Association. (2003). Beyond 2000—Teachers of science speak out: An NSTA lead paper on how all students learn science and the implications to the science education community. NSTA Position Statement.

 National Science Teachers Association (2003). NSTA Standards for science teacher preparation.

 National Science Teachers Association. (2004). Scientific inquiry. NSTA position statement.

 National Science Teachers Association. (2005). Responsible use of live animals and dissection in the science classroom. NSTA position statement.

 National Science Teachers Association. (2007). The integral role of laboratory investigations in science instruction. NSTA position statement.

Nawwab, I. I., Speers, P. C., & Hoye, P. F. (1980). *Aramco and its world: Arabia and the Middle East.* Dhahran, Saudi Arabia: Arabian American Oil Company.

Nesbit, J. C., & Adesope, O. O. (2006). Learning with concept and knowledge maps: A meta-analysis. *Review of Educational Research, 76*(3), 413–448.

Niguidula, D. (2005). Documenting learning with digital portfolios. *Educational Leadership 63*(3), 44–47.

 Nobel e-Museum. (2000). Press release: The 2000 Nobel Prize in Physics.

Nolen, J. (2002). *Plantzilla.* San Diego: Harcourt.

Norton, P., & Wiburg, K. M. (2003). *Teaching with technology: Designing opportunities to learn* (2nd ed.). Belmont, CA: Wadsworth/Thomson Learning.

Novak, J. D. (1991, October). Clarify with concept maps. *The Science Teacher,* 44–49.

Novak, J. D. (1992, March 23). *The current status of Ausubel's assimilation theory of learning.* Paper presented at the 65th annual meeting of the National Association for Research in Science Teaching, Boston, MA; personal communication, same date.

Novak, J. D., & Gowan, D. B. (1984). *Learning how to learn.* Cambridge, MA: Cambridge University Press.

NRC report suggests ways to improve teacher education. (2000). *NSTA Reports!, 12*(2), 6.

NSTA and NOAA present new SciGuide for exploring coral ecosystems. (2006). *NSTA Reports, 18*(4), 9.

NSTA Reports. (2004). Science de-emphasized in elementary ed, says study. *NSTA Reports!, 16*(1), 9.

Numeroff, L. J. (1985). *If you give a mouse a cookie.* New York: Harper & Row.

 Office of External Affairs, Health Sciences Division. (2002). Eric Kandel wins Nobel prize in medicine. *Columbia News.*

Okey, J. R., & Gagné, R. M. (1970). Revision of a science topic using evidence of performance on subordinate skills. *Journal of "Research in Science Teaching, 7*(4), 321–325.

Olien, R. (2005). *The water cycle.* Mankato, MN: Capstone Press.

Oppenheimer, T. (2003). *The flickering mind: The false promise of technology in the classroom and how learning can be saved.* New York: Random House.

Orlich, D. C., Harder, R. J., Callahan, R. C., Kauchak, D. O., Pendergrass, R. A., Keogh, A. J., & Gibson, H. (1990). *Teaching strategies: A guide to better instruction* (3rd ed.). Lexington, MA: Heath.

Ortega y Gasset, J. (1961). *Meditations on Quixote.* New York: Norton. (Original work published 1914).

Owston, R. D. (1997). The World Wide Web: A technology to enhance teaching and learning? *Educational Researcher, 26*(2), 27–33.

Padilla, M. (2005). Science and English-language learners. *NSTA Reports, 17*(1), 3-4.

Padilla, M. J. (1990). The science process skills. "Research Matters . . . to the Science Teacher." National Association for Research in Science Teaching.

Pajares, M. (1992). Teachers' beliefs and educational research: Cleaning up on a messy construct. *Review of Educational Research, 61,* 307–332.

Pallotta, J. (1986). *The ocean alphabet book.* Watertown, MA: Charlesbridge Publishers.

Pallotta, J. (1989). *The bird alphabet book.* Watertown, MA: Charlesbridge Publishers.

Pallotta, J. (1989). *The icky bug alphabet book.* Watertown, MA: Charlesbridge Publishing.

Parnall, P. (1986). *Winter barn.* New York: Macmillan.

Pauline, R. F. (1993). Microteaching: An integral part of a science methods class. *Journal of Science Teacher Education, 4*(1), 9–17.

Peck, J. (1998). *The giant carrot.* New York: Dial.

Penick, J. E., & Yager, R. E. (1993). Learning from excellence: Some elementary exemplars. *Journal of Elementary Science Education, 5*(1), 1–9.

Penner, D. E. (2001). Cognition, computers, and synthetic science: Building knowledge and meaning through modeling. In W. G. Seduce (Ed.). *Review of Research in Education* 2000–2001 (pp. 1–35). Washington, DC: American Educational Research Association.

Perkins-Gough, D. (2006). Understanding the scientific enterprise: A conversation with Alan Leshner. *Educational Leadership, 64*(4), 8–15.

Peters, L. W. (1988). *The sun, the wind, and the rain.* New York: Henry Holt.

Petheram, L. (2003). *Acid rain.* Mankato, MN: Bridgestone Books.

Phillips, L. (1991). *The million dollar potato.* New York: Simon & Schuster.

 Phoenix Mars Lander arrives in Florida. (2007). Jet Propulsion Laboratory News Release.

Piaget, J. (1964, 2003). Development and learning. *Journal of Research in Science Teaching, 2*(3), 176–184. (Reprinted in *Journal of Research in Science Teaching,* Suppl. 40, S8–S18.)

Pierce, W. (2001). Inquiry made easy. *Science and Children, 38*(8), 39–41.

Pilkey, D. (1994). *Dog breath.* New York: Blue Sky.

Pittman, K., & O'Neill, L. (2001). Using metaphors to evaluate ourselves. *Classroom Leadership, 4*(5), 1–3.

Playing to learn: Federation of Scientists supports "Edu-Gaming" in schools. (2006). *NSTA Reports, 18*(4), 1, 4.

Plitt, B. (2004). Teacher dilemmas in a time of standards and testing. *Phi Delta Kappan, 85*(10). 745–748.

Poetter, T. (2006). The zoo trip: Objecting to objectives. *Phi Delta Kappan, 88*(4), 319–323.

Polacco, P. (1988). *Boat ride with Lillian Two Blossom.* New York: Philomel Books.

Polacco, P. (1990). *Thunder cake.* New York: Philomel.

Popham, W. J. (2005). *Classroom assessment: What teachers need to know* (4th ed.). Boston: Pearson Education.

Powell, J. (2003). *Oil spills.* Mankato, MN: Bridgestone Books.

Prensky, M. (2005/2006). Listen to the natives. *Educational Leadership, 63*(4), 8–13.

Pringle, L. P. (2003). *Whales! Strange and wonderful.* Honesdale, PA: Boyds Mills Press.

Pringle, R. M. (2006). Preservice teachers' exploration of children's alternative conceptions: Cornerstone for planning science. *Journal of Science Teacher Education, 17*(3), 291–307.

Raskin, E. (1978). *The westing game.* New York: Dutton.

 Rebora, A. (2004, January 14). No child left behind. *Education Week on the Web.*

Reid, T.R. (2001, July). Thank you, Mr. Chips. *Reader's Digest,* 132–135.

Restak, R. (2003). *The new brain: How the modern age is rewiring your mind.* Emmaus, PA: Rodale Press.

Rey, M., & Rey, H. A. (1989). *Curious George goes to an ice cream shop.* New York: Houghton Mifflin.

Rice, D. C., Pappamihiel, N. E., & Lake, V. E. (2004). Lesson adaptations and accommodations: Working with native speakers and English language learners in the same science classroom. *Childhood Education, 80(3),* 121–127.

Richardson, D., & Richardson, D. (2001). *Can you dig it?* Colorado Springs, CO: Little Spirit Publishing.

Riddle, B. (2007). And then there were eight. *Science Scope, 30(5),* 78–80.

Ride, S. (2005). Igniting girls' interest in scientific careers. *Science Scope, 29(2),* 46–47.

Robertson, A., & Mahlin, K. (2005, November/December). Ecosystem journalism. *Science and Children, 43*(3), 42–45.

Robertson, B. (2006/2007). Getting past "inquiry versus content". *Educational Leadership, 64*(4), 67–70.

Rockwell, T. (2000). *How to eat fried worms.* New York: Random House.

Rommel-Esham, K. (2005). Do you see what I see? *Science and Children, 43*(1), 40–43.

Roop, P. (1985). *Keep the lights burning, Abbie.* Minneapolis, MN: Carolrhoda Books.

 Rose, L. C., & Gallup, A. M. (2004). The 38th annual Phi Delta Kappa/Gallup poll of the public's attitudes toward the public schools.

Rowan, K. (1999). *I know why I brush my teeth.* Cambridge, MA: Candlewick Press.

Rowe, M. B. (1974, 2003). Wait-time and rewards as instructional variables, their influence on language, logic, and fate control: Part one–Wait time. *Journal of Research in Science Teaching, 11*(2). (Reprinted in *Journal of Research in Science Teaching,* Suppl. No. 40, S19–S32.)

Rowe, M. B. (1978). *Teaching science as continuous inquiry: A basic* (2nd ed.). New York: McGraw-Hill.

Rowe, M. B. (1996). Science, silence, and sanctions. *Science and Children, 34*(1), 35–37.

Roy, K. (2004). Responsible use of live animals in the classroom. *Science Scope, 27*(9), 10–11.

Roy, K., Markow, P., & Kaufman, J. (2001). *Safety is elementary: The new standard for safety in the elementary science classroom.* Natik, MA: The Laboratory Safety Institute.

Ruby, A. (2006). Improving science achievement at high-poverty urban middle schools. *Science Education, 96*(6), 1005–1027.

Rush, C. (1996). *Levers.* Orlando, FL: Raintree Steck-Vaughn.

Russo, G. (2007, February 15). Broad sweep of genome zeroes in on diabetes. *Nature, 445*(668), 668.

Rutherford, F. J., & Ahlgren, A. (1990). *Science for all Americans.* New York: Oxford University Press.

Sagan, C. (1988). In S. W. Hawking, *A brief history of time.* (p. ix). New York: Bantam Books.

Sagan, C. (1989, September 10). Why we need to understand science. *Parade.*

Sagan, C. (1995). *The demon-haunted world: Science as a candle in the dark.* New York: Random House.

Sailor, W., & Roger, B. Rethinking inclusion: Schoolwide applications. *Phi Delta Kappan, 86*(7), 503–509.

Salinas, M. (2005). Scientist of the day. *Science and Children, 43*(2), 28–31.

Salkind, N. J. (1985). *Theories of human development* (2nd ed.). New York: John Wiley & Sons.

Samaras, A., Beck, C., Freese, A. R., & Kosnik, C. (2005). Self-study supports new teachers' professional development. *Focus on Teacher Education, 6*(1), 3–5, 7.

Sandall, B. R. (2003). Elementary science: Where are we now? *Journal of Elementary Science Education, 15*(2), 13–30.

Santrock, J. W. (2004). *Educational psychology* (2nd ed.). New York: McGraw-Hill.

 Scan of entire human genome finds unexpected new clues to Lou Gherig's disease. (2006, November 30). NMI Biochip Technologies.

Scardamalia, M. (1988). In *Tomorrow's schools, seminar one: Models of learning, a summary.* East Lansing, MI: The Holmes Group.

Schaffer, D. (1999). *Mealworms.* Mankato, MN: Capstone Press.

Schemo, D. J. (2006, October 25). Change in federal rules backs single-sex public education. *The New York Times,* A1.

Schibeci, R.A., & Hickey, R. (2000). Is it natural or processed? Elementary school teachers and conceptions about materials. *Journal of Research in Science Teaching, 37*(10), 1154–1170.

Schmidt, W. H. (2005, Winter). A mile wide, an inch deep. *Natural Selection, the Journal of BSCS,* 18–22.

 Schultz, L. (n.d.). Bloom's taxonomy.

Schütz, R. (2002). Vygotsky & language acquisition.

Schwarz, C. V., & Gwekwerere, Y. N. (2006). Using a guided inquiry and modeling instructional framework (EIMA) to support preservice K-8 science learning. *Science Education, 91*(1), 158–186.

Science for students with disabilities. (2007) *District Administration, 43*(2), 65.

Seda, I. (1991). Interviews to assess learners' outcomes. *Reading Research and Instruction, 31*(1), 22–32.

Selsam, M. (1959). *Seeds and more seeds.* New York: Harper & Row.

Selsam, M. (1966). *Benny's animals and how we put them in order.* New York: Harper & Row.

Selsam, M. (1980). *Eat the fruit, plant the seed.* New York: Morrow.

Selsam, M. E. (1983). *A first look at spiders.* New York: Walker.

Seuss, Dr. [pseud. for Geisel, T. S.]. (1949). *Bartholomew and the Oobleck.* New York: Random House.

Seuss, Dr. [pseud. for Geisel, T. S.], Prelutsky, J., & Smith, L. (1998). *Hooray for Diffendoofer Day!* New York: Random House.

Shaffer, D. W., Squire, K. R., Halverson, R., & Gee, J. (2005). Video games and the future of learning. *Phi Delta Kappa, 87*(2), 104–111.

Shapiro, D. (2006). School gardens grow science achievement score. *Science and Children, 17*(4), 5.

Shapp, M., & Shapp, C. (1975). *Let's find out about what's light and what's heavy.* New York: Franklin Watts.

Sharmat, M. (1980). *Gregory, the terrible eater.* New York: Simon & Schuster Children's.

Shaw, J. M. (1997). Threats to the validity of science performance assessments for

English language learners. *Journal of Research in Science Teaching, 34*(7), 721–743.

Shepardson, D. P. (1997). Of butterflies and beetles: First graders' ways of seeing and talking about insect life cycles. *Journal of Research in Science Teaching, 34*(9), 873–889.

Showers, P. (1961). *Find out by touching.* New York: Crowell.

Shulman, L. (1989). Address given to the annual meeting of the Holmes Group, Atlanta, GA.

Shulman, L. S. (1987). Knowledge and teaching: Foundations of the new reform. *Harvard Educational Review, 57*(1), 1–22.

Shute, N. (2007, January 8). Unraveling your DNA's effects. *U.S. News & World Reports, 142*(1), 50–54, 57–58.

Silverman, E., Coffman, M., & Younker, B. A. Cheep, chirp, twitter, & whistle. *Science and Children, 44*(6), 20-25.

Silverstein, A., Silverstein, V., & Nunn, L. S. (2002). *Cells.* Brookfield, CT: Twenty-First Century Books.

Silverstein, S. (1974). *Where the sidewalk ends.* New York: Harper & Row.

Simon, S. (1980). *Einstein Anderson shocks his friends.* New York: Viking Press.

Simon, S. (1981). *Einstein Anderson tells a comet's tale.* New York: Viking Press.

Simon, S. (1996). *The heart: Our circulatory system.* New York: Morrow Junior Books.

Siry, C., & Buchinski, C. (2005). A field guide of their own. *Science and Children, 43*(1), 36–39.

Sizer, T. (1985). *Horace's compromise.* Boston: Houghton Mifflin.

Slavin, R. E. (1994). *Educational psychology: Theory and practice.* (5th ed.). Boston, MA: Allyn and Bacon.

Sloane, E. (1966). *The sound of bells.* Garden City, NJ: Doubleday.

Snead, D., & Snead, W. L. (2004). Concept mapping and science achievement of middle grade students. *Journal of Research in Childhood Education, 18*(4), 306–320.

Sobol, D. J., & Andrews, G. (1984). *Encyclopedia Brown takes the cake!* New York: Scholastic.

Society for Neuroscience. (2002). *Brain facts: A primer on the brain and nervous system* (4th ed.). Washington, DC: Author.

Solano-Flores, G., & Nelson-Barber, S. (2001). On the cultural validity of science assessments. *Journal of Research in Science Teaching, 38*(5), 553–573.

Solso, R. L. (1988). *Cognitive psychology* (2nd ed.). Newton, MA: Allyn & Bacon.

Sparks-Langer, G., & Colton, A. (1991). Synthesis of research on teachers' reflective thinking. *Educational Leadership, 48,* 37–44.

Special education in the science classroom: Strategies for success. (2005). New York: Glencoe McGraw-Hill.

Starnes, B. A. (2006). What we don't know *can* hurt them: White teachers, Indian culture. *Phi Delta Kappan, 87*(5), 384–392.

Starr, M. L., & Krajcik, J. S. (1990). Concept maps as a heuristic for science curriculum development: Toward improvement in process and product. *Journal of Research in Science Teaching, 17*(10), 987–1000.

The state of teaching with technology. (2007) *NSTA Reports, 18*(9), 1.

Steenson, C. (2006). Learning logs in the science classroom: The literacy advantage. *Science Scope, 29*(7), 35–36.

Stefanich, G. P. (2005). The status of students with disabilities in science. *Proceedings of the RASEM—Regional Alliance for Science, Engineering and Mathematics Squared Symposium,* Las Cruces, NM.

Steinberg, E. R. (1989). Cognition and learner control: A literature review, 1977–1988. *Journal of Computer-Based Instruction, 16*(4), 117–121.

Stephens, N. (2006). *Plant cells and tissues.* Philadelphia: Chelsea House Publishers.

Steptoe, J. (1987). *Mufarro's beautiful daughters: An African tale.* New York: Lothrop, Lee & Shepard Books.

Stewart, M. (2002). *Sedimentary rocks.* Chicago: Heinemann Library.

Stice, C. F., & Alvarez, M. C. (1987, December). Hierarchical concept mapping in the early grades. *Childhood Education,* 86–96.

Stille, D. R. (2006). *Animal Cells: Smallest Units of Life.* Minneapolis, MN: Compass Point Books.

Stille, D. R. (2006). *Plant cells: The building blocks of plants.* Minneapolis, MN: Compass Point Books.

Stone, H., & Igmanson, D. (1968). *Rocks and rills—A look at geology.* Englewood Cliffs, NJ: Prentice-Hall.

Strauss, V. (2003, March 18). A radical formula for teaching science [Electronic version]. *The Washington Post,* A08. Accessed from *Access Research Network Library Files.*

Tal, T., & Morag, O. (2007). School visits to natural history museums: Teaching or enriching? *Journal of Research in Science Teaching, 44*(5), 747–769.

Tanaka, S. (2003). *New dinos: The latest finds! Tye coolest dinosaur discoveries!* New York: Atheneum Books for Young Readers.

Taylor, B. (1986). *I'm in charge of celebrations.* New York: Scribner's

Taylor, B. (1990). *Bouncing and bending light.* New York: Watts.

Taylor, B. (2001). *Oxford first book of dinosaurs.* New York: Oxford University Press.

Teale, W. H., Zott, N., Yokotam J., Glasswell, K., & Gambrell, L. (2007). Getting children in2books: Engagement in authentic reading, writing, and thinking. *Phi Delta Kappan, 88*(7), 498–502.

Technology training. (2000). *Kappa Delta Pi Record, 36*(4), 189.

Tekavec, H. (2004). *What's that awful smell?* New York: Dial Books for Young Readers.

Tekkaya, C., & Yenilmez, A. (2006). Relationships among measures of learning orientation, reasoning ability, and conceptual understanding of photosynthesis and respiration in plants for grade 8 males and females. *Journal of Elementary Science Education, 18*(1), 1–14.

Tharp, R. G., & Gallimore, R. (1988). *Rousing minds to life.* New York: Cambridge University Press. Cited in Slavin, R. E. (1997). *Educational psychology: Theory and practice* (5th ed.). Boston: Allyn & Bacon.

Therman, E. (1986). *Human chromosomes.* New York: Springer-Verlag.

Thier, M. (2003). Making the best of the wonder years: Parents as partners to link science and literacy. *Classroom Leadership, 7*(1), 1–2.

Thirunarayanan, M. O. (1998). An exploratory study of the relationships among science, technology and society (STS) issues as conceived by fifth grade students. *Journal of Elementary Science Education, 10*(1), 60–75.

Thomas, J. (2005). Calling a cab for Oregon students. *Phi Delta Kappan, 86*(5), 385–388.

Thomas, P. (1979). *There are rocks in my socks said the ox to the fox.* New York: Lothrop, Lee & Shepard.

Tobin, K. (1990). Research on science laboratory activities: In pursuit of better questions and answers to improve learning. *School Science and Mathematics, 90,* 403–418.

Tomlinson, C. A. (2001). Grading for success. *Educational Leadership, 58*(6), 12–15.

 Tomlinson, L. M. (1987). Locus of control and its effect on achievement. (ERIC Document No. ED276965)

Townsend, J., & Bunton, K. (2006). Indicators for inquiry. *Science and Children, 43*(5), 37–41.

Tran, L. U. (2006). Teaching science in museums: The pedagogy and goals of museum educators. *Science Education, 91*(2), 278–297.

Treaster, J. B. (2007). *Hurricane force: Tracking America's killer storms.* New York: Kingfisher.

Tyler, R. W. (1949). *Basic principles of curriculum and instruction.* Chicago: University of Chicago Press.

Tytler, R., & Peterson, S. (2004). From "Try it and see" to strategic exploration: Characterizing young children's scientific reasoning. *Journal of Research in Science Teaching, 41*(1), 94–118.

Ulerick, S. L. (1989, April). Using textbooks for meaningful learning in science. *Research Matters . . . To the Science Teacher.* National Association for Research in Science Teaching Newsletter.

Upadhyay, B. R. (2006). Using students' lived experiences in an urban science classroom: An elementary school teacher's thinking. *Science Education, 90*(1), 94–110.

 U.S. Department of Education. (1993). *National excellence: A case for developing America's talent.* Washington, DC: U.S. Government Printing Office.

 U. S. Department of Education (1999a). E-Learning: Putting a world-class education at the fingertips of children.

 U. S. Department of Education. (1999b). Preparing tomorrow's teachers to use technology (PT3).

 U. S. Department of Education. (2000). Revising the 1996 national educational technology plan.

 U.S. Department of Education (2002). *No child left behind.*

 U.S. Department of Education. (2005). *National education technology plan.*

U.S. Department of Education. (2004). *No child left behind: A toolkit for teachers.*

Using the National Science Digital Library. (2006). *NSTA Reports, 18*(2), 1,4.

Van Allsburg, C. (1981). *Jumanji.* Boston: Houghton Mifflin.

Van Allsburg, C. (1988). *Two bad ants.* Boston: Houghton Mifflin.

Van Frankenduyzen, G., & Van Frankenduyzen, R. S. (2001). *Adopted by an owl: The true story of Jackson the owl.* Chelsea, MI : Sleeping Bear Press.

Van Sertima, I. (1976). *They came before Columbus.* New York: Random House.

Van Sertima, I. (1988). *Blacks in science.* New Brunswick, NJ: Transaction Books.

van Zee, E. H. (1998). Fostering elementary teachers' research on their science teaching practices. *Journal of Teacher Education, 49*(4), 245–254.

Vancleave, J. (1996). *Janice Vancleave's ecology for every kid: Easy activities that make learning science fun.* New York: Wiley.

VanCleave, J. P. (1994). *Janice VanCleave's Dinosaurs for every kid.* New York: John Wiley.

Vanides, J., Yin, Y., Tomita, M., & Ruiz-Primo, M. A. (2005). Using concept maps in the science classroom. *Science Scope, 28*(8), 27–31.

Verplaetse, L. S. (1998). How content teachers interact with English language learners. *TESOL Journal, 7*(5), 24–28.

Vico, G. (1710). *De antiquissima Italorum sapientia.*

vonGlasersfeld, E. (1989). Cognition, construction of knowledge, and teaching. *Synthese, 80,* 121–140.

vonGlasersfeld, E. (1991). Knowing without metaphysics: Aspects of the radical constructivist position. In F. Steier (Ed.), *Research and reflexivity* (pp. 12–27). London: Sage Publications.

Vygotsky, L. S. (1934, 1986) On development of scientific concepts in childhood. In A. Kozulin (Ed.), *Thought and language.* Cambridge, MA: MIT Press. Cited in Ash, D., & Levitt, K. (2003). Working within the zone of proximal development: Formative assessment as professional development. *Journal of Science Teacher Education, 14*(1), 23–48.

Vygotsky, L. S. (1978). *Mind in society.* Cambridge, MA: Harvard University Press.

Wade, N. (1993, August 5). The good, bad, and ugly [Review of the book *Bad science:*

The short life and weird times of cold fusion]. *Nature, 364,* 477.

 Wade, N. (2000). Three share Nobel prize in medicine for studies of the brain. *The New York Times on the Web.*

Wade, N. (2006, July 21). Scientists hope to unravel Neanderthal DNA and human mysteries. *The New York Times,* A14.

Wade, S. (1990, March). Using think alouds to assess comprehension. *The Reading Teacher,* 442–451.

Waight, N., & Abd-El-Khalid, F. (2007). The impact of technology on the enactment of "inquiry" in a technology enthusiast's sixth grade science classroom. *Journal of Research in Science Teaching, 44*(1), 154–182.

Waldman, N. (2003). *The snowflake: A water cycle story.* Brookfield, CT: The Millbrook Press.

Walker, R. D. (2005). *Once upon a cloud.* New York: Blue Sky Press.

Walker, S. M., & Feldmann, R. (2001). *Levers.* Minneapolis, MN: Lerner Publishing Group.

Walsh, E. S. (1989). *Mouse paint.* San Diego: Harcourt Brace.

Walter, M. P. (1980). *Ty's one-man band.* New York: Scholastic.

Wang, J. (2001). TIMSS primary and middle school data: Some technical concerns. *Educational Researcher, 30*(6), 17–21.

Web-based education commission calls for "National mobilization" around Internet. (2001). American Association of Colleges for Teacher Education. *Briefs, 22*(1), 1.

Wechsler, D. (2003). *Bugs.* Hornesdale, PA: Boyds Mills Press.

Weiss, E. (2002). *The nose knows.* New York: Kane Press.

Weller, F. W. (1991). *I wonder if I'll see a whale.* New York: Philomel.

Wells, J., & Lewis, L. (2006). Internet access in U.S. public schools and classrooms, 1994–2005 (NCES 2007-020). U.S. Department of Education. Washington, DC: National Center for Education Statistics.

Westwater, A., & Wolfe, P. (2000). The brain-compatible curriculum. *Educational Leadership, 58*(3), 49–52.

Wheeler, G. F. (2006). Strategies for science education. *Educational Leadership 64*(4), 30–34.

White, E. B. (1945). *Stuart Little.* New York: Harper Trophy.

White, E. B. (1970). *The trumpet of the swan.* New York: Harper Trophy.

White, L. (1996). *Water: Simple Experiments for Young Scientists.* Brookfield, CT: Millbrook Press.

Wick, W. (1997). *A drop of water: A book of science and wonder.* New York: Scholastic.

Wilcox, J. (2007). NCLB on the eve of reauthorization. Calls for fundamental overhaul greet new congress. *Education Update, 49*(2), 1–2, 7–8.

Willerman, M., & MacHarg, R. A. (1991). The concept map as an advance organizer. *Journal of Research in Science Teaching, 28*(8), 705–711.

 Willett, W. C., & Stampfer, M. J. (2002). Rebuilding the food pyramid. *Scientific-American.com.*

Willis, J. (2007). Which brain research can educators trust? *Phi Delta Kappan, 88*(9), 697–699.

Willis, S. (1993, September). *Multicultural teaching: Meeting the challenges that arise in practice. ASCD Curriculum Update, 1–8.* Alexandria, VA: Association for Supervision and Curriculum Development.

Willis, S. (2006). Curriculum mapping on the edge. *Education Update, 48*(6), 5.

 Winebrenner, S., & Devlin, B. (2001). Cluster grouping of gifted students: How to provide full-time services on a part-time budget. (ERIC Document No. ED451663)

Winer, Y. (2002). *Birds build nests.* Watertown, MA: Charlesbridge Publishing.

Winer, Y. (2003). *Frogs sing songs.* Watertown, MA: Charlesbridge Publishing.

Wiske, S. (2004). Using technology to dig for meaning. *Educational Leadership, 62*(1), 46–50.

Wolfinger, D. M. (2005). Project produce. *Science & Children, 24*(4), 26–29.

Wolkstein, D. (1972). *8,000 stones: A Chinese folktale.* Garden City, NJ: Doubleday.

Women in engineering & related fields – Diversity analysis of students earning bachelor's degrees. (2006). Menlo Park, CA: *Engineers Dedicated to a Better Tomorrow D-E Communications—Critical Issues Series.*

Wood, J. (1990, March/April). *Implementing* *developmentally appropriate classrooms.* Paper presented at the 41st annual conference of the Southern Association on Children Under Six, Dallas, TX. (ERIC Document No. ED332789)

World Almanac. (2002). New York: World Almanac Books.

The World Almanac and Book of Facts. (2007). New York: World Almanac Books.

Worth, V. (1986). *Small poems again.* New York: Farrar, Straus & Giroux.

Wu, H.-K., & Krajcik, J. S. (2006). Inscriptional practices in two inquiry-based classrooms: A case study of seventh graders' use of data tables and graphs. *Journal of Research in Science Teaching, 43*(1), 63–95.

Yager, R. E. (1988). Differences between most and least effective science teachers. *School Science and Mathematics, 88*(4), 301–307.

Yager, R. E. (1993). The need for reform in science teacher education. *Journal of Science Teacher Education, 4*(4), 144–148.

Yager, R. E. (1994). Assessment results with the science/technology/society approach. *Science and Children, 32*(2).

Yager, R. E. (2005). Accomplishing the visions for professional development of teachers advocated in the National Science Education Standards. *Journal of Science Teacher Education, 16*(2), 95–102.

Yee, W. H. (2003). *Tracks in the snow.* New York: Henry Holt.

Yeh, S. S. (2001). Tests worth teaching to: Constructing state-mandated tests that emphasize critical thinking. *Educational Researcher, 30* (9), 12–17.

 Yerrick, R. K., & Ross, D. L. (2001, July/August). I read, I learn, imovie: Strategies for developing literacy in the context of inquiry-based science instruction. *Reading Online, 5*(1).

Yore, L. D., Anderson, J. O., & Shymansky, J. A. (2005). Sensing the impact of elementary school science reform: A study of stakeholder perceptions of implementation, constructivist strategies, and school-home collaboration. *Journal of Science Teacher Education, 16*(1), 65–88.

Zahorik, J. A. (1997). Encouraging—and challenging—students' understandings. *Educational Leadership, 54*(6), 30–32.

Zeldin, A. L., & Pajares, F. (2000). Against the odds: Self-efficacy beliefs of women in mathematical, scientific, and technological careers. *American Educational Research Journal, 37*(1), 215–246.

Zubrowski, B. (1979). *A Children's Museum activity book: Bubbles.* Boston: Little Brown.

Zull, J. E. (2004). The art of changing the brain. *Educational leadership, 62*(1), 68–72.

INDEX